Entrepreneurship, Creativity, & Organization

Entrepreneurship, Creativity, & Organization

Text, Cases, & Readings

JOHN KAO
Harvard Business School

Prentice Hall, Englewood Cliffs, New Jersey 07632

Library of Congress Cataloging-in-Publication Data

KAO, JOHN J.
  Entrepreneurship, creativity, and organization.

  Includes index.
  1. Entrepreneurship—Case studies. 2. Organization
—Case studies. 3. Venture capital—Case studies.
I. Title.
HB615.K36   1989   658.4′2   88-32101
ISBN 0-13-283011-6

Editorial/production supervision
  and interior design: *Edith Riker*
Cover design: *Lundgren Graphics, Inc.*
Cover photo: Published with permission of The Becket Paper Co.
Designed by Benchmark Incorporated. Photography by Bray Ficken.
Manufacturing buyer: *Margaret Rizzi*

     © 1989 by John Kao

Printed in the United States of America

10 9 8 7 6 5 4 3 2 1

ISBN 0-13-283011-6

Prentice-Hall International (UK) Limited, *London*
Prentice-Hall of Australia Pty. Limited, *Sydney*
Prentice-Hall Canada Inc., *Toronto*
Prentice-Hall Hispanoamericana, S.A., *Mexico*
Prentice-Hall of India Private Limited, *New Delhi*
Prentice-Hall of Japan, Inc., *Tokyo*
Simon & Schuster Asia Pte. Ltd., *Singapore*
Editora Prentice-Hall do Brasil, Ltda., *Rio de Janeiro*

For my teachers and my students

Contents

MODULE FOUR ENTREPRENEURSHIP IN THE ESTABLISHED FIRM

Preface

Entrepreneurs, people on fire with their ideas, have long fascinated me. Easy to recognize but hard to define, they are individuals whose zeal and passion make a difference. They almost willingly seek routes which put them in "harm's way." They frequently originate or catalyze the development of socially significant ideas. Their human qualities can be the decisive ingredients in the success of the organizations they create to pursue their vision.

Entrepreneurial organizations, with their volatility and flux, have also captured my attention. There is much to observe and learn in entrepreneurial environments, where standard operating procedures are lacking and organizational structure, culture, and leadership style are created anew each day. Like the art of Japanese ink-brush painting, developing entrepreneurial firms requires a sure and steady hand. They grow and evolve rapidly. A movement made too fast, and the ink will be too thin; too slow, and the ink will make an unsightly blot. The trick, simple to state but difficult to practice, lies in following the motion's natural course.

Entrepreneurship and creativity have interested me both academically and personally for a long time. I came to their study through an eclectic path. I have had a longstanding interest in human behavior in organizations, which led me to study behavioral science and philosophy in college. Training in medicine and psychiatry followed, as a way of applying knowledge about human behavior in a practical environment. Finally, I pursued graduate studies in management, which grounded my knowledge of human behavior in the business world. Hence, my interest in entrepreneurship and creativity, stemming from an early interest in human behavior in organizations, has led me to blend the intellectual and practical concerns of psychiatry and management.

Personally, entrepreneurship has also interested me as an important facet of my generational experience. Frequently, the rebel or truth seeker of the 1960s has become the entrepreneur of the 1980s. At one point in the film "The

Big Chill," one character turns to another and says, "Who would have thought that a couple of ex-revolutionaries could have made all this money?" Indeed, who could have predicted that the decade of the 1960s, characterized by revolution and "alternatives" to the status quo, could have led to the 1980s with its entrepreneurial and "young urban professional" culture? Self-expression, the culture of "doing your own thing," disillusionment with the establishment, all served as paths to an entrepreneurial career. Today, the drive for self-actualization, change, and independent expression often finds release on the canvas of business. Many of my friends went through such transitions, as did I.

My teaching in the area of entrepreneurship took specific shape in 1983, when the Harvard Business School sponsored a conference on entrepreneurship as part of its seventy-fifth anniversary celebration. Subtitled, "an agenda-setting colloquium," this meeting brought together some seventy academicians and practitioners to chart the future direction of entrepreneurship research and teaching at the School. It was a pivotal event for many, leading to the establishment of an entrepreneurship "interest group" with faculty members drawn from general management, finance, and organizational behavior areas who were challenged by the inherently interdisciplinary nature of entrepreneurship. New teaching materials were developed on the boundaries of these areas. This book is one of the first from that effort.

The impact of this conference can be judged in terms of a growing body of work. The teaching and research of entrepreneurship at Harvard, in itself an entrepreneurial endeavor, has increased significantly in recent years. From a relatively peripheral area of research and teaching, entrepreneurship in 1987 expanded to an endeavor involving five full-time faculty members and some 1,600 enrollments in entrepreneurship courses per MBA class of 800 students.

This expansion of interest is mirrored in other academic centers. In 1967, it was estimated that only ten academic institutions offered courses in entrepreneurship. By 1987, the number was estimated at 350, with more than 10,000 students enrolled. Such hypergrowth has led to the search for appropriate and up-to-date teaching materials. Because there are hazards in an overly academic and theoretical approach to an essentially experiential field, the case method of teaching has obvious advantages. For a field lacking a unifying theory, examination of cases goes far beyond the mere transmission of war stories, to the development of personal sensitivities and skills which are often invaluable to the practitioner.

One of the main questions raised by the Harvard conference was what concepts, skills, and attitudes ought to be developed in students of business who intended to pursue entrepreneurial careers. A number of these issues fell under a heading dubbed "the social psychology of entrepreneurship." So many such issues were identified that conference participants recommended the creation of a course in this area at Harvard Business School separate from the concerns of introductory organizational behavior courses.

This proposed course would encourage self and career assessment to identify realistically—while in school—the pros and cons of an entrepreneurial career in order to manage expectations of that career. Students would learn the importance of managing personal trade-offs in coping with uncertainty, failure, and success. Other desired skills would include interpersonal sensitivity within a partnership, delegation, managing human resources, leading a dynamic entrepreneurial firm, and managing a resource network outside of one's own firm. Conference participants also emphasized understanding the evolution of organizational structure in the entrepreneurial firm and the stages of venture development. An equally important topic was how to foster the entrepreneurial and creative spirit of the large and/or established firm.

Entrepreneurship, Creativity, and Organization, a MBA second-year elective, was developed to address these needs. Like any entrepreneurial venture, the course passed through several stages and addressed a number of challenges. At start-up, it involved taking the career risk of doing something new, operating in an interdisciplinary mode within an institution organized by disciplinary boundaries, and working long hours in the "garage." It required finding a champion, winning support among colleagues, and building a following in the student body.

Developing the new material for this course was intended to contribute to a better definition of the territory covered by the words "entrepreneurship" and "creativity." Creating this new course in the entrepreneurship "field" raised many questions for me. What *is* entrepreneurship? Is it a discipline? Is it even a subject? What is the body of theory that defines the field? What is its relationship to the notion of creativity? What is the base of research which supports it? Is entrepreneurship simply a set of mental attitudes? How do you teach it? Why should this sort of behavior be encouraged in students of business? What does entrepreneurship have to do with the mainstream of business? Why is it important? How will it help the practice of management? It is my hope that this textbook and the teaching experience it creates will lead to useful answers to these questions.

* * * * *

Harvard Business School proved to be a fertile and nurturing environment within which to incubate this venture in pedagogy. Many people contributed to the start-up. John McArthur, Dean of the Faculty at Harvard Business School, provided warm support and encouragement for the project. In many ways, he is the real champion of this corporate venture. Howard Stevenson, Sarofim-Rock Professor of Entrepreneurship, and Associate Professor Bill Sahlman, have been immensely valued colleagues and friends. Professors John Kotter, Michael Beer, John Gabarro, and Chris Argris, and Associate Professor Jeffrey Sonnenfeld from the area of organizational behavior have also given valuable feedback and encouragement. Other colleagues who provided valued help include Professors Chris Christensen and Abraham Zaleznik, Lecturer Pierre Wack, and Tony Athos. Professors Shervert Frazier, Fritz Redlich, and Thomas Detre of Harvard, UCLA, and Yale Medical Schools nurtured the development of my interest in psychiatric practice and research. The Harvard Business School Division of Research has also been supportive through the help of Professors E. Raymond Corey and Ronald Fox. Professor Jay Lorsch, my current research director, has encouraged the research agenda based on my course's concern. Several research assistants have made notable contributions, among them Marylou Balbaky, Susan McElroy, Hartley Rogers, Rick Stamberger, and Lee Field. Finally, as of this writing, nearly a thousand Harvard MBAs have taken the course, providing innumerable insights and sharpening my thinking. A number of students made noteworthy contributions, including Craig Knudsen, Deborah Goldberg, Jerry DeLa Vega, Dan Stern, Cella Irvine, and Audrey Dickason.

Entrepreneurs and entrepreneurial managers in a variety of settings also helped immeasurably in creating *Entrepreneurship, Creativity, and Organization.* They include Bob Norton and Bob Greber of Lucasfilm, Ltd; Lou Gerstner, Jerry Welsh, Kathi Kuhn, Fred Wilkinson, Jamie Dimond, and many others at American Express Travel Related Services Company; Ned Prebble and Tim Ferry of Synectics; Charlie Atkinson from The Whole Brain Corporation; Mitch Kapor, Janet Axelrod and Cathy Faulkner of Lotus Development Corporation; Wendell Butler of the Young Astronaut Program; Peter Ueberroth, Commissioner of Major League Baseball; Robert Saunders and Michael Cornfield of Robert Michael Companies; Linda Linsalata of Orange Nassau; Jim Morgan of Morgan Holland; Steve Ricci of The Palmer Organization; Art Snyder of U.S. Trust; Diana Frazier of BancBoston Ventures; Leo Castelli; Ron Shaich, Len Schlesinger and Louis Kane of Au Bon Pain; Nolan Bushnell, Larry Calof, and John Anderson of Catalyst Technologies; Ann Piestrup and Marcia Klein of The Learning Company; Peter Schwartz of Royal Dutch Shell Group; Jan Carlzon and John Herbert at Scandinavian Airline Systems; Al Vezza of Infocom; Bob Carpenter, David Housman and others at Integrated Genetics; Burt Morrison of the Ladd Company; Ted Turner of Turner Broadcasting Company; Akira Kimishima of Dainana Securities Company; Jerry DeLa Vega of Hot Rock; Jim Levy, Ken Coleman, Linda Parker, Brad Fegger, David Crane, Ralph Guiffre, Larry Hicks, Alison Elwers, and others at Activision. I have also learned a great deal from Pitch Johnson, Bobby Newmyer, Richard Rainwater, Tommy Taylor and David Wolff. Finally, Barbara Feinberg has made a fundamental contribution to this book as editor, colleague, and friend.

The opportunity to form intellectual partnerships with these outstanding people cannot be overvalued.

Entrepreneurship, Creativity, & Organization

Overview

Entrepreneurship has emerged in the 1980s as an important focus of attention for business students, practitioners, and academicians across the United States, indeed around the world. Much is happening on today's campus. Would-be entrepreneurs look for appropriate courses of study to prepare for their envisioned career. Groups of student entrepreneurs practice the ancient art of networking, enhanced by the advent of the personal computer. Entrepreneurial alumni return to campus to tell their stories before packed lecture halls. Established companies position themselves on campus as "entrepreneurial," "intrapreneurial," and "creative."

Such activity mirrors the world at large. The business press is replete with accounts of the most recent public offering, the newest mousetrap. New ventures are lionized as the source of new opportunities and new jobs. Major corporations experiment with ways of introducing the "entrepreneurial spirit" into the established environment. Their tools are new approaches to organizational structure, people management, and leadership. The flow of money continues to fuel the flames of initiative, with the formation of $20 billion of venture capital in the United States as of 1985. New streams of opportunity are evident everywhere. They come from new rules of the game such as deregulation and tax policy; they depend on new technology, exemplified by the microprocessor and recombinant genetic material. These opportunities are inspired by a significant shift in social values and career expectations. They are also fueled by a new willingness to experiment with public/private partnerships.

This current interest in entrepreneurship is appropriate. We need what entrepreneurs can give us: new products; new jobs; creative work environments; new ways of doing business. And yet, we should consider critically some of the ways entrepreneurship is being discussed today. Far from being easy, entrepreneurship is hard work, involving an unpredictable blend of calculation and luck; it is a tonic laced with the ever-present possibility of failure. Thus, it is important to put the current enthusiasm for entrepreneurship into perspective. As a nation we have spent a number of years questioning our basic business competence. Whether it be the Japanese challenge or our overvaluation of analytical management at the expense of common sense, we have had plenty of opportunity to doubt ourselves. In our search for answers, we must beware that entrepreneurship does not become a magic potion or a panacea. We do not yet know how to turn frogs into princes.

Keeping in mind, then, both the renewed attention to entrepreneurial and creative behavior and that it is not a cure-all, we can ask two questions: How do you "do" entrepreneurship well? What do you really have to know?

This textbook, and the course on which it was based, were developed to address these questions and fulfill a need. Existing entrepreneurship courses have tended to focus on technical skills: writing business plans; analyzing financial data; exploring legal issues. Yet entrepreneurship is fundamentally less about technical skills than about people and their passions. An old dictum of real estate holds that its three principles are "location, location, location." It could be said that the three principles of entrepreneurship are "people, people, people." Clearly, the entrepreneur must be skilled at identifying and pursuing opportunity. Yet, human issues are also predominant. Equally, the entrepreneur's task involves finding leverage through the efforts of others to amplify his or her own vision. Crusades are usually not entered into alone. Instead, the entrepreneur may find it necessary to enter into a partnership or start a new company. In creating the organizational means appropriate to pursuing a particular opportunity, the entrepreneur must work with and through people. By generating and communicating a vision of what is possible, the entrepreneur gathers together, leads, and inspires human beings.

The human issues of entrepreneurship also wear another, individual face. The entrepreneur must also manage him or herself effectively in dealing with the ambiguity and uncertainty which surround the creation of an idea and the organizational vehicle developed around it. The ability to take on such human challenges, indeed, to seek them out, is fundamental to entrepreneurial success and is emphasized constantly by those who have been through the process. Such knowledge is essential and complementary to entrepreneurial skills involving a mastery of technical subjects like finance, strategy, and marketing.

ENTREPRENEURSHIP, CREATIVITY, AND ORGANIZATION: GOALS AND PRINCIPLES

Entrepreneurship, Creativity, and Organization was originally an MBA elective developed for second-year students at Harvard Business School. Taught for the first time in 1984, it is directed to the needs of several groups of students:

- would-be entrepreneurs;
- would-be managers of entrepreneurial processes in established firms;
- would-be managers in creativity-driven businesses.

The material that makes up the course derives from field research questions, and the case study serves as the primary vehicle for the educational process. Students are introduced to a range of people, companies, and industries—some well known, others obscure. Because of the importance of these human stories, interview material appears from time to time. The use of video material, specifically developed for this course, is recommended as a means of making these human dramas more vivid and sharpening diagnostic and analytical skills.

Not all the course material chronicles success by any means, nor is there an underlying assumption that any one approach is "correct." Rather, the course presents students with a variety of people and situations from which they can extract general principles regarding the recurring issues and problems of entrepreneurs and entrepreneurial organizations.

Entrepreneurship, Creativity, and Organization's aim is *to contribute to the success* of the entrepreneurial and/or creative venture by helping students recognize—and anticipate—these recurring issues; to improve their sensitivity to human and organizational factors in the entrepreneurial environment; and to enhance their ability to make effective decisions and to find resolution of these issues. As a concentrated dose of preventive medicine, the course encourages a pattern recognition approach to learning, whose objective is an internalized sense of how things should be done. This does not derive from intellectualizing or theory but is lived; it is not free of charge but comes primarily from extensive and often painful personal experience.

The course is predicated on three underlying beliefs. First, entrepreneurship and creativity are seen as intimately related, timeless human qualities. Creativity implies generating new ideas and approaches. Entrepreneurial behavior involves the ability to identify opportunities based on these new ideas and approaches, and to turn them into something tangible. Outstanding organizations have always sought to mobilize both these qualities. Entrepreneurship and creativity are not topics of the moment but valuable corporate resources that can be managed for competitive advantage.

Second, the would-be entrepreneur needs facility in an array of human and organizational skills: self-understanding; interpersonal understanding; leadership; conflict resolution; stress management; tolerance for ambiguity; team and project management; creating appropriate rewards and incentives; and organization design.

Third, rigorous examination of entrepreneurial and creativity-dependent companies provides fresh insights into the relationships between organizations, strategies, and environments. Such companies operate in highly uncertain environments and exhibit great fluidity in their internal structure. Thus, they are continually challenged to generate mechanisms for fostering organizational integration and coherence. In addition, these firms evolve rapidly. Studying them reveals a panorama of the stages and dilemmas of leadership and organizational development. Put another way, they provide a significant laboratory for examining issues of generic importance to all managers.

Building on themes of basic organizational behavior and human resource management courses, *Entrepreneurship, Creativity, and Organization* poses some recurrent questions:

- What are the issues and concerns SPECIFIC to entrepreneurial companies?
- What is the impact on entrepreneurial organizations of:
  rapid growth;
  lack of established structure;
  balancing short-term and long-term decision making;
  shortages of resources such as managerial skills, time, and money;
  value conflicts between founders and newcomers;
  interaction patterns among functional groups in embryonic and rapidly changing organizations;
  the ongoing need to deal with stress and ambiguity
- What are the differences and similarities between entrepreneurial and managerial behavior at individual, group, and organizational levels?
- How do the human and organizational challenges of fostering entrepreneurship and creativity in large established firms and small entrepreneurial ones compare?

This course is organized around a process flow model. Four modules, each adopting a different point of view, and a group of related questions comprise the "golden thread" of this course. They are:

Managing creativity.   This module adopts the perspective of the manager of creative processes. It poses such basic questions as: Where do ideas come from? Which processes—individual and organizational—facilitate creativity?

The entrepreneur.   This module includes cases written from the entrepreneur's perspective. It allows students to clarify for themselves such issues as: What characterizes the person who recognizes the opportunity in an idea and translates it into reality? Is there a prototypical entrepreneurial personality?

The evolving organization.   This module also takes the entrepreneur's perspective. Once the idea and the people have been found, how can an appropriate company organization be developed and nurtured? How can the external environment influence the progress of an evolving firm? What are the predictable crises of organizational life which affect the viability of the enterprise?

The established organization.   This module adopts two related perspectives, that of the entrepreneurial leader/CEO and of the entrepreneurial middle manager.

When an organization is established in size, complexity, history, and corporate culture, how can the creative and entrepreneurial spirit be preserved and stimulated? What are the advantages and disadvantages of an established organization in pursuing these objectives? How do they influence the corporate or "internal" entrepreneur? What are important contrasts between bureaucratic and entrepreneurial organizations?

The four course modules suggest a number of additional questions specific to business students as they develop their career objectives and strive to achieve the highest possible level of professional effectiveness. These issues provide a subtext to the flow of course topics and include:

Managing creativity. How can I understand the creative process better in terms of my own experience? What facilitates or blocks it for me? How effective am I in managing creative people? How do I evaluate the quality of a creative environment? How can I enhance creative results in a given organization?

The entrepreneur. Where do I fall on a spectrum of entrepreneurial and managerial behavior? What aspects of my interpersonal and problem-solving style affect my potential as an entrepreneur or a productive member of an entrepreneurial and creativity-dependent organization?

The evolving organization. How do I assess the fit between myself and an evolving and dynamic organization? Am I comfortable with the ambiguity inherent in such an environment? What must I do to enter successfully such a company and manage my career within it?

The established organization. How can I create greater discretion for myself within the boundaries of an established organization? How do I gain the right to pursue entrepreneurial objectives? How do I make new things happen within the traditions and rules of an established company?

THE ENTREPRENEURSHIP, CREATIVITY, AND ORGANIZATION (ECO) ANALYTICAL FRAMEWORK

A basic assumption of this course is that entrepreneurship and creativity cannot be studied exclusively from one frame of reference such as the person or the organization, but must be dealt with more holistically. Entrepreneurship and creativity result from the interrelationship of three elements as shown in Figure 1:

- the person
- the task
- the organizational context

Figure 1 The ECO Analytical Framework

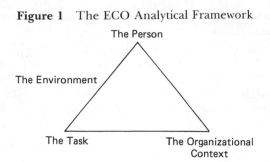

The first element, the "person," is obvious. New ideas are not generated or implemented by organizations or technology but come into being through the efforts of dedicated people. Thus, it is important to understand peoples' personalities, motivations, skills, levels of experience, and psychological preferences. It may be useful to know, for example, that someone has problems with authority stemming from previous relationships (personality issues); or is highly driven by a need for achievement (motivation); or has a particular facility with interpersonal relationships (skills); or has had work experience only in large bureaucratic organizations (level of experience); or finally, that someone prefers unstructured environments where intuition can be extensively used (psychological preferences).

The "task" is what a given group of people or an organization does. Tasks may be determined by an individual's personality or private vision. They are shaped by organizational strategy, as well as influenced by the external environment. For the entrepreneur, relevant tasks include generating new ideas or insights about new opportunities (creative tasks) and making those ideas come into some tangible form (operational/managerial tasks). As the entrepreneur develops an organization to serve as an appropriate lever for his or her vision, the nature and variety of tasks must inevitably change as the organization evolves and becomes more complex.

The "organizational context" is the immediate setting in which creative and entrepreneurial work takes place. Such issues as organizational structure and systems, the definition of work roles, and group culture affect significantly the nature of the creative or entrepreneurial environment. Such factors may limit or facilitate creativity and entrepreneurship, and become an increasing factor to contend with as the organization evolves.

Finally, these elements exist in an "environment," which refers to the outside world surrounding the organization. It is obviously significant as a source of external resources such as capital, people, information, and expertise, as well as various forms of professional services. It, too, can facilitate or impede creative and entrepreneurial endeavor to the extent that an appropriate infrastructure, for example, is either absent or present. The environment also defines the competitive situation, which may be composed of such factors as competitors, regulatory forces, and the development state of technology. Figure 2 summarizes the ECO analytical framework.

Figure 2 The ECO Analytical Framework

THE PERSON	THE TASK	THE ORGANIZATIONAL CONTEXT
Motives	What the person does	Structure
Personality	Inner/outer influences	Culture
Skills		Roles
Experience	Creative tasks	Policies
Psychological preferences	Operation/managerial tasks	Human resource systems
		Communication systems
		May limit or facilitate creativity and entrepreneurship
KEY ISSUE		
Modes of influence may change as the organization evolves	Nature and variety of tasks change as the organization evolves	Becomes more significant as the organization evolves
		Need for coordination, integration, and leadership increase

THE ENVIRONMENT

External resources
    capital
    people
    expertise
Infrastructure
Competitive pressures
Social values/mores
Regulation
State of technology

In general, the form an organization assumes and the tasks it undertakes are defined by and depend on both its strategy and environment.[1] Strategy gives shape to tasks by defining the overall goals and purpose of the organization. The environment's influence on tasks comes from the relative availability of resources and influences on the operating environment. An organization's viability depends significantly on how it fits with its strategy and environment.

Regardless of their strategy or environment, all organizations must address several basic challenges. First, they must handle information effectively. For some organizational theorists, such as Galbraith, organizations are information processing mechanisms whose central tasks include getting information, dissemi-

[1] John P. Kotter, "Organizational Design," *Organizational Behavior and Administration*, Paul Lawrence, Louis Barnes, and Jay Lorsch eds. (Homewood, Ill.: Richard D. Irwin, Inc., 1976).

nating it within the organization, and using it to make decisions.[2] Information processes define an organization's relative ability to interact efficiently with its environment and to pursue its specific goals.

Second, they must balance the need for what Lawrence and Lorsch[3] label differentiation and integration. Differentiation refers to diversity in cognitive and emotional point of view that characterizes people with different functional orientations. For example, software designers and marketing managers may see problems and priorities in a significantly different light. Integration means an organization's ability to effect needed collaboration between functional specialists and organizational units to meet the challenges of the environment. Achieving integration is a guiding objective of the entrepreneurial firm, where tasks are highly diverse, interdependent, and important. The more diversity and interdependence, the more potential for information and work overload and for organizational conflict, requiring different organizational strategies. Differentiation also affects the ability of an organization to respond to change. Specialization may lead to a decrease in flexibility at both individual and operating unit levels. Changes in the environment, strategy, and available resources can also cause difficulty in achieving a required level of integration.

Third, organizations must achieve a degree of structural formality appropriate to the degree of uncertainty and ambiguity which characterize their key tasks. For example, a high degree of task certainty encourages the development of formal structures to attain operational efficiency. On the other hand, a high degree of task uncertainty suggests a need for flexibility and greater informality. Obviously, entrepreneurial organizations are those with the highest degree of uncertainty and ambiguity, as Figure 3 indicates.

THE CRITICAL ROLE OF A HUMAN RESOURCE MANAGEMENT (HRM) PERSPECTIVE IN ENTREPRENEURIAL FIRMS

It is a basic orientation of this course that the concepts and skills represented by a human resource perspective are critical for the pursuit of creative and entrepreneurial objectives. The traditional entrepreneur's job description includes responsibilities like product development, business planning, and finance. But unless the company is a sole proprietorship, the entrepreneur quickly discovers that a substantial amount of time in the early phases of a company's life is taken up with human resource issues. The right people must be found, hired, and integrated into the organization; they must share the entrepreneur's vision of the future, be given appropriate direction, goals, and measures. The entrepreneur also must define agendas, make compensation deals and reward standards,

[2] Jay Galbraith, *Designing Complex Organizations* (Reading, Mass.: Addison-Wesley Publishing Company, Inc., 1973).
[3] Paul Lawrence and Jay Lorsch, *Organization and Environment* (Homewood, Ill.: Richard D. Irwin, 1967).

Figure 3 Sources of Uncertainty in Entrepreneurial Organizations

---

THE OPPORTUNITY

Market size
Pricing
Viability of original business idea
Customer response
Value of proprietary position/patents/know-how
Product/service life-cycle

EXTERNAL: THE EMERGING INDUSTRY AS ENVIRONMENT

Competitors
Regulation
Technology
Word-of-mouth information

INTERNAL: "THE ENTREPRENEURIAL SCRAMBLE"

The Organization

Fit between key people and organization
Access to key resources: capital, people

The Person

Management/leadership ability of founder(s)

Tasks

Identifying
Prioritizing
Executing
Ability to create product/service
Length of time to develop product/service

---

clarify responsibilities, allocate status, resolve conflict, manage interpersonal tradeoffs, as well as evaluate and develop key people.

What might be considered hard assets in a more established firm are to the embryonic firm often quite intangible. Technology may be in the process of development, finances contingent on performance, brand name unknown, comparative advantage and anticipated market position unproven. People are, on the other hand, among the most tangible and most expensive assets of the entrepreneurial company. One might think carefully about an investment decision involving a costly piece of equipment, yet in their haste to "get the job done," entrepreneurs are often less attentive to the managerial and financial implications of choosing and investing in people than they should be.

Difficulties in pursuing the human resource agenda may spring from an apparent tension between the "entrepreneurial spirit" and human resource management systems. The early-stage organization may be notable for its informality; people decisions like allocating responsibilities and rewards are made face to face. For some, creating human resource management systems may suggest the onset of bureaucracy. Such steps as hiring a human resource specialist, defining a human resources function, and embarking on human resource programs are often perceived, particularly by old-timers, as the imposition of unwanted structure on the company's free-wheeling entrepreneurial environment. It is often perceived, particularly by old-timers, as the imposition of unwanted structure on the company's entrepreneurial environment.

Yet, developing a human resource perspective is indispensible for the entrepreneur because it provides crucial leverage for influencing the development of the organization as well as the people in it. Human resource issues are important because entrepreneurs typically face an imbalance between the people resources at their disposal and the work that needs to be done. Hence, making the most of available human resources is clearly a central entrepreneurial challenge.

Growth provides another reason for valuing the leverage from effective human resource management. Growth rates of 50 percent to 100 percent per year are not uncommon as companies "ramp up" and attempt to win market acceptance. Early success, while ardently desired, can also lead to unique organizational risks and burdens for the entrepreneurial firm, which must maintain the flexibility and capacity to adapt to a changing and dynamic environment. To deal with emerging needs the firm must modify its organizational structure, find new methods of internal communication, develop new human skills, and assimilate new people into the organization.

Managing expectations is another human issue important to the entrepreneurial firm. First are the expectations of key people. A firm may be very dependent on the creative and/or technical talents of one or more "stars" who, in such high-tech areas as computer software and biotechnology may be responsible for a product's successful development. If retaining such people and maintaining their productivity are important, then they must be kept happy and their role continually developed in relation to the company's evolution. Second, there are the expectations of people who have been drawn to the entrepreneurial firm because of their perceptions of it: as a successful company; a vehicle for personal financial gain; an opportunity for advancement; an attractive company environment in which employees are treated well. Continually balancing expectations with reality is critical to maintaining a company atmosphere of excitement and productivity.

What specifically can a human resource management function do for an entrepreneurial company? Properly conceived, human resource management can be an important source of leverage for the entrepreneur in addressing the following key issues:

- Selecting the right person for the right job.
- Planning for change in a dynamic environment as both people and jobs evolve.
- Maximizing productivity through job design, clear expectations and performance appraisal, encouraging shared values, skill development and training, managing morale, managing nonfinancial incentives, encouraging communications within the company.

Human resources can influence each element in the ECO analytical framework. Clearly, the human resource function is critical in identifying and bringing the right people into the organization. It has a significant effect on people's progression in the organization through training, promotion systems, and career planning. HRM affects the task through job design and the creation of rewards appropriate to the behavior desired. It affects the organizational setting through such interactions as communication systems, counseling senior managers, managing company culture, and handling company climate. Figure 4 summarizes the role of human resource management as a source of managerial leverage and influence. Human resource management deals with each element by providing an answer to a key question:

- *The person:* Do we have the people we need today? Are we looking for the people we will need tomorrow?
- *The task:* Are tasks being defined to best satisfy individual and organizational needs?
- *The organizational context:* Is the organization developing so as to best support its strategy?

Human resource management acts on each element, but it is in the area of assuring fit that it realizes its greatest value: as a transmission system for linking the person, the task, and the organizational context. In this role human re-

Figure 4   HRM as a Source of Leverage and Influence

sources can buffer the effects of rapid or discontinuous change by operating in three critical dimensions:

- person-organization fit;
- person-task fit;
- task-organization fit.

Assuring fit between person and organization is critical to entrepreneurial and creative success. Variables such as personal style, needs, and ability to tolerate uncertainty may critically influence a person's ability to be successful in a given company environment. It is imperative that an organization understand itself in terms of culture and environment, and that it maintain a clear image of the type of person likely to be successful in it. Such an image increases the likelihood that the right people will be found through highly focused recruiting practices. It also determines the manner in which new people will be introduced to the norms and expectations of the organization. Finally, the fit between person and organization is dynamic, and influenced by change on both sides of the equation. Providing ways for both careers and organizational capabilities to develop will assure the continuous and mutual adaptation of person and organization.

Assuring person-task fit is also a critical responsibility of the human resources function. As an organization evolves, the nature and complexity of tasks to be accomplished will change. Developing people's skills through training and development allows them to keep pace with an organization's changing needs. Varying their opportunities to gain experience through job rotation and redeployment can lead to the development of critically needed skills.

Finally, achieving an ongoing fit between an organization's needs and the tasks to be accomplished is of fundamental importance. An organization must constantly ask itself whether the right things are being done relative to an organization's strategy and resources. Modifying the definition and design of jobs is an important way to redefine tasks as an organization's needs evolve.

Further issues of human resource management will be explored in each module note as it relates to specific issues of managing creativity, the entrepreneur, the evolving organization, and the established organization.

MODULE ONE

Managing Creativity

Understanding creativity provides a foundation for the modules on entrepreneurship that follow in this book. Central to the entrepreneur's role is the constant desire to create something: a new organization, new insights into the market, new corporate values, new manufacturing processes, new products or services, new ways of managing. All entrepreneurial activity unfolds around the birth of new ideas. Understanding how the creative process begins and evolves is therefore critical for entrepreneurial success.

Creativity is a topic relevant not only to the entrepreneurial start-up but to business in general. It is an important source of competitive strength for all organizations concerned with growth and change. For, to be responsive to change *is* to be creative: in such terms as perceiving the environment; developing new products and services; establishing new business procedures.

Creativity presents a variety of management challenges and it may require significant tangible investment. As an example, Hallmark Cards has spent substantial resources on an Innovation Center that houses several hundred employees involved with generating new product ideas. Creativity may be an integral part of a corporate culture that management wishes to instill. It may also determine organizational structure and human resource practices.

The management of creativity may proceed intentionally or by default. This module's purpose is to examine how to manage creativity *better* and to dispel the notion that it is simply brainstorming on a pink cloud.

Figure 1-1

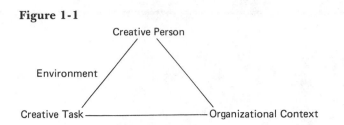

Creativity is a large and complex topic. In this book, it is considered from a managerial perspective, with the cases in this module revolving around what the manager must do to manage creativity effectively. In this module, three major issues are addressed: first, a working definition of creativity useful in business terms is established; second, the importance of managing creativity is demonstrated in terms of nurturing the competitive strength of a given organization; and third, a set of tools is presented for managers to influence the creative process. These tools reflect the importance of understanding creativity in both individual and organizational terms. Stated differently, the sections of this module note are entitled:

1. Creativity—What is it?
2. Managing Creativity—Why is it important?
3. Managing Creativity—How do you do it?

In seeking to foster creativity, the manager must differentiate among interventions which influence person, task, and organizational context. Figure 1-1 illustrates the model.

Appreciating the challenges facing creative individuals and their needs is an essential task for the would-be manager of creative process. Different interpersonal approaches to managing creative people are explored using such examples as Leo Castelli and George Lucas. Managers may influence the creative task through job design and the manner in which expectations and goals are communicated. At the organizational level, it will be shown that creativity, far from being unmanageable, is a resource deeply influenced by basic decisions about such organizational issues as structure, culture, and style of leadership. Such issues are taken up in the George Lucas case in this module, and in the Lotus Development Corporation case in the Module Three. Finally, managers must also be aware of the environment to the extent that it facilitates or hinders creative work through the availability of resources, supportive social values, and infrastructure.

CREATIVITY—WHAT IS IT?

Webster[1] defines creativity as "the ability to bring something new into existence." To others, it is a human process leading to a result which is novel (new), useful

---

[1] *Webster's Third New International Dictionary* (Springfield: G&C Merriam and Company, 1976).

(solves an existing problem or satisfies an existing need), and understandable (can be reproduced). But this tells us little about the process. A quote on creativity from Jasper Johns, a noted modern painter, captures this dilemma: "It's simple. Take something and do something to it and then do something else. Do it for a while and pretty soon you've got something." Pablo Picasso makes a wry distinction between technique and inspiration: "Some painters transform the sun into a yellow spot, others transform a yellow spot into the sun." The difficulty in defining creativity for the creative individual is highlighted in the article "On My Painting" by Max Beckmann which accompanies the Leo Castelli case in this module.

Creativity has a flavor of something revolutionary or subversive. For example, Degas once said that a painter paints a picture with the same feeling as that with which a criminal commits a crime. Creativity is intimately linked to the idea of change. "Every act of creation is first of all an act of destruction," says Picasso. Interestingly, the economist Shumpeter also referred to entrepreneurship as "creative destruction."

A most useful definition of creativity comes from a recent literature on social psychology. According to Amabile,[2] a product or response will be judged creative to the extent that it is a novel and appropriate, useful, correct, or valuable response to the task at hand, and the task is *heuristic* rather than *algorithmic*.

Algorithmic tasks are those governed by fixed rules. The path to a solution is clear and straightforward. Broiling a steak and repairing a carburetor are governed by specific rules. Painting a picture and designing a new computer chip, on the other hand, are heuristic tasks. They have not been done before; the task is not specifically defined, there is no established path to a solution. The algorithm must be developed from scratch, which involves a new interplay among a person, a task, and a social environment.

What are the characteristics of creative people? Can everyone be creative? While most would agree that the creativity of Mozart or Einstein operated at a high level sometimes described as "genius," others would argue that creativity is at least latent in everyone. The psychologist Maslow[3] writes that there is a type of creativity which "is the universal heritage of every human being" and strongly associated with psychological health. He distinguishes between "special talent creativeness" such as the musical talent of a Mozart, and "self-actualizing creativeness" which he believed originated in the personality and was visible in the ordinary affairs of life.

Many attempts have been made to list the attributes of the creative person. In reviewing the literature, Roe[4] offers the following:

- openness to experience
- observance—seeing things in unusual ways

[2] Teresa Amabile, *The Social Psychology of Creativity* (New York: Springer Verlag, 1983).

[3] Abraham Maslow, *Creativity in Self-Actualizing People, Toward a Psychology of Being.* (New York: Van Nostrand Reinhold Company, 1968).

[4] A. Roe, "Psychological Approaches to Creativity in Science," *Essays on Creativity in the Sciences,* ed. M. A. Coler and H. K. Hughes (New York: New York University, 1963).

- curiosity
- accepting and reconciling apparent opposites
- tolerance of ambiguity
- independence in judgment, thought, and action
- needing and assuming autonomy
- self-reliance
- not being subject to group standards and control
- willingness to take calculated risks
- persistence

Raudsepp[5] adds further attributes:

- sensitivity to problems
- fluency—the ability to generate a large number of ideas
- flexibility
- originality
- responsiveness to feelings
- openness to unconscious phenomena
- motivation
- freedom from fear of failure
- the ability to concentrate
- thinking in images
- selectivity

Other definitions of creativity come from an eclectic tradition of research. For instance, it is associated with neuropsychological theories which show specialization in the two cerebral hemispheres of the brain.[6] The left side of the brain is said to stress logical, rational, and analytical modes of thinking, while the right side governs emotional and intuitive experience. It is not a major leap to conceive in metaphorical terms of our left hemispheres as "managerial" and our right as "entrepreneurial."

Integrating these predispositions appropriately then becomes the central challenge. Logic without passion is sterile, while inspiration without analysis is often arbitrary or misguided. The bureaucrat without the taste for change and innovation is as stuck as the entrepreneur with brilliant ideas but limited management skills. Rothenberg has coined the term "Janusian thinking"[7] to refer to the capacity for "conceiving and utilizing two or more opposite or contradictory ideas, concepts, or images simultaneously." Janusian is derived from Janus, the two-headed god looking simultaneously into the future and the past, the god of beginnings. The idea of integrating apparent opposites is also contained in the

5   E. Raudsepp, "Profile of the Creative Individual," *Creative Computing,* August 1983.
6   H. Mintzberg, "Planning on the Left Side and Managing on the Right," *Harvard Business Review,* July–August, 1976.
7   A. Rothenberg, *Janusian Thinking in the Creativity Questions,* A. Rothenberg and eds. (Chapel Hill: Duke University Press, 1976).

Figure 1-2 The Process Approach to Creativity

CREATIVITY STAGE	ACTIVITY	PSYCHOLOGICAL STYLE
Interest	environmental scanning	intuition/emotion
Preparation	preparing the expedition	details/planning
Incubation	"mulling things over"	intuition
Illumination	the "eureka" experience	intuition
Verification	market research	details/rationality
Exploitation	captain of industry	details/rationality

notion referred to by Peters and Waterman as "simultaneous loose-tight properties."[8] This involves a process of controlling and not controlling, for example managing certain organizational agendas tightly while creating slack around others so that new initiatives can emerge.

Other disciplines have also explored creativity. Because it involves an interplay between a person, a task, and an organizational context, creativity has been the subject of extensive psychological research. Wallas,[9] an early American psychologist, described several stages of the creative process. For him, creativity begins with *interest:* There has to be something inherently compelling about the problem. This is followed by the stage of *preparation,* when the ensuing intellectual journey is planned, much as one would pack supplies for a voyage. *Incubation* then follows as an intuitive, "back burner," nonintentional style of working on the problem. *Illumination*—the intuitive, synthetic "ah-ha" experience—follows.

Finally, the results must be *verified.* Are they arbitrary or capable of replication and understanding? Subsequently the stage of *exploitation* or capturing value from the creative act has been added to Wallas' model. Figure 1-2 illustrates this process approach to creativity.

A central theme of this book is demonstrating the strong linkages between creativity and entrepreneurship. An entrepreneur can be defined as someone who is responsive to opportunity and has a sense of freedom both in personal and in organizational terms to act on that opportunity. Entrepreneurship connotes implementation, *doing.* While creativity implies a vision of what is possible, the entrepreneur translates that creative vision into action, into a human vision which guides the work of a group of people. If the term "innovation" suggests the implementation process by which creative inspiration leads to practical results, then entrepreneurship is the human and organizational process by which innovation takes place. Figure 1-3 illustrates the link between creativity and entrepreneurship.

[8] Thomas Peters and Robert H. Waterman, Jr., *In Search of Excellence* (New York: Harper and Row, 1981).

[9] Graham Wallas, "Stages of Control," *The Art of Thought* (New York: Harcourt Brace Jovanovich, 1926).

Figure 1-3 Entrepreneurial Capacity

		High	Low
Creative Capacity	High	③ Lotus Lucasfilm	① Think Tank Artists Coop
	Low	② Fast Food Franchiser	④ Mature Bureaucracy

Thus, while the concepts of creativity and entrepreneurship are highly related and overlap, they are not identical. The capacity to develop new ideas, concepts, and processes is not the same as the capacity to make things happen, to implement in practical terms. In the diagram above, we have four categories of companies differentiated by creative and entrepreneurial capacity. Capacity in this sense refers to all investment in people, infrastructure, or intellectual assets. Category 1 companies are high in creative resources but low in entrepreneurial resources. These might be think tanks or artists' cooperatives which are in the business of generating creative ideas without the responsibility of having necessarily to *do* anything with them. Category 2 firms are low in creativity, but high in entrepreneurship. These are companies involved in existing businesses, for example franchising fast-food businesses in a relentless and opportunity-driven manner. Category 3 involves firms well endowed with both creative and entrepreneurial resources, for example Lotus Development Corporation and Lucasfilm, Ltd. Finally, Category 4 refers to companies high in neither creativity nor entrepreneurship, for example, mature bureaucracies like the postal service.

This matrix also relates to the predispositions of individuals. Some people may be good conceptualizers or artists, adept at generating new ideas but weak in the areas of implementation. Others are entrepreneurial but not particularly creative. Like the owner of 20 McDonald's franchises, they may be able to spot opportunity and act on it with zeal but not be concerned about generating new kinds of businesses. It is important to keep in mind that the entrepreneur is not necessarily creative, but is able to recognize and take advantage of the creativity of others. Some people may be capable of both creative and entrepreneurial work, while others may have talent for neither and are content instead to work in a well-defined environment according to rules established by others.

There is a final distinction which should be made between creativity and entrepreneurship. Creativity may or may not be externally focused on the environment. Most painters will do whatever is required to pursue a personal vision. The creative process is inner-directed. The notion of doing market research to validate a creative vision is often anathema to people on the creative side of a business. This issue emerges strongly in the cases on the videogame industry in this module. On the other hand, the entrepreneur must keep at least one eye sharply focused on the environment if business success is to be assured. Ultimately what the entrepreneur accomplishes must be validated by a response from the "real world."

Again, managing creativity is a process, combining issues of the creative person, task, and organizational context. One could make a comparison between creative efforts in the organization and the biological process of conception, gestation, and birth. The act of inspiration, the "ah-hah" experience, is only the beginning: the combining of disparate elements in an act of fertilization. Gestation then requires a healthy environment, necessary resources, support without undue interference, patience with a natural evolutionary process, tolerance of anxiety, and other feelings that result from the uncertainty of the process, change, and adaptation in the host to accommodate development. When the creative product/organism is "born," the parallels continue. Does it fit with expectations when it sees the light of day? Birth raises a number of "parenting" issues. Who is to be responsible? What models and values of parenting seem most appropriate? Birth has an important impact on the environment. The experience of successful birth can validate a system in important ways. Conversely, birth can also bring with it the prospect of complications. How does one deal with something which doesn't turn out as expected? How does one deal with the attendant guilt, anger, or denial? How does one deal with grief over a "business death" from such causes as bankruptcy or premature project termination? Psychology gives us some important guidelines for dealing with such losses in ways that can contribute to growth. While not fully applicable, biological images can be a useful descriptive model for the task of managing creativity.

Creativity comes with a price. The costs within a competitive industry of maintaining a creative atmosphere and of retaining key personnel can be high. Top managers are increasingly aware of the extent to which "climate" and "corporate culture" can translate into expensive, tangible investment. Yet, the costs of failing to foster creativity can be significantly higher. Well-positioned indeed is the organization that facilitates the progress of its creative members toward the next "1-2-3," the next biotechnology breakthrough, the next Pac Man videogame, the next Macintosh computer, the next "Star Wars" movie. Thus, managing creativity can be seen as an important strategic dimension for long-term planning and decision making.

MANAGING CREATIVITY— WHY IS IT IMPORTANT?

To speak of "managing creativity" may sound paradoxical or even frivolous; the search for creativity has often been linked to magic, the demonic, or the divine. How could such a process be *managed*? But creativity is a central preoccupation of many managers every day in many types of firms: a biotechnology company where 50 percent of the employees are scientists; a financial services company that is constantly innovating in service and marketing strategies; a consulting firm continuously striving to develop new analytical tools; a real estate developer who designs original financings for unique opportunities. For companies in these situations, managing creativity is of critical competitive importance. Lucasfilm, Ltd., and the firms described in the videogame industry cases are only as secure as their most recent successes. Their business strategy requires them to maintain a constant flow of creative output. "Create or die" might be their motto.

Yet what does *managing* creativity mean? According to popular definitions of these words, "creativity" springs from the most inner recesses of human vision, the most intimate reaches of human experience. Creativity is thought by many to be "inspired," its comings and goings unpredictable and highly idiosyncratic. "Management" seems opposed to creativity, suggesting a valuation of collective attitudes above personal vision. The pragmatic, rational, and judgmental style frequently associated with business management seems at the outset inhospitable to creative efforts and threatens to dilute them.

Furthermore, creativity is commonly attributed primarily to artistic endeavor and the expression of cultural talent. Artists are by definition creative, it is believed. Something about their talent is innate; they are born and not made. But it is a guiding assumption of this book that far from being germane only to the arts, creativity is a resource important for the basic institutions of society: industrial and business organizations; educational institutions; social and community agencies.

In fact, there is no such thing as creativity divorced from a particular human group, from a particular set of political constraints. Creativity for *whom* is as important as the value-laden issues raised by the question of creativity for *what*. Indeed, creativity is latent in most collective situations, and the extent to which it is fully expressed determines whether a group reaches the fulfillment of its goals. Creativity and organizational processes then must engage, must mesh, if social institutions are to be fully productive. Seen in this way, creativity is not something for special people in special situations, but belonging to everyone.

Why is attention to the management of creativity important? As mentioned earlier, creativity is a competitive issue, not just something nice. It is a valuable resource that must be nurtured, not wasted, given the significant costs associated with creative talent and infrastructure supportive of creative work. Finally, managing creativity may require an experimental attitude towards developing new types of organizations. Many entrepreneurial organizations, in a sense, are laboratories in which the organizational structures appropriate to future business challenges are currently under development. How such organizations treat the question of managing creativity will be of considerable importance for their continued survival. New challenges will be faced by such organizations: managing explosive growth; dealing with greater work force diversity; establishing a culture supportive of creative activity; maintaining fairness.

This concern with managing creativity also tells a demographic story. In the 1980s new entrants to the workplace come with an expectation of more creative and fulfilling work. This "corporate new wave"[10] is concerned with self-

[10] John Kao, "The Corporate New Wave" in "Entrepreneurship: What It Is and How to Teach It," John Kao and Howard Stevenson, eds., Division of Research, Harvard Business School, 1984.

actualization, and the demands for creative work are higher. The pace of technological change is also relevant. Creativity is an important plane of competition, particularly in what Porter calls emerging industries.[11] The explosion of creativity which surrounds emerging industries involves not only new technology, but business practices and strategy. It frequently gives rise to a variety of organizational experiments in how to maximize creativity. The cases describing the range of companies placing bets on creativity in the videogame industry provide a dramatic illustration of this point.

Creativity, however, preoccupies more than start-up organizations. It is at the heart of much work on industrial policy at state and regional levels; it is also a challenge to established business organizations. Many significant experiments managing creativity are being carried out at considerable expense of resources, for example, the approaches of 3M, Hewlett-Packard, and IBM towards fostering innovation in established organizations. Other examples include such innovative organizations as MCC (Microelectronics and Computer Consortium), a joint venture of leading semiconductor and computer companies aimed at pooling knowledge and resources in a new fashion.

Meanwhile, managing creativity has become a highly visible topic of public debate in other parts of the world. Nowhere is this more apparent than in Japan. The president of Fujitsu Computers, Tuma Yamamoto, recently said: "The creativity of the Japanese people will be called into question from the latter half of the 1980s through the 1990s. The whole nation must work like one possessed to meet this great challenge."[12] Japan's MITI (Ministry of International Trade and Industry), in a recent report called *Vision for the 1980's,* urged Japanese industry to make the transition from imitation to creativity. As part of addressing this challenge, Japan has recently embarked on an ambitious national effort called the Technopolis Strategy,[13] a program of developing high technology zones or miniature Silicon Valleys all over Japan. This involves a massive investment in constructing environments conducive to industrial creativity. Will creativity become an explicit plan of global industrial competition in the future? Will "creativity gaps" emerge in the industrial societies of the future?

MANAGING CREATIVITY—HOW DO YOU DO IT?

The very management of creativity is heuristic and hard to reduce to a fixed set of rules. Yet, the goal of this module will be to provide tools for managers to apply in dealing with creativity.

We may learn more about creativity in a particular organization by understanding what facilitates or blocks its expression. Common sense tells us that to hinder creative expression we should:

- emphasize bureaucratic structures and attitudes
- pile on tradition and established culture

[11] Michael Porter, *Competitive Strategy* (New York: Free Press, 1980).
[12] Sheridan Tatsuno, *The Technopolis Challenge* (New York: Prentice Hall Press, 1986).
[13] Ibid.

- stress the importance of standard operating procedures
- suppress suitable role models for creative expression
- minimize the availability of needed resources
- ensure poor communication which blocks the flow of ideas
- have tight control systems which eliminate slack required for unofficial initiatives
- enforce strict penalties for failure
- omit rewards for success
- emphasize values which inhibit risk taking and questioning
- reinforce the expectation of external evaluation
- carry out surveillance of creative activity
- emphasize tight deadlines
- prefer specialization; emphasize authority over responsibility

On the other hand, a number of organizational actions can enhance creativity:

- create an open, decentralized organizational structure
- support a culture which provides leverage for creative experimentation
- encourage experimental attitudes
- circulate success stories
- emphasize the role of the champion
- provide the freedom to fail
- stress effective communication at all levels
- make resources available for new initiatives
- ensure that new ideas cannot be easily killed
- remove bureaucracy from the resource allocation process
- provide appropriate financial and nonfinancial rewards for success
- ensure a corporate culture which supports risk taking and questioning
- minimize administrative interference
- provide freedom from surveillance and evaluation
- loosen deadlines
- delegate responsibility for initiating new activity

As mentioned earlier the manager must consider several elements to gain perspective on the challenge of fostering creativity, including those outlined in Figure 1-4. Each of these elements provides an entry point for managerial intervention.

The manager influences creative people by selecting them, initiating them into the organization, and providing for their development. Through the medium of personal relationships, creative people can be motivated, their agendas clarified and adjusted, their connections to the organization fostered. The manager must be an astute psychologist, attentive to communication at all levels, sensitive to needs.

In managing creative people, managers need to be aware of their sources of leverage. Are they dealing with a uniquely talented individual or is the person replaceable? If replaceable, how easily? To what extent does the creative individual perceive you, the manager, as credible in your personal style, track record, or

Figure 1-4 Fostering Creativity

Person	Appreciating the creative person's process and the manager-creative person relationship
Task	Defining the creative task without stifling creativity
Organizational Context	Creating/influencing the organization in terms of structure and culture to maximize the creative atmosphere
Environment	Recognizing creativity as a resource influenced by competitive factors

technical expertise? To what extent do you, as manager, control resources which the creative individual needs, whether in terms of technology, money, management expertise, marketing clout, company reputation, or brand name? How much cooperation from creative individuals can be garnered through such sources of leverage?

The manager influences the creative task by defining it, setting expectations, and by providing goals and objectives. *He or she frames the problem.* Despite the heuristic nature of the task, he or she is nevertheless able to provide a map of what needs to be done. Hence, managerial style is important. The manager must be willing to practice "loose-tight" management. An excessive amount of evalua tion or surveillance of creative work will place an inhibiting burden on it. Yet, the manager must work within the world of budgets, resource allocation procedures, deadlines, market demands, and competitive pressures. Thus, the manager of creativity must become an integrator[14] between the creative and business priorities of the organization. He or she must know when to melt into the background, and when to push; when to leave expectations ambiguous, and when to clarify them. These skills involve the development of sensibilities rather than the memorization of rules. This is why studying the examples of such masters of creativity management as Leo Castelli can be so instructive.

Finally, the manager influences the organizational context by a range of organizational tools and "design factors." These include organizational structure and culture, human resource practices, and leadership style.

How an organization is designed is important: Relevant issues include organizable structure and the attendant communications network; physical layout; and resulting patterns of human interaction. Organizational systems for functions, such as resource allocation and formal communication between organization levels, can either support or inhibit creativity. It is important to foster the development of a corporate culture supportive of creativity, the freedom to question, and the freedom to fail. Many experiments in organization design have attempted to maintain the flavor of a creative "hot shop" within an established organization. In a sense, this means creating an officially sanctioned countercul-

---

[14] Paul Lawrence and Jay Lorsch, *Organization and Environment* (Boston, Mass.: Harvard Business School Press, 1986).

ture or a company within a company. Examples include the creation of the Convergent Technologies' laptop computer, and the design of the personal computer by IBM's entry systems group. At other times, creativity is maintained by delegating design tasks to outside firms. Apple, for example, delegated the design of the "mouse" for its Macintosh computer.[15]

Much managers' leverage in fostering creative efforts rests with the human resource management agenda. Seen in managerial terms, creative people are an important company asset: the "process" by which a creative "product" is developed or a creative "service" rendered. Managing this human process for maximum effect is vital. Reward systems are critical both in monetary and nonmonetary terms. "Signing the painting" is an important source of reward. For example, the Macintosh design team was permitted to sign their names inside the injection molded case of the computer.[16] Recognition programs are also important as with the IBM Fellows Program. Other areas for HRM intervention include evaluation and career development, perception of employee influence, participation in decision making, human resource planning, and job design. The theme of human resource management is carried forward in cases of other modules, including Lotus Development Corporation and American Express.

Another set of people-related issues involves dealing with creative talent. How should "mavericks" and "stars" be treated? How can creative success and failure be dealt with? The role of the "special person" must be clarified. While creativity may not be an outcome of democratic consensus, it is important that perceived fairness be maintained or that trade-offs around special treatment for some members of the organization be explicitly recognized.

In looking at creative people themselves, whether they be scientists, artists, engineers, or computer programmers, the manager is faced with a series of basic questions. What do they need to be most creative? How many of such people are needed, and how much will they cost the organization? How do you design jobs which will take best advantage of people's creative talents? What kind of leadership styles and role models best support an organization's creative needs? How much managerial latitude is provided in terms of the freedom to fail and/or to question? There are questions of what style seems appropriate to a given situation and set of needs. Many potential sources of conflict between managers and creative people exist stemming from the need for evaluation, resource allocation, planning, rewards, and standards of comparison. Classic situations include account executives and creative designers in advertising, scientists and marketing managers in biotechnology. Assumptions, perceptions, and feelings can easily become polarized. Which managerial interventions seem to work best? How far should management go to accommodate creative people? In this regard, Michael Eisner, president of Walt Disney, has remarked that "the only people I let roll around the floor having a tantrum are my three-year-olds."

---

[15] Michael Rogers, "Silicon Valley's Newest Wizards," *Newsweek,* January 5, 1987, p. 36.
[16] *In Search of Excellence: The Video,* produced by Nathan Tyler Productions, Waltham, Mass., 1985.

Managerial responsibilities are diverse in a creative organization. They include:

- creating and sharing a vision
- communicating clearly and flexibly
- providing interpersonal support
- cheerleading and coaching
- praising accomplishments—providing applause
- honoring failures
- using conflict resolution skills
- knowing when to open the process up and when to close it down
- balancing originality with resource constraints
- balancing vision with attention to detail

The manager orchestrates the creative process by organizing the flow of communication and human interaction around it. For example, the manager may wish to make use of creativity techniques which enhance creativity and allow it to emerge. Osborne[17] pioneered the technique of brainstorming, letting ideas emerge without substantial editing. Synectics[18] is a process of creative problem solving through attention to group process. De Bono[19] has developed the notion of lateral thinking as an anchor for training systems designed to foster creative thinking.

The manager must also be alert to questions of how the climate for creativity changes as an organization matures. How can it maintain creative excitement and productivity at later stages in its "life cycle"? What differences exist in managing creativity in the embryonic as opposed to the mature organization? What types of people are needed at what organizational stage? Can creativity be institutionalized? This issue of managing change is addressed through such cases as the Videogame Industry, Integrated Genetics, and Lotus Development Corporation.

Managing creativity in organizations brings a number of classic dilemmas and tradeoffs. Can you have creativity on demand? How do you balance the need for freedom in an organization with the need for structure? How can you balance the creative person's desire for unlimited development time with the manager's desire for deadlines? How can you reconcile the creative need for participation and informal communication with the management need for hierarchy and structured authority in more complex kinds of organizations? What kinds of systems for planning, resource allocation, and information flow are useful? If predictable conflicts arise between the managerial and creative sides of an organization, how can they best be managed? To what extent is there value for the organization in such conflicts?

[17] Alex F. Osborne, *Applied Imagination: Principles and Procedures of Creative Problem Solving* (New York: Scribner's Sons, 1979).

[18] George Prince, *The Practiced Creativity* (New York: MacMillan, 1970).

[19] Edward De Bono, *Lateral Thinking* (New York: Harper and Row, 1970).

THE CASES

Leo Castelli

This case permits a deeper exploration of creativity in terms of the relationship between creator and manager. Leo Castelli is the preeminent New York art dealer who has nurtured the careers of such modern artists as Jasper Johns, Roy Lichtenstein, Robert Rauschenberg, and Frank Stella. The case explores Castelli's development as an entrepreneur and catalyst, examines his personal style, and suggests a framework for looking at the creative process from the managerial perspective. The accompanying reading, "On My Painting" by Max Beckmann, introduces and allows an assessment of the world of the creative artist.

The Videogame Industry and The Videogame Design Process

These cases look at the specific issue of managing videogame designers within the broader contours of an emerging industry. They have general applicability since the explosive growth of the entertainment software industry shared characterics with the development of the television and automobile industries. The case on the videogame design process presents various approaches to managing creativity, some often contradictory. It allows for discussion of how a particular approach is shaped by specific organizational culture and strategy. Students consider such questions as: How does a firm establish and defend a guiding emphasis on creative quality? What are the appropriate incentives to sustain this focus? What happens to creativity in a volatile industry which suddenly experiences rapid decline?

George Lucas and Skywalking

This case presents an individual who has experienced exceptional success in turning his creative vision into a successful organization, Lucasfilm Ltd., to implement this vision. The company possesses both entrepreneurial and creative features, and appears skilled at dealing with ambiguity and human behavior. Analysis provides an opportunity to look at one person's concept of creativity and how this definition is translated into a company culture and operating system. In addition, individual and organizational issues are related to the question: What does this type of company have to do to manage the creative process successfully?

FOR FURTHER READING

ADAMS, JAMES, *Conceptual Blockbusting*. New York: W. W. Norton and Company, 1974.

AMABILE, TERESA, *The Social Psychology of Creativity*. New York: Springer-Verlag, 1983.

DE BONO, EDWARD, *Lateral Thinking*. New York: Harper and Row, 1970.

HERBERT, ROBERT ed., *Modern Artists on Art*. Englewood Cliffs, N.J.: Prentice-Hall, Inc., 1964.

JOHN-STEINER, VERA, *Notebooks of the Mind*. Albuquerque: University of Mexico Press, 1985.

KAO, JOHN, *Taking Stock of Creative Resources*. Working Paper 83-80, Division of Research, Harvard Business School, 1983.

KAO, JOHN, The Corporate New Wave, in *Entrepreneurship: What It Is and How to Teach It*, John Kao and Howard Stevenson, eds., Division of Research, Harvard Business School, 1984.

KIDDER, TRACY, *The Soul of a New Machine*. Boston: Little, Brown, 1981.

MAY, ROLLO, *The Courage to Create*. New York: W. W. Norton and Company, 1975.

PERKINS, DAVID, *The Mind's Best Work*. Cambridge: Harvard University Press, 1981.

POLLACK, DALE, *Skywalking*. New York: Harmony Books, 1983.

PRINCE, GEORGE, "Synectics," from Olsen, Shirley ed., *Group Planning and Problem-Solving Methods in Engineering*. New York: John Wiley & Sons, Inc., 1982.

RAUDSEPP, EUGENE, *How to Create New Ideas*. Englewood Cliffs, N.J.: Prentice-Hall, Inc., 1982.

RAY, MICHAEL, *Creativity in Business*. New York: Doubleday, 1986.

ROTHENBERG, ALBERT and HAUSMAN, CARL, *The Creativity Question*. Chapel Hill: Duke University Press, 1976.

Leo Castelli

Ask the international art community to name the single most important figure in the world of contemporary art and the overwhelming favorite would not be a painter, sculptor, critic, or collector. The likely choice would be New York art dealer Leo Castelli. His Castelli Gallery, founded in 1957, represented artists such as Jasper Johns, Robert Rauschenberg, Frank Stella, Roy Lichtenstein, Claes Oldenburg, James Rosenquist, Robert Norris, Ellsworth Kelly, Kenneth Noland, Cy Twombly, Donald Judd, Dan Flavin, Bruce Nauman, Richard Serra, and Andy Warhol, many of whom were not only successful proponents of their period, but also creators of an entirely new art movement (see *Exhibit 1*). Their contributions helped make New York the center of the art world. Leading them was the European-born Castelli, 50 years old at the gallery's inception.

Equally impressive was the longevity of Castelli's success and partnership with his artists. He remarked:

> Some other dealers have had a better eye or sense of discovery; yet they have failed while I have succeeded. I do attribute this in part to my background. To me, a business has to be treated with a certain seriousness. You can't live in a cloud and think that things will take care of themselves. The new, successful dealers understand this. They also seem to have an incredible talent for public relations.

Many of his artists no longer need an agent to sell their work; they are famous and in great demand. Yet they continue to sell work through Castelli Gallery, giving up some of their profit. What has Castelli done to inspire this uncommon loyalty? What must be done to manage successfully this creative process?

THE ART BUSINESS

While art may be plentiful, good art is rare; while beauty may be in the eye of the beholder, many mistrust their own eyes. Hence, for hundreds of years art

This case was prepared by Associate Professor John Kao, Research Associate Lee Field, and Terence Eagleton.
Copyright © 1986 by the President and Fellows of Harvard College, Harvard Business School case 9-486-071.

buyers have relied on experts to judge what was "good." Traditionally, these experts have been dealers and critics. With the increasing number and power of museums in the twentieth century, museum curators have been added to that list.

Once an expert labeled an artist or a group of artists and their works gifted, the market of supply and demand took over. The number of works an artist could produce in a lifetime was finite; the number of collectors who might desire one of those works was potentially much greater.

In the 1960s and 1970s, as wealth and inflation both increased, prices of old masters paintings skyrocketed, which created interest from a new segment of buyers—those seeking a good investment. This buyer relied to an even greater extent on experts. Further, rising prices of old masters spilled over to contemporary (living) artists. Would one of them someday be labeled a master? And who would first discover and aid the new talents and make them known to critics, curators, and collectors? Dealers.

The Dealers' Role

Art dealers have bridged the gap between artists and buyers. Ideally they make it easier for artists to produce their work by separating the business aspects of making a living from making art, thus freeing the artist to do more creative work. The association from the artist's viewpoint, however, has often been unpleasant. Marcel Duchamp, the French Surrealist, referred to dealers as "lice on the backs of artists—useful, but lice all the same." This characterization echoed the sentiments of many generations of artists who felt used or even abused by dealers. In fact, with some noteworthy exceptions such as Rembrandt, only recently (in this century) have artists actually made substantial amounts of money. Recently, the notion of "artists contracts" has been addressed as a mechanism whereby artists would share in profits from resale of their work as well as maintaining certain rights to it.

The basic strategy a dealer follows is to find an unknown artist or group of artists and make a market for him, her, or them. With success, the dealer then can attract new artists of increasingly high quality. At the same time, buyers will become interested in the other artists the dealer represents because the ability to judge good works has been proven.

Dealers provide several services. First, they set up shows for individual artists, averaging perhaps one show a month. Second, dealers obtain exclusive agreements with their artists or with a "stable" of artists. Commissions are usually 50-50, 60-40 (artist/dealer), or on occasion some other arrangement. A monthly allowance for the artist in the range of $1,000–$5,000 (or by negotiation) is not uncommon and is drawn against proceeds from sales. Third, the dealer publicizes the artist by finding buyers, soliciting museum acquisitions, and by ensuring reviews from appropriate critics and media. Finally, the dealer adds value to the buyer by providing him or her with art that appreciates in value and has investment qualities.

From the dealer's perspective, the relationship with the artist is important as well: Referrals to new artists often come through the artists whom he or she represents. The number of artists who have either shown in a gallery and/or were represented by a dealer grew from a few hundred in 1960 to almost 24,000 in 1985. The number of art galleries in New York City alone rose from a handful in the 1950s, to 450 by 1970, to over 650 in 1985.

The Price of Art

Overall, the price of art has risen dramatically in recent years. Alfred Taubman, chairman of the auction house of Sotheby, Parke Bernet, estimated that the total 1985 worldwide market sales of art and collectibles approached $25 billion. Resale prices of individual pieces indicate the trend. One early collector, for example, purchased a Jasper Johns' painting for $900; less than a decade later he had resold it at auction for $90,000. Records are constantly broken, a vivid example being the May 30, 1987, auction at Christie's in London, during which Van Gogh's "Sunflowers" fetched an astonishing $39.9 million, *triple* the price ever paid for a work of art at auction.

Prices vary for a new work, but a 20″ × 24″ painting by an unknown artist might sell in the $500–$1,800 range. If the artist has a successful first show, the price will rise by 20% and fluctuate with demand. If the demand exists, the artist's 2′ × 3′ canvas will rise to $10,000 in a few years, and after five or six shows to $20,000. The time needed to achieve a $20,000 price is a reflection of the dealer's judgment about how much exposure the artist can bear and how quickly, without saturating the market.

But as the prices of art have risen, the pool of interested buyers has also broadened. According to *The Wall Street Journal:*

> Art collecting has become a respectable, even trendy activity for rich American businessmen. Many have found that, apart from the investment value, buying a famous painting at auction can bring them a good deal of publicity. In addition, cheap dollars have made art increasingly attractive among European and, more prominently, Japanese collectors.[1]

Nonetheless, skyrocketing prices have brought concern that this burgeoning market will bottom out. Opinion is divided, as Klaus Perls, a New York dealer, notes:

> Anybody who says it [the art market] can't collapse wasn't there in 1930 to 1933. You couldn't sell anything. [Today] is a fantasy world like 1929, when people didn't want to believe that another group of suckers wasn't going to bail them out tomorrow. I think it can crash completely from here, or go sky high. It's anybody's guess.[2]

[1] *The Wall Street Journal,* May 19, 1987.
[2] Ibid.

CASTELLI BEFORE THE GALLERY

Born in 1907 in Trieste (part of the Austro-Hungarian Empire until ceded to Italy in 1919), Leo Castelli was from a privileged and cosmopolitan family. (See *Exhibit 2* for a time line.) His father rose in business to become the chief executive of a leading Italian bank. Moves to Austria and back led to a succession of larger villas and greater family comfort. The middle child (with a younger brother Giorgio and an older sister Silvia), Castelli remembered "lots of pretty girls, tennis, swimming, and things like that." Schooled in Austria, he developed a great fondness for literature, especially German, and sports. When not reading current novels (in English, French, German, and Italian, his first language), he was skiing in the Alps or mountain climbing in the Dolomites. He said: "I worried about being small, especially when I was younger. Therefore, I indulged in sports. I wanted to be, if small, strong. It has obviously played an important role in my life."

After four years at the University of Milan, Castelli graduated with a law degree in 1924 "without great enthusiasm. I was really more interested in literary cultural pursuits." Not wishing to practice law, he accepted a job with an insurance company in 1931. He recalled the circumstances of his employment.

> My father had a great deal of local influence, directorships and so on. I was totally reluctant. But my father's friends were very lenient and did not ask me to do anything. It was a bad situation. After a year I wanted to leave . . . go abroad and study comparative literature. My father said he would support me if I would first try business abroad. He arranged a job for me with the same insurance company, but in Bucharest. I agreed . . . went to Bucharest . . . still disliked my job intensely but got involved with a group of amusing people. I found the social situation very lively.

It was in Bucharest that Castelli met Ileana Shapira, daughter of a very wealthy Rumanian industrialist. They were married in 1933. After marrying, Castelli traded jobs—insurance for banking—and in 1935 moved to Paris, aided by his father-in-law. He recalled, "We had more than a comfortable life . . . and banking somewhat interested me, as it related to art and literature. As a young idealist, I did not really want to work. But from my father I did absorb what for him was a puritan work ethic and for me, an interest in economics."

Paris was exciting for the Castellis, . . . ("great parties . . . interesting people"). One new friend was René Drouin, an interior and Art Deco furniture designer whose wife was from Bucharest. In 1939 Drouin persuaded Castelli to become his partner in a gallery that would show furniture, objets d'art, and paintings. The financing came from Castelli's father-in-law. The Galerie René Drouin occupied an elegant space on the Place Vendôme, sharing a garden with the Hotel Ritz, next door to the fashion house of Schiaparelli. Castelli recalled, "I started this business without any idea of what I was doing. I did, however, have a certain feeling for bizarre objects, serendipitous things." Ileana was the Castelli who had spent the most time in museums. But her husband did know Leonor Fini of Trieste, a member of the Paris Surrealist group that also included Max Ernst, Pavel Tchelitchew, and Salvador Dali.

The opening exhibition was dominated by Fini and the Surrealists. In fact, no paintings were even shown. It was all fantasy objects, armoires with wings, mirrors with hair carved in wood, unusual sculpture. Castelli remembered, "Le tout Paris came . . . very chic. Thank God the war came before I turned into God knows what."

When the war broke out, the Castellis moved to the Shapira summer villa in Cannes. After France fell, the family (which now included three-year-old Nina) fled to escape Nazi persecutions of Jews. They migrated to the United States by way of Algeria, Morocco, and Spain, arriving in New York in March 1941. Shapira, already in New York, set them up in an apartment on Fifth Avenue until the townhouse he had purchased at 4 East 77th Street was remodeled for his family. The Castellis occupied the fourth floor.

In the meantime, wanting to do something both practical and intellectual, Castelli entered Columbia University and studied for a graduate degree in economic history. He joined the Army in 1943, gained U.S. citizenship in 1944, and was sent to Bucharest as an interpreter for the Allied Control Commission. While there, he located his sister Silvia and found out that his parents had died for lack of proper medical attention during the war. The news hit hard. He had lost touch with his family during the war. Ileana recalled: "Leo admired his father tremendously. Ernesto had a high position, was kind to and loved by everyone. He was an ideal for Leo."

On leave in Paris in 1945, Castelli discovered that the Galerie René Drouin was still open and showing a group of new artists—Kandinsky, Dubuffet, de Stael, Mondrian, Pevsner—but no one was buying art then. When he returned to the United States in 1946, he went back to Columbia University but did not finish the economics degree. Again, his father-in-law set him up in business—this time in a sweater factory—but as he recalled, "The only useful thing I did, when I was occasionally there, was fold sweaters during a rush."

After the war, however, Castelli did not want to depend on his father-in-law and the remains of the once-great Shapira fortune. He began to act as an agent in New York for Drouin's gallery and others. He would receive rolled-up Kandinsky paintings from the artist's widow and usually sell them to the Baroness Hilla Rebay, director of the Guggenheim Museum.

On a trip to France to sell the Shapira villa in Cannes, Castelli decided to end his partnership with Drouin. Because his father-in-law had put up the money for the gallery, Drouin split with Castelli some of the gallery's inventory—a Léger, three Dubuffets, a Kandinsky, and a Pevsner. Today, these works are worth many millions; unfortunately, not all are in Castelli's possession.

NEW YORK ART SCENE
AND THE CASTELLI GALLERY

When Castelli arrived in New York, his Paris reputation—news of his gallery (albeit short-lived) and his first show—had preceded him. Thus introduced, he quickly became involved with the very small New York art world. Castelli described the situation:

> I had a great enthusiasm for art. It was like a religious experience, not mystical at all, but once I got involved it became an important cause. Artists and writers had always been my heroes. The intellectual exercise of their work, not unlike great generals or statesmen, excited me. I liked getting to know these important people. They were my friends and I believed in them.

Jackson Pollock, Willem de Kooning, Franz Kline, Mark Rothko, Robert Motherwell—second-generation Abstract Expressionists—were all befriended by the Castellis. Parties at the Castelli home, gatherings at The Club (a bar/hangout on East Eighth Street in Greenwich Village), and summers in the Hamptons (the de Koonings stayed with the Castellis one whole summer) solidified their relationships. Castelli also developed friendships with important dealers/collectors such as Julian Levy, Peggy Guggenheim, and Sidney Janis, the art scholar turned dealer. With Janis, he organized his first New York show in 1950, a comparison of French and American artists. He also spent much time at the Museum of Modern Art (MOMA), furthering his education.

This relationship with the art community led Castelli to help with a show, held in 1951 in Greenwich Village on Ninth Street. He spent $600 to produce an advertising flyer and to buy white paint to clean up the building (even today he continues to give each of his exhibitions a "fresh start" by applying a coat of white paint to gallery walls before the opening of a new show. He is given credit by many for inaugurating this custom. The show included all the local artists, famous and unknown, and was a rousing success. Alfred Barr, the renowned curator of the Museum of Modern Art, and other major figures were impressed not only with the breadth and quality of the art shown but also with the efforts of the organizers, mainly Castelli.

About this time some of Castelli's friends encouraged, virtually demanded, that he become a dealer. But he was reluctant. He recalled, "Besides the fact that I considered it ungentlemanly, I didn't have the courage to become a dealer at that time." He did, however, continue to trade pictures on a small scale, which provided a moderate income and kept him involved in the art world. Much of this was done with Janis, who with Castelli's encouragement began showing the most important European artists and later the American Abstract Expressionists. This pairing brought visibility and new credibility to the Americans and helped escalate prices of their work. Castelli was satisfied with the arrangement, which provided him with a modest income and Janis' MOMA connections and knowledge. There was even talk of a partnership.

By 1955, however, the relationship had changed. Working as an agent for Janis, Castelli would scout art works and potential clients. When he brought in a picture and Janis sold it, Janis would take 10 percent as a commission. In the mid-1950s, Castelli brought in a Klee that was sent out to a client who already had on consignment another Klee from the Janis gallery. The client purchased Castelli's Klee and returned the other to Janis. Janis felt he had lost out on a sale because of Castelli's painting and took an additional 10 percent commission (charging a total of 20 percent of the sales price) from Castelli as compensation for the foregone sale. This was an arbitrary action, done without Castelli's approval or consent. When Castelli questioned him on this, Janis replied that he had lost a Klee sale of his own because the client wanted Castelli's painting instead; therefore, he lost out on 10 percent. It was not the idea or the reasoning that upset Castelli, but the fact that Janis had done it without consulting him. It was also difficult to accept what amounted to a 100 percent increase in the service charge. Castelli did not like terms and conditions arbitrarily dictated by someone else. Also at this same time, partnership talk ceased because Janis decided to keep the business in the family, saving it for his sons. Castelli stated:

> Since this thing with Janis couldn't go on, I lost my security. I had to do something to earn a living [Castelli was no longer connected with the textiles business] and stay in touch with the art community. Also, the environment was changing quickly. Prices were going up, to the point where I could not afford to buy. I *had* to become a dealer. It was the only way to stay in touch. Yes, it was a bit distasteful and I was apprehensive, but not because I was worried about the financial risk. I had no money to lose. My fear of failure was associated with feelings and pride. But I challenged this fear by doing it.

In matters pertaining to his career, Castelli was an empiricist. He stated, "If you examine my career over 30 years, you would find everything that I have done has been extremely tentative and has depended largely on whatever circumstances I was surrounded by and good or bad decisions that I made." For example, even though the decision was made in 1955, Castelli did not open his gallery until 1957 at the age of 50. Unsure how to begin, he went to Europe to explore the climate there and sell a few paintings to raise capital. He was certain about two things, however. He did not want to represent artists from an earlier period. While the Abstract Expressionists were his friends, they were all connected to other galleries and he did not relish the idea of raiding. He would give them shows, but he wanted to embrace new horizons, new trends. Having always been interested in the importance of art history, Castelli saw this possibility as a way to make his own impression on history and thus become an equal of his heroes.

He also decided to incur as little initial overhead as possible. Therefore, the first Castelli Gallery was located in his apartment on 77th Street. On February 1, 1957, the Castellis had their first show, a comparison of well-known European and American artists. Some works were borrowed, but most were from their own collection. Some of the pieces from the Castelli collection were from the group he received from Drouin when they split up the gallery inventory.

Johns and Rauschenberg

Of all the artists Castelli came to represent, two names stood out: Jasper Johns and Robert Rauschenberg. Castelli first saw Rauschenberg's work in the Ninth Street show in 1951, but had been most impressed with Rauschenberg's 1954 "Red Show," which Castelli referred to as an "epiphany." Castelli's other memorable event was the first time he saw a Jasper Johns painting. Ileana is quoted as saying that Castelli was so awestruck after returning from a show where a Johns painting was exhibited that he sat and talked about it for hours. He knew he had found something very different (*Exhibit 3*).

He was at Rauschenberg's apartment looking at paintings when he discovered that Johns lived downstairs. Castelli was so excited that he asked Rauschenberg to introduce him. The next moment Castelli was in Johns' studio, amazed by a room full of wonderful works. On the spot he offered to represent Johns, who accepted. Johns' first show, in January 1958, was the sensation of the art world and sold out quickly. Rauschenberg's first show with Castelli, however, was a flop. But Castelli supported Rauschenberg's cause and stuck with him. This vote of confidence was vindicated in 1964, when Rauschenberg won the International Grand Prize for Painting at the Venice Biennale, the first time in its history that an American had won. This enhanced not only Rauschenberg's international reputation but the price of his paintings.

MANAGING RELATIONSHIPS

"Each one of my relationships with artists is different and individual, just like the artists' personalities," Castelli remarked during an interview. This statement was clearly demonstrated during the next few minutes as he answered phone calls. Besides the many languages he used, Castelli used a distinctly different tone and style with each call to an artist. One conversation was bubbly and carefree; another was stern and fatherly.

Castelli also pointed out that the business was much different in 1986 from the 1950s. "Back then it was a shoestring corner store operation. Now, it's a supermarket." Castelli was probably the first dealer to put his artists on a monthly salary or stipend. "I tried to give them not only confidence, enthusiasm, and moral support, but also eliminate the worry of paying the rent."

> When I see something of Jasper Johns, for example, that I particularly find impressive, I go off the deep end . . . but then his new paintings are sometimes very, very difficult to accept . . . the fullness is marvelous, but you then don't

know what the content is. Jasper came out with what was certainly at [one] time really bizarre: he introduced out of the blue that cross-hatch motif. Everybody asked themselves "what the heck is that?" I just stood there and said, well let's hope for the best.

What happened is that a great collector came in, saw the painting and says "wonderful, how much is it? I'll buy it." This was Johns' first vote of confidence for the crosshatch . . . There is always somebody who comes to the rescue, some incredibly enthusiastic collector who has been waiting for a Jasper Johns painting for the past years and never got one. Then, a painting comes along which I consider really difficult or bizarre, and the collector comes in and sees it and says can I have it!

Regarding his relationships with collectors, Castelli remarked:

I have never picked up the phone and said, "Look, I have this special painting here now and I think you should buy it." I have never solicited the collectors. They have learned to be after me; some phone every day. Perhaps I would have done better if I had cultivated them, but I trust them to trust my good taste and support my artists' work.

Castelli had turned the tables: collectors came to him, not vice versa.

In addition, Castelli recognized early on the importance of creating a network of dealers throughout the United States to provide a broader audience for his artists. He commented: "It was financially better to sell for less profit than to have the art lying around unsold in New York. The art needed to be spread around, and every means was good. If I am guilty of propaganda, so were the apostles."

Values

Susan Brundage, who started working at the gallery in 1972 and whom Castelli called "my right hand" (see *Exhibit 4*) had this to say about Castelli Gallery and her boss:

This place is like a little museum. It records, preserves, and disseminates information and has continuous exhibitions. Many people pass through these doors every day. We are beset by more requests than we can accommodate because we have important artists from all the important periods of the last 25 years.

The gallery is certainly well organized and runs like an official business. Leo delegates a lot of authority; everyone has his or her specific tasks and responsibilities—it's very democratic. I'm accessible as the practical person, I'm sort of the resident complaint department. If [artists] want something, they can ask me; if they don't like the way things are going, they can also call and complain. They know if they talk to me, whatever they say or want will get back to Leo. I'm an expediter: I make their requests heard and they get done. Leo is always open to new or differing opinions and viewpoints.

Leo has never compromised on doing things for or spending money on his artists. He is generous to the maximum. This is one of the reasons why the artists respect him and have stayed with him. Leo also has great faith in his artists and their ability to create and will help them do whatever they want. Loyalty is very important to him. He always comes through and does what he says he will do. Therefore, the artists have confidence in him. Leo is also uncritical. He sees his role as the ultimate, unquestioning supporter or patron.

He has even commissioned public works by his own artists. Many times he might like to say "no," but he doesn't. And the smart people know to go to Leo if we have been firm on a price or have said no to a request. He enjoys being the person to say "yes." It's not that his is the ultimate veto; it's more like the ultimate give-in. Because of his personality, Leo is never sorry that he made something possible or gave somebody money or said yes. He has created close bonds with the artists. It's a very familial relationship.

It is very important, of course, to be able to sell the work. In this respect, Leo sees that it is his job to get the art out into the world, to place it with good collectors and museums. Some galleries might make more money, but none places more contemporary art.

I think one reason for the success of this gallery, besides the fact that we have very important artists, is that Leo made the gallery itself important and the center of a lot of activity. The gallery is the focus; not just a few artists. Castelli Gallery is high-profile and people are attracted to it. You can see this as a problem with some of the new galleries that are low-profile and with just a few major names. If they lose that name artist, they're in trouble. Therefore, you work at promoting yourself—your gallery—which differentiates you from the competition. The artists also enjoy the prestige associated with the gallery name. Leo does an interview at least once, sometimes twice a day. He makes himself and the gallery very accessible to the media. Castelli Gallery has cultivated an important image through Leo, and vice versa. He is as famous as his artists. The gallery is an embodiment of him, and I don't think he has any intention of its continuing after he is gone. I certainly don't expect it to.

Another reason for Leo's success goes back to his placement of priorities. He is more interested that the art gets sold and placed with good collectors than in squeezing the last ounce of profit out of a sale. [Unlike some dealers who use their galleries as a culling tool for their own collections, Leo did not keep the best paintings for himself. He has also passed up opportunities to buy back works of his artists and to make a quick profit.] I've often seen him take less on a sale if it meant a better placement. And rather than diminish the artist's profit, he deducts the discount from his commission. Most artists know this and appreciate it. [Jasper Johns gave Leo's son a very valuable drawing for his twenty-first birthday. Another artist once gave Leo a Maserati he had won.] Similarly, he has consistently maintained good relationships with his network of dealers in other regions by providing them with quality work, work that could easily have been sold here, which also reduced his profit.

Exhibit 1 Leo Castelli 25th Anniversary lunch, February 1, 1982, The Odeon, New York. *Standing left-right:* Ellsworth Kelly, Dan Flavin, Joseph Kosuth, Richard Serra, Lawrence Weiner, Nassos Daphnis, Jasper Johns, Claes Oldenburg, Salvatore Scarpitta, Richard Artschwager, Mia Westerlund Roosen, Cletus Johnson, Keith Sonnier. *Seated left-right:* Andy Warhol, Robert Rauschenberg, Leo Castelli, Ed Ruscha, James Rosenquist, Robert Barry. (Source: *Gentle Snapshots*, Bischofberger, Zürich, Switzerland. Reprinted with permission.)

Exhibit 2 Leo Castelli *Time Line*

Birth	1907
Earns law degree	1924
Joins insurance firm	1931
Moves to Bucharest	1932
Marries Ileana Shapira	1933
Moves to Paris	1935
Forms Drouin Galerie	1939
Moves to New York	1941
Joins U.S. Army	1943
Gains U.S. citizenship	1944
Father dies	WWII
Organizes Ninth Street show	1951
Decides to become a dealer	1955
Opens Castelli Gallery	1957
First Jasper Johns show	1958
Makes history at Venice Biennale	1964
Receives New York City Mayor's Award of Honor	1977
Celebrates 25th anniversary of gallery	1982

Exhibit 3

At home with Jasper Johns' "Fool's House", 1975. (*Jill Krementz*) (Source: *Gentle Snapshots*, Bischofberger. Zürich, Switzerland. Reprinted with permission.)

Exhibit 4 Staff of the Leo Castelli Gallery, March 1982. *Standing front row left-right:* Betsy Cahen, Mimi Thompson, Debbie Taylor, Patty Brundage, Michelle Dreyfuss, Mame Kennedy. *Back row left-right:* Susan Brundage, Terry Wilson, John Good, Tom Pelham. (*Glenn Steigelman*) (Source: *Gentle Snapshots*, Bischofberger. Zürich, Switzerland. Reprinted with permission.)

The Videogame Industry

The videogame, a curiosity that first appeared commercially in 1970, spawned an industry whose 1983 revenues of $10 billion were greater than the record and motion-picture industries combined. Videogames have elicited reactions ranging from interest in their potential educational and medical applications to worry about their contribution to delinquency and moral decay. One view on the industry was expressed by Ronald Reagan in March 1983 in a speech at Walt Disney's EPCOT (Experimental Community of Tomorrow) Center.

> Many young people have developed incredible hand, eye, and brain coordination in playing these games. The Air Force believes these kids will be outstanding pilots should they fly our jets. The computerized radar screen in the cockpit is not unlike the computerized video screen. Watch a 12-year-old take evasive action and score multiple hits while playing Space Invaders, and you will appreciate the skills of tomorrow's pilot.[1]

WHAT IS A VIDEOGAME?

The videogame married two key pieces of modern hardware: the computer and the TV set. The videogame industry included several distinct businesses covering both hardware and software applications.

Videogame Hardware

There were three basic types of hardware. The first was dedicated game-playing equipment designed for public places or specialized facilities such as restaurants or arcades. These machines carried retail prices of about $2,000 to $3,000 and were typically owned and operated by specialized distributors who divided game profits with the proprietors of specific locations. A second type of hardware was for home use, such as the Atari (VCS) or Mattel (Intellivision) game consoles. Third, nondedicated hardware,

This case was prepared by Associate Professor John Kao.
Copyright © 1985 by the President and Fellows of Harvard College. Harvard Business School case 9-486-011.

including mainframe and personal computers, could be programmed for videogames.

The following describes the "anatomy of a videogame":

What goes on inside a Pac Man arcade game—or any video arcade game, for that matter—that manages to turn a color video screen into an addictive adventure?

Perhaps not surprisingly, the inside of an arcade game, with its single main logic board bearing dozens of circuit chips, resembles the electronic section of a personal computer. In fact, the Z-80a microprocessor chip that operates the game is used as a central processor by Radio Shack, Sinclair, and numerous small-business microcomputer systems. Unlike a general-purpose computer, which has the flexibility to execute a wide variety of tasks depending on what programs are loaded into it, an arcade game's computer is a dedicated system. Serving as a responsive intermediary between humans and video screen is its only duty. Freed from the necessity of dealing with data from a keyboard, human-oriented languages, mass-storage devices such as disk drives and links to a printer, a video arcade game can employ integrated circuits (Pac Man has 84 on its main logic board) to create more detailed video images, versatile animated characters and complex sound effects.

The images on an arcade game's video screen are generated by two integrated circuit chips known as character ROMs. These read-only memory chips are permanent repositories for the program instructions defining the boundaries of screen images and their relative positions. Each chip stores 4,096 words of instruction. One chip provides the instructions for displaying the maze and the blockshaped figures that travel through it. The other contains the details needed to redraw these blocks into Pac Man and his four pursuers.[2]

Videogame Software

The software side of the business involves the computer program creating the videogame scenario. It could be: (1) a dedicated piece of computer memory contained in an arcade game; (2) a dedicated piece of memory in the form of a game cartridge, which can be plugged into a game-playing machine or; (3) a diskette or cassette. A typical game cartridge consisted of packaging plus a computer ROM (read-only memory). Typical manufacturing costs were around $6.00, while the cartridge itself retailed for $25 and $45.

But what actually was a videogame? It could be compared to a miniature movie; their similarities prompted some industry experts to dub California's Silicon Valley "Hollywood North." Videogames had characters, a plot, special effects, and a soundtrack. Some even had dialogue by way of speech synthesis technology. Unlike films, however, videogames were participatory. By pressing buttons, manipulating control levers or "joysticks," or rolling "Trak-ball" controls, players entered the videogame's action and influenced its outcome. As Sudnow and others point out, videogame practice led to a phenomenologically complex set of skills.[3]

Videogames employed numerous themes. Classic examples included Space Invaders, Pac Man, and Donkey Kong. In Space Invaders, rows of alien creatures attempted to land on a planet, which the player defended with a laser base. In Pac Man, cute little creatures chased a Pac Man character around a maze. If Pac Man ate "power pills," he could turn the tables on his pursuers and eat them. Donkey Kong presented the player with a skyscraper that a small video man had to climb to rescue a "fair maiden" from an uncooperative gorilla, hurled balls of fire at the video man.

Recent videogames were remakes of entertainment products popularized in other media. Atari reportedly paid $21 million for the rights to make the movie *E.T.* into a videogame.[4] Disney Studios' feature film *Tron*, and its videogame came out at the same time. Other adaptations included games based on the films *Star Wars, Return of the Jedi,* and *Rocky,* the TV shows "Mash" and "Nine to Five," the characters Cookie Monster, Snoopy, and the Pink Panther, and the rock group Journey.[5] As one industry executive put it, "They've licensed everything that moves, walks, crawls, or tunnels beneath the earth."[6] (See *Exhibit 1*.)

Individual videogames had both arcade and home forms. Successful arcade games were often later sold in home versions, as with Pac Man or Galaxian. Journey's Escape videogame was the first to reverse the sequence. Another example of videogame product extension involved a report that MCA-TV acquired the rights to the videogame Donkey Kong for development as an animated children's TV series.[7] Joint ventures between entertainment companies such as MCA and Atari supported this trend.[8]

Videogame Trends

Videogames became a public-policy concern in the 1980s. Their habit-forming nature caused a number of municipalities to pass ordinances either prohibiting adolescents from arcades during school hours or outlawing the games entirely in public places. Several countries, notably Taiwan, completely banned the games out of concern they were a waste of time and a corrupting influence on youth. Numerous examples of petty theft by children or spending lunch money on videogames were reported in the press.

Another issue was product safety. Arista released videogames based on the horror films *Halloween* and *The Texas Chain Saw Massacre*. Others marketed X-rated games. As of 1985, no research existed on the psychological effects of videogames or protracted game playing. A conference on videogames sponsored by Atari and the Harvard Graduate School of Education, however, yielded a number of impressionistic reports.[9]

In several academic centers, videogames were used experimentally as adjuncts to medical diagnosis, treatment, and rehabilitation.[10] As the basis of new educational programs, they were said to help the development of a variety of cognitive skills.[11]

Another important trend concerned the competitive environment for videogame companies. The life cycle of a successful videogame grew shorter as the field became saturated with product. Technological advancement also contributed to commercial obsolescence. Innovations include new player

controls, game architecture, speech synthesis, and 3-D effects.[12] One industry
source stated:

> Arcade games of even greater complexity are already in the testing stages.
> Features include stickless control mechanisms that register hand or eye
> movements as input; detailed graphics that rival the quality of live video; voice
> recognition, and voice-synthesis abilities that allow the game to conduct a
> conversation with the player; and hardware and software that is sophisticated
> enough to make strategy rather than hand-eye coordination the key to playing
> the game.[13]

Other predicted innovations included videogames linking computers
with optical videodiscs and use of holography for enhanced realism. Designers
were said to be dreaming of games controlled not with a joystick, but with eye
movements or brain waves.[14]

Technology resulted in ever-expanding uses. Videogames were used to
train army tank crews, as aids in flying instruction, and as diagnostic tools in
medicine to help brain-damaged patients. Games were also directed toward
more specialized markets. Ms. Pac Man, for instance, was allegedly the first
game designed for women instead of the usual adolescent male audience.
Games reported in development included those targeted to small children and
audiences age 45 and older.

THE INDUSTRY

Gagnon cites Willy Higinbotham as the first videogame inventor who in 1958
constructed a tennis game on an oscilloscope screen at Brookhaven National
Laboratory.[15] The first widely known videogame, Space Wars, was born on a
PDP/1 mainframe computer in 1962 in Cambridge, Massachusetts by a group
of Harvard students at the Littauer Statistics Laboratory. Small rocket ships
firing laser missiles could be guided around a video universe by players who
were to avoid such hazards as "heavy gravity."[16] However, the first
commercial videogame, Computer Space, was not released until 1970.
Commercialization depended on the significant drop in price of integrated
circuits in the late 1960s.

Atari

In 1972 Nolan Bushnell, an electronics engineer and former employee
of Ampex Corporation, founded a company called Atari with $500 in capital.
The word "Atari" comes from the Japanese strategy game Go and is a polite
way of telling the opponent, "You are about to be engulfed." Atari's first
product, a video version of the game of ping-pong, generated $3 million in
sales in its first year.

The next few years saw many new entrants into the industry. One major
competitor, Midway, licensed videogames designed in Japan, including Space

Invaders, Galaxian, and Pac Man. Pac Man itself deserves some special attention. Estimates counted 7 billion coins that by 1982 had been inserted into some 400,000 Pac Man machines worldwide, equal to one game of Pac Man for every person on earth. U.S. domestic revenues from games and licensing of the Pac Man image for T-shirts, pop songs, to wastepaper baskets, etc. exceeded $1 billion.[17]

Bushnell sold Atari to Warner Communications, Inc. for $28 million in 1976. The changeover occurred during considerable internal strife. Emanual Gerard, a Warner executive and Harvard MBA who engineered the acquisition, said, "They [Atari] really had no manufacturing, no sales, and no advertising or marketing expertise. Everything but research was lacking. It was amateur night in Dixie."[18] Dan Valentine of Corporate Management Services, an early Atari investor, put it in another way. "The state of the company in the mid-1970s was absolute chaos."[19]

Under new management, Atari profits mushroomed, so much so that Atari itself, as a division of Warner, ranked in the *Fortune* 500. In 1981, the division was responsible for 50 percent of Warner Communications' operating earnings. It recorded 100 percent growth in its second consecutive year.[20] (See *Exhibit 2.*)

After Warner's acquisition, Bushnell remained for a while as chairman of Atari. However, something reportedly changed in his management style. But so had the industry. According to one expert, "Bushnell started Atari with a 'We're all brothers' attitude, greeting each new employee with a power handshake and a smile. Then competitors began rushing out imitations of Atari's games, some of them very likely gleaned from spies in Bushnell's own plant. Now Atari owns paper shredders and a secret lab in the mountains and it's tough to get any kind of a handshake out of Bushnell."[21]

He did not stay long. There was disagreement whether he resigned or was fired, but the conflict between Warner and Bushnell was unmistakable. "There's a difference between having fun and running a company," said one Warner executive. "Nolan is a creator, a dreamer, a pie in the sky thinker, but he operated in a 'Hey, man,' kind of way."[22]

Warner brought in Ray Kassar, a Brooklyn-born Harvard MBA who had been a marketing executive at Burlington Industries for 25 years, to run the company. His regime was described in the following way:

> Kassar set about changing Atari. "I knew I had a consumer-marketing company, and I had nobody who understood the consumer business," he says. He brought in new people experienced at working in large organizations. He also established normal reporting procedures and financial controls, set specific sales and marketing goals, and tightened security measures to protect confidential information. Kassar put his stamp on the corporate culture as well. "Things were kind of casual here," he recalls. "People didn't work very hard." He made it clear that he expected people to be at work at 8 a.m. sharp, to answer the phones promptly, and to wear ties and jackets instead of T-shirts.
>   Kassar generated considerable resentment. "Ray is very structure-oriented and very elitist" says former Atari executive Gene Lipkin. "If he didn't like what you looked like, he wouldn't talk to you." In time, most of the key executives

from the Bushnell regime left. Kassar also antagonized some engineers who had been treated royally under Bushnell. After a newspaper story quoted Kassar comparing engineers to operatic divas, T-shirts emblazoned with the words, "I'm just another high-strung prima donna for Atari," became popular in the company's research labs.[23]

A heavy turnover in key Atari employees accompanied the change in corporate climate. Some left with entrepreneurial ambitions of their own. Others stayed but were unhappy with the new style. One Atari executive who had begun his professional life at IBM resigned from Atari after six years. He said, "Atari was a whole new world for me. Unlike IBM, it was fun to work there. But when Warner took over, I felt like I was back at IBM. The reason I went to Exidy [another videogame company] was because it reminded me of my early days at Atari."[24]

Since Atari

Other entrants in the videogame business began to make inroads on Atari's market (*Exhibit 3*). The most rapid growth was in home videogame software by new companies employing a "razorblade" strategy—making software for another company's hardware, mainly Atari and Mattel.

One of these new companies, Activision, founded by former recording company executive James Levy and four ex-Atari designers, started with $700,000 in venture capital. In its first year, 1981, it had sales of $6.2 million, $66 million in 1982, and anticipated revenues of over $170 million in 1983. It earned $744,000 in 1981, $12.9 million in 1982, and anticipated $22 million and $24 million for 1983.[25] Unlike many of its competitors, Activision did not rely on external sources of financing beyond its initial venture-capital infusion. It also did not license videogames from outside sources.

Activision exuded a distinctive philosophy directed at building involvement and motivating creative people. According to Levy, "the guys who design games are not [just] engineers or programmers. They have as much creative talent as any performing artist or author."[26] Activision heavily promoted designers as part of the product. The game instruction booklets carries pictures of the designers and tips about how to play the games. The company reportedly received several thousand letters a day addressed to individual designers. Designers were sometimes recognized and greeted by fans in public areas.[27]

Imagic, another Atari spin-off, was founded by William Grubb, former marketing vice president for Atari, in June 1981. It shipped 2.5 million cartridges in its first seven months of production.[28] Imagic allowed its nineteen designers to earn bonuses up to $1 million if a game earned more than $50 million at wholesale (three to four million copies).[29] Its three top designers created six of the first seven games. They, along with the company's president, anticipated becoming instant multimillionaires when the company went public. At an estimated $15–$17 per share issuing price, two of the designers would get $6.8 million and the third $11.8 million. The president of the company would own about 14 percent of the shares worth more than $34 million.[30]

Other firms, including large ones like Twentieth Century Fox Film Corporation, General Foods, Coleco, Paramount Pictures, CBS Inc., and Milton Bradley, as well as smaller start-ups, also threw their hats into the videogame business. They were attracted by the explosion in sales volume of videogame cassettes (*Exhibit 4*).

Promotion budgets increased markedly. According to *Fortune,* $200 million would be spent on videogame advertising in 1982, mainly for TV; 50 percent by Atari and Mattel alone.[31] Promotion budgets for individual games told the same story: Parker Brothers spent $4.5 million to advertise the Empire Strikes Back videogame and $5 million on Frogger.[32] The business also became riskier and the stakes higher: a losing game could cost at least $150,000, while a hit could earn up to $100 million in sales.[33]

But success was difficult to predict. Videogames were described as "a hits-driven" business (*Exhibit 5*). Ten percent of game titles accounted for 75 percent of sales.[34] Five games popular in arcades before they came into the home, including Pac Man, sold over five million copies.[35]

Competition led one industry expert to dub the state of the industry as "software wars." In early 1983 about 400 videogame titles were available and 200 were in preparation.[36]

Moreover, the competition for videogames included other entertainment products. Given the similarity between videogames and films, it was reasonable to assume some cannibalization of sales. This became particularly significant for the videogame industry when the film industry had a banner year, as in 1982 with *E.T.* and other films. Reports of increased spending for record albums in 1984 suggested another source of competition for the consumer entertainment dollar.

The Shakeout of 1982

In late 1982 investors in Warner Communications Inc. suffered a loss of about $1.1 billion in the market values of their shares. The reason? Atari's sales in both home video and arcades were far below expectations due to fierce competition, a recession, and disappointing product quality.[37] Its widely touted E.T. cartridge, for which it had paid substantial licensing fees, sold well below expectations. Warner lost almost half its market value in a few days as its shares slid from $51.875 to $35.125 in December 1982. Following on the heels of Warner's decline, Mattel also reported bad news: a fourth-quarter loss.

Another distress signal came from the arcade segment of the industry. In 1981 players put an estimated $7 billion in quarters into arcade videogames. Machine sales increased from virtually nil in 1978 to about $900 million in 1982, representing about 450,000 units at a price of $2,000.

Business Week reported in 1982 that a shakeout among arcade operators was already underway and indicated that due to distributor overstock, sales would be flat in 1983.[38]

Despite the reverses of late 1982, the industry still remained a juggernaut. It generated over $10 billion a year in revenues. An estimated 15 million U.S. homes had home videogame machines, representing a sixth of all U.S. households with TV. The market for consoles and games was about $3.8 billion for 1982.[39] Industry sources estimated that another ten million consoles or game-playing home computers would be sold in 1983. Thirty million game cartridges were sold in 1981, 65 million in 1982. Industry officials estimated that 1983 sales of game cartridges would approach 110 million units at a retail cost of about $2.4 billion.[40]

The shakeout of 1982 was viewed philosophically by industry leaders. Said one, "It will take the industry nine to twelve months to go through this purge and stabilize. But the thing that fortifies us is that technology and creativity can unlock the market again."[41]

REFERENCES

1. RONALD REAGAN, remarks to students and guests during a visit to Walt Disney's Epcot Center, March 8, 1983, from the Administration of Ronald Reagan, U.S. Government Printing Office.
2. STEVE DITLEA, "Inside Pac Man," *Technology Illustrated,* January 1983.
3. DAVID SUDNOW, *Pilgrim in the Microworld* (New York: Warner Books, 1983).
4. ALJEAN HARMETZ, "Makers Vie for Millions in Home Video Games," *New York Times,* January 13, 1983.
5. Ibid.
6. Ibid; see also Tim Ferris, "Solid State Fun," *Esquire,* March 1977.
7. "MCA-TV Acquires Rights to 'Donkey Kong' Series," *Daily Variety,* May 11, 1983.
8. "MCA Unit and Atari Join in Videogame Venture," *Daily Variety,* May 8, 1983.
9. FOX BUTTERFIELD, "Video Game Specialists Meet at Harvard to Praise Pac-Man, Not to Bury Him," *New York Times,* May 24, 1983.
10. WILLIAM LYNCH, "TV Games as Therapeutic Interventions," a presentation for the American Psychological Association's symposium: "Rehabilitation of Post-traumatic Brain-damaged Patients," Aug. 24–28, 1981, Los Angeles, California.
11. DIANA GAGNON, "Arcade Videogames," (unpublished manuscript).
12. DITLEA, "Inside Pac Man."
13. Ibid.
14. TEKLA PERRY, CAROL TRUXAL, and PAUL WALLICH, "Videogames: The Electronic Big Bang," *IEEE Spectrum,* December 1982.
15. STEVEN BLOOM, *Video Invaders,* (New York: Arco Publishing, 1982).
16. Ibid.
17. COLIN COVERT, "Video Gamesmanship, The Rise and Fall of Atari," *Detroit Free Press,* August 1982.
18. PETER W. BERNSTEIN, "Atari and the Video-Game Explosion," *Fortune,* July 27, 1981.

19. Ibid.
20. FERRIS, "Solid State Fun."
21. BERNSTEIN, "Atari and the Video-Game Explosion."
22. Ibid.
23. Ibid.
24. BLOOM, *Video Invaders.*
25. ANDREW C. BROWN, "Cashing In on the Cartridge Trade," *Fortune,* November 25, 1982.
26. DAN DORFMAN, "Is the Video Game Fad Cooling Off?" *St. Louis Post-Dispatch,* September 19, 1982.
27. "The Riches Behind Video Games," *Business Week,* November 9, 1981.
28. PERRY et al., "Videogames: The Electronic Big Bang."
29. THOMAS HAYES, "Imagic Scores in Video Games," *New York Times,* November 22, 1982.
30. PETER NULTY, "Why the Craze Won't Quit," *Fortune,* November 15, 1982.
31. HARMETZ, "Makers Vie for Millions."
32. JEANNETTE DE WYZE, "The Inter Workings of Videogames," *The LA Reader,* August 20, 1982.
33. "The Video Game Explosion," *New York Times,* December 7, 1982.
34. Ibid.
35. HARMETZ, "Makers Vie for Millions."
36. LAURA LANDRO and SUSAN FEENEY, "Fierce Competition in Video Games behind Dive in Warner Stock Price," *Wall Street Journal.*
37. "Arcade Video Game Start to Flicker," *Business Week,* December 6, 1982.
38. NULTY, "Why the Craze Won't Quit."
39. BROWN, "Cashing in on the Cartridge Trade."
40. "Arcade Video Games Start to Flicker," *Business Week.*
41. BLOOM, *Video Invaders.*

Exhibit 1   The Videogame Industry (Reprinted with permission of Lucasfilm, Ltd. Source: Parker Brothers.)

BECOME A JEDI MASTER
WITHOUT EVER LEAVING HOME.

In the STAR WARS®JEDI ARENA™, perfecting the skills needed to become a JEDI MASTER takes concentration and practice.

Use your LIGHTSABER to direct the attack of the whirling SEEKER. But stay alert, your adversary can attack at any time. So follow

your instincts. In no time at all you'll be a JEDI MASTER, ready to go saber to saber against any opponent who dares to do battle with you.

Play the STAR WARS JEDI ARENA home video game. Alone or head-to-head. The challenge awaits you.

⊚ PARKER BROTHERS

® TM & © Lucasfilm Ltd. 1982 Parker Brothers authorized user.   © 1982, Parker Brothers, Beverly, MA 01915

Exhibit 2 Warner Communications: Summary Statement

Years Ended December 31 (000s)	1982	1981	1980	1979	1978	1977	1976	1975	1974	1973
Operating Revenues:										
Consumer electronics	$2,008,805	$1,227,135	$512,743	$238,056	$177,947	$150,327	$35,541	—	—	—
Recorded music and music publishing	752,317	811,257	805,732	725,323	617,068	532,359	406,062	313,787	291,653	235,992
Filmed entertainment										
Theatrical distribution	338,635	439,897	869,647	433,746	261,329	253,574	221,649	202,333	275,497	152,718
Television distribution and production	355,453	315,278	299,287	175,944	131,687	99,599	63,540	53,582	43,499	56,744
Direct response marketing	445,927	359,401	—	—	—	—	—	—	—	—
Publishing and related distribution										
Domestic operations	88,848	84,185	72,005	74,948	55,103	52,235	48,407	40,189	45,698	40,795
Foreign operations	—	—	—	—	—	—	—	21,803	32,967	35,877
Total operating revenues	$3,989,985	$3,237,153	$2,559,414	$1,648,027	$1,243,134	$1,088,094	$775,199	$631,694	$689,314	$522,126
Operating income (Loss):										
Consumer electronics	$328,288	$286,553	$69,929	$6,233	$(2,677)	$(6,144)	$174	—	—	—
Recorded music and music publishing	58,656	85,014	82,902	81,706	92,557	84,041	68,299	50,212	46,921	41,576
Filmed entertainment	101,796	24,748	60,832	117,570	79,914	57,990	42,227	41,704	57,677	31,093
Direct response marketing	26,158	30,979	—	—	—	—	—	—	—	—
Publishing and related distribution										
Domestic operations	12,518	14,867	10,782	18,073	9,561	7,197	5,504	(2,009)	9,725	6,669
Foreign operations	—	—	—	—	—	—	—	(2,642)	(14,600)	(491)
Total operating income	527,416	442,161	224,445	223,642	179,355	143,084	116,204	87,265	99,723	78,847
Unallocated (Expenses) and Income										
Corporate general and administrative expenses	(75,446)	(58,991)	(41,983)	(35,350)	(30,217)	(25,127)	(21,706)	(17,884)	(17,893)	(11,707)
Interest expense	(96,314)	(69,643)	(36,217)	(42,834)	(33,267)	(27,428)	(20,464)	(19,557)	(24,754)	(16,702)
Dividend, interest, and other	29,244	51,666	44,946	19,615	12,918	12,742	13,559	13,538	11,399	14,032
Total unallocated expenses, net	(142,516)	(76,968)	(33,254)	(58,619)	(50,566)	(39,813)	(28,611)	(23,903)	(31,248)	(14,377)
Income from continuing operations before income taxes	384,900	365,191	191,191	165,023	128,789	103,271	87,593	63,362	68,475	64,170
Provision for income taxes	(127,089)	(138,700)	(154,100)	(55,965)	(96,592)	(36,057)	(29,724)	(17,587)	(27,355)	(22,159)
Gain on sale of 50% of cable operations (less applicable income taxes of $44,352)	—	—	100,000	91,689	—	—	—	—	—	—
Income from continuing operations	257,811	226,493	137,091	200,747	32,197	67,214	57,869	45,775	41,120	42,011
Discontinued operations	—	—	—	—	5,224	3,867	3,693	(37,471)[a]	5,540	1,282
Net income	257,811	226,493	137,091	200,747	37,421	71,081	61,562	8,304	46,660	43,293
Preferred dividend requirements	—	—	—	(22)	(383)	(1,118)	(1,265)	(1,467)	(1,584)	(1,591)
Income applicable to Common and common equivalent shares	$257,811	$226,493	$137,091	$200,725	$37,038	$69,963	$60,297	$6,837	$45,076	$41,702

Exhibit 3 Company Proliferation (Reprinted with permission of IEEE/Spectrum. From "Videogames: The Electronic Big Bang," Perry, Tekla, Truxal, Carol and Wallich, Paul, IEEE Spectrum, December, 1982.)

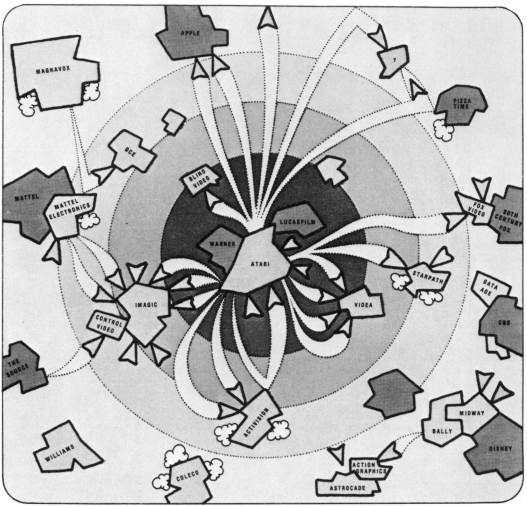

The expanding universe of video games. Experts calculate that the big bang occurred about 1972, and since then, the industry has grown to include dozens of companies, some of which are depicted as asteroids on the "screen" above. The size of each asteroid corresponds roughly to the size of its company. Overlapping or touching asteroids represent subsidiaries or joint endeavors; for example, Atari is a multibillion dollar subsidiary of Warner Communications and Midway worked with Disney to produce a game based on the movie Tron.

Atari's growth over the past 10 years has been impressive—from a $500 investment in 1971 to a company controlling 70 percent of the $10 billion video games market—but perhaps more remarkable still has been the rate at which it has spawned other game companies. Former Atari employees have founded such companies as Activision, Imagic, and Videa; on the screen, those companies that split off earliest have naturally "traveled" farther from Atari than those formed recently.

Each spaceship in the drawing represents a video-game designer or executive whom Spectrum discusses in this special report. Spaceship trails show the person's movement from company to company. For example, one ship flying from Atari to Activision and back to Atari represents designer Larry Kaplan; flying from Atari to the edge of the screen but turning back is designer Allan Alcorn.

The tendency of spaceships and their cargo of ideas to shuttle from asteroid to asteroid has displeased many an asteroidal satrap, leading to the barrage of lawsuits and accusations represented here by puffs of smoke. Of course, some designers have left the industry completely, as shown by the ships leaving the "screen" for hyperspace.

Companies represented by light-colored asteroids are involved primarily in video games, whereas darker asteroids show companies with other main missions. The asteroid marked with a "?" represents the company that Joe Keenan, Nolan Bushnell, and Mr. Alcorn, three of the founding figures of Atari, intend to form when their contract not to compete with their former company expires in October 1983.

Exhibit 4   A Heady Future for Sales of Videogame Cassettes (Source: *Business Week.*)

1979	100,000 units	1982	1,200,000 units
1980	200,000 units	1983	1,800,000 units
1981	750,000 units		(est.)

Exhibit 5   The Videogame Industry. (Source: *Electronic Games* magazine.)

☆Most Popular Videogame Cartridges ☆

This Month	Last Month	Game	System	Manufacturer
1	1	Pitfall	Atari 2600	Activision
2	2	Donkey Kong	ColecoVision	Coleco
3	—	Ladybug	ColecoVision	Coleco
4	12	Venture	ColecoVision	Coleco
5	—	Defender	Atari 2600	Atari
6	3	Donkey Kong	Atari 2600	Coleco
7	8	Zaxxon	ColecoVision	Coleco
8	5	Demon Attack	Atari 2600	Imagic
9	—	Megamania	Atari 2600	Activision
10	—	E.T.	Atari 2600	Atari
11	10	Berzerk	Atari 2600	Atari
12	—	Raiders of the Lost Ark	Atari 2600	Atari
13	14	Star Master	Atari 2600	Activision
14	—	Turbo	ColecoVision	Coleco
15	6	Frogger	Atari 2600	Parker Brothers

☆Most Popular Computer Programs ☆

This Month	Last Month	Game	System	Manufacturer
1	2	Pac-Man	Atari 400-800-1200	Atari
2	1	Star Raiders	Atari 400-800-1200	Atari
3	8	Centipede	Atari 400-800-1200	Atari
4	3	Castle Wolfenstein	Atari 400-800-1200, Apple II	Muse
5	5	Choplifter	Atari 400-800-1200, Apple II	Broderbund
6	—	Protector II	Atari 400-800-1200	Synapse
7	—	Gorf	VIC-20	Commodore
8	7	Missile Command	Atari 400-800-1200	Atari
9	4	Jawbreaker	Atari 400-800-1200	Sierra On-Line
10	—	Frogger	Atari 400-800-1200	Sierra On-Line

☆Most Popular Coin-Op Videogames ☆

This Month	Last Month	Game	Manufacturer
1	1	Donkey Kong	Nintendo
2	2	Tron	Bally/Midway
3	3	Zaxxon	Sega
4	5	Dig-Dug	Atari
5	10	Donkey Kong, Jr.	Nintendo
6	4	Ms. Pac-Man	Bally/Midway
7	6	Robotron	Williams
8	—	Tempest	Atari
9	9	Joust	Williams
10	—	Centipede	Atari

The Videogame Design Process

The videogame industry depended on game designers who combined creative artistry with technological sophistication. A typical game could take from 6 to 18 months to complete.

The design process resembled the creative people who carried it out. David Crane, a well-known and idiosyncratic designer, put it this way in a *Wall Street Journal* article: "Most of the time we're joking. Only one out of 50 crazy ideas will ever become anything. A tree falls down, try to get out from under it—obviously, nothing will come of that. But that's how we come up with the original game ideas."[1] This same article stated:

> Each designer has his own particular work habits and creative techniques. David Crane always starts by creating visual images after thinking of an idea for months—or getting struck by one overnight. He rushed back from a Chicago business trip to start work on the game Freeway after he saw a befuddled man trying to run across busy Lake Shore Drive in rush-hour traffic.
>
> Mr. Miller, on the other hand, starts with concepts. "There's a lot of discussion among the designers about what might make a good game, and we have a list of maybe 40 to 50 ideas," he says. "Yet most of the games we do aren't on the list. They come about because a designer gets inspired."
>
> Armed with an idea, Mr. Miller does some rough sketches of what he wants the playing fields of a game to look like, and he writes a brief description of how it is supposed to play. Then he retires to the mostly unfurnished living room of his nearby home, gets comfortable in a padded rocking chair, and spends days alternately staring out the window at trees and painstakingly writing an initial 10 to 20 pages of detailed computer code on small sheets of green paper.
>
> "Writing code for me is like writing English," Mr. Miller said. "I'm fluent in about a dozen computer languages." Each of Mr. Miller's late games had about 2,000 to 3,000 separate instructions which were eventually "burned" onto a computer chip to provide the look and playing features of the games.
>
> The designer spent two months writing and rewriting computer codes, producing about 200 pages of handwritten notes, and a five-foot stack of computer printouts. Then, after getting suggestions from other designers, he programmed his work into Activision's main computer to generate mountains, tanks, and other visual features and colors on-screen. For the next two months, he worked on playability, making the video and audio features of the game challenging without being impossible.

This case was prepared by Associate Professor John Kao.

For the last two months, Mr. Miller and his colleagues played the game for hundreds of hours to debug and polish it. "After I finish a game, I really hate it, and I don't want to see it again for months," Mr. Miller says.[2]

Atari came up with its own way of dealing with the creative process. One industry historian recalled, "Many of the best times occurred not in Sunnyvale, but at Atari's think tank in Grass Valley in the Sierra foothills, where Nolan Bushnell, founder of Atari, sent his brightest employees to consider the company's future. Hot tubs, pot, and private shuttle flights between the two valleys were the modus operandi there—or so legend has it."[3] One designer described Grass valley as "a place to dream up new ideas in a very unstructured work environment. It's very imaginative. Most of Atari's best ideas came from there."[4] Nolan Bushnell spoke about Grass Valley in these terms: "The basic architecture for everything came from there. Oddly enough, the engineering department at Atari was constantly sniping at the Grass Valley operation, and vice versa. They basically detested each other. According to the Sunnyvale crew, Grass Valley was full of prima donnas who couldn't make anything work—which was true in part, but they happened to be good technologists. Excuse me—great technologists."[5]

Bushnell, who planned a comeback in the videogame business when his noncompetition agreement with Atari expired, commented on Atari's design process: "Atari's done everything right in manufacturing and marketing. But it's done poorly in designing. Their current equipment is obsolete because it was designed nearly eight years ago and hasn't changed at all." Atari's approach, as he saw it, lay in creating better games and graphics for more exciting games. But that was not a strategy, declared Bushnell. "That's 'innovate me some more like you did last year' and that's wrong. They should be doing what I'm going to do.[6]

David Sudnow described the creative environment at Atari in the following terms:

> There I was on the Atari premises, and here were these rather speedy and excited young guys and gals in jeans and sneakers with Rembrandt prints and psychedelic posters in their offices, pianos and guitars lying about, Bartok coming out of this room, the Stones out of that, more TV sets going at once than in ten Sears, Roebucks put together, more technology and color and instruments and charts and sounds and knobs and controls and computers of every conceivable description than you'd ever see under one roof outside Silicon Valley, programmers literally sleeping in vans in the parking lot so they'd stay close to their consoles. And with the enthusiasm and animation any corporate manager would give away his American Express card for, they're laying out the lovely little grammars of these microworlds for me, speaking with such expertise and command and exhilaration as we went through the rundown of strategies and angles and hints, I figured myself in the presence of an artist's colony of the first magnitude, Black Mountain of the eighties, everyone working their brains off, chipmunks chipping away colors, movements and sounds into a whole marvelous assortment of new instruments.[7]

Lee Hauck, a noted game designer with Gremlin Industries, had his own point of view on the game design process:

He learned what didn't work—brainstorming sessions, for instance. "They've been absolute disasters. Games by committee are like most things by committee." He had a concept of what made a good game designer. "A lot of them come from computer disciplines. But they might come from other places, too, like people who write cartoons." The ability to work within the limitations of the medium is critical. "A movie screenwriter probably wouldn't work out, because in movies he doesn't have the problem of making it run on cost-effective hardware. Anything you want to do in a film you can do. But here it's gotta be achievable at low cost."

Hauck said Gremlin has a number of company game design groups. "But mainly we're looking to our programmers to supply ideas. If anybody even looks like he has an aptitude for games, we give him his head, let him do whatever he wants for a while." He estimated that ninety-five percent of such efforts hadn't succeeded. "But you only need a few winners to justify it. The trouble with creativity is that you can't teach it and you can't schedule it."

Hauck had strong convictions about those things that historically had fueled his own creativity. "I'm a big believer in the subconscious. The times when I've created the best is when I'm working the hardest doing the most. Going to seminars, reading books. Listening to jazz. Talking to people. Walking around arcades. The more inputs you can cram into your subconscious, the more it works for you, and pretty soon the ideas start coming."[8]

Alan Alcorn, one of Atari's original designers, felt that constraints stimulated creativity. In his words, "you get more juice out of a lemon when you squeeze it."[9]

According to an article in *Business Week* on the videogame design process:

Ideas begin in brainstorming sessions, normally held somewhere away from the company. No idea is too far-fetched, because no one knows what crazy idea will set off sparks in someone else and ignite the next hit game. "We talk about a Halley's comet game, for example," says Siu Kuen Lee, an Atari designer, "that would show a black screen and once every 76 years a light would flash across." This may sound far-fetched, but so did a multisegmented worm—an idea that led to one of the top games of 1982, Centipede.

Ideas can also come from other games, noted Larry Kaplan, a vice president at Atari. "To write a good game is difficult. It takes a long time, a lot of test marketing."

Robert Brown, vice president of engineering for Starpath in Santa Clara, California, said, "One way we choose games to design is by seeing what categories are popular in coin-op [arcade] games and trying to develop something in that category that is a new twist."

Game ideas also come from movies—directly, as when Disney got in touch with the Midway Manufacturing Co. of Chicago, a Bally subsidiary and asked it to design a game based on the movie *TRON*. "It gets to the point where you can't get through a movie without thinking, "Boy, that would make a good game," observed Bill Adams, director of games development for Midway.

Game ideas also come from real-life situations, particularly sports. "Sports games are easier to do," said Bob Whitehead, cofounder of Activision, "because they are well defined. A more original game has to evolve, so it takes more time."

Reality can also present a pitfall for a game designer, because mistakes are obvious. At Atari, a game nicknamed Foul Ball reached the marketing testing stage before anyone discovered that the designer, who did not understand the rules of baseball, was treating strikes as balls.

Some designers start with a picture rather than a concept for game play, then think of ways to interact with their graphics.

"I got interested in drawing pictures," said John Perkins, who designed Artillery Duel for Astrocade, Inc., Columbus, Ohio. "I started out with a desert and put cactuses all over it, then I drew a hill and put rocks on it, then trees. The idea for the game, shooting over the mountain, evolved as a way to interact with the scenery."

One complaint of game designers who left Atari is that too many game ideas were originating in the marketing department. "A videogame is a creative thing, like an artist with a palette full of colors," said Mr. Alcorn, who is still under contract to Atari, but on the inactive roster. "The artist has control of the medium; I can smear paint on a canvas, and it's not going to look like a picture. Take a marketing guy, someone who is nontechnical and doesn't understand the medium, he tries to design a game, and it's inefficient."

One example of a marketer's idea for a game, Mr. Kaplan says, is Polo, designed by Carol Shaw, a former Atari designer who is now with Activision. Mr. Kaplan related, "Ray Kassar [president of Atari] was into cosmetics. 'Hey,' he said, 'cosmetics is a $4 billion industry. Why can't we get a piece of that with videogames?' Warner commissioned clothing designer Ralph Lauren to come up with a perfume and put his name on it and call it Polo. They had a line of cosmetics and wanted this Polo cartridge as a come on in the stores." The perfume was not a hit on the market. The videogame was not sold.

If marketing people cannot always identify a good game, engineers are quick to admit that they cannot either. Engineers often love games that the public hates, and are bored by games—like Pac Man—that the public loves.

After ideas are generated and a priority list is drawn up, designers choose or are assigned an idea from the list. Perhaps half of the ideas are eventually attempted as games, says Lyle Rains, an Atari vice president for coin-op. Half of those or less are completed, he says and half again are produced.

Graphics artists become involved, doing storyboards for game ideas and working with designers to develop the graphics that will be put up on the screen. In the early days, artists were not necessary—paddles and a ball did not take much artistic ingenuity—but game graphics today have much more detail. Some programmers are artistically talented and will design their own graphics, and this can work very well, because they know the limitations of the system. But Roger Hector, president of Videa and a graphics artist, says it is difficult to find people who are both technically competent and artistically creative. The solution lies in a team approach.[10]

VIDEOGAME DESIGNERS

In a review of videogame designers, the editors of an engineering industry publication wrote:

The videogame industry is a test bed for engineering design in which there is no cookbook to design from. The research-and-development cycle must be kept short—under six months. Designs are personal. Designers admit they sometimes cannot read each other's code or even each other's schematics.

According to industry sources, there were only 100 full-time videogame designers, and of those, only about 20 in the United States were considered superb.[11]

What made a good videogame designer?

"You have to be a good engineer," said William Grubb, president of Imagic. "You have to have specific knowledge of that microprocessor you're working with and that comes from formal education and experience; it takes time to learn the idiosyncracies of the system. And you have to be able to combine art with engineering, to be able to understand what is fun, what will titillate your markets. Not every engineer used to thinking logically has that ability."

Donna Bailey, who designed Centipede for Atari . . . agreed, saying, "There's a lot of trendiness and pop culture that goes into games. Many programmers have trouble with that so they can't do games."

According to an Atari promotional videotape, a designer had to be an engineer who was also an artist and a musician. "You can't do games if you are a scientist type; you have to think artistically of what the computer can do," one Atari designer said. "I'm creating a world in which my game will live."

People moved into the games industry from many engineering places—automotive, electronics, instrumentation, larger computer systems, defense, and semiconductors to name a few. Many engineers joined the industry straight out of college.

Game designers were difficult to stereotype. "This industry takes all kinds," said Alan Alcorn. "You must have the ability to work with some very perverse people, because the best take strange forms."

On the one end, he said, are people like Steven Jobs, now president of Apple Computer. "He showed up on our doorstep, and the personnel lady said we should either call the police or hire him, because he's brilliant," Mr. Alcorn recalled.

Harold Lee, who designed the first game on a single chip for Atari, "came out of the hills of Los Gatos dressed in leather like a Hell's Angel and said he was going to work with us," Mr. Alcorn continued. "He drove a chopper to work and drank Ripple wine."

On the other end of the spectrum were people like Robert Brown, a former Atari employee and executive vice president of Starpath. He had a Ph.D., was bespectacled, and a very straight guy, Mr. Alcorn noted.

Once designers got into the games industry, it was hard to imagine them doing anything else. Brian Johnson, a designer with Fox Video Games, said, "I've thought it might be fun to come back in the next life as a rock 'n' roll singer, and videogames seemed as close as I'll get to that in this lifetime."

Were videogame designers the new generation of pop stars? Activision promoted its designers heavily. Jim Levy said he considers game designers "rock stars."

Atari, on the other hand, never willingly released the names of its game designers, some said for fear that they would be hired by another company. The Atari designers liked a little recognition, so they often buried their names in their games. It took work and memory that would have been used for additional game features, but they considered themselves artists, and artists signed their creations. Atari used to review games and take the signatures out; they have stopped that policy.

Designers learned to hide their tracks and beat the censors anyway.

Larry Kaplan, Atari vice president of product development, said he designed Superbreakout for the Atari 800. After a certain sequence of keys, the screen displayed: "I love Suzie and Benji too." He listed other signed games for the Atari VCS: Adventure with Warren Robinett's signature in a secret room; Yars Revenge with Howard S. Warshaw's initials appearing at one point and ending the game; Defender with the attackers turning briefly into Bob Polaro's initials very late in the game; and Missile Command, with Bob Fulop's initials appearing if the player loses the game immediately in game 13.[12]

Perhaps the most divergent approaches to dealing with and motivating creative people were those of Imagic and Activision.[13] Imagic stressed team projects and market testing. Designers wrote computer motion and control programs, but graphics and sound effects were created by other specialists. Imagic also emphasized interaction between marketing and design staff. Product development made use of collective brainstorming sessions followed by concept testing, in which storyboards and game descriptions were produced and tested with a group of young players. Activision, on the other hand, stressed the independence of the creative designer. Fewer than ten nondesigners had access to the design lab. Each designer was responsible for all aspects of game creation, although designers frequently consulted with each other.[14]

Many other philosophies existed about how to select and motivate talent. For example, Namco, a Japanese videogame company, had an unusual approach to finding the people it needed. It advertised in magazines for reformed juvenile delinquents and grade-C students. Masayo Nakamura, president of the company, stated, "For game designers, the knowledge acquired in school is not so helpful. I want people who think in unusual ways, whose curiosity runs away with them, fun-loving renegades."[15]

On the topic of creativity, Nolan Bushnell stated, "I believe that there is no real correlation between hard work and good results. I think good work is an effective blend of leisure and work. You need leisure for perspective and work for execution, but all execution and no perspective will give you a bad product. I want all my engineers to have that perspective, even more than I want them to work hard—which may be a funny thing to say."[16]

An important trend in videogame design rested with the increasing sophistication of frameworks aimed at explaining the psychological phenomena common to all videogames. Chris Crawford of Atari described key variables in terms of pace, endowing the computer with the ability to produce "reasonable behavior" in response to human opponents, and limiting the information that is available to the player.[17] Malone of the Xerox Research Center spoke of variables such as the meaningfulness of game goals, the uncertainty of outcomes, the multiplicity of goal levels, the randomness of the program, the use of hidden information revealed selectively, fantasy, surprise, and appeals to curiosity.[18] Definitive studies on videogame psychology awaited the next generation of research.

The future of videogame design may be profoundly affected by new technology. Reports indicated that software to help players design their own games is now available. One such product, The Arcade Machine, was a software package for the Apple and Atari home computers that retailed for $59.95. A "shape creator" developed visual images in various colors. The program also created "explosions" and defined the playing field through a routine called the "path creator." Time limits and target scores could be altered. A "load save" feature allowed the weary game designer to break for food and sleep.[19]

REFERENCES

1. STEPHEN J. SANSWEET, "Designers are Stars in Video-Game Field; Some Get Fan Mail," *Wall Street Journal,* January 19, 1983.
2. Ibid.
3. STEVEN BLOOM, *Video Invaders* (New York: Arco Publishing, 1982).
4. Ibid.
5. Ibid.
6. DAN DORFMAN, "Is the Video Game Fad Cooling Off?" *St. Louis Post-Dispatch,* September 19, 1982.
7. DAVID SUDNOW, *Pilgrim in the Microworld* (New York: Warner Books, 1983).
8. JEANNETTE DE WYZE, "The Inner Workings of Videogames," *The LA Reader,* August 10, 1982.
9. TEKLA PERRY, CAROL TRUXAL, PAUL WALLICH, "Videogames: The Electronic Big Bang," *IEEE Spectrum,* December 1982.
10. "The Riches Behind Video Games," *Business Week,* November 9, 1981.
11. PERRY, et al., "Videogames: The Electronic Big Bang."
12. "Creating Video Games that Score," *Business Week,* April 4, 1983.
13. Ibid.
14. STEVE LOHR, "Japan's New Nonconformists, Technology Spurs Change," *New York Times,* March 8, 1983.
15. Ibid.
16. BLOOM, *Video Invaders.*
17. CHRIS CRAWFORD, "Design Techniques and Ideals for Computer Games," *BYTE,* December 1982.
18. THOMAS W. MALONE, "What Makes Computer Games Fun," *BYTE,* December 1981.
19. ERIK SANDBERG-DIMENT, "The Imaginative Path to Designing Games," *New York Times,* May 24, 1983.

George Lucas (A)

At age seventeen, weeks before the end of his senior year in high school (whether he would graduate was still too close to call), George Lucas was seriously injured in a near-fatal auto accident. On his way home from studying, he was broadsided after an illegal left turn by a friend's Impala. Lucas' Fiat Bianchina rolled five times before smashing into a walnut tree on his family's ranch. Rollbars, installed months earlier, kept the car from flattening, and the racing seat belts, anchored to the floor with steel plating, failed—miraculously snapping at the base—allowing him to be thrown from the roof. Lucas stated:

> You can't have that kind of experience and not feel that there must be a reason why you're here. . . . I realized I should be spending my time trying to fulfill it. . . . The fact is I could never have survived that accident if I'd been wrapped around that tree. . . . Actually, the seat belt never should have broken, under any circumstances. . . . All of this affected me seriously. . . . The accident made me more aware of myself and my feelings. . . . I began to trust my instincts. I had the feeling that I should go to college, and I did. I got the same feeling later that I should go to film school, even though everybody thought I was nuts.
>
> I had the same feeling when I decided to make *Star Wars*, when even my friends told me I was crazy. These are things that have to be done, and I feel as if I have to do them.[1]

One of three children and an only son, Lucas was a disinterested student who had a D+ grade average. "I lived for cars, summer vacations, and shooting out windows with BB guns."[2] Fragile even before the accident—5′7″ and thin—some classmates referred to him as a "nerd." Diabetes kept him out of Vietnam. He did, however, enjoy fantasy—comic books and later TV—curled up with his black cat Dinky. Home life was easy if not stimulating. His father, a prosperous merchant of a stationery and office supplies store in Modesto, California, spent more time with the business and part-time walnut ranch than at home. Lucas, Sr. was a firm believer in old-fashioned virtues: Be true to yourself, work hard, and be frugal. But he thought his son never paid any attention. He recalled, "Scrawny little devil . . . never listened to me. He was his mother's pet. Always dreaming."[3] Lucas recalled, "Before the

This case was written by Research Associate Lee Field, under the supervision of Associate Professor John Kao.

accident I never used to think. Afterward, I realized I had to plan if I was ever going to be happy."[4]

During a two-year stint at Modesto Junior College, Lucas discovered special effects filmmaking. "We did trick animation, ran our movies backwards."[5] With the help of cinematographer Haskell Wexler, a friend from his race car days, Lucas entered the University of Southern California (USC) film school. Classmate John Milius said of Lucas, "He played with the concepts; he was free. He felt he was going to change everything and make the greatest art."[6] Before graduation in 1966, Lucas went to Warner Bros. for a six-month internship.

> From my point of view the film industry died in 1965. The day I walked onto the lot was the day that Jack Warner left and Seven Arts took over. The industry had been taken over by people who knew how to make deals and operate offices but had no idea how to make movies. When the six months was over, I never went back.

THE FILM BUSINESS

The movie industry has had a volatile history. Its golden age began in the 1920s and culminated in 1946 with 4.1 billion tickets sold. The introduction and popularity of television, however, helped the industry into a 30-year slump which hit the bottom in 1971 with 820 million box office tickets sold. But the industry picked up in the 1970s when hits such as *Star Wars, The Empire Strikes Back, Raiders of the Lost Ark, Jaws,* and *E.T.* each grossed more than $100 million (see *Exhibit 1*).

Nonetheless, the industry was still plagued by problems: Production costs were accelerating faster than revenues. In 1975 the average film cost $3.1 million to produce; by 1981, the average cost had risen to $10 million. After marking expenses and distribution fees, a $10 million film needed $30 million in box office revenues to break even. The production cycle often ran as long as 24 months for feature films. During that time two potential hazards awaited a new film's release. First, movie audience tastes might change, and second, a similar film by a competitor could be released first and lessen the impact of later releases.

The odds of success (here defined as achieving a return on investment of 15 percent) were poor. Statistics showed that six out of ten movies made lost money, two broke even, and two were profitable. Only one in every 250 films was a blockbuster. Movie-making was, therefore, a speculative business.

Movie-making was sequenced in distinct phases: preproduction, production, and postproduction. During preproduction, a team of people necessary for the project was pulled together, a script developed, the production process planned, and the cast and crew hired. These tasks were handled by studio executives and/or the film's producer.

During the production phase other temporary employees were hired—office help, technicians, and other talent groups—who were tightly scheduled and used (and paid) only for the time needed. The film's director was the key to this segment of production; he or she coordinated all the work teams and managed the creative people.

Postproduction involved new technical people—editors, sound technicians, and special effects experts. The finished product could depend on many variables: the intent of the director; the influence of the producer; or the involvement of the financial backers. In recent years, some films have been prescreened to sample audiences with different endings or effects and finished depending on the most favorable audience response.

Even before a film could be made, however, someone had to put together and contract the four key elements necessary for success in the film business:

1. A network of creative people to produce the product
2. Production controls
3. Access to the distribution channel
4. Financing

This role of "deal maker" was played by many different people—some were major studio executives, others independent production companies, agents, directors, producers, or star actors. Managing relationships with all the potential key players in a deal was the critical attribute of a successful dealmaker.

Two major changes had occurred in the movie business since World War II. Spiraling costs and the risks of production led to a conservative attitude at most major studios. And most major studios sought deep-pocket financial support. As of 1985, five of the eight major studios had been acquired by conglomerates; the others had either diversified independently or arranged additional private and public financial backing.

A PROMISING YOUNG FILMMAKER

In 1967 Francis Ford Coppola, respected director of films such as *The Godfather* and *Apocalypse Now* and himself a USC graduate, hired Lucas as an assistant for *Finian's Rainbow*. As director Roger Corman had done for him, Coppola took an interest in promising USC students and paid them with experience. The following year Lucas was allowed to film a documentary of Coppola directing *The Rain People,* and he repeated the format by documenting Carl Foreman making *McKenna's Gold.* Impressed by Lucas' technical ability, Coppola brought him in as a founder of American Zoetrope, a San Francisco-based production company intent on establishing a northern California film center to counterbalance Hollywood and its southern California power.

The friendship and collaboration grew. Coppola produced and helped Lucas obtain funding for his first feature, *THX 1138,* released in 1971 by Warner Bros. A remake of a student film festival winner that Lucas had made while at UCS, the story was a grim view of the future, filmed in the unfinished BART subway tunnels in San Francisco.

While Lucas enjoyed total control during the creative process, this was not the case for the finished product. Executives at Warner Brothers, who thought *THX 1138* was "unreleasable," ridiculed the film and gave it to an in-house editor to salvage. Only four minutes were cut, but Lucas, deeply hurt and insulted, remarked, "It was a very personal film. . . . I was completely outraged."

Many critics, however, recognized Lucas' potential. Kenneth Turan in a *Washington Post* review of April 17, 1971, saw Lucas' strength as "a very personal vision" that could "transform a collection of cheap effects into a visually gratifying science-fiction film." *Newsweek* (April 3, 1971) described the movie as "an extremely professional first film." *THX 1138,* however, with lackluster studio support, failed at the box office. Lucas commented on this experience:

> I realized I had to make entertaining films or back off and release through libraries. I didn't want to struggle to get $3000. It was too limiting and I didn't want my wife to support me forever. I decided to make a rock 'n' roll cruising movie.[8]

Called *American Graffiti,* the film was released in 1973, and produced by Coppola. "We cooked up a lot of good stuff together," remarked Coppola, "and on a certain type of movie, it would be great."[9] Once again, there were differences with the Hollywood powers, this time Universal Pictures. Even after the studio cut the film, one executive still refused to release it. Only Coppola's bluff tactics saved *Graffiti.* As the story goes, Coppola jumped up at the studio screening, checkbook in hand, and offered to buy the movie on the spot himself if Universal did not want it. He also chastised the executives for being cruel and insensitive after this boy had "put his heart" into this project. Flush from his *Godfather* success, Coppola turned the tide. But Lucas and Coppola also had some philosophical differences. Lucas recalled, "He (Coppola) wanted to be a mogul. I wanted to make more movies and help young filmmakers develop. But first I'd build a solid base for financial security."[10]

THE STAR WARS SAGA

Seven million dollars in personal profits from *American Graffiti* was the start, and it also bought Lucas some time. For three years, eight hours a day, he worked on a science-fiction saga called *Star Wars,* a romantic fantasy adventure laced with the mythic themes of good versus evil and a young man's coming of age. Lucas initially had problems securing a backer. He remembered the time spent writing as excruciatingly painful and difficult. For ideas and relaxation, he read books by Jung and Castaneda's *Tales of Power.* The financial success of *American Graffiti,* however, (cost: $750,000; two-year gross: $50 million) convinced Twentieth Century Fox to invest in Lucas' *Star Wars* script. Released in 1977, it added close to $12-million net profit ($40-million paper gross less taxes and profit sharing for cast and crew) to the Lucas bank account. When ancillary rights such as videocassettes, television rights, books, licensing, and merchandising were taken into account, *Star Wars* would eventually become a billion-dollar product.

Rather than retire to a life of coupon-clipping, however, Lucas determined that the best investment he could make would be in the sequel to *Star Wars,* the second film in a projected trilogy, called *The Empire Strikes Back.* Lucas used savings and $15 million in theater prepayments as collateral for the $30-million budget. Because he had retained all sequel rights to *Star Wars,* Lucas was able to negotiate a very favorable agreement with Twentieth Century Fox for *Empire.* Lucas' pretax profits from *The Empire Strikes Back* (1980 release) were $51 million.

With a secure financial base, Lucas made the last of the trilogy, the 1983 release, *Return of the Jedi.* Initially called *Revenge of the Jedi,* Lucas subsequently renamed it, at considerable expense, when he realized that "Jedi are not vengeful." It was made at a cost of $32.5 million, funded internally, through Lucasfilm Limited, a corporation he had founded to handle all filmmaking operations as well as R&D, contract work for other filmmakers, and new businesses. By 1981, Lucasfilm Limited had relocated all operations and corporate headquarters to Marin County in northern California. Besides film rentals, Lucasfilm had other important sources of revenue including merchandising profits, since it controlled the rights to licensing of all *Star Wars*-related products. With the release of *Return of the Jedi* and ten years after Lucas' personal *Star Wars* saga began, he was anxious to move on to other things.

Between *The Empire Strikes Back* and *Return of the Jedi,* Lucas originated the story for Lucasfilm's production of *Raiders of the Lost Ark* (1982 release) in conjunction with director Stephen Spielberg. He also coproduced the 1984 sequel, *Indiana Jones and the Temple of Doom.* Other Lucasfilm activities included creating special effects for films such as *Star Trek* and *Back to the Future,* developing a high-tech ride at Disney World, producing further Indiana Jones sequels with Spielberg and designing videogames. Lucas also admits that two other trilogies based on *Star Wars,* set in a time prior to and following the original, may someday be made.

LUCASFILM, LTD.

Five years after *Star Wars,* Lucasfilm Ltd. had grown from 40 to 400 employees, with a $16 million annual overhead. Yet, Lucas repeatedly insisted that he did not like business; nor did he like having his business in

Hollywood. After completing *The Empire Strikes Back,* in May of 1978, Lucas bought the 1,882-acre Bulltail Ranch in Marin County, California, north of San Francisco. During the next two years he purchased an additional adjoining 1,100 acres; total cost was around $3 million. Skywalker Ranch, its new name, was intended to be a movie think tank, not a studio.

One of Lucas' pet projects was Industrial Light and Magic (ILM), located at the ranch, which had state-of-the-art special effects equipment and artists. ILM did work for Lucasfilm and other quality film companies. In 1980 Lucasfilm had operating revenues of $350 million. Its main products were *Star Wars* and *Empire* and the newly emerging licensing fees and royalties from *Star Wars*-related merchandise. Profits from the films and merchandising subsidized the ranch's operating expenses.

At this time, Lucasfilm headquarters was located in Los Angeles in a converted warehouse near Universal Studios. Charles Weber, chief executive officer, had managed Lucasfilm's growth into a successful mini-conglomerate. Weber, who thrived on growing businesses and being in Hollywood, ultimately clashed with Lucas over the future of the company. Lucas, who had gladly given Weber complete business control, now wanted headquarters and control located in Marin County, with him. He wanted the business to fund his movie ventures, not vice versa.

Lucas agonized over the problem but ultimately decided to centralize all operations at Skywalker Ranch, fire Weber, and cut the size of the business staff. Only 34 of the 80 L.A. employees were invited to relocate. But Lucas offered generous cash settlements, six months severance pay, and vocational counseling for terminated employees. Bob Greber, former chief financial officer, became chief operating officer, while Lucas assumed the role of president and chief executive officer.

VALUES AND PRIORITIES

> A lot of the stuff in there is very personal. There's more of me in *Star Wars* than I care to admit. I was trying to say in a very simple way, knowing that the film was made for a young audience, that there is a God and there is both a good side and a bad side. You have a choice between them, but the world works better if you're on the good side. It's just that simple.[11]

"The key to his success," said one of Lucas' associates, "[is] that he cannot be turned from the vision inside his head or corrupted by outside influences."[12] Yet adherence to personal values and priorities has also resulted in professional and financial loss for Lucas. For example, Lucas resigned from the Directors Guild because they fined him for placing Irving Kershner's directorial credit at the end of *The Empire Strikes Back* instead of at the beginning. He also gave up membership in the Writers Guild over a similar dispute. Lucas described his rationale:

> The Hollywood unions have been taken over by the same lawyers and accountants who took over the studios. The union doesn't care about its

members. It cares about making fancy rules that sound good on paper and are totally impractical. They said Lucasfilm was a personal credit. On that technicality they sued me for $250,000. You can pollute half the Great Lakes and not get fined that much. I consider it extortion. The day after I settled with the Directors Guild, the Writers Guild called up. At least their fine didn't all go into the business agents' pockets. Two-thirds went to writers.[13]

His former wife Marcia (they were married in 1969 and divorced amicably in 1983) commented on Lucas' values and creativity: "He is methodical and ritualistic. He loves to feel safe and secure. Any kind of threat would make him so uneasy and uncomfortable he couldn't work. Even when he's silly, nothing is simply a fun moment. Everything gets logged."[14] Not surprising, the word most often used to describe Lucas is "serious."

Asked if Lucas believed in The Force (from the *Star Wars* movies, a universal power originating from faith), Marcia remarked, "I think deep down, part of his subconscious believes in it."[15] Lucas himself, admitting to his own belief in a "destiny of sorts," said, "I'm trying to set up an alternative filmmaking that allows me to do what I want, within certain parameters. We're trying to make a company that will respect the personality and individuality of filmmakers."[16]

Lucas was not known as a man of leisure. In Marcia's words: "You've heard of nine-to-fivers. George is a five-to-niner. He's up at five, leaves at five-thirty, and comes home at eight-thirty."[17] Lucas describes his workaholism thus:

> Ever since I was in film school I've been on a train. Back then I was pushing a 147-car train up a very steep slope—push, push, push. When *Star Wars* came along in 1977 I reached the top. I jumped on board and it's been downhill ever since. I've had the brakes on trying to stop the train on this steep slope, with the wheels screeching all the way. It's been work, work, work.[18]

His favorite fairy tale was *The Ant and the Grasshopper,* a story of an ant who could move bigger loads than a grasshopper because it worked harder and had confidence. Lucas continued: "I took the day off yesterday. I saw dailies at 9:00 a.m., had a meeting from 10:00 to 12:00, saw more film, had another meeting. I worked eight hours on my day off."[19]

Lucas described himself as someone with "simple wants and needs," and Mark Hamill, who played Luke in *Star Wars,* remembered being invited out to dinner and ending up at Taco Hut: "I should have known that George wouldn't go to a place with tablecloths and waiters."[20] Lucas agreed: "Francis [Coppola] accuses me of not knowing how to spend money. Francis is right."[21]

But Lucas has given percentage profit points in his movies to key employees and donated $5.7 million to the USC film school. However, when Coppola was in financial trouble after his $28 million electronic movie *One From The Heart* flopped, his associates were miffed with Lucas for not offering to bail Francis out. "I didn't ask him," said Coppola. "I don't think George is wired that way. Part of friendship is understanding what the limitations are. We're all products of our background."[22]

REFERENCES

1. DALE POLLOCK, *Skywalking* (New York: Harmony Books, 1983).
2. *Time,* May 23, 1985.
3. *American Film,* June 1983.
4. Ibid.
5. *Time,* May 23, 1983.
6. Ibid.
7. *American Film,* June 1983.
8. Ibid.
9. POLLOCK, *Skywalking.*
10. Ibid.
11. Ibid.
12. *American Film,* June 1985.
13. Ibid.
14. Ibid.
15. Ibid.
16. *Current Biography,* 1978.
17. *American Film,* June 1985.
18. POLLOCK, *Skywalking.*
19. Ibid.
20. *Time,* May 23, 1983.
21. POLLOCK, *Skywalking.*
22. Ibid.

Exhibit 1 Motion Picture Revenues

Top Money Makers

1. E.T. The Extra-Terrestrial (Universal, 1982)	$209,567,000
2. Star Wars (20th Century-Fox, 1977)	193,500,000
3. Return of the Jedi (20th Century-Fox, 1983)	165,500,000
4. The Empire Strikes Back (20th Century-Fox)	141,600,000
5. Jaws (Universal, 1975)	133,435,000
6. Raiders of the Lost Ark (Paramount)	115,598,000
7. Grease (Paramount, 1978)	96,300,000
8. Tootsie (Columbia, 1982)	94,571,613
9. The Exorcist (Warner Bros., 1973)	89,000,000
10. The Godfather (Paramount, 1972)	86,275,000
11. Close Encounters of the Third Kind (Columbia, 1977/80)	83,452,000
12. Superman (Warner Bros., 1978)	82,800,000
13. The Sound of Music (20th Century-Fox, 1965)	79,748,000
14. The Sting (Universal, 1973)	79,419,900
15. Gone with the Wind (MBM/United Artists, 1939)	79,700,000
16. Saturday Night Fever (Paramount, 1977)	74,100,000
17. National Lampoon's Animal House (Universal, 1978)	74,000,000
18. Nine to Five (20th Century-Fox, 1980)	66,200,000
19. Rocky III (MGM/United Artists, 1982)	65,763,177
20. Superman II (Warner Bros., 1981)	65,100,000
21. On Golden Pond (Universal/Associated Film Distribution, 1981)	63,000,000
22. Kramer vs. Kramer (Columbia, 1979)	61,734,000
23. Smokey and the Bandit (Universal, 1977)	61,055,000
24. One Flew Over the Cuckoo's Nest (United Artists, 1975)	59,204,793
25. Stir Crazy (Columbia, 1980)	58,408,000

Note: United States and Canada only. 1) Figures are total rentals collected by film distributors as of Dec. 31, 1982. 2) Figures are not to be confused with gross box-office receipts from sale of tickets. Source: *Variety*.

On My Painting

MAX BECKMANN

Max Beckmann (1884-1950), the great independent among German expressionists, did not attempt to explain his art, nor art in general. *On My Painting* is a beautiful extension in words of the haunting world of his paintings, one of the rare instances in which an artist has succeeded in putting into words the sense not just of his paintings, but of their genesis. It is probably more accurate to call it a prose poem, rather than an essay.

On My Painting was a lecture given by Beckmann at the New Burlington Galleries, London, in 1938. It was published in 1941 by the late Curt Valentin, in New York, and I am indebted to Ralph F. Colin, executor of the Valentin estate, for permission to use it here. Mrs. Max Beckmann, working from the original German manuscript, provided me with a number of corrections, especially in the "Song" toward the end of the text. With the greatest goodwill and patience, she checked and rechecked the revisions, and I offer her my sincerest thanks.

Before I begin to give you an explanation, an explanation which it is nearly impossible to give, I would like to emphasize that I have never been politically active in any way. I have only tried to realize my conception of the world as intensely as possible.

Painting is a very difficult thing. It absorbs the whole man, body and soul—thus I have passed blindly many things which belong to real and political life.

I assume, though, that there are two worlds: the world of spiritual life and the world of political reality. Both are manifestations of life which may sometimes coincide but are very different in principle. I must leave it to you to decide which is the more important.

What I want to show in my work is the idea which hides itself behind so-called reality. I am seeking for the bridge which leads from the visible to the invisible, like the famous cabalist who once said: "If you wish to get hold of the invisible you must penetrate as deeply as possible into the visible."

My aim is always to get hold of the magic of reality and to transfer this reality into painting—to make the invisible visible through reality. It may sound paradoxical, but it is, in fact, reality which forms the mystery of our existence.

What helps me most in this task is the penetration of space. Height, width, and depth are the three phenomena which I must transfer into one plane to form the abstract surface of the picture, and thus to protect myself from the infinity of space. My figures come and go, suggested by fortune or misfortune. I try to fix them divested of their apparent accidental quality.

One of my problems is to find the Self, which has only one form and is immortal—to find it in animals and men, in the heaven and in the hell which together form the world in which we live.

Space, and space again, is the infinite deity which surrounds us and in which we are ourselves contained.

Reprinted with permission of the estate of Max Beckman, from *Modern Artists on Art*, Robert L. Herbert ed. (Englewood Cliffs NJ: Prentice Hall, 1964).

That is what I try to express through painting, a function different from poetry and music but, for me, predestined necessity.

When spiritual, metaphysical, material, or immaterial events come into my life, I can only fix them by way of painting. It is not the subject which matters but the translation of the subject into the abstraction of the surface by means of painting. Therefore I hardly need to abstract things, for each object is unreal enough already, so unreal that I can only make it real by means of painting.

Often, very often, I am alone. My studio in Amsterdam, an enormous old tobacco storeroom, is again filled in my imagination with figures from the old days and from the new, like an ocean moved by storm and sun and always present in my thoughts.

Then shapes become beings and seem comprehensible to me in the great void and uncertainty of the space which I call God.

Sometimes I am helped by the constructive rhythm of the Cabala, when my thoughts wander over Oannes Dagon to the last days of drowned continents. Of the same substance are the streets with their men, women, and children; great ladies and whores; servant girls and duchesses. I seem to meet them, like doubly significant dreams, in Samothrace and Piccadilly and Wall Street. They are Eros and the longing for oblivion.

All these things come to me in black and white like virtue and crime. Yes, black and white are the two elements which concern me. It is my fortune, or misfortune, that I can see neither all in black nor all in white. One vision alone would be much simpler and clearer, but then it would not exist. It is the dream of many to see only the white and truly beautiful, or the black, ugly and destructive. But I cannot help realizing both, for only in the two, only in black and in white, can I see God as a unity creating again and again a great and eternally changing terrestrial drama.

Thus without wanting it, I have advanced from principle to form, to transcendental ideas, a field which is not at all mine, but in spite of this I am not ashamed.

In my opinion, all important things in art since Ur of the Chaldees, since Tel Halaf and Crete, have always originated from the deepest feeling about the mystery of Being. Self-realization is the urge of all objective spirits. It is this Self for which I am searching in my life and in my art.

Art is creative for the sake of realization, not for amusement; for transfiguration, not for the sake of play. It is the quest of our Self that drives us along the eternal and never-ending journey we must all make.

My form of expression is painting; there are, of course, other means to this end such as literature, philosophy, or music; but as a painter, cursed or blessed with a terrible and vital sensuousness, I must look for wisdom with my eyes. I repeat, with my eyes, for nothing could be more ridiculous or irrelevant than a "philosophical conception" painted purely intellectually without the terrible fury of the senses grasping each visible form of beauty and ugliness. If from those forms which I have found in the visible, literary subjects result—such as portraits, landscapes, or recognizable compositions— they have all originated from the senses, in this case from the eyes, and each intellectual subject has been transformed again into form, color, and space.

Everything intellectual and transcendent is joined together in painting by the uninterrupted labor of the eyes. Each shade of a flower, a face, a tree, a fruit, a sea, a mountain, is noted eagerly by the intensity of the senses to which is added, in a way of which I am not conscious, the work of my mind, and in the end the strength or weakness of *my soul*. It is this genuine, eternally unchanging center of strength which makes mind and sense capable of expressing personal things. It is the strength of the soul which forces the mind to constant exercise to widen its conception of space.

Something of this is perhaps contained in my pictures.

Life is difficult, as perhaps everyone knows by now. It is to escape from these difficulties that I practice the pleasant profession of a painter. I admit that there are more lucrative ways of escaping the so-called difficulties of life, but I allow myself my own particular luxury, painting.

It is, of course, a luxury to create art and, on top of this, to insist on expressing one's own artistic opinion. Nothing is more luxurious than this. It is a game and a good game, at least for me; one of the few games which make life, difficult and depressing as it is sometimes, a little more interesting.

Love in an animal sense is an illness, but a necessity which one has to overcome. Politics is an odd game, not without danger I have been told, but certainly sometimes amusing. To eat and to drink are habits not to be despised but often connected with unfortunate consequences. To sail around the earth in 91 hours must be very strenuous, like racing in cars or splitting the atoms. But the most exhausting thing of all—is boredom.

So let me take part in your boredom and in your dreams while you take part in mine which may be yours as well.

To begin with, there has been enough talk about art. After all, it must always be unsatisfactory to try to express one's deeds in words. Still we shall go on and on, talking and painting and making music, boring ourselves, exciting ourselves, making war and peace as long as our strength of imagination lasts. Imagination is perhaps the most decisive characteristic of mankind. My dream is the imagination of space—to change the optical impression of the world of objects by a transcendental arithmetic progression of the inner being. That is the precept. In principle any alteration of the object is allowed which has a sufficiently strong creative power behind it. Whether such alteration causes excitement or boredom in the spectator is for you to decide.

The uniform application of a principle of form is what rules me in the imaginative alteration of an object. One thing is sure—we have to transform the three-dimensional world of objects into the two-dimensional world of the canvas.

If the canvas is only filled with a two-dimensional conception of space, we shall have applied art, or ornament. Certainly this may give us pleasure, though I myself find it boring as it does not give me enough visual sensation. To transform height, width, and depth into two dimensions is for me an experience full of magic in which I glimpse for a moment that fourth dimension which my whole being is seeking.

I have always on principle been against the artist speaking about himself or his work. Today neither vanity nor ambition causes me to talk about matters which generally are not to be expressed even to oneself. But the world is in such a catastrophic state, and art is so bewildered, that I, who have lived the last thirty years almost as a hermit, am forced to leave my snail's shell to express these few ideas which, with much labor, I have come to understand in the course of the years.

The greatest danger which threatens mankind is collectivism. Everywhere attempts are being made to lower the happiness and the way of living of mankind to the level of termites. I am against these attempts with all the strength of my being.

The individual representation of the object, treated sympathetically or antipathetically, is highly necessary and is an enrichment to the world of form. The elimination of the human relationship in artistic representation causes the vacuum which makes all of us suffer in various degrees—an individual alteration of the details of the object represented is necessary in order to display on the canvas the whole physical reality.

Human sympathy and understanding must be reinstated. There are many ways and means to achieve this. Light serves me to a considerable extent on the one hand to divide the surface of the canvas, on the other to penetrate the object deeply.

As we still do not know what this Self really is, this Self in which you and I in our various ways are expressed, we must peer deeper and deeper into its discovery. For the Self is the great veiled mystery of the world. Hume and Herbert Spencer studied its various conceptions but were not able in the end to discover the truth. I believe in it and in its eternal, immutable form. Its path is, in some strange and peculiar manner, our path. And for this reason I am immersed in the phenomenon of the Individual, the so-called whole Individual, and I try in every way to explain and present it. What are you? What am I? Those are the questions that constantly persecute and torment me and perhaps also play some part in my art.

Color, as the strange and magnificent expression of the inscrutable spectrum of Eternity, is beautiful and important to me as a painter; I use it to enrich the canvas and to probe more deeply into the object. Color also decided, to a certain extent, my spiritual outlook, but it is subordinated to light and, above all, to the treatment of form. Too much emphasis on color at the expense of form and space would make a double manifestation of itself on the canvas, and this would verge on craft work. Pure colors and broken tones must be used together, because they are the complements of each other.

These, however, are all theories, and words are too insignificant to define the problems of art. My first unformed impression, and what I would like to achieve, I can perhaps only realize when I am impelled as in a vision.

One of my figures, perhaps one from the "Temptation," sang this strange song to me one night—

Fill up again your pumpkins with alcohol, and hand up the largest of them to me. . . . Solemn, I will light the giant candles for you. Now in the night. In the deep black night.

We are playing hide-and-seek, we are playing hide-and-seek across a thousand seas. We gods, we gods when the skies are red at dawn, at midday, and in the blackest night.

You cannot see us, no you cannot see us but you are ourselves. . . . Therefore we laugh so gaily when the skies are red at dawn, at midday, and in the blackest night.

Stars are our eyes and the nebulae our beards. . . . We have people's souls for our hearts. We hide ourselves and you cannot see us, which is just what we want when the skies are red at dawn, at midday, and in the blackest night.

Our torches stretch away without end . . . silver, glowing red, purple, violet, green-blue, and black. We bear them in our dance over the seas and the mountains, across the boredom of life.

We sleep and stars circle in the gloomy dream. We wake and the suns assemble for the dance across bankers and fools, whores and duchesses.

Thus the figure from my "Temptation" sang to me for a long time, trying to escape from the square on the hypotenuse in order to achieve a particular constellation of the Hebrides, to the Red Giants and the Central Sun.

And then I awoke and yet continued to dream . . . painting constantly appeared to me as the one and only possible achievement. I thought of my grand old friend Henri Rousseau, that Homer in the porter's lodge whose prehistoric dreams have sometimes brought me near the gods. I saluted him in my dream. Near him I saw William Blake, noble emanation of English genius. He waved friendly greetings to me like a super-terrestrial patriarch. "Have confidence in objects," he said, "do not let yourself be intimidated by the horror of the world. Everything is ordered and correct and must fulfil its destiny in order to attain perfection. Seek this path and you will attain from your own Self ever deeper perception of the eternal beauty of creation; you will attain increasing release from all that which now seems to you sad or terrible."

I awoke and found myself in Holland in the midst of a boundless world turmoil. But my belief in the final release and absolution of all things, whether they please or torment, was newly strengthened. Peacefully I laid my head among the pillows . . . to sleep, and dream, again.

Creating Video Games That Score

One Startup Stresses Team Efforts, Another Creative Freedom. Both Are Winners.

In one corner of Imagic Inc.'s Los Gatos (Calif.) headquarters is an area nicknamed "the zoo." Inside, behind locked doors, are Imagic's 30 video-game designers, most of them young men in their 20s. There are few rules in the zoo. Designers work any hours they choose. Some dress in shorts and T-shirts. One wears three earrings.

Activision Inc., in nearby Santa Clara, has a similar lab. It, too, is a distraction-free haven for game designers. Fewer than 10 nondesigners have access to the lab. No memos are ever delivered to it. The telephones there don't ring—they simply flash a small light.

If Imagic and Activision pamper their designers, it is with good reason. These small, elite groups are at the heart of the companies' product development efforts in the video-game software business, a cash mill that generated $1.4 billion in sales last year and may top $2 billion this year as game machines and home computers proliferate. Unlike other leading competitors, such as Atari Inc., these two stunningly successful startups rely entirely on internal development for their game ideas. But their approach to game design could hardly be more different.

Arts and sciences. Reflecting nearly opposite philosophies of product development, Activision tries to give individual designers as much creative freedom as possible, while Imagic emphasizes team projects and market testing. Says James H. Levy, Activision's president: "Creative businesses aren't factories. To be successful, you must deal with and live with uncertainty and surprises. If you try to make it too predictable, you squeeze all the life out of it."

Imagic comes at it from the other side. "Product development is not one artist creating something all by himself," says President William F. X. Grubb, who, at 38, is the oldest member of Imagic's management. "Here, the designer is more like an orchestra leader."

Activision's 31 designers, for instance, choose their own projects with no interference from the marketing department. In fact, Activision does no market research on a game until the designer is completely finished. "Market research will kill as many good games as bad ones," says Levy. Instead, during the game design process, which typically takes about six months, a designer constantly tries out new ideas on his fellow designers and on Activision's creative-development managers. These managers serve as sounding boards for ideas and as liaison with the rest of the company.

Business Week, April 4, 1983. Reprinted with permission.

But for the most part, design at Activision is a one-person process. Each designer is responsible for all aspects: selecting the idea, writing the computer programs that control objects on the screen, and adding sound and background graphics. Activision managers believe team projects cut creativity. "Very few novels are written on an assembly-line basis," says Thomas M. Lopez, vice-president for editorial development. Says designer Steve Cartwright: "I wouldn't want to let someone else do my work. I'm the only one who will put in enough effort to make it right."

Toothpaste to the rescue. Cartwright has designed several of Activision's hit games, including Megamania, and has just finished Plaque Attack, set for release this summer. Rather than have the player fire missiles against a spaceship, this game calls for shooting a jet of toothpaste to defend a set of teeth against advancing columns of hamburgers, French fries, and ice cream cones. Cartwright spent months revising his original idea. "You go through hundreds of different combinations. There's a fine line between something that's challenging and something that's frustrating."

Throughout the long process of designing a game, Activision officials avoid imposing deadlines. "Time pressure makes the designer take short cuts," says Lopez. "It could turn a mega-hit into an average game. The game might lose that indescribable something that tickles neurons in millions of people."

At Imagic, designers write the computer motion and control programs that form the heart of the game, but in many cases a specialized artist designs the game's graphics, while another adds sound effects. This specialization is made possible, in part, by software tools developed at Imagic that

make it easier to program a computer to perform special tasks. For instance, Imagic has developed a program called Da Vinci, which assists in designing graphics, and another called Handel, which helps create sound effects.

Imagic promotes close collaboration between the marketing and design staffs. Marketing managers even sit in on the designers' twice-a-year "game-storming" weekends and sometimes throw out ideas of their own.

The Imagic product development process begins with those weekend meetings. After each one, designers draw up a list of 100 or so game ideas, then whittle that down to 30 or 40, and present these to the marketing department. Marketing produces story boards and game descriptions for each idea and then runs a "concept test" with about 100 teenagers. The results can influence the designer's approach to the game. One game originally involved a mouse trying to pick up cheese while being chased by a cat. Concept tests showed that teenagers preferred a game in which a prince tries to pick up treasures while being chased by a dragon. The designer followed the market feedback, and the game, called Dragonfire, is now a hit.

With Stock Options and Incentives, Top Designers Can Become Multimillionaires

Designer Rick Levine got the idea for his new game, Truckin', during one of his regular 800-mi. round trips on California's Highway 5 to visit his girlfriend. Market research showed children preferred a truck game to a car game. The player learns about U.S. geography as he guides the truck around the country, making deliveries on a tight schedule.

Imagic designers do not have to use all

concept-testing results in their games. "We like to see engineers follow about 80% of the results," says James H. Goldberger, vice-president of marketing. But if concept scores are very high or low, "we lobby very hard," he adds.

Licensing devotees. Most of the half-dozen other leading companies in the videogame software business hew to a product development approach totally different from those practiced at Imagic and Activision. They rely largely on licensing well-known arcade games and movie titles and converting them to home games. Atari's hugely successful Pac-Man, for example, was based on a license from Bally Mfg. Corp.

Coleco Industries Inc. attributes its zoom from zero to 8 million game cartridges sold last year to the "prerecognition" of its games drawn from arcade hits, such as Donkey Kong and Turbo. Releases for 1983 include licensed games based on the movie *Rocky* and the cartoon characters, the Smurfs. Coleco President Arnold C. Greenberg insists: "The real weak area [in home videogame sales] is the multiplicity of nonlicensed titles." But Activision and Imagic disagree; both believe that in the long run, internal development of original games will be the best way to survive.

Until recently, explains Levy of Activision, product development played only a modest role in the game software business. "The consumer developed a voracious appetite that couldn't be satisfied," he says. "To a certain extent, products sold no matter how good they were."

E.T. stays home. The seller's market fizzled last year when supply caught up with demand, and weaker software products no longer sold well. Earnings fell below esti-mates at several companies, including industry leader Atari, which was hurt by defections of key designers to Activision, Imagic, and elsewhere. One of Atari's most spectacular losers was a game based on a coveted license that seemed like a certain winner: the movie *E.T.* Atari paid $22 million in licensing fees. Thinking it could sell 4 million cartridges, it reportedly produced that many. It sold only 1 million—potential buyers found the game dull.

The supply of movie and arcade properties suitable for conversion to video games is limited, says Levy. "Each year, 100 titles will drive the business," he predicts. "The arcade business can provide 6 or 10 titles a year. Only a half-dozen movies could be the conceptual basis for video games. Where will the other 85 come from? They will be original product designed for the medium."

So far, that thinking has worked, and the payoff for Activision and Imagic has been remarkable. At Activision, founded in 1979, revenues for the nine months ending Dec. 31 topped $100 million. Imagic, which shipped its first product in March, 1982, sold more than $75 million worth of game software in its first year of business. Its Demon Attack won the-game-of-the-year award from *Electronic Games* magazine last year. And in recent months two cartridges from Activision, Pitfall and River Raid, have occupied the first and second positions on the top 10 chart published by *Billboard* magazine. "When it comes to creative games, Activision and Imagic are definitely the leaders," says Michael J. Blanchet, who writes a syndicated column on video games for a variety of papers.

Thoroughbred talent. For the designers, too, the rewards stretch well beyond the freedom of "the zoo" and a phone-free lab. Both Activision's Cartwright and

Imagic's Levine, for instance, receive royalties on games they have designed. And if, as expected, Activision and Imagic go public later this year, both men will become multimillionaires through their stock holdings.

Such incentives have helped Activision and Imagic attract the cream of the industry's design talent, giving them both a big advantage. "Design is the cornerstone of success in video games," notes Arnie Katz, editor of *Electronic Games* magazine. "If you don't have the horses, you can't run."

George Lucas—Skywalking

DALE POLLACK

The flow takes Lucas to an anonymous business district in nearby San Rafael, site of the nerve center of Lucasfilm. The casual passerby has no inkling that five white stucco buildings, marked with orange trim and pseudo-Mediterranean tile roofs, and inconspicuously lettered A, B, C, D, and E, are a magician's lair. They include the Kerner Company Optical Research Lab, better known as Industrial Light and Magic, and, in an adjoining building is the computer division. Cheerful greenery surrounds the buildings. Inside, the walls feature original production sketches, paintings, and posters from Lucasfilm productions. There are also displays of bizarre offerings from *Star Wars* fans, the people who make this all possible.

These buildings, Skywalker Ranch, and Parkhouse comprise "Lucasland," a term that makes Lucas bristle, although his friends and employees often use it. Lucasland is a self-contained community, a new version of the nineteenth-century company town. Last Thanksgiving, the paternal owner gave away turkeys to his employees, 431 ten-pound birds in all. In 1979, the number of employees and family members attending the annual July Fourth picnic at the ranch was less than fifty; by 1980, it had grown to three hundred, and then to nine hundred in 1981.

On July 4, 1982, more than one thousand people showed up for an all-day-and-night celebration featuring barbecued hot dogs and hamburgers, beer and wine, organized softball, volleyball, and croquet games, plus bocci ball and horseshoes. There was swimming at the lake (lifeguards present), followed by a dance featuring a rockabilly band. Horse-drawn surries and haywagons shuttled Lucaslandians to and from the parking lots, and a brass band played in the meadow. Walt Disney couldn't have done it better.

Disney's dreams came true because his brother Roy ran the business and paid the bills. Lucas has no sibling to turn to, although Marcia, his wife, acts as his counselor and confidante. George sets the direction for Lucasfilm and makes everyone believe that he knows what he's doing. Richard Edlund likens it to working on a special effects sequence with Lucas: "You may not understand the sequence yet, but you know that *he* does. By talking with you, he's building his understanding and yours at the same time."

Lucas reluctantly accepts his role as chairman of the board of Lucasfilm Ltd. He started paying himself a salary only at the end of 1981. Lucasfilm has average annual revenues of more than $26 million, a number that can multiply quickly when a hit movie is released. Lucas keeps his company private so that he doesn't have to tell anyone how much he makes (except the government). But being a successful executive is not his idea of fun.

"Running the company to me is like mowing the lawn," Lucas says, coming full circle from age eight to thirty-eight. "It has to be done. I semi-enjoy it, once in a while." As a child, Lucas found a way out of his dilemma; he saved his money and bought a power mower. He'd love to make Lucasfilm a self-propelled machine—but for now, he must push it.

Pushing it means showing up at President Bob Greber's office for his twice-weekly meetings. He speaks and meets with Greber and his executives at other times, but this ritual might be called "George Needs to Know." Present are Greber, vice president and chief operating officer Roger Faxon, finance vice president Chris Kalabokes, vice president and general counsel Kay Dryden. They have a direct line to Lucas. They are his extensions, doing what he can't do. Lucas is pulled in so many different directions that he has little time to spend with his employees. "They're just going to have to do it on their own," he says. "Everybody can't have me."

For four hours each week, Lucasfilm has Lucas. The meeting is informal; George leans back on the couch, his arms outstretched. Greber, serious but relaxed, sits on his desk—in his mid-forties, he is the oldest person in the company. Faxon, a former congressional budget analyst, has his glasses perched on his nose and a yellow legal pad on his lap. Dryden also has a legal pad, on which she takes copious notes. There is no formal agenda, but Greber keeps things moving. Items are discussed briefly with occasional humorous asides; the atmosphere is relaxed and open.

The renovation of a Lucasfilm-owned office building is brought up, and George looks around the room. "What do you recommend?" he asks. When everyone agrees on a decision, he nods his head: "That's my

mind on it, too." Imperceptibly, Lucas is in charge—he rattles off questions about earthquake liability and insurance like a seasoned corporate analyst. When he's made his decision, he invariably says, "My feeling is. . . ." Told that someone needs to fly to Japan on business, Lucas jokes: "This is how deals are made—all to get a free airline ticket." Then the smile disappears. "Get the specifics of exactly why this trip is necessary," he instructs Greber.

Those close to Lucas agree that he has gradually become a happier, more relaxed person; he is less shy, if still not outgoing. In Greber's office he is open and communicative, expressing his thoughts without hesitation or reserve. Lucas still shuns the limelight—a request that he autograph one hundred raiders story records elicits a look of wide-eyed disbelief. "What?" he exclaims, amazed that Faxon would dare make the request. Ascertaining that it was not for charity, he dismisses the idea with a wave of his hand. These are the times, Greber says later, that Lucas would rather be somewhere else. "He would prefer never to speak to people like me if he could get away with it," Greber states.

Lucas possesses the instincts of the natural businessman, a trait rare in filmmakers. He has the ability to make decisions and to anticipate their consequences. "Most people pass the buck," says Michael Levett, head of Lucasfilm merchandising—he is not a person who floats through life. He lays a foundation for his thoughts and then methodically builds on it. "His business acumen astounds me," Greber attests.

Lucas smiles when he hears these compliments—he almost flunked math in eighth grade. He may not understand tax shelters or oil depreciations, but as he says, "We can manage very well with things I *can* understand. If it makes sense to me, then it's okay." Lucas's business philosophy is dollar-in, dollar-out, the legacy of George, Sr.

"Survival of the fittest," Lucas is fond of saying. "I'm glad I have this simple-minded, small-town, conservative business attitude. I'm just like a small shop-keeper." Minding a $26 million candy store, he might add.

Lucas has mixed feelings about the rest of his patrimony. It wasn't fun having to buy clothes out of an allowance, or having the cost of undone chores deducted each week. "It straightened me out, so I've sort of done all right in my life," he says of his practical upbringing. "But sometimes I wonder if it was really worth it—if I've turned out that much better as a result." Lucas is tired of the hard work, perseverance, and patience that have made him a success.

Surprisingly, his father has the same doubts. "I'm kind of a perfectionist, I guess," says George, Sr., echoing his son. "To some extent I neglected my family. For years, I was at work at seven A.M., six days a week. I wouldn't quit until I had done something to *my* satisfaction, and I never wanted to lose. I was a loner—I didn't want to take anyone else on, because if I got into trouble, I'd bring them down with me." Lucas worries about the same things, an inheritance he'd rather do without.

It's 6:00 P.M. when George goes next door to the offices of Industrial Light & Magic. The company's identity is revealed by an elaborate circular logo above the receptionist's desk: a magician in full tuxedo and tails, black top and white gloves, a red rose in his lapel, a wand in one hand, surrounded by a machine gear and the curved letters ILM. Security is tight. There are two receptionists in the foyer and foreboding signs warning visitors to check in. The precautions are necessary: ILM is where Lucas's imagination becomes real. Spaceships dangle from the ceiling, rock music blares in a room lined with hundreds of model airplane and tank kits. A poster on the wall shows Sinbad flying on a celluloid carpet. In four sealed vaults lie the crown treasures:

models and miniatures of the *Millennium Falcon,* the Death Star, the Snow Walkers, even Luke, Han, and Leia. "This is where the future is made," says ILM manager Tom Smith.

Lucas comes to ILM every evening when a film is in or nearing production. Walt Disney strolled down Dopey Drive and Goofy Lane to visit with his animators; Lucas spreads his pollen from department to department at ILM. The illustrators, monster makers, and costume designers would like to see him more often but, as Lucas says, "There aren't enough hours in the day for me to do everyone I have to do."

Joe Johnston and George Jensen are working diligently at drafting boards as George enters the storyboard room and takes off his leather jacket. He picks up a red marking pen and both illustrators groan. The walls are lined with thumb-tacked drawings of each shot in the climactic battle sequence in *Return of the Jedi;* Lucas immediately sees that one shot is missing. He unpins the illustrations and moves them around, projecting the moving in his head. The storyboards not only give him a sense of how a scene fits together but enable him to reject specific shots before they are filmed.

When the red marker comes out, there's no doubt whose point of view will prevail. Lucas has the last say on everything. He is brutal about what he doesn't like: large red marks obliterate several carefully rendered drawings. Lucas grunts, "Let's eighty-six this one." The goal is a smooth flow of images. "I want it all to be *action!* No waiting time!" If Lucas criticizes, he also exhorts. "This is it, come on guy, we've got to get serious about this. The time is now!" The pep talk always works—Lucas drums up as much enthusiasm as a revival preacher. "Great," he says with satisfaction as he surveys a wall blotchy with red Xs.

As Lucas picks up his jacket and heads

for the door, Johnston jokingly calls after him, "If you need us around midnight, we'll still be here." Lucas laughs, but the comment disturbs him. He is halfway down the stairs when he turns and goes back, sticking his head into the room. "Will you really be here that late?" he asks—his concern for their welfare seems genuine.

As Lucas proceeds through ILM, his invariable greeting is "How's everything goin'?" said in a toneless murmur. "The fact that I don't say hello and smile and be friendly doesn't mean I don't care," Lucas says in his own defense. "If anything, I care too much." But he seems uneasy around his employees, and they are unsure of how to approach him. Distance, not intimidation, defines the relationship, and both sides maintain it. Lucas's inability to accept his position is evident when he enters a recently completed dubbing stage and a carpenter approaches him for an autograph. Lucas is taken aback, but reluctantly complies. "I didn't ask to be famous," he says later, standing in the parking lot. He looks at his feet and mutters, "But I guess that's all part of it."

George Lucas has coped with whatever "it" is, changing little in dress, attitude, or philosophy. But when he walks through an office, an imperceptible wave goes through the room, and a small entourage amorphously accumulates around him, as if he were too special to be related to on a normal level. "I know a lot of people who are afraid to talk to him. They just don't know what to say," Joe Johnston states with a shrug. Lucas can be intimidating to those who don't know him. Jane Bay once hired a receptionist and Lucas didn't speak to her for three months, not even to ask her name.

His demeanor has improved since then. "I think he's just more comfy on the planet now," says Bill Neil, who has known Lucas since The Rain People in 1968. George thanks people for their contribution and oc-

casionally chats with them on his rounds. He is sparing in his compliments—marketing chief Sidney Ganis remembers receiving only two in three years. "I think George would like to freeze a lot of people and bring them out only occasionally," observes a bitter Anthony Daniels. Lucas is sensitive to people's emotions—anyone who could create a Wookiee and R2-D2 can't be all bad. "George isn't a person who physically expresses his affection for people, but he definitely feels it," insists Jane Bay.

Sometimes Lucas's uncommunicativeness confuses his associates. When the computer building was under construction, Lucas questioned the placement of a door. The next day the door was moved to the other side of the room. Lucas was bewildered. "I didn't ask for this door to be over here," he said. The next day the door was moved back to its original location. Ed Catmull, head of the computer division, says, "People take him very literally."

* * *

I don't make pictures just to make money. I make money to make more pictures.

Walt Disney

After *Empire,* Lucas had to decide what to do with all the money he hadn't lost. In May 1978, George and Marcia formed a company that purchased the one hundred-year-old Bulltail Ranch in Nicasio, just north of San Anselmo. Set on 1,882 acres of rugged brown hills and deep valleys, Bulltail was once a thriving cattle and dairy ranch. Within two years, Parkway Properties bought thirteen parcels adjacent to Bulltail, including Big Rock Ranch, which climbed the nearby hills. The total spread came to 2,949 acres and cost Lucas $3 million. (The price was cheap because of county requirements that the land be kept agricultural, which scared off condominium developers.)

Skywalker Ranch promised to fulfill many of Lucas's long-standing goals: It would give him a headquarters unlike that of any other movie company. It would be a motion picture think tank, where movies would be conceptualized, rather than physically made. It would be neither a film studio nor a film campus, but something in between—exactly what, Lucas still doesn't know. Even the huge profits of *Star Wars* and *Empire* weren't sufficient to build and operate the ranch. But using merchandising as its base, Lucasfilm could expand into nonfilm investments that would guarantee Skywalker's completion whatever Lucas's future success in the movie business. Lucas liked the idea of confounding Hollywood again—his films would subsidize the ranch, not its owner.

Chris Kalabokes, the financial analyst who had reluctantly approved *Star Wars* at Fox, joined the company when he heard Lucas describe Skywalker. "That was a vision I could trust," he recalls. Other associates thought the decision was alarmingly irrational. Where would the money come from? Was George serious?

Lucas listened to his inner voice again. "I don't know why I'm building the ranch," he admits. "It's coming up with an idea and being committed to it without any logical point of view, I know. But it's just a feeling I have."

To realize his dream, Lucas knew that somebody had to take charge of his company, and he didn't want the job. "I needed a businessman," Lucas says. Charles Weber, the slim, soft-spoken corporate executive who had specialized in high-finance real estate ventures, was his choice. Weber's professional confidence impressed Lucas and soothed his worries about money matters. He gave Weber a simple directive—Charlie could run Lucasfilm, and if he made money, he could run it as he saw fit. If he didn't make money, he was out of a job. "Leave me

out of it," he told Weber, who was skeptical that Lucas could remove himself from his own company.

Lucasfilm found a home in the shadow of Universal Studios, an old brick-faced egg and dairy warehouse next to the Hollywood Freeway. When the purchase was finalized, Lucas confided to Richard Tong, "One of these days, Universal is going to really want this piece of property and I'm really going to make them pay for it."

Lucas was reluctant to set up corporate headquarters so close to Hollywood. It meant flying regularly between San Francisco and Burbank, a trip he loathed. He wanted to base Lucasfilm in Marin. But Weber, permanently settled in L.A., persuaded him that it was best to stay near Fox, which still controlled the only income-producing activity for the company, the merchandising. An ambitious remodeling program was begun on the old warehouse, renamed the Egg Company; the cost quickly went from $200,000 to $2 million.

George felt his by-now familiar premonitions of doom, as the Los Angeles staff expanded from five employees to fifteen, then fifty, then almost one hundred. "I wasn't happy with it ever," Lucas now says. But he rarely expressed his displeasure to Weber other than to remind him that Lucasfilm should be kept small and intimate. Weber patiently explained that if the company was going to pay for the ranch, he needed to expand.

Lucas wanted the Egg Company to be an ideal environment for creative and business people. The original skylight was buttressed with giant oak rafters; beneath it, an indoor courtyard was filled with tables, director's chairs, and hanging plants. George laid out the large, roomy offices, and Marcia designed the stunning interiors: dark green walls with burnished trim, antique desks and tables, and a polished oak balcony overlooking the courtyard. "I remember working at Sandler Films, sitting in a dark cubicle," Marcia says. "I want every employee to have a decent place to work.

George Lucas may have brought Hollywood to its knees, but he has also kept it alive. *Star Wars, Empire,* and *Raiders* have removed more than $150 million in profits from the coffers of two major studios that have had to content themselves with distribution fees. Tom Pollock says, "George has siphoned money out of the system that cannot be used again to make movies, other than his own." Lucas is the biggest profit participant in the history of the film business. Hollywood has benefited from his successes, however. Many movies rode the profitable coattails of Lucas's string of blockbusters. Without Lucas, the movie business might have fallen on even harder times. The success of *Raiders* allowed Paramount to make twelve less successful films.

"George Lucas is *not* what the rest of the business is about," says Ned Tannen. "Nobody has ever done what he has done. Nobody. George Lucas is over there, and the rest of the business is over here." Lucas is the man who got away, who beat the system by building his own system. "The studio system is dead," Lucas insists. "It died fifteen years ago when the corporations took over and the studio heads suddenly became agents and lawyers and accountants. The power is with the people now. The workers have the means of production."

Can that be George Lucas, the conservative businessman from Modesto, spouting socialist Hollywood rhetoric? Of course not. Lucas is talking about the *creative* power of the independent writer, director, and producer, a goal to which he has dedicated his career. With power comes the envy of those who do not possess it. Lucas and Hollywood have taunted each other for more than a decade; he finds Hollywood crooked and sleazy, while the film industry

resents his success and arrogance. "They don't care about movies," George says. "The advantage I've also had over the studios is that I do care. . . ."

Lucas can't wholeheartedly embrace business practices that he considers unfair and unscrupulous. Those who violate the basic tenets of morality (honesty, fairness, generosity) are eventually undone, Lucas believes. He is so honest that during the ICM arbitration over *Empire,* his staff was instructed to tell ICM's lawyers *everything,* even if it was harmful to his case.

Lucas wants the kind of ethical company that does not exist in Hollywood. His father's employees stayed with L. M. Morris for as long as twenty years, and George wants to develop that same loyalty in Lucasfilm. He tries to set a moral example. When you have someone over a barrel, don't push your advantage. When you negotiate a deal, be tough and demanding, but never unreasonable or unfair. When you have a success, share the profits. "It's just a matter of doing what's right," Lucas says.

*   *   *

Han Solo: I never would have guessed that underneath the person I knew was a responsible leader and businessman. But you wear it well.

Lando Calrissian: Yeah, I'm *responsible* these days. It's the price of success. And you know what, Han? You were right all along. It's overrated.

From *The Empire Strikes Back*

Lucas's worst fears about what could happen to Lucasfilm came true after *Empire* was released in 1980. The *Star Wars* profits had been invested and the dividends were not only paying for the company's overhead, but also freeing George from having to make movies and providing the financial base for Skywalker Ranch. Charles Weber had turned Lucasfilm into a thriving, successful miniconglomerate—*too* successful, as far as its chairman was concerned.

When Lucas extricated himself from the financial mess of *Empire,* his small, familial company of twelve people had become a well-heeled corporation with an annual overhead of $5 million, and 280 employees spread across California. His plans to consolidate the company in Marin seemed to have been forgotten. Most of Lucasfilm was already in Northern California, but the headquarters remained in Los Angeles, a community George despised.

Lucas always came back from Los Angeles feeling angry and frustrated. The Egg Company had originally had ten offices to house executives, secretaries, and receptionists. Now the building was enlarged, middle-management executives were driving Mercedes-Benzes and Porsches leased by Lucasfilm (annual cost, $300,000), and the Los Angeles staff was requesting its own cook. "It got totally out of hand," Lucas complains. "We were one step away from the delivery boy having a company Porsche. We were up here living in poverty row and they had a palatial estate."

Lucas saw the corrupting influences of Hollywood at work: His executives joined civic organizations, went to cocktail parties, and became what George had always vowed never to become—part of the industry. "I always felt a little uncomfortable being in the Hollywood community as a representative of Lucasfilm," says Weber. "I was constantly being told by George that nobody should be in Hollywood." Lucasfilm was a Marin County operation as far as Lucas was concerned. He had to get his people out of L.A.

Chronically unable to confront difficult problems, Lucas searched for a way out. He had never taken Lucasfilm seriously, allowing executives to tell him what they thought he wanted to hear. Remembers Weber, "From the day he hired me, I was a

foreign entity. He was the filmmaker, and we were the business people." Lucas's daily contact with his Los Angeles office consisted of a forty-five-minute phone conversation with Weber; he usually contributed a "Yeah" or "No" to the list of questions and issues Weber had prepared. What Lucas never said was "Stop it right now. This company is getting out of hand," which is what he was thinking.

As always, it was a question of control. "While I'd been saying, 'Charlie, this is your company,' when it came down to it I realized it was my money and I cared a lot more about how it was spent than I had in the beginning," Lucas admits. The matter came to a head when Weber wanted to borrow $50 million to turn Lucasfilm's passive investments into majority ownership in a variety of companies, from DeLorean automobiles to communications satellites.

Weber also wanted Lucas to bring other movie and TV producers into Lucasfilm, lending them his name and expertise. "Charlie is a businessman, and he doesn't realize how hard it is to come up with a creative thing, not to mention *consistently* creative things," Lucas says. Like Walt Disney, Lucas didn't want his name on anything he couldn't personally supervise. When Weber suggested that the ranch represented too much of a cash drain, Lucas had enough. "The ranch is the only thing that counts," he told Weber. "That's what everybody is working for. And if that is getting lost in the shuffle, then something's terribly wrong here."

George suffered sleepless nights, chronic headaches, and bouts of dizziness throughout the fall of 1980. "I'm not very brave about these situations," he said. "I'm somewhat insecure and slightly a coward." When he came back from Los Angeles just before Thanksgiving, he was stricken with stomach pains. Medical tests showed he had an incipient ulcer, which disappeared when medicated. Lucas internalized himself right into the hospital.

There was no one to turn to other than Marcia. It was a painful process for both of them as Lucas grappled with his dilemma. The conclusion was unavoidable: He was going to have to let half of the Los Angeles staff go, move everybody else up north, and pare Lucasfilm to a manageable size. Weber was called up to San Francisco and Lucas, sweating profusely, his voice hoarse and hollow, told him of the decision. Weber, usually impassive in business situations, was shocked. He had hoped to renegotiate an already generous salary package, and now he was told that Lucasfilm was being snatched from him.

George wanted Weber to stay with the company—he still admired Charlie and he felt guilty as hell. Weber agreed to moderate his demands and drove to the airport. Half an hour later, he was summoned back to Parkhouse. Lucas had decided that Lucasfilm couldn't be his and Weber's company at the same time. Accountant Richard Tong called George just after Weber left and recalls, "He sounded like he'd been through the wringer. Talk about ill, he sounded like he was dying." Lucas's sole comment on the firing of Weber is, "The one thing I regret is I didn't do it earlier."

When the Los Angeles staff returned to the Egg Company following the Christmas holidays, they were given the bad news. Only thirty-four of the eighty employees were asked to make the move north. There were bruised egos and bitter recriminations, mostly directed at Lucas. George felt terrible about disrupting people's lives, and went to great lengths to ease his conscience. Laid-off employees were given six months to find new jobs and generous cash settlements. Lucas even hired a vocational counselor to help them.

In a strange way, the experience was cathartic for Lucas. Marcia thought George learned one of life's valuable lessons: "When a situation is not working out, you confront that situation and you fix it. This was an uncomfortable situation for George, and he didn't confront it. In his reluctance to confront it, it just got worse and worse." By regaining control of Lucasfilm, George was again the center of his universe.

On May 28, 1981, Lucasfilm Ltd. officially relocated its corporate headquarters from Los Angeles to Marin County, completing what a press release called "the long-planned consolidation of the company." Mistakes had been made, money had been lost, dues had been paid. Changes of direction are expensive, but Lucas knew where he wanted to go.

Bob Greber, who had been chief financial officer, was made executive vice president and chief operating officer. Lucas initially kept Weber's title of president and chief executive officer (he has since given it to Greber) as well as retaining his own position as chairman. Greber's background was similar to Weber's—he had managed $60 million worth of Merrill Lynch's investments. But Greber accepted a condition that was unacceptable to Weber: "Basically, I implement those things George wants done."

Greber had some conditions of his own. Lucas had to openly and directly express his feelings about Lucasfilm. Greber told him, "You've got to tell me whether you like something or not. You just can't sit there and take it." Greber prepared a report that explained just how much money Lucasfilm had, how much it was spending, and how much was left over. Lucas was pleased: "Before, I'd gotten a seventy-five-page report that didn't say anything." He wanted to know the bottom line: cash-in, cash-out. Greber told him and won Lucas's trust.

Greber is accommodating, but he isn't a yes-man. Lucasfilm is not a company where orders are issued and the troops snap to attention. At times the atmosphere seems unnaturally idyllic: bright, motivated people all roughly the same age, with many of the same interests. The top executives are men, with the exception of Kay Dryden and Merchandising vice president Maggie Young, but many of the middle-management jobs (publishing, merchandising, fan club) are held by women. These employees share Lucas's parsimonious philosophy: "They're looking to save every dime they can," says Charles Weber.

Lucas's belief in corporate ethics, group decisions, and a family atmosphere filters down from the top. He has instilled a sense of pride in his employees through his own example. "The best boss and fellow workers a person can have," fan club president Maureen Garrett says in earnest. "I can't put it any other way." Secretaries and stage technicians are made to feel as if *they* are the artists. Because they share George's dream, they want to help him make it come true. Lucasfilm attracts the best people because of this reputation. What other filmmaker shares the wealth of his films with *all* his employees? "One act of kindness can carry you through a year of hell on a production," says librarian Debbie Fine. "The loyalty that man engenders is incredible."

As Lucas increasingly becomes a corporate overseer, his personal contact with his employees diminishes. At the 1981 Christmas party he had no idea who most of the one thousand guests were. His friends worry that he has been consumed by the corporation, which is fast becoming a new sea of faceless workers. Lawrence Kasdan senses an "IBM military" feel to Lucasfilm's corporate offices, nicknamed The Tower, after the evil-looking black administration building at Universal Studios. If a filmmaker screens a movie at Lucasfilm, he gets a computerized bill charging him for the projection room and any telephone calls he made, just like at Universal.

As the company grows, so does the internal bickering and division between the "haves" and the "have-nots." The production staff feels bullied and slighted; once again, they see executives driving around in company-leased Mercedes. And although ILM is completely unionized, as are the construction crews at Skywalker and Sprocket Systems, Charles Weber is among those who foresee problems: "People are going to think since they work for George Lucas, why is there any limitation to what they can make?" Lucas bristles at such criticism—Lucasfilm's annual overhead is $9 million, most of it in salaries. He calls the average wage scale at his company "awesome," the result of periodic surveys that ascertain the going rate in Hollywood. But three years between movies is a long time, and Lucasfilm has had to diversify to pay for all this. The company has invested $10 million in oil and natural gas wells, and owns $5 million worth of real estate in Marin County alone. Other properties include office buildings in San Francisco and the Egg Company in Los Angeles, now leased to filmmakers like Randal Kleiser. There are plans for a new commercial development in the Bay area that will combine a marina with a shopping center, a first-class restaurant, and condominiums. Greber expects Lucasfilm's passive investments to grow and speaks of profit centers and the prospect of creating TV programs. "If we can take care of that dream that George and Marcia have, it would be wonderful—as long as it's sensible," Greber says. That kind of talk was one reason Charles Weber lost his job.

Outside of passive investments and the movies themselves, Lucasfilm's only consistent source of profit is merchandising. There are literally hundreds of licenses for toys, decorator telephones, talking clocks, bicycles, lunchboxes, letter openers, children's and adult's underwear, pinball machines, video games, bumper stickers, candy, and ice cream and the bowls to eat it from. Lucasfilm also supervises the publication of novalizations, children's books, souvenir books, and comic books based on the *Star Wars* and Indiana Jones films. The record group oversees sound-track albums, story records, and jazz and disco spinoff albums. The in-house art department designs some of the merchandise and creates stationery and company logos. No ad is done without Lucasfilm's approval, no license granted before careful scrutiny of the manufacturer and distributor. Lucas's philosophy of responsibility and control has become corporate policy.

From May 1977, when *Star Wars* was released, through May 1983, merchandising of Lucasfilm products approached $2 billion in retail sales, *before* the release of *Return of the Jedi*. The company gets a royalty of between 1 and 7 percent on most items, although on products like T-shirts, Lucasfilm's share is closer to 50 percent. Lucas always recognized the potential in merchandising, but even he never imagined that a *Star Wars* label could mean a 20 percent increase in sales.

Lucas's personal beliefs suffuse the merchandising. Exploitative items are not sold, whether vitamins (he doesn't want to encourage kids to pop pills) or Princess Leia cosmetics (makeup can be harmful to children's skin). South Africa is boycotted in every respect but film sales, which are under Fox's control, because Lucas disagrees with the country's apartheid racial policies. He reviews every prototype toy (if Kenner Toys sold nothing but *Star Wars* merchandise, it would be the fifth largest toy company in the world) and maintains a veto power on all food tie-ins. Sugar cereals are verboten, but Hershey bars, Cokes, and milkshakes are okay. That was the stuff Lucas lived on as a kid—it's part of the American way of life.

*   *   *

There will be no one to stop us this time.

Darth Vader in *Star Wars*

When the term "software" came to mean everything from movies and TV programs to floppy computer disks and video games, Lucas hated it. But he soon realized that he could become one of its premier suppliers. A new era was dawning and, ever the pragmatist, Lucas planned to take advantage of it. . . .

Lucas also wanted to develop a complete computerized postproduction system: editing, sound editing, sound mixing, and film printing. It let him rationalize developing computer games, computer animation, and computer simulation (recreating images) at the same time. An outside firm constructed a computer-simulated spaceship battle, and the results looked as good as anything ILM had photographed. The process was costly and not yet economically feasible, but it *could* be done.

Starting a computer company from scratch is expensive and time-consuming. Lucas has already spent $8 million and still hasn't completed his postproduction system, which will revolutionize the mechanics of making movies. The drudge work will be done by the computer, leaving the filmmaker to think about how the movie fits together. Lucas wants to be on the cutting edge of film technology. People expect the creator of *Star Wars* to be ten steps ahead of the next guy.

Ed Catmull, the young director of the company graphics department at the New York Institute of Technology, became Lucasfilm's resident electronic genius. Catmull resembles the traditional technofreak: long hair, thick glasses, and a Ph.D. in computer science. Lucas told him to spend a year studying how to marry film to computers and how much it would cost. "Trust me," Lucas said. "We'll have our computer division."

In one of Lucasfilm's nondescript buildings, Lucas's promise is coming true. Bicycles line the building's hallway; the rooms are cooled by special air conditioners that maintain the optimum temperature for computers. At the end of one hall is a room filled with twenty-five minicomputers, equipped with $1,100 circuit boards that do the work $250,000 computers used to perform. In an adjoining laboratory red, green, and blue laser beams zip around a $100,000 laser table, a prototype system built at Lucasfilm with the help of outside consultants. In the graphics room, computers generate "calculated synthetic images:" a landscape of tall mountains topped by fluffy clouds is invitingly realistic; close examination reveals it consists of millions of tiny computer dots. No one wears white lab coats—the usual outfit is jeans, sneakers, and work shirts. These people *are* creating the future.

MODULE TWO

The Entrepreneur

The entrepreneur is central to this textbook and the course it embodies, for without the key individual who makes things happen, there can be no creative or entrepreneurial result. Timmons writes that "the eventual success of a new venture will depend a great deal upon the psychological make-up and determination of the lead entrepreneur. Venture capitalists have learned from experience that there is something (about) a (successful entrepreneur) that is different."[1]

In this module, traditional concepts of entrepreneurship will be assessed, and current mythologies discarded whenever possible. It may well be that no ONE, all-encompassing entrepreneurial profile exists; rather, a range of entrepreneurial types and behaviors may emerge through discussion. The module therefore introduces a variety of entrepreneurs with whom students may compare and measure themselves. Although different, these people share certain basic characteristics, understanding of which is facilitated by case discussion. The module also encourages a comparison of the entrepreneurial and managerial roles and continues to explore the themes introduced in Module One of personal and interpersonal creativity. The role of the entrepreneur in newly emerging and established organizations will be considered in Modules Three and Four.

In stressing a management perspective, the module is intended to increase one's ability to manage one's self and others. Students will better recognize the

[1] Jeffrey Timmons, *New Venture Creation* (Homewood, Ill.: Richard D. Irwin, 1985).

entrepreneurial potential in themselves and others as well as become more adept at fitting themselves with particular organizational environments and challenges. The goal of this module is to create a framework for understanding and to generate personal flexibility through the ability to use skills appropriate to different situations, people, and environmental demands. In this note the following topics are discussed:

1. Entrepreneurship—What Is It?
2. The Entrepreneurial Environment
3. The Entrepreneurial Task
4. The Entrepreneurial Personality
5. The Entrepreneurial Career

ENTREPRENEURSHIP—WHAT IS IT?

Entrepreneurship is elusive, difficult to define. The word itself is derived from a French root meaning "to undertake." Peter Kilby in his writings on entrepreneurship has compared it to the heffalump of Winnie the Pooh fame.[2] The heffalump is a large, self-important creature whom many claim to have seen though none can identify his characteristics with certainty. Similarly, there seem to be as many definitions of entrepreneurship as there are pundits or practitioners of the art. Entrepreneurship has been defined as "adventurism," "adrenaline-addiction," "risk-taking," and "thrill-seeking." While colorful, such definitions frequently reflect personal assumptions and are often contradictory.

How can we begin to define entrepreneur in a more satisfying manner? Certainly they are catalysts. They make things happen. They use creativity to conceive new things and zeal to implement them. Thus, the entrepreneur is both a creator and an innovator. He or she both generates the new idea and serves as the human vehicle by which implementation of that idea occurs. He or she takes the ball and runs with it, overcoming obstacles in the way.

At a recent research conference on entrepreneurship, the following definition was adopted:

> Entrepreneurship is the attempt to create value through recognition of business opportunity, the management of risk-taking appropriate to the opportunity, and through the communicative and management skills to mobilize human, financial, and material resources necessary to bring a project to fruition.[3]

The challenge of defining entrepreneurship is compounded by several factors. First, our understanding of entrepreneurship is often personal: Like creativity or love, we all have an opinion about it. Second, "entrepreneurship" is

---

[2] Peter Kilby, "Hunting the Heffalump," in *Entrepreneurship and Economic Development*, ed. Peter Kilby, (New York: The Free Press, 1971).

[3] John Kao and Howard Stevenson, eds., *Entrepreneurship: What It Is and How to Teach It*, Division of Research, Harvard Business School, 1984.

Figure 2-1

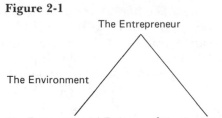

increasingly synonymous with "good." To the extent that entrepreneurs are viewed as the new cultural heroes, critical examination of their characteristics can be obscured by media hype or collective beliefs. Third, while "entrepreneur" has some tangibility because it refers to a person, "entrepreneurship" is more difficult to define because it is an abstraction. Fourth, our definitional challenge is also intensified by the current paucity of well-designed and controlled research studies to date on the entrepreneur. Finally, definition is difficult when it is assumed that entrepreneurship is something opposed to or divorced from management—that the entrepreneur and the manager are two different species of business person. Understanding the commonalities as well as differences in the entrepreneurial and managerial roles is central to our discussion.

Previously we introduced the idea of interrelating person, task, and organizational context to discuss creativity. In this module the framework will again be adopted in considering entrepreneurship. See Figure 2-1.

Collective values and available infrastructure which make up the entrepreneurial environment exert a powerful influence on the character of entrepreneurship: They either support or inhibit its emergence. The environmental challenges confronting the entrepreneur differ greatly in the United States, Japan, or Sweden, for example. Attitudes towards self-employment, wealth, and risk, and the availability of investment capital are only some of the relevant factors.

The first leg of our conceptual tripod relates to the tasks which face the entrepreneur. What does the entrepreneur do? What is his or her role in the organization? What business should he or she be in? What technology should be developed? What resources marshalled? Let us say that the business is to be convenience foods. What kind of company should be founded? What organization should be developed? How should the service be rolled out? What type of information is required to support decision making? What kind of people are needed? What marketing strategy should be adopted? Answering these and scores of other questions define the task of the entrepreneur.

The second leg involves the person, and his or her motives, style, and skill. Motives are those personal factors driving the individual towards a particular goal. They make up the factors "under the hood" that create motion. They are the source of "entrepreneurial zeal."[4] Style refers to social interaction, the inter-

---

[4] A favorite term of noted venture capitalist Pitch Johnson, founder of Asset Management Corporation.

Figure 2-2   Module Two—The Entrepreneur—Key Issues

Person	Understanding his/her personality and skills
Task	Defining a vision
	Marshalling resources
	Providing leadership
Organizational Context	Created depending on who the entrepreneur is, what the task is, and what leverage is required
Environment	Exploiting the availability of environmental resources, including:
	Capital
	People
	Infrastructure

face between self and others. It determines how one is perceived. It is an important means by which the entrepreneur achieves his or her goals through others. Finally, the variety of skills employed range from intuition to analytical ability. Individuals must also be considered in terms of their developmental history. Many of the cases in this book describe a personal story that gave significant shape to the individual entrepreneurial career. In short, it is important not simply to make do with a one-dimensional view of the entrepreneur: We need to keep many factors and perspectives in mind. Finally, our conceptual model includes the notion of organizational context, which is bracketed in this module. Obviously, the entrepreneur stands alone, initially. It is his or her task to create an organizational context which fits best with personal vision and sense of purpose, with the key tasks which must be accomplished for the enterprise to succeed, and finally with the environment which has the capacity to facilitate or hinder the new enterprise. This organizational context is latent in the entrepreneur's vision and requires realization. The challenge of developing an appropriate organizational context will be the subject of Module Three in the evolving organization. The issues of Module Two are summarized in Figure 2-2. The next three sections maintain this multidimensional perspective in expanding on the discussion of the entrepreneurial task, environment, and individual.

THE ENTREPRENEURIAL ENVIRONMENT

Entrepreneurship is environmentally determined. For example, our colloquial understanding of the term is very much a reflection of the values and traditions of the United States. When we examine the values that guided the founding of this country, when we read such classic works as Ralph Waldo Emerson's essay on self-reliance,[5] we are struck by the importance of independence, self-determi-

[5] Ralph Waldo Emerson, "On Self-Reliance," *Essays*, ed. Irey, Eugene F., (New York: Garland Publishing, 1981).

nation, and the rewards of initiative. This is eloquently captured by Kaplan:[6]

> Words matter. Americans believe that their country is great because it is good; in the 1980s they believe it is good because it is entrepreneurial. And so the controversy about what entrepreneurs are is far more than a debate about how to run a business. It is about how to lead and who is to lead. It is a discussion, a discussion about what businesses always are, about what America is and what Americans are.

If entrepreneurship is "as American as apple pie," then current events conspire to expand its definition, for in the 1980s, entrepreneurship is undergoing global expansion, and in previously unprecedented ways.[7,8] For example, entrepreneurship and creativity are hot topics of discussion in Japan, whose culture is known for its emphasis on consensus and group behavior. In Japan in the late 1980s, the Japanese executive may find it easier to overcome a need for company loyalty and security and start something independently. The case on Akira Kimishima in this book is relevant in this regard. In Europe, the 1980s have witnessed the explosion of venture capital, the prominence of successful venture companies (e.g., Benetton, Virgin), a trend toward the privatization of industry, increasing media attention, changing attitudes towards independence and money. Even in the People's Republic of China, entrepreneurial activity is enjoying a resurgence.[9]

What are the ingredients that influence an entrepreneurial environment? A number of factors are relevant, whose combination creates a "critical mass" necessary for entrepreneurial activity to flourish. Obviously, capital availability is essential. The "golden rule" applies here as well: Those with the gold make rules. Mechanisms for realizing value are also important. There is little point in making money if it cannot be accumulated and directed towards new objectives. The "harvest" for the entrepreneur may occur through, for example, sale of stock in capital public markets or private placements. If appropriate public markets for unlisted securities are absent or if tax regulations are punitive, the entrepreneur's zeal may be dampened by an inability to harvest.

Availability of other resources is also important. These include human resources with the necessary experience and skills, experts in such areas as law, information resources such as libraries and data banks, and infrastructure resources such as inexpensive space. Other factors influence the environment. Media attention is important, particularly as a means of publicizing the stories of appropriate role models and success stories. Idea-generating institutions are also important. Leading corporations such as Control Data and Hewlett-Packard have taken a role in fostering entrepreneurship through educational and invest-

[6] R. Kaplan, "Entrepreneurship Reconsidered: The Antimanagement Bias," *Harvard Business Review*, V. 65, no., 3, 1987.

[7] Sabin Russell, "Now It's the World's Turn," *Venture Magazine*, September 1984.

[8] John Kao, ed., *Global Entrepreneurship*, (forthcoming).

[9] Howard Chao and Paul Theil, "Entrepreneurship in the People's Republic of China," ed. John Kao, *Global Entrepreneurship*, (forthcoming).

ment programs. Universities are also valuable, as sources of technical opportunity and expertise. Finally, the environment is in a sense composed of the streams of opportunity available to the entrepreneur. New technological breakthroughs are likely to fuel a large amount of entrepreneurial activity.

The environment also exerts a significant influence in dictating the choices available to the would-be entrepreneur. In many societies, for example, access to mainstream jobs in established companies is blocked or hampered for certain groups such as minorities and immigrants. Individuals from such groups will be forced by circumstance to create their own economic platform by starting their own businesses. The drive towards social assimilation will stimulate such efforts.

Finally, the cultural environment is influential. Entrepreneurship in the 1980s is different in style from its manifestations in other historical periods. In this decade, the time between the creative idea and the corporate institution is swift; in no other era have the dynamics of organizational growth been more compressed. And as if in response, a group of young people and the organizations they have founded appear inherently supportive of entrepreneurial activities that seemingly thrive on rapid, volatile change. Names like Apple, Celestial Seasonings, Lotus—these conjure up a new spirit of entrepreneurship, which I call "the corporate new wave."[10] This corporate new wave is not only responsible for creating an economically significant group of companies (and entire industries) with aggregated annual net revenues in the billions, it has been considered trend-setting by both the popular and business press. Sharing the cultural heritage of the 1960s, which has somehow informed their business values, these young founders have established organizations that embody a new corporate role and new patterns of organizational responsibility. Many of the cases in this textbook—Janet Axelrod, Managing Change at Lotus Development Corporation, The Young Astronauts Program—illustrate this "new wave" ethos.

THE ENTREPRENEURIAL TASK

What do entrepreneurs do? Basic to the entrepreneurial role is the ability to recognize and exploit opportunities. In fact, Stevenson has defined the task of the entrepreneur as "the relentless pursuit of opportunity."[11] He sees opportunity as the recognition of a desired future state involving growth or change, and a belief that achievement of the state is possible.

As Drucker and others have pointed out, opportunity may come from many sources: the unexpected; incongruities in the relationship among industries and customers; process needs; changes in industry or market structure; changes in perception technology; government regulation; demographic shifts; and competitive pressures. Examples of factors which may create new opportunities for the entrepreneur include diplomatic relations with China (the unex-

---

[10] John Kao, "The Corporate New Wave," in *Entrepreneurship, What It Is and How to Teach It*, John Kao and Howard Stevenson eds., Division of Research, Harvard Business School, Boston, 1984.

[11] Howard Stevenson, personal communication.

pected); breakdown in the relationship between brokers and purchasers of securities (incongruities in the relationships among industries and customers); robotics (new process needs); the growing importance of home video relative to movie theaters (changes in industry or market structure); gourmet fast foods (changes in perception); genetic engineering (technology change); banking and airlines (deregulation); herbal teas and other health foods (demographic shifts); the personal computer industry (competitive pressures).

Implicit in the definition of the entrepreneur's role as the perception and pursuit of opportunity are a number of *psychological tasks*. They are captured by Schwartz's elegant description of the entrepreneur as "a dreamer who does."[12] The entrepreneur must be skillful to see opportunities where others do not. It is as though the entrepreneur has more finely tuned antennae. To the extent that an opportunity is latent in a given situation or implies a desired view of the future, the entrepreneur must use *intuition* effectively. Psychologists define intuition as the ability to find a meaningful pattern in an assortment of disparate data, to rely on knowledge derived from within. The entrepreneur often knows something with conviction when others do not, or when factual data are lacking to back up the claim. The entrepreneur will often say "Aha!" when others are still scratching their heads.

The entrepreneur must also be an implementer. This means an *ability to attend to details,* to be operationally oriented, to "take care of business." The entrepreneur must be responsive to objective knowledge derived from the environment. Thus, implicit in the entrepreneurial role is the notion of psychological balance between personal or intuitive and external or objective knowledge. Stereotyping the entrepreneur as an impractical dreamer or as a tough-minded seeker of personal advantage through the mastery of details is inaccurate.

The entrepreneur is faced with a number of *interpersonal* tasks as well. To marshall needed resources, the entrepreneur must work with many external constituencies; bankers, lawyers, public relations companies, consulting firms, government agencies are only some examples. It is part of the entrepreneur's job description that he or she must be comfortable working with a wide range of people. This *extroverted* style must be balanced by an ability to be alone to pursue *creative* tasks. It is only in the solitude of the entrepreneur's own thoughts that the creative vision about a new business possibility can be worked out completely. Thus, the extroversion of working through people must be balanced with the *introversion* of creative thought.

Unless the plan for a new enterprise will work through a sole proprietorship, the entrepreneur must work with and through people to build an organization suited to implementing the perceived opportunity. Thus, the entrepreneur must be a *leader,* able to define a vision of what is possible and to attract people to rally around that vision and transform it into a reality. The entrepreneur's leadership tasks are complicated by the inherent nature of the new enterprise. Typically, resources are scarce and the organization has no track record. Thus, the entrepreneur cannot attract people to the enterprise because of current

---

12   Robert Schwartz, personal communication.

financial rewards, or the stability and prestige of the organization. Rather, to paraphrase Charles Revson, the entrepreneur offers hope—hope that the vision will be realized, that future rewards will be obtained.

The entrepreneur often motivates others by charisma, the ability to exert an influence on others solely because of who one is. Entrepreneurs like Steven Jobs (Apple Computers) or Fred Smith (Federal Express) are frequently described as charismatic. Charismatic authority is personal and unstable, suited to times of change; hence, entrepreneurs frequently use their charisma to get things done through people in situations where usual incentives are unavailable or difficult to apply. They embody a cause which attracts the loyalty of those people needed for the success of the new enterprise.

Thus, the entrepreneur's tasks are diverse: to see an opportunity; marshall human and other resources necessary to pursue it; and transform the opportunity into a tangible result. Their job description includes creative, operational/ managerial, interpersonal, and leadership tasks.

THE ENTREPRENEURIAL PERSONALITY

Various scholarly lenses have been held up to the entrepreneurial individual. Numerous attempts have been made to identify essential characteristics of entrepreneurs, using a trait approach; other research examines the entrepreneur's personality and is based in large measure on psychoanalytic or depth psychological theory.

Entrepreneurial Traits

In a recent and comprehensive review, Timmons and his colleagues summarized characteristics on the entrepreneur distilled from 50 research studies. These traits include:

- Total commitment, determination, and perseverance
- Drive to achieve and grow
- Opportunity and goal orientation
- Taking initiative and personal responsibility
- Persistent problem solving
- Realism and a sense of humor
- Seeking and using feedback
- Internal locus of control
- Calculated risk-taking and risk-seeking
- Low need for status and power
- Integrity and reliability[13]

---

[13] J. Timmons, et al., *New Venture Creation* (Homewood, Ill.: Richard D. Irwin, Inc., 1985).

Several of these characteristics have been studied in greater detail. For example, many accounts of the entrepreneur portray an impulsive, gambling adventurer, intoxicated by his or her own adrenaline. Certainly, entrepreneurs frequently place themselves at risk. Liles has described these risks in terms of financial security, career opportunities, family relationships, and personal well-being.[14] Yet research also shows that the entrepreneur is more a risk manager than a risk-seeker. Brockhaus used standardized measurements of risk to study entrepreneurs and found little to distinguish risk-taking propensity of entrepreneurs from that of managers.[15] Stevenson has characterized the entrepreneur's attitude towards the risk-reward relationship as "You take the risk, I'll take the reward."[16]

McClelland's[17] work on achievement motivation also contributes to the literature on entrepreneurship. From his social psychological perspective, human beings are seen as driven by three motives: the need for achievement (accomplishing things); for affiliation (being with others); and for power (controlling others). Of these the need for achievement ("n Ach") was seen as most relevant for understanding the entrepreneur.

McClelland characterized individuals with high need for achievement as preferring to be personally responsible for solving problems, setting goals, and for reaching these goals by their own efforts, as well as strongly desiring some measure of their accomplishments. He suggested a link between a high "n Ach" and an entrepreneurial bent.

This trait approach to describing entrepreneurship evolved in response to practical needs. It was considered desirable to develop a profile of the entrepreneur to identify those who might become successful entrepreneurs. Hence, we do not know which are necessary, as opposed to sufficient, conditions for entrepreneurship nor which characteristics are uniformly associated with success.

Overall, the trait approach is far from satisfactory; many traits used to describe entrepreneurs could just as easily apply to many managers. The trait approach also lacks specificity, refers largely to men, and is not applicable in all cultures. It has also been observed by Timmons and others that certain personality characteristics of entrepreneurs, if taken to an extreme, can be a drawback to a successful enterprise in the long run (e.g., extreme self-sufficiency could prevent the founder from delegating authority and using others' help). Hence, even so-called entrepreneurial traits must be present at an optimum level for entrepreneurship to occur. A final difficulty with the trait approach is that the traits listed are usually positive, a further move towards making the terms "entrepreneur" and "good" synonymous. For example, turn around the qualities men-

---

[14]   P. R. Liles, *New Business Ventures and the Entrepreneur* (Homewood, Ill.: Richard D. Irwin, Inc., 1974).

[15]   Robert Brockhaus, "Risk-Taking Propensity of Entrepreneurs," *Academy of Management Journal*, Vol. 23, No. 3, 1980.

[16]   Howard Stevenson, personal communication.

[17]   David McClelland, *The Achieving Society* (Princeton: D. Van Nostrand Company, 1961).

tioned in the beginning of this section which Timmons used to define the entrepreneur. No one would want to be:

- Lacking commitment
- Lacking drive to achieve
- Avoiding personal responsibility
- Not oriented to problem solving
- Unrealistic and overly serious
- Avoiding feedback
- Driven by demands of others
- Not a manager of risk
- Needing status and power
- Lacking integrity and reliability.

Personality Studies

Two key efforts to explore the personality of the entrepreneur come from Collins and Moore's[18] studies and Zaleznik's writings.[19,20] Each is based on a central assumption, stated in the words of Collins and Moore, that "The act of entrepreneurship is an act patterned after modes of coping with early childhood experiences."

The Collins and Moore study, published in 1964, was based on interviews and psychological testing of successful male manufacturing entrepreneurs in Michigan. The keystone characteristic of the entrepreneurs studied was a high need for autonomy, independence, and self reliance. The implicit psychological theory underlying the study was psychoanalytic: The entrepreneur was seen as driven by unresolved conflicts around authority stemming from the early relationship with his parents. A tremendous ambivalence surrounded parental authority, which could be neither rejected nor accepted. In the entrepreneurs studied, the fathers were typically unsupportive and absent failures; the mothers were long-suffering and devoted to the son, ready to rely on him rather than the father.

For Collins and Moore, the entrepreneurs' ambivalence about authority resulted in an ability either to completely accept or reject parental norms. There was a corresponding inability either to express resistance to authority or to accept it in a mature fashion. Authority was often dealt with by avoidance or a need to escape. In practical terms this accounted for the observation that entrepreneurs frequently could not function comfortably in a bureaucratic organization unless they headed it, and that they had difficulties in relinquishing possession of authority and in forming long-lived partnerships.

---

[18] Orvis Collins and David Moore, *The Enterprising Man* (East Lansing, Mich.: MSU Business Studies, 1964).

[19] Abraham Zaleznik, *Power and the Corporate Mind* (New York: Harper and Row, 1976).

[20] Abraham Zaleznik, *The Entrepreneur and the Juvenile Delinquent* (unpublished manuscript cited with permission).

This ambivalence was also linked to the entrepreneurs' ability to function well in adversity, to accept failure and rise again, to stage successful comebacks. It was based on "anxiety over success; guilt over replacing the father." At its most extreme it constituted a real weakness: the tendency to fail repeatedly.

Collins and Moore observed that an entrepreneur's story was often linked to an early crisis or dramatic vivid event—frequently an economic crisis—a dangerous and difficult situation from which the entrepreneur could survive only by relying on himself.

The Collins and Moore entrepreneurs adhered to common American success values such as honesty, hard work, self-sacrifice, competitive spirit, winning, going it alone, determination. They displayed a lack of socially upward mobility, being more interested in their achievements than in "making it" in society. They pursued hard work and chronic fatigue—for their own sake—as a personal control mechanism, balancing, striving, and exhaustion. They were described as restless and dissatisfied.

The authors observed patterns in the entrepreneurs' ability to work with others. Such individuals often exhibited patriarchal or patronizing attitude toward subordinates, and projected their own resisted vices such as sloth and rebelliousness onto others. There was a high need to dominate and a fear of being dominated. This led to difficulty in establishing or maintaining partnerships.

Collins and Moore also explored motives. The most important drive in the entrepreneurs studied was for autonomy. Money was important insofar as it ensured independence, authority, and freedom from the frustrations and dependency of poverty. But it was not considered a primary motivator. Entrepreneurs used money to achieve more—not to retire. Many of these people became entrepreneurs when their advancement in organizations or the professions was blocked.

Another psychoanalytic view of the entrepreneur comes from the work of Abraham Zaleznik and his colleague Manfred Kets de Vries. Like Collins and Moore, they see the entrepreneur as a person deeply influenced by a turbulent and disrupted childhood. Their lives are frequently suffused with themes of real or imagined poverty, deprivation, death of significant others, and loneliness. Zaleznik and Kets de Vries view the entrepreneur as motivated by "persistent feelings of dissatisfaction, rejection and powerlessness" stemming from conflicted relations with parents, typically in the form of a remote, rejecting father and a domineering mother. It is the aching psychological need for restitution, for relief of these painful conflicts, which can lead either to self-destructive and impulsive acting out or to creative and innovative efforts associated with developing a new enterprise.[21] It is perhaps for this reason that Zaleznik has remarked, "To understand the psychology of the entrepreneur it is necessary to study the juvenile delinquent."[22]

[21] Abraham Zaleznik and Manfred Kets de Vries, "Myths and Realities of Entrepreneurship," *Power and the Corporate Mind* (New York: Houghton Mifflin Company, 1975).

[22] Abraham Zaleznik, The Entrepreneur and the Juvenile Delinquent (unpublished manuscript, cited with permission).

Elsewhere, Kets de Vries sees the entrepreneur as operating through a sense of "entrepreneurial theater."[23] Characteristics of this theater include a need for control, a tendency towards suspicious thinking, a need for applause and the use of various psychological defenses including projection (externalizing internal problems) and splitting (seeing the world in black and white terms).

Kets de Vries, in examining the making of the entrepreneurial personality sees six principal elements:[24]

- environmental turbulence
- struggles around issues of authority with one's parents
- a feeling of rejection
- painful feelings of anger, hostility, and guilt
- identity confusion (identification with the person causing the hurt)
- adopting the "reactive" mode to painful feelings (guilt, rebellion, impulsiveness)

These authors also deal with the issues of company succession which are often materially affected by the entrepreneur's personality. To the extent that entrepreneurs identify closely with their enterprise and depend on it as a source of self-esteem, their need for control over the enterprise may conflict with its need for the sharing of authority by a larger group. If the firm is to grow, it may come into conflict with the entrepreneur's rigid or inflexible behavior. At times, the succession of new leadership or abdication by the entrepreneur may become the only options. For this reason, Kets de Vries describes the leadership style of the entrepreneur as "self-limiting."[25]

Typologies of Entrepreneurs

Because current definitions of entrepreneurship are frequently one-dimensional, it is important to develop typologies or different categories of entrepreneurs. Timmons mentioned a few differences; for example, product-oriented businesses may require different skills from service-oriented businesses, and high-tech entrepreneurs may have different educational attainments from nontechnical or service-oriented entrepreneurs.

A useful distinction may also be made between *creative* and/or *charismatic* entrepreneurs who are commercially innovative as well as entrepreneuring, and *conventional* entrepreneurs who want to own and develop their own businesses but who stick to conventional product/service ideas. Although creative people and successful entrepreneurs share certain characteristics (for example, independence and tolerance of ambiguity), not all creative people are entrepreneurs nor are all entrepreneurs creative. The key to great entrepreneurial success may

[23] Manfred Kets de Vries, "Can You Survive an Entrepreneur?" (HBS Case Services, #9-484-081, Boston, 1984).

[24] Manfred Kets de Vries, "The Entrepreneurial Personality," *Organizational Paradoxes* (London: Tavistock Publications Ltd., 1980).

[25] Ibid.

involve possessing a unique constellation of traits which includes creativity and entrepreneurial drive. A corollary distinction should also be made between entrepreneurs who are keen on fast growth and expansion—like Fred Smith, the founder of Federal Express—and those who are content to remain with viable small businesses.

In general, the literature on entrepreneurship shows a need for integration and developing useful typologies of entrepreneurs. Classic motivational theories, especially the psychoanalytic, are in some ways "deficit" models. But the "drive" for creativity and freedom may reflect "higher level" human needs that have developed out of health and sufficiency, and from a positive desire for self-actualization rather than from deficiency.[26]

Entrepreneurs and Managers

The literature also reveals few systematic comparisons of the characteristics distinguishing entrepreneurs from managers, although Stevenson has contributed to our understanding of the contrast with his differentiation of the promoter and the trustee.[27] Prompters make new things happen without regard for the resources currently controlled, while trustees maintain the status quo and emphasize ownership of resources. Nonetheless, in general, "entrepreneur" and "manager" are widely and freely used, as if we all understood their "differences."[28]

Using the framework of task, environment, and person may help to resolve some of these semantic issues. In fact, one of the goals of this module lies in dispelling the myth of *the* manager and *the* entrepreneur as distinct species within the business world. It aspires, rather, to introduce the idea of a spectrum of styles and predispositions, and to eliminate artificial distinctions. People may behave in a managerial or entrepreneurial fashion depending on the lens used to examine them. They may be able to array themselves by choice on a behavioral spectrum according to the demands of the task, the characteristics of the environment, and their own personal predispositions.

In general, the entrepreneurial position involves putting one's self at risk for the sake of the venture. Entrepreneurs may jeopardize their financial security and the security of others in order to get started; they may also put marriages and friendships at risk through neglect and the prospect of business failure. The entrepreneur's central question is "What can I do?" He or she does not live with the status quo, but works to change it in accordance with his or her personal vision and values.

---

[26] Abraham Maslow, "Towards a Psychology of Being," *Self Actualization* (Princeton: D. Van Nostrand Company, 1962).

[27] Howard H. Stevenson, "A Perspective on Entrepreneurship," (HBS Case Services, Harvard Business School, #9-384-131, Boston, 1983).

[28] John Kao, "Entrepreneurs and Managers: Are They Different?" Working Paper, Division of Research, Harvard Business School, 1986.

By contrast, the manager is motivated more by externally imposed goals and rewards, is less tolerant of uncertainty or ambiguity than the entrepreneur, and less oriented towards risk. Managers have chosen the relative safety of salary and position over the uncertainty of a new venture with its potential for failure and financial loss. For the manager, the operant question is, "What should I do in this situation?" The manager accepts most existing values and can create additional ones; he or she can also make new rules and has the option to change some existing ones.

The roles of entrepreneur and manager suggest different types of personal skills. We customarily think of the entrepreneur as skilled in intuition (envisioning possibilities) and emotions (appealing to others to "join the cause"). Managers, on the other hand, are seen as preferring to use rational and detail-oriented skills. Each set of skills has its appropriate place. For example, we would not wish to rely on intuition or emotion to fly an airplane or perform brain surgery. Nor would we be empathic to the needs of others or write poetry based on rational skills alone. Different tasks require different skills.

Different environments also require different skills. A bureaucracy like the post office is less likely to tolerate innovative or unusual behavior, while loosely structured, participative organizations such as entrepreneurial start-ups tend to be allergic to rigidity, whether expressed in behavior, structure, or management systems.

Different personality profiles also lead to the use of different skills. The willingness of an individual to become involved in a given type of situation depends significantly on personal preference. Someone with an obsessional style steeped in details and logical thinking may feel anxious in the unstructured environment of the start-up. Similarly, someone comfortable with emotion and intuition could feel stifled and frustrated in a rule-governed, highly structured environment. Again, the key involves an understanding of range and fit; what skills and psychological style fits with what situation.

The roles of entrepreneur and manager clearly overlap. Entrepreneurs who start companies must use managerial skills to implement their vision. Managers must use entrepreneurial skills in order to manage change and to innovate. The issue involves the combination of managerial and entrepreneurial traits in response to a given personality, a given environment, and a given set of opportunities.

THE ENTREPRENEURIAL CAREER

Our model of task, person, and organizational context is also relevant in considering the nature of an entrepreneurial career. Clearly, if the would-be entrepreneur has no opportunities to pursue, there is no entrepreneurial task, and hence no career. The environment is a factor to the extent that it facilitates or hinders the pursuit of opportunity. Finally, personality dictates what kind of environment the would-be entrepreneur is more or less likely to feel comfortable in, and

Figure 2-3

No Go	Go
Financial obligations	Financial resources available
Need for security	Desire for self-actualization
Family obligations	Family support
Inexperience	Relevant experience

hence what type of company the entrepreneur feels comfortable working in or desires to found.

The entrepreneurial career has several distinct phases. The decision to embark on an entrepreneurial career can be influenced by a variety of factors, some personal and some environmental. Collins and Moore commented on the motivation towards entrepreneurship as coming from "blocked opportunity." They observed that entrepreneurs often start their own businesses because they are high achievers who are blocked in terms of significant advancement in large organizations or in the professions. This suggests that social conditions support increase in entrepreneurial activity among such groups as women, minorities, and academics. Our current social values encourage (allow, necessitate) women and minorities to achieve significantly while opportunities for advancement in large organizations are narrowing. For example, many academics are crossing the boundary into entrepreneurial work when academic advancement in universities has become increasingly constricted and financially unrewarding. The emergence of the biotechnology industry, with its many professor/entrepreneurs, is an indication of this trend.

Clearly, however, entrepreneurs are not only those whose prospects for advancement have been curtailed by society. Stevenson, in his study on the self-employed, found, surprisingly, that an increasing percentage of graduates from Harvard Business School undertook entrepreneurial careers.[29] Frequently, students decide to work for established organizations to continue the learning process and gain further experience in a "tuition-free" environment. As their contacts, resources, and experience increase, they may be more able to take the leap of starting their own businesses. On the other hand, obligations to spouse, children, or employers can adversely influence the entrepreneurial decision. Financial needs are obviously important. Conversely, having a supply of "walk-away money" in the bank can provide a useful comfort level. Figure 2-3 presents a "balance sheet" approach to making the entrepreneurial career decision.

Brockhaus has discussed the role of job dissatisfaction in the decision to start a business.[30] In fact, it is well known that large companies often "put entrepreneurs into business" by blocking their path towards realizing a personal

[29] Howard Stevenson and Paula Duffy, "Who are the Harvard Self-Employed?" Division of Research, Harvard Business School, 1984.

[30] Robert Brockhaus, "The Effect of Job Dissatisfaction on the Decision to Start a Business," *Journal of Small Business Management*, V. 18, #1, January 1980, pp. 37–43.

vision. Steven Jobs and Steven Wozniak initially offered their personal computer to Hewlett-Packard Corporation, which turned it down. Mitch Kapor held a short-lived position at Digital Equipment Corporation but quit because he perceived slim chances of advancement. Eventually he started Lotus Development Corporation. George Lucas turned to his own company when Universal Studios offended him by cutting a token amount of footage out of his film and asserting their "creative control" over the project. Jerry Sanders of Applied Micro Devices started his own company out of a desire to "get even." Departed executives from Baxter Travenol have been responsible for a dozen startups in the biomedical arena. To the extent that established companies fail to provide avenues for their talented individuals, they may lose valuable human resources and even create their own competition. Some of these issues relating to preserving entrepreneurship in the established organization will be addressed in Module Four.

THE CASES

Janet Axelrod

Janet Axelrod was the first employee to join Lotus Development Corporation, a rapidly growing software company that achieved early success with its "1-2-3" program. The case shows her role as the vice president of human resource management.

Axelrod began without any existing structure or resources in place, she had only her personal vision. Her task lay in breathing tangibility into this vision. Early experiences with activist causes may have influenced the missionary quality of her subsequent work with Lotus. She leveraged her vision by developing the company's human resource function.

This case provides a look at the nature of entrepreneurship in personal terms. The class discusses such issues as Axelrod's style of doing business (the person), the role of social concerns and values in her professional outlook (the environment), and her influence on the company's development (the task).

Ted Turner

Turner, one of the most visible and flamboyant of a new generation of entrepreneurs, has a unique style. It is arguably one of his greatest assets and requires further analysis. Working constantly to redefine the rules of the game, Turner rides out on a white horse to face new challenges: He loves being on the cutting edge. An Atlanta billboard shows him proclaiming, "I was cable before cable was cool." In his style and beliefs, he fits with classic American dreams and with the stereotypical view of the entrepreneur.

Turner's personal background, developmental history, and relationship to his father are presented. They stimulate a discussion revolving around the questions: What are the personal and psychological issues that shape the motivations and interpersonal style that we have identified as entrepreneurial?

Akira Kimishima

In the Japanese business environment, Akira Kimishima would be considered very entrepreneurial, yet this description might be less accurate in the West. This case examines the influence of culture (the environment) on the definition of entrepreneurial behavior as well as those aspects of entrepreneurship that are independent of culture. Also, using the lens of culture, students explore Kimishima's task (starting new ventures) and his personality (such as his personal values and relationship with his father).

Paul Lutwak, Deborah Goldberg, Craig Knudsen, Audrey Dickason: The Entrepreneurial Career

These four caselets reveal different facets of the decision to embark on an entrepreneurial career path. Paul Lutwak, Deborah Goldberg, Craig Knudsen, and Audrey Dickason are recently graduated MBAs, each struggling with the choice of an exciting but risky venture versus a more traditional job opportunity. The Paul Lutwak and Deborah Goldberg cases also explore the question of responsibilities to a family business. The practical and personal factors important in choosing between an entrepreneurial and an established career path are elucidated.

FOR FURTHER READING

COLLINS, ORVIS, F. and MOORE, DAVID G., *The Enterprising Man*. East Lansing, Mich.: Michigan State University Business Studies, 1964.

KAO, JOHN, "Managers and Entrepreneurs, Are They Different?" Division of Research, Harvard Business School, Boston, 1986.

KOTTER, JOHN, *The General Managers*. New York: The Free Press, 1985.

McCLELLAND, DAVID, *The Achieving Society*. Princeton: D. Van Nostrand Company, 1961.

STEVENSON, HOWARD, "Perspective on Entrepreneurship," Division of Research, Harvard Business School, Boston, 1985.

WILLIAMS, CHRISTIAN, *The Story of Ted Turner: Lead, Follow or Get Out of the Way*. New York: Times Books, 1981.

ZALESNIK, ABRAHAM, *Power and the Corporate Mind*. New York: Harper and Row, 1972.

Janet Axelrod

There's no one in the company who does exactly what I do. *I articulate values,* keep the values, remind Mitch (Lotus' chairman and founder) of values when necessary and inject values into our daily operations. It is a tremendous responsibility that sometimes scares the piss out of me.

> Janet Axelrod
> VP of Human Resources
> Lotus Development Corporation

THE PERSONAL COMPUTER SOFTWARE INDUSTRY

Software programs are the instructions that tell the hardware what to do. For mainframe computers, software was usually individually written for particular end-users and to their specifications and needs. The mainframe manufacturers and a few independent specialists (Cullinet, for example) wrote the programs.

The advent of personal computers (PCs) changed this situation. PCs first appeared in the 1970s, although they did not really boom until the 1980s, when, in 1982, 5 million PCs were in consumers' hands. The projected growth rate through 1990 was 18 percent. This ever-increasing base of installed PCs created an ever-increasing demand for software. Programs did not need to be customized either, as was the case for mainframe users: One program could be duplicated for use on thousands of PCs. In 1980 there was no PC software industry. By 1983 software revenues totaled $2.2 billion. Estimates for 1988 approached $12 billion. In 1983 the PC software segment comprised 4 percent of the total market; the estimate for 1988 was 15 percent.

This case was prepared by Associate Professor John J. Kao.

Copyright © 1986 by the President and Fellows of Harvard College. Harvard Business School case 9-486-013.

LOTUS DEVELOPMENT CORPORATION

Lotus Development Corporation was founded by Mitchell Kapor in 1982. Kapor, a former software designer who had nearly completed an MBA from MIT, had an idea in 1981: Rather than only design software, why not create a company, based on advanced PC products and technology, that would design, produce, and market its applications packages? His first major product idea was a combined business and productivity tool—one housing spreadsheet, graphics, and database in a single program—that would use the new IBM PC. The product, 1-2-3, was shipped in January of 1983. An instant success with business users, 1-2-3 dovetailed with the sale and penetration of the IBM PC in the business market.

First-year sales for Lotus were $53 million; two years later they were $225 million and Lotus was the software industry kingpin. Subsequent products included Symphony, an upscale, integrated package, and Jazz, a package for the Apple Macintosh, as well as foreign versions of others.

In 1981, even before Kapor had his business revelation, he hired his first employee to help with Micro Finance Systems, his growing software design business. This employee, who later suggested the name Lotus, was Janet Axelrod.

AXELROD'S START

This is the most hysterical story. I worked for five years at Haymarket (a Boston cooperative) as a cofounder. Raising money, reviewing proposals, setting up whatever organizational systems we needed—including nine boards across New England—setting the philosophical tone, articulating the politics, dealing with the very rich and the very poor. That was a different start-up situation; now Haymarket is a ten-year-old, half-million-dollar-a-year operation. I loved it and learned a lot. I got to act out a lot of things that I had only thought about.

But when I decided it was time to leave, I did something that I would never do again. I left Haymarket before I had another job. With only a B.A., I had no idea what I wanted to do. I just drifted. This was 1980. I had just produced a huge benefit concert featuring Bob Marley and the Wailers for the liberation of South Africa. Twenty thousand people came. It was a big success, and we had a great time. But that was the end to my Haymarket career. I left, with no visible or physical means of support, and no idea what I was going to do. I got a part-time job in a nutrition and social agency program, and that was how I lived—from hand to mouth.

Depressed, I didn't know which end was up or what to do next. It was a crisis. A friend of mine, Shelly, had a man walk into her office in Central Square, observe her for a while, and say, "I need somebody like you to help me run my business." She said, "Well, I happen to know someone who is almost exactly like me, and she is really looking for a job. Why don't you call her?" Amazingly enough, he followed up on this thing. The man was Mitch Kapor.

He called me up and said, "Shelly told me to call you. This is who I am; do you want to talk?" I was at the end of my rope—I would discuss anything. I said, "You should know that I don't know shit about your business. You should also know that I can probably learn it." He came over to my house, we started talking, and he found that we knew a lot of the same people from New Haven and had been through a lot of the same experiences. We liked each other a lot. I think that was really when the deal was sealed, when we realized a mutual "I like you. I can work with you. I feel good about that trust." We had a series of meetings, then I went to Brazil for a month. I said I would think about this when I was away. What were my options? Work or do not work. Work is better, and a paycheck comes in. He offered me $17,000 a year, which was more money than I had ever made in my life. Whatever there was to be done, we would do it together.

He wrote up a job description for me which I still have. It was hysterical. Remember, I did not know him from a hole in the wall. He could have been a complete creep. All I cared about was that I was going to have a job five days a week, and he was going to pay me to work there. He was a nobody who had written software, and I did not know what the hell that was either.

The office was his house in Belmont, and I had a little desk. He had a bookkeeper/consultant once a month, a wonderfully sweet, smart Jewish yenta, who immediately took me under her wing and said everything would be all right. We started looking for office space. Mitch was throwing all this literature to me: "Here is the industry; learn it." I started reading industry publications, and figured out that this could be something big. I met people in the business and leaned heavily on one of my friends who had done the same thing. She found us the insurance vendor, the real estate guy, and all of the backup work that I needed. We still use a lot of the same services that she turned me on to in the first few days. I spent a lot of the time kind of pulling things together, making sure everything was set up to start running the business, something I had never done. I had stationery made up, designed the logo—the things you do in any organization. This was just for profit instead of not-for-profit. We found a place on Franklin Street and moved, just the two of us.

We had a semblance of an organization, but we didn't have a product. We did not know what we were doing. The only other person we hired was Todd, a 14-year-old. Todd was working with us in the summer full-time, and in the winter part-time. He would come by bus from Newton, because he did not have his license yet. He still works here. Todd had written a program with Mitchell called EBS—executive briefing system. It was written for the Apple II. It worked decently, but it did not break any records. That was our only product.

I was not "invested" in the company—there was nothing to invest in. It was just a job. I was not thinking "What is Mitchell going to do?" I didn't care, as long as I had a job. Gradually the company grew, and as my life became more and more intertwined with the growth of this place, I got more and more invested in it. Problems would come up and I would go to Mitch and say, "This is not working right. What are we going to do about it?" Through that process—realizing that there were problems and issues to deal with along the way, and seeing them first and bringing them to him—we worked out a style of relating that was very comfortable for both of us. That solidified our relationship, which is seen as the primal relationship in the company. We fought then and we continue to fight now. But there is a bedrock of respect. We have been through a lot together.

Another important thing about this place is the absence of sexist bullshit; whenever it raises its head, it is immediately put down. At first, it was only me. Now it is not. Women around here know that if somebody makes a comment that doesn't reflect the inclusion of women, I do not care who it is, they are to be corrected. That is an important thing to me personally and to the women who work here. We have a lot of women in important positions in this company. The sense that there is respect for women, that people understand the contribution that we are going to make to this company, is important. It really does a lot for our personality and our presence.

In Mitchell's speech today, he said, "We are so successful, it is like 'Star Trek,' we are going where no man has ever gone." Immediately my head echoes to myself, "or woman" and Mitchell said, "or woman" before I said anything.

Anyway, we had this little organization. We sat in one big room and shouted at each other. We would take turns answering the phone. Everybody washed their own dishes. It was like SDS—everybody doing their work. We had meetings once a week and figured out who was going to make supper. It was great fun. We were all making a living, didn't know where we were going, but that was OK. As time went on, we attracted more people. But we had not started figuring out, What are we going to do now?

Then in the summer of 1981, Mitchell met John Sachs. Mitchell and I went out for a Chinese lunch one day. He said, "I have met this guy who I think is really important to our future. I am going to offer him a job and pay him a lot of money, more than you make, more than I make. We are going to get him." I felt, "What has he got that I haven't got?" What he had was the beginning of 1, 2, 3. Mitchell had the wisdom to see that this guy was really on to something. He brought John to meet us—a very retiring, shy programmer type—very sweet, not obnoxious at all (unusual in a person like that). I liked him.

That was when we started to check people out with my gut instincts. This is an important thing that we do; it is a lot of why I am in this chair. I get a very quick take on people. I have developed that ability over the years; I think the fact that we have a lot of good people working here is due, to some degree, to the exercise of that gut. If somebody can't look me in the eye, something is wrong and I don't want to work with them.

AXELROD'S ROLE

To a certain extent it is easy: notices on affirmative action, ensuring that people participate in the process. The interests of workers and managers often diverge. All of this talk about worker participation and worker control can boil down to a very nice little PR campaign for the manager.

So I worry. Is this the right thing to do? Are we heading in the right direction? Do our efforts add up to something really meaningful? How are we going to institutionalize *real* influence, power, and controls? These are the questions that wait for us in the future which we are trying to work out as we go along.

Mitch and I talked from the first day about how we were going to bump up against these contradictions. "We are going to have to figure out where we stand personally on them and where the company stands on them and fit all that to the prevailing wind. How are we going to do that?" These kinds of questions—philosophical stuff that gets translated through various ways across the company—are, to a large degree, in my domain.

I used to spend a lot of time talking to Mitchell about these things when we were younger. We don't discuss them as much any more. Now I talk with our VP of marketing. It's funny, because we don't share the same political outlook, but he is sensitive to the issues. Maybe that's because of where he came from, how old he is.

I bounce things off of people. Then I go to Mitch and say, "The time to start thinking about this issue is *now*." Today I went to Mitchell and told him, "This is our next project. We have to start thinking about it." We're this $30-million company, X number of employees, and we are fabulously successful. So what? This is the existential life of an intellectual corporation. What are we doing and why are we doing it? Why are we in this business? We have to come up with personal answers to satisfy ourselves, but we have to bring those personal answers to a corporation discussion. Is it enough to produce quality? Is it enough to make money? Is it enough to employ 200 people? What is the meaning of all this?

Another part of what I do is to be the mommy. That means people come in here and talk to me about whatever's going on in their lives and in their work. This is an important role to me and will be important as we get larger. It is a role I really do not want to give up. I am good at it, and I like it. It also gives people the sense that there is somebody sitting in a corner office who has Mitchell's ear, was closer to the president than anybody else in terms of history, etc. This is a person who wields power, and when you are not happy and you have complaints, you have somebody to go to.

It's a critical role—to make people feel that something is going to happen if they can convince you that the problem is serious.

The other thing I do is guide the development of this department. I say guide rather than manage. I am not a professional human resources manager. I do not have a degree, nor do I know the buzzwords, but I hire people who do. I just hired a woman who has a lot of experience in high-tech companies to be our compensation/benefits manager. Compensation/benefits is something very difficult to understand—very convoluted and arcane. It is not something I want to spend a whole lot of time learning about, but it is extremely critical.

The bottom line in any company is how much people get paid and how much respect they get. I don't care what you say, but those two things are linked. Everything else is really crap. "Put it in the paycheck." That has become clearer and clearer to me. I am not a person who gives a shit about money. I can't even spend all of my salary, but that is how you measure: It is one lesson you learn in corporate America. So I guide the development of this department, figuring out where our needs are hiring those people bringing them on.

More than anything I feel I am like an icon. Mitchell made this rap this morning about arrogance—how it's important not to be arrogant. One of the guys who works in the warehouse, a Haitian immigrant who is not a major player in the company, but a nice guy, came up to me and said, "I really think that was a good speech Mitchell gave this morning and I think it is important that he keeps doing that." As the elevator doors closed, he said, "And, I know you put him up to it." This guy does not know me, but there is a perception of where these issues are coming from, which is correct. The fact that Mitch is into it—the fact he is willing to do it at a moment's notice—is also critical.

What else do I do? I plan events. I do a lot of thinking about our direction, a lot of talking to people about our direction and how they are feeling about what we are doing. I do a lot of administrative day-to-day stuff. I keep the database on the employees. I do not want to give that up, because it keeps me in touch with who is here. I try to remember who everybody is. I do a lot of walking around, trying to get to all the floors a few times a day. I just want to be out there so people can talk to me and give me input. That is critical stuff.

Also, I do a lot of work setting up the physical plant, where we live. I chose most of the furniture and made most of the design decisions for this building. That's fun—bringing together what people need. One of my values is that, in order for something to be perfect, it has to be both beautiful and functional. This building does that; it's beautiful and works very well. It meets people's needs. There are some problems, like these glass front doors in their offices. When we first told them they were getting glass fronts on their offices, people lost it; they just were so upset. We had to say, "What are you going to do in your offices? Are you sitting in there beating off or something?"

People feel like our office on Franklin Street was the beginning of something. It was saying we are not going to do things like people have always done them. We are going to do things the way we want to do them. We are going to make the rules. I think that an important part of our personality at Lotus is maintaining this balance between a company and 157 people, and saying "We are going to be aggressive about using power." We have worked hard. We deserve it. We are good people. We are going to use it in better ways than it has been used before. We are going to trust that we know what those ways are. I think that whole ability to move in and take control, at this age, really has its roots in what we were saying earlier, the days of the sixties, student politics, organizing, that stuff.

We have two older managers. One, in his mid-forties, is a finance guy. Coming into this setting has set him free. The same is true of our vice president of operations. They observed what was going on in the 1960s from their Eisenhoweresque position, and how we matured and created structures that they could fit into. They came in, and they liked it. We are casual; there is very little bullshit, minimal politicking, and almost no ass-licking. It is a different kind of setting. And there is respect for knowledge. People really want to listen to you. Lotus is a hard school. You really have to prove yourself. You have to have good ideas, keep a very, very quick pace, but if you can do that, it is a nice environment to work in. You can be yourself. That is really what has fed me, and I think it has fed Mitch. I think it feeds these older guys, too. For the first time, they do not have to play stupid games.

For younger people, I found that some are in awe. I am like their grandmother. "What do you mean? I am only 30 years old, give me a break." It's scary. I find myself getting into this nostalgic trip when I talk of the way it used to be. It is funny, to grow old. Some people think we're aging hippies who don't know how to act in the real world. But on the other hand, they see our tremendous success.

This is a good environment to work in. Some people come here from other companies and they are very, very suspicious at first. "You are telling me that I am going to have a piece of this pie? Other places have really bullshitted me and I have been burned." It takes a couple of months to get used to the fact that they are really hearing the truth, that their questions are answered to the best of our ability, that they don't have to read between the lines. What they are hearing is what is happening.

From the very beginning, Mitchell and I talked about the importance of honesty and dealing straight with one another. We did not want to create an environment where we had to go around bullshitting each other. This is where the issue of "Why are we doing this?" comes into play. Clearly, part of the reason is to create a comfortable working environment that meets our personal needs. Both of us are ethical people, and we clearly believe that what goes around, comes around.

If you treat people like shit, you are going to get shit. It is common to every philosophy, religion, and culture that has ever flowered. You have to do unto others as you would have them do unto you. Mitch and I really believe [that]. If you expect to get something out of a situation, you have to put into it in a positive way. Going around and screwing people is not going to do it. Somehow, you are going to pay. There is no guarantee that if you treat people right, they will treat you right, but you do not have a chance of getting paid back well if you're going to treat people lousy. I think that concept, articulated as karma in our generation, is important.

Another question that is always in the back of our minds is who are these people we are hiring? Where are they coming from? Have they been exposed to this kind of situation before? How can we fill in our experience by hiring people different than we are? That is a very important concept both of us agreed on from the beginning: The richest kind of environment is one that incorporates many different schools of thought. That is something I believe without question. It is an article of faith for me, a religion. I have seen it in a lot of different settings. When you have people coming from completely different places, the result is a rich mixture; you do not want to limit yourselves to people just from your own background, affirmative action stuff notwithstanding. On the other hand, Mitchell and I and a lot of the other people around here share this similar New York, Jewish, intellectual *quasi*-left sentiment. For that reason Mitchell and I can talk shorthand or Yiddish or whatever, and that makes things easier. So there is a balance.

MANAGING TRADEOFFS

Mitch decided we had to have some business guy in here. One guy we talked to was this guy Mitchell had done a lot of work for and trusted and liked. I was not nuts about him, but I did not really care. Then there was another guy who lived around here, already a multimillionaire—young, our age. Mitchell brought him in and he glowed red. "Don't go near this guy. He is dangerous." He was like a shark, in my opinion. I did not feel like I knew where I was when I talked to him. I felt he was playing a political game with me. He made me nervous. I told Mitchell, "This is not the guy for us. He is not going to work out." Mitchell had the same feeling. Then Alan came along. Mitchell said, "I think we can talk him into coming here. What do you think?" I said, "I don't know; I have to meet him. What are his qualifications? What is the story on him?" He told me what Alan had done and who he was. He seemed on paper to be a very good, logical choice. We committed a "folie à deux": [we thought] that we would never find someone that was really like us, and that we liked, who also knew what they were doing in business. Horse shit.

I was feeling anxious. What am I doing here? This is going to be a corporation? This is going to be a company? How can I trust this when my orientation for my entire life has been to question these structures and to build something else in their place? I was really torn. Could I trust myself? I was trying to work in Lotus' interest, but I really did not know what [that] was. I had a lot less confidence in myself than I do now. I was not tested. We did not have the kind of success that we have now. Now I know you can do it the way I do it and win.

Mitchell brought Alan in. We had dinner together. He was this short, roly-poly, Midwestern, swaggering business type, our age. He was remarkably like the images of the businessmen that you have in your head—wearing cowboy hats, going to trade shows. I thought, "This is the kind of person we need now, because neither of us is like this." But we had to figure out how to relate. We went to his room at the Hyatt afterwards for drinks and started talking. I raised my bellwether issue, which is Cuba and where I've been. I do not expect people to agree with my thinking, but I just want to see who they are, where they stand. Have they ever given this issue any thought? "How do you feel on this?"

He was a reactionary. I did not like that, and I did not think he had much respect for women, either. I did not like him. The next day Mitch said, "What do you think?" and I said I did not like the guy. He said, "Well, you have to go and talk about this fucking Cuba thing all the time." He was really mad at me. "Where do you get off, raising these political issues with somebody you are trying to bring to the company? You might have blown it." I tried to explain to him that it was a diagnostic thing, but he did not believe it or else he did not care. I probably would not be the same way today.

Mitch, however, had made up his mind. I said, "Look, Mitchell, you know a lot more about business than I do. If you think that this guy is what we need, I will live with it." But I did not like him. He brought him in and Alan made a fabulous deal for stock with Mitchell. He also called Mitchell and said it would not look good if he came in only as a VP, so "You have to make me an EVP." Mitchell went for it. This guy was setting himself up in a position of power. It put me at a distance from Mitchell. I did not know how much of that was my own ego and how much was the real truth and concern for the company. I said, "OK, we will see what happens."

The policy-making committee of the company then became the three of us. Alan was much more money-oriented, more of a traditional businessman. "Let's get this product out the door. We have to sell and sell and make money." The concerns that Mitchell and I had always talked about—how people felt about their work, what kind of environment this was—started taking second place. Both of us bought into that.

Mitchell has a habit of putting people on a pedestal. He has to readjust when he realizes the person is not superhuman. It is something that the person who is being pedestalized has to realize. You have to say, "Oh well, fall-from-grace time." You have to be able to say, "I am not a superman or superwoman." Alan thought he was superman.

Lotus started being unpleasant. There was backbiting; I started getting very upset. Alan would come into my office and say, "Mitch does not trust me. What should I do?" Then he would turn around and stab me in the back to Mitch. All of our relationships were in flux.

Alan played tons of games and I did not have power to do anything about it, much less to see what was going on very clearly at all. I felt I could not go to Mitch and say, "This guy has to go. He is ruining the organization." At that point, I felt maybe I was ruining the organization. I did not know. Was I the one with off-the-wall ideas? Maybe in business you are just not supposed to pay any attention to how people feel. Maybe I was wrong? Maybe I am going to have to quit. Maybe contradictions are starting to come down. Those were always very real options to me. I did not know how long this would last. I knew I was not going to sell out on all the things that I believed in to keep this job. It was a very, very tough time for us, very stressful. Everybody was walking on eggs.

All of the company reported to Alan. I kept on reporting to Mitch. I think Mitchell basically just could not tell me, "You are going to report to Alan." I just would have been such a bitch.

Alan and Mitchell started having weekend meetings and I was not involved. I was just going to become some kind of a drone. I was really getting isolated. That was the way Alan wanted it.

It was about this time that Mitchell kept giving me raises out of nowhere. My field of influence expanded, and I was carving out what I am doing now. I realized, "All right, I have this title now—human resources. This is where my ambition stops. This is the place where I want to be." I went into Mitchell's office and said, "I just want you to know I have reached the limits of my ambition and I am in the right place now. You can rely on me staying here and not playing games, to be my old self in this capacity all the time." That was an important realization to me. I think it was also important for him to hear.

Then these consultants came in. Lotus was the smallest company they had ever agreed to deal with. Why they took us on I do not know. I do not understand how they could see that Lotus was going to be an important force, but they did see it. Jim, one of the consultants, turned out to be an absolute jewel. A good consultant is worth a lot, because he ferrets out what everybody is feeling. How was everybody feeling? Insecure, upset, and most of it traced to Alan. Jim started talking to Mitch about this; he had been talking to me about it all along. We struck up a very good relationship right from the beginning, and he used me a lot as a testing board. "What do you think is going to happen here?" He respected my gut and also provided for me a model of a business person who respected the things I respected and gave me a sense of my own value in this company. It was a very important turning point for me.

Finally it became clear to Jim and to me that Lotus was going down the drain unless Alan got out. I got sold on that pretty easily. I knew that if I felt as badly as I did, other people were not going to be happy either. I knew there was a tension in the air which was terrible. Jim, through a series of long and painful discussions with Mitchell, also convinced him.

Mitchell had brought Alan from this computing software company, paid him lots of money, uprooted his whole life, and felt a responsibility to this guy. What he was not seeing—and this is the blind spot in Mitchell—was the responsibility that he had to all the other people at Lotus, which more than outweighed the responsibility to Alan. Jim kept hammering at Mitchell that he had to get rid of this guy. "I do not know how you should do it. I am telling you that the fate of the company rests on this one thing." Jim really believed that. I do not know if I would have put it in such extreme terms, but I have come to believe he was right. Mitch and I started talking again in the ways that we had before; this crisis brought us together. He said, "Jim thinks I have to get rid of him. What do you think?" And I said, "I think so too. I thing he is a dog. Any way I can help you, I would be glad to."

This was basically a struggle that Mitchell had to go through himself. I think it was probably the most painful struggle he has ever had. He was a mess for a couple of weeks; he was not sleeping. It was horrible. He was really in agony. He had to renege on promises that he made to Alan. This really upset him. He just does not like doing that. He had to admit he had made a big mistake. He is not used to making big mistakes, either. He had never made another mistake that big, as far as I know. Also, he was going to have to take business responsibilities for the company. I think he was really frightened of that; he did not know if he could really do it. I think he did not really believe that he could lean on me yet. I did not really believe it either; I still was thinking I was just a schmuck. He did not really believe that I had the capability to do a lot of the things it later turned out I could. He felt isolated, freaked-out and scared about this whole thing.

Alan knew that something was rotten in the cotton. Alan would come to me and say, "Do you know what Mitchell is feeling?" He tried to pick my brain, to be very straightforward, but it was bullshit. Finally Mitchell decided he had to go. So he did.

Having figured out, after the fact, that the information that my gut was passing to my head about these people turned out to be right—that was the major clue for me. Also seeing how certain decisions that I had made with my heart worked out all right. Shall I talk to this person about this issue? Should we move into this building? I think there is just no substitute for experience—making decisions, making them right, and knowing that you can do it. At the same time you have to be very careful because there is a kind of naivete that you lose when you start knowing that you know what you are doing, a naivete which can be very valuable. There are questions that you ask that are sometimes very important. Later on, you just don't ask.

LOTUS' HUMAN RESOURCE SYSTEM

There is a system, but this is an area in which I feel uncomfortable. To me, these are the things that you owe employees. We have not done as much as I feel we should. My anxiety about being legitimate as a businessperson has been replaced by, "Are we legitimately providing what we ought to be providing?"

At the same time that we had the consultants in to do an appraisal of the company, I got my own consultant to do personnel and human resources planning assistance. That was terrific for me. She was a really nice woman. I liked her a lot and she liked me and we had a giggle about everything, a really fun experience. She was the one who turned me on to the fact that there are things you are supposed to do, like getting job grades. That was a rude awakening. It was not an issue that I was worried about. She and I sat down and we concentrated on issues. We wrote up a whole bunch of stuff like, What are the human resources issues facing Lotus right now? What do we have to do immediately?

The first thing we had to do was to institute a system of writing job descriptions. We were already growing at a very rapid rate, but it was before the most intense staffing. It was already clear that things were totally out of control. We started writing up job descriptions. I had to fight people, saying, "We have to get some damn organization in this place." I had a big struggle with a lot of people around the organization. There was a real tendency toward anarchy, which is something I cannot stand. I really hate it.

I also have a real problem with people who act like prima donnas. I have been in a lot of organizations that have been destroyed by people who were unwilling to play by the rules. It makes me really mad. I get very emotional about a lot of this. I took it personally, got pissed off, and ranted and raved at Mitch. All of it worked out in the end. We instituted job descriptions and a system of attachments to job descriptions that said "I need to hire somebody. This is what they are going to do. This is what I want to pay the person." It is an approval system which has been a problem since the day it was instituted. One of the major problems we have here is that everything is moving so fast that people just think this is useless bureaucracy. They do not understand the necessity for control. That is a big problem.

Systems are really important. They do away with so much mushiness; that frees you to do the creative work. I believe that anarchy is a kind of tyranny. Organization sets you free. To people here, when I say something like this, sometimes they think, "What is this, 1984?" I believe that; an organization that runs easily gives you the time, energy, and space to do stuff that you really want to do.

I don't know how much of it is manageable, because of the kind of speed we are in. But I am working on the system. It turns out that our job grade structure is suddenly not big enough; we have to redevelop it. Evaluation systems have been even less satisfactory. For a long time I would talk about the different ways of evaluating numbers, and issues connected to raises. It is very complex. We made some proposals and we took them to the policy committee. Every time we went over there, they said, "No, it is too complicated, people will not do it." Back to the drawing board. We came up with nothing that worked. It has been sitting there in my mind ever since, worrying and upsetting me. In the meantime, people do these half-ass reviews. Sometimes they happen when someone gets angry enough to say, "I have been here six months and nobody has ever told me a word about my performance." That is really unfair. It is really inexcusable.

One of my new people, in her first week here, did a survey. She gave people five examples of evaluations. She knew in her mind which one she wanted. She asked 35 people at random all over the company, "Which ones do you like? How would you like to be evaluated? And how would you like to evaluate?" The answer came back resounding—the one that she wanted. Surprise, surprise. She got a chance to tell people what counts. I did an evaluation yesterday using her model and it was so great. I love it. Now I send out every month a list of who needs evaluating, either because they are passing through a probationary period or because they have been here for a year. I have not gotten to the six-month level yet. How we are going to tie those evaluations into raises or what is going to constitute a merit increase, etc., I do not know.

The other thing is profit sharing. At this stage of our lives, we are so profitable we have to figure out ways to spend our money. I just feel like it would be a really good investment, on a lot of levels, to give it to the people who are making it in the form of raises or bonuses, so that some day when we are not so flush, and we can't give raises and bonuses, people will say, "While we were flush we shared in that."

We have an orientation procedure that is better than it was but still not good enough. It gives them all their papers and tells them what is going on here. They do it in a group that they can relate to. Everyone gets introduced at the weekly staff meeting. What we don't have are things like employee handbooks. We haven't written it yet. Nor a handbook of policies. It's kind of amazing that people have as good a feeling about this place as they do.

I also want to get into the issues of philanthropy because we are in a position to give away some money. Philanthropy is something that I know about; it seems like a natural place to put some energy. So I'm going to be doing that. That's in addition to restructuring the organization so people feel like they belong here.

We have these jackets you see everyone wearing—black satin, on the back it says Lotus and on the front it has your initials embroidered in red. It has a red satin lining and they're really sharp. Every single person gets one of those when they pass a three-month probation period. So, these are the kinds of things . . . that really make people feel like the company cares. We're constantly trying to keep on top of ways that we can give to people.

PERSONAL HISTORY

OK, I was born in New York City—Harlem—and I lived for the first five years of my life in the Bronx. My father is a professional, he runs a series of health clinics in Chicago now. He used to run a health plan at Yale when we were there. By the time I was born my father was just getting his degree on the GI bill. My father's father was a tailor, a socialist who left the Soviet Union before the Revolution. Leftism is historically based in my family. My mother was good-natured, not sophisticated politically, but sensible and a very strong thinker. She was a value transmitter and he was the intellectual thinker. So in my lifetime we went from being marginally OK to being pretty successful and having some money. There was never any doubt that my sister and I would go to college. She's the oldest. That kind of fits in with the middle-class Jewish upbringing. It was clear that if they had to hock the house we would go to school.

I went to public school and had a lot of community experiences throughout my life. We belonged to the Y and I did a lot of stuff there with a lot of people like us, politically and socially. Another very important influence on me was that I went to one of these leftist camps in upstate New York. Kids from all walks of life came. I went to the one that was particularly political, that was really consciously trying to build organizers.

At this camp I learned a lot of the basics of right and wrong and how you organize people and take responsibility for your actions, just an unbelievable education on how you run your life according to the rules and regulations that are set down by yourself. This was really a valuable thing and I went there for like five years and I loved it.

I went to college in 1969, Barnard, class of '73. Mitchell, who is 33, and I have the same birthday, which is kind of amazing, one year apart. When he told me his birthday was November 1; I thought he was shitting me, I thought he had seen my birthday somewhere. We're both left-handed, as are six out of seven VPs here. It's so weird. We're doing a study of how many people are left-handed. So anyway, I went to college and learned a lot. I'm one of the only people I know who really feels good about their college education. It was a great time for me. My family had enough money, so I didn't have to work. I did a lot of political stuff, helped found the women's center.

PUTTING IT ALL TOGETHER

This has been an odyssey, really getting into business, learning, dressing for success, and all that kind of crap.

In my more paranoid moments I think to myself, "Some of the people here must really think I'm out of my mind." Because people know where I stand on every single issue. I'm an open book, and to look at my situation— what I believe, who I am—and see where I'm working and where I'm putting most of my energy—there are real serious contradictions and conflicts.

The whole concept of purity is one that has dropped from my vocabulary. Even the pretension that I can decide what's pure or not pure has just vanished. If you're not flexible in this business you do not last. If you can't live with ambiguity, you cannot live with change; it's impossible.

I cannot tell you how important it was to appreciate all the stuff I learned, largely in the women's movement, that let me respect my way of dealing with the world, that allowed me to say, "Yeah, I depend on some sixth sense that I get, not measurable. It's called instinct; it's called woman's intuition. I depend on that and know it's the right thing to do." And suddenly, in the bastion of what has opposed that way of operating, instinct becomes appropriate and correct.

Ted Turner (A)

"Just call me Ted, I ain't no mister."[1]

To act on one's convictions while others wait
To create a positive force in a world where cynics abound
To provide information to people where it wasn't available before
To offer those who want it a choice
For the American people, whose thirst for understanding and a better life made
　　this venture possible
For the cable industry, whose pioneering spirit caused this great step forward in
　　communications
And for those employees of Turner Broadcasting whose total commitment to
　　their company has brought us together today
I dedicate the News Channel for America, the Cable News Network . . .

Read by Ted Turner, at the dedication[2]

Will the real Ted Turner please stand up? Is he "Captain Outrageous"
or a devoted family man? The "Mouth of the South" or a Southern folk hero?
Ardent supporter of conservative political and religious personalities such as
Jesse Helms and Jerry Falwell or duck-hunting buddy of Fidel Castro?
Military school graduate and war historian or nuclear disarmament advocate?
Corporate czar or environmental protectionist? Is he a flash in the pan or a
significant long-term contributor to American business? Is Ted Turner fact or
fantasy?

It depends on whom you ask. Credentials, however, are not debatable:
Turner rebuilt his failing family advertising/billboard business into a cash
machine. Next, he leveraged those proceeds into a multimillion-dollar
conglomerate including several radio and television stations. One station,
WTCG—now known as the Superstation, WTBS—was the first independent
television station to broadcast via satellite, reaching homes throughout the
country.

---

[1]　*New York Times,* July 21, 1985.

[2]　Christian Williams, *Lead, Follow, or Get Out of the Way* (New York: Times Books, 1981).

This case was written by Research Associate Lee Field, MBA '85, under the supervision of Associate
Professor John Kao.

Turner acquired the Atlanta Braves baseball team, the Atlanta Hawks basketball team, and TV rights to the Atlanta Flames hockey team as well as rights to many reruns of network programs and a library of 2,700 old movies.

He created the Cable News Network (CNN) in 1980, vying for a piece of the TV news market, 24 hours a day. The cost: $51 million a year initially, $100 million in 1985. Total investment to date: $220 million. So far, CNN has beaten its only competitor in the 24-hour news game, Satellite News Network, a joint venture of ABC and Group W-Westinghouse. In 1982, he premiered CNN2, a 24-hour headline news service.

Besides his business successes, Turner is also a champion sailor. Winning skipper of the America's Cup in 1977 with his boat *Courageous,* Turner was a survivor and the winner of the 1979 Fastnet Race with his boat *Tenacious* near Ireland (where a storm killed fifteen). He is the unprecedented three-time winner of the "yachtsman of the year" award, and coauthor of the sailing tactics and philosophy book *The Racing Edge.*

HISTORY

Robert Edward Turner III was born in Cincinnati, Ohio, on November 19, 1938, His father Ed, had lost his Mississippi cotton farm during the Depression and moved north to work as a salesman. Ted's mother Florence, was the granddaughter of the first owner of chain grocery stores in Cincinnati.

Turner rarely spoke about his childhood; others, however, remembered him as a mischievous child who took frequent "trips to the woodshed." One unhappy incident that Ted did recall was being left at a boarding school at age six while his mother and younger sister Mary Jane (who later died from lupus) accompanied his father on a World War II navy assignment in the Gulf of Mexico.

A family friend, Dr. Irving Victor, commented on the relationship between father and son: "Ed idolized Teddy who was his whole life. . . . He bought him guns, boats. Yet he was tremendously difficult with him. I think he took out a lot of hostility on Teddy."[3] Ted's first wife, Judy Nye Hallisey, offered another explanation for Ted's stringent disciplining. "Ed wanted Ted to be insecure because he felt that insecurity bred greatness. If Ted was insecure then he would be forced to compete."[4] Turner talked about his father:

> My father could be absolutely charming or he could be a complete horse's ass. He could be the kindest, warmest, most wonderful person in the whole world, and then go into a bar, get drunk, and get into a fist fight with the whole place.
> He was a rugged individualist. It's an old phrase, but it describes him well, because he was a throwback to the past. He didn't have a whole lot of fear, but sometimes he did have remorse—for the things he had done. He had a bad

[3] Ibid.
[4] Ibid.

habit . . . saying exactly what he thought, without being diplomatic at all. That got him into a lot of trouble, along with the drinking.

I've tried to learn from that. Maybe I tend to be outspoken myself, but he was so outspoken that it cost him friends and money. He would have gone a lot further if he hadn't been so controversial.[5]

After successfully building a billboard business from scratch in Ohio, his father bought an outdoor advertising firm and relocated the family to Savannah, Georgia when Ted was nine. Ted worked for Turner Advertising Company during the summers. He recalled:

One summer I made $50 a week (cutting grass around billboards and creosoting the poles) and my father charged me $25 a week rent. I asked him if that wasn't a little high. He said if I could do better than that for food and lodging seven days a week, I could move out.[6]

Although he attended public school in Ohio, Ted was sent to military schools after the move south—Georgia Military Academy near Atlanta and McCallie school in Chattanooga, Tennessee. At the former, he battled familiar labels of show-off and smart-ass. There was a new albatross as well: being a Northerner. Following a rumor that he had said an unkindness about Robert E. Lee, Turner remembered "about 40 kids in Confederate grey uniforms running after me yelling, 'Kill the Yankee bastard!'"[7] At McCallie, described as a college preparation school with a Christian environment for boys from Chattanooga and the South, Turner was remembered as "Terrible Ted." One of his teachers described him as smart but high-strung. Hoping to calm him down, the master assigned Turner to an older boy's dorm. He became their leader, however.

Despite his mother's report that he "hated" McCallie, while there, Turner acquired a fondness for history and the classics—"grandeur and tradition, glory and beauty," and an interest in nature. He grew real lawn grass in his room, which he clipped with manicure scissors, and he gave refuge to stray or injured dogs, birds, snakes, and anything else he could find. He also developed competitive skills and became Tennessee state high school debating champion.

Early on, Turner came to the painful realization that he had no natural talent with traditional sports. And he said, "I tried and tried, but I couldn't make a contribution."[8] So, along with turning to books and nature, he sought out and excelled in sports and contests that required mental, not physical, expertise. Known in Savannah sailing circles as "Turnover Ted" or "The Capsize Kid" because he was forever pushing his 11-foot Penguin over the edge, Turner quickly attained superior sailing skills.

---

[5]   Ibid.

[6]   Ibid.

[7]   Ibid.

[8]   Ibid.

College Years

When it came time to decide on a college, Ted wanted to try for an appointment at the Naval Academy, but Ed wanted his son properly trained for a future business career. So, having been turned down by Harvard, Turner was sent to Brown University in Providence, Rhode Island. Looking back on this choice, Turner said, "If I had gone to Annapolis I would have done great, and I'd be an admiral now. But no one would have heard of me."[9]

Once at Brown, Turner chose to major in classics, a decision probably reflecting not only a genuine interest in the subject, but an urge to rebel against his father. Influencing his choice as well was his friendship with teacher/mentor John Rowe Workman, a classicist whose interest centered on "disaster" and the thesis that disaster usually followed human progress.

When Turner informed the family of this choice, his father fired back the following letter:

> My dear son:
>
> I am appalled, even horrified, that you have adopted Classics as a major. As a matter of fact, I almost puked on the way home today. I suppose that I am old-fashioned enough to believe that the purpose of an education is to enable one to develop a community of interest with his fellow man, to learn to know them, and to learn how to get along with them. In order to do this, of course, he must learn what motivates them, and how to impel them to be pleased with his objectives and desires.
>
> I am a practical man, and for the life of me I cannot possibly understand why you should wish to speak Greek. . . . These subjects might give you a community of interest with an isolated few impractical dreamers, and a select group of college professors. God forbid!
>
> It would seem to me that what you wish to do is to establish a community of interest with as many people as you possibly can. With people who are moving, who are doing things, and who have an interesting, not a decadent outlook . . .
>
> It isn't really important what I think. It's important what you wish to do with your life. I just wish I could feel that the influence of those oddball professors and the ivory towers were developing you into the kind of a man we can both be proud of. I am quite sure that we both will be pleased and delighted when I introduce you to some friends of mine and say, "This is my son. He speaks Greek . . ."
>
> If you are going to stay on at Brown, and be a professor of Classics, the courses you have adopted will suit you for a lifetime association with Gale Noyes. Perhaps he will even teach you to make jelly. In my opinion, it won't do much to help you learn to get along with the people in this world. I think you are rapidly becoming a jackass; that the sooner you get out of the filthy atmosphere, the better it will suit me.
>
> Oh, I know that everybody says that a college education is a must. Well, I console myself by saying that everybody said the world was square, except Columbus. You go ahead and go with the world, and I'll go it alone.

[9] Ibid.

I hope I am right. You are in the hands of the Philistines, and dammit, I sent you there. I am sorry.

Devotedly,
Dad[10]

Turner's initial response to this letter was equally harsh—he had it printed in its entirety in the campus newspaper. Later, however, he changed his major to economics. But Professor Workman remarked, "We didn't really lose him. The real humanist will always go out of his way to be different."[11]

At Brown, Turner maintained his competitive excellence in debating and in the sport he had learned as a child—sailing—considered in the Northeast, however, as anything but child's play. Attesting to his skill, a Connecticut yacht club offered him a summer job and a chance to represent it on the regatta circuit. In response, Turner's father insisted that he come home and help with the now multicity family business. That summer, rather than sailing and sunning in Narragansett Bay, Turner sold billboard space out of an office in Savannah.

The heat and humidity of a southern summer, combined with a growing resentment of his father (and an imminent divorce at home), pushed Turner near his boiling point. Close enough, in fact, that he was willing to forego a $5000 reward from his father if he refrained from taking a drink of alcohol until he was 21. When he returned to Brown in the fall, he became involved in an alcohol-related brawl at a nearby women's college. As a result, Turner and some friends were suspended from school. After a six-month tour of active duty in the Coast Guard—arranged by his father—Turner returned to Brown. Not long after he was asked to leave permanently for breaking a rule against overnight female dorm room guests.

A Return to the South

After another cruise with the Coast Guard—for the summer—Turner returned to Georgia to manage the Macon branch of Turner Advertising Company. Two years later, in 1962, Ed Turner, already a millionaire, fulfilled another lifelong dream and acquired a significant base in Atlanta with the purchase of General Outdoor Advertising Company, the largest in the country. In doing so, however, he became financially overextended, and mounting pressures persuaded him to initiate plans to sell out. But he encountered a formidable, tenacious obstacle in Ted, who had become the zealot of the family business and whose appetite for growth and challenge was whetted by the risky Atlanta acquisition. Ed was now faced with competition from his own son whom he had prepared for greatness.

Six months after the Atlanta business purchase, on March 5, 1963, Ed Turner killed himself with a pistol in his South Carolina plantation. Turner commented:

[10] Ibid.

[11] Ibid.

(My father and I) loved each other and yet we were so cruel. He was a hard man, and I tried to please him . . . but we had terrible, terrible fights. It was after one of those fights—we disagreed about how the business should be run—that he blew his brains out.[12]

In the following days, after Turner learned that the business and properties had been left to him, he halted the uncompleted sellout transactions, sold off the two plantations in Georgia and South Carolina to raise cash, and regained control (through roughhouse tactics and complex financings) of the businesses already sold. In one instance, Turner convinced a buyer to tear up the sale agreement for $200,000 in cash, later negotiating the cash into stock. This later became a favorite Turner financing ploy.

By 1985, Turner's business had become an advertising/broadcasting conglomerate known as Turner Broadcasting Systems (TBS). Its stock, traded publicly, with 82 percent held by Turner himself, had a market value of $400 million. The principal holdings and investments of TBS were in cable television stations and CNN, the Cable News Network, begun in early 1980. CNN offered 24-hour news coverage, challenging the major networks in the TV news business. Turner's main cable station, WTBS in Atlanta, also challenged the networks by offering alternate programming that WTBS beamed via satellite to cable subscribers throughout the United States.

Cable's inroads in the television market have been substantial. CBS Broadcast Group president Gene Jankowski predicted that by 1990 cable's time share of viewers with cable availability would reach 43 percent. Furthermore, CNN's only competitor thus far in 24-hour news competition, a joint venture of ABC and Group-W Westinghouse, folded in 1983 after less than one year of operation.

TURNER'S BUSINESS STYLE

Turner had a unique business philosophy that was built, in large part, on disdain for traveling the safe or established path:

Business is full of lawyers and advisers, and you've got to remember, whatever you're doing, that these guys are trying to keep you from getting burned. That's their job. So if you get a new idea, don't expect everyone to say, "Let's go." You're the one who says that. I don't believe in marketing studies. Do you want to do it? Are you committed to making it work? Then it will, or at least it'll have the only chance it ever had. The reason nothing gets done in this country anymore is that there are so many committees. It just has to be you. Like McDonald's says, "You—you're the one."[13]

Regarding his principal competitors, the television networks, Turner offered this vivid remark:

---

[12] Ibid.
[13] Ibid.

Do you know why we're going to be such a big success and why I'm going to make a billion dollars? It's because people know things are screwed up, and they're looking for a change. It's not that I'm a genius, it's that television is lousy, and the three networks have it all to themselves and they want to keep it lousy. The networks are like the Mafia. The networks ARE the Mafia. Do you know they spent a quarter of a million dollars in Washington trying to stop my Superstation from showing movies and sports in people's houses? Well, their day is finished now. It's over. They've made unbelievable profits, and what have they brought us? Mr. Whipple squeezing the toilet paper. *The $1.98 Cheap Show. The Newlywed Game. Love Boat.* The networks are run by a greedy bunch of jerks that have hoodwinked the American public, and now I'm riding in on a white horse. I'm telling you, the networks are scared. But they can't stop me, because people are demanding—they're insisting—on alternatives.

OTHER VIEWS OF TED TURNER

In his personal as well as business life, Turner had an unwavering commitment to goals. Jane Smith Turner (Janie) recalled her first impressions of Turner and their early days of marriage:

> We met at a party . . . My first impulse was to run as fast as I could the other way . . . He was a divorced man . . . and he came on so strong . . . telephoned every day. He had this Ferrari and every night he came to take me to dinner in the Ferrari. I thought, "Oh boy, this isn't for me . . . He was crazy." But there was no getting away. And my father liked him. He said, "Ted's the most amazing young man I've ever met." He finally wore me down. When Ted was courting me, he was very bored with the office . . . The billboard companies (were) going real well, and he used to sleep until ten-thirty or eleven in the morning. Sailing became everything. My own babies came along (Ted's two children from his first marriage lived with them also) and I was left alone. I was miserable a lot of the time. Three times Ted was away from home sailing over Christmas. One Christmas I was so pregnant I couldn't go home to my parents so I just stayed in Atlanta. I cried and cried.[14]

Christian Williams, author of the Turner biography, characterized Turner as a

> dizzying mixture of fierce pride, nonstop, high-decibel speech-making, philosophical gloom, nightmarish evocations of a ruined earth populated by homo sapiens gone to seed, utter candor, and a sense of personal destiny that is easy to recognize, and he makes no attempt to hide it: he will remake the world of commercial television, dominate international yachting, and simultaneously maintain a nineteenth-century Southern agrarian home life to which he can return periodically for sustenance.[15]

[14] Ibid.
[15] Ibid.

Akira Kimishima

At the time this case was written, Mr. Kimishima was 49 years old, married and the father of two children. He was serving as executive vice president and chief operating officer of Dainana Securities Company, a medium-sized investment bank located in Tokyo, Japan. In 1984, Dainana maintained five offices, all located in the metropolitan Tokyo area.

JAPANESE CULTURE IN CORPORATIONS

The culture of Japanese corporations is markedly different from that found in American companies in many important ways. To begin with, major firms and government agencies hire once a year, in the spring, when students graduate from junior and senior high schools and universities. Those who do not pass on to higher levels of education enter the work force as laborers. Large corporations and government agencies hire graduates from Imperial Universities and a few prestigious private colleges for managerial training positions. Once hired, a new employee can depend on lifelong employment with the firm until the mandatory retirement age of 55; an employee will be terminated only for a major criminal or other grave offense. Unemployment among young people is almost nonexistent.

Historically, there has been very little job-hopping in Japanese corporations. This has partly been because Japanese cultural values favored loyalty to family and associations. It has also been the result of the career path in Japanese companies and the advantage of seniority. While job switching has been on the rise in recent years, it is nowhere near the magnitude of U.S. corporations.

Seniority has always played an important role in the management of Japanese companies both emotionally and functionally, for senior Japanese managers were usually the most experienced. This system concentrates wisdom in high places and also saves other senior people from having to suffer the humiliation of reporting to someone younger. The most senior official is usually in charge of personnel.

This case was prepared by Assistant Professor John Kao.

Copyright © 1985 by the President and Fellows of Harvard College. Harvard Business School case 9-485-131.

Japanese companies pay their employees with salary plus a bonus which is not contingent on individual performance but rather on the overall performance of the firm. Management also encourages group activities, even unionization, as ways of solidifying group loyalty. Blue and white collar employees could be found in the same company in the same union.

Confrontation and open disagreement in the workplace are rare. Most managerial decisions are made by consensus in group circles and major deadlocks can occur when one member refuses to go along with a decision.

KIMISHIMA FAMILY HISTORY

Why was I able to do what I did? I think maybe it's something I inherited from my father. He is a very aggressive guy. He is still living, and is 83 years old. He is a very interesting man. My father was born at the end of the nineteenth century in Japan, the son of a poor Shinto priest. He really wanted to be a doctor but my grandfather did not have any money. So he became a school boy and lived in a doctor's house, and studied medicine very hard. At the time the Japanese medical system did not require university graduation, rather, passage of a state examination to get a doctor's certificate. My father studied and worked very hard, night and day. He passed the examination in his twenties. This was exceptionally young at the time, the average age for passing the examination was around 25. Then he decided to go abroad.

At the beginning of the twentieth century, it was very hard to get the chance to go abroad in Japan. So he went to a small island called Oshima, 100 kilometers from Tokyo, a kind of fisherman's port. He had a small office there and made a little money. Then he moved to another island farther away in the south, where he had a small office. Then he went to Manila, where he worked for a Japanese doctor and got a lot of money. Finally, he went to Germany and ended up at Berlin University. There he got the title of doctor. He came back to Japan, became an assistant to a professor at the medical school, and opened a medical office in Tokyo. At this time he was still young—30. He married my mother and I was born. Gradually he got frustrated staying in Japan after spending so much time abroad. He closed down his office and went to Hong Kong; he became the family doctor of a chief of the Chinese government who came from Canton.

I am the oldest son, and therefore my father expected me to be a doctor. Unfortunately, I did not want to be a doctor—I went to premedical school but changed my mind. I really hated to be a doctor, sitting in the clinic seeing patients from early morning to late at night. My two brothers and a sister became doctors. The problem is my two brothers do not have children. There is a succession problem. I asked my son to be a doctor. He was born in the United States and brought up in London and spent quite a long time in Paris. He entered medical school this spring in Japan and I am quite happy about it.

The reason why I wanted to enter Keio University is that the school culture is quite independent and a lot of businessmen came from this school. I admired the school and culture of Keio University. I did not have any idea of what I wanted to do. But at the time my family was happy, because my father thought I was going to the medical department, and Keio has one of the best medical schools in Japan. I worked very hard and finally I entered premedical school. Two years later I changed direction and went into business.

I had been brought up in a foreign country and many times I wanted to go abroad, particularly during the 1950s and 1960s, because in those days the Japanese living standard was so poor. When we saw American movies we really wanted to go abroad. I was lucky—immediately after graduation I was assigned a job in the United States. It was a very good time for the United States—the time of President Kennedy, the New Frontier spirit. ·

I really wanted to go to the U.S., so I applied to my boss to go. At the time the investment securities business was concentrated in the domestic market, no foreign operations existed within the organization. Most of the people could not speak English of course, I could not speak English either. But the boss said OK and I came to the States in 1961. I was 24.

UNITED STATES

At that time the Japanese government issued a national bond on Wall Street. We were a syndicated group of underwriters, we tried to sell Japanese bonds to the public. But nobody was interested in Japanese bonds then—Japan was still an underdeveloped country. We realized we must have a series of retail shops all over the States. Underwriting is good business, but at the same time we needed retail business. We tried to establish a subsidiary company in Los Angeles because there were so many Japanese living there and they preferred to invest in Japanese securities.

I did not know how to build up a company! Fortunately I could buy a paper company of a Japanese securities firm which had been built before the war. Because of World War II this company only existed on paper. I bought this paper company and opened an office in L.A. I was the CEO, and we had about 20 employees. At the time I did not know much about American regulation. One day I was asked to come to the SEC office and was asked a lot of things about my office and business. I could not reply and I was very embarrassed! SEC regulations are very tough. At the time our company was very small and I had a lot of inventory. We had to immediately improve it otherwise we would have had to close the office. At the age of 24 I was very scared, but on the other hand it was rather fun!

We continued to sell Japanese securities through a retail security firm. The New York office engaged mainly in the underwriting business, and the California office acted as a retailer of securities to the public. I was six months in New York, then another six months in California. It was a very busy time.

Then we had the problem of the interstate equalization tax. This was 1963, and President Kennedy issued a new tax which meant that anyone who wanted to invest in foreign securities had to pay a surcharge tax of 15 percent. This killed investment and our business began to decline. I tried to move to handle American securities. In California we handled a lot of American securities in the over-the-counter market. I had a very close relation to Sumitomo Bank of California and Bank of Tokyo of California. I tried to sell the stocks of these Japanese banks. This business went very well. Also, some American people were interested in purchasing stocks of Japanese banks.

At this time, a Japanese securities company became a member of a syndicate of a secondary offering of Ford Motor Company shares. The Ford Foundation wanted to sell 2 million shares of Ford Motor to the public. Securities companies tried to make a kind of consortium, and we became a member of this consortium and bought 80,000 shares of Ford Motor from Ford Foundation. We signed the contract on the morning of November 22, 1963. We had already gotten purchasing commitments from prospects, and it seemed things were going well. But later that morning President Kennedy was assassinated. All the stocks on the stock exchange fell. The opening price of Ford was 41¾, then all of a sudden the price came down to $38. All prospects cancelled their orders. I did not know what to do, I was very confused.

We had signed the contract with the Ford Foundation, but due to the cancellation of the purchasing orders of our prospects, we had to hold all the shares ourself. We did not have enough money by that time. I tried to call Japan but in those days the international communication system was not so convenient, usually a call to Japan took two to three hours. And at the time the president was assassinated, all lines were occupied by press people. All listed stocks on the New York Stock Exchange declined heavily and the exchange closed to avoid confusion. It was Friday and all weekend I could not sleep at all. On Monday morning the stock exchange was opened but prices still came down. Around noontime they gradually recovered and by closing time of Monday afternoon they recovered to their original price. I really relaxed. It was a very exciting time. I realized that the investment security business was a risky and out of control business! I did not like this kind of speculation, and I thought it might be better to change jobs. Also, I wanted to know about manufacturing and trading.

JAPAN

Soon after that, I got married to a Japanese girl in the United States. We had our first boy in the States in 1963. Because I was the eldest son, my father wanted me to come back to Japan—he wanted to see his grandson. I had already been in the U.S. many years and I thought this was long enough. So I made up my mind to go back to Japan. I asked my boss to send me back, but

he said it might be better to stay in the U.S. because at the time—1966—
Japan was suffering from serious business stagnation. Finally I came back
to Japan; I realized that the living standard in the U.S. was far better than
Japan. We were very depressed and disappointed at the living standard
in Japan. When we were in the U.S. we had two cars, enjoyed life, but in
Japan it was impossible to have even one car! Also, salary-wise, it wasn't
attractive. It was a very difficult time for me to survive, in Japan.

I lived there for three years, then I tried to change jobs. Coincidentally,
at that time Xerox Corporation established a Japanese venture company—
jointly owned with Fuji Film—so-called Fuji-Xerox. I was invited to be
manager of the corporate planning department for Fuji-Xerox. I was very
glad to be in that position. When I was in the States I had met Joe Wilson,
the founder of Xerox. This was the beginning of the 1960s—a time when
Xerox just took off. Joe Wilson came to Wall Street once a month. He had
luncheon meetings with security analysts quite often and tried to explain what
Xerox intended to do and what their current status was, so I was quite
familiar with the organization of Xerox and his business philosophy. I joined
Xerox in Japan and immediately I was transferred to London to Xerox
International headquarters, at my request.

LONDON

I was in London from 1969 to 1974. All the family enjoyed their life over
there; it was the most peaceful time of our life. When we were in London, the
U.K.'s general economic and social situation was not so bad. So I really
enjoyed life in London, but my five years there was nothing exciting for my
private or my business life. In the Xerox International HQ I was in charge of
subsidiaries and later, product planning. During my stay in London I was also
in charge of planning new products in which Japanese technology was quite
advanced. I think I did quite well, so Xerox asked me to move from London
to Stamford, Connecticut where Xerox had corporate headquarters. I was
very glad to move back to the U.S., but suddenly Japanese Xerox was strongly
against this move, because according to them, I originally belonged to
Fuji-Xerox. Without any prior consensus with Fuji-Xerox no one could ask
me to move to the U.S. I was very embarrassed; I had to decide whether or
not to move to the U.S. or go back to Japan.

Then a representative of Mitsubishi Corporation came to see me in my
office in London. Mitsubishi wanted to go into the office automation product
field. Nobody had experience with this product group and the market, so
Mitsubishi was looking for someone and they asked me to join them. It was
not a bad offer; salary-wise, it was very attractive. They wanted me to be
stationed in Europe and to develop a sales network all over Europe. This was
good, so I decided to move to Mitsubishi. I went back to Tokyo in order to be

a formal staff member of Mitsubishi. I was given an orientation in Tokyo for six months and went back to London. My first assignment was to build a new company in France.

FRANCE

Every day at Mitsubishi France we talked about what was the best way to develop the market. Finally we decided to take over a French company, not a big company but with enough sales force and service network—about 400 or 500 employees. At the beginning we took only 50 percent of the equity; the other 50 percent was kept by the French owner. This was a typical French company—owned by a French family, run the French way. Everybody enjoyed their life in the company very much like a family, but the business was not going very well because there was no control system in the organization—no reporting system and no budgeting system—in short, a kind of "laissez-faire" style. Even so, the company was making profit because of a lot of person-to-person relations with major customers. When doing business in France the important thing is to establish good relationships on a person-to-person basis.

I tried to implement a management accounting reporting and budgeting system in the company. I asked all branch managers and corporate staff to come to Paris and I explained our business goals and our purpose in implementing this new system and so on. Everyone said they understood and agreed with me. Then I put together a package of reporting systems and I asked them to send it back to me every month. Almost two months later, nothing had happened. I tried to call every branch manager, but at the time I could not speak French at all. So I visited the branches and asked the branch managers why they had not sent back the reports. They said there was no time to prepare. I was really embarrassed and I tried to explain again. Again they agreed with me and for the next two months reports began to come to my office. I checked them one by one and realized there were inconsistencies and inaccuracies. I asked my secretary to ask every branch manager how they got the figures. They replied that the secretary prepared the report and they did not know how to get the figures. This kind of thing—back and forth, back and forth—were the usual daily matters.

At the time I suffered very seriously from the French way of life—long lunch times, etc. I enjoyed our private life but I was very frustrated at work. Every Saturday and Sunday I went to the office to collect information and prepare corporate reports for Tokyo. It was a fascinating and exciting time—four and a half years living in Paris. It was a completely new experiment in my life compared with living in London for five years. It seemed that the French were less interested in developing markets or finding new business than in enjoying life. Business was only a tool for enjoyment. It's a completely different concept from the Japanese. Now I think the attitude of the French people was very right!

In those days I had to fight every day with French people to modernize the company. Finally we decided to separate from the French partner. Fifty-fifty looks nice, but nobody makes decisions. The Japanese company—Mitsubishi—took over 20,000 shares of the French company and owned 100 percent of the equity. We tried to implement our philosophy, our way of management in the company and I tried to rationalize everything. When the French problem was settled, Mitsubishi asked me to go to Hamburg where Mitsubishi had a European headquarters. I suddenly realized I had a family problem. My first son was 15, the second was 7. The first son was born in the U.S. and had gone from city to city—London, Paris, etc. He could speak English and French very well as well as Japanese, but he could not read or write Japanese at all. I realized he was gradually losing his identity as a Japanese, and as you may know, the entrance examination to Japanese university is tough. So my wife and I decided it was time to go back to Japan. I asked Mitsubishi if I could go back to Japan to the head office. After a struggle with the head office, they agreed for me to come back to Japan sometime in the future.

THE ALTMAN SYSTEM

One of the American consulting companies contacted me. They asked me if I was interested in moving to another company and I said, "OK, I'm interested in an offer. I asked them what kind of business it was and they explained that a German company wanted to establish an operation in Tokyo. They were looking for the president of the company. Sounded interesting. They explained the nature of the business, but I did not understand what kind of business it was! What would I do in Japan? They tried to explain many times but I still couldn't catch on. I told them the terms and conditions sounded very interesting to me but I did not understand them, therefore I was not interested.

Weeks later I received a letter from this company—called Universe AG—Hamburg. The letter stated, "I just received your name from Booz Allen and I am very much interested in your prospects and your career, therefore if you have time please come to see me in Hamburg." The air ticket was enclosed! I was curious so one day I went to Hamburg. I visited the head office and met the CEO of this company. It was not a big company—only 500 people. He explained the nature of his business which is a kind of *matchmaking* business.

The background of this business was interesting. Germany suffered very seriously from WWI and WWII, and from a demographic point of view there was a big imbalance between males and females. Marriage had become one of the most serious social issues in Germany. Also, a lot of younger people came to the big cities such as Munich, Hamburg, Frankfurt, and tried to find jobs.

There were many job opportunities, but these people who came from the countryside had no contact with other people and they were quite isolated in the city; the modern industrial structure is such that male jobs and female jobs were separated, therefore men and women did not have many chances to meet each other. Under these circumstances, once they meet by chance, they got married immediately. But almost all of them had no compatibility, so they separated easily. If this kind of situation continued, it would be a very serious social problem for Germany. If the family was unstable, the social environment might be very unstable in the future. Therefore, one of the most important things was to create stable and sound families.

The basic "service" of the company was to diagnose compatibility. A professor at the University of Kiel established a theory about the compatibility of males and females in the couple relation. The business was based on the theory which is called the "Altman System" in Germany. The company was established 25 years ago; at the time the computer was not developed, although it's essential to this kind of matchmaking. The business in West Germany was not going so well: German young men and women gradually were losing an interest in getting into marriage. Most people preferred to spend their money to travel. The CEO thought that this system might be adaptable for Japanese society because in Japan there is already a system called "omiai" which means arranged marriage through a go-between. After World War II this system gradually lost popularity because young people prefer falling in love on their own. But the German guy thought this might be an interesting business if it were implemented in Japan; he wanted someone to conduct the business in Japan.

When I heard this story, it seemed interesting, but I rather hated this kind of business. This was a completely different business from my career, and particularly in Japan, the prestige of this kind of business was not very high. I was used to working for first-class companies. But, it sounded very interesting so I made several suggestions to him about launching this kind of system in Japan and left. Immediately after, he wrote to me to consider this position. I said, "No, I have no reason to leave Mitsubishi." One year later I received a letter from him which stated that he had made up his mind to launch this business in Japan, and he wanted me to really think about the business. I said OK after a long negotiation of the terms and conditions. Mitsubishi had finally agreed with my moving to the Tokyo head office as a deputy general manager of the general merchandise department. But I was anxious. Housing was difficult in Japan. Houses are so expensive, and it is very hard to get a Western living standard. So I asked the German management—would you furnish us a nice house and give me double the salary of Mitsubishi and a car and so on. He said yes.

So, I established a new company in Japan, the so-called Altman System International. The German company had already established a market research company in Japan, but their capitalization was very small because it was only for market research. When I arrived in Tokyo I was very embarrassed because of insufficient operating funds in the bank account. I visited several investment bankers and commercial banks; I explained the nature of the business, but nobody trusted me. Some banker said, "This is a silly business, are you really thinking about it seriously?" I thought at the time that as a German company, their credibility with Japanese people was not very high. I thought that if a reliable and important Japanese company invested in us it would increase our credibility. So I went to Japan Airlines and explained the whole story. Japan Airlines showed an interest in the proposal because we were creating married couples and I promised to send couples created through our system to Japan Airlines for a honeymoon tour. Honeymoon trips are really big business for them; nearly 50 percent of profit for package tours comes from this. So Japan Airlines decided to invest a small amount of money in this company. The important thing for me was their prestigious name as shareholders. I did not need the money; the name was much more important. I told many bankers, "Look, even Japan Airlines is a shareholder!" Finally, the biggest bank gave me an overdraft of 50,000,000 yen, which was not a big amount, but enough to start our business in Japan. I made huge advertisements in lots of newspapers and magazines and so on. At the time, we were a marketing research company which employed around ten people.

When I started this business in 1957, revenue was only 100,000,000 yen. Three years later it was six hundred million and 6 years later annual revenue became ¥5 billion. It grew quite steadily and very fast. I had a lot of experience in trading companies and manufacturing concerns, and in these businesses the important things were to watch inventory and accounts receivable. But in this company there was no inventory, no accounts receivable. I felt very scared and uncertain. What shall I watch? I was very confused. This was a fascinating experience for me. But the company grew very fast; from the very beginning it was a very profitable company because there was no huge advance investment. We were just selling a service.

This is a labor-intensive business. The number of employees increased very rapidly. Now we have 500 employees and most of them are system counselors. System counselors are very similar to service personnel; they explain the system and advise members. Once a week we send data to all outstanding members. Our membership circle right now is 35,000. In terms of accumulation it's nearly 70,000. The outstanding number is 35,000, which means 35,000 have left the members circle because of getting married and expired membership. In consequence the marriage rate of all members is 50 percent. So there are already many Altman System babies in Japan—more than 200.

Once a male and female get into marriage, the first important event is that people are usually invited to a big hotel for a wedding ceremony. Fifty percent of Japanese hotel revenue comes from this. After that, they honeymoon, which makes a great contribution to the traveling service industry. Then, after that, the new family would like to buy furniture, electric home appliances, a house, and so on. So many people are interested in our business and they asked us to work with them—hotels, travel agencies, real estate firms, and so on.

MANAGEMENT PHILOSOPHY

I have worked for several companies since graduating from college in 1957 and throughout my career have spent much time thinking about, "What is management?" The philosophy of management is a most important concern in my life. Is the goal of management to increase profits or market share or to achieve a high growth rate? I don't think so. Since graduation from college I have worked in Japan, the United States, England, and France. In addition to that, I have built a company with some German people in Japan. So I have worked in five different places and the purpose of management in each place was completely different. My conclusion is that it is management's job to make people happy. This is the only purpose of management. The company will run continuously if supported by people of good faith. For example, a company has many relations with customers, shareholders, and employees, and if we only concentrate on increasing profits then maybe the customers or the employees are not happy. From my point of view this is not fair. The purpose of management is related to the happiness of people within the company. This is my philosophy, and I have been thinking about these kinds of things for the past 20 years.

I am interested in creating something and I think that management itself is a kind of art. Creating art is quite similar to building up a new business. However, once I create something new I lose interest in it. In France I worked very hard from early morning to late night Saturdays and Sundays; I tried to build up an effective organization and control system. But once I completed my assignment, I lost interest. This is my nature—I try all the time to change things. I built up a small business in California. That was the beginning of my challenge. Then I tried to build an organization in France and then in Japan. I always tried to build up a business based on the goodwill of human beings.

I learned a lot of things through this new business in Japan. For example, I think the nature and character of the management of business ought to change from time to time, depending on its stage of development and growth. There is the foundation period, the growing period, and the maturing period—this is the process of a growing business. I ask myself always, "Am I a good CEO through all phases of business growth?" I believe that every phase of business expansion might need a different character of management. My personality and my nature is good for the foundation period and the growing period of a company, but in the mature period perhaps I would kill the business. Some people can perform very well during the foundation period, but during the growing period and in the maturing period most people do not do very well.

When I am in the very early developing stage of business I am very active and positive. However, during the mature phase, the important thing is how to maintain the business, and I feel bored. So it's almost impossible for me to stay in such a stable environment for a long time. I always try to challenge something. In the mature phase of business, people tend to get very conservative. In this stage, I always have conflict with people, I try to build up something further, to achieve something, to enter into new businesses. This is my inclination, but most of my subordinates and employees do not like this, particularly at the stage of maturity. They would rather stay in a nice stable environment with nothing to do other than enjoying a high salary without hard work. From my past experience, I always get into this kind of problem with my subordinates. I understand the attitude of people: once they reach a kind of wealthy stage they like to keep things as they are. This is human nature. However, I do not like it!

If someone is in the position of director, he may have done very well, but once he is promoted to vice president sometimes he creates a problem. I have seen this kind of thing quite often. In Japan many companies have shown very fast growth in the past decade. A company may be growing very fast (20 percent or 30 percent per annum), but the capacity of the people—particularly of managers—cannot keep up with the growth of the company. This discrepancy between the development of human capacity and the growth of an organization creates a lot of tragedy under the lifetime employment system in Japan. The company grows very fast and management must grow very fast, i.e., it must have a bigger role, and bigger involvement in all ways to adjust to the growth of the company. In most cases, the growth of people's capacity and the growth of the organization do not meet each other, there is no correlation.

This lack of fit between a staff's capacity and the organization will generate many problems if the company's philosophy is not clear for everybody. The important thing is, what is the goal of the organization? What is the important thing? Growth? Profits? Human beings? I do not know. I am still seeking the goal of business, the goal of life itself. I try to find the right answer. We are always trying to find out the correct answer to uncertainty, but it is difficult.

Most American people trust in it—it's American enterprise. This might be changing with the individual and the social environment, however, most American management people still stick to short-term profit. That is important but it's human beings that are most important. In this country human beings are treated as a kind of resource. Everyone says "human resources." From my point of view people are not "resources." Organizations will have to be conscious of human beings, without human beings there *is* no business. Most people think that management comes first and people second. Particularly with a big organization, there are many conflicts between humans and profit. Therefore I would like to establish an ideal organization which is for human beings first and the rest second.

An individual in an organization must have a very clear identity. Particularly in Japan most employees do not have any identity as individuals. I really hate it—the Japanese company. These days everybody is talking about Japanese competition. The Japanese system is good for mass production industry because it is the kind of organization which keeps discipline like an army organization. Western European or American industry is slightly different. I think both the Japanese system and the American system have good points; I would like to combine the strength of them both. However, I think that management and employee are the same people and must have the same rights—only their function is different.

When I started my business in Japan I tried to build this kind of organization. I promoted a lot of women to managers which is quite rare in Japan. And wages and salary were made completely the same—no discrimination. But some Japanese people do not like to be under the control of women managers. At the very beginning most of the men showed strong resistance to this. But after six months to a year they accepted it. So I think not 100 percent but 40 percent of my dream of an ideal organization structure was actually realized during my stay in Japan.

A major task was educating my own employees. Creating an ideal organization, a business, is a kind of art. If I were an artist I could paint an item on the canvas myself and I would not need any collaboration or support. But in creating an organization the important thing is how to get people to understand my philosophy, my way of life. This is a very important but hard job. Communication is very difficult. When I started the Altman business there were only ten people working for us. From the very beginning I tried to let them understand what I was thinking. I spent a lot of effort on this, sometimes it was person-to-person communication and sometimes it was in groups. I spent most of my days for that purpose, because the purpose of this kind of service business is to sell my philosophy to the public. I tell people, "Please do not think about working for the company; you should think that you are working for yourself." Otherwise things do not go well. The identity of the individual as a human being is the most essential thing. I do not know whether or not they really understood what I was telling them. But this is a small experiment in Japanese society.

I had nice executive offices in a skyscraper in Tokyo, and I was in the office all the time and talking with our employees, trying to be in touch as much as possible with a lot of people. This was fun for me and I think most of the employees enjoyed working with me. I tried to let my employees understand my philosophy; I also tried to explain my way of thinking to outside people. Some of them agreed with me but most of them did not understand what I told them. I think that creating a new business is really fascinating. Just like falling in love.

I think that the most important thing for business in the future is that business must sell a kind of ideology to the public. Particularly in the case of service businesses, many people try to offer services to meet the need of the market. This might be good for a while, but in the future individual values will be so varied that it will be impossible to meet the needs of a lot of the people in the market. These days we can summarize market demands based on the lifestyle of people, but in the future individual values might vary more and more. This change will be very important in service businesses, because if the purpose of the business is to meet market demand, it will be impossible as a business to cover so many market segments.

I think when we establish a business, the important things are, first of all, to make the ideology and philosophy of the business clear. Then we have to sell the philosophy to people. If someone agrees with our business ideology, they can come see us. If not, they are not our customer and market. In the process of establishing business, the important thing is how to *educate* the market and the people. In the future, particularly from the demographic point of view, business will change day by day. For example, manufacturing businesses are declining from the point of view of labor force distribution. Less than 30 percent of the population is working in manufacturing. Even in Japan, more than 50–60 percent of the population is working in service industries; more and more people attempt to offer a wider range of services to people.

I think that ordinary people are not interested in the selling of a concept or ideology; however, most of my concern is selling an ideology, and a philosophy which may lead us to the ultimate end of human life. I must say this is a new business!

How to establish better communication among people is essential, particularly in the society of the future. Let people understand each other—this is the most important job, the most important business. I would like to put most of my energy into building good relationships, good communication among people.

Most people are very conservative. Once he or she is in a nice environment, he or she will not try to run away from the nice environment. Lao-Tse, in his way of life which I like very much, said only people who are not yet rich are radical. Rich people are conservative. Only poor people become radical and take risks. I think this is the nature of the human being. From my point of view I am not very rich but reasonably rich compared with most Japanese people. Therefore, I am not worried about life or family. Even if I lost my job, my family would be able to survive for the next few years without working. This is very important to me, otherwise I could take risks.

I do feel fear all the time. I always think about the risk. But I like to give myself stimulation, I rather enjoy putting myself in such an environment. I always want to put myself to a challenge. It's not a problem of age. Once people lose philosophy, perspective, and some kind of passion, even a young person is young no more. Therefore, I try to keep myself young. I like to challenge myself.

When companies are growing fast, their managers have difficulty. Most managers do not realize the growth of the company is reality, and they behave based on their experience. I admire the attitude of Mr. Honda, the founder of Honda Motors. He is a kind of a crazy guy. He has no normal common sense even though he owned such a big company in Japan. He never put on a tie. He always put on funny clothes. But he knew what the problem was that Honda Motors faced right now, and one day suddenly he decided to leave the company. Honda Motors was founded and developed by Mr. Honda and his partner Mr. Fujisawa. Mr. Honda was mainly involved in the engineering R&D aspect of the company. And Mr. Fujisawa came from Mitsubishi Bank. Fujisawa looked after the administration and marketing aspects of the company. Neither had any education from the Japanese point of view. Both worked very hard and Honda became a nice company but Mr. Honda and Mr. Fujisawa realized in 1974 that it was not an era for both of them. And all of a sudden they left the company. In Japan when the president leaves his position usually he becomes the chairman, but Mr. Honda left completely. They then elected a very young fellow to be the president and CEO. This was quite extraordinary in Japanese society. He is a great guy and his way of thinking is very different from other Japanese.

Most entrepreneurs *are* kind of eccentric people. But I am not very eccentric as you can see! This is my problem, I think! I really enjoy challenge, but all the time I think I should be more fanatic, more eccentric in order to build a new venture.

It's just like I am playing in the palm of Buddha! There is a very old Chinese story, a very famous story. It's very long but I like it. There is a naughty monkey—very mighty and a kind of Superman. The monkey was able to run at high speeds riding on the clouds. One day he had a problem with Buddha. Buddha asked "If you are Superman, if this is so and you are going to the far West, there are five totem poles that are standing. Can you reach them?" And the monkey said, "That is easy." Then he called a cloud and rode on the cloud to the west. He found the five totem poles and he signed his name on them. It was easy for him. Finally Buddha said OK, and he showed the monkey's mark on each one of his fingers! The monkey thought that he had run far away, but actually he was only playing on the palm of the Buddha.

I always try to jump out of the palm. I think I can jump from the palm of the Buddha, but still I am playing on the palm.

Audrey Dickason

I suppose what attracts me to venture capital and small companies is the opportunity you have to help them grow up. It's almost like raising a child.

Audrey Dickason should know. She had a 5½ year old son, John. As a single parent—her HBS application and divorce papers were processed about the same time—Dickason faces additional worries and constraints in the job search process. She remarked:

Some jobs and locations are eliminated immediately. I can't see my raising John in New York, for instance. Or taking a job that involved long hours in the office every day or extensive travel. I have to be around for my son.

My father (a former military officer) was very distant, both literally and figuratively when I was growing up. He still works for Rockwell. We lived in Columbus, Ohio, but my father was always gone, off at a project site. He was surprised when I majored in engineering—his discipline—at Case Western. I really created my own major—biochemical engineering—the first one at the school. This was 1981, about the time Genentech started, so it was a totally new field.

After two years with Diamond Shamrock's chemical business and a market research job for a consortium of MIT and Harvard biology and chemistry faculty members, I landed a job with a start-up biotech firm in Boston, Genzyme Corp. This was an interesting place, and I organized many different projects before starting my first year at HBS.

Last summer I worked for Collaborative Research, Inc. identifying potential partners and ideas for biotech research. I'm considering going back there or to another biotech firm. I'm also talking to Bank of Boston about a position in high-tech lending. It would be a great challenge and a lot of fun to be entrepreneurial in that framework. That's also an appealing alternative because of the security involved. And I like Boston very much. I've lived here for three years. John also has quite a few friends here. But I'm not a risk-averse person. I think I'm more of a calculated risk-taker.

Venture capital is also appealing as a job possibility. The financial upside is better than at a bank or a company where I didn't get equity. But I also wonder how many good deals will be around in the future.

I'm also looking at a biotech start-up company. In fact, I'm doing some consulting work for them now. This would really allow me to build on my past

This case was prepared by Research Associate Lee Field and Associate Professor John Kao. Copyright © 1986 by the President and Fellows of Harvard College. Harvard Business School case 9-487-034.

experience and what I've learned at HBS, primarily in finance. But there are drawbacks. The hours could be long, there might be more travel than I want and then there's the financial risk.

I suppose someday I'd like to have my own company. My ex-husband started his own business after our divorce and while I was in the first year. He was unemployed a lot during our marriage. Just as I'm sure he wanted to show me he could do it, I think a motivating factor for my degree and future success is to prove that I can do it also. My parents didn't wholeheartedly approve of our marriage, so it would be nice to prove to them as well that I can succeed. And then there's Johnny. I have to do well for him, too.

Exhibit 1 is a copy of Dickason's resume.

Exhibit 1

AUDREY L. DICKASON
15A Soldiers Field Park
Boston, Massachusetts 02163
(617) 498-8985

education
1984–1986 **HARVARD GRADUATE SCHOOL
OF BUSINESS ADMINISTRATION**   **Boston, MA**
Candidate for the degree of Master in Business Administration, June 1986. Emphasis in entrepreneurial finance. Member of the Corporate Leadership Forum, Venture Capital, and Health Industry clubs.

1977–1981 **CASE WESTERN RESERVE UNIVERSITY**   **Cleveland, OH**
Bachelor of Science degree in chemical engineering, with Honors, May 1981. Technical sequence in biology. Elected President of CWRU Mortar Board. Awarded Rockwell International Management Club scholarship.

**business
experience**
Summer **COLLABORATIVE RESEARCH, INC.**   **Lexington, MA**
1985 **Market Analyst.** Identified potential joint venture/research contract partners for biotechnology research projects. Contacts included Fortune 500 chemical and pharmaceutical firms. Assessed market value of technologies through interviews, market data, and literature review. Worked directly with senior scientists to evaluate technical concerns of clients. Proposed new project ideas based on industry and market analysis.

1983–1984 **GENZYME CORPORATION**   **Boston, MA**
Program Manager. Managed project planning and implementation for the clinical diagnostic enzyme division. Coordinated production, marketing, and research departments with project management and critical path analysis programs. Initiated and installed sales forecasting, production planning, and inventory management systems which tripled operating efficiency.

1983 **BIOINFORMATION ASSOCIATES**   **Boston, MA**
Marketing Consultant. Conducted market research and performed economic feasibility analyses of biochemical products for this consortium of MIT, Harvard, and Whitehead Institute faculty members. Presented recommendations to senior officers of client, Genzyme. Performance resulted in offer of full-time employment as client liaison and program manager.

1981–1983 **DIAMOND SHAMROCK**   **Cleveland, OH**
Chemical Engineer, *New Business Development.* Analyzed potential venture capital investments, corporate R&D projects, and technology licenses. Designed system and received capital appropriation for laboratory-scale enhanced oil recovery model.

personal Interests include scuba diving, sailing, swimming, racquet sports, running, dance, and theatre.

references Available upon request.

October, 1985

Deborah Goldberg

For Deborah Goldberg, two years at Harvard Business School passed into history a few short days following the 1985 graduation ceremonies. Now, as she consulted European air travel schedules for a long-awaited vacation, she could not put some extremely difficult career decisions out of her mind.

Fortunately, she had narrowed her options to four possibilities: (1) working in her family's business; (2) joining a venture capital firm; (3) working at a company in the same industry as her family's; (4) starting her own company. Goldberg had studied American history as an undergraduate at Boston University and then did some graduate work in American Studies. For a while, she worked at a department store company and then went on to law school at Boston College, before entering Harvard Business School in the fall of 1983.

THE FAMILY BUSINESS

Goldberg's grandfather was Sidney Rabb, founder of the Stop and Shop Companies, Inc., a major food, drug, and discount chain. They were very close. In her words, "The three generations in my family were more like a single unit. My level of commitment is very strong to the family business; there's no separation of church and state with us. Furthermore, I am the oldest sibling in my immediate family."

Stop and Shop had always been a family-run business. Goldberg's mother, the youngest of two daughters had visited stores with Rabb when she was a child. Currently, she was senior vice president and COO of Stop and Shop; her husband served as president and CEO.

Part of Goldberg's concern about joining Stop and Shop involved its sheer size: a huge company with $3.5 billion in sales and 40,000 employees. She described herself as a freewheeling person, one who sometimes likes to shoot from the hip. She recalled her typical HBS attire as jeans, cowboy boots, and a raccoon coat. As she put it, "I prefer the peer dynamics of a nutty

This case was prepared by Associate Professor John Kao.
Copyright © 1986 by the President and Fellows of Harvard College. Harvard Business School case 9-487-033.

start-up, where people love me for my crazy personality. The traditional environment isn't me. I'm not sure I want to be part of this industry. Also, people from HBS don't start as vice presidents at our company. My mother and father, for example, worked their way up from the bottom.

THE VENTURE CAPITAL OPTION

Goldberg had been considering a career in venture capital for some time. During law school, a close friend's father, a successful high-tech entrepreneur and venture capitalist, had been a significant influence on her. High tech was new to Goldberg's family and she felt that she could be successful in her own niche away from the family business. She also felt that there would be a good fit between the industry and her freewheeling and independent personality. Previous operations experience (real estate and managing a catalogue sales start-up) and her network of business relationships persuaded her that she could be an effective venture capitalist working with developing companies. HBS had also been an important step toward a career in venture capital, because it gave her financial experience as well as an edge as a woman in a male-dominated industry. She saw venture capital going through a transitional stage, but still thought that her timing would still be right. At a time when people were less enamored of the field, she saw considerable career opportunity. She had considered "old-line" venture capital firms with a small number of partners and an intimate, collegial atmosphere.

WORKING IN A COMPANY RELATED
TO THE FAMILY BUSINESS

During her job search, Goldberg had consulted a family contact, the chairman of a major retailing firm. In the course of giving her career advice, he offered her a position as assistant to the president of the marketing services division working for a 36-year-old superstar. The job amounted to an opportunity to serve the entire company as an internal strategic consultant. The scope and challenge of the job appealed to her; it seemed like an opportunity for her to do what she felt came naturally to her.

STARTING HER OWN BUSINESS

Goldberg also gave a lot of thought to starting her own business. She had serious reservations about the idea of working for someone else. On the other hand, she had some concerns about starting her own business as long as the Stop and Shop issue remained unresolved. There were times when she felt she needed to deal with that first, before considering the idea of an independent business career.

The risk of starting her own business did not frighten her, but rather, appealed to her. She felt well prepared for an entrepreneurial endeavor and had experience at building effective teams. She also had an inventory of personal contacts from which she could readily select. She saw herself as good at developing concepts, raising capital, and writing business plans. One possibility she considered involved specialty retail, for example a women's clothing store like Ann Taylor. Goldberg thought that while there were a million women's stores, there were also a million women out shopping and that she would have a flair for coming up with a winning concept. She also thought about food retailing. She felt that such businesses came naturally to her. Lastly, she was very opportunity-driven, and would be receptive to exciting deals that might come her way.

So, as Goldberg prepared for her flight to Europe for the traditional post-graduation vacation, she tried to put career thoughts on hold. She did not want to deal with them, tried not to think about them. Yet she felt a sense of what she termed "ominous responsibility" towards her family.

Craig Knudsen

Craig Knudsen, on educational leave from IBM, owned a $20,000 piece of equipment in his dorm. Not a high-powered microcomputer; but an organ: an electronic keyboard that produces music. This, however, was not an average organ. But then Knudsen was not an average Harvard Business School student.

After discovering the keyboard at a friend's house, Knudsen started playing and studying the organ at the age of five. By age seven he was considered a child prodigy, improvising music and giving recitals. As Knudsen, the youngest of three boys, recalled:

> Music has always been an enjoyable diversion. It was also very easy for me. Then, and now, I spend hours every day practicing, not because I have to, but because I want to. It's fun.

At fifteen, he gave his first concert. Two years later he started working for Wurlitzer as their concert artist, a job he expanded to product development and sales training consultant in a few years. He remarked:

> I remember after one of those concerts my father, who was very proud and happy, said, "I hope you don't enjoy this applause too much." He thought that the performing world was unreal.

Knudsen's father, (one of the few people to beat cancer, 23 years ago) now the successful owner of an executive recruiting firm, started with IBM and became a branch manager at 25, still something of a milestone. Knudsen commented:

> Even though my dad went on to work for Control Data and Telex and then started his own business, he is still a vocal supporter of IBM. In fact, after I received my deferred admit to HBS, it was my father who suggested I talk to IBM about a job. So, I worked for IBM during the week, and did concerts (really promotional appearances and demos) for Wurlitzer on the weekends. During my last months at IBM, I played the organ full-time at IBM recognition events all over the country.

This case was prepared by Research Associate Lee Field and Associate Professor John Kao. Copyright © 1986 by the President and Fellows of Harvard College. Harvard Business School case 9-487-035.

After I came to HBS I continued to play for Wurlitzer on the weekends—about two a month—just as I had done at Northwestern as an undergraduate. By now, I was starting to feel topped-out. The concerts were no-brainers. But they did pay for my education and keep me in spending money. It was a very personal satisfaction, though, one that I was sort of embarrassed to share with my peers. "You play the what? Oh, yeah, well I'll come to church and hear you some time."

Between first and second year, I went back to IBM—one of the leave stipulations—and worked on a software project and played concerts on the weekend. But my main interest that summer was learning the intricacies of a new organ I had bought in May—just after the POM final—a Yamaha FX-20, the new state-of-the-art. During my last months I wanted to switch to Yamaha, so I bought the machine ($20,000 depreciable over three years), got to know it, worked up a show, and tried it on some Florida dealers at the end of the summer. They were enthusiastic, called Yamaha, who then called me. Now I'm Yamaha's concert artist/sales training specialist. I'd been around long enough to know that Yamaha needed a demonstration of my commitment to their product. And I am. Finally, I can do things that I want to show to my peers.

As for post-graduation, I don't want to waste my talent, but I feel there's too much chance involved in becoming a star—too much beyond my control. That's why I haven't jumped in with both feet. I am however actively pursuing start-up music businesses, even though to most music industry people an MBA doesn't mean anything. They're more apt to say, "That's nice, but can you play an F minor 7th with a flatted 5th?" I think my business education gives me a competitive advantage. I know the industry well—from many different perspectives—and I'd like to be involved in all phases of the business. But there's a creative dilemma here. I could take a traditional job—IBM, consulting—and still play the organ on weekends. If I work in the industry, however, I might not be able to do that.

Exhibit 1 is Knudsen's resume; *Exhibits 2* and *3* are reviews of concerts he has given on the Wurlitzer and Yamaha organs respectively.

Exhibit 1

CRAIG ARTHUR KNUDSEN

Morris B1-3   1211 West 22nd Street
Harvard Business School   Suite 900
Boston, Massachusetts 02163   Oak Brook, Illinois 60521
(617) 498-5651   (312) 789-8977

education
1984–1986   **HARVARD GRADUATE SCHOOL**
            OF BUSINESS ADMINISTRATION   **Boston, MA**
            Awarded deferred admission to Class of 1986 while a senior in college.
            Candidate for Master in Business Administration degree, June 1986.
            Selected by faculty to tutor Management Communications.

1978–1982   **NORTHWESTERN UNIVERSITY**   **Evanston, IL**
            Earned Bachelor of Arts degrees in Economics and Biology, each *with
            distinction*. Elected to *Phi Beta Kappa, Mortar Board, Kappa Alpha Pi* and
            Phi Eta Sigma honorary societies. Dean's List every quarter for final
            GPA of 3.9/4.0.

            Waa-Mu Show Staff Writer, performer, co-chairman. Appointed to the
            Executive Board Junior and Senior year. Premier *University Jazz Ensem-
            ble* 1978 to 1982 Section Leader. Elected Assistant Social Chairman of
            Theta Chi fraternity.

**business
experience**
1977–1985   **SELF-EMPLOYED CONSULTANT**   **United States/Canada**
            Business has operated continuously since 1977, concurrent with
            professional employment and with undergraduate and graduate
            studies. Concentrated in the electronic organ industry as a Sales Train-
            ing Specialist. Initiated, developed, and conducted presentations
            throughout the United States and Canada to aid retailers in developing
            their staff's sales and demonstration abilities. Undertook responsibility
            for introducing to dealers and customers several new lines of instru-
            ments for the Wurlitzer Company over this period. Collaborated on
            user documentation and supporting marketing material. Represented
            the company at all trade shows. Consulted, on a continuing basis, with
            engineering department on product enhancement and development.

summer   **INTERNATIONAL BUSINESS**
1985   **MACHINES, INC.**   **Minneapolis, MN**
            Summer Intern in newly-formed business unit. Developed integrated
            demonstration of newly-announced products, now used in regional
            field sales efforts. Supervised regional summer assistants. Advisor/In-
            structor for Corporate Training Program.

1982–1984   **INTERNATIONAL BUSINESS MACHINES, INC.**   **Chicago, IL**
            Marketing Representative. Completed year-long Corporate Training
            Program. Graduated with rank of #1 in CCM and ADM classes. Wrote
            system proposals for customers and assisted Branch Manager on spe-
            cial projects. Member of team that exceeded sales objectives in 1983.
            IBM Performance Plan evaluation of "1" on a scale of 1-5. 1983 Branch
            Manager's Award from Chicago West branch.

            NAD Player. One of twenty IBM employees on a special assignment to
            represent IBM on staff at 1984 Corporate Recognition Events held in
            Bermuda, Miami, and Los Angeles.

community
1971–1976   **BOY SCOUTS OF AMERICA**
            Eagle Scout

personal   Have travelled extensively throughout the United States, Canada, and
            Europe. Am interested in running, snow skiing, and water sports.

references   Personal references available upon request.

                                                           October, 1985

Exhibit 2 A Newsletter for Musical Friends and Families

VOLUME 1 NO. 1

The
Music Stand

DECEMBER 1983

KEYBOARD NOTES
— A NEWSLETTER FOR MUSICAL FRIENDS AND FAMILIES —

MUSIC STAND ORGAN CONCERTS A HUGE SUCCESS

What an evening it was!!

The place? Downtown Oakville. The time? November 19th at 7:30 p.m. At that time a young 22 year old musician gave a fabulous concert on the new dynamic Wurlitzer Omni keyboard computer. His name is Craig Knudsen and he absolutely amazed the packed audience with his style, personality and talent.

Craig began the evening with a tremendous show of digital dexterity with Herb Alpert's "Rise". He could undoubtedly become a gifted surgeon with those fast fingers. His great sense of humour and his Chicago charm filled the gap between numbers. He played a beautiful rendition of "Wave", which he mentioned was one of his mother's favorite numbers. For the younger generation, he amazed them with his version of Christopher Cross' "Sailing". The audience's favorite number seemed to be his "Phantom of the Opera", where he conducted various instruments on the organ while standing 5 feet away! The country steel guitars and picking banjos had the audience clapping to the country classic "I Walk the Line". Craig ended the concert with everyone reminiscing with the Big Band Brass playing "Moonlight Serenade".

For the first encore The Music Stand surprised everyone with having talented

7 year old Jean-Marc St. Pierre play the Omni. Jean-Marc showed signs of a professional dressed in his tuxedo and playing the pedals as a seasoned master. This was truly amazing, as Jean-Marc is shorter than the organ, and was playing standing, as he can't reach the pedals while sitting.

Craig was back with the second encore, playing "Tico-Tico" faster and better than I've ever heard it played. This was well applauded by all the Wurlitzer enthusiasts.

The evening concluded with everyone enjoying delicious fresh pastries, coffee and lots of friendly conversation. It was obvious from the concert that Wurlitzer has done it once again, presented an organ line with incredible tone and versatility.

Several visitors took the Music Stand up on their fabulous offers on the Wurlitzer organs at the concert.

The night before Friday, Craig was put to work for a similar concert organized by Mr. Del Mott, the manager of the Markham Music Stand. This concert took place at The Parkway Inn. The concert was also a great success as the audience responded with enthusiasm at hearing Craig perform.

If you attended either concert, we know it was a thrill for you to hear Craig Knudsen play. If you missed it, all we can do is hope you don't miss the next occasion. Look for news of it in the future issues of the "Keyboard Notes" or keep in touch with your local Music Stand: Burlington, Oakville or Markham for further details. See you soon.

Douglas Jones
Manager
The Burlington Music Stand

ON A LIGHTER NOTE:

"Do you like Brahms?" asked the young piano student of her date.

"I dunno, I've never had them" replied the boy.

Exhibit 3 *Sound Hound,* November/December 1985

FX-20 GOES TO HARVARD

Craig Knudsen and the Yamaha FX-20 Electone Keyboard received a standing ovation at the end of a program for the Harvard Graduate School of Business' Orientation for the class of 1987. Knudsen is an MBA candidate, who plans to receive his degree from Harvard in June. He began the program with three complete "concert" numbers, and then during the presentations, which included skits and speeches, he was asked to replace the orchestra during excerpts from last year's variety show.

The Harvard student newspaper said, "He captured the audience from the start. The Yamaha presentation was the highlight of the show, and Knudsen turned the Yamaha into a veritable orchestra."

Paul Lutwak

Paul Lutwak sat in Aldrich 111, surrounded by a heated debate on the respective definitions of "managers" and "entrepreneurs," and on the role of semantics in management education. He could not help relating the discussion to the question of his own career.

For two years after undergraduate school, Lutwak had worked at an investment bank. He felt he had the skills and temperament to pursue a successful career in this field and make a great deal of money after graduation from HBS. However, his investment banking experience had been "fun in prestige terms," "doing big deals," but not very happy. For Lutwak, the personal happiness or lack thereof which his investment banking colleagues enjoyed was "frightening." They made a lot of money for other people and themselves, but had no time to enjoy it. What was the point of having a big boat if there was no time to sail it? Thus, he was giving serious consideration to two other options: working for himself or working for an entrepreneur.

PERSONAL BACKGROUND

Paul Lutwak grew up in Ohio in a "pleasant but sheltered" environment. His father started his first business in automobile retailing at age 35 after leaving the Navy and working in several sales-related jobs. Lutwak remembers always looking up to and trusting him for his skill and integrity. He never felt disappointed by his father, whom he feels would be surprised at his choice of HBS with its emphasis on big business. Lutwak's father went into businesses he was unfamiliar with, and some of his projects failed. Yet the ups and downs of business life left little mark on the quality of Lutwak family life, although they were not "incredibly wealthy." His father's schedule was flexible, and he was able to separate the challenges of business from family life. Lutwak feels similar to his father. In his words, "I don't see myself getting super elated or depressed by business activities. What's done is done." Both parents spent a lot of time with Lutwak and pushed him to excel in academics. An only child, he remembers his mother devoting herself to him in many ways which occasioned some resentment at her overprotectiveness.

This case was prepared by Associate Professor John Kao.

Copyright © 1986 by the President and Fellows of Harvard College. Harvard Business School case 9-487-032.

Lutwak's father never expressed an overt desire for him to go into the family business. They never talked about it, although they'd talk about general business matters from time to time. He remembers his father as not trying to direct him into a particular career.

In 1978, Lutwak's mother died, and his father passed away in 1980. He was left alone with a moderate inheritance which included a small commercial real estate development company run part time by his father. Lutwak disposed of company assets and shrank the business, aiming eventually to halt it. He felt that entry barriers were not strong in this business, and that no inherent advantage lay for him to staying in Ohio.

THE CAREER DECISION

For Lutwak, an important criterion for his career involved life style. He related this need to his father's life style which combined total business control with total flexibility over his schedule.

Thus, he was attracted to the flexibility of working for himself. He thought of opening a retail store, or developing a unique marketing idea which would rock the world. For Lutwak, the type of business was not very important. In his words, "One business is the same as another. I don't know what the idea would be. It could be something very small. I want to gain some experience and then grow my business idea. My background is not that technical or focused. It will be difficult to pick an industry to go into."

At age 25, Lutwak also perceived risks in starting something on his own related to his lack of experience. He felt he didn't have much to offer in the way of technical or specialized skills. Furthermore, he had no family to go to for career guidance.

He thought of working for another entrepreneur to gain experience and looked through *Forbes* and *Fortune* for entrepreneurs to contact. However, there were not many people for whom he could muster a great deal of respect. He had some reservations about this option, perceiving entrepreneurs as having unique and strong personalities. "Is working for an entrepreneur the best way to become one?" he wondered. Lutwak was also concerned about the possibility of a negative influence; the idea of working with someone like Ted Turner who demands total control could be difficult for him. While Lutwak perceived entrepreneurs as wanting to mold their employees, he said, "I don't want to be molded." Working with someone else might be an opportunity to understand the entrepreneurial mind up front. "But how do you know what the entrepreneur will choose to show you?"

Lutwak also considered working for someone he knew. For example, one of his friends was president of a manufacturing concern in the consumer goods area which also involved two siblings and their father. But he wondered about the risk of straining a personal friendship. Would it be a growth experience? Would there be competition? What would happen if differences of opinion emerged about the direction of the business?

Exhibit 1

PAUL LUTWAK

<table>
<tr><td>

education
1984–1986

</td><td>

**HARVARD GRADUATE SCHOOL
OF BUSINESS ADMINISTRATION**   **Boston, MA**
Candidate for Master in Business Administration degree, June 1986. General management curriculum with concentration in finance. Member of Finance Club. Intramural Athletics.

</td></tr>
<tr><td>

1978–1982

</td><td>

CORNELL UNIVERSITY   **Ithaca, NY**
Awarded Bachelor of Science degree, with Highest Honors, May 1982. Majored in Hotel Administration. Recipient of Dean's Merit Award. Elected to Hotel Honor Society.

As an independent research project, developed the Cornell School of Hotel Administration's course in *Intercultural Communication.* Teaching assistant for *Effective Communication.* Appointed Student Advisor and Freshman Orientation Counselor. Big Brother Program. Mobile Meals for the Elderly Volunteer. Intramural Athletics.

</td></tr>
<tr><td>

business
experience
summer
1985

</td><td>

CITICORP   **New York, NY**
Summer Associate, Real Property Services/Project Development. Analyzed the finances, operations and competitive position of an unprofitable subsidiary to determine its long-term viability. Developed a turnaround strategy and marketing plan. Presented analysis and recommendations to Citicorp senior management. Strategy incorporated in subsidiary's 1986 budget and operating plan.

</td></tr>
<tr><td>

1982–1984

</td><td>

THE FIRST BOSTON CORPORATION   **New York, NY**
Analyst, Public Finance Department. Provided investment banking and financial advisory services to hospitals, housing authorities, and state and local governments. Senior analyst on financial advisory team for the City of New York. Structured a variety of tax-exempt financings including the refunding of outstanding debt. Prepared new business proposals, presented innovative financing alternatives to clients, and coordinated document sessions. Performed extensive computer-based analysis and supervised the development of a computer model which projects cash flows for hospital equipment loan programs.

</td></tr>
<tr><td>

part-time
1980–present

</td><td>

MOTORS, INC.   **Akron, OH**
President. Upon death of my father, I became president of the company he founded. Managed commercial real estate holdings and other investments of corporation. Negotiated sales and leases. Evaluated potential acquisitions. Directed activities of the company's four employees. Current involvement is primarily that of consultant.

</td></tr>
<tr><td>

publications
1983–1984

</td><td>

Wrote monthly article for *Hospital Bottom Line,* an independent health care finance newsletter. Column detailed developments in the tax-exempt health care market.

</td></tr>
<tr><td>

interests

</td><td>

Enjoy tennis, skiing, photography, and travel.

</td></tr>
<tr><td>

references

</td><td>

Personal references available on request.

</td></tr>
</table>

Can You Survive an Entrepreneur?
MANFRED KETS DE VRIES

Peter Star had come to the Salar Corporation as vice president of operations after a period of intense courtship by its president, Lester Milton. An entrepreneur with ambitious ventures in mind for the future of his company, Lester had painted a bright picture of its prospects and the opportunities Peter would find to exercise his managerial skills. The sky seemed the limit as Lester projected them. And when Peter first came to work, it was obvious that his arrival created a lot of excitement and anticipation. He had worked hard, put in long hours, and for over three months had been in almost daily contact with his boss. But suddenly, all that had changed. After being treated like a long-awaited hero, Peter had to face the realization that the honeymoon was over—he had little to do and Lester hardly had time to see him. He had to admit he felt let down, and wondered if he should have taken this job in the first place.

His first assignment had been to set up a new budgeting system. It was an idea he had come up with after looking at the old system and seeing how outdated it was for Salar's current operations. When Peter had pointed out to Lester how little information the old system gave them and outlined his plan for revising it, Lester had been so enthusiastic in his response, that he wanted it done yesterday. Lester was not a patient man, Peter reflected now. You never had to wait long for his answers; he was a person who operated on hunches and impressions. He liked dramatic, instant action.

Peter realized in hindsight that the system he had installed might have been too sophisticated for Salar, but nevertheless, it was a good system. The message he was getting now from the president, of course, was quite different. After installing the system, Peter had discovered paradoxically enough that the Salar Corporation had actually been losing money. His boss had not taken that piece of information lightly. He turned on Peter as a messenger of bad news. Peter found to his great surprise, that of all the people responsible, he was being blamed for the company's losses. Basically, he was told that things were out of control because his budget changeover had "thrown things into confusion."

Peter knew that the changeover had little to do with it. A previous vice president had made some serious merchandising errors; her key mistakes had been faulty pricing decisions and large raw material purchases that turned out to be wasteful. Judging by the stories going around the office, she had certainly fooled Lester with her forecasts of how profitable the various product lines were going to be. She seemed to have been one of the few who could wind

This note has been prepared by Visiting Professor Manfred F. R. Kets de Vries.

the president around her little finger. In any case, the results of all of Peter's efforts were that his responsibilities had been curtailed and he was excluded from a sizeable part of top management decision making. Planning had been taken abruptly out of his jurisdiction and given back to a colleague who was an old-timer. To add insult to injury, he was the last person to be informed.

During the five months he had been with Salar, a number of things he observed had troubled Peter. The culture was a sharp contrast to that of the publicly owned corporation that he had come here from. The differences all seemed to center around trust. He was beginning to wonder if Lester Milton really had much faith in anyone. One symptom of his lack of confidence in his people was his insistence on being kept informed of the tiniest details of the operations. Peter would get annoyed at being asked repeatedly, as other subordinates were also, to come to Lester's office to explain trivial decisions. It was disrupting to the flow of work in the office. And you had little choice: if you didn't keep Lester informed and something went wrong, hell would break loose. If it was bad news, the unexpected was definitely not welcome. Subordinates would often paint a too rosy picture after agonizing over how to present

unpleasant information, which inevitably led to distortions and created false optimism. Peter felt that although Lester's controlling style may have been useful when his company was smaller, it was now seriously getting in the way of sound decision making. As he looked around, Peter questioned how much tolerance his boss really had for independent thinking. Colleagues who were old-timers seemed extremely subservient, too eager to please Lester. If they had opinions of their own, they were unwilling to stand up for them.

Peter had not paid much attention at first to Lester's description of himself as a workaholic. He had been caught up in the excitement of working with him, and in the possibilities he saw for Salar's growth and expansion as well as for his own career. He wondered now how Lester could have any family life, considering the long hours he spent at the office and the time out on business trips. And he expected his key executives to be similarly dedicated and available at all times. If Peter ever refused to be available, it was interpreted as insubordination. He soon learned it would produce outbursts of anger. Lester's leadership style—erratic, impulsive and extreme—made Peter wonder if the job was worth the strain. He might as well start looking for another job.

THE ENTREPRENEURIAL THEATRE

Peter Star's experience is not an unusual example. Much as there is to admire in the character of entrepreneurs, working for them is another matter. Entrepreneurs create an atmosphere of enthusiasm, they convey a sense of purpose, and they make us feel that we are where the action is. They seem to give an organization its momentum. But along with the mystique of entrepreneurship, their personality quirks make

them difficult people to work for. As Derek du Toit, an entrepreneur himself states:

. . . The entrepreneur who starts his own business generally does so because he is a difficult employee. He does not take kindly to suggestions or orders from other people and aspires most of all to run his own shop. . . .

His idiosyncrasies do not hurt anybody so long as the business is small, but once the business gets larger, requiring the support and active cooperation of more people, he is at risk if he does not change his approach. It has been correctly stated that the biggest burden a growing company faces is having a full-blooded entrepreneur as its owner. . . .[1]

His comments raise questions about the kinds of characteristics we should be attuned to when working for an entrepreneur. What are the elements of their style which can cause problems? Are there any pitfalls to avoid? What are the implications for our own needs of an entrepreneur's style of management? What should we know about ourselves if we are considering joining an entrepreneurial firm?

In answering these questions we have to keep in mind that entrepreneurs do not necessarily make up a homogeneous group. Most likely there exist different types of entrepreneurs, each with their own specific characteristics.[2]

Need for Control

A major theme in the life and personality of many entrepreneurs is the need for control. Their preoccupation with control inevitably affects the way entrepreneurs deal with power relationships and their consequences for interpersonal action. Entrepreneurs relate to power with striking degrees of ambivalence; in their view, power seems to possess a Janus face. On one hand, it is associated with omnipotent thinking and such themes as influence, control, and authority, but it

also awakens thoughts of helplessness. Entrepreneurs experience a lurking fear that their grandiose desires will get out of control and place them at the mercy of others in a position of helplessness. The reasons for such fears are probably manifold. Most likely, the explanations have to be found in early life experiences. Child observation studies and clinical research have shown that these feelings can originate from early developmental failures, especially the inability of parents to deal age-appropriately with the demands of the maturing child.[3] Whatever the exact reasons, entrepreneurs do experience serious difficulties in addressing issues of dominance and submission. They are suspicious about authority; they cannot easily accept control. This attitude toward authority is quite in contrast to that of managers. One of the main characteristics that distinguish managers is their ability to identify in a positive, constructive way with authority figures, using them as role models. This pattern is largely absent in entrepreneurs. The manager's fluidity in being able to change from a superior to a subordinate role seems to be lacking. Instead, an entrepreneur has a great inner struggle with issues of authority and control. Structure can be experienced as stifling, making it very difficult to work with others in structured situations. Frequently this seems possible only in those instances when the entrepreneur created the structure; if the work is done on his or her terms.

Listening to entrepreneurs' case histo-

[1] Derek F. du Toit, "Confessions of a Successful Entrepreneur," *Harvard Business Review*, November–December 1980, pp. 3–4.

[2] See for example Norman R. Smith, *The Entrepreneur and His Firm: The Relationship between Type of Man and Type of Company* (East Lansing: Michigan State University, Graduate School of Business Administration, 1967); Edward B. Roberts and Herbert A. Wainer, "Some Characteristics of Technical Entrepreneurs," *Research Program on the Management of Science and Technology*, Massachusetts Institute of Technology, 1966, pp. 145–166; and John A. Hornaday, "Research About Living Entrepreneurs," in *Encyclopedia of Entrepreneurship*, eds. Calvin A. Kent, Donald L. Sexton and Karl H. Vesper (Englewood Cliffs, NJ: Prentice-Hall, 1982).

[3] See, for example, Heinz Kohut, *The Analysis of the Self* (New York: International Universities Press, 1971).

ries, we find many situations where it was their inability to submit to authority and accept organizational rules and regulations that drove them to become entrepreneurs in the first place. In a sense, they were "misfits" who had to enact their own environment.[4] The deference we can expect to find in power relations between superior and subordinates seems suffocating to this type of person. Perhaps, it revives old sensations of previously encountered states of intense helplessness when they had no control over their destinies. It is as if they have told themselves that they never again want to be in a vulnerable position; they don't want to be at the mercy of others. Even if they have moved away from these old controlling influences, the concern lingers on. Many entrepreneurs seem to be preoccupied with the threat of being subjected to some form of external control or some external infringement on their will.

Individuals who are preoccupied with issues of control often have a low tolerance for subordinates who engage in independent thinking. In an organizational context, this desire for control can go to extremes. One symptom is the need many entrepreneurs feel to be informed about every minute operation of the company. Such behavior creates a ready-made atmosphere for sycophants. Moreover, the excessive concern with detail that may have been appropriate in a start-up phase for a company will increasingly turn into a burden as it stifles the information flow in the organization and hampers decision making.

To illustrate such behavior, we can take the extreme of one entrepreneur who was responsible for a $20 million consumer product operation. Every morning he used to open not only his personal mail but all mail directed to his company. In addition, this man had instituted a policy that all requisitions, no matter how small, must be approved by him. He said it gave him a "feel" for the operation. The effect of this, not surprisingly, was that his subordinates, although they admired many of his qualities, deeply resented being treated like incapable children. In addition, necessary information for decision making did not circulate because accountability was lacking, endangering the future growth of the enterprise.

A Sense of Distrust

Closely related to the entrepreneur's need for control is a proclivity toward suspicious thinking. Again, this tendency is often a legacy of developmental failures. What we can observe is the strong distrust which many entrepreneurs have for the world around them. Many live in fear of being victimized. They want to be ready for an emergency, as if they expect disaster to strike at any moment. Paradoxically, entrepreneurs may feel at their best when their fortunes are at their lowest. When they are successful and stand out, they can imagine themselves incurring the envy of others. No wonder that they respond by saying that business is only "so, so" or "not too bad," when they are asked how things are going. But if their fortunes turn and they are close to bankruptcy, it is as if they have paid the price; they have done their penance. Their predicament can actually have a positive effect, because it produces a sense of relief. With the alleviation of anxiety, a base is created to start anew. The release of new energy renews their enthusiasm and sense of purpose.

Because entrepreneurs have pervasive

---

[4] See, for example, Orvis F. Collins and David G. Moore, *The Organization Makers: A Behavior Study of Independent Entrepreneurs* (New York: Meredith, 1970) and Manfred F. R. Kets de Vries, "The Entrepreneurial Personality: A Person at the Crossroads," *Journal of Management Studies*, 1977, 14(1).

fears of being victimized, they are continually scanning their environment for something to confirm their suspicions. There is a constructive side to this behavior pattern, however; it makes them alert to developments in the industry, to every move made by competitors or the government. Anticipating the actions of others keeps entrepreneurs from being taken unaware. But it can also make them lose any sense of proportion. Focusing on certain trouble spots and ignoring others may cause trivial things to be blown up. No longer do they see events in the context of the reality of the overall situation.

Suspicious thinking and the need for control reinforce each other. When a strong sense of distrust takes over, it has serious consequences for the organization. Sycophants set the tone, independent action is discouraged, and political gamesmanship is rampant. The quality of management and the soundness of decision making deteriorate.

One entrepreneur who hired a consultant to develop and implement a strategic plan for his company refused to provide him with the financial statements he needed to assess profitability by product line. The entrepreneur was afraid the information could be used to help his competitors. How he expected the consultant to develop a realistic plan was another question. The same person also refused to sell goods-in-progress to a noncompeting business at a time when his company's machines were idle and employees had been laid off. He argued that he had once been hurt when a competitor used his goods-in-progress to manufacture a line of products that competed with his own.

Another entrepreneur in the home furnishing industry went so far as to install two television cameras to monitor both front and back entries at his plant and his office building. On his desk he kept two consoles which he could watch constantly to alleviate his suspicions that his employees were stealing from him. What such action did to company morale is another matter.

The problem in contending with this distorted form of reasoning and action is that, behind the false perceptions that lead to fear and suspicion, one can always find some reality. If we look hard enough there is always, somewhere, some confirmation of the entrepreneur's suspicions. Unfortunately, he ignores the price to be paid in deteriorating morale, low employee satisfaction, and decreasing productivity.

The Need for Applause

A common myth starts with the hero's miraculous but humble birth, his rapid rise to prominence and power, the conquest over the forces of evil, his fallibility to the sin of pride, and his fall through betrayal or heroic sacrifice. The basic symbolic themes here, of birth, conquest, hubris, betrayal and death, are relevant for all of us. And, as we have seen, the entrepreneur is no stranger to these crises and transformations. It often appears that entrepreneurs act out exactly the same myth, against a background of a Greek chorus applauding their achievement, but warning them against the sin of pride. Perhaps the myth explains why so many entrepreneurs live under a great tension. Their feeling of brinkmanship is related to their fear that success will not last. Symptomatic of this anxiety is their need for control and their sense of distrust, but along with it is their overriding concern to be heard and recognized. Entrepreneurs experience a strong urge to show others that they amount to something, that they cannot be ignored. A good illustration of this phenomenon was described to me in a dream an entrepreneur experienced over and over. In the dream, he would be standing on a balcony, looking down, to see a group of women looking admiringly at him. The same man would recall dreams of himself as a swaggering cowboy riding up an ever-narrowing trail to the top of a mountain. The wishes and fears in this symbolic statement are not hard to decipher. One of the more obvious messages is that grandiosity is fraught with dangers.

The need for applause can be viewed as a reaction against the feeling of being insignificant, of being a nothing. Many entrepreneurs seem to experience an inner voice telling them that they will never amount to anything. But, whoever put the idea into their minds, entrepreneurs do not want to be listeners; they are the rebels. They can rally enough inner strength to prove the messenger wrong, and show the world that they amount to something. They will ride to the top in spite of all its dangers; they will try to master their fears.

A manifestation of this inner need is the interest entrepreneurs show in building "monuments" as symbols of their achievements. Sometimes the monument is an imposing office building or production facility; sometimes it is a product which takes on a specific symbolic significance.

For example, in the reign of the first Henry Ford, the Model T was untouchable. Unfortunately, the applause he received for his unique achievement in making a car for the masses changed when some of his darker sides came to the fore. His statement, "any color as long as it is black" had more than one meaning. Its implicit threat was: don't touch the car. If you want to make changes, change the assembly line. The Model T had turned into a holy grail. Whatever its direct symbolic significance was to Henry Ford,[5] his refusal to let anyone tinker with his Model T had important stra-

tegic implications. The most important consequence was that the car came from the assembly line basically unaltered for a period of 19 years in spite of changing consumer needs and the great inroads made by General Motors. When his grandson took control of the organization after World War II, the company was almost bankrupt.

Another entrepreneur almost invited bankruptcy by building an imposing head office and new factory building during a period of economic decline, against all advice to the contrary and in defiance of the fact that off-shore production was the only viable alternative in that industry. However mistaken his judgment was, he showed people in the section of town where he grew up that he amounted to something. The contrast between his buildings and the decrepit surroundings was striking. This again illustrates how intensely entrepreneurs crave applause and need witnesses to attest to their achievements.

Defensive Operations

Character is largely determined by the way a person balances his or her internal view of the environment with external reality. Character implies relatively enduring, pervasive patterns of behavior. Analyzing character brings us into the domain of personality defenses and leads to the question of how individuals deal with the stress and strain of daily life. All of us need our defenses to cope with the vicissitudes of existence. The kinds of defenses we rely on predominantly as individuals will determine the kinds of relations we develop with others.

Entrepreneurs often resort to *splitting* as a way of coping with life. This is the ten-

---

[5] For a greater elaboration of the personality dynamics of Henry Ford, see Anne Jardim, *The First Henry Ford: A Study in Personality and Business Leadership* (Cambridge, Mass.: The MIT Press, 1970).

dency to see everything as either ideal (all good) or persecutory (all bad). What is noticeable to an observer in this behavior is the lack of balance in perception. Affective and cognitive representations of one's self and others become so dramatically oversimplified that the person fails to appreciate the real complexity and ambiguity of human relationships. A preference for extremes comes to the fore in attitudes toward other people. Some are idealized and put on a pedestal, others are vilified. And the attitudinal pendulum easily shifts from one extreme to another.

To take an example: one entrepreneur made a point of hiring young MBAs just out of school. He would marvel at their mastery of the latest management techniques and hold up the new executive as the example for employees to emulate. He would tell them that this was the kind of manager they all needed for the future success of the company. Not only did his lavish praise stir up an enormous amount of envy among the other employees (with the predictable spiteful consequences), but the president's infatuation with his latest recruit would soon exhaust itself. No new recruit could live up to his exaggerated expectations. Inevitably, disappointment would set in. An exodus of young MBAs became a pattern in that company.

Another kind of defense quite common to entrepreneurs is *projection,* the tendency to externalize internal problems. An internal threat that the person has experienced seems to become more manageable if he attributes it to some other person or to an external event. Scapegoating is one outcome of managing stressful events in this way; never to find blame for mistakes in oneself becomes a personality characteristic. Individuals inclined toward this behavior experience little sense of personal responsibility. They are always looking for victims. One danger of this kind of thinking is that it con-

tributes to political infighting, passing on responsibility in an atmosphere of insularity and factionalism. Moreover, it leads to further distortion of reality by encouraging subordinates—out of self defense—to tell the entrepreneur what he likes to hear, instead of the facts of the situation.

One entrepreneur, known for his outbursts of anger when he was confronted with bad news, managed to create a climate of false optimism that the business was doing well at a time when sales were dropping rapidly and the bank was ready to pull the plug on the company. The president kept on arguing that the new product line had miraculous potential, blaming any adverse indications on the government's or customer's malice instead of recognizing that they resulted from mismanagement on his own factory floor and in his design department. Nobody in the company was bold enough to contradict his statements. Instead, his subordinates continued reassuring each other that the president's opinion must be correct.

Finally, many entrepreneurs have the inclination to *turn the passive into the active,* a characteristic which is related to their efforts to manage tension. As they try to steer between their fear of success and fear of failure, it is almost as if they ask themselves if they deserve to be successful, and if so, will it last? They may be concerned—perhaps not consciously—that they will suffer the fate of the mythical hero. They cannot wait passively for doomsday; the work of worrying is far too anxiety-provoking. Entrepreneurs prefer to act, even if they act impulsively without giving due consideration to facts. Passivity has its attractions for them, but perhaps they fear more strongly that being passive would make them overdependent and in the end fall victim to control by others. So they behave counterdependently.

There is, however, a delicate balance

between passive longing and active striving. In many entrepreneurs this shows up in their predisposition to mood swings. When things are going well, everything is "terrific," but when they can no longer maintain this artificial high, when the bubble bursts, the pendulum often swings completely in the other direction. Then, we hear complaints that everything is terrible; that the situation is hopeless. They talk as if bankruptcy is just around the corner.

At one point, one entrepreneur compared himself to the mythological King Midas, implying that everything he touched turned into gold. He would describe at great length how fantastically successful and profitable his company was. In this state of mind, of wanting to see only what he wanted to see and using all the defensive patterns I have described, he didn't really bother to read the various sales and financial reports. If anyone questioned him about that, he would say his reporting system was the least of his worries; he was convinced beyond any doubt that everything was fantastic. Only when his auditors were drawing up a financial statement for tax purposes and pointed out that the company had suffered a loss over the last quarter was he finally aroused from his self-deceptive state. Needless to say, he didn't take this news with equanimity. All of a sudden, he felt that he had gotten himself into a hopeless situation and began to worry that he was going bankrupt. It took some time and effort to pull himself together.

WHERE DO WE GO FROM HERE?

I have described some of the darker sides of entrepreneurship. Although the extremes stand out and are most noticeable, most situations do not go that far. The many positive contributions made by entrepreneurs are often due to their visionary abilities and leadership qualities that make it possible for managers to transcend petty concerns and accomplish good work. When the entrepreneurs radiate confidence and purpose, they can be extremely contagious. This mobilizes energy, creates momentum, and has a positive effect on the culture of the enterprise, making for better morale, motivation, and productivity.

Some of the darker notes of entrepreneurship, however, are quite real and pose serious quandaries for those working for them. Apart from the better-known high dramas in entrepreneurial firms—the crises surrounding succession and growth—more immediate problems created by the kinds of personality quirks I have described are constantly arising. How to manage these is no easy matter.

Any subordinate working for an entrepreneur is in a vulnerable position. Very often he or she appears to be there at the pleasure of the entrepreneur. There may be times when the subordinate can bring about a change in the entrepreneur's attitude, but these changes tend to be modest. Whatever behavior modifications take place, the subordinate is up against the economics of power. The entrepreneur controls the company in more than one way. More often than not, he is a major shareholder, and subordinates will have to take the consequences of his ownership position. The realization that he might lose his company can suddenly motivate him to do something about his personal style and to take remedial action.

Individuals attracted to firms run by the kind of entrepreneur I have described are often self-selected: many among them don't mind working under a strong leader. If they are searching for a symbolic father figure, the entrepreneur is there to oblige. Instead of feeling held back or even misled by the peculiar behavior patterns of the entrepreneur, some individuals identify with him and draw strength from his leadership. This interface can contribute to a constructive, synergistic relationship whereby the entrepreneur's vision and drive becomes translated into effective and efficient organizational functioning.

If anyone can influence the entrepreneur's leadership style, it is usually an outsider. Someone not heavily exposed to the organization's culture has the greatest impact. Such a person, a consultant or a member of an advisory board, often has enough distance to see things in perspective and to discount the drama and tension common in entrepreneurial firms. Such a person can play the role of confidant and use the entrepreneur's ambition to effect constructive change.

But even then, we have to keep in mind that the entrepreneur's personality quirks may have been a key factor for his success. Thus, instead of discounting these idiosyncracies as completely negative, we should also look at them as a challenge to build on, if it can be done constructively. There is a Chinese proverb, "He who rides a tiger cannot dismount." That is what the entrepreneur is all about. The simultaneous desire for danger and opportunity is what makes for the entrepreneurial spirit, which in the end is the life blood of society.

A Perspective on Entrepreneurship
HOWARD H. STEVENSON

The term "entrepreneurship" has entered the business vocabulary as the 1980s' equivalent of "professionalism," the managerial buzzword of the 1970s. Many individuals aspire to be entrepreneurs, enjoying the freedom, independence and wealth such a career seems to suggest. And larger corporations want to become more "entrepreneurial," their shorthand for the innovative and adaptive qualities they see in their smaller— and often more successful—competitors.

Our purpose in this chapter is to shed some light on the concept of entrepreneurship. We will define entrepreneurship as a management process, and will discuss why we believe encouraging entrepreneurial behavior is critical to the long-term vitality of our economy. Finally, we will suggest that the practice of entrepreneurship is as important, if not more important— to established companies as it is to start-ups.

INCREASING INTEREST IN ENTREPRENEURSHIP

It would be difficult to overstate the degree to which there has been an increase in the level of interest in entrepreneurship. A strong indicator of such interest is provided by the unprecedented rise in the rate of new business formation. The number of annual new business incorporations has doubled in the last ten years, from annual rates of about 300,000 to over 600,000.

These trends are mirrored in the capital markets that fund these start-ups. The decade 1975–1984 saw explosive growth in the amount of capital committed to venture capital firms in the United States. There was a concurrent dramatic increase in the amount of money raised in the public capital markets by young companies.

In addition to interest on the part of individuals who wish to become entrepreneurs and investors who wish to back them, there has been a wave of interest in what some refer to as "Intrepreneurship," or entrepreneurship in the context of the larger corporation. In addition to the wealth of books and articles on the subject, some large firms seem to have recognized their shortcomings on certain critical dimensions of performance, and have structured themselves in an attempt to be more innovative.

Indeed, we believe that the strengthening of entrepreneurship is a critically important goal of American society. The first thirty years of the postwar period in the

Professor Howard H. Stevenson prepared this note as the basis for class discussion.

United States were characterized by an abundance of opportunity, brought about by expanding markets, high investment in the national infrastructure, mushrooming debt. In this environment, it was relatively easy to achieve business success, but this is no longer true. Access to international resources is not as easy as it once was; government regulation has brought a recognition of the full costs of doing business, many of which had previously been hidden; competition from overseas has put an end to American dominance in numerous industries; technological change has reduced product life in other industries; and so forth. In short, a successful firm is one that is either capable of rapid response to changes that are beyond its control, or, is so innovative that it contributes to change in the environment. Entrepreneurship is an approach to management that offers these benefits.

DEFINING ENTREPRENEURSHIP

As we have discussed, there has been a striking increase in the level of attention paid to the subject of entrepreneurship. However, we've not yet defined what the term means.

As a starting point, it may be helpful to review some of the definitions scholars have historically applied to entrepreneurship. There are several schools of thought regarding entrepreneurship, which may roughly be divided into those that define the term as an economic function and those that identify entrepreneurship with individual traits.

The functional approach focuses upon the role of entrepreneurship within the economy. In the 18th century, for instance, Richard Cantillon argued that entrepreneurship entailed bearing the risk of buying at certain prices and selling at uncertain prices. Jean Baptiste Say broadened the definition to include the concept of bringing together the factors of production. Schumpeter's work in 1911 added the concept of innovation to the definition of entrepreneurship. He allowed for many kinds of innovation including process innovation, market innovation, product innovation, factor innovation, and even organizational innovation. His seminal work emphasized the role of the entrepreneur in creating and responding to economic discontinuities.

While some analysts have focused on the economic function of entrepreneurship, still others have turned their attention to research on the personal characteristics of entrepreneurs. Considerable effort has gone into understanding the psychological and sociological sources of entrepreneurship— as Kent refers to it, "supply-side entrepreneurship." These studies have noted some common characteristics among entrepreneurs with respect to need for achievement, perceived locus of control, and risk-taking propensity. In addition, many have commented upon the common—but not universal—thread of childhood deprivation and early adolescent experiences as typifying the entrepreneur. These studies—when taken as a whole—are inconclusive and often in conflict.

We believe, however, that neither of these approaches is sound. Consider, for example, the degree to which entrepreneurship is synonymous with "bearing risk," "innovation," or even founding a company. Each of these terms focuses upon *some* aspect of *some* entrepreneurs. But, if one has to be the founder to be an entrepreneur, then neither Thomas Watson of IBM nor Ray Kroc of McDonald's will qualify; yet, few would seriously argue that both these individuals were not entrepreneurs. And, while risk bearing is an important element of entrepreneurial behavior, it is clear that many entrepreneurs bear risk grudgingly and only after they have made valiant attempts to get the capital sources and resource providers to bear the risk. As one extremely successful entrepreneur said: "My idea of risk and reward is for me to get the reward and others to take the risks." With respect to the "supply side" school of entrepreneurship, many questions can be raised. At the heart of the matter is whether the psychological and social traits are either necessary or sufficient for the development of entrepreneurship.

Finally, the search for a single psychological profile of the entrepreneur is bound to fail. For each of the traditional definitions of the entrepreneurial type, there are numerous counter-examples that disprove the theory. We simply are not dealing with one kind of individual or behavior pattern, as even a cursory review of well-known entrepreneurs will demonstrate. Nor has the search for a psychological model proven useful in teaching or encouraging entrepreneurship.

ENTREPRENEURSHIP AS A BEHAVIORAL PHENOMENON

Thus, it does not seem useful to delimit the entrepreneur by defining those economic functions that are "entrepreneurial" and those that are not. Nor does it appear particularly helpful to describe the traits that seem to engender entrepreneurship in certain individuals. From our perspective, entrepreneurship is an approach to management that we define as follows: the pursuit of opportunity without regard to resources currently controlled.

This summary description of entrepreneurial behavior can be further refined by examining six critical dimensions of business practice. These six dimensions are the following: strategic orientation, the commitment to opportunity, the resource commitment process, the concept of control over resources, the concept of management, and compensation policy.

We shall define these dimensions by examining a range of behavior between two extremes. At one extreme is the *"promoter"* who feels confident of his or her ability to seize opportunity regardless of the resources under current control. At the opposite extreme is the *"trustee"* who emphasizes the efficient utilization of existing resources. While the promoter and trustee define the end points of this spectrum, there is a spectrum of managerial behavior that lies between these end-points, and we define (overlapping) portions of this spectrum as entrepreneurial and administrative behavior. Thus, entrepreneurial management is not an extreme example, but rather a range of behavior that consistently falls at the end of the spectrum.

The remainder of this chapter defines these key business dimensions in more detail, discusses how entrepreneurial differs from administrative behavior, and describes the factors that pull individuals and firms towards particular types of behavior.

STRATEGIC ORIENTATION

Strategic orientation is the business dimension that describes the factors that drive the firm's formulation of strategy. A promoter is truly opportunity-driven. His or her orientation is to say, "As I define a strategy, I am going to be driven only by my perception of the opportunities that exist in my environment, and I will not be constrained

Figure 1

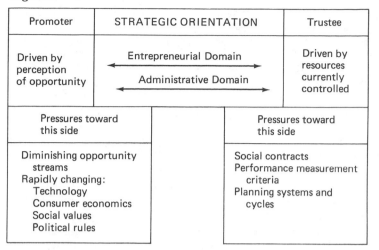

Promoter	STRATEGIC ORIENTATION		Trustee
Driven by perception of opportunity	Entrepreneurial Domain ←——————→ Administrative Domain ←——————→		Driven by resources currently controlled
Pressures toward this side		Pressures toward this side	
Diminishing opportunity streams Rapidly changing: Technology Consumer economics Social values Political rules		Social contracts Performance measurement criteria Planning systems and cycles	

by the resources at hand." A trustee, on the other hand, is resource-driven and tends to say, "How do I utilize the resources that I control?"

Within these two poles, the administrator's approach recognizes the need to examine the environment for opportunities, but is still constrained by a trustee-like focus on resources: "I will prune my opportunity tree based on the resources I control. I will not try to leap very far beyond my current situation." An entrepreneurial orientation places the emphasis on opportunity: "I will search for opportunity, and my fundamental administrative task is to acquire the resources to pursue that opportunity." These perspectives are represented on Figure 1.

It is this inclination that has led to one of the traditional definitions of the entrepreneur as opportunistic or, more favorably, *creative and innovative*. But the entrepreneur is not necessarily concerned with breaking new ground; opportunity can also be found in a new mix of old ideas or in the creative application of traditional approaches. We do observe, however, that firms tend to look for opportunities where their resources are. Even those firms that

start as entrepreneurial by recognizing opportunities often become resource-driven as more and more resources are acquired by the organization.

The pressures that pull a firm towards the entrepreneurial range of behavior include the following:

- Diminishing opportunity streams: old opportunity streams have been largely played out. It is no longer possible to succeed merely by adding new options to old products.

- Rapid changes in:
  Technology: creates new opportunities at the same time it obsoletes old ones.
  Consumer economics: changes both ability and willingness to pay for new products and services.
  Social values: defines new styles and standards and standards of living.
  Political roles: affects competition through deregulation, product safety and new standards.

Pressures which pull a firm to become more "administrative" than entrepreneurial include the following:

- The "social contract": the responsibility of managers to use and employ people, plant, technology and financial resources once they have been acquired.

- Performance criteria: How many executives are fired for not pursuing an opportunity, compared with the number that are punished for not meeting return on investment targets? Capacity utilization and sales growth are the typical measures of business success.

- Planning systems and cycles: opportunities do not arrive at the start of a planning cycle and last for the duration of a three- or five-year plan.

COMMITMENT TO OPPORTUNITY

As we move on to the second dimension, it becomes clear that the definition of the entrepreneur as creative or innovative is not sufficient. There are innovative thinkers who never get anything done; it is necessary to move beyond the identification of opportunity to its pursuit.

The promoter is a person willing to act in a very short time frame and to chase an opportunity quickly. Promoters may be more or less effective, but they are able to engage in commitment in a rather revolutionary fashion. The duration of their commitment, not the ability to act, is all that is in doubt. Commitment for the trustee is time-consuming, and once made, of long duration. Trustees move so slowly that it sometimes appears they are stationary; once there, they seem frozen. This spectrum of behavior is shown on Figure 2.

It is the willingness to get in and out quickly that has led to the entrepreneur's reputation as a gambler. However, the simple act of taking a risk does not lead to success. More critical to the success of the entrepreneurs is knowledge of the territory they operate in. Because of familiarity with their chosen field, they have the ability to recognize patterns as they develop, and the confidence to assume the missing elements of the pattern will take shape as they foresee. This early recognition enables them to get a jump on others in commitment to action.

Pressures which pull a business towards this entrepreneurial end of the spectrum include:

- Action orientation: enables a firm to make first claim to customers, employees and financial resources.

Figure 2

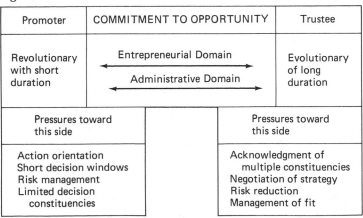

Promoter	COMMITMENT TO OPPORTUNITY		Trustee
Revolutionary with short duration	Entrepreneurial Domain → Administrative Domain →		Evolutionary of long duration
Pressures toward this side		Pressures toward this side	
Action orientation Short decision windows Risk management Limited decision constituencies		Acknowledgment of multiple constituencies Negotiation of strategy Risk reduction Management of fit	

- Short decision windows: due to the high costs of late entry, including lack of competitive costs and technology.
- Risk management: involves managing the firm's revenues in such a way that they can be rapidly committed to or withdrawn from new projects. As George Bernard Shaw put it, "Any fool can start a love affair, but it takes a genius to end one successfully."
- Limited decision constituencies: requires a smaller number of responsibilities and permits greater flexibility.

In contrast, administrative behavior is a function of other pressures:

- Multiple decision constituencies: a great number of responsibilities, necessitating a more complex, lengthier decision process.
- Negotiation of strategy: compromise in order to reach consensus and resultant evolutionary rather than revolutionary commitment.
- Risk reduction: study and analysis to reduce risk slows the decision-making process.
- Management of fit: to assure the continuity and participation of existing players, only those projects which "fit" existing corporate resources are acceptable.

COMMITMENT OF RESOURCES

Another characteristic we observe in good entrepreneurs is a multistaged commitment of resources with a minimum commitment at each stage or decision point. The promoters, those wonderful people with blue shoes and diamond pinky rings on their left hands, say, "I don't need any resources to commence the pursuit of a given opportunity. I will bootstrap it." The trustee says, "Since my object is to use my resources, once I finally commit I will go in very heavily at the front end."

The issue for the entrepreneur is: what resources are necessary to pursue a given opportunity? There is a constant tension between the amount of resources committed and the potential return. The entrepreneur attempts to maximize value creation by minimizing the resource set, and must, of course, accept more risk in the process. On the other hand, the trustee side deals with this challenge by careful analysis and large-scale commitment of resources after the decision to act. Entrepreneurial management requires that you learn to do a little more with a little less. Figure 3 addresses this concept.

On this dimension we have the traditional stereotype of the entrepreneur as tentative, uncommitted, or temporarily dedicated—an image of unreliability. In times of rapid change, however, this characteristic of stepped, multistaged commitment of resources is a definite advantage in responding to changes in competition, the market, and technology.

The process of committing resources is pushed towards the entrepreneurial domain by several factors:

- Lack of predictable resource needs: forces the entrepreneurs to commit less up front so that more will be available later on, if required.
- Lack of long-term control: requires that commitment match exposure. If control over resources can be removed by environmental, political or technological forces, resource exposure should also be reduced.
- Social needs: multistaged commitment of resources brings us closer to the "small is beautiful" formulation of E. F. Schumacher, by allowing for the appropriate level of resource intensity for the task.
- International demands—pressures that we use no more than our "fair share" of the world's resources, e.g., not the 35 percent

Figure 3

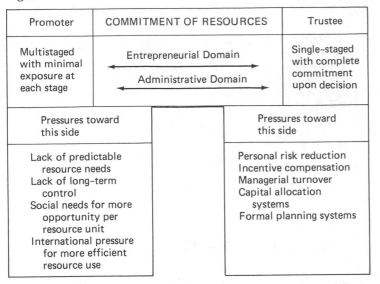

Promoter	COMMITMENT OF RESOURCES		Trustee
Multistaged with minimal exposure at each stage	Entrepreneurial Domain ←——————→ Administrative Domain ←——————→		Single–staged with complete commitment upon decision
Pressures toward this side		Pressures toward this side	
Lack of predictable resource needs Lack of long-term control Social needs for more opportunity per resource unit International pressure for more efficient resource use		Personal risk reduction Incentive compensation Managerial turnover Capital allocation systems Formal planning systems	

of the world's energy that the United States was using in the early 1970s.

The pressures within the large corporation, however, are in the other direction—toward resource intensity. This is due to:

- Personal risk reduction: any individual's risk is reduced by having excess resources available.
- Incentive compensation: excess resources increase short-term returns and minimize the period of cash and profit drains—typically the objects of incentive compensation systems.
- Managerial turnover: creates pressures for steady cash and profit gains, which encourages short-term, visible success.
- Capital allocation systems: generally designed for one-time decision making, these techniques assume that a single decision point is appropriate.
- Formal planning systems: once a project has begun, a request for additional resources returns the managers to the morass of analysis and bureaucratic delays; managers are inclined to avoid this by committing the maximum amount of resources up front.

CONTROL OF RESOURCES

When it comes to the control of resources, the promoter mentality says, "All I need from a resource is the ability to use it." These are the people who describe the ideal business as the post office box to which people send money. For them, all additional overhead is a compromise of a basic value. On the other hand, we all know companies that believe they do not adequately control a resource unless they own it or have it on their permanent payroll.

Entrepreneurs learn to use other people's resources well; they learn to decide, over time, what resources they need to bring in-house. They view this as a time-phased sequence of decisions. Good managers also learn that there are certain resources you should never own or employ. For instance,

Figure 4

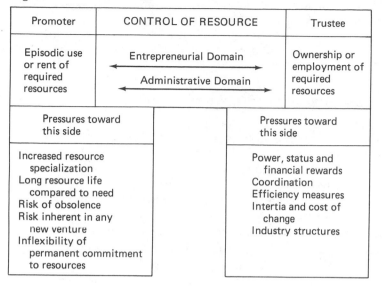

Promoter	CONTROL OF RESOURCE		Trustee
Episodic use or rent of required resources	Entrepreneurial Domain ←————→	Administrative Domain ←————→	Ownership or employment of required resources
Pressures toward this side		Pressures toward this side	
Increased resource specialization Long resource life compared to need Risk of obsolence Risk inherent in any new venture Inflexibility of permanent commitment to resources		Power, status and financial rewards Coordination Efficiency measures Intertia and cost of change Industry structures	

very few good real estate firms employ an architect. They may need the best, but they do not want to employ him or her, because the need for that resource, although critical to the success of the business, is temporary. The same is true of good lawyers. They are useful to have when you need them, but most firms cannot possibly afford to have the necessary depth of specialization of legal professionals constantly at their beck and call. Figure 4 illustrates this dimension.

The stereotype of the entrepreneur as exploitative derives from this dimension: the entrepreneur is adept at using the skills, talents, and ideas of others. Viewed positively, this ability has become increasingly valuable in the changed business environment; it need not be parasitic in the context of a mutually satisfying relationship. Pressures towards this entrepreneurial side come from:

- Increased resource specialization: an organization may have a need for a specialized resource like a VLSI design engineer, hi-tech patent attorney or state-of-the-art circuit test equipment, but only for a short time. By using, rather than owning, a firm reduces its risk and its fixed costs.
- Risk of obsolescence: reduced by merely using, rather than owning, an expensive resource.
- Increased flexibility: the cost of exercising the option to quit is reduced by using, not owning, a resource.

Administrative practices are the product of pressures in the other direction, such as:

- Power, status and financial rewards: determined by the extent of resources ownership and control in many corporations.
- Coordination: the speed of execution is increased because the executive has the right to request certain action without negotiation.
- Efficiency: enables the firm to capture, at least in the short run, all of the profits associated with an operation.

- Inertia and cost of change: it is commonly believed that it is good management to isolate the technical core of production from external shocks. This requires buffer inventories, control of raw materials, and control of distribution channels. Owner-ship also creates familiarity and an identifiable chain of command, which become stabilized with time.
- Industry structures: encourage ownership to prevent being preempted by the competition.

MANAGEMENT STRUCTURE

The promoter wants knowledge of his/her progress via direct contact with all of the principal actors. The trustee views relationships more formally, with specific rights and responsibilities assigned through the delegation of authority. The decision to use and rent resources and not to own or employ them will require the development of an informal information network. Only in systems where the relationship with resources is based on ownership or employment can resources be organized in a hierarchy. Informal networks arise when the critical success elements cannot be contained within the bounds of the formal organization. Figure 5 illustrates this range of behavior.

Many people have attempted to distinguish between the entrepreneur and the ad-ministrator by suggesting that being a good entrepreneur precludes being a good manager. The entrepreneur is stereotyped as egocentric and idiosyncratic and thus unable to manage. However, though the managerial task is substantially different for the entrepreneur, management skill is nonetheless essential. The variation lies in the choice of appropriate tools.

More entrepreneurial management is a function of several pressures:

- Need for coordination of key noncontrolled resources: results in need to communicate with, motivate, control and plan for resources *outside* the firm.
- Flexibility: maximized with a flat and informal organization.
- Challenge to owner's control: classic ques-

Figure 5

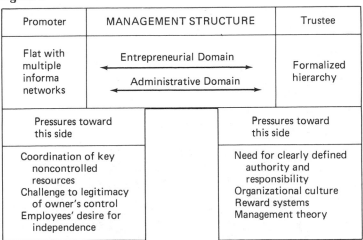

Promoter	MANAGEMENT STRUCTURE		Trustee
Flat with multiple informa networks	Entrepreneurial Domain		Formalized hierarchy
	Administrative Domain		
Pressures toward this side		Pressures toward this side	
Coordination of key noncontrolled resources Challenge to legitimacy of owner's control Employees' desire for independence		Need for clearly defined authority and responsibility Organizational culture Reward systems Management theory	

tions about the rights of ownership as well as governmental environmental, health and safety restrictions, undermine the legitimacy of control.

- Employees' desire for independence—creates an environment where employees are unwilling to accept hierarchical authority in place of authority based on competence and persuasion.

On the other side of the spectrum, pressures push the firm towards more ad-ministrative behavior. These include:

- Need for clearly defined authority and responsibility: to perform the increasingly complex planning, organizing, coordinating, communicating and controlling required in a business.
- Organizational culture—which often demands that events be routinized.
- Reward systems—which encourage and reward breadth and span of control.

REWARD PHILOSOPHY

Finally, entrepreneurial firms differ from administratively managed organizations in their philosophy regarding reward and compensation. First, entrepreneurial firms are more explicitly focused on the creation and harvesting of value. In start-up situations, the financial backers of the organization—as well as the founders themselves—have invested cash, and want cash out. As a corollary of this value-driven philosophy, entrepreneurial firms tend to base compensation on performance (where performance is closely related to value creation). Entrepreneurial firms are also more comfortable rewarding teams.

As a recent spate of take-overs suggests, more administratively managed firms are less often focused on maximizing and distributing value. They are more often guided in their decision making by the desire to protect their own positions and security. Compensation is often based on individual responsibility (assets or resources under control) and on performance relative to short-term profit targets. Reward in such firms is often heavily oriented towards promotion to increasing responsibility levels. Figure 6 describes this dimension.

The pressures that pull firms toward the promoter end of the spectrum include:

Figure 6

Promoter	REWARD PHILOSOPHY		Trustee
Value-driven Performance-based Team-oriented	Entrepreneurial Domain ← → Administrative Domain		Security-driven Resource-based Promotion-oriented
Pressures toward this side		Pressures toward this side	
Financial backers Individual expectations Competition		Societal norms Impacted information Demands of public shareholders	

- Individual expectations: increasingly, individuals expect to be compensated in proportion to their contribution, rather than merely as a function of their performance relative to an arbitrary peer group. In addition, individuals seemingly have higher levels of aspiration for personal wealth.
- Investor demands: financial backers invest cash and expect cash back, and the sooner the better. Increasingly, shareholders in publicly held firms are starting to press with a similar orientation.
- Competition: increased people competition for talent creates pressure for firms to reward these individuals in proportion to their contributions.

On the other side, a variety of pressures pull firms toward more trustee-like behavior:

- Societal norms: we still value loyalty to the organization, and find it difficult to openly discuss compensation.
- Impacted information: it is often difficult to judge the value of an individual's contributions, particularly within the frame of the annual compensation cycle performance review that most firms use.
- Demands of public shareholders: many public shareholders are simply uncomfortable with compensation that is absolutely high, even if it is in proportion to contribution.

SUMMARY

These characteristics have been gathered onto one summary chart (see Figure 7). In developing a behavioral theory of entrepreneurship, it becomes clear that entrepreneurship is defined by more than a set of individual traits and is different from an economic function. It is a cohesive pattern of managerial behavior.

This perspective on entrepreneurship highlights what we see as a false dichotomy: the distinction drawn between entrepreneurship and intrapreneurship. Entrepreneurship is an approach to management that can be applied in start-up situations as well as within more established businesses.

As our definition suggests, the accumulation of resources that occurs as a firm grows is a powerful force that makes entrepreneurial behavior more difficult in a larger firm. But the fundamentals of the behavior required remain the same.

Still, our primary focus will be on the start-up. The situational factors that define a start-up situation do much to encourage entrepreneurship. As we look at the start-up process, however, it is worth keeping in mind that many of these lessons can be applied equally well in the large corporate setting.

Figure 7

Pressures toward this side	Promoter	Key business dimension	Trustee	Pressures toward this side
Diminishing opportunity streams; Rapidly changing: Technology, Consumer economics, Social values, Political rules	Driven by perception of opportunity	Entrepreneurial Domain ↕ Administrative Domain — STRATEGIC ORIENTATION	Driven by resources currently controlled	Social contracts; Performance measurement criteria; Planning systems and cycle
Action orientation; Short decision windows; Risk management; Limited decision constituencies	Revolutionary with short duration	Entrepreneurial Domain ↕ Administrative Domain — COMMITMENT TO OPPORTUNITY	Evolutionary of long duration	Acknowledgement of multiple constituencies; Negotiation of strategy; Risk reduction; Management of fit
Lack of predictable resource needs; Lack of long-term control; Social need for more opportunity per resource unit; International pressure for more efficient resource use	Multistaged with minimal exposure at each stage	Entrepreneurial Domain ↕ Administrative Domain — COMMITMENT OF RESOURCES	Single-staged with complete commitment upon decision	Personal risk reduction; Incentive compensation; Managerial turnover; Capital allocation systems; Formal planning systems
Increased resource specialization; Long resource life compared to need; Risk of obsolescence; Risk inherent in any new venture; Inflexibility of permanent commitment to resources	Episodic use or rent of required resources	Entrepreneurial Domain ↕ Administrative Domain — CONTROL OF RESOURCES	Ownership or employment of required resources	Power, status and financial rewards; Coordination; Efficiency measures; Inertia and cost of change; Industry structures
Coordination of key noncontrolled resources; Challenge to legitimacy of owner's control; Employees' desire for independence	Flat with multiple informal networks	Entrepreneurial Domain ↕ Administrative Domain — MANAGEMENT STRUCTURE	Formalized hierarchy	Need for clearly defined authority and responsibility; Organizational culture; Reward systems; Management theory
Individual expectations; Competition; Increased perception of personal wealth creation possibilities	Value-based; Team-based; Unlimited	Entrepreneurial Domain ↕ Administrative Domain — COMPENSATION/REWARD POLICY	Resource-based; Driven by short-term data; Promotion; Limited amount	Societal norms; IRS regulations; Impacted information; Search for simple solutions for complex problems; Demands of public shareholders

177

MODULE THREE

The Evolving Organization

This module examines the characteristics of evolving organizations: those undergoing rapid growth and change. Its cases reflect a process of organizational development; they portray the challenges of managing a start-up and examine some of the predictable crises associated with rapid organizational growth. Section 1 of this note discusses the transitions typical of a rapidly evolving firm. Sections 2 and 3 define and assess the distinctions associated with rapid growth. Finally, Section 4 discusses concepts and tools relevant to *managing* rapid growth.

DEVELOPMENT TASKS OF THE EVOLVING ORGANIZATION

Like individual human beings, organizations go through a life-cycle of characteristic stages.[1] Many developmental tasks must be accomplished for the organization to be successful. Obviously, they begin when a founder or founding team initiates a start-up: A vision of company purpose must be established, and company direction set. Then the appropriate resources must be marshalled to transform this vision into reality. In these early stages, the identities of the founders and their firms are often hard to separate. This can be a positive factor when

---

[1] John Kimberly, et al., *The Organizational Life Cycle* (San Francisco: Jossey-Bass, Inc., 1980).

leadership is capable but is often a negative when individual and organizational needs become entangled to mutual detriment.

As an organization evolves, it becomes more complex in size, diversity of constituents, and range of professional functions housed under one roof. Systems must be put into place to handle functions like human resources, finance, control, and strategic planning. Conflict often emerges between the informality of the start-up environment and the perceived formality of such management systems. In Japan, the notion of "kan-ban" or "just-in-time" has been developed to enable highly efficient manufacturing processes. A similar notion can be applied to management systems in the entrepreneurial firm. Systems may be necessary, but they should be developed and instituted "just in time," and "at the right time."

This passage from organizational infancy to adulthood is often described as the "entrepreneurial-managerial" transition.[2,3] As Greiner[4] has pointed out, the informality of the start-up soon gives way to crises of control and direction in which needs for systems and "professional" or "technical" management are exposed. This poses a dilemma: how to maintain entrepreneurial zeal while installing structure and systems which may contribute to an increasingly impersonal organizational climate. This also poses dilemmas for the founder(s) of the organization. On the one hand, their entrepreneurial qualities keep them on center stage; they are guardians of the organizational vision, keepers of the flame. On the other hand, these very qualities may create friction with key managers or business problems for the organization. Transitions between entrepreneurial and managerial leadership have both been orderly (Lotus Development Corporation) and traumatic (Apple Computer Corporation).

Learning at several organizational levels must accompany the growth process. Typically, individual skills are lacking in relation to responsibilities assumed. For example, the founders of a software company may literally have had no previous business experience. A biotechnology company may have two dozen senior scientists with Ph.D.s, none of whom has ever managed other people, carried out a performance appraisal, or learned basic supervisory skills. Senior managers may be new to an entrepreneurial environment or to working with creative people. They may need to learn about the industry or be responsible for people vastly different in age or underlying values from themselves. Effective responses to a wide range of unprecedented situations must also be learned at group and organizational levels. For example, as they evolve, organizations must deal with the implications of achieving (or not achieving) their goals. Success can be as burdensome as failure.

Ambiguity is a hallmark of the evolving organization's internal operating environment. The ambiguity associated with evolving organizations is often in-

[2]   Eric Flamholtz, *How to Make the Transition from an Entrepreneurship to a Professionally Managed Firm* (San Francisco: Jossey-Bass, 1986).

[3]   Michael Roberts, *The Entrepreneurial-Managerial Transition,* Dissertation, Division of Research, Harvard Business School, 1987.

[4]   Larry Greiner, "Evolution and Revolution as Organizations Grow," *Harvard Business Review,* 50:4, July-August, 1972.

tensified by their external environment. Start-ups are common in emerging industries such as biotechnology, personal computer software, and superconductors. As described by Porter[5] and others, emerging industries share the characteristic of uncertainty in such fundamental terms as technology, marketing strategy, customer needs, and concept of service. Industry structure and the rules of the game await definition. Emerging industries often resemble a casino where a range of bets are placed on different strategies, entrepreneurs, or organizational approaches. Sahlman[6] and Stevenson have described the phenomenon of "capital market myopia," where a plethora of competing and often redundant companies are created by the pressures of capital availability and investment community ambitions. An example is the creation of multiple companies in the disk drive industry for personal computers. Such capital market myopia can also provide a fascinating laboratory for observing the effects of different types of organizational assumptions on performance. Evolving firms make a wide range of often critical organizational choices which can determine their fate competitively. By making the right choices, evolving firms can create barriers to competitors which come, in Porter's words, "less from the need to command massive resources than from the ability to bear risk, be creative technologically, and make forward-looking decisions to gain input supplies (people) and distribution channels."[7] In other words, HRM and organizational factors are frequently decisive for an organization's ability to compete.

In sum, the evolving organization must literally create for itself a style of doing business, shared values, a strategy, and guiding assumptions about key success factors in the business. The traditions, habits, and standard operating procedures of an established organization are completely absent. Everything is up for grabs. Thus, the evolving organization must deal with a high degree of uncertainty both internally and externally. At the same time, and equally importantly, it must provide an environment in which the creative and entrepreneurial energies of its people are allowed to emerge.

RAPID GROWTH

Rapid growth presents a difficult set of challenges. There is an old Chinese curse which says, "May you live in interesting times." Change and dynamism are sometimes seen as obstacles to the peace of mind which brings wisdom. Yet the progress they imply is widely sought after in the world of entrepreneurial business.

Certainly interesting times are part of the life of an entrepreneurial firm and can be both a curse and a blessing. Many recent roller-coaster stories such as those of Osborne Computer Company[8] and Atari[9] provide a high-tech historiog-

[5]   Michael Porter, *Competitive Strategy* (New York: The Free Press, 1981).

[6]   William Sahlman and Howard Stevenson, "Capital Market Myopia," *Journal of Venturing*, 1986.

[7]   Michael Porter, op. cit.

[8]   Adam Osborn and John Dvorak, *Hypergrowth, The Rise and Fall of the Osborne Computer Company* (Berkeley: Idthekkethan Publishing Company, 1984).

[9]   Scott Cohen, *Zap: The Rise and Fall of Atari* (New York: McGraw-Hill Book Company, 1984).

raphy of how rapid growth can lead from euphoria to nightmare in a short period.

Managing rapid growth successfully is a complex and ambiguous task. To quote a recent HBS visitor to "Entrepreneurship, Creativity and Organization," the initial task of the entrepreneur is "to turn chaos into mere disorder." Another entrepreneur routinely differentiates among "hypergrowth," "explosive hypergrowth," and "merely explosive growth." Such "terms of art" underscore the approximate and uncertain nature of the task.

What *is* rapid growth? Three years in the history of Lotus Development Corporation provide a useful example that may help us recalibrate our measuring instruments. This software company started in 1982 as the legendary basement operation with a handful of young founders. By 1983, it consisted of 500 people and at the third quarter of 1985 crossed the 1,000-person mark. In that same period, revenues climbed from $174,000 in the company's first nine months of operation, to $53 million in 1983, to $225 million in 1985. By late 1985, the company was operating in sixteen locations and four countries.

What do companies experience during such convulsive growth and change? Which skills must they master? What are the pitfalls? Can some be avoided? What issues are relevant for all companies, not just high-tech start-ups? This module explores these issues. Classical dilemmas of rapid growth will be considered in an effort to evaluate some of the responses that companies have developed through the school of experience.

The Dilemmas of Rapid Growth

Even when results in business terms are positive, rapid growth creates many organizational problems. The following are some primary examples:

A. Growth covers up problems. Rapid growth and business success can cover up a variety of underlying problems of organizational development. Profitability can provide an apparent cushion for wasteful decisions regarding the allocation of financial, human, and other resources. The excitement of growth can mask inadequacies in leadership or management skills. Growth can forgive a lack of planning or an inadequate orientation towards long-term issues. Success can excuse a variety of shortcomings while breeding a dangerous form of arrogance. The logic assumes that since *we* are successful, *we* must be doing something right. "Don't tell *us* what to do because *we* are writing the book." Such an attitude of hubris and group-think can lead to a dangerous sense of complacency, strategic surprise, or even disaster. By the time problems turn into recognizable crises which flash on the corporate radar screen, it may be too late: The opportunity for corrective action may have passed. It is easy to become blindsided in the hubbub of rapid growth by focusing on internal challenges to the exclusion of external ones. Internal absorption may crowd out environmental scanning, with unfortunate consequences.

B. Dilemmas of leadership.   The tasks of leadership become more complex as an organization grows rapidly.

For example, communication among organizational levels becomes difficult and problematic. It is harder to project a sense of vision and shared purpose in the organization as its constituencies increase in size and points of view. This is a critical problem since a company's central vision is an important institutional anchor, providing a motivating force and a raison d'être for activity at all levels.

Also, rapid growth tends to dilute the effectiveness of leadership. Many entrepreneurial organizations initially mobilize around the leadership and charisma of a central figure—Steven Jobs at Apple Computer Company and Mitch Kapor at Lotus Development Corporation are the classic examples. In the face of growth, there is simply less of the leader's time to go around on a pro rata basis.

In the early stages of a company's development, much communication occurs informally, with "walk around management" an important element in the leader's repertoire. As the organization grows, new mechanisms may be needed to amplify the effectiveness of leadership and market the central values of the organization. Companies deal with this challenge through a variety of formal and informal means. Newsletters, events, meetings, videotaped orientation materials, written communications from top management all can augment the shared culture and perception of leadership in the organization. These manufactured events typical of a larger firm contrast with the spontaneous "happenings" of an earlier and more informal phase in the organization's life. They require resources and determination to develop.

Preserving two-way, up-down communication becomes an important challenge. Without appropriate communication channels, company leadership may lose valuable opinions, insights, and feedback from the rest of the organization on a variety of issues. It is difficult to "stay in touch" as the firm becomes more complex.

C. Loss of focus in company mission.   In a rapid growth situation, the number of short-term tactical issues that must be addressed increases relative to the major strategic issues that require broad-stroke thinking. The pressure of events allows less time for strategic thinking, for stepping back and looking at the big picture. Yet, this is precisely what is required in the dynamic situation of rapid growth. Stable businesses need maintenance thinking. Their course is clear; only minor adjustments are required from time to time. Dynamic entrepreneurial situations, on the other hand, require constant reevaluation and adjustment of strategy and tactics. When everyone is busy and on "crash-dive" programs, the essential ingredients of quality time and communication are in short supply. It is impossible to prioritize one's work with perfect foresight—too much is unknown. Rather, intuition and feelings become important guides to establishing priorities and designing agendas.

The pressured environment of the rapidly growing company encourages the loss of focus in other ways. When immersed in fire-fighting and reacting, a company may deviate from its original mission for impulsive reasons. Or, suffering from its own omnipotence, it may believe it can handle anything. Given the fragility of the embryonic firm and its limited resources, deviating from an original sense of mission can be extremely hazardous.

D. Communication becomes harder. Another difficulty for the evolving firm involves developing communication channels able to keep pace with organizational evolution. It is difficult to preserve the "small town" character of the early organization in which information is shared informally and intensely. Distance between people emerges as an organization grows both vertically and horizontally. Increased task complexity, interdependency, and specialization also lead to communication barriers.

As an organization grows, communication often becomes harder in other ways. For people in the rank and file, the problems can become severe as the organization grows from a tribal to a corporate environment. In the informal stage of development, everything and everyone seems to have its place. One knows where to go for things. People may have clear formal roles, but equally important, their *informal* roles are clear. With growth, however, the informal, commonly known roles lose their coherence and shared importance.

The problem is aggravated by the emergence of internal subgroups who often interpret company history, industry, and mission very differently. For example, subgroups of old-timers and newcomers often develop. Those close to the founding of the organization may share a bond. The first hundred employees at many companies such as Apple, for example, form a distinct subgroup. They share the "honor" of having double-digit ID numbers and may be accorded special status by others in the organization. Complaints about bureaucratization from this group may have diagnostic significance for the organization's continued success.

It is quite common in rapidly growing firms to have distinct morale differences among different subgroups depending on how long they have been in the organization. Such "micro-demographics" may tell an interesting story. Old-timers may have high satisfaction because they are close to the founding of the company, may have more company stock, and know more about the intimate details of company history. They have been through the "Declaration of Independence" and "Valley Forge" periods. Newcomers also may have high morale because they are excited about the company and eager to embark on the honeymoon stage of their careers. It is people in an intermediate group, having benefits of neither "new" nor "old" status, who may feel the most difficulty in maintaining a high degree of zeal.

Subgroups also emerge between insiders and outsiders. People who have access to key leaders or resources differentiate themselves from others without such access. Finally, subgroups may emerge which define themselves by technical and functional specialization. The perennial conflict between "creative" and "business" types, or between product development and marketing, are well known.

With the presence of strong subgroups and in the absence of a strong central culture, power dynamics will emerge.[10]

[10] John Kotter, *Power and Influence* (New York: Free Press, 1985).

Establishing or maintaining effective communications within evolving organizations often requires professional skills and experience which original team members may not possess; the advantage of being "in on the beginning" does not assure the skill base needed to manage in an environment that demands more sophistication, particularly when organizational devices such as matrices and project teams are used. Training, leadership behavior, and human resource practices can all help to mitigate these communication problems, however.

E. Inadequate human resource practices. In a situation of rapid growth, human resource practices often receive inadequate attention. The problem is exacerbated when one area, such as marketing or research and development, receives more management attention because of its strategic importance. Emphasis on how people are recruited, assimilated, trained, and developed is critical for the evolving organization. This is true both for acculturating new employees as well as making the best use of people in a changing environment. It is also in fitting an individual's skills with the requirements of their job, a difficult task because jobs and the skills they require can change rapidly.

F. Management skill and organizational needs. Imbalances between an organization's needs and the human skills available can lead to problems. "Entrepreneur's disease" can be particularly hazardous. The entrepreneur who wishes to retain decision making and power as a "closely held" function, may be unwilling to delegate to key managers. It is precisely when the pace of change quickens that the entrepreneur's anxiety and consequent unwillingness to delegate may increase. This is a severe problem when the entrepreneur becomes a bottleneck for the quantity and quality of decision making required.

Critical imbalances may also occur when people find it increasingly difficult to expand their responsibilities. When their skills are out of step with the requirements of their role, effective action may be impaired.

G. The emergence of stress and future shock. As psychologists well know, the continued loss of the familiar leads to stress. Alvin Toffler, in his book *Future Shock*,[11] describes how acceleration of the pace of events and the rate of environmental change can lead to individual alienation and "dis-ease." Relationships become more superficial, or to use his term, "disposable," and the ability of organizations to create meaning and engender loyalty can be severely diluted.

Any change involves the human experience of loss, and contributes to the build up of stress. The evolving organization is all about change: change in status, responsibilities, roles, requirements. Hence, on a human level it is inherently stressful. The entrepreneurial environment is one in which rapid change and uncertainty exist constantly. The individual is exposed not only to a number of different experiences but to a large percentage of *new* or *novel* events relative to the whole. Everything, in a sense, is a new experience in a start-up situation, requiring a fresh outlook and effective decision making. If the pace of events

---

[11]   Alvin Toffler, *Future Shock* (New York: Bantam Books, 1971).

Figure 3-1

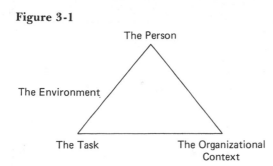

becomes too much to handle, stress and burnout[12] may result, with ominous consequences for the organization.

The notion of stress, however, is double-edged. Without it, the environment would be boring and routine; the quality and quantity of work would decline. But too much stress would lead to a drop in productivity and a deterioration in the quality of decision making. Stress is like an inverted U-shaped curve: Productivity declines when there is either too little or too much. It is therefore the responsibility of leadership to manage stress by titrating the amount of uncertainty and novelty in the environment with people's perceived ability to handle it.

MANAGING RAPID GROWTH

Managing rapid growth in an evolving organization may benefit from thinking in terms of the opportunities for intervention represented by task, person, and organizational framework. Figures 3-1 and 3-2 review the framework in relation to the evolving organization.

The Organizational Context

Developing an entrepreneurial organization often depends on the degree to which appropriate values and attitudes are inculcated in the organization's members. Developing a corporate culture which fosters the achievement of organizational goals is a central task. Some of these values and attitudes include: expecting the unexpected; anticipating the end of rapid growth; assessing the meaning of growth for the firm and maintaining focus; developing sources of objectivity; thinking like a small company; developing appropriate leadership; and fostering company culture through constant affirmation of company mission.

Expecting the unexpected.   Anything can happen in an entrepreneurial organization and it probably will. Maintaining a flexible attitude is paramount

---

[12]   Dennis Jaffee, *From Burnout to Balance* (New York: McGraw Hill, 1985).

Figure 3-2 Module 3—The Evolving Organization—Key Issues

Person	Understanding the entrepreneur's motives, personality, skills, fit with organization.
Task	Creating the minimum critical structure needed, managing growth, decreasing ambiguity and uncertainty, maintaining focus, coordinating the entrepreneurial scramble; juggling creative operational/managerial, interpersonal/leadership tasks.
Organizational Context	Creating/influencing the organizational context: structure, culture, systems.
	Dealing with fluidity, informality, and change.
	Assessing the interplay between the entrepreneur's personality and the organization's style.
Environment	Dealing most effectively with environmental constraints and opportunities:
	Regulatory issues
	Competition
	Labor pool and other inputs.

for individuals as well as organizations. A useful image comes from the old Chinese proverb about the supple bamboo plant which is able to sway in any wind without breaking, while the rigid tree is toppled by the sudden storm. Such flexibility comes from, among other things, the *expectation* that the organization will change continually to accommodate new needs.

Anticipating the end of rapid growth. It is easy to be seduced into thinking that growth will never end. After all, growth is exciting, like an adrenaline high. One gets a great deal of feedback from the marketplace, colleagues, the business press, and friends, all confirming how good one is. In times of success, the entrepreneur resembles a tightrope walker looking for ways to top the last stunt while the crowd oohs and aahs.

But explosive growth inevitably slows down at some point. This may occur for a variety of external reasons: market maturation or saturation; product or technology obsolescence; and the emergence of strong competition. It may also come from internal sources. The organization may be unable to marshall its resources and sustain further growth. Or its central values may require the limiting of growth. Such organizations as Lucasfilm, Ltd. have made a conscious effort to limit their growth to a fixed ceiling of employees in order to maintain the creative energy of their internal environment.

There is much that a company can do to anticipate slowdowns and to help its members make necessary adjustments. Understanding that slower growth is not necessarily *bad,* nor rapid growth always *good,* is helpful, particularly when such attitudes are modeled by those at the helm of the organization.

Assessing the meaning of growth for the firm and maintaining focus. Traditional business views growth as something sacred. According to this standard, growth is good and more growth is better. It is by such measures that American management has been evaluated and on which shareholders make known their judgments of a company through demand for its stock. Maintaining earning trends and steady growth are important from a capital markets perspective.

But there are other ways of looking at growth. Growth involves important tradeoffs and may occur at the expense of organizational coherence, motivation, and individual well-being. This issue is found in Tolstoy's short story called "How Much Land Does a Man Need." Growth is particularly problematic when it is fueled by the personality of an entrepreneur or a group who uses it as a source of continued self-esteem. The entrepreneur may feel impelled to pile up accomplishments as tangible evidence of achievement in order to project an image seen as acceptable to others. This was certainly the theme for many entrepreneurs who grew up in the depression era and whose concerns about upward mobility and status became a means to overcome their humble and frequently immigrant origins.

Growth via the right kind of creative focus is also important, and the "right" kind of focus inevitably changes. Many entrepreneurial firms must cope with organizational tensions like keeping one eye on R&D and another on the marketplace. Creativity for its own sake can lead to wasteful investment in activities which do not make profits available to fund the future. Conversely, mere focus on profitability without a sense of the creative obviously limits innovation. Focus on markets and customers, then, is the litmus test of acceptance for a company's creative activities.

Finally, the rapidly growing company must avoid overextending itself and maintain a strategic view consistent with its resource base. It must continuously anticipate future needs in such terms as supplies, manufacturing capacity, money, space and people.

Developing sources of objectivity. Rapid growth can be intoxicating. Like a revolutionary cell, the entrepreneurial organization works feverishly to create the future in the present. Greiner refers to this organizational phase as "growth by creativity."[13] This early period is characterized by informality, high energy, commitment, and boundless zeal on the part of a company's people.

It is in precisely such periods that companies are in greatest danger of losing objectivity. Where does leadership go for a different perspective? Internal signals are important as are systems for informal communication. Lotus Development Corporation, for example, instituted a "grapevine" system which allowed anyone to communicate with anyone else in the company to discuss any topic anonymously.

[13] Larry Greiner, op. cit.

Other sources of objectivity include directors, suppliers, distributors, colleagues, and friends. Maintenance of outside perspectives discourages "star syndrome" attitudes and promotes a more objective point of view. It is more important to know the difference between reality and hype than to believe one's own press releases.

Monitoring the competitive environment either formally or informally is critical, and infinitely preferable to flying blind. Procedures for environmental scanning can be beneficial. Finally, attention to strategic planning that is neither overly rigorous nor loose will help preserve a sense of objectivity and reality-testing in a dynamic environment.

Thinking like a small company. Redundancy is one of the benefits of working in a large company. Restrictive bureaucracies often contain slack which can cushion the impact of failure and provide multiple pathways for problem solving. In an entrepreneurial firm, the resource base is typically much thinner; backup systems and redundant resources are not available in the same quantity and quality. A jumbo-sized safety net waiting below to support risk-taking individuals and groups does not exist.

This becomes an important issue when bringing in people from other company environments and explains why many entrepreneurial old-timers are suspicious of people with large company or "organization man" backgrounds.

Leadership. The leadership of a rapidly growing organization must be honest with itself and constantly ask the question, "Do I/we have the skills and expertise to continue to be effective?" One option is to limit growth to fit leadership capabilities. Others involve bringing in new people or replacing those at the top.

The issue of an evolving leadership function is important because it is the source of vision and strategy for the organization, the locus on which core values are established. Leadership also provides an important mechanism for grounding these values through direct example, providing positive motivation and encouragement to employees, and monitoring and managing the culture of the firm.

The leader can also champion new projects, establish an "express lane" for their development, and provide creative direction and support for new initiatives.

Culture—constantly reaffirming company mission. Corporate culture provides insight into understanding how an organization's belief system, social norms, and values function. Managing corporate culture allows the entrepreneurial firm to grow and innovate more effectively.

Culture commonly refers to a sense of social reality created collectively by a particular group over time. Thus, implicit in the notion of culture as manageable is a paradox. Yet, for the entrepreneurial firm, culture is something which must be managed actively: There is no time to wait for culture to emerge. It must be marketed internally to smooth organizational development by sharing desired values and communicating a useful sense of leadership.

The mission of a company as expressed by its culture is its spiritual blueprint, its raison d'être. It should shape decisions, guide action, and provide a context for planning. It should be a source of direction to newcomers as well as middle managers who are struggling with increased ambiguity, time demands, and tough decisions around allocating scarce resources.

The marketing of culture is amenable to the traditional analysis of money, motive, means, and message. A variety of corporate communication channels, even human resource systems, are important potential means for inculcating company values and mass producing their acceptance. For example, American Express refers to a recent recruiting video as its "culture video."

Culture is also transmitted by example through influential people within the organization. The case "Janet Axelrod" in Module One shows the guiding influence of one of the company's founders on the entrepreneurial sense of mission. In her role as head of HRM, she continually thought about values such as "What are we doing and why are we doing it? Why are we in this business? Is it enough to produce quality? Is it enough to make money? What is the meaning of all of this?"

Adhering to the original commitments of the organization in areas like human and social values, product quality, or customer service is vital. It preserves the spiritual strength of the organization and should not be compromised by short-term business pressures.

The Person

Human skills—minding the store.   As an organization grows, it needs the appropriate balance between entrepreneurial and managerial attitudes. Business discipline, in areas like planning and fiscal control, is important to enable growth. It should provide optimal conditions for entrepreneurial creativity, not inhibit it. Ideally, the organization develops a culture that balances the intuition and emotion of the entrepreneur with the rationality and systematic thinking of the manager. Achieving this requires constant attention to maintaining the diversity of people within the organization, to developing a culture which explicitly recognizes the importance of such diversity, and to establishing integrative roles throughout the organization which recognize the importance of such diversity.[14]

People—managing human resources.   HRM actions are needed at critical junctures of a rapidly growing firm's development.

Recruiting.   Recruiting is critical for the growing organization since the consequences of a bad hire in an evolving situation are much worse than in a

[14]   Paul Lawrence and Jay Lorsch, *Organization and Environment* (Homewood, Ill: Richard D. Irwin, 1963).

stable one. A "bad apple" can demoralize working groups, sabotage communication links, or make decisions with fateful consequences.

Recruiting is also important to assure person/company fit. An entrepreneurial company is looking for, in the words of entrepreneur Sheldon Breiner, people who can "hit the ground running." Self-starters need little training to be effective in their work, assimilate quickly, find a sense of consonance between their values and the culture of the company, and are comfortable with ambiguity, challenge, responsibility and growth.

Assimilation. HRM is an important mechanism for communicating values and socializing new employees once they have joined a company. The original vision, values, and priorities of the founders are a valuable resource for the organization. Like a Declaration of Independence or Magna Carta, they provide principles by which people can live in a day-to-day world, a map through a maze of ambiguity. Culture creates the environment for work. New employees must learn this culture effectively and rapidly, because in a hypergrowth environment people have no time to explain things completely. The company's environment is also growing in complexity so that informal explanations are no longer as satisfactory. Efforts must be made to systematize the assimilation process, mass producing it for the needs of new entrants. CEO and/or founder involvement is clearly desirable in the process.

Career planning. This is important in establishing a sense of an organization's "people inventory" which can help it make rational job allocation decisions and enhance the possibilities for cross-functional communication. It contributes to the development of people with diverse experiences who are better rounded and can therefore make a greater contribution to the future growth of the company.

Information gathering. HRM can be an important mechanism for enhancing informal, top-down and bottom-up communication. It can also serve to gather information and monitor the internal health of a company. Techniques include such devices as grapevines and suggestion boxes, important as "distant early warning" and monitoring systems and thus beneficial for managing employee expectations.

Reward systems. The rapidly growing organization must always ask itself, "Is the right kind of behavior being rewarded? Is risk-taking encouraged in an appropriate fashion? Are intrinsic as well as financial rewards being used in the most effective manner?"

Human resource planning. HRM is important to the overall planning process. People not only "make things happen," they are critical to the organization's scarce resources. Human resource planning can also help the organization through rough transitions. For example, Activision survived major personnel cutbacks in part because of an HRM system which enabled it to function reasonably and fairly so that company morale and reputation in Silicon Valley were maintained.

Balancing human skills with growing complexity. A rapidly growing company must be strong-minded enough to replace or reassign people when their jobs have outstripped their capabilities. Career development and planning must be made a critical issue for the organization. Old-timers may find their responsibilities outstripping their skills, but their experience with the organization is a vital asset. Ways must be found constantly to *reassimilate* them into the organization. Hiring practices, training, and career mobility systems will all help address the issues of balancing skills and job responsibilities in a dynamic environment.

THE TASK

In an evolving organization, it is difficult to define with precision the nature of tasks to be accomplished, the manner in which they should be pursued, or their desired sequence. The situation in the evolving organization has been described by an eminent venture capitalist as "an entrepreneurial scramble." The entrepreneur works long hours: 5 to 9 as opposed to the typical 9 to 5. It is often difficult to be orderly in organizing one's time. New information must constantly be assimilated into the overall picture, new events dealt with, new challenges met. The nature of the entrepreneurial task in the evolving organization is fundamentally heuristic; that is, it is not amenable to analysis by a given set of rules or procedures. The path towards addressing the task must be developed from scratch. Furthermore, the tasks are diverse and constantly changing. Continual effort must be given to assuring fit between the organization's people and its key tasks.

THE CASES

Hot Rock

This case shows three young business school students embarking on a start-up in the exciting and potentially lucrative area of music retailing using advanced telemarketing methods. It enables a discussion of what human and organizational requirements must be satisfied to get underway.

Catalyst Technologies

Catalyst Technologies is in the business of providing a complete environment for the start-up company, including physical space, infrastructure, financing, and services. In a sense it is a venture for manufacturing ventures. Such "venture incubators" package under one roof a range of start-up companies services need and have attracted much attention as vehicles for community development and as venture opportunities in themselves. Analysis of Catalyst's "operating system" and "service concept" clarifies the critical ingredients necessary for the growing start-up company.

Managing Change at Lotus Development Corporation

In Lotus Development Corporation case (and the Activision cases that come later) students consider the importance of human resource managing in the entrepreneurial situation.

Lotus is an example of what its founder, Mitchell Kapor, calls "explosive hypergrowth." This case zeros in on how such growth can be managed through an approach to human resource practices and corporate culture that is both flexible and paced with the organization's development. It discusses how the human resources function at Lotus has evolved, and presents the company's values and leadership style. Students are asked to analyze Lotus' success in supporting and preserving its values and organizational culture, to project how much further growth the company can sustain, and to consider how its human resource practices must adapt to maintain future growth.

Integrated Genetics

This case follows Integrated Genetics, Inc. a biotechnology company, from inception to the present. This four-year period contains several milestones, including growth in numbers of people, success at raising capital, and progress on the scientific front. The case highlights the ways in which creative resources have been managed as the company has evolved. Students are encouraged to identify with the issues facing the CEO, Bob Carpenter, as he deals with the challenge of managing human and organizational processes.

Infocom

Infocom, a young computer software company, has experienced market acceptance and rapid growth. The case is set at a time when the company is considering a major reorganization to accommodate a new product line—a departure from its traditional business. This has considerable implications for the spirit of entrepreneurship at the company and for the evolving roles of the company's founders. Organizational design options are evaluated in light of company history, present needs, and future plans. This case also emphasizes the leadership dilemmas in an entrepreneurial firm, as well as the risks that arise when strategic and organizational focuses are not maintained.

The Young Astronauts Program

The Young Astronauts Program, another example of an evolving entrepreneurial organization, contains a twist; it portrays a nonprofit organization. It enables an analysis of the differences in handling a start-up in the nonprofit sector, seen in such terms as motivating people, and handling specific leadership challenges, and financing.

The Learning Company

The Learning Company was founded by two women with diverse abilities, one more "creative," the other more "managerial." This case examines the team's history, key assumptions, and approaches to organization and management. It also provides students an opportunity to explore the individual and organization skills involved in handling uncertainty, leadership questions, and the entrepreneur-venture capitalist relationship in a climate of organizational change.

Three Myths, and How Much Land Does a Man Need?

This material focuses on questions of values and personal trade-offs in the entrepreneurial career. How does one create an appropriate balance between personal and professional demands? What are the limits of ambition? How can one balance success with humility? With humanity? How does one guard against hubris, narcissism, and greed?

FOR FURTHER READING

DAVIS, STANLEY, *Managing Corporate Culture*. Cambridge, Mass.: Ballinger Publishing Company, 1984.

DEAL, TERRENCE and ALAN KENNEDY, *Corporate Cultures*. Reading, Mass.: Addison-Wesley Publishing Company, 1982.

FLAMHOLTZ, ERIC, *How to Make the Transition From an Entrepreneurship to a Professionally Managed Firm*. San Francisco, Calif.: Jossey-Bass, 1986.

McCASKEY, MICHAEL, *The Hidden Dimension*. Marshfield, Mass.: Pittman Press, 1982.

MORITZ, MICHAEL, *The Little Kingdom*. New York: William Morrow, 1984.

OSBORNE, ADAM and JOHN DVORAK, *Hypergrowth: The Rise and Fall of Osborne Computer Company*. Berkeley, Calif.: Idthekkethan Publishing Company, 1984.

PENROSE, EDITH, *The Theory of the Growth of the Firm*. New York: M. E. Sharpe, 1980.

ROBERTS, MICHAEL, *The Transition from Entrepreneurial to Professional Management, An Exploratory Study*, Doctoral Thesis, Harvard University, Boston, 1986.

Hot Rock, Inc. (A)

When, on July 17, 1983, Hot Rock, Inc. received its 50,000th phone call, its founders—Michael Wigley, Jerry DeLaVega, and David Ishag—did not have time to celebrate. They were too busy answering telephones and filling orders. Seventeen days earlier Hot Rock had aired its first television advertisement on the cable music television channel MTV.

For the start-up trio, social lives, sit-down dinners, and eight hours of sleep were things of the past. Stress and 20-hour days were the new status quo. Wigley's weight, 220 lbs and rising—helped along from too much fast food and too little exercise—was getting out of hand, and his cigarette consumption had risen to three packs a day. DeLaVega was almost as bad, with a newly acquired two-pack a day habit. Ishag, looking pale and pasty, had lost his usual smile and upbeat demeanor. Hot Rock had clearly turned their lives upside down. While other first-year classmates and friends at the Harvard Business School were busy with summer internships, career networking and socializing, these three entrepreneurs were betting on changing the way consumers bought records.

INDUSTRY OVERVIEW

Musical recordings had been available since the late 1800s when Thomas Edison invented the Victrola. As consumers spent more disposable income on entertainment, record sales grew. The baby boomers in particular spurred a dramatic growth in the recorded music market from 1968–1978. During that period sales grew at the compounded rate of 12.75% per year to $4.2 billion in 1978. Sales declined through 1982 to $3.4 billion but rebounded to $3.8 billion the following year. Two main channels of distribution accounted for a majority of sales volume in the recorded music industry: retail stores and mail order clubs. The retail record outlets fell into four main categories. *Specialty stores* catered to the traditional music buyer, and accounted for almost 50 percent of the sales in this segment. They provided full selection, knowledge,

This case was prepared by Research Associate Lee Field, under the supervision of Associate Professor John Kao.

Copyright © 1986 by the President and Fellows of Harvard College. Harvard Business School case 9-487-045.

and instant gratification to the buyer. The *department stores* sold on impulse. Located in high traffic floor areas, these department stores usually offered limited selections volume. *Discount stores* aimed for the price-sensitive buyer also often had limited selections. They sold approximately 28 percent. The remaining sales were categorized as *other retail outlets*. These four store groups accounted for roughly 71 percent of all sales in 1985.

Mail order clubs sold the remaining volume. Often these were affiliated with one of the record producers or offered selections of a particular style such as Classical Clubs or Jazz Clubs. These groups often operated like book-of-the-month clubs, sending items that members kept or returned. While the clubs tended to have a national distribution, the retail outlets, other than department stores, were mostly local or regional and highly fragmented. No single, powerful national distributor controlled any segments of the market.

HOT ROCK'S GENESIS

Michael Wigley and Jerry DeLaVega met as sectionmates at Harvard Business School during the first year of the MBA program. The two not only sat next to each other in class but had similar values and philosophies of hard work, hard play, respect for others, and taking responsibility. Their friendship flourished, in and out of the classroom. Like other married students at HBS they joined the Partners Club, an organization designed to assist married couples returning to school. The club sponsored many social activities and the Wigleys and DeLaVegas became good friends.

In February of 1983, Wigley and his wife, Barbara, had driven DeLaVega to Logan Airport to pick up his wife, Debbie. During the wait they passed the time talking about their Christmas vacations. While home in San Antonio, Texas, DeLaVega had been amazed to find many of his friends absorbed in MTV. This infant cable channel, which played videos 24-hours-a-day, was already being hailed as the savior of the ailing recording industry. Wigley and DeLaVega were music lovers who each owned over 500 record albums, but neither had been active buyers for the past couple of years due to time constraints. With increasing excitement, they discussed the MTV phenomenon and its potential effectiveness as a marketing vehicle. How could one exploit MTV's hypnotic success? Were there enough people out there like themselves who might comprise a new consumer group? Remembering a recent marketing case detailing telemarketing, they wondered if advertising on MTV using a toll-free number might be a new and profitable way to sell records. Wigley wondered if a gigantic untapped market of buyers like DeLaVega and himself who didn't have the time, inclination, or opportunity to shop in a record store existed. If so, perhaps a phone-in, 24-hour music store could provide the convenience, selection, and service to bring these people back into the market.

Further brainstorming resulted in the concept of a toll-free 24-hour music store offering wide selection, prompt delivery, superior customer service, and reasonable prices. After additional research, "Hot Rock, your 24-hour music store . . . call 1-800-HOT ROCK," evolved as the concept with an easy-to-remember image and phone number. The idea hinged on making the delivery system as easy as possible for the consumer.

For the next six months, Wigley and DeLaVega researched the idea between classes and on weekends, not sure how to proceed. DeLaVega had never considered starting his own business. In fact, his only previous jobs had been in the public sector. As for the Hot Rock idea, he envisioned developing the concept and selling it to an established company with the resources, skills, and time to make it work.

Wigley, however, had other ideas. He convinced DeLaVega that the prospects were too exciting and promising not to pursue Hot Rock themselves, at least through the summer. Besides, they might get university funding through the Lebor Fellowship, which provided up to $10,000 for students to work with developing companies. The two hoped to stretch the intent of the fellowship to include summer work "developing a company." The March 15 application deadline imposed the discipline to do the research and get the concept down on paper. Unfortunately, they did not receive the fellowship.

Undiscouraged, the pair had thought of another option. Earlier Wigley had described the plan to another classmate, David Ishag, a successful entrepreneur in his own right. Ishag loved the idea and was anxious to invest. From his classroom impressions, however, he appeared opinionated, arrogant, and temperamental in DeLaVega's opinion. Ishag had tremendous energy, enthusiasm, and some money, but could they work with him? DeLaVega expressed these worries to Wigley at the first of many round-table discussions at the DeLaVega home. They decided to ask him.

At another round-table meeting, including Jerry, Michael, Debbie, Barbara, and Ishag, Jerry took the lead and said, "David, I don't know you very well except for what I see in class. To make this thing go, we will have to all work very closely together. Can you work with us?" Sensitive to their concerns, Ishag remarked that much of his class behavior was showmanship. He assured them that he would adapt to their style and fit in as needed. Ishag made it clear, however, that he did not want to be as involved in the day-to-day business, preferring to be an active investor with no line responsibility. He offered $10,000 for an equal equity stake with Wigley and DeLaVega, who contributed $2,000 each.

After polishing the business plan, the three enlisted the aid of attorney and classmate Liz Dodge. Hot Rock, Inc. was incorporated on May 5, 1983. At one of the organizational meetings Dodge asked for a list of the officers in order to file the proper documents. "I want to be president," Wigley announced. This was something he had thought long and hard about. After all, he felt, Hot Rock, Inc. was the result of his creativity and work.

Ishag was startled by Wigley's proclamation. He had not expected him to be so aggressive or blurt it out so quickly. Recovering, Ishag remarked that as he came on board late and would not be active in daily affairs, consequently he did not want to be president. DeLaVega noted that Wigley had "presidential qualities" and supported him for the post. Ishag and DeLaVega became executive vice presidents. While the functionality of the roles was as yet undefined, they all agreed that the titles were in name only, because decisions would still be made democratically—one person one vote. See *Exhibit 1* for the organization chart.

The Principals

Wigley. Michael Wigley had an imposing physical presence. A solid 6'3" by 220 lbs, he also possessed academic credentials to back him up: B.S. and B.C.E. degrees from the University of Minnesota and an M.S. from Stanford. He had a take-charge personality and optimism that infected all around him. While running for section office during the first week of classes at Harvard, Wigley gave an indication of things to come with a campaign speech. Lumbering down from his skydeck seat, he bellowed at the class, "I'm a big, bad, mean son-of-a-bitch who never backs down. Believe me: I won't be afraid to fight for you!" Not surprisingly, during the semester he earned his classmates' confidence with his tenacious drive, keen negotiating skills, and sharp, analytical mind.

Wigley's self-confidence was not solely the result of bravura or an M.S. from Stanford. He had owned and operated his own retail record and stereo store, was a director of a software development firm, and general partner in a real estate development company. He had also managed various energy-related projects. Throwing his heart and soul into a project, Wigley was competitively driven: He hated to lose. He also liked to motivate people. He remarked, "I think I'm good at providing a vision of how the world could be and helping people define the specific steps necessary to make things happen."

DeLaVega. The first in his south Texas family to graduate from college, Jerry DeLaVega received a B.A. from Boston University and joined the staff of a Massachusetts state senator. Later, he continued his government career with the Economic and Employment Policy Administration. His last job before business school was managing a $10 million youth program for the Department of Labor in his home town of San Antonio. His family was very proud of his acceptance to Harvard Business School; therefore, graduating was his number one priority.

DeLaVega was very much a "process person." He strongly believed in building commitment through personal involvement. While he possessed an eye for detail and general management skills, these were overshadowed by his rapport with people. Sensitive and honest, he had a calming, motivating influence on others, he was good at smoothing ruffled feathers. While his unselfish nature made him a great team player, one never knew exactly what he was thinking—except when it concerned his family and their security.

Ishag. An Englishman, David Ishag had founded a company that provided touring services for visitors to England. With the substantial profits from that enterprise, he gained a law degree from the London School of Economics and later formed an import/export business in California which brought British tableware into the United States and sent electronic products to Britain. His international experience was consistent with his manner: sophisticated, arrogant, calculating, and keen. An instinctive gambler and born salesman, Ishag knew just how to strike a deal. A loner at heart, he thrived on action and loved making money. With his flamboyant style, he too, was not one to back down or accept no for an answer.

In class, Ishag often played devil's advocate, taking an outrageous position just to shake up his classmates or move the discussion to a higher level. To him, class—like business—was nothing personal.

See *Exhibits 2–4* for the resumes of the three Hot Rock principals.

THE START-UP

In May, the hard work devoted to the business plan began to pay dividends. Although MTV was successful in attracting millions of viewers and subscribing stations, the Warner-Amex joint venture was not yet profitable. It was difficult to sell the vast inventory of commercial time. Hot Rock's persuasive partners and slick documentation coincided with MTV's need for advertisers and opened the door. Wigley took the lead in negotiations that lasted three weeks.

MTV began by insisting on a six-month deal at a flat rate per commercial. Knowing that Hot Rock could not afford any fees now, nor fixed rates during the start-up, Wigley countered with a plan for MTV to accept a percentage of sales during the first six months. The two sides finally agreed to a percentage arrangement for three months (later extended) with a flat fee thereafter. For their six commercials per day, Hot Rock received exclusive privileges at a rate of 10 percent of gross sales, a substantial discount.

With MTV now on board, Hot Rock needed to raise money for inventory and working capital. A marketing case taught earlier in the year had described a local Boston bank—Coolidge Bank & Trust—as "aggressive and supportive of promising entrepreneurial ventures." The team made an appointment to meet with bank representatives. Unfortunately, the only available slot was on the afternoon after a final exam. Dressed in suits and ties, they rushed from their four-hour exam to the bank, armed with the MTV contract and the Hot Rock business plan. Following a professional presentation, the impressed bank officials awarded Hot Rock, Inc. an initial $25,000 line of credit. A week later, Hot Rock signed agreements with the major record labels. Through a private placement of 11% of company stock to family and friends, the partners raised $90,900. This offering, which was oversubscribed, valued the company at $8 million.

The next step was to select an advertising agency to conceive the commercials for the MTV spots. After taking suggestions from classmates and reviewing presentations, one agency stuck out in Ishag's mind. Saatchi & Saatchi had done an incredible job with Prime Minister Margaret Thatcher's rise to power in Britain and its promotion of British Airways in the United States. After a meeting in New York, Ishag negotiated their representation on the account, complete with deferred billings—until a time when Hot Rock could afford to pay. (*Exhibit 5* is an example of Hot Rock's print advertising.) DeLaVega took charge of operational necessities. A few days later an office and warehouse was leased in Woburn, an attractive location because of its proximity to Boston, low rents, and Cable TV. Naturally, the three wanted to monitor their ads and the MTV station.

The three partners relied on friends and family for more than initial start-up capital. Ishag convinced an award-winning London filmmaker friend to produce Hot Rock's first commercial. DeLaVega's wife assumed the role of customer service manager, while Wigley's wife became vice president of human resources in September, leaving a Boston company with a similar position. Wigley and his wife had worked together before at the record store and as house parents for a group home for behavior problem adolescents, and were very comfortable with the idea. DeLaVega privately had reservations. He hoped that friendship, trust, communication, and better judgment would help resolve any potential conflicts. Two of Wigley's good friends, James DeLay and Joe Sodd, came on board as vice president of operations and product manager, respectively. Another old friend also joined as assistant buyer, and Wigley's brother and two friends agreed to spend the summer handling operations and buying.

On the day before Hot Rock's first commercial would air, the phones had not been installed and there was no inventory. The phones made it in time for the first day's 2,000 calls but the inventory did not. The team, however, had a contingency plan for this event: filling orders by buying from wholesalers and local stores. The inventory arrived a few days later. Hot Rock kept its promise and delivered within one week of the initial orders via UPS.

Backroom HRM

Recalling the staffing responsibilities, DeLaVega remarked, "Luckily, Mike's wife Barb had a Master's in human relations so she took over that area completely. We told her what we needed: salespeople with musical knowledge. She delivered."

Ads in the Boston Globe such as, "If you like music call us, we have a job for you," attracted students from Berklee and other schools of music in the area, as well as an eclectic group of music lovers.

Once hired, the new employee was introduced (which always was followed by a round of applause) and then started a training program. In the beginning days of Hot Rock, the training was simple and quick: Role play a few scripts of hypothetical dialogue and then sit with a veteran (or one of the principals) to listen and learn for half a day. Then you were on your own.

As time passed, the training program became more sophisticated. After introductions, a new hire now received a training manual and time to read it. Next, a supervisor went over the manual and answered questions. Role-playing was followed by a stint with an experienced salesperson for a couple of days. Once on their own, the new employee was actively monitored by a supervisor for a few more days.

In the beginning all salespeople were on a straight salary. Later, however, the pay structure evolved to 70 percent in commissions after a period of adjustment. Other mechanisms for employee motivation included sales contests for albums, concert tickets, and weekend trips. Sporadic at first, the contests became a regular feature later on.

Wigley would also personally challenge some of the salespeople to selling contests. Even though he and the other principals had managerial tasks, they all worked the phones. In fact, Wigley consistently made the Top 10 in sales, which were posted monthly showing each employee's sales volume. At Hot Rock, everything was shared: the work, fun, and decisions. This relaxed, family atmosphere was probably in part responsible for the low employee turnover.

Because of the 24-hour operations, it was impossible to have a meeting with everyone present. Therefore, communications were primarily written and distributed in a rack of folders for each employee.

Growth Phase

MTV aired 24 hours a day, 7 days a week; Hot Rock thus operated 24-hour, 7-day weeks. The agreement for air time called for a 24-hour rotater schedule. Therefore, Hot Rock only had one day's advance notice as to when a commercial would run. With 24 incoming WATS phone lines, Hot Rock processed 3,000 calls per day average during the first four months. Volume swelled to 15,000 calls per day after six months.

As set forth in the business plan, Hot Rock's strategy was geared toward direct-response telemarketing. Statistics showed a conversion sales rate average of 60–80 percent of calls answered over a broad range of similar direct-response television marketeers. At a 60 percent sales/calls rate, Hot Rock's pro forma income sheet was highly profitable. Break-even was 10 percent.

As volume expanded, capacity was increased to handle the growth. Fixed costs rose as more equipment and staffing were needed. By November of 1983, the company had grown to 82 employees and revenues in excess of $200,000 per month.

At an executive meeting in mid-December, however, some interesting points were made and questions asked:

1. Sales had flattened, while call volume was dramatically increasing. Why?
2. Blockages (busy signals) were increasing. Should capacity be increased further?
3. Prank calls were increasing. Why? What could be done?

4. Even after attempts to hold down costs, the company was still losing money. Why?
5. How soon would the company need more money? How much?
6. Rapid growth had led to more formal reporting relationships and responsibilities. At what cost?
7. Ishag was experiencing severe burnout from his combination Hot Rock duties and second year at HBS. What should he do?
8. Direct mail marketing tests to date had been successful and profitable. How should the company proceed with this opportunity?
9. Overall management frustration brought on by the continual problems was high and company morale was low. What actions needed to be taken to fire up the troops and regain commitment?

As December waned and their friends at HBS worried about final exams, vacation plans, and second semester course schedules, the three partners focused on other matters. See *Exhibit 6* for Hot Rock's income statement and *Exhibit 7* for its balance sheet.

Exhibit 1 Hot Rock, Inc. (A), *Organizational Chart,* July 29, 1983

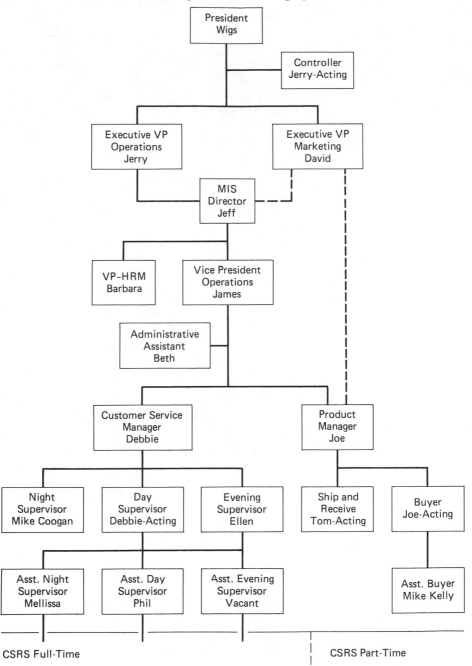

Exhibit 2

GERARDO DELAVEGA
9 Kensington Park #3
Lynn, MA 01902
(617) 581-953

education

present **HARVARD BUSINESS SCHOOL**   **Boston, MA**
Candidate for the Degree of Master in Business Administration, June
1986.

1974–1978 **BOSTON UNIVERSITY**   **Boston, MA**
B.A., Political Science, Cum Laude, Martin Luther King Award for
Academic Achievement.

experience

1980–1982 **DEPARTMENT OF EMPLOYMENT
AND ECONOMIC DEVELOPMENT**   **San Antonio, TX**
Program Manager. Monitored the implementation of six million dollars in program budgets; assured compliance with federal, state, and
local regulations.

1978–1980 **EMPLOYMENT AND ECONOMIC
POLICY ADMINISTRATION**   **Boston, MA**
Department Manager. Designed and implemented program review
procedures and policies. Conducted system integrity reviews, and internal investigations.

1977–1978 **MASSACHUSETTS STATE SENATE**   **Boston, MA**
Research Assistant. Summarized pending legislation for Judiciary
Committee Chairman.

November, 1985

Exhibit 3

DAVID ISHAG

2 Soldiers Field Park
Apartment 813
Boston, Massachusetts 02163
Phone: (617) 498-8771

Permanent Address:
17 The Drive
Wembley Park
Middlesex, England

education

1982–1984 **HARVARD GRADUATE SCHOOL
OF BUSINESS ADMINISTRATION**   Boston, MA
Candidate for the degree of Master in Business Administration in
June 1984. General Management curriculum in the first year. Second-year emphasis in marketing, real estate, entrepreneurship and
competitive analysis. Elected President of the Management Consulting Club.

1978–1981 **LONDON SCHOOL OF ECONOMICS
UNIVERSITY OF LONDON**   London, England
LLB.-Law Degree. Graduated with Honors. Specialized in Tort, Con-
tract, Property, Mercantile and Criminal Law.

business experience

1981–1983 **CROWN SILVER, INC.**   Los Angeles, CA
President. Handled formation, coordination and implementation of
policy. Company started early 1981. Imports British made silver flat-
ware. Distribution—national, through manufacturers' representatives.

1978–1983 **ZADEX INTERNATIONAL, LTD.**   London, England
Director and Chairman. Importer of electronics, dealer in general
import/export particularly with commodity goods to Africa and the
Middle East. Much of the day-to-day responsibilities during my absence were delegated. I primarily dealt with the creation and development of initial contacts as well as any major decisions in policy. Sold to
Inchstar Ltd., London.

1978–1979 **DEVEX-ASCOT INTERNATIONAL LTD.**   London, England
Director and Chairman. Company started in response to growing
demand from foreign visitors, particularly Middle Eastern, for a comprehensive service to meet their daily requirements, ranging from
entertainment guidance to house purchase. Proved extremely successful but time consuming. Sold to Dukes of London, England.

References furnished upon request.

October 1983

Exhibit 4

MICHAEL ROBERT WIGLEY
16 Mead Street, 3rd Floor
Allston, Massachusetts 02134-1140
(617) 254-8097

education

1985–1986 **HARVARD GRADUATE SCHOOL**
OF BUSINESS ADMINISTRATION   **Boston, MA**
Candidate for Master in Business Administration degree, June 1986.
First-Year Honors.

1978–1979 **STANFORD UNIVERSITY**   **Stanford, CA**
Bachelor of Civil Engineering Degree with Distinction; December
1978. **Bachelor of Science** Degree in Geology with Distinction; August 1978. Geology Field Camp Scholarship.

experience

1979–1982 **BATTELLE MEMORIAL INSTITUTE**   **Columbus, OH**
Manager-Design Analysis Group: Line responsibility. Managed and
marketed professional management and engineering staff with annual budget of $6.3 million.

Lead Project Manager: Staff position reporting to Divisional VP. Organized and directed three extremely successful special problem task
force groups, utilizing both internal and external personnel.

Project Manager: Line management. Performed engineering and scientific analyses.

1978–1979 **STANFORD GEOTHERMAL PROGRAM**   **Stanford, CA**
Research Assistant. Performed laboratory and numerical analyses.

1975–1979 **GROUP HOMES, INC.**   **St. Paul, MN**
Live-in Houseparent: Administered individual treatment programs
for ten behavior problem adolescents.

references Personal references available upon request.

November 1985

Exhibit 5

YOU'RE LOOKING AT
THE WORLD'S NEWEST
MUSIC STORE

Now for the first time ever, your telephone is also your personal music store.

Because now you can order any records or tapes you want *any time* simply by dialing 1-800 HOT ROCK. We have the world's largest music selection. And we'll deliver right to your door in less than one week.

Use Visa, MasterCard or American Express. With the holidays coming we'll even gift wrap your order. And with any 3 albums, we'll give you a free, very hot HOT ROCK T-shirt.

This is the number that's sweeping the nation: 1-800 HOT ROCK. Your 24 hour Music Store.

THESE HOT SPECIALS ARE NOW ONLY $6.99 EACH.

Dial 1-800 HOT ROCK
Your 24-hour Music Store

Exhibit 6 Actual Income Statement for Six Months Ending December 1983

	July	Aug.	Sept.	Oct.	Nov.	Dec.
Net Sales	$26,212	$52,962	$79,287	$213,217	$203,653	$202,483
Cost of Sales	15,287	29,659	42,283	101,319	94,699	93,976
Gross Margin	10,925	23,303	37,004	111,898	108,954	108,507
Operating Expenses:						
Rent	2,172	2,172	2,172	2,172	2,172	2,172
Salaries & Wages	16,025	26,235	32,573	61,015	66,504	47,705
Telephone	8,018	12,886	15,010	35,023	34,733	29,145
Advertising	2,067	13,030	8,620	64,354	90,197	70,254
Postage & Shipping	2,295	7,621	8,977	37,805	32,399	36,993
Other Expenses	3,432	7,968	8,059	10,830	13,965	14,256
Total	34,009	69,912	75,411	211,199	239,970	200,525
Income (loss) from operations	($23,084)	($46,609)	($38,407)	($ 99,301)	($131,016)	($ 92,018)
Taxes	10,070	21,394	17,667	45,678	60,500	42,331
Net Income (loss)	($13,014)	($25,215)	($20,740)	($ 53,623)	($ 70,516)	($ 49,687)
STATISTICS						
Expenses as a % of Net Sales						
Purchased Merchandise	58.32%	56.00%	53.33%	47.52%	46.50%	46.41%
Rent	3.74	4.10	2.74	1.02	1.07	1.07
Salaries & Wages	61.14	49.54	41.08	28.62	32.66	23.56
Telephone	30.59	24.33	18.93	16.43	17.06	14.39
Advertising	7.89	24.60	10.87	30.10	44.29	34.70
Postage & Shipping	8.76	14.39	11.32	17.73	16.15	18.27
Other Expenses	13.09	14.36	10.10	5.08	6.86	7.04
Total Gross Margin	41.68	44.00	46.67	52.48	53.50	53.59
Total Operating Expenses	129.74	132.00	95.11	99.05	117.83	99.03
Monthly Growth in Sales	—	102.05%	49.71%	168.92%	(4.49)%	(.57)

Exhibit 7 Actual Balance Sheet as of Six Months Ending December 1983

	July	Aug.	Sep.	Oct.	Nov.	Dec.
ASSETS						
Current Assets:						
Cash	$ 44,603	$ 29,627	$ 17,283	$221,394	$158,805	$116,537
Accounts Receivable	947	16,011	59,474	157,114	202,547	235,336
Inventory	17,700	35,537	40,785	121,413	220,591	173,371
Pre-paid expenses	467	1,246	896	727	558	1,065
Total	63,717	82,421	118,438	500,648	582,501	526,309
Non-Current Assets:						
Net Fixed Assets	56,062	56,184	65,533	72,368	89,241	89,143
Deposits	15,400	15,400	15,400	18,693	18,693	18,693
Organizational Costs	33,315	39,634	38,952	81,264	79,846	78,427
Total	104,777	111,218	119,885	172,325	187,780	186,263
Total Assets	$168,494	$193,639	$238,323	$672,973	$770,281	$712,572
LIABILITIES						
Current Liabilities:						
Accounts Payable	21,672	54,701	114,128	270,013	441,547	415,800
Payroll Payable	2,384	7,719	12,474	32,651	35,136	21,350
Taxes Payable	(10,070)	(31,464)	(49,131)	(94,810)	(155,310)	(197,640)
Bank Note—current	30,371	39,111	58,720	58,720	128,475	203,316
Other	0	0	0	0	14,500	14,500
Total	44,357	70,067	136,191	266,574	464,348	457,326
Non-Current Liabilities:						
Bank Note	27,251	26,551	25,851	25,141	24,141	23,141
S/H Note	5,000	30,350	30,350	28,950		
Total	32,251	56,901	56,201	54,091	24,141	23,141
Total Liabilities	76,608	126,968	192,392	320,665	488,489	480,467
EQUITY						
Common Stock	104,900	104,900	104,900	464,900	464,900	464,900
Retained Earnings	(13,014)	(38,229)	(58,969)	(112,592)	(183,108)	(232,795)
Total Equity	91,886	66,671	45,931	352,308	281,792	232,105
Total Liabts & Equity	$168,494	$193,639	$238,323	$672,973	$770,281	$712,572
STATISTICS						
Quick Ratio	1.07	0.68	0.58	1.43	0.78	0.77
Current Ratio	1.48	1.20	0.88	1.89	1.26	1.15
Working Capital	$20,552	$13,646	($16,460)	$235,368	$118,941	$69,765
Debt to Equity Ratio	0.67	1.41	2.48	0.32	0.54	0.97
Inventory Turnover	0.86	0.83	1.04	0.83	0.43	0.54

Catalyst Technologies

> I'm sort of a honeybee. I like to fly from flower to flower and pollinate them.
>
> Walt Disney as quoted by
Nolan Bushnell

> Nolan walks in the front door with that smile on his face and puffin' on that pipe, and it's like a whirling dervish walked in. People's hair stands on end. Their eyes get like saucers. And they flock around him like J.C. the Man just walked in.
>
> A formal Bushnell colleague

> My name is Nolan Bushnell, but I'm not God.
>
> Nolan Bushnell

NOLAN BUSHNELL

Nolan Bushnell, founder of Catalyst Technologies, has been described by more than one observer as the heir apparent to the throne left vacant by the death of Walt Disney. Bushnell has been involved in a wide range of post-1960s entertainment companies whose products and services range from videogames, to domestic robots, to add-on card sets for the Trivial Pursuit game that sported such novel titles as "Vices" and "Rich and Famous." Unifying most of Bushnell's business activities has been the desire to blend technology and entertainment values in startling, new, and unreservedly commercial ways.

Bushnell was born in Clearfield, Utah. He was educated at Utah State and at the University of Utah where he studied economics, engineering, philosophy, mathematics, and business. He spent summers in charge of the games department at a local amusement park. Turned down for a job at Disney, Bushnell moved to Santa Clara County, California, where he worked as an electrical engineer at Ampex.

Late at night, in a home lab carved out from his daughter's bedroom, Bushnell developed a videogame called Computer Space. In 1971, he incorporated himself, first under the name Syzygy, Inc. and subsequently as

This case was prepared by Associate Professor John Kao.

Atari. ("Atari" is a Japanese term from the game of "Go" which roughly corresponds to the concept of "check" in chess.) Bushnell then hit upon the idea for a videogame version of the classic game of ping pong. Pong was an overnight success. The fledgling Atari had sales of over $3 million in 1973 and it proceeded to grow by leaps and bounds as the videogame industry mushroomed.

Bushnell sold Atari to Warner Communications in 1976 for $28 million, a spectacular return on his initial $500 investment in his start-up. His personal net worth at the time was estimated at $15 million. A key condition of the sale bound Bushnell to a seven-year noncompetition agreement. In 1979 he was ousted from Atari because of "management differences."

Bushnell's life-style was fast and well publicized. Divorced in 1974, he took to flying around the country in his Lear jet and sailing on his yacht which sported the name Pong. He bought a 16-acre northern California estate equipped with riding stables, a swimming pool, and tennis courts. He also acquired homes in Paris and Aspen, Colorado. By the early 1980s, his net worth was estimated in the range of $70 million.

Bushnell's first major venture after Atari was Pizza Time Theatre, a concept restaurant chain founded in 1978, which expanded so rapidly that it twice made *Inc.* magazine's list of the 100 most rapidly growing companies. The concept for Pizza Time involved animated robots with names like Chuck E. Cheese, Pasqually, Jasper Jowls, and Madame Oink. Near the dining and theatre area stood the Fantasy Forest Game Preserve—a vast selection of arcade and amusement games. Patrons could play videogames with Chuck E. Cheese tokens while they waited for their pizza. They could also spend real money on an array of merchandise, including Pizza Time Theatre T-shirts, Chuck E. Cheese sunvisors, and theme toys. In 1980, the restaurants grew in number from seven to 88. Half were company owned, the rest were franchises. In 1981, sales were $36 million and the company went public, issuing 1.1 million shares at $15. Company growth continued. By 1982, there were 204 outlets in 35 states as well as Canada, Australia, and Hong Kong. The stock doubled in price. But in 1983, Pizza Times sales ran 20 percent lower in average store sales. Caught in the videogame slump and plagued by customer complaints about food quality, Pizza Time began to hemorrhage money, at a rate estimated by one business periodical as $20 million per month by the end of 1983. In March 1984, Pizza Time Theatre filed Chapter 11.

During this period, Bushnell was involved in numerous other projects in such areas as interactive videodisks and advanced videogame technology. But perhaps his fondest vision lay in the notion of "personal robots," the business of another Bushnell company, Androbot, which was the first company to be included under the Catalyst Technologies umbrella. Bushnell was quoted as saying:

> I'm mad for robotics! . . . Robots are good company. Nice to have somebody around the house. Suppose you're watching a football game on TV and you

don't want to walk into the next room to get your pipe or a beer. You don't
want to press a button for one of the servants, either. So you get the robot to do
it. And then there's the ego thing. Wouldn't you like someone to come into your
room in the morning and say, 'O great and omniscient one, are you ready for
your coffee?'

Bushnell predicted a "new Victorian era" whose civility and leisure would be a
direct result of the home robot revolution. Recommended by Merrill Lynch in
the summer of 1983 as a hot new issue, Androbot, was in a product
development phase and operating at a loss. Caught in the sea of red ink that
bathed the consumer electronics industry in general and the videogame
industry in particular, the offering was called off.

CATALYST

Nolan Bushnell started Catalyst Technologies in late 1981 with two partners
from his Atari days, Larry Calof and John Anderson. Bushnell was chairman
of Catalyst, Calof served as Catalyst's president, and Anderson as executive
vice president. Catalyst's goal was to provide start-up and development-stage
ventures with capital, essential services, management training, and suitable
facilities. This would decrease costs, increase speed, and avoid the pitfalls of
the business formation and development process. The following comments
came from the company's statement of concept:

> It has been the perception of the Principals that, in many cases, the primary
> reason many start-up and development-stage companies are unable to reach
> potentials which could be expected based solely on technological criteria, is the
> entrepreneur's lack of knowledge and experience in developing and managing a
> business. In many instances this lack of business acumen and experience alone
> may result in failure but, in any event, will be a source of distraction to the
> development team and may result in delays of six months or more in the
> development effort. In high-technology industries such delays often mean the
> difference between success or failure because companies that first introduce a
> new technology or product have a distinct advantage in the marketplace.
>   The traditional venture capital operating model does not adequately deal
> with these problems of the start-up or development-stage venture. In that model
> the venture capital investor provides equity or debt financing to a portfolio
> company and periodic advisory services, most frequently through representation
> on the board of directors or in periodic consultation. The day-to-day aspects of
> running and developing the business are left in the hands of the entrepreneurial
> group.
>   The Catalyst Technologies concept differs greatly from this traditional
> model, by providing on-site facilities and continuous on-site services and
> training. Substantially all Catalyst Technologies services and training are
> rendered in its own facility, which is occupied by the companies using its
> services. Thus, the Catalyst Technologies facility, located in a 50,000 square foot
> building in Sunnyvale, California serves as the incubator for start-up companies.
> It is intended that these companies will remain in the Catalyst Technologies
> facility until such time as they are ready to commence manufacturing, a period

expected to be 12 to 24 months, although Catalyst Technologies may continue to provide some services to a company even after it has moved to its own facilities.

The Principals believe that substantial benefits have been and will be derived from the close interaction of a group of very talented technologists under one roof. Although the companies using Catalyst on-site facilities and services remain separate entities, in many instances they encounter common technological and managerial problems in product development and are able to assist each other without the risk of losing control of proprietary information or aiding a competitor. This synergy of entrepreneurial talent with Catalyst experience, services and training substantially enhances the timing and effectiveness of the development efforts of all participating companies.

The Catalyst Technologies approach involves four general categories. First, Catalyst Technologies provides leased space on a short-term basis to start-up and development-stage companies. The space can be customized to the individual company's needs, including office use, product development and assembly of prototypes and preproduction units.

Second, Catalyst Technologies leases or arranges for the lease of equipment for its participating companies. Equipment which is likely to be used by a number of companies, such as test equipment and computers, is acquired by Catalyst Technologies and provided on a time-sharing basis. Specialized equipment is obtained directly for individual companies.

Third and most important, Catalyst Technologies provides extensive management, professional, and office services, consulting and training to its member companies. In addition to normal office services, such as secretarial assistance, telephone and duplicating facilities, the following consulting and training services are or will be provided.

- Accounting and financial statement preparation
- Personnel
- Purchasing
- Material control
- Engineering services (including engineering design)
- Business planning and strategy formulation
- Cash management
- Budgets and forecasts
- Contacts with professional service organizations
  accountants
  investment brokers
  attorneys
  banks
- Assistance in seeking additional capital
- Marketing and technical assistance
- Assistance in seeking additional management and facilities
- Engineering library

In addition, Catalyst Technologies provides on-site seminars and similar educational programs in order to train the management teams of the participating companies in many of those management skills which will continue to be their individual responsibilities and essential to their continued growth when they leave the Catalyst Technologies facility.

All facilities, equipment and services are provided to participating companies at rates that are generally below prevailing market rates in the area.

Finally, where they believe participating companies offer significant investment potential, the Principals participate in seed capital and later-stage financings for such ventures. The Partnership has been organized primarily to participate in such investment opportunities.

Bushnell described the process in the following terms:

No one has ever done this before because it's easier to simply invest and wait for things to happen. We think that the housing of a group of very talented people under one roof, and providing them with services they need, makes a tremendous amount of difference in product development. We think of the Catalyst as the ultimate incubator, or fertile environment, for the transformation of new ideas into tangible companies producing marketable products. Catalyst provides an environment in which the creative process is fostered and transformed into the productive process. Basically what we hope to accomplish here is to take talented people with good ideas and put them into a framework which can result in economic success.

Which Xerox-type machine do you buy? Well, a technologist can get fascinated with the intricacies and the engineering that go into the machines and spend three weeks making his decision. It'll be the right decision, but he'll spend too much time making it. Our product at Catalyst is essentially to provide the entrepreneurial team with the key to the door. They walk into their office and, lo and behold, there's a desk and a chair and a telephone system that works; there's a full accounting system, purchasing, receiving; there's a stack of papers on the desk; and when the leader gets through signing his name 35 times, he's incorporated, he's got employee benefit plans, he's got insurance, he's got the whole works, he's got his patent-secrecy forms—everything he needs—and he can devote his efforts to the development process as opposed to making mistake after mistake.

As of early 1985, Catalyst Technologies companies and alumni included Androbot; ByVideo, an interactive videodisk point-of-purchase promotion company; Timbertech, a sophisticated computer camp for children; Cinemavision, a large-screen television company; Axlon, which designed an unsuccessful data communications device but is now in the electronic toy business; IRO, a color consultation computer for cosmetology and fashion; and Etak, a company developing an on-board computer navigation system for cars.

LARRY CALOF

"The president's role at Catalyst is less function- than title-oriented. Catalyst is a proprietorship. It's the organization by which we provide the accounting, legal counsel, staff, and other services to our companies. Running it involves making sure we do things like billing and getting leases signed. It's an overall responsibility for administration. This kind of service company is at best a break-even operation. It is difficult to make the service organization profitable, unless you were setting up an incubator-type facility funded by the public sector for small, and not necessarily entrepreneurial, businesses. A lot of cities, for example, are taking some of the areas near universities which are run down, renovating buildings, and renting them out without providing much management help. We're up to something different here.

"How does Catalyst work? Assuming we've decided we're going to go forward with company X, we'll enter into a lease with them—a sublease of our space here. It will cover the space they need and allocation of common area space, basic telephone service and the related equipment, security service, the cost of reception, the Xerox machine, and other general types of services. They'll also enter into an agreement covering direct charges: long distance telephone charges, specific Xerox charges based on the number of copies they run, express mail. They'll probably enter into some sort of equipment lease with us. They can also get equipment from us directly if we have it around. We have scopes and other hardware, but they may need some specialized engineering equipment which we may be able to get for them. Then there will be a management services agreement that covers our providing management services to them—the four of us plus accounting and other general office services.

"We have about 20 people involved in Catalyst Technologies. We've got the management group: the four of us—Nolan, John, Perry, and myself. We then have an analyst level. Right now we only have one analyst, although we typically have had more than that. One is now running a division of Axlon and another has gone over to Etak, which is what we wanted our analysts to do. Since we don't have any other companies in the hopper now, we haven't replaced the people who have moved into operating roles. Analysts spend a lot of time working on business plans for the start-up companies. They look at business plans that come over the transom, that we may have an interest in investing in. They spend a lot of time in day-to-day liaison with the various companies, which is how they end up moving into operating roles. The next level we have is the accounting staff, which depends on how many companies we have. We will have anywhere from four to five up to eight people doing that. This level also involves handling Catalyst Ventures and other administrative matters around here, and accounting for Nolan as well. The rest are building people, the receptionist, and secretaries. At capacity, we have supported 10 companies with over 200 people in them.

"We have done some training and organizational work with our companies at Catalyst but not a great deal recently, primarily because we have shifted from the concept of developing the entrepreneurial engineer into the president, we now prefer to bring in somebody with the right skills and experience. We have worked to develop some skills in our entrepreneurs—accounting knowledge, protecting proprietary technology. We get somebody from our accounting firm or our law firm or just ourselves, and we hold a session for our people and videotape it, so it is available in our library.

"We are the management and the board, when we start one of these companies. When we originally started this process, we brought in a team of engineers, one of them would be president and we would monitor product development and provide general advice. We thought we could make good entrepreneurs. One of the things we found out is that, by and large, engineers or people with big company backgrounds may be pretty good at managing a development group, but they may not be the right CEO. We have made a number of changes in the senior management of our companies.

"When you bring in a professional manager to act as president and chief executive of a company, it can be a terrible ego blow for the founders. When we set up these companies, we said, 'Alright, you're president, but you're not really president. Don't get married to that title because you don't have the skills necessary for that, and we may need to bring in a businessman later to make this successful.' And our person said, 'Oh I understand, that's great.' Then it comes time to say 'You're no longer president.' And all hell breaks loose. So to get around that problem, when we brought in or built an engineering team around an idea, nobody in that team had the title or function of chief executive. We'd have Nolan or Perry or John or me in that role, it didn't matter who. We effectively were operating management and we controlled the company's board.

"Nolan, John, Perry, and I are also general partners of the Catalyst Venture fund. It is a limited partnership funded primarily by institutional investors. The fund is designed to invest, alongside the general partners, in seed-stage Catalyst companies. We each bring to it something a little different because we all have skills in different areas. We start Company A here and Catalyst Venture puts in money. Noland and the rest of us also put in money personally. Catalyst Technologies provides services, as a sole proprietorship, and money flows back to Nolan. So it's not quite in and out of the same pocket. Later rounds can vary, but the initial positions are equal, to avoid conflict of interest problems.

"We get a management fee which is capped and figured on the basis of net cost. So there's a minimum and a maximum. The maximum is based on asset value. We also have the normal carried interest. Our management fee is higher than most because we have a relatively small fund, a start-up fund. We're not trying to make the service organization a profit center. The profit for us comes from the capital gains we are going to make on our investments.

"We had some early losses. We've got two or three companies that look like they're on a growth curve. The fund has been in existence now for about a year. It was easy to cut out two or three companies in the beginning, and we've done that. We've aggressively written down the value of companies that were going in a direction that we weren't happy about. It's too early to tell about the ones we just started and invested in. If you project the numbers out based on where we are today, I think the fund is going to be significantly profitable, but it is not there yet.

"We're being conservative in doing any further investing in start-ups right now. We do provide our companies with a lot of assistance. When we get to the point where we've got something to show we put deals together for further financing. We have good contacts in the venture business. However, venture financing is tough to get today. In looking at the reasons why, it is necessary to examine the IPO market and the lower levels of current financing. The IPO market and the mezzanine round have disappeared for now. When the mezzanine round disappears, everyone in traditional venture capital has to put their money not only into the companies they've got trouble with, but into the ones that are doing well and need more working capital. They're not yet quite bankable, which would open up other capital sources from Europe, the Middle East, and major institutions here. There's a lot less capital available today, a lot less being allocated for first-round financing of companies by venture capitalists. There are two reasons for that: one, because their money is going to good companies that they wouldn't have otherwise had to finance; two, there are a lot of companies in trouble and that requires money, but more importantly—people, everybody is people short.

"You take a prototypical venture capital firm, five or six partners and 65 investments. Say you get fifteen companies, five in serious trouble and 10 wavering a little bit, and you've got to save them or kill them. That takes personnel. So you've got your staff trying to save what you consider worth saving and then kill a few. When you do that, you don't have people around who can do the analysis, due diligence, *and* spend time preparing to commit time to new companies. As a result, it's been very tough to raise second-round financing, and we've been reluctant in recent months to say we want to commit to a new business if we're going to have to turn to the venture capital community to provide that next round of financing. Right now, we believe that if later financing isn't going to be there, we're going to run into a brick wall. Obviously, these things do run in cycles.

"You've got to be able to fund your companies. We had one last year that we started that we thought had a tremendous amount of promise. It has developed an interactive cable television system, a good idea. We put the money in, got the prototype developed, and then the cable television industry had an awful year. We ran into a brick wall trying to finance it. We found an investor who's going to come in and take over, but everyone's going to suffer a tremendous amount of dilution. You've got to avoid doing that very often. Everybody's still excited about the technology, but you don't want to pour any more money into it unless you can see your way clear to profit. We were the only ones around to finance it, and we decided we weren't going to do it.

"You've got to have the team as well as the product well in place when you go for outside financing, but it's harder to draw the good people out to form these companies during a period of time when a lot of start-ups are going out of business and there's no clear window to leave a reasonably good job to come in and take some high risks. We take our people risks at the beginning of our companies, and that's something we feel pretty good about, because we're here and we can see what they're doing. But you've got to be able to pull people out of secure positions. There are a lot of people wandering around this valley who'd be happy to come in and do something, but are concerned about risks. The good engineers are easily employed, so it's tougher to get them during times when financing is more difficult, compared to what it was a year or so ago. You don't want to lose people, so you've just got to be more careful. Our fund is designed to put in that first $500,000 or

$750,000 and then get out, not in terms of liquidating our position, but not participating in any further financing. We've got our position, we'll take the dilution that we expect, and we go on with it. Then we do another deal. If we get into the situation where we've got to continue to finance one of those companies, then we run out of money. So, we want to make sure we're doing things in a fashion where we have as much assurance as we can that the second round will feed it.

"We've been hurt by Pizza Time and Androbot. The Androbot story rests on the fact that we believed that our underwriters could get us public. And I think that was realistic. When they pulled out, the offering was already oversubscribed at retail. But they didn't want to take it solely at retail. A lot of that had to do with their internal situation. Then part of it was that we were coming out just when Atari, TI, and Mattel announced their enormous losses. It blew the market out. We had been ready to go. We weren't delayed. We followed our time schedule almost down to the day. We cleared the SEC and were ready to go. If we had been able to do it quicker, conceivably we would have been out. Had Androbot been public, the stock may have been down in the dumps, because high-tech stocks went down that way. Androbot certainly had not performed, but it would have had $15 million, and it would have had time to get its products on the market. Instead, when that fell away, Nolan provided the financing and it became a scramble. Businesspeople do better when they can plan and avoid having to act in a completely scramble mode. That really changes the way you do business.

"Finding the people to make it happen is the absolute critical element for our business. One of the problems I think we had in Androbot was not enough engineering talent and not enough management of the engineering team. So we got a long way down the road and were not anywhere near where we ought to have been. I think the other thing we have learned is to look for open niches to create new technologies and new industries, or applications of existing technologies without having to do the kind of basic scientific research which increases market risk. Androbot is a clear example of that risk. ByVideo was another. You get an idea, and everybody says without any reservations it is going to happen. But all of a sudden we find ourselves three to five years ahead of the time that it will happen, either because of cost considerations or technology or markets. Building the market for something new is more difficult than many people expect. Pong and the videogame industry took off so fast that I don't think they provided realistic examples of what it takes to open a brand-new market. I think we have come to a realization that being early can be just as bad as not getting the technology there. I think those are our principal lessons."

JOHN ANDERSON

"I was in financial accounting at Atari. Then I moved into administration and eventually I was vice president of administration there. At Catalyst what I do here is mostly day-to-day administrative and financial operations. I spend a lot of time on financial transactions: banking relationships, managing assets. When you have things wrapped together in a sole proprietorship, you have to keep things separated and trackable. We are either starting or running or closing a business, or trying to figure out what we should do next. So it involves a continual review process. Right now, for example, there are three projects that I am giving a fair amount of my time to, trying to be like a shepherd of the projects. Perry has his projects. And Larry has his. I also act as liaison to the various companies that I have worked in or have responsibility for; I function as the chief financial officer. Our accounting department does the accounting for all the companies as well as Catalyst.

"We're always running out of cash. You're always running out of cash in the future; you always have a need to finance. I figure out the financial strategy. Then I figure out how we are going to get there and how we are going to justify it. Do we wait? Do we raise the price? Can we stretch it that long? Should we take our money now and make sure?

"We have an informal management group. No one runs it. Larry and I organize it. We run Catalyst. Nolan suggests and creates and strategizes the companies. We meet as needed and a lot of our work is done over the phone. Three of the four of us meet quite a bit. We don't sit down on a regular basis—maybe once every two weeks, when there are a couple of critical issues that need to be addressed. The four of us will sit down either here or at Nolan's house or mine. Nolan likes to have breakfast meetings at his house. Ultimately, Nolan makes most decisions, but he has to be informed of the pros and cons of what we are going to do.

"Most of what we do here is Nolan's idea, within some framework. Almost everything we have done here has been an internally generated idea from people who come on our staff, throw out a bunch of ideas, and then go off and form a company around it. Or ideas that we have kicked around on various fronts with various people. The time may be right and we like that person and that project and off they go. A case in point would be IRO. Larry, Nolan, and I were talking about it two years ago. What's hot? What is it that people are spending money on? What's new in the consumer world? What has high margins? People are interested in finding out what colors suit them best. What about the technology requirements? Maybe we could use a computer, we could wave around a wand. Having your colors done with a little bit of technology on some kind of a Mary Kay, Avon, Tupperware party basis—it seemed like a do-able business. We had a lady who'd worked with Nolan for several years who had a good perspective on design and fashion. She was working with another one of our companies called ByVideo. She decided that there weren't any opportunities for her there and wanted to do something on her own. Nolan gave her IRO. He said, 'Here, you got it. Here is what I want it to be. Let's get together once in a while. You need to decide on hardware. We've got to design the color scheme and the software. We have to think about how we are going to market this thing.' Unfortunately, she didn't run it as well as she could have. She's gone now, and we have someone else in charge who is reconfiguring the hardware and software, and getting the marketing effort off to an effective start. We are now making some money on this idea.

"People inventorying is an important concept. People are out there that have certain talents, people in our companies as well. We are able to assemble packages of people. For example, our trivia card project involved our being able to call in three or four strong marketing people, a couple of technologists, and a guy who used to be CEO of one of our companies.

"I'm not sure we have a formal conflict management procedure here. A traditional venture capitalist will go to board meetings and then on behalf of the company, talk to people from time to time. We have the advantage of being in the building; we know everybody who works for the company. We can walk through the room, every day, several times a day if we need, to just see what is going on. Is there a team here? Are they working in the same directions? Are they all off to lunch all day long? Or do they get in late and go home early? Is the guy who is supposed to be in charge, really in charge? Or is he just sitting in his room working on something else? Or is he dreaming about God knows what? All those incidents you don't see unless you are physically there. So our work is a daily process of constantly refining, redirecting, supporting, challenging, advising, strategizing. A lot of it relates to how the Catalyst notion is perceived by the various companies. Some are not very experienced. They may ask us a lot of questions that we may not have the answers to, but we discuss them. Or we bring somebody in who can give us input, from the inventory of people that are around. We are always bending over backwards to serve our entrepreneurs' needs. They don't stroke each other very often. Sometimes it is tough to keep them all happy.

"Our CEOs have autonomy. The companies are theirs to run. But we have an active role as well. 'You know, you don't seem to be really getting to where you are supposed to be going. What are your problems? Some technician isn't doing the job? Why don't you get rid of him?' Then you might suggest that he go talk with one of our other people who is hanging out upstairs with some office space working on their own project. Let's bring him down and pay him some consulting fees for a couple of days and see what the problems are. So Catalyst is constantly shifting, depending on which of its companies has the problems. We follow financials closely, but we don't want to strap a lot of administrative burdens on people. We have a lot of back and forth with our people.

"People look to Nolan for inspiration because he is perceived as having the answers, particularly on technical, marketing, and strategic topics. I am the answer man on financial matters. Larry is the answer man on negotiations and legal matters. Perry, when he is here, is the answer man in operational and marketing situations. Nolan is the ultimate answer.

"We've gotten rid of more than one or two CEOs. It is not easy. Our basic approach is to try to find the right people who can handle the challenge. We also have the pressure of external as well as internal financing, getting outside venture capitalists onto our company boards. We are becoming a little tougher; we will give you some time, but we won't give you forever. We may give less time than we did in the past. If it doesn't work out, we'll put you back in the inventory pool where you'll either be on salary to the company or to Catalyst in addition to retaining whatever equity interest you may have accumulated.

"Let's suppose I was to have an idea on the way to work. OK, I'm going to ask Nolan for $100,000. OK, I am going to move into an office. The first thing that happens is that we all meet the players and come up with a skeletal business plan. I hate the term; but it's needed. I prefer to call them executive overviews. What's the plan? What are we doing here? Who's going to develop the product? How are we going to market it? Lots of work goes to budgeting. What are the time constraints? What year do I plan to get things done in? How many critical tasks are there? What sequence do I have to accomplish them in? Do I have the production capacity? How can I take advantage of internal resources? There are a lot of people here at Catalyst who can be extremely useful to talk with. How are we going to organize all this? Are we going to do this as an R&D partnership? As a sub-S corporation? As a straight corporation? As a sole proprietorship? Then we structure the deal. How much do you own? How much do they? What are you going to keep in reserve? This can take several weeks. Then you come to a focus with a plan. We review the critical tasks. Gradually we work things out and come up with the people we need and the resources which we can't get in Catalyst itself.

"Facilitating internal communications in Catalyst is what we try to do—trying to get people together with other people. You never know who around here might really be able to help you. I spend a lot of my time just developing relationships, telling someone what another person is going to come to see them about. Encouraging someone to go see somebody and talk about what they are doing. Or helping people with their needs. We answer questions, prepare people, head them in the right direction or say, 'I don't know.' Or say, 'That's what you were hired for. You figure it out.' It's a good place to work. It isn't heavily and rigidly structured.

"So we capitalize the company—half ours and half venture funds at a seed level, maybe $60,000. Now we are going to put in a quarter of a million dollars. You don't have to worry about money here up to that amount. You do have to think about marketing expenses. Three million dollars? How do we get it? How much do we need to put in? Where can we get the rest? What should the valuation of the company be? Do we talk to R&D people? To venture capitalists? Almost always it winds up being venture capitalists. Which ones? Larry and I will make introductions, and build relationships. So the venture capitalists come in, stock is issued, people come on board, you get a lot of de facto outside consultants. You like to get good people on board. Then you have to deal with growth. More space. More equipment. We provide what is required. Another PC? Access to a VAX computer? Maybe we have some of that stuff around. Maybe someone is unloading equipment so we can buy it at a discount. What kind of people do you need? Do we have this person around at Catalyst? If not, can we get them?

"Sometimes things are quiet around here, sometimes they're not. But you can always sense the enthusiasm and energy. In part, it comes from just being here and getting the resources and advice you need. Making your own presence felt. We have lots of exchanges, occasionally arguments. We try to make sure that everybody knows everybody else. We used to have monthly meetings. 'Grand Council of Empire' is what we used to call it. All the company presidents would come for beer and to talk about anything. These meetings don't happen as often as they used to. Everybody got too busy for one reason or another. Our process has become a lot more informal.

"This building is full now. It was full before, but in between being full then and now, it was almost empty. Ideally you don't have everyone move out at once. It has happened that a company has returned to Catalyst. They may have moved out too early and then collapsed. One of the reasons they may have collapsed was because of this huge overhead they had to pay every month called rent. If they are here and they can't pay rent, we don't shoot them. After all, it is our money."

Managing Change at Lotus Development Corporation

> The people of Lotus, far more than anything else, have made the company what it is today—a very special place to work. We believe strongly that people count, and we are committed to fair treatment for all and the creation of opportunity for greatest professional growth and contribution.
>
> Mitchell Kapor, CEO and chairman,
> from *An Introduction to Lotus*, 1986

> We have a problem in this company. The problem is that we're too successful.
>
> Mitchell Kapor, CEO and president
> Lotus Company Meeting, 1983

From a humble beginning in the spring of 1981, Lotus Development Corporation in 1986 had emerged into adulthood as a leader in the personal computer software industry. In 1985, revenues of $225 million earned profits of $38 million and the company had a market value of approximately $400 million (assuming a share price of $25). (See *Exhibit 1*.) On February 21, 1986, the company announced a buy-back of up to 10 percent of its stock. (See *Exhibit 2*.) From a small, informal band of founders who included an ex-disc jockey and a former radical philanthropist, the company had grown to 1,160 people stationed around the globe whose dress and demeanor were the very essence of professionalism. (See *Exhibit 3*.)

This case describes Lotus' industry and company history, and then considers its approach to managing people and developing its organization.

LOTUS' INDUSTRY

The microcomputer software industry had grown with the proliferation and rapidly advancing price/performance ratio of personal computers. As the hardware technology increased in speed and flexibility, more sophisticated software applications were possible. The introduction of the IBM 16-bit personal computer (PC), and its significant penetration of the personal

This case was prepared by Associate Professor John Kao.

Copyright © 1986 by the President and Fellows of Harvard College. Harvard Business School case 9-487-036.

computer market, created a large market for IBM compatible software. (See *Exhibit 4* for software product market share data.)

In this evolution Lotus perceived an attractive opportunity; there was no integrated software package targeted to the productivity needs of business and professional users (or soon-to-be users). Its package, *1-2-3,* was developed to serve these productivity needs and to take advantage of the new generation of speedy and powerful 16-bit computers.

LOTUS COMPANY HISTORY

Mitchell Kapor, founder and chairman of Lotus, first thought of an integrated software package—one combining spreadsheet, graphics, and database—in 1981 while using an Apple II. Creating software programs was not something new for Kapor. As a student at MIT's Sloan School of Management in 1979–1980 (he earned three-quarters of an MBA before business interests pulled him away), he created Tiny Troll, a program that allowed microcomputers to convert the mainframe financial modeling program Troll. At this time he created a company called Micro Finance Systems, Inc. (MFS), to develop and market Tiny Troll. He left school, moved to Sunnyvale, California, and became a contract software writer. Subsequently, he developed another graphics-oriented program called VisiPlot/VisiTrend (later renamed VisiTrend/Plot). Quickly tiring of the Silicon Valley scene, Kapor moved back to Boston, continuing as a contract writer, yet eager to build MFS into a viable software development business.

In May 1981 Kapor hired Janet Axelrod as MFS's first employee. By July, the VisiTrend/Plot program sales started to boom, generating substantial royalties. In the fall, Kapor sold VisiTrend/Plot to VisiCorp for $1.5 million and used some of the proceeds to create Lotus Development Corporation. The idea was not to design software—he had done that—but rather to create a major company based on an advanced product and technology.

During the summer of 1981 Kapor met Jonathan Sachs, a programmer who was developing sophisticated spreadsheets, and hired him to work on an integrated productivity tool. The result, *1-2-3,* was introduced at a New York press conference in October 1982, demonstrated at a trade show in Las Vegas in November, and shipped on January 26, 1983. Instantly becoming the number-one-selling business software package, *1-2-3* had stayed on top ever since. In that first year of sales, Lotus earned $14 million on revenues of $33 million.

Subsequent Lotus products included *Symphony,* a multifunction upscale package and *Jazz,* an integrated package for the Apple Macintosh, as well as French and German versions of *1-2-3* shipped from a new Dublin manufacturing facility. A Japanese version was due out in 1986.

In 1985 Lotus acquired Dataspeed, of San Mateo, California, formed the Lotus Information Network Corporation, and announced that unit's first product, Signal, in October. Signal received market quotations via FM radio and fed them into *1-2-3* and *Symphony* spreadsheets. (See *Exhibit 5* for an official company history.)

MANAGING GROWTH AT LOTUS

By 1986, the evidence of growth was everywhere. Kapor described the process as somewhere between "hypergrowth" and mere "explosive growth."

Outgrowing an obscure basement location in Cambridge, Massachusetts, the company was now housed in several offices in the Cambridge Kendall Square area; a building that it had renovated on First Street, the Badger building, and its Smith Place facility. In April 1985, the company moved into a large new building on the banks of the Charles River, "The Lotus Development Building." Dominating the Kendall Square skyline, the building felt "huge" to many employees who lost the sense of company growth into space "wherever we could get it." "Office consciousness" increased, with limited space allocated by need, based on a rule of 50 percent in offices and 50 percent outside in cubicles.

In addition to its Cambridge facilities, the company had sales offices in New York, Chicago, San Francisco, Los Angeles, Dallas, Atlanta, Seattle, Washington, D.C., Detroit, Houston, Philadelphia, and Cleveland. It also had a marketing presence in London, Munich, and Paris, as well as manufacturing facilities in Puerto Rico and Ireland.

While the company still maintained the custom of regular staff meetings and preserved such customs as introducing new people at these meetings, it now had to rent a ballroom at the nearby Sonesta Hotel to fit in all of its employees.

There were also changes in company leadership. Kapor, the company's founder, became chairman and CEO with responsibilities for overall company direction and new product development through the chairman's Research and Development Group. Jim Manzi, former McKinsey consultant and Lotus vice president of marketing, became president and COO. (His management style is illustrated in memos included as *Exhibit 6*.) A number of founders and insiders, including Jonathan Sachs and Meade Wyman, were gone. (For further background on the founders of Lotus, see the case "Janet Axelrod.")

The company was reaching out for a new sense of identity to keep pace with its growth and success. Attempts to focus this new sense of the organization included such notions as "paradox, loose, tight, diversity, focus, adult, bottom line, enable, building, mean and lean, clarity." These focus themes had originated from Kapor who was concerned about developing a respect for structure and procedures as the vehicle for individual freedom and responsibility at the company. It was a process, as he put it, of providing the "skeleton for the flesh." One Lotus insider described this search for identity as the signs of growing up and of instilling discipline.

In 1985, the company had developed a "Lotus Corporate Values Statement." Vice presidents had direct reports about perceptions of core company values, and then had worked with Kapor through a series of management meetings to develop a values credo which was finalized in tasteful poster form. (See *Exhibit 7*.) But not every employee or organizational need could be satisfied at all times. And this was difficult in light of the company's traditional concern for people.

THE HUMAN RESOURCES FUNCTION AT LOTUS

Human Resources at Lotus also reflected the larger organizational changes. In 1986, it was a department consisting of 23 people. Janet Axelrod remained vice president of Human Resources Management (HRM) with a direct reporting relationship to the president and a continuing personal relationship with the chairman. Reporting to her were four functions. These were:

1. A human resources manager with responsibility for the company's employee database, compensation and benefits, human resource information system, and recruiting. Reporting to this manager were a compensation and benefits manager, to whom reported a compensation analyst and a benefits administrator. This group also included several recruiters and one administrative assistant, and an administrative supervisor with several database administrators providing support for the entire organization.

2. An employee relations manager. Reporting to this person were two employee relations representatives, an administrative assistant, and a training manager who was supported by two assistant trainers. The training functions' first responsibility was developing a "Managing at Lotus" seminar. Held over a period of five days offsite, the course trained managers in interpersonal and supervisory skills. Groups of 12 to 20 people were included in each session. It was intended ultimately that all 160 Lotus managers would take the course. Other course offerings focused on business writing and interviewing skills. Efforts were also underway to help employees "manage diversity." The company felt it was important to consider explicitly the implications and challenges of having a highly diverse work force. Employee relations was also responsible for a company attitude study, a study of management succession, and organizational development.

3. A special projects manager. This person had been with the company since its beginning. She had responsibility for such areas as policy manual development, company parties, the Lotus jacket program, the company newsletter, employee sports events, a lunchtime program, the aerobics program, diet programs, and a Smokenders program.

The jacket program was an example of a special Lotus custom. New employees, once they had passed a three-month probationary period, were given a "sharp" satin jacket with "Lotus" stitched on its back. The jacket program was highly popular but ended, due to its cost, when the company had reached 500 employees. (These handmade jackets cost $90.00 each.) Examples of special events included such celebrations as parties at Spit, a local new-wave nightspot in Boston.

4. Grants administration. This person administered the Lotus philanthropy programs in cooperation with a philanthropy committee drawn from employees around the company which voted on grants of software and money to deserving organizations.

The philanthropy program brochure stated, "We at Lotus believe that success is most satisfying when it is shared, particularly with those who have been denied equal opportunity and, as a result, have been unable to achieve their full potential." Lotus' philanthropy program involved an annual allocation by its board of directors; it included software donations and project grants with a focus on either computer-related skill transfer or antiracism themes. Awards were given out three times per year. Lotus also had a policy of matching, two for one, donations by Lotus employees to nonprofit tax-exempt organizations up to a maximum Lotus contribution of $200 per employee, per year.

A great deal of communication were the norm in the human resources department. Axelrod met with her direct reports for at least two hours most Friday afternoons. Every other week there were meetings of the recruiters and administrative staff, and employee relations reps met weekly. Every quarter the department would go out to dinner. Sometimes informal lunches were organized.

The emphasis on communication extended to the rest of the organization. One of the more unusual methods HRM developed to encourage informal communication within the company was the Lotus "grapevine system." An extension of the suggestion box idea, the grapevine gave every employee a vehicle for communicating in writing to any other person in the company on any topic. Forms were available which could be "posted" in grapevine collection boxes. The "grapes" would then be distributed to the appropriate recipient. "Grapes" could either be signed or anonymous. For a time, the company had an informal award, such as a bottle of wine, for the "grape of the week" which would be circulated throughout the company. Selection criteria included whether a "grape" was brilliant, could be implemented, or was well thought out. The grapevine provided a sensitive barometer to company mood. New or controversial initiatives in the company might be greeted with a barrage of "grapes" to offer advice or express concern or give encouragement.

The company also maintained an employee referral program. Thirty percent of Lotus employees were said to have been referred by other employees. The company paid a bonus of $500 for each new employee who stayed with the company at least 90 days. (See *Exhibit 8*.) A popular T-shirt at the company, developed for the program, read, "Good fortune is worth sharing."

EMPLOYEE BENEFITS

The company administered a wide range of employee benefits. Lotus was self-insured because it wanted to provide maximum benefits without restriction. Insurance benefits included without charge: life insurance and accidental death insurance at 2½ times salary with a $50,000 minimum, short-term disability at full salary up to four weeks, 67 percent until 90 days at which time long-term benefits would apply, and long-term disability equal to 67 percent of salary until age 65.

The company's medical plan was also comprehensive. Coverage, at no charge, provided for choice of one's own physician, and second opinions, with deductible. Specific medical coverage included one annual physical, up to $200; office and home visits, up to $200; hearing plus equipment; vision plus equipment; prescription drugs subject to a $1 deductible; mental health benefits at 80 percent and a generous dental plan.

A tuition reimbursement program covered two courses per semester, books, and fees, again without charge. Vacation times could be taken after six months and amounted to three weeks per year on an accrual basis. The company covered 12 paid holidays, five personal days, and five sick days. Other company benefits included two paid memberships in professional organizations, free parking if available on a seniority basis, and a subsidized Mass Pass $48/month for public transportation.

The company offered a pension program with vesting in four years as well as profit sharing (5 percent of the company's gross income in 1984). The company also had a $401,000 deferred compensation scheme (before tax money), whereby Lotus matched .25-1 percent up to 7 percent of annual salary.

The company was committed to the concept of child care. It worked through a child care information and referral service, provided by the Child Care Resource Center (CCRC), a local independent nonprofit organization. This organization maintained a database on 3,000 child care providers licensed in eastern Massachusetts. Interested employees could receive free personal consultation and referral services by appointment. The company also made available to its employees a detailed educational brochure called "How to Select Child Care" which was prepared by CCRC.

Lotus employees were eligible for participation in a sophisticated credit union, the PCU Federal Credit Union System. (See *Exhibit 9*.)

Lotus created an Affirmative Action Advisory Committee (AAAC) with the goal of "providing a diverse work environment that encourages everyone to grow and succeed." The committee was made up of employees from a wide range of company positions. Its mandate was "advising and implementing policies, procedures and/or programs that reinforce Lotus' corporate values." In addition, the AAAC was to work with the human resources department in "developing and implementing effective recruitment, hiring and training programs, as well as responding to all affirmative action/equal employment issues and concerns of any Lotus employee." Other projects of AAAC as of 1985 included (1) a recruitment outreach program aimed at minority candidates; (2) a Lotus scholarship program supporting minority students in engineering programs, (3) a summer youth employment program; (4) sensitivity seminars on multicultural issues; (5) a community service program that would support organizations fostering racial harmony, crime prevention, aid for the poor, homeless, and battered; and (6) a program seeking credible minority vendors to work with Lotus.

AN ORIENTATION TO LOTUS

By its own description, the company did a "reasonable" job of assimilating new employees. How were Lotus new employees received on their first day of the job? An actual account follows.

The Lotus building's formidability, somewhat heightened by ground-floor security guards and a strict sign-in procedure was quickly eased by the warm greeting of the new employee's supervisor. Traveling the elevators, walking the halls, or just observing people in the cafeteria, one was struck by the happy, and pleasant atmosphere. People were smiling and friendly, and it was not insincere.

After a personal escort to their new locations, coffee, and introductions to fellow workers, the new hires were again escorted to the orientation conference room on the fourth floor and introduced to the employee information officer who was leading the orientation (one of four who rotate). The room was a mix of comfortable, functional elegance; the chairs and other furniture and fixtures, like the rest of the building's contents, are custom designed and built.

When all scheduled attendees were present, the meeting began with the showing of a film called *Working On Lotus,* a company portrait of the people who are Lotus. A well-made film with a jazzy score, it started orientation off with an upbeat note. New employees were then asked to introduce themselves and to tell where they would be working. Then necessary forms were handed out and explained. The pace of the meetings was not at all rushed, and the overall atmosphere was friendly, relaxed, and helpful. Even though this orientation leader repeated this process continually, she did not appear bored.

A handbook called *The User's Guide to Lotus* was given to each person. A three-ring binder, this book, not unlike a software user's manual, could easily accommodate updates and changes. The guide included such items as a brief history on Lotus, letters from the chairman, president, and vice president of human resources, and information about the company. (See *Exhibit 10.*) The book also covered benefits in great detail.

The orientation leader reviewed all the benefits, which are substantial. She even went so far as to tell the people in attendance if they thought of anything that was not covered to let her know, because Lotus wanted to cover every possible need of their employees.

After the benefits review, each person was asked to read and sign their employee agreement (*Exhibit 11*). Next, the leader talked about the Lotus philanthropy program and the Affirmative Action Advisory Committee. At this point, a person from pension and profit sharing briefed the newcomers on Lotus programs.

The orientation lasted about an hour and a half. But before the leader escorted the new employees to get their I.D. badges, she presented everyone with a gift—a Lotus key chain.

Exhibit 1 Consolidated Operating Statements

CONSOLIDATED STATEMENTS OF OPERATIONS
(In thousands, except per share data)

	THREE MONTHS ENDED	
	December 31, 1985	December 31, 1984
Net revenues	$71,847	$50,432
Income before provision for income taxes	19,708	18,915
Provision for income taxes	8,294	7,113
Net income	$11,414	$11,802
Net income per share:	$0.70	$0.73
Weighted average common shares and share equivalents outstanding	16,341	16,194

CONSOLIDATED STATEMENTS OF OPERATIONS
(In thousands, except per share data)

	TWELVE MONTHS ENDED	
	December 31, 1985	December 31, 1984
Net revenues	$225,526	$156,978
Income before provision for income taxes	67,403	65,538
Provision for income taxes	29,253	29,492
Net income	$ 38,150	$ 36,046
Net income per share:	$2.31	$2.24
Weighted average common shares and share equivalents outstanding	16,532	16,065

Exhibit 2 (Reprinted Courtesy of *The Boston Globe.*)

Lotus plans buyback of up to 10% of stock

Lotus Development Corp., the Cambridge software company, said yesterday it will buy back up to 1.65 million shares, about 10 percent, of its outstanding common stock.

The company's strong cash position and relatively weak stock price were the chief factors behind the buyback, said Lotus spokesman Bruce Rogers. Lotus had about $90 million in cash and its equivalent at the end of 1985, Rogers added.

Wall Street analysts agreed with Lotus' assessment that its stock is undervalued, and investors apparently were heartened by Lotus' announcement, as the company's stock closed at 24¼, up 2¼, on the over-the-counter market yesterday.

"I'd be more comfortable with it at about $35," said Curt A. Monash, a securities analyst with Paine Webber Mitchell Hutchins in New York.

Lotus is considered underrated because it is viewed as a one-product company, its software primarily functioning as spread sheets for personal computers. But Lotus has superior technology on the way, Monas said, and much of the earlier skepticism resulted from the inability of Lotus' Jazz and Symphony software to eclipse the success of its popular 1-2-3 program.

In its most recent quarter, which ended Dec. 31, Lotus posted sales of $71.85 million, a 42 percent increase over the previous year, but earnings of $11.41 million, yielding a 3 percent decline. The lower earnings chiefly resulted from a writeoff that the company took for promoting its Jazz software, analysts said.

GREGORY A. PATTERSON

Exhibit 3   The User's Guide to Lotus—Structure

ORGANIZATIONAL STRUCTURE

The company at this time is organized with four departments and four divisions, each headed by a vice president who reports directly to the president, and a research and development group that works directly with the chairman of the board.

CHAIRMAN'S RESEARCH AND DEVELOPMENT GROUP

Departments

Corporate Communications
Corporate Public Relations
Creative Services
Investor Relations
Trade Shows and Special Events

Finance and Operations
Data Processing
Finance and Administration
   Budgets and Analysis
   Control
   Corporate Policies and Procedures
   Library
   Treasury
Legal Counsel
Operations
   Corporate Services
   Manufacturing
   New Products
   Production
   Security

Human Resources
Compensation and Benefits
Corporate (Philanthropic) Giving
Employee Relations
Employment
Training

Sales and Service
Customer Support
Regional Sales (New York Region)
Regional Sales (West/New England Region)
Sales Operations
Sales Planning
Technical Marketing
Training

Divisions

Business Products Division
123/Symphony Development
Documentation
Jazz Development
Manufacturer Relations
No Comment Development
Product Marketing
Product Planning
Quality Assurance Testing
Technical Marketing

Engineering and Scientific Products Division
Marketing Programs
Product Marketing
Product Planning and Development

Information Services Division
Information Services Development
Lotus Information Network Corporation

International Division

Lotus Publishing Division
Circulation
Editorial
Production
Promotion

September, 1958

Exhibit 4   Software Product Market Share Data

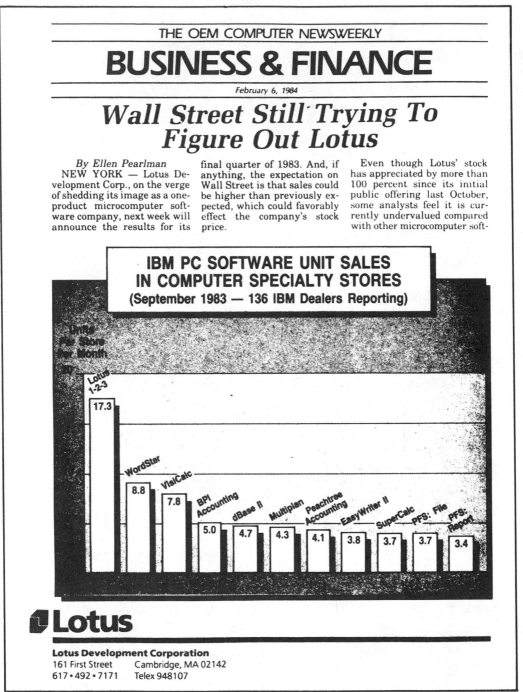

THE OEM COMPUTER NEWSWEEKLY

BUSINESS & FINANCE

February 6, 1984

Wall Street Still Trying To Figure Out Lotus

By Ellen Pearlman

NEW YORK — Lotus Development Corp., on the verge of shedding its image as a one-product microcomputer software company, next week will announce the results for its final quarter of 1983. And, if anything, the expectation on Wall Street is that sales could be higher than previously expected, which could favorably effect the company's stock price.

Even though Lotus' stock has appreciated by more than 100 percent since its initial public offering last October, some analysts feel it is currently undervalued compared with other microcomputer soft-

IBM PC SOFTWARE UNIT SALES IN COMPUTER SPECIALTY STORES
(September 1983 — 136 IBM Dealers Reporting)

Units per Store per Month

Lotus 1-2-3	WordStar	VisiCalc	BPI Accounting	dBase II	Multiplan	Peachtree Accounting	EasyWriter II	SuperCalc	PFS: File	PFS: Report
17.3	8.8	7.8	5.0	4.7	4.3	4.1	3.8	3.7	3.7	3.4

Lotus

Lotus Development Corporation
161 First Street   Cambridge, MA 02142
617 • 492 • 7171   Telex 948107

Exhibit 5   The User's Guide to Lotus—History

A BRIEF HISTORY OF LOTUS

July, 1978

Mitch Kapor, now chairman of Lotus's board and chief executive officer, buys an Apple® II and begins tinkering with software and microcomputers. Feeling that micros are the challenge he has been looking for, he becomes a founding member of the Boston Computer Society.

1979–1980

Mitch enrolls in MIT's Sloan School of Management, having decided he wants to write software. During his coursework there, he uses "Troll," a mainframe financial modeling program. Mitch writes a software program that will convert Troll for use on a microcomputer. He forms Micro Finance Systems, Inc., to develop and market "Tiny Troll," a business graphics package written for the Apple computer. Personal Software, Inc. (PSI), the company that would later become VisiCorp, publishes it. Mitch makes the decision to leave school and become a contract software writer for Personal Software, in Sunnyvale, California.

Spring, 1980

Mitch begins development of another graphics-oriented program, called VisiPlot/VisiTrend, that is of great interest to PSI. They strike a deal with Mitch to distribute it. He discovers that he and Silicon Valley don't mix and that, more importantly, he wants to be his own boss.

Spring, 1981

Mitch moves back to Boston, but continues working as a contract writer with VisiCorp and finishes what is finally named VisiTrend/Plot™. Using his royalties from the product, Mitch sets to work building Micro Finance Systems (MFS) into a viable software development business.

May, 1981

Janet Axelrod becomes MFS's first employee, joining Mitch as office manager/Jack of all trades. Ezra Gottheil (as of 7/85 a member of the Chairman's Research and Development group) and Celia Hollander (Documentation) join the company's staff soon thereafter.

July, 1981

VisiTrend/Plot begins to sell, generating substantial royalties. Mitch meets Jon Sachs, who is developing a spreadsheet compatible with an idea that Mitch is working on for an integrated productivity tool (later to become 1-2-3®). Jon joins the group to work with Mitch on design of the new product.

Exhibit 5   The User's Guide to Lotus—History (*Continued*)

Fall, 1981

Mitch sells his right to VisiTrend/Plot to VisiCorp and uses some of the proceeds to start what is officially to become Lotus Development Corporation. (The company's name is Janet's idea.)

As a sideline, Mitch begins Professional Software Technology to publish the products created by Micro Finance Systems.

April, 1982

Ben Rosen, a venture capitalist with Sevin, Rosen, Partners, Ltd., shows support and interest in Mitch's product ideas.

Rosen's group, along with Kleiner, Perkins, Caulfield and Byers invest $1 million in Lotus. The company incorporates as Lotus Development Corporation. Mitch begins discussing his idea for an integrated software product with IBM.

June, 1982

The now sixteen employees that comprise Lotus outgrow their Cambridgeport office space and move to 55 Wheeler Street in West Cambridge.

Mitch sells Professional Software Technology, the company formed to publish Lotus products, and Lotus begins to do its own publishing.

October, 1982

1-2-3 is introduced at a press conference at New York's World Trade Center in the first major Lotus public event.

November, 1982

The first hands-on product demonstrations of 1-2-3 are held at Comdex™ in Las Vegas. Lotus sends half its 32 employees to the show to help introduce 1-2-3 to the industry and to the world.

December, 1982

Crown Associates joins Sevin, Rosen, Partners in a second round of venture financing of $3.7 million.

Lotus contracts with McKinsey and Company to provide management and organizational consultation. The team includes Jim Manzi, who consults with Lotus for about three months. Mitch, recognizing a good thing when he sees one, begins negotiating for Jim to join Lotus on a permanent basis.

January 26, 1983

1-2-3 is shipped on time, as promised, by 34 employees.

Exhibit 5   The User's Guide to Lotus—History (*Continued*)

Lotus's commitment to innovative marketing materials begins with the Lotus Dealer Preview Kit (created by Marv Goldschmitt and Joyce Bartlett), sent to 1,000 dealers before 1-2-3 ships to give them a preview of the product and its capabilities. The kit includes instructions for copying the Tutorial diskette and distributing it to prospective customers.

March, 1983

1-2-3 becomes the number one (best-selling) business microcomputer package. It has stayed at the top of the charts ever since.

May, 1983

Jim Manzi joins Lotus as director of Marketing, where he focuses on building a strong sales and service organization and on creating Lotus's unique marketing strategy.

June, 1983

Lotus ships a new release (Release 1A) of the IBM version of 1-2-3. Although it includes only a few new features and the list of supported devices for graphics output is expanded, the main point of the release is a code reorganization that allows 1-2-3 to be ported more easily to other machines.

September, 1983

Lotus international operations gets underway with the creation and shipment of a version of 1-2-3 adapted for the United Kingdom.

October, 1983

Lotus goes public, offering 2.6 million shares of stock at $18 per share. The stock is traded on the NASDAQ national market. In 1983, Lotus earns $14 million on sales of $53 million.

February, 1984

The second major Lotus product, Symphony®, is announced at a press conference at the Hotel Pierre, in New York.

Symphony combines spreadsheet, word processing, business graphics, forms-oriented database, and communications in one package. Other features include window management and a command language. The program is designed to be open-ended, allowing third party developers to produce application packages (add-ins).

Symphony is demonstrated to the public at Softcon, in New Orleans, where we also offer a sneak preview of Jazz™, a product for the Apple® Macintosh™ computer. Jazz combines many of the features of 1-2-3 and Symphony.

Exhibit 5   The User's Guide to Lotus—History (*Continued*)

May, 1984

At Comdex®, Lotus announces that it will discontinue its Corporate Accounts Program, through which it sold directly to volume purchase end users. Lotus now relies on a network of key dealers to sell to such accounts, though the company itself continues to supply support and training services directly, as well as through our dealers.

June, 1984

Symphony ships, again on time as promised. Market acceptance of the product is very favorable, keeping Symphony consistently at the top of the charts.

October, 1984

The Lotus Board of Directors announces the appointments of Mitch Kapor as chairman and chief executive officer, and Jim Manzi, previously vice president of Marketing and Sales, as president and chief operating officer.

November, 1984

Lotus receives the award for Product of the Year from Softsel for Symphony, repeating the 1983 accomplishment, when Lotus received the award for 1-2-3.

December, 1984

Oxfam/America and the Christian Relief Development Association receive Lotus's first Philanthropy Committee donation, $10,000, to help fund a locally organized effort to send a planeload of supplies to famine victims in Ethiopia.

February, 1985

Jim Manzi announces a reorganization that includes the formation of the Sales and Service department that covers all field activity and customer support and service, the Marketing department that includes technical marketing and all product marketing, and the entirely new Engineering and Scientific Products Division.

Lotus sets up an alliance with Arity Corporation in Concord, Massachusetts, founded by Peter Gabel and three other former Lotus software developers. The company is working to develop business software for personal computers that uses artificial intelligence.

Former Lotus software developer Ray Ozzie and his newly formed software company, Iris Associates, Inc., agree to develop a new line of integrated business software, giving Lotus exclusive rights to license, market, and support Iris products.

Exhibit 5 The User's Guide to Lotus—History (*Continued*)

March, 1985

In an ongoing effort to form strategic alliances with other companies, Lotus announces it will work with Cullinet Software, Inc., makers of mainframe software, to provide a much-needed software link between mainframes and personal computers. Symphony Link™, developed by Lotus, and Cullinet's product (to be developed), joined with mainframe software, will connect Symphony to a mainframe.

April, 1985

Lotus begins cracking down on "gray marketers," the unauthorized resellers and mail-order houses that deplete software sales.

With the introduction of serial numbers on our products and distributors providing Lotus with lists of authorized dealers, the Sales department begins tracking and policing product sales in unauthorized channels.

A major step is taken toward diversification when we sign a letter of intent to acquire Dataspeed, a company that makes products to distribute real-time financial data. One such product is a small, hand-held device that broadcasts stock and futures trading via FM band radio frequencies. The second product sends the financial information directly to the subscriber's personal computer. Lotus and Dataspeed begin working on a software program that will feed financial information directly into 1-2-3 and Symphony spreadsheets and automatically recalculate the value of the user's portfolio.

In addition, Lotus announces acquisition of Software Arts, which includes purchasing VisiCalc®, TK!Solver®, an engineering equation program, and Spotlight®, a desktop management product. Daniel Bricklin and Bob Frankston, co-creators of VisiCalc and founders of Software Arts, join the company after the merger to work with Mitch in his Chairman's R&D Group.

May, 1985

We attend Comdex ready to show the business world that we are successfully positioning Lotus in a newly expanded role in the information industry.

Expansion to the Far East becomes a reality when we sign a letter of intent with Kanri Kogaku Kenyusho Ltd., a Japanese software company, to form a long-term development partnership. The company will work with Lotus to translate our products into Japanese.

May 16th is an important day for Lotus as the one-millionth package of software, a package of 1-2-3, rolls off the line at the distribution center and is presented to Massachusetts Governor Dukakis.

On May 27th, Jazz ships to an expectant public.

Exhibit 5 The User's Guide to Lotus—History (*Continued*)

June, 1985

French and German versions of Jazz ship from the new manufacturing subsidiary in Dublin, Ireland, making this plant the principal supplier of Lotus products to European markets.

August, 1985

At the corporate staff meeting, Jim announces a major reorganization of the company into five business divisions, in keeping with the growth and expansion of our operations. They are Engineering and Scientific Products, Business Products, Information Services, Publishing, and International.

Lotus currently employs about 975 employees at its headquarters in Cambridge, and in regional offices in major cities throughout the United States and Europe. Lotus has moved from the status of a small, unknown start-up company to a position of leadership in the industry.

To quote Mitch on Lotus's progress, "We have come a long way in just three years. The alliances we have formed, the new products we have and are developing, and the creative power of our employees are making Lotus a leading player in the information industry."

Exhibit 6 Jim Manzi's Management Style

To: All Lotus Employees
From: Jim Manzi
Subject: Paper

Every day at Lotus we defoliate a small forest in our process of sending memos.

Personally, I get dozens of multipage memos a week and do not know why I am getting them. I would guess many of you are in the same position.

Let me suggest some recommended steps for keeping Vermont green:

1. Never send a memo if the distribution list is longer than the message.
2. If it fits on one page, put it on one page.
3. Don't write memos that don't fit on one page (see #2 above).
4. Review the standard memos and status reports you generate and make sure everyone to whom you send it, wants it.
5. If you get a memo that you don't want or need, write "RETURN TO SENDER" in block letters and get rid of it (see #4 above).

Thanks for your help on this.

(Please do not write RETURN TO SENDER on this note. Just this once).

Exhibit 6 Jim Manzi's Management Style (*Continued*)

January 13, 1986

To: All Lotus Employees
From: Jim Manzi
Subject: Internal/external communications

At an offsite meeting last week, all Department heads and Divisional General Managers agreed that we should rededicate ourselves to improving the way we serve and support our customers, the press, investment community, vendors and fellow employees and to begin to take concrete steps to make suggested improvements a reality.

Starting immediately, we all should

1. Respond to **all** mail within 48 hours of receipt. We may not be able to provide the sender with a full response to an inquiry but we should send, at a minimum, an acknowledgement of receipt of his/her letter and identify a time at which a full response will be forthcoming.

2. Call back **anyone** who has telephoned us within 24 hours of receiving the phone call. No one should leave work with a single, unanswered phone message—not to mention a pile of them—on his/her desk before leaving for the evening—unless, for some reason, a disproportionate number of calls came in at the end of the day.

3. Transfer a caller to someone else's phone mail **only after asking the caller** if he/she would like to leave a message on phone mail. In the event that the person to whom you are referring the call does not have phone mail, take the message and personally relay it to the appropriate person for response. **No one should be transferred to phone mail without first being asked if they approve and no calls should be transferred back to the company console operators.**

4. **Answer any and all ringing phones** that are uncovered, even if you just happen to be walking by and then take a message and leave it taped to the appropriate person's phone.

In addition to the above, all department heads will be working out procedures so that no phones in their departments will ever again be uncovered. This will include plans for the phones of all secretaries and administrative assistants to be forwarded and/or part of a "pick group."

Since some of our problems are associated with the phone system itself, we have also commissioned an internal task force to look at what other company-wide improvements are possible over the next few months.

Exhibit 6 Jim Manzi's Management Style (*Continued*)

If we all pay attention to this, we will be making great strides in improving our external relationships and in making it a lot easier for people to do business with Lotus. When we review this issue three months from now, we would all like to think that the level of frustration for people calling Lotus will have been cut to zero and that we are much more efficient and responsive to each other in fulfilling our individual responsibilities.

If you need assistance on implementing this within your own department, please call Judy Giordano at 8010.

Thanks for your cooperation.

Exhibit 6 Jim Manzi's Management Style (*Continued*)

March 19, 1986

To: All Lotus Employees
From: Jim Manzi
Subject: Meeting Mania

Does the phrase *"take a meeting"* mean anything to you?

It doesn't mean anything to me either but as long as we're on the subject of meetings, I thought I'd share a few observations. There is an explosion of "meetingitis" at Lotus. It's a serious ailment that's hard to cure once the real damage sets in.

Meetings are usually, after all, incredibly boring events and should be avoided at all costs.

First of all, there are the small annoyances like too few chairs and not enough coffee.

Then there are the larger annoyances like no agendas; no one remembering who called the meeting; no one knowing why the meeting was called; or no one understanding the objectives of the meeting.

Finally, there are the very large annoyances like not remembering the results of the last meeting; not understanding why you're sitting in a room with five or ten people you have never seen before; not knowing how you're going to get out of the next meeting; and worst of all, walking into the room, being handed a fifteen page, single-spaced document and being asked for immediate comments so that you and everyone else can "buy into" the process.

Some meetings are, of course, very important (e.g., my meetings) and attempt to improve information sharing and facilitate decision making. Others are relatively painful and unproductive because of a general failure to follow one or two simple guidelines.

After years of personal research on the subject, I have developed the five following rules that I thought might be worth passing along:

1. Never call a meeting without knowing what you're trying to accomplish.
2. Never attend a meeting when someone else has not done Number 1.
3. Always ask why you were invited and what is expected of you (if you don't get satisfactory answers to the questions, you can gracefully bow out and spend your time polishing up on your skills at writing shorter memos).
4. Never attend more than three two-hour meetings in one month—more than three can be life threatening.
5. Never let anyone talk for more than three minutes unless they know what they are talking about.

I'll see you at the next staff meeting.

Exhibit 7   The User's Guide to Lotus—Corporate Values

Corporate Values

Quality is paramount at Lotus; we will strive to achieve the highest level of quality in every aspect of our business.

We will deal with our employees fairly within a system where rewards are based on merit. Lotus will strive to provide equal opportunity in employment and in compensation. We seek to build a diverse work force where the dignity of each individual is respected and valued.

Lotus people will bring the greatest degree of honesty, ethical behavior and personal responsibility to our jobs in order to maintain the overall integrity of the company, our products and the individuals working here.

Teamwork and cooperation are essential ingredients in the work environment at Lotus. Each employee is expected to be not only an individual contributor, but also a contributor to the efforts of the group. No one individual is or can be responsible for our success.

Lotus people must have the flexibility to respond quickly to situational changes, and be open to adjusting behavior accordingly, without compromise to our other fundamental values.

We place a high value on creativity, innovation and initiative; those characteristics will be eagerly fostered. We will strive to maintain an atmosphere where risk taking is encouraged and consideration of new ideas is supported at all levels of the organization.

A sense of humor is an important asset. It is indicative of the way individuals look at themselves, and reflects how they deal with other people. It is important that people not take themselves too seriously, as they may be the only ones that do so.

Exhibit 8 Lotus Employee Referral Program

MEMORANDUM

TO: All Lotus Personnel

FROM: Marilynn Considine

SUBJ: Guidelines For The Employee Referral Program

DATE: January 18, 1984

To qualify for the $500 "bounty" paid to employees at Lotus for all successful hires in the Employment Referral Program:

1) The employee must submit the candidate's resume directly to the Recruitment Administrator (Chris Bresnahan) who will process it before the recruiters can review it for possible openings.

2) The attached form will be circulated throughout each department and should be attached to the front of the resume. Space is provided should additional suggestions/comments be necessary.

3) Recruitment will review all resumes and route those deemed qualified.

4) We will no longer accept as valid Employee Referrals those resumes that are not forwarded to the Recruitment Office for review.

5) In cases of multiple Employee Referrals of a candidate, the referral selected for the "bounty" will be the one that is first logged in the Recruitment Office.

6) Agency Referrals that are logged in Recruitment before Employee Referrals will supercede the Employee Referral.

All employees submitting resumes will receive notification from the Recruitment Office indicating receipt of same. Employees and their referrals will be notified as soon as our review is completed.

Should you have any questions, please contact Chris Bresnahan.

KEEP THOSE GREAT REFERRALS ROLLING IN. . . .

Exhibit 9 PCU Federal Credit Union System

Share Programs.

PCU's Share Program includes a variety of accounts designed to accommodate the savings needs of our members.

The Regular Share Account.

This is PCU's standard savings account. It is a flexible account that pays a better than average dividend and allows members to deposit and withdraw at any time. A minimum balance of $5 (the value of a share) must be maintained.

ShareDraft (checking) Account.

One of the most unique of all PCU services is the ShareDraft account. It combines the convenient features of checking with the earning power of a savings account.

When you open a PCU ShareDraft account we'll order you a supply of share drafts which look like personal checks and may be used in the same way: to obtain cash, make purchases, pay bills, and for other purposes. You are not required to maintain any minimum balance in your ShareDraft account. There are no service charges regardless of how many drafts you write. Best of all, the unused funds in your ShareDraft account will earn the same high dividends as your regular Shares.

Club Savings Accounts.

PCU Federal Credit Union offers a number of special savings programs designed to help members budget for special purposes. Club Savings Accounts earn the same generous dividends as our regular share accounts. Deposits are made by means of a convenient payroll deduction, cash, check, or money order. Since these accounts are perpetual, they renew themselves automatically once you have received your annual payment. There is no need to fill out further paperwork.

PCU offers a Christmas Club, Vacation Club, and All-Purpose Club.

Certificate Accounts.

PCU Certificate Accounts pay an even higher rate of return than our regular Share Accounts, in exchange for your agreement to leave a specific minimum amount of money on deposit for a specific minimum period of time. Certificate Accounts represent an excellent choice for those members looking for a high-yield, flexible investment option. You may borrow against these account balances at a special low interest rate, thus offering an alternative to costly penalties for early withdrawal. Federal regulations require a substantial tax penalty for early withdrawal of certificate funds other than dividends.

Individual Retirement Accounts (IRA).

This savings plan is designed to furnish members with a tax shelter, and a supplement to future retirement income. Any working individual can have an IRA regardless of their involvement in company pension plans. Because PCU understands that all savers are not alike, we offer three IRA options. As with our savings programs, PCU's IRA rates are competitive with those offered by banks and other institutions.

To protect your retirement investment, IRA accounts are insured to $100,000 by NCUA.

Lending Programs.

Flexibility is the basis of our approach to designing loans to suit members' borrowing needs.

Unsecured (Signature) Loans.

As a PCU member, you may borrow money on the strength of your good name alone;

Exhibit 9   PCU Federal Credit Union System (*Continued*)

no additional collateral is required. Depending upon your credit worthiness and ability to repay, you may borrow various funds on your signature. Signature Loans are considered fixed rate loans.

Line of Credit. This special loan program is designed to provide our members with the easiest and fastest way to borrow. Once your application is approved, you are assigned a credit limit up to $5,000. This line of credit is considered part of your total unsecured loan funds. You may obtain advances up to the available limit on your line in person, by mail or by phone. Loan drafts, are accessible to those members who prefer to use them. The interest rate for this type of loan is variable.

Secured Loans. PCU offers members a complete range of secured loans at competitive interest rates.

Automobile Loans. New and used automobile loans are used to purchase a car, truck, or motorcycle. Terms for new and used loans are 48 and 36 months respectively. You can borrow up to 90% of the purchase price, at a fixed rate.

Boats and Recreational Vehicle Loans. You may borrow up to 80% of the purchase price and repay the loan over a ten year period. These types of loans are offered at a variable rate.

Stock Loans. Under this program, by pledging your stock as collateral, you can borrow up to 70% of the current value of your stock over a period of 10 years. The interest rate for a stock loan is variable.

Share Secured Loans. By pledging your shares as security, you may borrow up to the full balance in your savings account at a special low interest rate. You will continue to earn dividends on your savings while your loan is in effect, thus reducing the effective cost of your loan even further. Salary and other personal information are not required for this loan, and approval is automatic. These variable rate loans can be extended for up to 120 months.

Mortgage Programs. Your credit union offers a Mortgage Program with competitive market rates. The credit union processes your loan from application to closing, and provides you with a convenient payment schedule. Ask your PCU Loan Officer for loan details.

First Mortgages. First mortgages are available for owner-occupied houses and condominiums. As a member you can choose from a variety of competitively priced first mortgages with down payments as low as 5%. And, you can choose a fixed or adjustable rate, with terms ranging from 15-30 years.

Second Mortgages. A Second Mortgage from PCU is an excellent way to make major purchases or meet expenses by putting the equity you've built in your home to work for you. Second Mortgages are available for any amount provided that the total of your first and second does not exceed 80% of the value. You can take up to 12 years to repay. These loans are offered at a variable rate.

FHA Title 1—Home Improvement Loan. Under this program, you can borrow funds for any work which alters, repairs, or improves your home. These fixed rate loans and the rate charged is determined by the duration of the loan.

Educational Loan Programs. When it comes to financing education, PCU can assist you with a variety of flexible loan programs designed to help pay the costs of schooling at the lowest possible rates.

Guaranteed Student Loans. As an agent for Massachusetts Higher Education Assistance Corporation, PCU offers students and parents two government-backed, low-interest programs: HELP and PLUS.

HELP (Higher Education Loan Program). This program helps students finance undergraduate and graduate costs. Interest is subsidized by the government and repayment begins after

Exhibit 10   The User's Guide to Lotus—Introduction

⬛Lotus®

Introduction

The people of Lotus, far more than anything else, have made the company what it is today — a very special place to work. We believe strongly that people count, and we are committed to fair treatment for all and the creation of opportunity for greatest professional growth and contribution.

The success we have experienced and the growth which has followed have resulted in continuous change. At times, Lotus can be a bewildering place to work. This "User's Guide to Lotus" has been designed to provide a helpful hand by collecting and organizing a wide variety of information to make your day-to-day activities simpler and more efficient.

In a well-run organization, policies and procedures should help provide standard ways of getting things done, leaving more time and energy for creativity and individual contributions. If we work together, we can have a strong business, one based on teamwork and respect for each and every individual. Your effort and commitment is needed to make this happen.

Mitchell Kapor

Mitchell Kapor
Chief Executive Officer
and
Chairman of the Board

⬛Lotus®

What are we trying to accomplish as a company and how will we know whether we are successful?

We intend to become and remain the worldwide leader in our industry. However, leadership is not solely defined by the innovativeness and widespread appeal of our products. Nor just by the proven capability of our marketing. Nor by the strength of our balance sheet.

We want our industry leadership to be as much defined by the way this organization treats its people as by anything else Lotus does. Lotus, like any organization, is only a collection of individuals, and as such, how this organization treats its people is synonymous with how we treat each other.

This is a highly-charged, fast growth atmosphere, which we both enjoy immensely and suffer through. Teamwork, cooperation and flexibility, therefore, are absolutely critical to our success.

In addition, let all of us be known, both inside and outside Lotus, for the honesty, integrity and professionalism with which we deal with each other and with our suppliers and customers.

We will all be asked to make hundreds of decisions, both large and small, during our work at Lotus. If we are dedicated to the successful completion of our individual responsibilities as well as to assisting, whenever possible, others in being successful, we will be on the way to success as a company.

Jim Manzi

Jim Manzi
Chief Operating Officer

Exhibit 10   The User's Guide to Lotus—Introduction (continued)

Dear Lotus Employee,

This booklet is designed to help you to use your health benefits easily, and to answer any questions you might have about coverage for you and your family. We have made it as simple as insurance language permits; and Pat Kiernan, Lotus Benefits Coodinator, is available to clarify any aspects you may want to discuss further.

I cannot stress strongly enough that, given the depth and comprehensiveness of these benefits, it is my hope that you will make full use of them. Much is asked of you at Lotus, in time, energy, and commitment. The company's commitment to you and to your health is nowhere illustrated as completely as in the scope of benefits that cover you. Please use this plan whenever you are unwell and also to ensure, through the coverage for your yearly physical exam, that nothing is going untreated.

This year, in response to an often expressed wish by employees that we raise the Mental Health benefit, we have so. As of January 1, 1985 you have $1,250 a year to spend for this treatment, where you were covered for $750 in 1984.

Also, we have included orthodontia for adults in the plan, where before the benefit was extended only to children.

In addition, we are beginning to address the issue of child care this year in recognition of changing workforce demographics. Lotus has contracted with Child Care Resource Center, Inc., 552 Mass Ave., Cambridge, MA (02141) to provide our employees with information and support in locating quality child care of all types. A call to them will put you in touch with the best network available for this service. Details on this are found on page 41 in the booklet.

Finally, I want to remind you to be certain to report any job related accident or illness to your supervisor so that he or she can have the Human Resources Department begin to process a Workers Compensation claim on your behalf. While I certainly encourage everyone to take full advantage of the benefits described here, my real hope is for a very healthy year for you and your family.

Please take good care.

Sincerely,

Janet Axelrod
Vice President,
Human Resources Department

Exhibit 11   Employee Agreement

LOTUS DEVELOPMENT CORPORATION
One Broadway, Cambridge, MA 02142
(617) 494-1192

LOTUS DEVELOPMENT CORPORATION
EMPLOYMENT AND CONFIDENTIALITY AGREEMENT

In consideration of my employment or continued employment by Lotus Development Corporation ("Lotus") and in recognition of the fact that as an employee of Lotus I will or may have access to Confidential Information, I agree with Lotus as follows:

1. Lotus' Relationship to Employees: Lotus is a computer software firm dedicated to the development and marketing of computer software which is creative, functional, and easily used. Lotus is committed to quality in every aspect of its business and looks to and expects from its employees a high level of competence, cooperation, loyalty, integrity, initiative, and resourcefulness. Lotus, in turn, tries to offer its employees an atmosphere where these personal qualities can flourish and grow, and asks of each of its employees that the employee contribute what she or he can to our mutual effort to make Lotus a good place to work, and a successful firm.

2. Employment Status: I hereby accept Lotus' offer of employment as provided in this Agreement. I understand that I am employed for an indefinite term and that either Lotus or I may terminate our employment relationship at any time pursuant to Paragraph 7 hereof.

3. Duties of Employee: I shall be performing the duties of the job title listed on Schedule "A" and such other or additional duties and responsibilities as may be assigned to me from time to time by persons in authority at Lotus.

4. Compensation and Benefits: I shall receive the compensation listed on Schedule "A" and, in addition, I may participate in such employee benefit plans and receive such other fringe benefits as are afforded other Lotus employees in my job with the same job tenure. I understand that these employee benefit plans and fringe benefits may be amended, enlarged, or diminished by Lotus from time to time.

5. Employee Performance: I shall use my best efforts to perform my work diligently, loyally, conscientiously, and with reasonable skill, and shall comply with all Lotus' rules, procedures and standards governing the conduct of employees and their access to and use of Lotus' property, equipment and facilities. Lotus will make reasonable efforts to inform me of the rules, standards and procedures which are in effect from time to time and which apply to me.

6. Management of Lotus. Lotus may manage and direct its business affairs as it sees fit, notwithstanding any employee's individual interest in or expectation regarding a particular business program or product.

7. Termination of Employment: My employment may be terminated by Lotus or me at any time, without cause, on two weeks prior written notice, or by Lotus on payment of two weeks severance pay in lieu of notice. Lotus may terminate my employment for cause at any time without prior notice. Cause includes, but is not limited to, failure to comply with rules, standards or procedures promulgated by Lotus, neglect of or substandard performance by an employee of assigned responsibilities, breach of the terms of this Agreement, falsification of Lotus records or documents, or any other act of dishonesty on the part of an employee.

Exhibit 11   Employee Agreement (*Continued*)

8. Agreement Not to Compete With Lotus: As long as I am employed by Lotus, I shall devote my full time and efforts to Lotus and shall not participate, directly or indirectly, in any capacity, in any business or activity that is in competition with Lotus. For a period of one year after the termination of employment with Lotus for any reason, I shall not attempt to hire, or hire any employee of Lotus, or assist in such hiring by anyone else, or encourage any employee to terminate his or her employment with Lotus.

9. Unauthorized Disclosure of Confidential Information: While employed by Lotus and thereafter, I shall not, directly or indirectly, disclose to anyone outside of Lotus any Confidential Information or use any Confidential Information (as hereinafter defined) other than pursuant to my employment by and for the benefit of Lotus.

The term "Confidential Information" as used throughout this Agreement means all data or information not generally known outside of Lotus whether prepared or developed by or for Lotus or received by Lotus from an outside source. Without limiting the scope of this definition, Confidential Information includes any technical data, design, pattern, formula, computer program, source code, object code, algorithm, subroutine, manual, product specification, or plan for a new or revised product; and any business, marketing, financial or sales record, data, plan, or survey; and any other record or information relating to the present or future business or products of Lotus. All Confidential Information and copies thereof are the sole property of Lotus.

10. All Developments the Property of Lotus. All Confidential Information and all other discoveries, inventions, processes, methods and improvements, conceived, developed, or otherwise made by me at any time, alone or with others and in any way relating to Lotus' present or future business or products, whether or not patentable or subject to copyright protection and whether or not reduced to tangible form or reduced to practice, during the period of my employment with Lotus ("Developments"), shall be the sole property of Lotus. I agree to, and hereby do, assign to Lotus all my right, title and interest throughout the world in and to all Developments. I agree that all such Developments shall constitute works made for hire under the copyright laws of the United States and hereby assign to Lotus all copyrights, patents and other proprietary rights I may have in any such Development.

Integrated Genetics

Sometimes I wake up in the middle of the night wondering if those little
molecules really do the things the scientists say they do.

Robert Johnson, president of Angenics

Late in 1983, Bob Carpenter was looking forward to the next few months.
Integrated Genetics (IG), the fledgling genetic engineering company of which
he was president, hoped to begin field trials soon of its first diagnostic test to
detect the presence of salmonella bacteria in food products. If all went well
the test would be marketed in early 1984. Prototype test kits had been
designed, testing of the kits had just begun, and IG was gearing up for
production and marketing. The whole company, but especially the top
management team, eagerly awaited their first product on the market.

Carpenter felt pressured by difficult operational and people problems
that he could not easily resolve. They were clearly the reason he had trouble
sleeping. Getting the salmonella test out into field trials would help. A
product on the market would bring in revenues and demonstrate to the
investment community that IG was a viable enterprise. IG had gone public
with its stock in July; ever since then Carpenter had felt that he and IG were
in the public eye.

When he got to his office one day, one of the scientists told him bad
news. The salmonella tests, run the night before, were a disaster. Although
the diagnostic test had often been performed successfully, when new vials
were used this time, all the polyvinyl filters had dissolved. None of the
scientists knew why. The problem could take one day to solve or an indefinite
amount of time. It was a definite setback and Carpenter settled into his chair
feeling discouraged.

Although it was a minor problem (since the scientific staff would surely
find the trouble eventually), it meant that the test's marketing would be
further postponed. Carpenter thought about the other problems he had to
contend with and would discuss with his afternoon visitors, one of whom was
a friend and early consultant to IG.

When his guests arrived, Carpenter ushered them into his office looking

This case was prepared by Research Associate E. Mary Lou Balbaky, under the supervision of
Associate Professor John Kao.

somewhat more harried and weary than usual. He immediately told them about the dissolving filters. "It's the first time it's ever happened and nobody can figure out why!" Carpenter's guests wanted to know about the major problems and issues he faced as president of a start-up firm so dependent upon scientific creativity. Ironically, Carpenter said: "I spend maybe 75 percent of my time on people problems. They won't go away, some are very sensitive, and there are no easy solutions."

COMPANY BACKGROUND

Integrated Genetics was founded in February 1981 to develop, manufacture, and market diagnostic and therapeutic products. Using proprietary techniques based upon recombinant DNA technology, IG's strategy was to develop products that provided near-term revenues and would enable it to build manufacturing and marketing capabilities necessary to support long-term growth.

David Housman, who began the company, was a large, friendly, slightly heavy-set man, youthful in appearance due to a casual, graduate-student manner of dressing. Known for his enthusiasm and a tendency to try to do many things at once, he was described as an intuitively brilliant scientist. He saw himself as a biologist skilled at genetic engineering. He believed that being strong in theory and technology was a "key to significant contribution."

By 1976 Housman and many others involved in developing recombinant DNA technology saw its potential for uses beyond answering fundamental questions. Housman developed his thinking about various practical uses of the technology when he was called upon to defend DNA research before Cambridge residents in the mid-1970s. By 1978 he felt even more strongly that something both beneficial and commercial should be done with the technology. On the advice of a friend who worked for a major company producing vaccines, he wrote to its vice president in charge of new-product development to suggest products that could be developed through recombinant DNA techniques. He got no response from the company. "This marked the point when I knew that I ought to do something commercial in this area," he says.

The Genentech public stock issue in 1980 stirred the investment community to see that, as Housman said, genetic engineering was "for real and not some flaky thing. The Genentech public issue had a tremendous impact. . . . It opened the doors [for others]. . . . It seemed to me that [forming my own company] was the way to go. I saw that the American pharmaceutical industry was very conservative and [that big companies were] not really geared to pick up on new technology quickly."
Housman also said:

> The advantages of my being able to be directly with the science and the development of a company were very attractive. This issue came up again when we were getting investors: whether we wanted big corporate investors or pure

venture capital investors. I knew that I was not a businessman and didn't have the experience to go out and run a business. But I wanted to have a small enough structure so that I did not have the ponderous weight of the decision-making process that every major corporation seems to have [and] that gets in the way of actually getting things done. . . . What is really most frustrating to me (in a university lab) is when we get sucked into the big bureaucratic structure—when we want to get something installed, for example, and have to go through two levels of bureaucracy and several offices and even then can't get it done correctly. . . . That is not the way I like to do things. [I have been more concerned with] what kind of structure would feel right than [the question]: Is this going to be more profitable than that?

Housman described the steps of the company's formation:

I had a group of colleagues that I'd worked with and been in touch with for a long period of time, going back to when I was a post-doc. I was very comfortable with them. Art [Skoultchi] and I had shared a lab bench together. Bernie [Forget] was at Children's Hospital, but we were closely in touch. The fourth person who came in was a student of mine in Toronto and MIT who went to Mass General. . . . A very important part of doing science is *talking* science. This group I felt most comfortable talking with and collaborating with. . . . So I got them together, had a couple of meetings, and we decided to do it [form a company]. . . . In the group there are very different personalities and styles. Each brings different things. Art is a very careful and thorough person: he wants to see that every point has been covered. I'm more helter-skelter. I may see something intuitively, but Art will want to work through it point by point. Bernie brings a whole medical orientation plus knowing the technology really well.

Housman pointed out that Bernie Forget was also skilled at the interface of two fields—basic academic research and clinically oriented research. "This is a very important aspect of what I think we are good at," he said.

So the four of us got together and tried to define what it was that we as a group were most interested in and most capable of doing scientifically and how we could make that into a venture. Two areas of strength were genetics and diagnostics, and we had all worked in areas related to hematology—basic blood products. We looked forward a few years down the road, and we looked at what the problems were with the technology as it existed in the fall of 1980. At that time the only genetic engineering systems were in bacteria. We felt it would be possible to develop mammalian cell systems to do genetic engineering. . . . So those three areas basically started us off. We decided to focus on things that had a real market as opposed to things that were speculative. We also looked for something that would be hard to do, so that by the time we got this whole thing rolling it wouldn't already have been done by five other groups. We knew the hemophilia factor was going to be technically difficult, but it has a very defined market. People need it and there are very serious problems with the current form of the product. We said: "Let's not be me-toos!"

The founders did experience time pressure.

The things we chose were two or three years down the road. We tried to pick things that would be in a time frame that while not leisurely would be reasonable. If we had tried to get into the growth hormone business with

Genentech, we would have been under intense pressure. . . . However, we had to get things rolling as quickly as we could.

Once Housman and his partners decided to do a freestanding start-up rather than become the genetic engineering department of a big company, they needed to find out how to do it.

Basically, each of us had a contact of one sort or another. Bernie came in contact with Don Hudson, who became a founder of the company. Don had been in medical electronics and was interested in helping to start a company in genetic engineering. He was a Yale alumnus living in New Haven, and he decided to knock on doors at Yale. Somebody at Yale pointed out Bernie's door to knock on. Don had an interview with Bernie just at the time we were talking about forming the company, and Bernie suggested Don come up and see me, the first time in October 1980. Hudson made the initial contact with Bill Draper at Sutter Hill [a venture capital company]. Around Thanksgiving Jim Gusella and I met Bill Draper for breakfast, had a more extensive meeting four weeks later, went to Palo Alto, and "closed the deal." At that time I did not realize exactly what I was doing.

One reason we chose Sutter Hill was "experience." Two, I guess we were really impressed with the intellectual caliber of the people. They were people who asked the hardest questions. Three, Sutter Hill had played an active role in developing management teams for start-up companies. I did not want to run a business. I wanted to be able to contribute to the technical management but did not want to count pennies or write salary checks. They gave us the names of all the companies that they started or invested in and said we were free to call them and ask what it was like working with Sutter Hill. We did call four or five and asked whether they had been helpful. We got a uniform answer that Sutter Hill had been extremely helpful. The last point was that they had been involved with Hybritech, so they were not complete novices in the biotechnology area.

The deal with Sutter Hill did not give us the largest sum of money that we could have gotten. But the key to it was a conversation I had with Bill Draper in which I asked, "What is going to happen when we need more capital?" His answer was that no company they had ever started had failed for lack of capital. "If you are doing OK, we will be able to get the capital you need." He is a very trustworthy person. . . . What made the difference was the sense of commitment and experience of the people involved.

Housman had a clear conception of what he wanted his company to become.

My vision is that I would like to become a major force in the world of biotechnology and health care. . . . I do not want to become the R&D of somebody else's big company. Our strategy is to build a freestanding enterprise and build it as high as we can, one step at a time.

THE MANAGEMENT TEAM MEMBERS

The administrative and management staff reported to IG's president, Bob Carpenter, age 38; the scientific staff, including a number of outstanding scientific consultants, reported to Robert Erickson, age 41, vice president and technical director. (*Exhibit 1* is a list of IG's directors and officers.)

Bob Carpenter

Carpenter remembered his decision to join the company:

It was amazing. I always had the idea that being my own boss and the clear leader was something that I wanted . . . but I never had any good ideas, and I was always afraid about the money until this golden opportunity. . . . But I *did* jump. I had all the things you're not supposed to have—a mortgage and kids and a very good future at Baxter. I think I'm a person who likes change or maybe likes risk-taking occasionally. For example, I was kind of eager to go to Vietnam.

Dave Anderson of Sutter Hill contacted Carpenter and interviewed him on the phone. The first meeting between Carpenter, the five founders, and Draper took place at La Guardia airport. "We all flew in from different places and met there for an hour," Carpenter recalled:

I knew nothing about DNA; the only thing I knew about was markets, and the markets they were talking about were pretty good. I was impressed by the scientists, but they were incredibly naive businesswise. Sutter Hill was putting in $500,000 with a provision that they would put in another $500,000 if all things went well. I probably made up my mind at that first meeting that this was something I wanted to do.

Carpenter and his wife made a formal decision to accept, negotiated the salary, and came to Boston on April 19, 1981. When he arrived there was no place to work and no full-time employees. The founders were going to be involved only part-time. He got together with Hudson and began the difficult task of finding laboratory space.

Carpenter described the difference between running IG and his former job.

We have thousands of opportunities and lots of people going off in different directions. How to pull things together, focus our efforts, and get something done is more difficult here than at Fenwal. . . . And picking people is a much bigger problem. At Fenwal you had an ongoing operation. So you had to replace and occasionally add new people. But it wasn't a situation where you are constantly trying to recruit 10 or 20 people a month.

Asked what it took to succeed in this business, Carpenter answered without much hesitation, "A single-minded fixation on getting things done! Actually lots of creativity comes up when you are driving for a goal."

Carpenter tells the following story about this determination to get things done:

The new building that is going up could have been held up because the manufacturer of the glass front of the building told the contractor and Tom Smith, our vice president of operations, that the window would not be ready for 14 weeks instead of the promised 6 weeks. Everyone said nothing could be done about it. I said, "What do you mean that nothing can be done? Call the president of the Libby-Owens Ford!" I knew from being president of Fenwal that if a customer called *me* on a problem I'd sure get on it. The point is: you exhaust every avenue. You think of every possible answer or solution. The same is true of the scientific problems.

Bob Taber

Around 1970 Bob Taber became very good friends with Housman and Art Skoultchi but moved away, first to teach at the University of Massachusetts Medical School and finally coming to a faculty/administrative appointment at the University of California in San Francisco with an office in Palo Alto and connections to Stanford. His job involved putting together big grants and organizing new projects. Taber had begun to get involved in a start-up when he heard that Housman and Skoultchi were putting a company together. He said:

> I started checking around with all my friends about Sutter Hill and found they were first-rate. Then they hired Bob Carpenter. Housman said, "Come and talk to Carpenter." Carpenter was like the ideal guy. I thought, "This guy is going to make the difference." I talked to him for two or three hours right at the beginning and it just blew me away. He was smart and knew what he was doing. The deciding factor was Carpenter, because he was a guy who was really able to start a company and pull it off. Bob made me an offer.

Taber talked about his strengths and weaknesses in relation to the company and the team.

> My strengths are that I am a fairly clever person. I know almost everybody. I can put things together. We have some people coming in this afternoon who are with another company. If we can pull something together that we really need, we can do a terrific deal. I have lots of contacts and I am not afraid to call people up. I am good at that and I am good at recruiting. What I am bad at is anything that requires attention span. I ran diagnostics for six months and I was at the end of my rope: I hated it. I started out by doing a terrific job. The last two months I did a lousy job because I just did not pay enough attention to details, nor did I want to. I do not want to manage people; I do not have the concentration. Carpenter does. He is good at sticking to a problem. He will sit and quiz somebody until he has found out every possibility. That bores me. I would rather be planning or lining up new projects. That is where I fit into the whole thing.

Taber reflected on his future with the company.

> I think in three years there is not going to be a place for me in this company. It is going to be a more market-driven company. Someone like me will be a luxury. They will not need the skills I have as much. Plus, I do not think it will be as much fun for me. I want to start my own company or get involved in another start-up, because I'm good at that. I can hire people and get things off the ground. I'd like to get in a little bit earlier, get a little more equity, do it over again. That is my personality type. I do not ever want to be president of a company, but I want to do a start-up again. I'd enjoy that.

Bob Erickson

Erickson, IG's technical director, was formerly with Miles Laboratories as vice president of research in the biotechnology group. He said:

> I recognized that recombinant DNA technology would revolutionize the business I was in, and I knew that you had to move very quickly with this new technology or you would be left behind.
>
> I was contacted by David Housman, who was coming to Chicago and was willing to drive out to see me. I met David but was not enthusiastic. I was at a stage in my life when my kids were just about to go to college, and I felt that I needed some security. Then I got a call from Carpenter. After talking to Bob I knew I had to see what the company was about. I flew to Boston and spent a day talking to him. I was impressed by his enthusiasm and by his business skills. I liked the strategy he had for developing the business. After about a month or six weeks of negotiations, I finally agreed to come on board in March 1982.

Erickson had many of the characteristics that Carpenter was looking for in a technical director: He had a lot of experience in corporate life and with large-scale industrial fermentation, and he knew how to interact with the Federal Drug Administration.

Describing himself as low-key, Erickson talked about his motivations for coming to IG and what his first few months were like. "I recognized the excitement and challenge of the area," he said, "and I thought that in a big organization where decisions take so long to be made I would mostly be doing politics and not really participating in the science."

One thing Erickson had not expected when he came to the company was a feeling of insecurity that lasted about three months.

> Leaving such a secure company and such a secure position, I came here and realized how fragile an organization is in its early stages. First of all there was the limited amount of funds that we had at first. We would sit down and calculate how long we'd be around if we were unsuccessful. Second, the company was all based on the scientific expertise of the people in the lab. Knowing that and trying to keep the people working as a team and not losing some key people was a serious concern. It's difficult because you hire someone and get him working and it takes probably a commitment of a year to see if you hired the right person. If you haven't, it is a major event to terminate somebody. You have to take a guess if a person is going to fit into an organization like this.

Erickson's role at IG was a key one: he bridged the gap between the scientists and business managers. He said, "I try to be a spokesman for the scientists and protect them from some of the pressures. Under too much pressure you start doing bad science. So my role is to try to preserve an environment in which they can do good science."

Pat Connoy

The youngest member of the top management team, Connoy found the idea of getting an equity position in a start-up venture was very interesting to him. "It was clear," he said, "that there were going to be a number of successful companies and also a number of failures because too many firms started too quickly." Connoy came to Boston twice to meet with the scientific advisory board members and the management team. "During the interim," he said, "I did quite a bit of checking on the individuals through contacts at AHS and at their previous companies."

One potential problem was that the company had no big-name, Nobel-prize-winning scientists to attract other top scientific talent by reputation alone. Connoy went on to say that Carpenter was a key selling point in his coming to the company.

> He's a very open guy, very easy to talk to. He also sets a good example by being such a hard worker. I liked the fact that Bob was looking for someone to be fully responsible for sales and marketing and that he wouldn't be heavily involved in all the small decisions. My previous boss kept his fingers in everything and as a result he squelched a lot of good ideas and decisions.

Connoy described his own method of decision making:

> One of the things I have been trying to do from a marketing standpoint is to make sure people are aware of the decisions that are being made. I may make the final decision, but I try to get the management team's input. I'd like to have them all feel that they are involved in the sales and marketing aspects. The entire company got involved in picking a trademark name for our diagnostic products. I had a contest for everybody in the company to submit names and had a free dinner for the winner. Over 200 names were submitted. I picked the ten best ideas and let the management team vote on them. Everyone liked "Gene-TRAK." They all felt more ownership of the name than if I had just chosen one.

Connoy enjoyed developing the new sales and marketing system and felt real excitement in starting fresh.

> The role I see for the sales and marketing group (when it is formed) is to be responsible for seeing market needs quickly and recognizing the size of potential markets. We will go to the management group and say, for example, "We ought to develop a test for herpes. There is a big market. We've got the kind of distribution network to get to the customer, and the competition doesn't look too strong."

Tom Smith

Smith came to IG as vice president of operations from Abbott Labs, where he had been the operations manager for the diagnostics division. He had an unusual variety of experience in big companies. In addition to Abbott (which had about 30,000 employees), he had also been at Baxter Labs, in the Navy with the *Polaris* missile program, and, as a chemist, in a research lab at Anaconda. "I have been a plant manager, quality-control person, materials manager . . . a lot of different things," he said. "It is a crazy background, but a good one for this job." Smith had also done a lot of work on productivity programs and organizational change. He was a member of the National Advisory Committee on Productivity and was a leading expert on innovative work programs.

Smith described the interesting way in which he joined the company:

I knew Bob Carpenter from several years ago. I looked at the list and saw Bob's company in the portfolio. So I called Carpenter to check out the venture group, and he said, "Oh, they're real good but never mind that. How would you like to come out and work for me?"

What brought me here, besides knowing Bob Carpenter? I could spend the rest of my life making other people wealthy or I could grab a share of it myself at a start-up level. Isn't that what most of us in these kinds of businesses are motivated by?

When I first came here I said, "At last! There's no politics. At last! There's no backbiting! Imagine how productive I can be." And you find out there really is politics—that you are never without politics. The pressures, the urgencies are there just like in a large company, but the decision making is *so* much easier and so much less cumbersome. I find it very exciting because there is no back-up for your decisions. Here you can make the wrong decision and really get everybody in trouble, and that makes it a little more exciting.

The attribute that I felt most needed changing around here was that everything was done one-on-one. The group process was entirely missing. I'm naked without the group process. Bob is a one-on-one kind of guy.

So that was the number one problem I saw. The second was the lack of planning. The strategy of the company is in the mind of Bob Carpenter. There are no goals; there are no MBO approaches; and performance reviews have never been written and are kind of "Atta boy, you're doing a good job and we'll see you tomorrow." Nobody knows how they stand. But that's a start-up.

This had worked well when it was all science development, but bringing me on board meant that it was time now to commercialize the product. So besides the science there is now a need to talk about inventory and blueprints, specifications and plastics technology, production and equipment. We have to build a factory, buy some equipment, put in a fermentation process, and all that.

Team Structure and Process

The upper-level management team had a weekly meeting, usually every Monday morning. Each member updated Carpenter on his particular work, and the group discussed decisions that had to be made. Carpenter said:

My team has now expanded from two people to half a dozen, and it *is* more difficult making sure that everyone is informed, that they are all pulling together in the same direction and not taking shots at each other.

We have a rule that we are going to be open and candid in our meetings. What I've done in the last month or so is to simply say: "I'm not going to tolerate sniping. If you think there is a problem, don't come to me with it. Go to the guy you have the problem with. We are all good people trying to make this thing go. Let's solve the problems rather than do big-company technique. We can't have a win-lose situation in this company."

THE SCIENTISTS

Scientific Advisory Board

An element of IG's development had been its Scientific Advisory Board (SAB), comprising four scientist/cofounders of the company. Each SAB member met one day a week or more with IG's full-time scientists and management to review ongoing and proposed scientific activities. They also helped recruit scientific personnel. SAB's members were:

- **David E. Housman,** Ph.D., age 36, associate professor of biology at MIT since 1975, noted for his development of recombinant DNA applications to human genetics and work on red blood cell formation.
- **Bernard G. Forget,** M.D., age 44, a professor of medicine and human genetics and chief of the Hematology Section, Yale University School of Medicine, noted as a member of the first group to isolate human hemoglobin genes by recombinant DNA methods.
- **Arthur I. Skoultchi,** Ph.D., age 42, an associate professor of cell biology at the Albert Einstein College of Medicine in New York City, noted for his work on the transfer of the human hemoglobin genes into mouse tissue culture cells.
- **James F. Gusella,** Ph.D., age 30, an instructor in neurology at Harvard Medical School and an assistant in genetics in neurology service and children's service at Massachusetts General Hospital, whose work involved the application of recombinant DNA techniques to the study of neurogenic disorders, particularly Huntington's disease.

There were two levels of Ph.D.s at IG—research scientists and senior scientists—and below them, three grades of technicians with various types of advanced training. Above the senior scientists were only the Scientific Advisory Board and Erickson, the technical director.

When IG was formed, three established senior scientists with extensive laboratory experience were hired at fairly high salaries and given generous amounts of stock. One had been at Oak Ridge National Laboratories for seven years. The staff scientists, mostly young, postdoctoral people, were added gradually at roughly two-thirds the salary of the senior scientists and given stock on an individually negotiated basis.

According to Housman, the work of the scientific staff required significant thought and creativity. Erickson agreed. "Competition in the industry is such that our processes and products must be uniquely different and better than others," he said. "Our success depends a lot on our creative abilities."

Everyone in IG recognized that the company scientists were extremely hardworking and committed. "There are some experiments that take 14 to 16 hours, no matter what," Housman explained. "And you have to do something at every point along the 16-hour timeframe."

PROJECTS

Products in Development

IG was developing products for major health-care markets, including diagnostic tests for infectious diseases and genetic disorders and therapeutic proteins for the treatment of human infertility, blood protein deficiencies, and cardiovascular disorders. IG expected to complete development and commercialization of its first product, a diagnostic test for salmonella bacteria, during the first six months of 1984. (*Exhibit 2* has a description of IG's products.)

IG's scientific work was organized into projects of many phases requiring a great variety of skills or components—cloners, expression people, purification people, people with bioengineering skills. A project leader was responsible for organizing and coordinating other people's work. Five to fifteen people might work at different times on one project. Service-function specialists worked on two or three different projects at a time. Erickson assigned priorities among the projects when there was competition for the technicians' time, although the staff knew in general which projects had highest priority.

In the past the project leader had been the person with the most direct experience in the area. Now the leader was usually the person showing the most organization skills. Carpenter said that scientists "were not used to getting things done on time schedules or interacting with people so that work came together in the end."

Marketing and Competition

IG's marketing strategy identified specific market opportunities appropriate for its combination of scientific expertise, market size, product development timing, and other factors. Its main markets were those in which a relatively small number of customers accounted for a large proportion of the market. These included major food-processing companies, blood collection centers, hemophilia treatment centers, clinical laboratories in large hospitals, and major private clinical laboratories. IG was considering marketing its products through a direct sales organization to maximize profit potential and achieve market leadership. It decided to concentrate its initial direct marketing in the United States.

IG competed with biotechnology companies, pharmaceutical and chemical companies, and other large industrial firms diversifying into biotechnology. The newer biological products would compete against existing traditional products. Many companies had substantially greater financial, marketing, and human resources than IG. (*Exhibit 3* has a discussion of risk factors associated with the company.)

REWARDING THE SCIENTISTS

The recognition of the scientists' need for people and project-management skills and management's attempt to reward these strengths both caused some dissension among the scientists. Problems had begun to surface among the scientists when some staff scientists were promoted to senior-scientist level. The promotions were given when Carpenter became aware of growing dissatisfaction among the junior people. One of the more highly qualified staff scientists had left IG for a job with a $10,000 salary increase. Carpenter felt he left also because he was a high performer and key contributor and yet had been paid less and had received much less stock than the senior scientists. (In July 1983 IG made a public stock offering of 1,600,000 shares of common stock at $13.00 per share. Proceeds to the company were $19,344,000. See *Exhibit 4* for financial information as of July 1983.)

Erickson was also concerned with the problems of rewarding and recognizing scientists' achievements. He said:

> Rewarding these people is difficult. Title has a little bit to do with it. If they think they are one of the best scientists in the company, they would not want people with higher titles over them. That was one of the problems initially in the company. . . . Most of the scientists claim that money alone is not the right way to reward them either.

Recognition of achievement was a very important reward for the scientists. Hence one method of rewarding to promote younger people to senior scientist status. According to Erickson, another way was to give them independence to have outside contacts with consultants of their own. Most scientists saw that the best way to reward them was to give them a good environment in which they could do excellent work. They wanted to be proud of the science they were doing even though there were deadlines to meet.

Employee Compensation and Stock Plans

Carpenter and Dave Housman decided the firm's first compensation strategy. They thought it important to offer the scientists salaries at least equal to what the market demanded, at that time up to $45,000 a year for a senior Ph.D. scientist.

In the beginning, stock was offered as an additional incentive to join the company and the amount determined was individually negotiated. This led to perceived inequities among the scientists. Stock options were used as a way to even these inequalities out. (See *Exhibit 5*, Employee Stock Purchase Plan.) Claimed Carpenter, "At the beginning the scientists did not clearly appreciate the value of the stock they received; they were more concerned with salaries and job responsibilities than how much stock they got. Now it's become a very tangible thing. Everyone watches the stock market."

Schedules and Deadlines

At IG, unlike an academic setting, progress had to be made within specific timeframes particularly with work done under contract. Management generated milestones for the projects, but the more difficult the project, the more difficult it was to set any deadlines. Every experiment had a level of uncertainty; setting deadlines on such a process was chancy at best.

Erickson thought working under deadlines and tight schedules was a problem for some of the academic scientists. He said:

> Most of them come from backgrounds where they did not have any hard deadlines, but they loved the science so much they would work 12 to 14 hours a day. Even now, though the problems are more applied and there is less freedom to explore, most are really excited about the challenge. They respond fairly well to pressure. But we have to be careful not to give them deadlines that they can't meet, and they need to be involved in the process of setting those deadlines.

One of the younger scientists saw this as a problem in communication: "The biggest problem is communication. A lot of times people feel they are not consulted. Contracts are made and deadlines are expected when the science just isn't that far. It is the business needs (the contracts) vs. reality."

Taber believed in the value of Socratic dialogue as a way of keeping the scientists on track. Scientists needed someone to pursue the details of their experiments, to question the logic of the choices made. "You have to keep people thinking," Taber said.

Edelman suggested that "committees should devote two hours a week to sitting down and thinking out the other scientists' problems with them." These ad hoc committees of peers would be motivated by a real concern to help the other scientists. "The only way we are going to compete with Genentech," he said, "is if we all really get in this thing together."

Housman also saw dialogue and communication as key elements in an environment conducive to scientific creativity and productivity. "It is important to have people talking so that they are being intellectually stimulated," he said.

Erickson and Edelman both observed that ideas were born and emotional paralysis avoided through seemingly random talk. "A lot of times, when sitting on the Scientific Advisory Board," Erickson said, "I have thought there was a lot of random talk going nowhere until I saw how it occasionally really sparked an idea in someone's mind."

A new building, under construction, was designed to foster interaction. Comfortable and inviting spaces for talking were included in the halls. Spaces for retreat were also included.

Management encouraged scientists to go to professional meetings where they talk with peers outside the company and make new contacts. They were also encouraged to publish papers on patented work and thus enter into public dialogues. Management also tried to give the scientists as much freedom and responsibility as possible for how they approached and planned their projects. (Initially, the SAB had set the direction for the projects.)

THE CULTURE OF THE SCIENTISTS AND MANAGING SCIENTIFIC CREATIVITY

When he was being recruited, Connoy, the vice president of marketing, considered what it would be like working in a heavily scientific environment. "I knew it would be different with so many Ph.D. scientists around," he said. "The pleasant surprise is that I find them fun. They are excited . . . enthusiastic about what they are doing and very interested in my aspect of the business as well."

About differences in values and expectations between scientists and the business managers, Erickson said, "The scientists really, for the most part, want to do *good* science—to approach the problems in a systematic manner. What this requires is time and a significant amount of patience on the part of the administration."

Sally Dole, one of the new senior scientists, said that she was motivated by the need "to do the best job that I can do. I felt that even as a postdoc. It certainly isn't money; I've always worked hard. I want to get the job done and do it as well as I can. I think that motivates a lot of scientists."

Barry Edelman, one of the first Ph.D. scientists to join the company, also agreed that "money is not what makes people work. You want to be the first to do something no one else has done," he said.

Building Team Spirit

Edelman believed that building team spirit in IG's projects was very important, but other scientists resisted it.

> They hate it. People go into science because it is a career that allows you to spend long hours by yourself doing something that you think is great. Scientists are deeply egotistical people. It is not the kind of career you go into because you want to do teamwork. You sacrifice large parts of your life so that you can play with test tubes all by yourself. It is an individual enterprise, and everybody likes to get the highest score. And then they like to go and tell somebody about it. That's the reward.

Erickson also saw a need to stimulate more team feelings among the scientists. He observed, without any negative evaluation:

> Scientists are very egocentric people. There is always competition between scientists, and people tend not to share ideas. We also have a peer review, in which each scientist has to go in front of six of his peers and present his project to them. That initiates discussion and gets good feedback. We also have what is called a "journal club," where the scientists get together every week, usually on

Friday afternoon, for socializing. Everyone is invited and scientists are selected or invited to give talks on whatever they want to talk about. It usually stimulates good conversation.

Concerning competition for rank, Edelman thought that promotions and rewards were part of the problem and should be downplayed. Striving for promotions prevented people from interacting. The dilemma of promotions was accentuated by the fact that the scientists, and especially the technicians, wanted some clear form of career progression and promotional opportunities.

Carpenter had felt it necessary to thrash out the problems in the Salmonella test with the group. Among many other problems, the group was trying to do a scale-up of the process and had not appreciated how difficult it was going to be. Carpenter's view of what happened was that: "We went through a period of about a month when there was such intense effort—meetings and critical questioning—that everyone was getting discouraged. So we backed off and let the scientists try to solve it by themselves."

MANAGING GROWTH/MANAGING THE TRANSITION

As of July 1983, IG had 69 full-time employees, 50 of whom were engaged in R&D. Seventeen employees were Ph.D.s, and four held other advanced degrees. The company had entered into agreements with major health-care companies, including Serono Laboratories Inc. (a U.S. subsidiary of a Dutch company and the largest producer of fertility hormones worldwide), and Toyobo Co., Ltd., a major Japanese company. From inception to March 31, 1983, IG spent $2,795,846 on R&D and received $975,000 in revenues from sponsored research.

The company was now in an important transition and growing rapidly. It had been leasing about 17,000 square feet of space in Framingham, Massachusetts; it now purchased a 3.5-acre facility, using the original site for pilot-production. The new site housed multiproduct manufacturing facilities.

"We are no longer just a research and development company," said Pat Connoy. "We are turning into a business." He discussed what this transition meant:

> We are going to sell a product and have got to get things off the lab bench and out on the market. This is hard for some of the scientists to accept. They definitely feel the pressure. They are not used to setting specific goals within a timeframe. This is a real challenge for the scientific group.

A number of people anticipated that changes would be necessary in managing the transition to a company producing and marketing products as well as doing science. The growth IG people worried about was not so much any cultural change as: (1) extra stresses on the already overburdened scientific staff; and (2) the need for new skills in translating bench science to a production process that had to work perfectly all the time.

The greatest growth-related issue facing IG was recruiting—finding the right people for the company—as fast as possible. Managing growth and recruiting were almost synonymous.

Recruiting

Taber said:

> In a company like this, the only way we are going to survive is to get in the market first and get good penetration and identification. And there is a direct relationship between how fast you do it and how many good people you have. We do not yet have enough good people. So we are making a big push for hiring. We did not hire many people last year, and now we need at least ten more PhDs.

Carpenter explained the hiring hiatus which the company went through:

> We felt we were fairly well staffed for the projects we had under development at the time, and I didn't know where the next money was coming from. I was worried about overstaffing the company until we had some money coming in—some products out the door. Now I think I should never have let up on hiring. I didn't realize we were going to have a boom in the stock market. Our original plan was not to raise this kind of money from a stock offering. Our expectation for product introduction was much slower, so I thought "We don't need to hire any more people until we get the products out." Now, since we went out, got a lot of money, and need to rapidly grow the company, the pressure is on. But we've not been successful at hiring people. We've had a lot of people coming through, and we either don't like them or they don't take our job. I can't tell if this is right or wrong. We need the bodies, but one thing I've read is that in fast-paced organizations you should be very selective in your employment and only hire good people. We weren't as selective in hiring some people in the past, and we recognize that they are not going to be major players in the company down the road.

Housman said there was always a trade-off.

> It is always a problem to get people of the caliber that you want. You not only want people of the highest caliber, you want them instantly. There is always a trade-off between wanting someone who is the best possible person and having someone who will be there tomorrow. A person who is going to join in two years, who is the best possible person, is not going to help you to get a product out that has to be done next year. This is a major issue.

In charge of recent recruiting, Taber said that his inclination was to wait longer and get better people. He found recruiting difficult for several reasons. There was incredible competition from companies looking for exactly the same people, and there were not a lot of highly qualified people left in the job market. Not having a well-known scientist in the company made recruiting a little harder, as did the fact that IG was located in Framingham, Massachusetts rather than Cambridge, which had a number of biotechnology companies and was considered a more exciting community.

Exhibit 1   Management

Directors and Officers

The Directors and officers of the Company are as follows:

Name	Age	Position
Robert J. Carpenter	38	President, Chief Executive Officer and Director
David E. Housman	36	Chairman of the Board of Directors
Patrick J. Connoy	33	Vice President—Sales and Marketing
Robert J. Erickson	41	Vice President—Technical Director
Evan M. Lebson	40	Treasurer
Thomas A. Smith	45	Vice President—Operations
Robert L. Taber	40	Vice President—Corporate Development
Thomas C. Chase	40	Secretary
David L. Anderson	39	Director
F. Donald Hudson	49	Director
Gordon F. Kingsley	54	Director
Peter P. Phildius	53	Director

Mr. Carpenter has served as President, Chief Executive Officer and a Director since May 1981. Prior to May 1981, Mr. Carpenter was employed for more than five years by Baxter-Travenol Laboratories, Inc., most recently as President of the Fenwal division. Mr. Carpenter holds a B.S. degree from the United States Military Academy at West Point, an M.S. degree in Computer Science from Stanford University and an M.B.A. degree from Harvard University.

Dr. Housman is a co-founder of the Company and has served as Chairman of the Board of Directors since March 1981. He is and has been for more than five years an Associate Professor of Biology at Massachusetts Institute of Technology. Dr. Housman holds a B.A. degree in Biology and a Ph.D. degree from Brandeis University.

Mr. Connoy has served as Vice President—Sales and Marketing since January 1983. Prior to January 1983, Mr. Connoy was employed for more five years by American Hospital Supply Corporation, most recently as Vice President, Marketing, Nursing Products Division of the American Pharmaseal division. Mr. Connoy holds a B.S. degree in Business Administration from the University of Minnesota.

Dr. Erickson has served as Vice President—Technical Director since March 1982. Prior to March 1982, Dr. Erickson was employed for more than five years by Miles Laboratories, Inc., a subsidiary of Bayer AG, most recently as Vice President, Research and Development for the Biotechnology Group. Dr. Erickson holds a B.A. degree from Wabash College, an M.A. degree from Wesleyan University and a Ph.D. degree from the Waksman Institute of Rutgers University.

Mr. Lebson has served as Treasurer since May 1983. From May 1982 until May 1983 he served as Controller of the Company. Prior to May 1982, he was employed for more than five years by National Medical Care, Inc., most recently as Controller, Dialysis Services and, prior to that, as Corporate Director of Accounting and Reporting. Mr. Lebson, a Certified Public Accountant in Massachusetts, holds a B.S. degree from the University of Rochester and an M.B.A. degree from Harvard University.

Mr. Smith has served as Vice President—Operations since May 1983. Prior to May 1983, Mr. Smith was employed for more than five years by Abbott Laboratories, Inc., most recently as Operations Manager—Diagnostic Products and, prior to that, as Operations Manager—Physiologic Diagnostics. Mr. Smith holds a B.S. degree from the University of Michigan.

Dr. Taber has served as Vice President—Corporate Development since January 1983. From August 1981 until January 1983 he served as Director of Planning. Prior to August 1981, Dr. Taber was Associate Director of the Northern California Cancer Program in Palo Alto and a faculty member of the Department of Pharmacology at the University of California at San Francisco School of Medicine. Dr. Taber holds a B.A. degree from Harpur College and a Ph.D. degree from the University of Pittsburgh School of Medicine.

Mr. Chase has served as Secretary since February 1981. He is and has been for more than 10 years a partner of Gaston Snow & Ely Bartlett, Boston, Massachusetts, counsel to the Company, and holds a B.A. degree from Bowdoin College and an LL.B. degree from Harvard University.

Mr. Anderson has served as a Director of the Company since March 1981. Mr. Anderson has been a general partner of Sutter Hill Ventures, a venture capital investment partnership, since 1974. Mr. Anderson is also a director of Activision, Inc., Apollo Computer Inc., Hybritech, Inc. and Dionex Corporation. He holds a B.S. degree in electrical engineering from Massachusetts Institute of Technology and an M.B.A. degree from Harvard University.

Mr. Hudson is a co-founder of the Company and has served as a Director since March 1981. He has held various positions with the Company since February 1981, most recently as Director of Marketing—International. Prior to February 1981, Mr. Hudson was employed by Norlin Corporation, most recently as Vice President, Planning and Development. Mr. Hudson holds a B.E.E. degree from Yale University and an M.B.A. degree from New York University.

Mr. Kingsley has served as a Director since August 1981. Mr. Kingsley has been President, Chief Executive Officer and a Director of Haemonetics Corporation since 1971. He holds a B.S.M.E. degree from Northwestern University and an M.B.A. degree from Harvard University.

Mr. Phildius has served as a Director since September 1981. Mr. Phildius was President, Chief Operating Officer and a Director of Delmed, Inc. from 1981 until June 1983. From 1978 to 1981 he was President, Chief Operating Officer and a Director of National Medical Care, Inc. Mr. Phildius holds a B.B.A. degree in Business Administration from Hofstra College.

Exhibit 2 Products in Development

DNA HYBRIDIZATION TECHNOLOGY: DIAGNOSTIC TESTS

All of the company's diagnostic tests are based upon its proprietary technology in the area of DNA hybridization. This technology involves the use of genetically engineered DNA fragments which can quickly and accurately identify the presence of infectious organisms such as viruses and bacteria. (The genetic information encoded by the DNA of each species is unique and as such can be used to identify that species. Furthermore, knowledge of specific sequences of DNA can be used to identify abnormalities in organisms resulting from alteration in genetic structure.) DNA hybridization technology has been used successfully as a tool in research laboratories for several years. The commercial application of the technology provides an entirely new method for diagnosing infectious diseases and offers many advantages over traditional tests. The currently used tests are time-consuming, expensive and labor intensive. The products which IG has concentrated on developing are intended to be faster, more sensitive, and more specific than existing conventional tests, and should be readily acceptable to clinical and industrial laboratories. It is believed that the present market in the U.S. to which DNA hybridization technology can be applied is several hundred million diagnostic tests annually.

The diagnostic tests include:

Salmonella. Salmonella bacteria are a frequent cause of gastrointestinal disease and are ordinarily transmitted through contaminated food products. Under federal regulations, certain classes of food products are required to be tested for the presence of Salmonella before distribution to consumers. In addition, patients suffering from severe intestinal disorders are generally tested for Salmonella in the clinical laboratory. Current tests are time consuming, expensive, labor intensive, and not readily adaptable to automation. IG believes it can reduce the testing time from 5–7 days to less than three hours, thus reducing inventory, labor, and handling costs of tested foods. The current cost of testing is as high as $15 per test, and several million such tests are performed annually in the U.S. The company is working with Silliker Laboratories of Chicago, a leading independent food products reference laboratory, to develop a test to detect Salmonella.

Cytomegalovirus (CMV). CMV infections can lead to serious illness or death if occurring in infants or immunologically compromised individuals. The company believes that current testing methods for this disease are inadequate and that the potential U.S. market exceeds two million tests annually.

Hepatitis B. Hepatitis is a serious viral disease of the liver, affecting millions of people worldwide. Currently available tests are not sufficiently sensitive. Some contaminated blood products are not identified and as a result are transfused and may cause serious disease in recipients. IG believes it can develop a much more sensitive test. The company anticipates that it will begin full field trials of its test in 1984. Demonstration of appropriate test sensitivity during field trials and FDA approval (which the company expects will take at least one year from filing with the FDA) will be required before full-scale commercialization.

Tests for genetic disorders. Members of the company's scientific advisory board are recognized experts in the application of recombinant DNA techniques to human genetic diseases; the company has made a major commitment in this area. IG believes that testing for disorders such as cystic fibrosis, muscular dystrophy, and Huntington's disease will represent a rapidly expanding market during the 1980s, and it has initiated a research program on cystic fibrosis.

Therapeutic products. Integrated Genetics has also performed extensive research which may lead to the development of commercially valuable and medically significant therapeutic products which are expensive to produce from traditional human sources. The company believes it has made substantial progress in developing improved production ("expression") systems to produce these products commercially by genetic engineering technology. These expression systems have been developed in genetically engineered yeast and mammalian cells and offer certain potential advantages over traditional sources or expression systems developed in genetically engineered bacterial cells.

Therapeutic products under development include:

Fertility hormones. Production of these hormones through recombinant DNA technology could eliminate several problems with hormones which are conventionally derived from human urine. It is thought that the current worldwide market for these products exceeds $20 million annually and could increase substantially with the development of genetically engineered products.

Blood products. Factor VIII. Factor VIII is a blood-clotting protein used to control bleeding in hemophiliacs. Natural Factor VIII, derived from human plasma is expensive and a potential source of infection. IG believes that the current worldwide market for Factor VIII exceeds $200 million annually and that a genetically engineered product would gain wide acceptance. However, the production of Factor VIII by recombinant DNA technology is a formidable technical challenge and will require several years of research and development and testing. The expertise of the Scientific Advisory Board of the company has allowed IG to devise unique strategies for the isolation of the Factor VIII gene which the company is currently implementing. A recognized expert in the molecular structure of Factor VIII has been hired as a consultant to the project.

Tissues Plasminogen Activator (TPA). TPA is a clot-dissolving enzyme applicable to the treatment of a wide variety of severe cardiovascular disorders including heart attacks and arterial blockages. Current treatment methods are expensive or have undesirable side effects. The company believes that these problems can be eliminated and that the potential worldwide market for TPA could exceed $400 million annually.

Exhibit 3 Risk Factors

The following factors should be carefully considered in evaluating the Company and its business before purchasing the shares offered by this Prospectus.

Recently commenced commercial operations. Integrated Genetics was organized in February 1981. Most of the products which the Company is pursuing are currently in the laboratory research phase and will require extensive further development and investment prior to commercialization. All of the Company's revenues to date (other than interest income) have been derived from payments under two research and development contracts, both of which are cancellable upon short notice without significant penalty to the sponsor. No products developed by the Company through sponsored or its own research have yet become commercially available. The Company's revenues to date have not been sufficient to cover operating expenses. Net losses for 1981, 1982 and the first three months of 1983 were $526,679, $1,761,658 and $564,693, respectively. At March 31, 1983, the Company had an accumulated deficit of approximately $2,881,171 and it expects to continue to incur substantial losses in 1983. During the next several years, while Integrated Genetics is engaged in extensive product development and commercial scale-up, operating losses are expected to continue.

Product development. In order for the Company to achieve profitable operations, the Company must complete the development of several products and must successfully introduce and market these products. While Integrated Genet-

ics is developing several clinical products for diagnostic and therapeutic purposes, there is no assurance that these products will perform in accordance with the Company's expectations, that the Company will receive timely approvals from the United States Food and Drug Administration ("FDA") or that the Company will be able to successfully produce and market these products in commercial quantities.

Uncertainty of financial results and capital needs. Because the timing and receipt of revenues from the sale of products, and currently from contract research, are tied to the achievement of new product development objectives, which cannot be predicted with certainty, there may be substantial fluctuations in the Company's results of operations. Furthermore, in addition to expending substantial funds on its ongoing product research and development programs, Integrated Genetics expects to spend significant amounts in the near future in pursuit of regulatory clearances, and in continuing to build the Company's production and marketing capabilities. In addition, certain of the Company's products and processes are being developed under contracts with other companies. The companies hold licenses to make, use and sell such products and processes, and the revenues derived by the Company therefrom will depend upon the extent to which such other companies determine to exploit commercially such products or processes and the success of such commercialization. If revenues do not grow as rapidly as planned, or if research, development and clinical programs require more funding than originally anticipated, Integrated Genetics may have to scale back product development efforts and undertake additional financings. There can be no assurance that such financings, if available, will be on terms favorable or acceptable to the Company.

Government regulation. Integrated Genetics and its contract customers plan to manufacture and sell many products which may require regulatory approval. In particular, products involving pharmaceutical and biological applications are subject to the approval, prior to marketing, of the FDA in the United States and comparable agencies in foreign countries. The Company and its contract customers have not sought regulatory approval for any of its products under development. The process of obtaining such approvals can be costly and time consuming, and there can be no assurance that the necessary approvals will be granted to Integrated Genetics or its contract customers. The extent of adverse government regulation which might arise from future local, state and federal legislation or administrative action cannot be accurately predicted.

Patents and proprietary technology. The Company has filed several patent applications in the United States, based on inventions made in the course of its research and development activities. There can be no assurance that any patents will be issued or that, if issued, the Company's patents would effectively protect its proprietary technology. The Company intends to rely substantially on its unpatented proprietary know-how, and there can be no assurance that others will not develop such know-how independently or otherwise obtain access to the Company's technology. Universities and

other public and private concerns have filed for, or have been issued, patents on inventions, some of which have been licensed by the Company and others, which, if valid, would require the Company to obtain additional licenses if the inventions are used in the course of its product development activities. Except to the extent set forth in "Business—Patents and Proprietary Technology", the number, scope and validity of any such patents and patents applications, the extent to which the Company may be required or may desire to obtain additional licenses thereunder, and the availability and cost of such licenses are presently unknown. Certain of the Company's consultants have developed portions of the Company's proprietary technology at their respective universities or in government laboratories. There can be no assurance that the government or the universities may not assert rights to intellectual property arising out of university- or government-based research conducted by the Company's consultants.

Competition. Competitors engaged in all areas of biotechnology, and specifically genetic engineering, in the United States and abroad are numerous and include, among others, major pharmaceutical, energy, food and chemical companies, specialized biotechnology firms, universities and other research institutions. The Company expects that competition will increase with the perceived potential for commercial applications of biotechnology. In addition, the greater availability of capital for investment in these fields and the potentially greater funding of industrial research in these fields by foreign governments will likely result in increased competition.

Exhibit 3 Risk Factors (*Continued*)

Many of the large corporations which are involved in or are expected to become involved in biotechnology have substantially greater resources than the Company and have the capability of providing significant long-term competition.

Technological change. The field of biotechnology has undergone, and is expected to continue to undergo, significant and rapid technological changes. Although the Company continually seeks to expand its broad base of technological capabilities, there can be no assurance that research and discoveries by others will not render the Company's products or processes obsolete.

Retention of key personnel. Because of the specialized nature of the Company's business, it is necessary to attract and retain personnel with a wide variety of management and scientific capabilities. Competition for such personnel is intense and is expected to increase in the future. While the Company considers its

compensation and other benefit programs, as well as its corporate and research environment, to be attractive, there can be no assurance that the Company will continue to be able to hire and retain personnel of high business and scientific caliber.

Possible volatility of stock price. Because of the factors discussed above, the market price of the Company's Common Stock may be highly volatile. Additionally, factors such as announcements of technological innovations, new commercial products, patents, the development of proprietary rights by the Company or others, or public concern over the safety of the Company's activities or products may have a significant impact on the market price of the Common Stock. In addition, the market price may be significantly affected by future sales of shares by existing stockholders pursuant to registration rights or pursuant to Rule 144 under the Securities Act of 1933. See "Shares Eligible for Future Sale."

Exhibit 4 Integrated Genetics

| | February 3, 1981 (inception) to December 31, 1981 | Year Ended December 31, 1982 | Three Months Ended March 31, | |
			1982	1983
Statement of Operations Data (1):			(unaudited)	
Revenues from sponsored research	$ 75,000	$ 600,000	$150,000	$300,000
Interest income	50,651	460,298	87,608	104,881
Total revenues	$125,651	$1,060,298	$237,608	$404,881
Research and development expenses	$232,871	$1,898,277	$321,524	$664,698
Net loss	(526.679)	(1,761,658)	(387,503)	(564,693)
Net loss per common share	(0.27)	(0.63)	(0.15)	(0.19)
Weighted average number of common shares outstanding	1,986,291	2,778,990	2,548,968	2,913,483

| | March 31, 1983 | |
	Actual	As Adjusted (2)
Balance Sheet Data:	(unaudited)	
Working capital	$4,221,989	$23,240,989
Total assets	9,063,070	28,082,070
Long-term debt, including capital lease obligations	3,339,859	3,339,859
Stockholders' equity	5,099,917	24,118,917

(1) From its inception through March 31, 1983, the Company had total revenues of $1,590,830 and net losses of $2,853,030.

(2) Adjusted to reflect the sale of 1,600,000 shares offered hereby and the initial application of the net proceeds to working capital as set forth in "Use of Proceeds."

All information relating to the Company's Common Stock contained in this Prospectus, except that contained in the financial statements and net loss per common share information, reflects the conversion of all outstanding shares of the Company's Class A and Class B Preferred Stock into Common Stock on the date of this Prospectus (unless the context otherwise requires). All share and per share data in this Prospectus have been adjusted retroactively to reflect a 3-for-1 stock split effected in May 1983.

Exhibit 5 Employee Stock Purchase Plan

Under a 1981 Employee Stock Purchase Plan, IG could sell an aggregate of 926,250 shares of common stock to employees at the fair market value of the stock at the date of issue.

Substantially all of the common stock was issued through agreements which contained restrictions on resale. Certain shares issued to employees vested over a five-year period. The company reserved the right to purchase that percentage of shares not vested upon termination.

The company has two "Incentive Stock Option Plans." All options under these plans expire ten years from the date of the grant. The 1982 Common Stock Option Plan allows for the granting to employees of options to purchase up to 400,000 shares of common stock at the fair market value of the shares on the date of the grant. The 1982 Preferred Stock Option Plan allows for the granting to employees of options to purchase up to 150,000 shares of Class B preferred stock at the fair value of the shares on the date of the grant.

A 1983 Employee Stock Purchase Plan made all full-time employees, who have been employed by the company for more than six months, eligible for grants of options to purchase up to an aggregate of 200,000 shares of common stock at purchase prices equal to 85% of the lesser of the fair market value of the shares.

Infocom, Inc. (A)

You enter the office of Albert Vezza, CEO of Infocom, a dynamic Cambridge software development company known for its hot line of interactive fiction games. You are the consultant.

You ask the CEO what's going on in the company. Vezza tells you they are growing fast and it's causing problems. Top management is stepping on each other's toes. Roles are unclear. He is doing too many things. They need to reorganize to accommodate an ambitious new business product line but are not sure which way to go to keep down the conflict. Can the company be held together? He wants some answers and he wants them soon. Your job—analyze the situation and make recommendations to the board.

You walk out of the office and run into a man in a bright Hawaiian shirt. In an office on your left you see several casual fellows in work shirts and Levi's hanging over computers. A group of worried-looking men in coats and ties troop out of an office on the right leaving a large board filled with schedules. Two young women in classic business dress walk hurriedly past talking about PR. You think: "Where do I start? And, what are the issues around here?" Type in your answer now!

INFOCOM, INC.

Infocom was a leading developer of entertainment software for personal computers. It popularized a form called "interactive fiction" in which a computer user takes a role such as adventurer, detective, or star voyager; a story's plot unfolds on the computer screen as a result of the player's decisions.

Infocom was formed in June 1979 by ten computer scientists who worked together at the Laboratory for Computer Science at MIT. They decided to develop and market interactive fiction games and other software, using programming techniques developed in MIT's computer labs. All the scientists at first served as consultants and advisors to the company in the development of software tools and products.

The first interactive fiction computer game—a treasure hunt through labyrinthine caves—was created in the mid-1970s by computer buffs in

This case was prepared by Associate Professor John J. Kao.

Copyright © 1986 by the President and Fellows of Harvard College. Harvard Business School case 1-487-015.

Cambridge and at Stanford University. In 1977, a group of MIT students—including Marc Blank, who later became vice president of product development at Infocom—developed their own adventure "story" called Zork, using MIT's mainframe computers. The game was then converted to personal computer format by Infocom.

Zork I came on the market in December 1980 and quickly shot up to the top of the best-selling entertainment software lists, adding a new genre of computer games which was Infocom's distinctive niche. Zork itself became something of a cult item. A "Zork users group" was formed to provide hints on how to penetrate the many layers of the game and gain access to new adventures and new treasures.

In June 1981, after graduating from MIT's Sloan School, Joel Berez, one of the ten founders, became Infocom's first full-time employee. In January 1982, the second founder Marc Blank, became the third full-time employee to join the company. In June 1982, the company consisted of Joel Berez as president and CEO and Marc Blank as vice president of product development. (The second full-time employee had left the company.) Albert Vezza was chairman of the board (see *Exhibit 1* for resumes). The company had three products on the market—Zork I, Zork II, and Deadline, all of which stood in the top 30 adventure games on Softsel's best-seller list of entertainment software. Four more entertainment products were under development.

THE ENTERTAINMENT SOFTWARE INDUSTRY

The recreational or entertainment software market was volatile and competitive. Success in the market was reflected in a slot on the weekly "Softsel Hot List" published by one of the world's largest computer software distributors. In 1982 most of the best-sellers on the list were "zap and escape" arcade-style games such as Pac Man and Choplifter. By 1984, however, half of the top 30 required brain work much more than dexterity. Users of increasingly sophisticated computers wanted increasingly sophisticated programs and designers strained to produce more elaborate graphics and more challenging (and addictive) programs.

In 1984 the best-sellers were games that stretched the imagination and taught while they amused. Sublogic's Flight Simulator II and Microsoft's Flight Simulator which allowed players to practice a close to life experience were high on the charts for months.

After spectacular beginnings in the early 1980s, many of the entertainment software manufacturers experienced hard times—leading to rapid revamping and switching of product lines. The software entertainment industry was often noted for its likeness to the record business. A company cannot rest for long on one hit record, but must keep coming up with new hits constantly. And the new hits must show variety; at first several companies made major mistakes in bringing out a series of clones of previous best-sellers.

The most successful companies in this industry had not followed the pack. Infocom was one of the few companies that had not only not followed the pack, but had in fact established a niche in which it had almost total dominance—the text adventure niche. Starting with Zork in 1980, Infocom created, developed, and popularized the genre of interactive fiction, appealing to sophisticated, intelligent, and literate adults who loved games but who were not attracted to the run of the mill arcade-style games. Infocom's audience was composed heavily of computer hackers and buffs, and the company was not keen on altering and simplifying its games in order to attract a mass market. Infocom's conservative market strategy was lauded as one of the components of its success. Though the company felt that it had a tendency to underproduce and underpromote, on this basis it was able to earn over $500,000 in profits on $6 million in sales in 1983.

Another unique aspect of Infocom's strategy which set it apart from its competitors was the attention it paid to creative packaging and supplementary materials such as books of clues and hints that provided the user with a complete environment, adding to the hypnotic realism of the games.

The company also showed unusual flexibility in redesigning its trademark packaging to fit more easily onto dealers' shelves and, in a sharp departure from industry practices, pricing its titles according to their varying level of difficulty.

One of the ironies of success in the entertainment software business (as in computer software in general) was that it could stimulate a host of competitive products leading to a glut in a given category. As of mid-1984 at least three other companies (Spinnaker, Epyx, and Imagic) had entered the interactive fiction genre, although none had emulated Infocom's particular style. The one rule that could be counted on in the software industry was constant change—ever-new developments.

Diversification

In September 1982, Infocom decided it was both possible and important to diversify into the business software market and sought $2 million in equity financing for expansion. As a result of negotiations with potential investors, it was decided that the chairman of the board, Albert Vezza, should be brought into the company on a full-time basis as CEO. Vezza brought with him the maturity and experience gained as associate director of MIT's Laboratory for Computer Science that investors thought the company needed. Joel Berez continued as president of the company since this was his perceived role in the marketplace, and his credibility and contacts might be affected if his title were to change. However, some ambiguity developed around the definition of Vezza's and Berez's role and responsibilities.

Another element of complexity was that at MIT Vezza had been Blank's and Berez's faculty supervisor and his role relation to them had been a somewhat paternalistic one. At Infocom, although he was in the chief executive's seat, Vezza was a newcomer to an established group and was a co-owner with the other two. Vezza there sat on the board and had input into key decisions. Vezza also had concerns about how to develop a strong corporate image and felt that the company had to become more businesslike. He wanted to hire people with strong business experience who did not belong to the MIT computer network, who were more mature, *and* who had a keen concern for the bottom line. Vezza had a strong feeling of responsibility for making the company successful, and took seriously the idea that "the buck stops with me."

Berez had come from a family of successful businessmen and tended to be quiet, low key, and very attuned to the subtle communications of deal making. Blank was the creative leader of the game developers; he was frequently impatient with restrictions on the freedom that seemed to nourish his intuitive brilliance.

DEVELOPMENT OF THE COMPANY

At the end of 1982 Infocom employed 12 people and had $1.662 million in revenues and a net income of $336,000. By the end of 1983 the company had almost tripled in size to 32 employees and had five new products. Revenues in 1983 reached $6.052 million and net income was $526,000. Zork I, the company's first product, remained at the top of a popular best-seller list for 12 straight weeks. It was anticipated that the company's first business product would be on the market in late 1984, as well as five new games for the year (see *Exhibits 2* and *3*).

Since a considerable number of new hires were anticipated for 1984, a personnel assistant was recruited from the ranks of the office staff. Her job consisted primarily of recruiting and interviewing new people, passing on good candidates to those who had made hiring requests, orienting new employees, and administering payroll and benefits. The personnel assistant was worried that the personnel job was beginning to outgrow her skills. Rapid advancement to higher level managerial positions was occurring in a number of areas, bringing with it the problem of having people in key functions with limited formal managerial training or experience. One employee, for example, had been an original company employee and had shown great energy and flair for handling multiple functions, running the office, and acting as an administrative assistant to Berez as president. She knew everything about the company, had performed well in a variety of functions, and showed a talent for sales. Still in her mid-twenties, she was a key person in the company but suffered considerably from the ambiguity about what her role would or could be in the future.

In late 1982 and early 1983 a group of people were brought in to Infocom to develop the new business product, a data base management system. The business product, or BP developers were different in style and culture from the older consumer products or games people, and subtle antagonisms and conflicts began to arise. In 1984, a group of people responsible for marketing business products came aboard and exacerbated the problem.

The consumer products (CP) or games designers and testers were highly independent and eclectic in style. Most of them worked long hours but preferred the freedom of working late into the night and on weekends if they wished rather than following a conventional schedule. Most preferred to dress informally in work shirts, jeans, and tennis shoes and feared the increasing bureaucratization and "blue suit" mentality that they saw coming with increasing growth. They treasured the intimate, personal, creative, and "fun" atmosphere that had characterized the company in its early days.

The BP development and marketing people exhibited a different culture from the CP developers. The style of dress of BP people was more conventional; conservative business shirts, ties, and sweaters were standard attire. The BP people were also physically separated from the CP people; each group worked on a different floor and had little occasion to run into each other casually. The games designers and old-timers in the company tended to hang out together, to discuss business over lunch or dinner or have beers outside the company. New people coming into the company had to learn these informal modes of communication and negotiation or be treated to a certain amount of razzing. One new professional in the company was used to writing informal memos to other employees as a way of communication. She was first lightly lampooned in "Infodope," the company's underground newsletter and then a ludicrous phony memo was distributed in her name.

The professionalization of the company or the "blue suit" mentality was seen by some as a threat to the essential values of the company—including the emphasis the games designers placed on quality and uniqueness of products. They worried that if business products were developed too rapidly and compromises were made on product quality or marketing strategy, Infocom's established reputation as a leader in high-quality, high-value, top-of-the-line software might be affected. One person commented that Infocom was the "Rolls Royce" of recreational software and that some of the new people would tend to let quality slip in their emphasis on productivity and penetration of new markets. Others felt that this was completely untrue. Some argued that the company was and would have to be a market-driven company. Others said it was and would have to stay R&D-driven.

Several of the key games designers had begun to question whether rapid growth was desirable and necessary. The CP group felt that the profits generated by their side of the business were being used to subsidize and partially finance business product development. Many had doubts that a new data base management system could succeed in its highly competitive segment of the market. The CP people also resented the drain on their financial and people resources, which they said curtailed their own developmental work. "CP was being bled by BP," one designer commented. In fact, financial support for each group was roughly equal. In addition, competition arose over an important shared resource—the microcomputer programmers who translated programs developed on the mainframe computer to programs for various personal computers.

Thus, as the company grew and as new people were hired into the business product side of the company, tensions mounted. The company was seen as divided variously into old-timers versus new professionals, creative types versus business-oriented professionals, and BP people versus CP people.

ASSESSING ORGANIZATIONAL STRUCTURE

Early in 1984 as the sense of conflict increased and role ambiguity at the top developed, a large investor and director suggested that Vezza bring in a consultant to assess the climate of the company and make recommendations, in particular about the appropriate organizational structure. Key questions were: Should the company have a divisional structure or a functional structure with two product lines sharing most functions? Was there any chance of a split in the company between the two product lines and their champions? What would be needed in the company if it continued to grow at the current rate?

The consultants interviewed all of the senior management of the company and distributed a climate assessment questionnaire to all employees. (See *Exhibit 4* for the questionnaire.)

The interviews revealed a wide spectrum of opinion on how the company should be structured and what the key issues were. Examples of what emerged were: cultural conflict, managerial inexperience, normal growing pains, conflict over resources, the cohesiveness of top management, a need for better communications and conflict resolution skills, a need for better coordination between departments. (Selected summaries of the interview results are in *Exhibit 5*.) In spite of the company's problems, it was in general viewed as an exciting, caring, and frequently fun place to work. One competitor remarked in a news article that Infocom was not only a formidable force in the recreational games market but it also "seemed to have a lot of fun doing it."

Interviews in the company reflected a great variety of opinion about the ideal organizational structure for Infocom at this time. Everyone agreed that the organizational structure as it stood early in 1983 was ambiguous and contributed to problems around departmental coordination and communication. The interviews also revealed no clear consensus about which sales or marketing or other functions were shared. There were also many opinion about how similar or different the product lines were. Arguments in favor of product line divisions were as follows:

1. The CP and BP product lines were separate without many similarities.
2. A product line organization would foster more profit responsibility and motivation towards the achievement of financial goals.

3. A product line organization favored a balanced allocation of resources. (In a functional structure the most successful product line had first priority over resources.)

Arguments against a strict divisionalization of the company included:

1. The product line markets were not as dissimilar as they seemed. The business product could be marketed as a sophisticated consumer product for the intelligent upper-level personal computer market. Thus there was the potential for similar end users and some distribution channels.
2. A strict divisionalization would divide the product groups further and could potentially split the company apart.
3. The company could not afford the functional redundancies of a product division.
4. The divisional structure encouraged individual product lines to pursue their own goals without regard for overall company values and goals other than financial ones.
5. There was a need for *one* company to face the world, not two. Strategies and practices of the two sides needed to be congruent and the business product had to maintain the Infocom quality image with no compromises.

Shared areas between the two products at the time included: public relations, the ad agency, marketing, and product testing. It was clear that a decision needed to be made about the potential market for the data base management system with corporate clients, value-added retailers, and the sophisticated home user. There was also considerably divided opinion about what the role relationships and responsibilities of the top management group should be. Many feared too much centralization of decision making.

The consultant's job was to find an organizational structure that was acceptable to all and which would not create conflict for the future.

Exhibit 1 Resumes of Key Infocom Executives

JOEL M. BEREZ

EDUCATION

1979–1981 M.I.T. SLOAN SCHOOL OF MANAGEMENT   Cambridge, MA
S.M. in Management
Concentration in Marketing. Thesis entitled "An Investigation of the
Decision Hierarchy for the Selection of Motion Pictures."

1972–1976 MASSACHUSETTS INSTITUTE
OF TECHNOLOGY   Cambridge, MA
S.B. in Computer Science and Engineering
Thesis entitled "A Dynamic Debugging System for MDL," published
as TM-94, M.I.T. Laboratory for Computer Science, January 1978.

EXPERIENCE

June 1981–   INFOCOM, INC.   Cambridge, MA
Present   President
Managed firm through transition into full-scale business operation.

July 1979–   INFOCOM, INC.   Cambridge, MA
May 1981   Consultant
Designed and/or implemented software tools for the creation of new
products, including parts of a development system for the creation of
machine-independent games for microcomputers. Supervised corporate product development activities. Managed general business functions including sales, purchasing, accounting, and customer service.

Summer   DIGITAL EQUIPMENT CORPORATION   Hudson, NH
1980   Principal Operations Analyst
Constructed a computer model for the creation, maintenance, and
evaluation of long-term financial plan for the Government Systems
Group.

October   ACTION INDUSTRIES, INC.   Cheswick, PA
1977–   Operations Research Analyst
June 1979   Analyzed operational problems in business, proposed possible solution, and supervised implementation of selected alternatives. Projects
included selection and installation of company's first on-line computer system for program development and immediate user data access; major restructuring of merchandise tracking procedures from
purchasing through sales; and revision of cost accounting systems in
manufacturing operation.

June 1976–   M.I.T. LABORATORY FOR
September   COMPUTER SCIENCE   Cambridge, MA
1977   Research Staff
Participated in development of databased message system for U.S.
Naval Department. Designed and implemented virtual terminal inter-
face modules of message system.

Summers,   ACTION INDUSTRIES, INC.   Cheswick, PA
1972–1975   Various summer jobs:
1. Programmer
Designed and implemented system for scheduling promotions
among 10,000+ retail stores with minimal conflicts.
2. Buyer
Purchased housewares for Far East, inspecting and selecting merchandise, negotiating prices and terms, and scheduling shipments.
3. Analyst
Recommended and supervised installation of in-house graphic
arts facility including photography, typesetting, and ad layout.

Exhibit 1   Resumes of Key Infocom Executives (*Continued*)

MARC S. BLANK, M.D.

EDUCATION

ALBERT EINSTEIN COLLEGE OF MEDICINE
M.D. degree received June 1979

MASSACHUSETTS INSTITUTE
OF TECHNOLOGY   Cambridge, MA
S.B. degree received June 1975. Major field was biology with minor in economics.

Elected to Phi Beta Kappa, 1975
Elected to Phi Lambda Upsilon, 1974

EXPERIENCE

1982   INFOCOM, INC.   Cambridge, MA
          Vice president for product development
          Responsible for the design and development of new products for Infocom, including both simulation games and business software.

1979–1981 INFOCOM, INC.   Cambridge, MA
           Consultant
           Designed and developed a machine-independent development system, based on the MDL language, to run on microcomputers. Designed and developed prose simulation games based on this development system and supervised the introduction of versions on a number of different computer systems.

1980–1981 M.I.T. LABORATORY FOR
           COMPUTER SCIENCE   Cambridge, MA
           Research Associate
           Designed and led the development of a machine-independent MDL for use on mainframe and minicomputers.

1979–1980 MASSACHUSETTS GENERAL HOSPITAL-
           LABORATORY OF COMPUTER SCIENCE   Cambridge, MA
           Research Fellow, Department of Medicine
           Worked on user-interfaces and display graphics for the COSTAR system—a medically oriented data base system developed at MGH.

1975–1979 MIT LABORATORY FOR
           COMPUTER SCIENCE   Cambridge, MA
           Consultant
           Numerous projects had included MDL language development and maintenance, the design and implementation of an MDL disk-resident database system designed for use in message systems, message system implementation, and general system utility and maintenance programming.

PUBLICATIONS

"ZORK: A Computerized Fantasy Simulation Game." *IEEE Computer*, Vol. 12, No. 4, April 1979, p. 51.

Programming Technology Division Document SYS. 11.24, Marc S. Blank, "Abstr. User's Manual," September 1975.

Exhibit 1   Resumes of Key Infocom Executives (*Continued*)

ALBERT VEZZA

HOME ADDRESS: **OFFICE ADDRESS:**
                                              Laboratory for Computer Science
292 Winter Street   Massachusetts Institute of Technology
Weston, MA 02193   545 Technology Square
                                                        Cambridge, MA 01139

EDUCATION
              NORTHEASTERN UNIVERSITY   Boston, MA
              M.S., Electrical Engineering Department, 1966

              ROCHESTER INSTITUTE OF TECHNOLOGY   Rochester, NY
              B.S. Electrical Engineering Department, 1962

EXPERIENCE
1982 to   MASSACHUSETTS INSTITUTE
Present   OF TECHNOLOGY
            LABORATORY FOR COMPUTER SCIENCE   Cambridge, MA
            Senior Research Scientist, and Acting Associate Director

1980–1982   MASSACHUSETTS INSTITUTE
            OF TECHNOLOGY
            LABORATORY FOR COMPUTER SCIENCE   Cambridge, MA
            Senior Research Scientist

1978 to   MASSACHUSETTS INSTITUTE
Present   OF TECHNOLOGY
            LABORATORY FOR COMPUTER SCIENCE   Cambridge, MA
            Lecturer, Department of Electrical Engineering

1978–1980   MASSACHUSETTS INSTITUTE
            OF TECHNOLOGY
            LABORATORY FOR COMPUTER SCIENCE   Cambridge, MA
            Research Associate

1974 to   MASSACHUSETTS INSTITUTE
Present   OF TECHNOLOGY
            LABORATORY FOR COMPUTER SCIENCE   Cambridge, MA
            Group Leader, Programming Technology Group

1976–1978   MASSACHUSETTS INSTITUTE
            OF TECHNOLOGY   Cambridge, MA
            Research Associate, Department of Electrical Engineering and Com-
            puter Science

1974–1976   MASSACHUSETTS INSTITUTE
            OF TECHNOLOGY   Cambridge, MA
            Lecturer, Department of Electrical Engineering and Computer Sci-
            ence

1970–1974   MASSACHUSETTS INSTITUTE
            OF TECHNOLOGY   Cambridge, MA
            Deputy Leader of Programming Technology Group Project MAC

1969–1970   MASSACHUSETTS INSTITUTE
            OF TECHNOLOGY   Cambridge, MA
            Research Staff, Project MAC

1964–1969   MASSACHUSETTS INSTITUTE
            OF TECHNOLOGY   Cambridge, MA
            Research Staff, Electronic Systems Laboratory

Computers

Putting Fiction on a Floppy

Software bestsellers let players write the plot

Mrs. Robner says she loved her murdered husband, but you know she is lying. The proof is in the love note you just intercepted. Ask her about the man who wrote it, and she says she never heard of him. Confront her with his letter, and she changes her tune. "You have certainly stooped to a new low, Inspector, opening other people's mail!" Then she spills her story.

Not all mysteries these days appear in paperbacks or movies. The tale above scrolled up the screen of a personal computer. The story, titled *Deadline*, is part of the latest craze in home computing: programmed fiction. Machines that were used mainly for blasting aliens and calculating monthly budgets are now also churning through adventure tales and murder-mystery plots. "It's like reading a novel, only you are the protagonist," says Science Fiction Writer Linda Bushyager. While arcade-style games like Pac Man are losing popularity, these complex programs are winning more and more fans.

In *Deadline*, one of ten computer "novels" produced by Infocom, a Cambridge, Mass.–based software publishing house, the player is given a casebook of evidence, a floppy disc containing the plot, and twelve hours to unravel the mystery. If the murderer is not found in the allotted time, a character named Chief Inspector Klutz takes the player off the case. The program shuts down automatically and must be replayed from the beginning.

As *Deadline* opens, a wealthy businessman has been found dead in the library of his mansion from a mysterious drug overdose. The player, who takes the role of inspector, has been called in to investigate. He types commands into the computer, and the machine responds with descriptions of people and places and snatches of dialogue that develop the story. Suspects duck in and out of rooms; clues appear and disappear; characters lie low or kill again, depending on the player's actions. The story can unfold in literally thousands of ways. A typical investigation, including starts and restarts, can run 40 hours or longer. "It takes me three to six months to get completely through one," says Craig Pearce, 31, a building manager from Berwyn, Ill. "It's unbelievable how you can get hooked on these things."

The concept of interactive fiction is not totally new. The hit of the Czechoslovak pavilion at Expo 67 in Montreal was an experimental movie that let the audience vote on the course of the action. But it took the computer, with its awesome power to store and sort text, to turn the concept into a popular art form.

Author Berlyn and Programmer Blank team up to play Suspended

Two hit novels: Infocom's *Deadline* mystery and *Zork* adventure
"You have certainly stooped to a new low, Inspector."

The first participatory computer tale. *Adventure*, was created in the mid-1970s by computer researchers in Cambridge and Stanford. It involved a treasure hunt through a labyrinth of caves and dungeons and soon attracted a cult following. Miniature versions that ran on microcomputers were available in the late 1970s.

There are now two types of interactive stories on the market: high-resolution ones that display colorful pictures on the screen, and text-only games that show just words. Judging from recent sales, the text programs are more popular. *Deadline*

(price: $49.95) has sold more than 75,000 copies since it was released by Infocom almost two years ago. The company's three-part fantasy adventure, *Zork*, is doing even better. The first episode, *Zork I*, is the bestselling piece of recreational computer software on the market, with sales of 250,000 copies. It is currently outpacing the home versions of such arcade hits as Zaxxon and Frogger. "Whiz-bang graphics may be easier to sell to the uninitiated, but they are being replaced by games that give a sense of realism," says Marc Blank, the 29-year-old M.I.T. alumnus who wrote *Deadline* and is co-author of *Zork*.

The key to interactive fiction is the parser, the part of the computer program that interprets the player's commands. Parsers originally accepted only one- and two-word commands ("Take sword, Kill troll"), a most frustrating limitation. In 1977, a group of M.I.T. graduates, including Blank, began working on more powerful parsers. Using programming techniques developed at the university's artificial-intelligence laboratory, they added adjectives, prepositions and compound verbs, allowing such full sentences as "Pick up the red bomb and put it in the mailbox" and "Where is the missing will?"

Their first game, *Zork*, was developed on one of M.I.T.'s huge mainframe computers. The next task was to squeeze the program down so that it would run on a microcomputer with one-thousandth as much processing power. Blank, who had been studying medicine when he helped write *Zork*, did the necessary programming while serving his internship.

With *Zork* and *Deadline* already big hits, newer and more colorful computer novels are appearing on the software bestseller lists. Stuart Galley, an Infocom programmer, has written a detective story, *The Witness*, in the hard-boiled style of Raymond Chandler. *Infidel*, by Michael Berlyn, is an archaeological adventure set in modern Egypt. *Planetfall*, by Steven Meretzky, is a science-fiction comedy that co-stars a robot named Floyd.

By literary standards, Infocom's stories are crude. The characters are two-dimensional, plots are forever clunking to a halt, and the writing tends to be sophomoric. Perhaps the best computer thriller to date is *Suspended*, also by Berlyn, a published author with several science-fiction books to his credit. With computer novels selling better than many hardcover books, it may not be long before the new genre attracts an Isaac Asimov or a Stephen King. —*By Philip Elmer-DeWitt. Reported by Jamie Murphy/Cambridge*

76   TIME, DECEMBER 5, 1983

The Evolving Organization   **285**

Exhibit 3 Software "Hot List" for Week of September 5, 1983 (Copyright 1983 by Softsel Computer Products, Inc. Reprinted by permission.)

SOFTSEL ®

This Week	Last Week	Weeks on Chart	RECREATION
1	2	50	**Zork I** · Infocom · AP, AT, CP/M, IBM, C64, DEC, TIP
2	1	25	**Zaxxon** · Datasoft · AP, TRS, AT
3	4	50	**Frogger** · Sierra On-Line · AP, AT, IBM, C64
4	3	51	**Choplifter** · Broderbund · AP, AT
5	5	50	**Temple of Apshai** · Epyx · AP, VIC, AT, IBM, C64
6	11	50	**Deadline** · Infocom · AP, TRS, AT, CP/M, IBM, C64, DEC, TIP
7	7	25	**Fort Apocalypse** · Synapse · AT, C64
8	6	22	**Jump Man** · Epyx · AT, C64
9	12	23	**Miner 2049er** · Big Five · AT
10	13	48	**Zork II** · Infocom · AP, AT, CP/M, IBM, C64, DEC, TIP
11	21	40	**Zork III** · Infocom · AP, AT, CP/M, IBM, C64, DEC, TIP
12	9	8	**Survivor** · Synapse · AT, C64
13	18	37	**Castle Wolfenstein** · Muse · AP, AT
14	8	52	**Wizardry** · Sir-Tech · AP
15	15	41	**Starcross** · Infocom · AP, TRS, AT, CP/M, IBM, C64, DEC, TIP
16	19	8	**Witness** · Infocom · AP, TRS, AT, IBM, C64, DEC, TIP
17	10	5	**Blue Max** · Synapse · AT
18	22	34	**Miner 2049er** · Micro Lab · AP
19	20	21	**Suspended** · Infocom · AP, AT, IBM, C64, DEC, TIP
20	23	37	**Flight Simulator** · Sublogic · AP, TRS
21	25	37	**Ultima II** · Sierra On-Line · AP, AT
22	32	22	**Necromancer** · Synapse · AT
23	14	9	**David's Midnight Magic** · Broderbund · AP, AT, C64
24	31	23	**AE** · Broderbund · AP, AT
25	24	37	**Flight Simulator** · Microsoft · IBM
26	27	51	**Knight of Diamonds** · Sir-Tech · AP
27	38	7	**Telengard** · Avalon Hill · AP, TRS, AT
28		8	**Juice** · Tronix · AT
29	28	14	**Dig Dug** · Atari · AT
30	33	4	**Dreibs** · Synapse · AT

Exhibit 4 Infocom Questionnaire

1. What are three words that best describe the company's goals for you?
2. What are three words that best describe the company's values for you?
3. What are the company's three greatest strengths?
4. What are the company's three greatest problems?
5. What are you particularly concerned about as the company grows and changes?
6. What are three words which describe how you would like the company to become?
7. What are three words or phrases which describe what it was like to work in this company?
8. Are you satisfied with your progress in the company?
9. Are you satisfied with the pay you are receiving?
10. What three personal goals would you like to achieve at Infocom?
11. How much supervision does your job entail? (circle one)

    Lots   Some   None

12. What problems do you experience in the way you are managed or supervised? What could be done to improve things?
13. What problems do you experience in supervising or managing others?
14. Do you get enough information on what was happening in the company—or in your own area—to do your job effectively or to satisfy your "need to know?"
15. What other observations would you like to make on organizational issues which may affect the company's success?

Exhibit 5 Presenting Problems/Issues

The company needs a reorganization to clarify the relationship between the two product lines.

Top management roles need to be clarified: People are "stepping on each others toes." Vezza: "I am doing too many things."

ORGANIZATIONAL STRUCTURE

- Structure was inadequate to deal with multiple product line company
- Organizational structure was perceived as unclear by company members
- Large gap exists between formal and informal organization (executive committee)
- Limited mechanism for integration and conflict resolution
- Structural problem increases role ambiguity
- Key positions unfilled

"Frustration comes when the lack of departmental coordination results in people being defensive of their own space, several people doing small parts of one job and therefore overlapping, lack of knowledge about

Exhibit 5   Presenting Problems/Issues (*Continued*)

what was going on on a day-to-day basis, etc. More attention to be paid to various departments working together to get things done or to keep things moving.

"As we grow, responsibility for the product was spread out over many people, some who can't stick to their guns, who are lazy but who say, 'That will do, or that doesn't matter, it won't show.' We can command a high price for our games because we are the Rolls Royce of recreational software, not because we let things slip by. Maybe we need some motivational speakers to come in occasionally and remind everyone where we are and who we are and how we got here."

ROLE CLARIFICATION

"At the level of top management: As expected we found ambiguity in the way top management roles were defined and carried out. Role ambiguity exists at other levels of the company also. Role ambiguity results in diffusion of responsibility and interpersonal conflict."

COMPANY CLIMATE

ATMOSPHERE OF CONFLICT

- Between key individuals
- Between product groups
- Between functional gaps

MORALE

- Creativity
- Participation
- Poor communication

COMMUNICATION

"Bringing in new personnel and letting them stake out territory without checking on the situation and discussing it with current personnel can lower morale quickly and deeply."

"Communication *must* improve, starting with the top levels."

"Information was not always passed along in a timely fashion for use at the proper levels. This causes frustration for some and anxiety for others."

"Many people feel that important or useful information was being concealed from them."

Exhibit 5 Presenting Problems/Issues (*Continued*)

POSITIVES

"Everyone at Infocom was so confident and positive. It's a great feeling to be part of a growing company."

"I think this questionnaire was an indication that the company wants to be aware of employee concerns."

"The quality of Infocom's people was the greatest asset."

MANAGEMENT SKILLS

"Greatest problem in the company was poor management skills—especially the management of people."

"Managers don't have good management skills

- They don't deal with conflict
- They don't coach subordinates enough."

(Board member) "There was a great need for managerial skills development."

CURRENT PERSONAL PICTURE

- A good orientation system for new employees
- Procedures had been established for:
  - requisitions for new hires
  - internal job posting
  - raises
  - performance evaluations
- Some job descriptions had been done
- Some policies are in the process of being written
- Compensation has been established on an ad hoc basis by board decisions, negotiations with desired employees, comparisons with current hires. Perceived internal equity seems good. External equity was perceived to be poor
- Some employees dissatisfaction with benefits
- No training or development programs exist although tuition reimbursement was offered

Au Bon Pain

> I want Au Bon Pain to be the highest quality retail food company in the world.
>
> Ron Shaich, President and CEO

HISTORY

Au Bon Pain, which translates "Where the Good Bread's At" debuted in Boston's Faneuil Hall, in 1977, as a marketing tool for a French company, Pavailler, interested in selling ovens and other bakery equipment in the United States. In 1978, Louis (French pronunciation) Kane, a prominent and successful Boston businessman, bought the store and the rights to the concept. He was fascinated with the idea of creating a chain of retail outlets. Expanding to locations in Boston's Prudential Center and the Burlington Mall, each unit operated as a self-contained production bakery in the back room with a retail store in the front. Approximately 200 other French bakeries operated similarly in the United States in 1979. The Faneuil Hall and Prudential shops also produced fresh breads daily for Boston restaurants such as Locke Ober, Pier 4, Maison Robert, and Jimmy's Harborside as well as for the Copley Plaza and Sheraton Boston Hotels. This wholesale business alone provided steady cash flow of $750,000 to $800,000 per year.

The retail operations however were another story. While sales were good by industry standards—$7,000 per week per store average by 1980—break-even was $9,000 per store. Each location employed bakery-chefs responsible for the delicate, demanding process of rolling croissants and baking breads. Croissants, done in the classic French style, were created by hand. A rolled rectangular piece of pastry dough layered with butter was folded like a business letter, forming three layers of dough and two layers of butter, turned and rerolled.

The process was repeated a minimum of four times, sometimes more, with careful monitoring of dough temperature and consistency. If the mixture became too warm, the dough required refrigeration before the process could continue. Each turn tripled the number of layers, therefore,

This case was written by Research Associate Lee Field, under the supervision of Associate Professor John Kao.

Copyright © 1986 by the President and Fellows of Harvard College. Harvard Business School case 9-486-100.

five turns would produce 243 paper-thin layers of dough and butter. The dough was then cut into triangles, rolled up and baked, expanding in the process to produce the light and fluffy texture. While unit time of cutting, forming and baking croissants was not long, under an hour, the early phase of making the dough could take twelve hours or longer. Some chefs insisted that the dough cool and rest for an hour in between each turn. Therefore, product quality at each location depended on the moods and attitudes of the bakers. (One Au Bon Pain insider remarked that strung-out bakers were not known for consistency.) Controls, training, and selection of sales personnel also varied per location, decided by each store manager.

In August of 1980, Ron Shaich (rhymes with CAKE), owner of The Cookie Jar at 52 Winter Street in downtown Boston, approached Louis Kane for help with a problem. Witnessing significant morning traffic on the sidewalk outside his store but no cookie sales inside, Shaich persuaded Kane to grant him a license to sell Au Bon Pain products at his store. Intrigued by the challenge and opportunity at Au Bon Pain, and believing he could make a significant contribution, Shaich, four months later, convinced Kane to merge their businesses and become equal partners. Kane, who had never considered operations a strength or a joy, was impressed with Shaich's credentials, enthusiasm, and apparent operational prowess. Adding The Cookie Jar, Au Bon Pain now operated four stores in the greater Boston area, had attractive locations, but, as the principals agreed, risked bankruptcy unless fundamental operating changes were made and a viable concept defined.

By January 1986, Au Bon Pain had prospered and aggressively expanded to 36 locations in 10 states and the District of Columbia, employing over 900 people; 1985 system revenues were well over $20 million, and the company had $4 million cash in the bank. In 1985, Shaich and Kane also added another partner, Len Schlesinger who left the Harvard Business School as an associate professor to become Au Bon Pain's executive vice president and treasurer. Now the recognized leader in its industry segment, Au Bon Pain was the envy of many food service companies and the recipient of 50 unsolicited franchise requests per week. What transpired between 1981 and 1986, the people who made it happen, and the outlook for the future is the rest of the story.

THE INDUSTRY

In the early 1970s, French breads were strictly a wholesale product found on supermarket shelves. Consumers wishing to purchase croissants could only do so in elegant restaurants and hotels. Availability of these specialty items was a direct reflection of demand; there was not much. By 1984, however, the situation had changed. That year customers spent approximately $1 billion on French breads and $700 million for croissants, a 31 percent average revenue increase from the year before. This surge in sales attracted a new participant in the bakery industry: the specialty French bread and croissant store.

Consumer demand came from changing preferences. An increased interest in good-tasting, nutritious foods first led to a surge in variety bread sales. From 1977 to 1982, wholesale French bread revenues increased about 40 percent. Consumer willingness to pay a premium price for perceived high quality, gourmet items led to entrepreneurial developments of both products and outlets. By 1983, there were over 300 specialty bakery locations, increasing to over 400 by 1984. As baby boomers entered the work force, they spent more money on all kinds of specialty products, including French breads and croissants.

Growing consumer demand for convenience, as witnessed in the splurge of fast-food businesses, supported the growth of French bakery specialty stores, especially in high traffic locations such as shopping malls. Changing eating habits of consumers also helped the market. No longer inclined to eat only at prescribed times of the day, the "grazers" as they were called, ate whenever and wherever they were hungry. To capitalize on changing demographics and capture a share of the fast-food market, some specialty bakeries expanded their menus to include sandwiches and stuffed croissants.

Two variables contributing to the success of an operation were location and product line. High-traffic stores could keep their menus simple, selling only croissants and a few breads. More sedate locations, however, depended on repeat customers. Their stores usually included a French cafe which served other simple foods besides bread products. By 1984, specialty retail sales were estimated at $139 million for breads and $84 million for croissants, 11 percent and 47 percent increases from the year before.

One of the first to pioneer the concept was Vie de France, founded in Washington DC in 1972. In 1984, with sales of $55 million, 18 wholesale and 45-plus retail outlets, Vie de France was the largest specialty producer in the industry. PepsiCo's foodservice unit started La Petite Boulangerie in 1984, planning 100 store openings that year and 2500 within the decade. Consolidated Foods Corporation's Sara Lee division, after a smashing success in the frozen-product supermarket segment, also intended a major move into the retail croissant market. What may have been deemed a fad in the beginning was now definitely an industry segment here to stay. As one industry participant observed, however, "Only the fittest will survive."

"THE SHAICH UP"

Recalling those first months at Au Bon Pain, Shaich explained:

> There were quite a few people working in the stores who didn't want to be there. One of the first things we did was ask (with some we told) those people who didn't care about creating something great, to leave. And a majority of our employees (28 out of 36) took the "out" option. Needing replacements, we searched for people who took care and pride in doing a job well; dependable and competent because it was their nature. We also organized an entry-level managers' orientation and training school.

Shaich identified an improvement in the quality of the people as the single most significant change in the company. Sales went up immediately. By 1985, revenues per store averaged over $15,000 per week.

The second major change was a decision to centralize production. "Our business was selling food products," Shaich remarked, "not operating individual restaurants." On one weekend, he fired 15 of the company's 18 bakers and centralized production at the Prudential Center location. As he remembered from his days at Harvard Business School (class of 1978), "If you decrease production costs and spread them out over many units, you lower your break-even." Centralizing production allowed the company to: (1) pay fewer skilled people more money and leverage their efforts over more units of croissants; and (2) reduce overhead and fixed-cost requirements at the retail level. As a result, the break-even point dropped from $9,000 to under $5,000 per store per week.

An added benefit of the decision to centralize was improved product quality. Shaich described:

> We kept our best three bakers: a French couple for croissants and a Portuguese man for breads. We increased their salaries and eventually bought them equipment, which ultimately improved the consistency and quality of the product.

Starting from a tiny space (20′ × 30′) in the back of the Prudential Center, production facilities underwent several enlargements. By April of 1983, all production had been centralized in a new South Boston facility. With the sophistication of a modern factory, products were made, frozen, and then shipped to retail locations for baking as needed. (Remarkably, the pastry dough was better frozen than fresh. This characteristic was the basis for manufacturing strategy and process modernization.) Plant capacity in 1986 (after enlarging the facility and adding a second shift) was over one million units per week.

Another major decision was made to focus on retail. "We were a second-rate wholesaler with first-rate retail locations," Schlesinger and Shaich decided. Therefore, all but a couple of wholesale customers were dropped. Dramatic as these changes were on the company's cash flow, Shaich and Kane were both confident in their ability to manage the company's operations, buoyed in part by Shaich's past experiences.

RON SHAICH'S BACKGROUND

The older of two children (a younger sister) Shaich, whose average physical size is enlarged by a forceful, energetic personality, remarked, "I grew up with a very strong tradition of values—respect and dignity, social justice and sensitivity in a liberal and politically active home in New Jersey." His grandparents were all Eastern European Jewish immigrants. His father, a self-employed, well-to-do accountant, cast a rather large shadow. Ron stated, "Even though he only wanted me to be happy, I wanted to prove myself and make him proud. He still is very motivating. Business success on my own has led to tremendous family respect." Shaich remembered his high school days. "Like most teenagers, I was trying to discover who I was. I found an identity in politics as a McCarthy-for-President chairman, and so on."

After acceptances to Princeton and Clark, high school graduation, and a year off in Washington working on Capitol Hill and running as a McGovern delegate, he went to Clark because "they didn't make me take courses not of my liking." He remembered being a "study freak" freshman year, concentrating on social, political, and leadership activities thereafter. Shaich recounted:

> Around this time some friend and I were falsely accused of shoplifting in a local Seven Eleven-type convenience store and thrown out. So I said "Screw these guys, let's start our own nonprofit store."

Aided by his influence as treasurer of the student body, he gained approval for the concept and led the start-up. His previous business experience—magazine sales and pizza delivery—while ambitious and successful, had not prepared him to run a store. Yet, as he recalled with a smile, "It worked because I cared enough to make it work. We kept lowering prices but still made $50,000 profit that first year. I liked winning—beating those guys who threw us out—and having fun. It was my creation and passion, but I loved the esprit de corps." (Shaich was honored at an alumni banquet for previous store managers in 1985, marking the eleventh anniversary of operations.)

Armed with the reputation of a savvy retail operator, he was hired for a summer job as assistant to the president of Store 24. He recollected:

> After two weeks on the job, I approached the president with a list of 200 suggestions for improving the stores. He said, "These are good, but I can't destroy my organization. Give it time, gain some credibility and then talk about changes."

During his senior year Shaich set up a business distributing surplus or damaged Hartz Mountain Flea Collars. "I sold to discount houses, department stores, and through flea markets and made a killing. I was running so much cash through my bank I'm sure they thought I was selling drugs."

The fall after graduation he continued his business pursuits academically and started his first year at Harvard Business School. He said:

> I was young, had to work hard, but I learned a lot about analytical skills and interpersonal abilities. I may not have liked it at the time, but it gave me 20 years' worth of experience I could not have gotten elsewhere. In between years, I was assistant to the vice president of Marketing at CVS.

After graduation Shaich took a job with the Original Cookie Co., a fast-growing regional chain of retail cookie stores owned by Cole National Corporation, as director of operations in charge of 17 stores. He related:

I did not know beans about making cookies, but I could motivate people. During this "third year" of my MBA I realized my time was not being leveraged in my financial best interest. So I left after one year.

Following a four-month hiatus in Boston, he took a job in Washington, once again seeking to fulfill his political "destiny." He worked for Matt Reese and Associates, a liberal-Democratic consulting firm. He recalled: "After a year and a half I was the number two man—calling the shots—but I became disillusioned. And like my previous job, I was not really making a difference. This was just another business, but more importantly, someone else's business. He described his feelings:

I guess I've always been driven to find a better path. It's fun—an intellectual turn-on. But I don't think I'm an entrepreneur because I don't have original ideas. I do, however, recognize good ideas and execute them better than most. Part of that is being open to self-criticism. For me creativity comes from self-criticism and examination.

In 1980, Shaich decided to start his own business. Since he knew something about cookie stores and how to operate them, he opened one. About this move, he explained:

Here I was, a Harvard MBA with a tiny cookie store in downtown Boston. Was I nuts? I wanted to make something happen—watch the meter rise—and my own business seemed to be the best vehicle. I was driven to prove I could do it. Six months later I was a partner in Au Bon Pain.

About Shaich, Louis Kane commented:

He was the first Harvard MBA I had worked closely with who was willing to get out from behind the desk, get his hands dirty, and get the job done. He was very sharp analytically, and his enthusiasm was tremendous. Ron has taught me to focus and be tougher before starting on something. He also has taught me to be more direct and face up to problems immediately, instead of going around them. He has also rejuvenated my understanding of the word commitment. Ron has been—is—very good for me. To the people in the stores and our plant, Ron Shaich *is* Au Bon Pain.

LOUIS KANE'S BACKGROUND

While Shaich shaped up operations, Kane scouted for new locations and arranged financing, proving very successful at both. His vast network of friends and business contacts developed over 25 years served him well.

From a family of old-line financiers, Louis Kane, the epitome of a handsome and sophisticated Boston Brahmin, graduated from Harvard College in 1953 and became an officer in Marine Corps reconnaissance. After the service he worked for the family-owned Kane Financial—which he later controlled—and founded Boston Partners, one of the early venture capital companies. Kane had a penchant for turning ideas into reality. Grinning, he remarked, "I'd get an idea and go do it." While his projects and interests were in private business, Kane was keenly aware of the public sector. His wife, Kathy, Boston's deputy mayor during the Kevin White era, had always been in politics. "Even during my time in the military, Kathy was on President Eisenhower's staff. But it didn't help me get promoted any faster," he told a local Boston paper.

Kane's ideas and deals led to a number of successful companies, including Healthco—nursing homes and health services; and Colombo—yogurt manufacturing. Both were later sold to larger companies after initial start-up and growth phase. It was during the installation of a frozen yogurt shop in Faneuil Hall that Kane discovered Au Bon Pain.

When it came time to expand Au Bon Pain, Kane was the man for the job. Given his instincts, experience, and network, he not only found the most promising locations, (like Harvard Square and Copley Place) but also knew whom to contact and how to make the deals. From the developers' perspective, it was ideal. They negotiated directly with the chairman, not some unauthorized agent. And this chairman had quite a track record. Kane was hardly an easy sell, however. He only negotiated exclusive leases at attractive rates. If Au Bon Pain signed on, it was guaranteed as the only French bakery cafe at that development.

On State Street in Boston's financial district, Louis Kane *was* Au Bon Pain. His credibility, due to previous successful ventures, proved valuable for Au Bon Pain's outside funding. Store construction financing and, later, Industrial Revenue bonds for the $1.28 million original plant construction and $2 million addition to the South Boston facility were granted after Kane's lobbying before the Massachusetts Industrial Finance Agency and the Boston Industrial Finance and Development Agency. Kane also spearheaded the placement of $11 million in equity to institutional investors in 1984. "Louis has made it possible because he can really sell," Shaich emphasized. "Around here, he's known as 'Mr. Magic.'" (For store locations and opening dates see *Exhibit 1*.) Articulating what Au Bon Pain meant in his life, Kane responded:

With some of my other businesses, I didn't have my heart in it. Healthco, for instance, was an extremely successful operation and the largest operator of nursing homes in the country. But I didn't enjoy the business, did not like going in the facilities, or relish the thought of making money from dying people, even though we provided a good service. Therefore, I took no pride in it, got no enjoyment out of it.

At Au Bon Pain, however, the situation is totally different. I get tremendous satisfaction being a part of this company. We are well respected and well known. We have quality products, attractive stores, and wonderful employees. I'm very proud, and I can't wait to get up in the morning and get here.

METAMORPHOSIS

While Kane was on the outside laying the expansionary groundwork as quickly as possible, Shaich was on the inside turning a bakery into a factory, a group of restaurants into a chain of fast-food businesses. A good example of the evolutionary process involved Gilbert Vidal, the French croissant baker. Shaich recalled:

> When I decided to fire most of the bakers, I had no idea how to run the operation. I did have good instincts, though, and Gilbert seemed to be the correct choice. He and his wife worked hard and cared a lot about the quality of their work. So, the night before we were to go with centralized production, he called me at 3:00 a.m. A sensitive young man, my age—then 27 or 28—he was upset because he felt responsible for the others getting fired. I reassured him that he was blameless. That first day Gilbert worked 21 hours as we went from a night to a day shift. He only took three hours off to sleep at my apartment. But he produced the product, and I made certain he got all the moral support needed. During the first six months I was very patronizing, almost to the point of calling every day making sure he had eaten three square meals. Gilbert the "chef" required pampering.
>
> I would go to Gilbert's house for dinner and parties, and he and his wife would come to mine. They would come home with me to New York at holidays and I would show them the city. I put them on a bonus plan after a time and they were making over $50,000 a year between them. The business was growing, we started mechanizing somewhat, and finally moved into the new plant. Before, Gilbert and I had been mutually dependent. By now, however, I had neither the time nor inclination to constantly hand-hold. At the old place, where it was basically a physical job, Gilbert was great. In the new plant, however, he could not handle the more complex managerial tasks and electronic controls, much less figure out decimal points. Deciding to bring in a professional manager, I hired a VP of manufacturing, Ted Borland, who had worked in large, high-volume bakeries for over 25 years and knew the business backward and forward. In retrospect, Ted is probably one of the greatest hires we have made. He is smart and tough, not petty or defensive, a team player and inspirational example.
>
> Rooting for Gilbert, I honestly hoped Ted could help him learn and manage. Unfortunately, the organization outgrew him. It wasn't just skill level either. He ran his territory like a club. "I like you, come on in. I don't like you, you're fired." We worked for over a year trying to get him to change. Finally, Ted and I had to ask for his resignation because he had become everything we opposed: emotional, inconsiderate, and a bad example. The moral of this story? There are two kinds of people who don't make it at Au Bon Pain: People who care but can't manage and grow, and people who can manage but who don't care enough. At Au Bon Pain we demand results and role models.

As the manufacturing operation took shape, Shaich concentrated more time and thought on store operations. Whereas he pampered the manufacturing people at first, the stores were a different story. "I ran them with an iron fist—really tight controls," he said. "So there was a double standard. But at the time I couldn't see it any other way." He also tugged with the problems of creating management systems and structures that could assimilate future growth. Shaich commented:

Early on we did a fairly good job of figuring out strategy, understanding the economics and discovering the key to success in this business: You had to have damn good store operations. And to do that you needed good, caring people, trained properly, so they could do it right. This passion for providing quality service unseen elsewhere is a very personal statement. What I tried and am still trying to do is institutionalize that passion and those values. I can't, nor do I want to do everything for everyone. It's physically impossible and emotionally draining. I can, however, try to institutionalize values and set good examples. There's not a floor I haven't mopped or a bathroom I haven't cleaned myself. But I want the people in this company to see for themselves what needs to be done, have the skills to do it, and deliver.

At first we just had to learn by doing it. Now, we have accumulated thousands of hours of learning how to operate these stores. In managers' meetings we have brainstormed and argued a million different operational improvements. But we don't want extensive discretionary creativity at the unit level. We're trying to find the right systems and get commitment to compliance to those systems; develop a system we know works and can take to the bank. We're not there yet, but almost.

TURMOIL

In the industry's eyes, by 1984 Au Bon Pain was the picture of success. The company was profitable and growing rapidly (a new store opened every ten days.) Company momentum was high and consumers liked the products and stores. The concept was so well received that new competitors entered the market. PepsiCo, for example, opened "La Petite Boulangerie" stores as rapidly as possible. Some large companies also made offers to buy Au Bon Pain. They were declined. Yet, while all the environmental elements were coming together, Shaich could not help feeling that operations were getting out of control. He recalled:

> We had $1 million in the bank yet couldn't pay our bills; the computer literally blew up; and our CFO was a wonderful guy but he couldn't do the job and I had to let him go.

Shaich's father, a CPA, had been helping out three days a week for over a year, but was no longer involved. Kane, the first to admit he was not an operations guy, had neither the time nor the desire to actively jump in and help Shaich. While Au Bon Pain preferred to develop and promote managerial talent from within, outside managers were hired. Some worked, some did not. Shaich stated:

> Our values are just different from, say, a McDonald's. One of their managers just can't step in here and automatically succeed. How do I know? Because I hired one as vice president of store operations, after spending over a year looking for the right person. The store managers had been promised someone who could help and teach them while making a long-term contribution to the company. This McDonald's person was a disaster. There was open dissent among managers and a great deal of hostility and resentment. He never earned

the managers' respect. Coming from a mature company where a missing pickle on a hamburger was cause for immediate dismissal, he was unable to adjust to our quickly evolving menu and operations. During his reign of terror, we suffered extremely high turnover throughout the company. It also took us two tries to get the right CFO and three attempts to find a good VP of construction.

In February of 1984 Au Bon Pain completed its first private placement of stock with a group of institutional investors, so now there were additional constituents to worry about. By December of 1984, as Au Bon Pain opened new stores ever other week, Shaich was feeling burned out. He said:

> Were we growing too fast? We could do it, but was it best? I was lonely, frustrated and unhappy. Feeling up against the wall, I had no one who could help me. So, I decided we had to slow down, and do it right.

WELLNESS PROGRAM

Shaich described this phase at Au Bon Pain as a "wellness program." Along with the decision to curb expansion, he was determined to get help running the company, or better yet, find another partner to share with, "like a brother." While continuing to look long term, he sought short-term consulting advice. "From an organizational perspective I was looking for a People Express kind of adaptation—a way to get people to understand and think about the business while psychologically and physically buying into it," he conveyed. Concerning this topic he asked a Harvard Business School classmate, now a faculty member, to recommend someone. The classmate advised him to call Len Schlesinger, an associate professor in the organizational behavior area.

LEN SCHLESINGER

A large, robust and sparklingly energetic man, Len Schlesinger, recalling his first encounter with Au Bon Pain, elaborated:

> In September or October of 1984 I got a call from Ron Shaich saying he was from Au Bon Pain and had been referred to me by a number of different people. He needed someone with an expertise in incentive systems, and asked if I would talk to him. A few weeks later I went out and he gave me the "Investment Banker" talk about how great everything was at Au Bon Pain and the big issue now was how to institutionalize all the good stuff here. I was mildly amused yet impressed with his earnest enthusiasm, and I kind of liked him. Instead of spending a few hours, we talked the whole evening.
>   After leaving the office and going out to dinner, Ron let his hair down. "We are opening a new store every ten days, this place is becoming more bureaucratic and ossified, stuff is falling through the cracks and the more successful we become the less good I feel about it! How do I deal with it?" I listened and talked to him as a friend, but very frankly.

Ron was aware of some structural and systems issues that were hampering the company. Their strategy at this time of intense growth was to throw bodies at problems instead of analyzing and developing action agendas. The company was full of young, vibrant, enthusiastic but very tired people.

At the end of the meeting and after some agreeing that he couldn't afford my consulting fees, I volunteered to do some work on this anyway. Without the slightest idea how to help them in a comprehensive manner, I thought the problem was intriguing.

We had three or four more dinner discussions during the next few months, after which I wrote up some reports and suggestions and scheduled a meeting. This was January of 1985. I walked into Ron's office, he opened up the folder of materials and said, "This is the same kind of crap I get from all consultants. If you know what's going on around here why don't you help me run it? Let's create the equivalent of People Express in the food business. Are you ever going to quit telling people how, and do something yourself? You want to, don't you?"

I thanked him for his offer but declined. I was close to a tenure decision at Harvard Business School, and wanted to finish that before considering anything else. But here I was thinking, "The chemistry is very good with Ron, the problems are intellectually challenging, but I can't take this seriously." Then Ron did a very shrewd thing; He planted a seed. Convincing me to agree not to say yes or no until after the weekend, he also asked me a final question. "Is there anything about your life right now you would like to change?"

Over the weekend I didn't think about the job offer but did consider the second question. With a wife and three children, I hated to travel. I felt guilty about being gone all the time. But that was the life of an HBS professor; everyone did research, consulted, and traveled. I called Ron back on Monday and mentioned the problem with travel. "That's not even an issue, Len. You wouldn't have to do much."

The more I thought about it, the more I got seduced. I did my own investigation—talked to a lot of company people, visited some stores, ran some numbers—and talked with my wife. What clinched it for us was a visit to the Au Bon Pain annual employees' meeting. After listening to various speakers describe the situation and objectives for the future, we both knew I could make an immediate, needed contribution to this company. As my wife Phyllis said, "You'd be crazy not to do it. You can do everything they need." This was such an exciting move forward in my life, I didn't even think about what I was giving up. It was a chance to be part of a group of people who truly cared about the institution they were building. The fact that I was given an equity stake was nice, but the psychological partnership—the critical responsibilities at an important time—was what excited me most.

About Schlesinger's decision to join Au Bon Pain, Shaich maintained:

He understood, both emotionally and intellectually, what we were about. Because of the type of guy he was, Len made Louis and me feel very comfortable with the thought of bringing on a new partner who wanted as much for this company as we did.

Schlesinger recalled a facetious comment from an Au Bon Pain employee, describing him after a few months on the job:

The guy said, "It used to be that Ron Shaich was always around and got involved in a lot of issues. Then he got spread too thin and he wasn't around as much. Now Ron Shaich has been cloned and there are two of them. They're everywhere!"

On that subject, Shaich countered:

He's much better than I ever was at some things. The values and vision are the same, and yes, he is another voice for toughness.

On Schlesinger's contribution to Au Bon Pain, Kane offered:

Len has been a great balance to Ron and me. He came in and very quickly earned tremendous credibility with everyone in the organization through his accessibility and keen problem-solving ability. He's a real doer who understands the company as well as anyone. Interestingly enough, he's become a strong champion for manufacturing, whereas Ron has always championed the stores. Most of all though, Len has helped this organization focus on the key issues, acting both as catalyst and energizer, to bring all areas of the company together, working toward one goal. He's proven to be a great operating manager and there's no question that he is an equal partner in this thing. He's earned it.

About his tenure thus far at Au Bon Pain, Schlesinger reported:

I don't consider myself entrepreneurial, nor this move risky. As for the experience since coming here, I've gained a lot of confidence in my ability to operate a real business and teach other people how to as well. That's what it's all about—educating people about the business, letting them run it, and pushing them to make decisions. I want people to know and understand the economics, buy stock in the company, and become emotionally committed.

I also want to insure everyone is thinking about the business from a big picture viewpoint. To do that takes time. We have a talented, dedicated, hard-working management group, but only two are MBAs. Most of the store managers and associate managers are high school and junior college graduates. But they are learning. Every time we get groups of managers together, which is at least six times a year, we take up something new, like explaining balance sheets, return on equity, or ratio analysis. Before long, they're going to see more clearly what we're trying to do, and why.

Commenting on the different styles of the partners, Schlesinger observed:

You go for an interview with Ron, he asked about your mother's child-rearing habits, when you were weaned, and how dedicated you are. Me, I want to know when you can report for work. Ron is also a detail person; he likes the i's and t's done perfectly. If the results are good, I'm happy.

HUMAN RESOURCE SYSTEMS AT AU BON PAIN

While the organizational leadership was now clearly a triumvirate, plans were underway to make Au Bon Pain operate like a large partnership. Institutionalized systems, structures and mechanisms were evolving, designed to increase employee ownership—tangible and psychological—in the company. From the beginning Ron Shaich knew, in his opinion, what was important at Au Bon Pain. He explained:

> Louis Kane made it possible, I whipped it into shape and now Len Schlesinger, our partner, is helping run it and plan for the future. But the people who work in the plant, and those who work in the stores and serve our customers, they are the ones who will decide if we become a quality company. It's our job—mine, Louis', Len's, and all the other senior managers—to make certain those people have every conceivable opportunity.

What was Shaich's definition of a quality company? He had talked about that subject and others at every new management orientation session of the last five years. His speech sounded something like this:

> What is Au Bon Pain all about? Quality. Quality products and quality people working to build a quality company serving quality customers. Who are the Au Bon Pain customers? They are people who view food as something more than just fuel, who recognize and appreciate a materially better product, who want it quick yet want to enjoy the experience. This customer has higher expectations and is more critical and selective than an average fast food buyer, but is willing to pay more for a quality product. This segment of the population, which recognizes positive price/value relationships, is the fastest growing in the retail food business today. Let me read you a letter—we get hundreds like this a month—from one of our customers.

> Dear Au Bon Pain,

> Having patronized your restaurant in several locations, I now feel some thanks are in order. Thank you for good food at a reasonable price, for general courtesy of staff, and most of all, thank you for the heavenly music which turns my steps to your door.

> Sincerely,
> Maggie Smith Dalton

> How do we define quality?

> **1. A quality company provides above-average financial rewards for its employees.** Although we pay competitive market salaries, we think there should be more. We want everyone who works here to have an opportunity to own a piece of it. We do that through stock options and a stock purchase plan. We want you to understand all about stock ownership, especially the risks involved, but we hope you will invest in your company. I promise you it will be worthwhile.

> **2. A quality company provides above-average return on investment to its investors.** We have some large, sophisticated institutions who believe in this company. General Electric, Harvard University, Allstate Insurance, Market Corp Ventures, and others have invested money because they think it will earn a better return with us, in the long run, than some place else. We must reward their faith with profitable operations, or we won't get another chance.

3. A quality company manages with clear principles based on respect for people. In 1983, the interdepartmental committee, at that time consisting of anyone interested in getting together at lunchtime to talk about the company, drafted a document called the Corporate Philosophy. This was not done for our customers' benefit, but for the people inside this company. You've all got a copy in your blue books so let's go through it together. (See *Exhibit 2* for Corporate Philosophy.)

4. A quality company meets customers needs and earns their respect. Do you know what a typical organizational chart looks like? There's usually the chairman at the top, then the president, vice presidents, district managers, local managers, and local store workers at the bottom. And who deals directly with the customers? Those at the bottom of the organization. (See *Exhibit 3*, Staffing.)

At Au Bon Pain we want to reverse the way we look at organizational structure. At the top are the customers, because we are nothing without them. Everything and everyone else in this organization should support those people who serve our customers. This is the key to our company. Which means we must focus on training to provide superior service.

I am the first to admit that training here has changed over the years. In the old days new managers got their initiation by being thrown into the heat of the battle—sink or swim. We've come a long way since then, and we're going even farther. We also have learned not to grow any faster than we can train and assimilate people. Look at our new competition—PepsiCo, Sara Lee—each is losing big money in this business. In fact, some companies have practically begged us to take failing stores off their hands. No investment on our part, just take them and try to make them work. But we said no. It would have put too big a strain on our organization. Our competition has grown too quickly without operations, infrastructure, people, or training. They just threw the stores up as fast as they could. We are not going to do that.

In 1986 we will triple the amount of money spent on training versus the prior year. We're also going to spend more time and resources on training our trainers. We have a lot invested in people already and will do even more in the future.

5. A quality company grows to provide opportunity for employees. We want all of you to think that Au Bon Pain means opportunity. If we grow and prosper, there will be abundant avenues for advancement. Almost everyone who is running this company today started out at one time in your shoes as an Associate Manager or a Crew Member. If not, they have at least been through this training program. Au Bon Pain wants each of you to succeed and will promise you every chance.

6. A quality company maintains a justified superior public reputation. At this point in time our company has a very good reputation. We feel we understand the business and are in control. We also have tremendous credibility with the developers. They know there is only one real player in our business. Besides, we operate well, our stores look good and do a lot of business, which, in turn, produces a lot of rent for the landlords.

You know, I have some friends who work for McDonald's. At parties and social gatherings they're embarrassed to tell other people where they work. We hope that each of you will be as proud of this company as those here now are. We hope that you care enough about yourselves, your coworkers and this company to make Au Bon Pain the very best it can be.

7. A quality company keeps control of its own destiny. As I said earlier, we have institutional investors, but the largest group of stockholders in this company is its employees with over 60 percent control. Each of you will have the option to buy stock. We intend to maintain majority ownership so we can pace ourselves, our way, according to our set of values, in the long-term best interests of this company.

8. A quality company honors commitments and delivers to: Its employees, its stockholders and its customers. This I promise: If we tell you we're going to do something, and we don't, pick up the phone, call me and say, "Ron Shaich, you lied to me." I, for one, do not want that to happen. But people in this company appreciate constructive criticism that an honest atmosphere encourages. We won't hide things from you, so don't you, from us. Always tell us what you think.

9. A quality company serves the local communities in which it operates. This company strives not only to serve our customers, but our customers' communities as well.

How does someone succeed at Au Bon Pain? You must: (1) be disciplined; (2) have some food sense; (3) be able to keep many balls in the air without dropping them; (4) have the capacity for hard work; (5) learn the way to communicate up, sideways and down; and (6) be able to manage and make decisions.

You would also do well to gain some credibility quickly, have a sense of humor, and be able to laugh at yourself. But most of all, you have to care enough to make things happen. When Hurricane Gloria was approaching Boston last year, we told everyone who worked at the plant to stay home. They all showed up anyway because they were concerned about helping out.

This is not easy work; it's tough, the hours are long and your bosses are demanding. But I promise you, it will all be worth it someday when you look back and can say, "See that great company Au Bon Pain, I helped build it."

Another example of a structural mechanism was the managers' meetings, held every eight weeks. District, general, and associate managers were each convened separately (district managers usually attended all three), and various headquarter staff conducted the sessions. (See *Exhibit 4* for an agenda and description of a February 1986 meeting.)

When asked about other institutional mechanisms used at Au Bon Pain, Schlesinger offered the following:

Communications Day—During the third week of each period, either Ron, Louis or Len met with every headquarters-based employee in the company by functional group. Each group was given a financial update, a special theme discussion (topics on understanding the business) and a question and answer opportunity.

Baker's Board—A bimonthly newsletter for the entire organization, it updated situations and information.

Leadership by Example—The senior management encouraged visibility throughout the company. As Len remarked, "There's nothing asked of others that we won't do ourselves. If customers need help when we're at a store, we work the counter. Or, if the bathrooms are dirty, we clean them."

Documentation—Managers were asked to provide and request hard copies on verbal agreements, so everyone would be better able to fulfill objectives and promises.

Culture Creation—The "Au Bon Pain Stories"—the old days and new, the good and the bad, the heroes and heels—were told and retold at every opportunity.

Task Forces—Voluntary groups studied and recommended changes on such topics as new products, purchasing, equipment, service, marketing, compensation, and training.

Roundtable Discussions—Frequently, senior managers convened groups of employees to discuss company status.

PLANNING FOR THE FUTURE

(See *Exhibit 5* For 1986 Priorities and Goals.)

As Kane, Shaich, Schlesinger, and other senior managers planned for the growth and evolution at Au Bon Pain, their worries did not focus on competitive business strategy or production management. Conceivably, the market offered nationwide potential, and the manufacturing process could add capacity if needed.

The primary concerns were threefold. First, could the company demonstrate consistent profitability and growth? Second, could Au Bon Pain dramatically enhance customer service? Finally, could the company break the cycle of failure, endemic to the retail food business, or would it flounder with a discontented work force like the rest of the industry? (See *Exhibit 6.*)

Exhibit 1 Au Bon Pain Locations as of April 1986

Owner-ship	Location	City	State	Year Opened	Square Footage
C	Faneuil Hall Marketplace	Boston	MA	1977	1,400
C	Burlington Mall	Burlington	MA	1978	1,400
C	Prudential Center[a]	Boston	MA	1985	3,000
C	Downtown Crossing	Boston	MA	1980	425
C	Logan Airport[b]	Boston	MA	1981	800
C	Filene's[c]	Boston	MA	1984	800
C	Filene's/Franklin Street	Boston	MA	1985	150
C	Filene's Basement	Boston	MA	1984	600
C	Filene's Basement/Subway	Boston	MA	1985	200
C	Harvard Square[d]	Cambridge	MA	1983	2,500
C	Fox Run Mall	Newington	NH	1983	500
C	Maine Mall	South Portland	ME	1983	500
C	Copley Place	Boston	MA	1984	2,500
C	Copley Place-Stuart Street[e]	Boston	MA	1985	1,000
C	Park Plaza	Boston	MA	1984	1,000
C	Arsenal Mall	Watertown	MA	1984	2,300
C	City Place	Hartford	CT	1984	2,400
C	Crossgates Mall	Albany	NY	1984	1,400
C	Crystal Mall	Waterford	CT	1984	600
C	Cape Cod Mall	Hyannis	MA	1985	1,000
C	Cherry Hill Mall	Cherry Hill	NJ	1984	1,000
C	2 Penn Center	Philadelphia	PA	1985	2,700
JV	Riverside Square[f]	Hackensack	NJ	1984	1,800
JV	Rockefeller Center[g]	New York	NY	1985	2,500
F	Pennzoil Building	Houston	TX	1983	1,800
F	The Park at Houston Center	Houston	TX	1983	1,200
F	Memorial City Mall	Houston	TX	1983	1,800
F	West Oaks Mall	Houston	TX	1984	1,900
F	First City Center	Dallas	TX	1984	2,300
F	The Citadel	Colorado Springs	CO	1984	1,100
F	National Place	Washington	DC	1984	1,400
F	L'Enfant Plaza/Metro	Washington	DC	1984	2,600
F	L'Enfant Plaza/Pavillion	Washington	DC	1984	1,000
F	2000 Pennsylvania Avenue[h]	Washington	DC	1984	2,100
F	Tabor Center[i]	Denver	CO	1984	2,500
F	St. Louis Union Station	St. Louis	MO	1985	1,000

C = Company-owned store.

JV = Joint venture.

F = Franchise.

[a] Replaced previous unit opened in 1979.

[b] Interior baking facility which presently services seven bakery carts and one bakery counter.

[c] Replaced previous unit opened in 1982.

[d] Does not include seasonal outdoor cafe with seating capacity for 140 persons.

[e] Does not include seasonal outdoor cafe with seating capacity for 150 persons.

[f] Replaced previous unit opened in 1978.

[g] Replaced a 900-square-foot unit owned by a corporation in which the company purchased a 25% interest in 1984.

[h] Does not include seasonal outdoor cafe with seating capacity for 80 persons.

[i] As of April of 1986, the company had three franchisees who owned and operated stores. Managers of these stores did not report to Au Bon Pain executives, but were trained in the company program.

Exhibit 2

CORPORATE PHILOSOPHY

1. Au Bon Pain believes that the company and its participants must all succeed together. We must not attempt to succeed by exploiting others within the company. We believe in maintaining a "you win, we win" orientation. Those who are legitimately made to feel as if they are winners will act as winners.

2. Enthusiasm and caring are criteria for advancement at Au Bon Pain. Four faults are inexcusable at Au Bon Pain: not caring, not learning from one's mistakes, dishonesty, and not supporting decisions made by the group.

3. There is no value in hiding the truth from people. Au Bon Pain believes that all employees should be continually informed about their performance and progress. We all have a need to know when our work is not up to standard, and to be counseled on ways to improve it. Of equal importance is informing those who are performing well of their success.

4. The final measure of success at Au Bon Pain is performance. We believe in rewarding employees with incentives, promotions and recognition based on equitable measures of their performance and on the consistency with which they meet their commitments. The best way to motivate is by providing both tangible and intangible rewards for superior performance. The purpose of these rewards is to assure that all Au Bon Pain people share the same goals; in this way, each of us becomes his or her own supervisor.

5. It is the policy of Au Bon Pain to attempt to develop and advance management from within the organization. Au Bon Pain strives to provide opportunities for rapid development. The foundation for this is a strong commitment to training. Au Bon Pain also recognizes the importance of job security. The effect of decisions on job security and perceptions of job security will be carefully considered.

6. All Au Bon Pain people must evince respect for one another, and for the limits of others' abilities and aspirations. We must all be truly sensitive to the needs, perceptions, and values of others. We must also remember that people know their own jobs better than anyone else. The successful Au Bon Pain employee must therefore genuinely listen and respond to those with whom he or she works.

7. Au Bon Pain exists to meet customer needs. We meet customers needs by creating and operating excellent retail stores. To do this, we must operate a superior manufacturing operation. The rest of the company exists to support these efforts.

8. Ours is a business of routine tasks and details. Success is achieved by all of us managing those details daily. Because of this, hard work and high productivity are prized. A high degree of discipline is expected and rewarded.

9. We are here to meet our objectives by working together as a team. Because we believe that we work best when we work together, we encourage a highly communicative and informal organizational style. Employees at all levels of the company must be accessible to each other. Open disagreement and discussion is encouraged as a method of identifying and solving problems and of resolving conflict; hiding problems is not acceptable.

10. Au Bon Pain believes in leadership by example. We believe that it is inappropriate to ask another to do what one would not be willing to do oneself.

11. Au Bon Pain believes that we can and should be the quality leader in whatever we decide to do. We will only pursue those tasks which are consistent with our overall strategy, and at which we believe we can excel when we exert our best efforts. This requires that we continually search for new opportunities, experiment with new products and procedures, and scrutinize our current operations for possible improvements.

au bon pain.
THE FRENCH BAKERY CAFÉ

Exhibit 3 Staffing[a]

Function	Number of Employees
Crew	600
Associate Manager	55
General Manager	21
District Manager	5
Associate Director of Operations	1
Loss Prevention	1
Purchasing	1
Construction	4
Wholesale	2
Financial Accounting	10
HRM Training	3
Marketing	2
G/A	10
Mfg., R&D, QC	60
Executive Vice President and Treasurer	1
President and COO	1
Chairman and CEO	1

[a] This was an April 1986 approximation. The company did not have a formal chart.

(1)	Easy Order Sandwich	Neal Yanofsky
		Louis Basile
(2)	Video Presentation	Sue Buerkel
		Neal Yanofsky
	B R E A K	
(3)	Cycle of Failure	Len Schlesinger
		Ron Shaich
(4)	Structural P&L	By District
(5)	Group Discussion	Jim Rand
(6)	State of the Company	Ron Shaich
(7)	Closing Comments	Louis Basile

EASY ORDER SANDWICH ROLL OUT

- Objectives of Program
- What the Easy Order Sandwich Is, What It Is Not
- Results from Park Plaza and Burlington Test Markets
- Roll-Out Procedure and Schedule
- Communicating the Program to Customers
- Communicating the Program to Crew
- New Register Board
- Mystery Shopping
- Keys to Making It Work

Description of the Manager's Meeting

The overall tone and mood at this meeting was relaxed, friendly and workmanlike. Humor, mixed freely throughout the day by executives and managers alike, good naturedly drove home many points. Another observance was the frank, honest feedback by both participants and leaders. The morning began with a presentation on Au Bon Pain's new store training program called "easy order sandwich," designed to decrease the time between sandwich order and delivery. Results of market tests, planned roll-out schedule, and training (every store would receive special training help, including scripts and role playing), and an incentive program for crew members (mystery shoppers would conduct tests, evaluate order takers, and either reward—a $10 bill—or offer regrets and reasons why the person did not receive the reward) were presented. The next section was a video presentation of customer focus groups, assembled and questioned on likes and dislikes about Au Bon Pain.

Before Len Schlesinger's presentation, Ron Shaich led everyone in singing Happy Birthday to Louis Basile, associate director of company operations, who received a cake with candles.

Len's presentation, involving everyone in the room like a Harvard Business School case discussion, addressed the cycle of failure. The participants discussed perceived differences between Au Bon Pain and other fast-food businesses (Example: Au Bon Pain had a 3-hour lead time from start of a frozen croissant to availability; McDonald's had 3-5 minutes. Customers perceived Au Bon Pain as fast food but it really wasn't).

Len also asked people what they didn't like about working at Au Bon Pain. The responses—quite frank—included:

- high standards, but vaguely defined
- company zeal for perfection, not incrementally better performance
- if you improve one thing, you catch hell for something else; not enough positive reinforcement
- no time to catch our breaths
- get new associate managers who don't know what to do . . . you take time to teach them (often months) and then they're whisked off to another store
- on-the-job training for crew is different from store to store
- too much time on details . . . working on the desserts and haven't perfected the meat and potatoes yet . . . like worrying about clean tables but ignoring customers, or requiring two people to go to the bank for $40 in quarters
- ignoring the big picture—customers—while worrying about the infrastructure
- no time to do the paperwork
- too much pressure on managers, who in turn, pressure the crews
- no feedback on promotions decisions
- the hours are too long (a frequent complaint)

After lunch the managers broke up into groups, led by a senior staff member, to work on suggestions to companywide problems, or improvements for existing systems. These mini-task forces were given different topics at each meeting. Results and recommendations were presented later that afternoon or at subsequent meetings.

The last speaker of the day before closing comments was Ron Shaich, who gave a status of the company report, including a review of the P&L.

Exhibit 5 1986 Priorities, Programs and Goals

PRIORITIES

1. Demonstrate an ability to generate attractive, sustainable rates of growth and profitability. Company executives candidly admitted that a profit level of over $2 million was needed before the company could go public with a stock issue.

2. Dramatically enhance service to the customer. As Ron emphasized to a manager's meeting, "Focusing on product and service needs of the customer is our most important objective. We need to lose some of our arrogance and let the customer define what's right and wrong. I'm telling you it is all right to break bureaucratic rules to serve customers. If we deliver the service, the economics will follow."

3. Fully utilize our people through human resource systems which increase their psychological and financial ownership in the company. Within this category specific programs and goals were proposed.

PROGRAMS AND GOALS

a) Selection and training was the number 1 commitment for 1986. Through questionnaires completed by every Au Bon Pain manager and data collected from industry-wide research, the company was designing, through a consulting firm, a series of psychological tests for job applicants. The company intended to use this information as a tool for the hiring process that would lead to lower employee turnover.

With a better funded and more sophisticated training program, Au Bon Pain planned to improve the learning process that gave people skills, provided direction, and let them do things on their own.

b) Break the cycle of failure. This goal attacked the problems of frustration, burnout and job dissatisfaction endemic to the industry. Au Bon Pain was insistent on finding a cure to this problem.

c) Encourage leadership. The company sought to decrease its dependence on any one person. As an example, Len recalled how the company was changing. "Before, when Ron or Lou were gone, things didn't get done. In November of 1985, however, when Ron was in Japan and Lou was traveling, they weren't even missed."

Exhibit 6 Towards a Comprehensive Human Resource Strategy at Au Bon Pain

"BREAKING THE CYCLE OF FAILURE ONCE AND FOR ALL!"

In 1985, the retail operations of Au Bon Pain confronted the set of human resource problems endemic to the fast food industry for the first time. Labeled by Ron Shaich as "the cycle of failure" these problems inter-related in a systematic pattern of poor performance at the store level. Foremost among these problems are:

(1) The sudden, and now continuing crew labor shortage (especially in Boston) despite the dramatic increases in hourly rate we have offered.

(2) The chronic shortage of associate managers which emerged in the late winter-spring of 1985 as an outgrowth of our first significant increase in voluntary turnover.

(3) Our continuing inability, despite an exhaustive and time-consuming selection process, to attract and select high-quality management candidates on a timely and highly accurate basis.

(4) The lack of depth provided by our training program and the consequent performance shortfalls at the retail level by inadequately trained management staff.

(5) Due to our management inexperience, the requirement of our district managers to play "super GM"; continuing to obsessively focus on follow-up of day-to-day actions (ostensibly a GM's responsibility) at the expense of clear definition of a DM's role.

(6) A significant degradation of the customer experience due to all of the above factors plus a lack of clearly articulated and understood quality and service standards.

If Au Bon Pain is to deliver in a consistent way on its objectives of a high-quality customer experience which results in sales and profitability (and consequently growth and development for our employees in extrinsic and intrinsic ways) we must break the "cycle of failure" once and for all. To do so will require a concerted effort to respond to these problems in a comprehensive and integrated fashion. To do any less is to put the company's future on the line.

The remainder of this memo is devoted to outlining our current problems and just such a coordinated response. To date, the human resource management activities at Au Bon Pain have largely been in the form of disconnected reactions to events within and outside the company. While this "fire fighting" does have some place in the organization, it is clearly not the way in which we will be able to make a significant difference in the company's success. Our view is that we must become more proactive and in this memo we seek to outline the steps we must take.

Exhibit 6 (*Continued*)

A FRAMEWORK FOR HUMAN RESOURCE MANAGEMENT

These are four generic processes or functions that are performed by a human resource system in any organization:

- selection
- appraisal
- rewards
- development

These four processes reflect sequential managerial tasks. The diagram below represents them in terms of a human resource cycle. Clearly the dependent variable is performance: The elements of the human resources system are to be designed to impact performance at both the individual and the organizational levels.

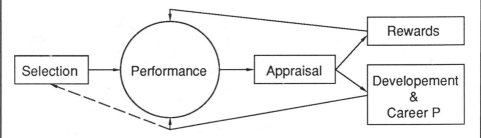

Performance, in other words, is a function of all the human resource components:

- selecting people best able to perform the jobs
- motivating employees via judicious rewards (monetary and recognition)
- training and developing employees for improved current and future performance
- appraising employees to justify the rewards

In addition, performance is a function of the organization context and resources surrounding the individual. Thus the operations organization impacts performance through the ways stores are designed, the structure of the service system, the magnitude and simplicity of the paperwork systems and through how well our products are planned to meet customer needs.

In order to outline these functions in the context of Au Bon Pain, we can distinguish among the time frames in which these human resource issues must be addressed.

- *Long Term (Strategic)*—Over the long term, we are concerned with policy formulation and overall goal setting around the human resource management agenda.
- *Medium Term (Managerial)*—Over the medium term, we are concerned with the availability and allocation of human resources to carry out our business strategy.
- *Short Term (Operational)*—Over the short term, we are concerned with our ability to carry out the day-to-day operations of the company. Ideally, these activities are carried out under the umbrella of the medium-term managerial plan.

The exhibit on the next page [6a] attempts to detail this action agenda for Au Bon Pain.

Exhibit 6a

Level	Recruitment and Selection	Rewards (Pay and Benefits)	Appraisal	Development	Career Planning
Strategic (long-term)	Specify the characteristics of people needed to run business over long term. Alter internal and external systems to reflect future	Determine how work force will be rewarded over the long term Link to long-term business strategy	Determining what should be valued in long term Develop means to appraise future dimensions. Make early identification of potential	Plan developmental experiences for people buying future business. Set up systems with flexibility necessary to adjust to change	Develop long-term system to meet individual and organizational needs for both flexibility and stability Link to business
Managerial (medium-term)	Validate selection criteria Develop recruitment marketing plan Develop new markets	Set up compensation plans for individuals Set up benefits packages	Set up systems that relate current conditions and future potential Set up assessment process for development	Establish general management development Provide for organizational development Foster self-development	Identify career paths Provide career development Match individual with organization
Operational (short-term)	Making staffing plans Make recruitment plans Set up day-to-day monitoring systems	Administer wage and salary program Administer benefits packages	Set up appraisal system Set up day-to-day control systems	Provide for specific job skill training Provide on-the-job training	Fit individual to specific jobs

The Young Astronaut Program

Our goal is to have a Young Astronaut Chapter available to every school-aged child in the U.S. by 1990.

Jack Anderson, chairman,
The Young Astronauts Council

The Young Astronaut Program was a nonprofit, private sector, educational initiative which sought to stimulate student interest, at an early age, in science, mathematics, and technology. Chapters of up to 30 members—girls and boys—were set up in schools or community organizations throughout the United States and abroad. The program, begun in 1984, had 13,000 chapters containing 320,000 members in 30 countries as of March 1987.

The core of the program was the space-related curriculum materials sent monthly to each chapter. Currently designed for ages six through sixteen, with a program for preschoolers to be implemented in the fall of 1987, the materials provided challenging, high quality, timely, and simplified teaching aids supplemental to standard school curricula.

The program was not only aimed at those students and teachers already interested and knowledgeable in math, science, and space, but to the average child and teacher, both in rural and urban environments. The Young Astronaut Council, which administered the program, was a privately sponsored, nonprofit, educational organization launched by President Reagan, the council's honorary chairman, in October 1984. The council's chairman was political columnist Jack Anderson who proposed and promoted the idea. T. Wendell Butler, a former White House staffer, served as executive director.

President Reagan, at a ceremony marking the first anniversary of the Young Astronaut Program, said, "In the short time since its inception, this splendid, private sector initiative has captured the imagination of thousands of students. . . . Educators, parents, business, industry, and professional groups have enthusiastically embraced this initiative to improve the scientific and mathematical skills of our nation's youth."

This case was prepared by Research Associate Lee Field, under the supervision of Associate Professor John J. Kao.

ORIGIN

As the father of nine children and the grandfather of seventeen (as of January 1987), Jack Anderson was always concerned about the future of children. In the 1970s and 1980s these concerns focused on children's education and motivation. Research indicated not only a decline in ability of American school children, especially in the hard sciences, but in interest as well. Research further indicated that outer space and everything about it fascinated young children. "Why not get them involved in the real thing, not just movies and video games, as a way to help with the educational dilemma? What about a high-tech, outer space focused program of some kind?" he thought.

In early 1984 Anderson approached President Reagan at a meeting in the Oval Office with the idea for the Young Astronaut Program. Reagan instantly expressed genuine interest in the proposal and promised to study it and get back to Anderson. T. Wendell Butler, the White House's educational specialist in the Office of Private Sector Initiatives, recalled, "If the President wanted it to happen, it was going to happen. It was not just an idea, but an opportunity."

A blue ribbon committee of science, mathematics, and space educators was convened to discuss the program and develop objectives. Among the committee members were Dr. Kerry Joels from the Smithsonian's Air and Space Museum, and Dr. Dan Kunz, educational director from Commodore Business Machines, Inc. (who both later became council staff members) and representatives from NASA, the Department of Education, the National Education Association, and other educational groups. Butler was the White House representative. After six weeks of study, the committee concluded that:

- student competencies were dropping in science and mathematics
- quality teachers were leaving math and science fields for industry jobs
- elementary teachers often lacked the training and interest to deal with these subjects
- while high-quality, curriculum materials had been developed before, these efforts had failed to increase interest in science and math, largely because:
  - the materials were textbooks and not timely
  - the materials were geared to students and teachers who were already interested in the subjects
  - materials distribution lacked marketing sophistication, expertise, and funding
  - the materials often attempted a complete curriculum revamping, which many schools were unable or unwilling to do

The committee made the following recommendations for establishing a Young Astronaut Program:

1. The program should be supported and administered by the private sector, not the government.
2. The council should become a solid educational organization that arouses interest through a classroom or "club" setting.

3. Materials should be flexible and supplementary; they should appeal to all students and be useful in stimulating interest in all subjects, not just math and science; they should be usable and straightforward to lay persons as well as teachers.

4. The program should use the theme of the totality of outer space—celestial events, astronomy, communications, and space exploration—as the vehicle for enhancing young persons' interests.

Under Butler's direction, the White House prepared for the media event of October 17, 1984, when the program was to be launched. Butler recalled:

> We had to create a White House event that would appeal to students, educators, business leaders, government officials and the media. Draft curricular materials were pretested in the classroom, T-shirts designed, and school kids invited to Washington from across the country. The program, however, had not gone beyond the conceptual stage, nor was I confident that it ever would.

After the program's formal introduction, Jim Coyne, Special Assistant to the President for Private Sector Initiatives and a Harvard Business School graduate, with Anderson's insistence, asked Butler to take over the Young Astronaut Program full time. Butler remembered:

> I was pretty skeptical, but he asked me to have lunch with Jack Anderson, who had been asked to serve as council chairman, and talk it over. Jack invited me to an upcoming shuttle launch. There, I saw the magic of the U.S. space program and its potential to excite kids and teachers. As the ground was shaking during the liftoff, Jack turned and asked if I would take the job. At that moment, I couldn't resist the challenge.

Said Anderson about the program and Butler's involvement: "I had the idea, but Wendell Butler deserves the credit for making it come alive. He runs the show and runs it well."

T. WENDELL BUTLER

The son of a rural Maryland tobacco farmer—one of eleven children—Wendell Butler graduated from an all-black high school in 1958. "I left the farm for Washington, D.C. and Howard University," he related. A member of the ROTC, Butler was commissioned in the Air Force after graduation and became an Air Force communications officer. "I didn't want to fly necessarily, but I liked planes," he continued. "I used to lie on my back in the tobacco field and watch fighter planes from nearby Patuxent Navel Air Test Center fly by. Later, I learned that Alan Shepard and the other original Mercury astronauts were in flight training there at the time." Butler spent five years in Italy and Greece as the commander of a processing center tracking Soviet tactical and space communications. Although enjoying his time with the Air Force, Butler recalled his decision to leave: "I was in Europe and missed a large part of a very important social event—the civil rights movement. I wanted to come home and participate in it, and to work for the Great Society programs."

Someone suggested to Butler on his return, that the Office of Management and Budget (OMB) was a good place to start. He became an OMB legislative budget analyst for two years and later worked his way up the civil service system to become a member of the Senior Executive Service. After a sabbatical at Harvard's Kennedy School of Government in 1975 where he received a Master's degree in public administration, Butler returned to Washington and worked up to Deputy Assistant Administrator at the Department of Energy. He remarked:

> I ran the petroleum allocation program, a huge and relatively unsuccessful regulatory program for crude oil and petroleum products. When Reagan took office, energy was decontrolled and the need for the office eliminated.

During this period awaiting another assignment, Butler read a *Time* magazine article about Reagan's Private Sector Initiative, a proposal to involve corporate and private America in quality of life programs handled in the past by the federal government. This spurred Butler's interest to get involved again with the private sector. After his Kennedy School stint in 1975, Butler had been a consultant for Xerox, designing and implementing an employment training program for inner-city children in 30 cities across the country. The program, which won Xerox a presidential citation, was ongoing in 1987. Butler, recalling that experience, stated, "The most rewarding thing for me was the chance to work with kids and give back some of my good fortune. It was the greatest joy that I have had professionally."

COUNCIL START-UP

After taking the executive director's job, Butler put together articles of incorporation and secured office space formerly used by the Los Angeles Olympic Organizing Committee. To his prospective landlord, a retired Air Force general, Butler implored, "We don't have any money to pay rent, but we will in about three months. Would you let us have it free now, and we can start paying later?" Butler got the new landlord to agree. He brought over two volunteers from the White House, Richard Funkhouser and Hamish Park, as the first staffers.

Butler remembered the existence of the Intergovernment Personnel Act (IPA) passed during the Kennedy administration. Under the act, government agencies loaned executives to other organizations (principally state and local government entities) for up to one year. Butler applied to the Office of Personnel Management (OPM) to have the council designated as an "IPA-eligible" organization. Following OPM approval, Butler identified several key executives in government agencies and had them loaned to the council. As of March 1987, seven of the council's sixteen professional staff were on loan from the government. In January 1985, the Young Astronaut Council began to function with about six people, four rooms and word processors donated by Commodore. The first order of business was to develop strategies for the creation and delivery of curriculum materials.

DEVELOPING THE EDUCATION PROGRAM

The primary objectives of the program were to:

- motivate young Americans to pursue educational endeavors related to mathematics, science, and technology
- increase young Americans' awareness of and appreciation for the United States' space program
- develop a more technologically proficient work force
- provide mechanisms for teachers to upgrade their personal skills in mathematics, science, and technology
- introduce young Americans to the variety of aerospace-related careers that would be open to them in the future

Key strategies included:

- Using the space program and its activities as the foundation for learning mathematics, science, and technology
- Motivating teachers to inspire and encourage their students to improve and develop knowledge and skills in mathematics, science, and technology
- Creating a Private Sector Initiatives program enlisting parents, schools, industry, civic groups, and other youth organizations to support the program

Program implementation would focus on chapters in schools, supervised by teachers, or chapters located in the community, supervised by adults with community-based institutional affiliations. Co-curricular or extracurricular materials would be provided by the Young Astronaut Council. Whenever possible, the substance would be extracted from appropriate existing materials developed by NASA, U.S. Department of Education, National Science Foundation, professional education associations, and other aerospace organizations. A Chapter Leader's Handbook was prepared containing an orientation to the program, classroom organization, activities, resources information, and recommendations for program extension activities such as Space Camp, field trips, private sector involvement, fairs, exhibits, and projects.

Through Butler's contacts with various school systems, the council gathered 50 schools and did its own test marketing in a few months. In return for previewing and critiquing materials specifically, and the program generally, these so-called "pilot chapters" got free membership in the program. Pilot chapters were still used in 1987. Their main job was to critique the materials packet that would go out monthly to each Young Astronaut Chapter.

Dr. Kerry Joels, director of curriculum, had primary responsibility for the development of the educational program. Working with the Education and Technology Advisory Board (ETAB) (see *Exhibit 1*), educational consultants and curriculum experts, a theme was determined for each school year. Monthly materials tied into that theme. For example, the theme for 1986–87 was Living in Space and the 1987–88 theme, Astronomy.

Final review and approval of all materials was given by the Education and Technology Advisory Board. Joels, commenting on the ETAB, said:

> The board not only gives approval of materials but also provides feedback concerning other aspects of our educational mission. If you have 30 educators who say, "No, this concept won't work," or "That proposal is bad from an educational standpoint," people listen and take note. The board is a good reality check.

After board approval, the materials were tested in the pilot schools, feedback recorded, final drafts modified, if necessary, reproduced and then sent out to club chapters. The materials were designed to teach through hands-on tasks, games, and activities that were challenging and fun. Regular features of the packets included sections titled: Toys That Teach, Physics of Fun, Recycled Science, and Space Watch. In addition, curricular activity packages, posters, contests and newsletters reflected current developments in space.

Activity-based instruction, not memorization, was the learning approach. Curriculum posters—actual photographs of space and space travel which changed bi-monthly—helped to focus and generate interest in the curricular activities found on the back of the posters. The curriculum had different levels of difficulty, and activities involved not only science and math but language and arts. Joels stated:

> Remember, these materials are designed to be flexible, supplemental and used only if desired. It is not a requirement or a necessity that every bit of material be used to keep up. This is an *enrichment* program, not a *core* curriculum; therefore, new materials are provided every month. Because NASA has been in the forefront of aerospace education, we work closely with them and utilize some of their best work for our program.

Butler reiterated:

> The purpose of the program is not to train kids to be astronauts. The goal is to prepare them for the twenty-first century and make them more aware of the world and its possibilities. Perhaps it can give them a few more tools and motivation to succeed in a high-tech world.

Other aspects of the program included:

Membership. There were three different categories of members: Trainees, Pilots, and Commanders. These titles reflected age and class levels of members: ages 6–8, 9–12, 13–16, or grades 1–3, 4–6, 7–9. Through the first two years of the program, boys outnumbered girls 3 to 2. The cost to join and receive two to three hours per week of materials was $20.00 per chapter per year in 1987. Each group named its own chapter, designed its own T-shirts, and planned its own field trips and activities. While meeting times and places were chapter-specific, most met approximately one hour each week during school. Students received membership cards and certificates and made a Young Astronaut pledge. (See *Exhibit 2*.) If no local chapter was available to an interested student, she or he could become a "satellite" member for ten dollars per year and receive approximately one-half of the curricular materials.

Mentoring.   Chapter leaders were encouraged to promote "mentoring," whereby older or more knowledgeable students aided and tutored younger, less skilled members.

Contests.   Joels revealed that one of the most challenging elements in the program was the nationwide contests for Young Astronauts. Thus far, contests had been held in designing Olympic games which could be played in a space environment, creating a learning center in outer space, and developing a Space Bill of Rights.

ASTRONET.   The council introduced both students and teachers to the practical applications of high technology via the council's computer program ASTRONET which linked chapters to the national office. This free computer service (donated by McDonnell Douglas) provided monthly space and curricular updates, space briefs, space adventure stories, and presidential messages.

Exchange program.   Butler stated that international exchanges represented a key element in the program. "Not only do student exchanges with like-minded youngsters in foreign countries provide an invaluable educational experience per se, but they constitute a means for building a better and peaceful world," he added.

Butler recalled that Jack Anderson had persuaded President Reagan to recommend an official and continuing exchange of Young Astronauts of America and Young Cosmonauts of the Soviet Union in his meetings with General Secretary Gorbachev at the Geneva summit in November 1985. The president had done so, and the highly successful two-way exchange of visits took place in October and November 1986 between ten Young Astronauts and ten Young Cosmonauts.

While the program was initially designed as a domestic one, there was unusual international interest. Over 1,000 inquiries from Americans and others living in foreign countries had been received from more than 80 countries by March of 1987. Chapters and satellites had been formed in 30 countries. (See *Exhibit 3* for details.) Furthermore, Canada and Japan instituted national Young Astronaut programs based on the U.S. version, and exchange visits and tripartite conferences by satellite took place. Private or governmental representatives in other countries, including Australia, India, West Germany, South Korea, and Taiwan were also experimenting with the program.

DEVELOPING A FUNDING BASE[1]

While Dr. Joels and staff were developing the educational program, Butler focused on acquiring working funds and building an organization. The initial fund-raising drive sought $25,000 donations from corporations. This attempt raised $150,000 in two weeks, but it was hard going. Butler recalled:

> We had to wait in the "donations" line, and it was long. We soon realized we were in the wrong line—dealing with the foundation side of the corporation—while the opportunity was on the marketing side.

Butler continued:

> I talked with Jay Morehead from the Los Angeles Olympic Organizing Committee—LAOOC—about the Olympic licensing program. Jay put us in touch with Peter Ueberroth who sent us to Joel Rubenstein, the LAOOC marketing head who orchestrated the LAOOC's licensing program. This was a turning point for the Young Astronaut Council. We learned about cause-related marketing, and its potential for our organization.

The task of creating a financial base sufficient to fund the Young Astronaut Program was large and complex. The council needed immediate financial support as well as long-term corporate sponsorship. Butler concluded that he needed to recruit a director of marketing who had the necessary business acumen, creativity, and contacts to develop and implement a fund-raising program that was suitable to the council's needs. He remarked:

> I needed a person who had a vision of what the Young Astronaut Program could be and the salesmanship to present it successfully to the corporate world. Most of all, I needed someone who could quickly change expressions of interest into cash commitments.

Butler recruited Paul Burke, who had worked with him as a senior executive in the U.S. Department of Energy. Butler remembered saying to Burke:

> Paul, this is an extraordinary opportunity that I would like to share with you. I know that the commitment requires taking a big chance, but I believe in the program. It's exciting work; let's do it together.

The first order of business required a marketing plan that focused primarily on licensing. Butler and Burke decided to establish relationships with select small manufacturers as well as *Fortune* 500 companies. They also concluded that to have an effective licensing program, the council needed to

---

[1] The U.S. Department of Labor awarded a grant of $300,000 (1985–1986) to target Young Astronaut materials to economically disadvantaged students; the U.S. Department of Health and Human services provided a grant of $125,000 to pilot Young Astronaut materials for preschool youngsters. About $27,800 was received in 1986; the balance would be received in 1987.

create attractive logos and themes that would enhance the image of the Young Astronaut Program. Burke said:

> We needed a symbol that would suggest adventure, action and patriotism, and appeal to both boys and girls. It also needed to be suitable for a wide range of materials. Not only would the symbol be used for educational purposes, it could also be displayed on consumer goods.

The council hired a firm to create the logo and image. Designs were developed, submitted and rejected during a painstaking process that took over a month. Burke managed the process which included separate reviews of all materials by himself, Butler, and Anderson. The goal was to have a symbol that would, in a few years, have instant recognition. The council finally selected the logos seen at the beginning of the case and in *Exhibit 2*.

The next step was to create informational brochures and begin the process of making sales calls on companies. The strategy was to select a single corporate sponsor in key categories of consumer goods, such as books, videos and apparel, games and toys. The council sought corporations with a vision of the program that involved a commitment beyond a profit. *Exhibit 4* is an excerpt from a brochure.

The search aimed for sponsorship companies which produced products that added to the excitement, awareness, and fun of being a Young Astronaut. The licensing agreements required an advance paid against future royalties to support the program during the start-up period. Additionally, each contract sought a multiyear commitment. Butler and Burke criss-crossed the country, selling the program and its educational purposes to corporate America. By October 1985, the Young Astronaut Council had entered into a dozen licensing and promotion agreements with leading corporations. The total value of contractual commitments to the council through 1988 exceeded $5 million.

Revenues derived from advances and royalties on products and promotions were used to finance the difference between the actual cost of developing and distributing the program's educational materials and the annual chapter membership fee. (Chapters paid twenty dollars per year for up to 30 students and received curriculum materials valued at two hundred dollars.) "There wouldn't be a Young Astronaut Program today without the backing and support of these corporations," said Burke. (See *Exhibit 5*.)

By 1986, Young Astronaut corporate sponsors had created new product lines for the program and presented them to the market. In the toy category, Coleco developed a Young Astronaut Cabbage Patch Kid in a space suit with appropriate "adoption" papers and space flight "qualifications." Monogram Models/Skilcraft marketed a Young Astronaut line of plastic model and science kits. The leader in optics products, Tasco, launched a full line of Young Astronaut microscopes, telescopes, and binoculars.

A comprehensive range of Young Astronaut clothing was also available. Adidas produced activewear garments, and Allison and Pilgrim marketed sleepwear lines for infants and toddlers. These clothing lines were featured in

Sears stores. Sports Specialties produced Young Astronaut caps, while Action Packets marketed the official Young Astronaut embroidered patches, and Lee Company produced belts and belt buckles.

The country's leading manufacturer of lunch boxes and insulated bottles, Thermos, provided a line of Young Astronaut school supplies. Marvel Comics produced a children's book series, and Bantam Books published the official *Young Astronaut Handbook.*

Royalties derived from the sales of these licensed products provided cash flow used to fund the monthly educational materials. Moreover, these sponsors' advertising publicized the program to children, teachers, and parents.

The Young Astronaut Program was also supported by these companies through national promotional campaigns. These promotions contributed to the financial base of the program but concentrated on membership growth.

- McDonald's ran a "Happy Meal" promotion in September of 1986 that generated thousands of dollars for the program; it was to be followed by promotions in 1987 of a similar magnitude.
- Pepsi offered a variety of benefits to chapters through their national bottler network in addition to their financial commitment.

A number of sponsors lent support through financial and in-kind contributions:

- Tymnet, a division of McDonnell Douglas, provided chapters free access to its computer network for accessing ASTRONET, the Young Astronaut electronic delivery system.
- Group W Television funded the production of two promotional videotapes, displaced in a number of leading aerospace installations, museums, and visitor centers.
- Martin Marietta designed and donated a computer system and staff training for maintenance of membership records, in addition to financial donations.
- Rockwell International contributed funds for the production of chapter materials.
- Safeway promoted the program on over 200 million shopping bags, milk cartons, and cereal boxes. A few times each year the store carried advertisements and information request forms on its grocer bags. Safeway also helped the council plan a balanced menu that was part of a nutrition-related activity package in the curriculum.

In February 1987 at Toy Fair, an industry trade show in New York, the council and Coleco introduced a major new toy line called STARCOM: U.S. Space Force. Future revenue plans included a Saturday morning television show, a monthly magazine, a depot for student purchases of council apparel and materials and other promotional activities.

LOCAL IMPLEMENTATION

The council determined that there were three key field-based groups essential to chapter growth and institutionalization: chapter leaders, local coordinators, and sponsors. Chapter leaders assumed local responsibility for organizing and implementing the program as outlined in the Chapter Leaders' Handbook. The council identified and supported these chapter leaders. Local coordinators, science or mathematics supervisors, curriculum directors, principals, or other appropriate institutional staff, organized new chapters, encouraged and supported existing chapters, and ensured continuing support for them. Council-developed guidelines for local coordinators facilitated consistency in chapters' development and expectations and protected the council from liability claims.

Sponsors were local businesses, PTAs, fraternities, sororities, clubs, and individuals who assisted local coordinators with financial support, speakers, or as field trip arrangers, assistants, and the like.

COUNCIL ORGANIZATION AND MANAGEMENT

Butler remarked on the council's staff and organization:

> I am trying to run a very lean organization. We add people only as absolutely needed. I don't want to create a far-flung bureaucracy; we have no regional offices at the present time. We believe that local input, ownership and support ensure successful program implementation; however, overall leadership, direction and curriculum design will be managed at the national office.

The Washington staff numbered twenty-two, with sixteen professionals and six support staff. (See *Exhibit 6* for an organizational chart.)

Butler added about the staff:

> I noticed one day that no one in this office smokes, and everyone is in good physical shape. These are just some of the shared similarities. Everyone here is also very concerned about the education of children; people become very proprietary with this program. We have a woman who runs the mail room where we receive about 800–1,000 letters a week. I was here one weekend and saw that so was she, with her son and his friend, all working on the mail. I asked her why she was here on the weekend, and she said, "Because I love my job and what we are doing." That's the kind of dedicated person we have working here. Most people get fervently involved in this cause, therefore, we must carefully share ownership in the program.

All council employees (except Butler) were covered by a bonus/reward system, depending on availability of dollars. Bonuses were determined by Butler after year-end evaluation.

He described his management style:

I like to call the plays, lay out the strategic objectives, but leave their execution to the person in the functional position. I was involved in everything at first; now I delegate extensively because I have confidence in the people making the decisions.

Our offices are designed for a lot of interaction. I have to pass by many people on the way to the coffee machines so I stop and talk a lot. I find out what's on people's minds; what they think and how they are doing.

Anderson recounted his own management role:

I make explicit suggestions to Wendell from time to time, and he takes most of my suggestions. But if he didn't, I wouldn't fire him. In fact, I lobbied hard for a staff person who Wendell just didn't think was working out. I wanted to keep him on; Wendell didn't. The person was fired. Wendell runs the operation and will continue to as long as he wishes and the results are so good.

Outlook

Between 1985 and 1987 the Young Astronaut Program had grown from an idea to over 13,000 chapters and 320,000 student members with the ultimate goal of establishing a chapter in every elementary and junior high school in America. The council focused longer term strategy on the following:

- improving delivery of the curriculum materials
- building and supplying membership

Improving material and delivery.   According to Lolita Hickman, the council's deputy director, "the primary complaints during our first two years of operation concerned missed or late mailings. As we grow geometrically, we are going to contract out with national, professional fulfillment houses to handle mailings."

Building and supporting membership.   During the first two years, most of the chapters originated in suburban and rural areas. Statistics showed, however, that the 20 largest school systems in the United States contained 80 percent of the students. Future targeting would emphasize these students. Dr. Shirley A. Jackson, educational specialist on loan from the Department of Education, developed a strategy to bring the program to major urban school districts, and by March 1987 more than 20 had been brought on board.

Another turning point in membership growth occurred when the Department of Health and Human Services asked the council to design a special program for Head Start, the nation's preschool program. A pilot project was developed and testing began in Florida in late 1986. The council expected to introduce the program to 25,000 Head Start centers in school year 1987–88.

The Challenger Tragedy

Perhaps the most critical and traumatic crisis the Young Astronaut Program faced was the Challenger tragedy, which claimed the lives of seven U.S. astronauts following an explosion just after liftoff on January 28, 1986. From its inception, the Young Astronaut Council was based on the successful U.S. space program as exemplified by the flights of the shuttle, with which every child in America was familiar. NASA's newly instituted policy of selecting, training, and sending non-aerospace civilians as members of mission flight crews provided role models for civilians nationwide. That the first selection of a civilian was a teacher who was to broadcast lessons to school children from outer space was to be a leap forward for the Young Astronaut Program. The council worked closely with Christa McAuliffe, the teacher selected, and arranged for her son and his third-grade chapter of Young Astronauts to attend the launch with the council's delegation.

After the catastrophe, the council expected that the reaction of children, parents, and teachers, would deal a serious blow to the program. Said Butler:

> What we failed to realize was the extraordinary resilience of, above all, the children. Our mail, both domestic and overseas, cascaded. Applications to join the program tripled. Chapters were signing up at the rate of 250 per month prior to the shuttle accident; following, that rate increased to 800 per month and remained at that level through most of 1986. Our conclusion was a new conviction that we were on the right road, that the need was there, and that space, the challenge of the future, was in good hands . . . those of our young.

Issues

While pleased with the progress of the council in its first few years, Butler could not help wondering if he and the other council members were doing everything they should or could to make certain the program would not self-destruct. These were some of the issues and questions the council faced in March 1987 as the program continued to grow.

- Would the private sector be able to continue funding the program, or would the council have to find other ways to raise funds or reduce costs? (See *Exhibits 7* and *8* for financial and membership data.)
- To what extent would increased or decreased public interest in the U.S. space program destabilize the Young Astronaut Program? Chapter registrations surged immediately after the Challenger disaster, but what would further setbacks or successes produce?
- How could the program maintain its unique attraction in a competitive and dynamic environment?
- To what extent would the council's efforts to institutionalize the program within the educational establishment, by committing school districts (superintendents) to the program, affect implementation?
- To what extent would international exchanges, symposia, and the formation of a world Young Astronaut movement contribute to program success?
- Was the council's internal organization equipped for the growth ahead? Should the structure remain national?

Exhibit 1 Education and Technology Advisory Board Association Members

American Association for the Advancement of Science
American Association of School Administrators
American Federation of Teachers
Association for Educational Communication and Technology
Association for Supervision and Curriculum Development
Association of Science and Technology Centers
Council of Chief State School Officers
Council of Greater City Schools
National Aeronautics and Space Administration
National Association of Elementary School Principals
National Association of Secondary School Principals
National Association of State Boards of Education
National Catholic Educators
National Council of Parents and Teachers
National Council of Teachers of Mathematics
National Education Association
National School Boards Association
National Science Foundation
National Science Teachers Association
United States Department of Education

Exhibit 2 The Young Astronaut Program

CERTIFICATE OF MEMBERSHIP

I pledge my best efforts to improve my grades
in science, mathematics and related subjects, to learn about space
and to help others towards these goals.

_____

(Name of member)

_____   _____

(Grade)   (School or Organization)

_____

(Date)

_____

(Teacher or Chapter Leader)

YOUNG **A**STRONAUT ™
PROGRAM
United States of America

Exhibit 3 International Year-End Summary (December 31, 1986)

1. Overseas Chapters: 67 from 18 foreign countries, NOT including 23 APO NY, mostly Germany, Spain; 6 FPOs Miami, mostly U.S. territories (Virgin Islands, Puerto Rico); 8 APO San Francisco, mostly U.S. territories (Guam, Truk, Saipan), Japan and Philippines.
2. By country: 26-Canada; 8-Australia; 6-Japan; 4-U.K.; 3-Mexico, Philippines, India, Saudi Arabia; 2-Kuwait, Zimbabwe; 1-Italy, Singapore, Indonesia, Taiwan, Ireland, Finland, Columbia.
3. Overseas Satellites: 74 from 22 foreign countries, NOT including U.S. possessions and APOs.
4. By Country: 36-Canada; 5-West German; 3-Japan, France, Australia; U.K., Finland; 2-U.A.E., New Zealand, Philippines; 1-Bahamas, Mexico, Ireland, Brazil, Saudi Arabia, Taiwan, Malaysia, Columbia, Uruguay, Turkey, Argentina, Austria.
5. Totals: 141 Chapters and Satellites from 30 foreign countries.
6. Foreign Inquiries: 1,065 from 82 foreign countries, plus 6 international organizations.

Exhibit 4 Excerpt From Brochure

Join the Space Team™ and KEEP AMERICA #1

The Young Astronaut Program is a privately sponsored, non-profit, educational organization established by the White House to develop and deliver high-quality curricular material to Chapters formed by schools and community groups. The purpose is to encourage students in elementary and junior high schools to study science, mathematics, technology and related subjects. By receiving information and activities related to the Space Program, Young Astronauts will gain the knowledge and skills they need for the coming decades.

All materials are reviewed by our Education and Technology Advisory Board, composed of representatives of all the major professional education associations as well as aerospace experts. These materials are then sent to classrooms across the country for additional review. In this way we ensure that learning and fun are effectively blended.

Why is this so critical?

As technological challenges have increased, the educational standing of young Americans has fallen. We put up the buildings, and we hand out diplomas by the millions. But the quality of education has declined.

Warns the National Space Commission: "An estimated 90 percent of America's high school graduates may not be capable of accomplishing even the most routine high-technology tasks. While up to 90 percent of high school graduates in other countries are proficient in math and science, a mere six percent of U.S. graduates attain the same proficiency."

If this trend isn't dramatically reversed, the United States could forfeit its technological leadership and lose its superiority in the factory and the field.

President Reagan established the Young Astronaut Program as a catalyst to prepare our children for the future. In the words of the National Space Commission, "The privately sponsored Young Astronaut Program is effectively reaching out to elementary and junior high school students to ignite their enthusiasm for studying science, mathematics and high technology."

Young people are fascinated by space. To channel that fascination into the hot pursuit of the studies required for the exploration and settlement of other worlds, to make school work less forbidding by dramatizing that it is the key to the universe beyond, to attract students to the disciplines that are prerequisite to tackling the challenge of the stars—these are the objectives of the Young Astronaut Program.

And...

- The Young Astronaut Program is designed for in-school activities to encourage further study in math and science.

- The curriculum is timely (within months of new breakthroughs), prepared by the finest educators from multiple disciplines, and piloted in school systems nationwide.

- The curriculum focus is *activity based*...doing is learning, and designed to involve the students.

- The curriculum is interdisciplinary; students use all learning skills.

President Reagan congratulates Executive Director Wendell Butler on YAC first-year accomplishments.

Exhibit 5 The Young Astronaut Program Board of Directors and Corporate Sponsors

YOUNG ASTRONAUT COUNCIL BOARD OF DIRECTORS

Honorary Chairman—Ronald Reagan
Honorary Vice Chairman—Senator Jake Garn
Honorary Vice Chairman—Senator John Glenn
Honorary Vice Chairman—Rep. William Nelson

Executive Committee:

Chairman—Jack Anderson
Vice Chairman—Hugh Downs
Secretary—Harold Burson
Executive Director—T. Wendell Butler

CORPORATE SPONSORS AND LICENSEES

Action Packets[a]	Pepsi-USA
Adidas-USA[a]	Pilgrim[a]
Allison[a]	Rockwell International
Bantam Books[a]	Safeway Stores
Coleco[a]	Sears
Group W Television	Sports Specialties[a]
Martin Marietta Corporation	S.P.M. Manufacturing[a]
Marvel Comics[a]	Tasco[a]
McDonald's	Tymnet
Monogram Models[a]	Thermos[a]

[a] Licensee.

Exhibit 6 Organization Chart, January 1987

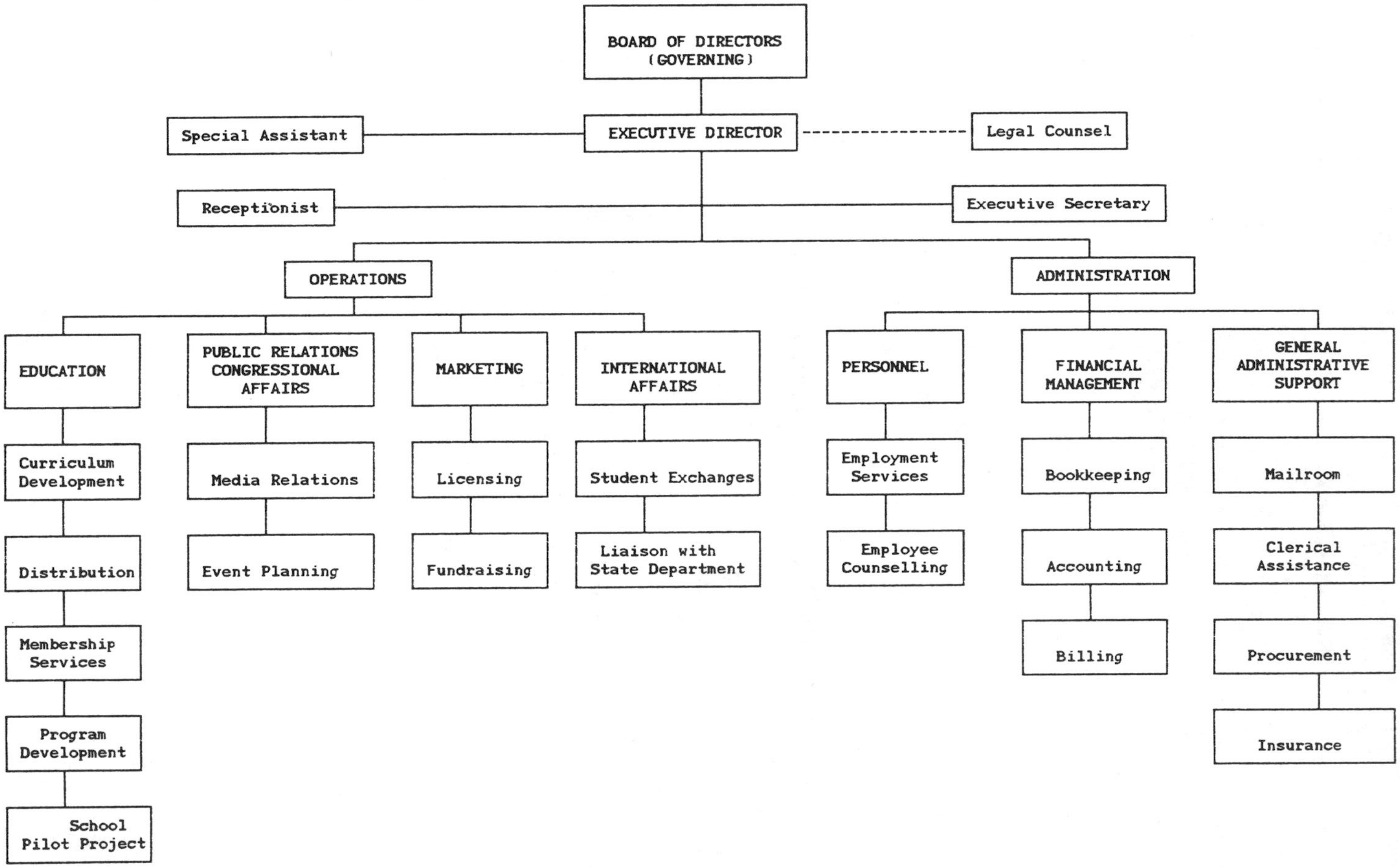

Exhibit 7 Income and Expenditure—1984–1986

	1986		1985		1984	
Income						
Direct Public Support	$ 147,003	8%	$ 529,542	37%	$118,605	97%
Government Grants	244,455	13	83,435	6	—	—
Membership Dues	201,608	10	93,101	6	3,326	3
Royalties/Other	1,350,471	69	727,881	51	—	—
Total	$1,943,537[a]		$1,433,959		$122,241	
Expenditures						
Curriculum Production and Communication	$1,942,490	83%	$1,029,603	79%	$ 89,214	80%
Overhead	409,684	17	276,120	21	22,745	20
Total	$2,352,174[a]		$1,305,723		$111,959	

[a] The $408,637 difference between Income and Expenditure represents accounts receivable from licensing agreements.

Exhibit 8   Membership Growth and Financial Requirements January 1987

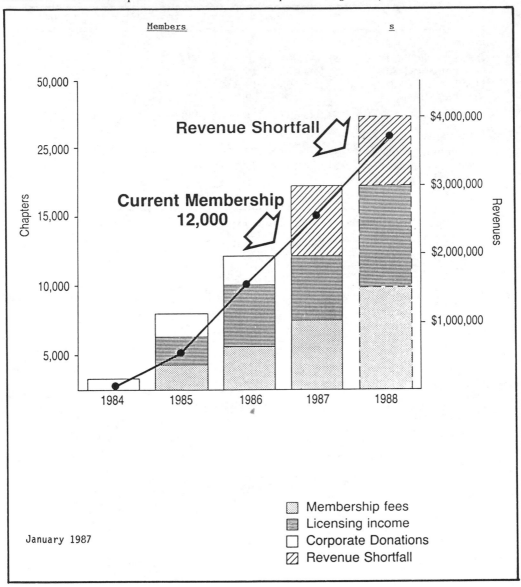

Members   s

Revenue Shortfall

Current Membership
12,000

Chapters

Revenues

50,000 — $4,000,000

25,000 — $3,000,000

15,000 — $2,000,000

10,000 — $1,000,000

5,000

1984   1985   1986   1987   1988

January 1987

☐ Membership fees
☐ Licensing income
☐ Corporate Donations
☐ Revenue Shortfall

The Learning Company (A)

Ann Piestrup, chairperson of The Learning Company, leaned back from her desk and smiled. Warm California sunshine played over the terrace outside of her window. Colorful pictures of cartoon raccoons and ducks, characters from the company's products, festooned the walls. "Life here is very exciting these days," she said. "We're evolving a distinctive way of doing things."

As I got up to leave, I said, "You are without a doubt the nicest company I've ever had dealings with. I wonder how you're going to stay nice in the future."

COMPANY OVERVIEW

Located in Menlo Park, California, The Learning Company developed and marketed interactive, graphics-based microcomputer software for children aged three and up. Its products presented basic concepts in mathematics, logic, language, and reading in a playful and challenging way. Its products were compatible with popular microcomputer systems from Apple, Atari, and Radio Shack.

The company was founded by Dr. Ann Piestrup in 1980 as Advanced Learning Technology, with grants from the National Science Foundation, the National Institute of Education, and the Apple Education Foundation. In January 1982, the company received $300,000 in funding from Melchor Venture Management. At this time, Marcia Klein joined the company as president and CEO. In April 1982, the firm's name was changed to The Learning Company. See *Exhibit 1* for landmark dates in the company's history. *Exhibit 2* provides further background on company senior management.

The company currently had 23 employees; its 1982 revenues were about $1 million. *Exhibit 3* presents an overview of the organization.

This case was prepared by Associate Professor John J. Kao.

Copyright © 1986 by the President and Fellows of Harvard College. Harvard Business School case 0-487-038.

PRODUCT PHILOSOPHY

The following comments were taken from The Learning Company's descriptive material:

> Expanding a child's potential for creativity through logical thinking is the cornerstone philosophy of The Learning Company. Its products reflect this by encouraging conceptual learning in an atmosphere of interactive play . . . The result is a new approach to early childhood learning. Instead of defining good performance and bad, right and wrong, this new learning concept challenges the child to reach what he or she is capable of learning.
>
> With The Learning Company's programs, a child learns to think logically by developing ideas out of experience. The building block structure of the programs guides the child through progressively more difficult adventures; the concepts learned early in the program are applied in later stages while new concepts are learned.
>
> This theme of progression also is carried out within a series of software, in which one program may be aimed at very young children and another program, based on the same concepts, may be targeted for use by ten to eighteen-year-olds.
>
> The programs use graphics, color and sound, and place the child in a stimulating, three-dimensional environment that maintains his or her interest for long periods of time.
>
> This theme of learning through colorful, picture-filled play is carried out in all of The Learning Company's programs. The programs, designed to be progressively more difficult, give the child a positive experience, are self-pacing, are nonviolent, do not allow for failure, and are easy to begin and end. Overall, the computer is seen as a friendly partner in a mental playground, rather than as a dehumanizing drillmaster. These programs will help today's youngsters function comfortably in tomorrow's computerized world.
>
> Each program includes clear, brief instructions that can be accessed at any time. Many feature a friendly, animal-like character that the child can identify with. The programs also encourage the participation of the child with things to build, patterns to create and music to generate.

Exhibits 4 and *5* present The Learning Company's brochure and product line description.

ANN PIESTRUP

"I do four things here. First, I point to the future, getting grants or somehow masterminding things that will take us into the future. I particularly do that through grants, because we want to be part of the academic community. We plan university-related activities in which we tie into Harvard, MIT, and other places with modems and networks. I also do special projects that relate to creating software that adds to TLC's future and to future business possibilities.

"The second thing I work on is product design for the company. I work with every product. I work with the people we bring in. Design is very important because our company philosophy is to have excellence in our products. As an educator and someone who is aware of what computers do, I look at outside products coming in, help design the flow of each product, and think of ways to make them more playful. I do specs for new products.

"The third function I do is public relations. I'm a spokesperson for the company. I do interviews, and appear on television. I go to a lot of conferences. I'm a keynote speaker at computer conferences and things like that. The fourth thing I'm involved with is strategic planning. And this is not in my written job description, but a lot of people come and talk with me about what's going on with their jobs. They say, 'I'm really concerned about this or that.' A lot of people touch base with me often. However, no one in the company has a line relationship to me except my assistant. I can't say you'll do it because I say so. Not that I would even if I were in a line position. I see myself on the organization chart as the concept person. And R&D is close to me. It's very exciting to have design sessions around here. A sixteen-year-old kid might have ideas and we might say fantastic—go for it!

"Our core values here involve our desire to prepare children for the computer age. We want to do that with technical excellence in computing. We want to use the very best mass market micros to do that, to do it playfully, engage the kids, involve them, get them excited about learning, give them an active goal so that it's not a sugar-coated pill where there's some dinky little reward or something. It's really involving children in a way that they become totally excited about learning and forget that it's a task. Using TLC programs is like building something with an erector set where you get totally lost in the process. So our goal is to offer that kind of learning on the computer specifically for skills that are needed in the future. No one is quite doing that, building thinking skills, ability to analyze, to construct, to approach things from different angles, to think flexibly, to reason carefully, and do that in a way that you're building something, not destroying it. A real explicit value is: We don't accept software that blows things up. We don't like blowing things up because they're aliens. We like finding out about aliens! There's a lot of belief about our work being good for people and that really drives us. It isn't just selling soap. There's a sense that we're offering something very fine and special that no one else has, and that motivates people a lot.

"We have human values too. I really love it that just about everyone in this company is producing to their maximum. They are challenged. They're carefully selected, and they terribly want to be here or they're not here. We have stacks of resumes that come in. Lots of phone calls. I love it that people are excited about what we're doing. There's a tremendous feeling of participation. There's a lot of ownership in the product by everyone. There's a lot of warmth here, compared to researchy types of places. There's a lot of personal caring. When I walk in, I am so excited to see people in the morning. There's a very explicit emotional bond among the people that are here, and the sense of 'We're doing it together.' There's an excitement about presenting ourselves here to the world as women. We're determined to be exceedingly successful to show that we can do it. It's so much fun to have it work. I don't think we have gender preferences. If we had a male and a female candidate, I think we might give preference to a male to get a little more balance. But I like our sensitivity.

"We're working on a development group that will have its own budget and office and manager. A separate entity financially. It will be called The Scientific Thinking Institute and will be organizationally a subsidiary of TLC. I will be principal investigator for an NSF-funded project, and we will have more basic development going on there. We're going to have a computer network tying people in Harvard, MIT, game designers, kids, kids in Harlem, in a barrio in Texas. It's an electronic university, a time-sharing research consortium with a specific purpose which is the development of new software. We're not going to do this in TLC because there we have to get products done in a shorter period. The Institute is going to be the future center, like Xerox PARC and the Atari Futures Product Group. It will build our long-term future. The downside is that it could be a drain. It could fail to produce anything. Our hope is that this is what will make TLC special. I think that people will work with us differently by having it organizationally separate. But the link through me and through our head of R&D will be very important."

MARCIA KLEIN

"My responsibility is to make sure that the best and most creative ideas are implemented. I look at things strategically and also make sure that we take care of business. Things like contract negotiations, business development and budgets. I spend about a third of my day responding to people's needs. One of the most important things I do here is to develop a sense of teamwork. I spend an enormous amount of time with the people here. Usually, most of my work happens after everybody goes home. In the morning, my out basket is full. I read my mail at night. I go over the status reports of people, react, say, 'Have you thought of this or that?' A lot of people like our lawyers and accountants know that if they need to reach me, after six is a good time. Last night I did a lot of budgeting. Stayed here until about 10:30. I try to save the day for people, personnel problems, hiring problems, and strategic issues. Because we're a small company, I'm involved with pretty much everything.

"When I arrived here, there were fourteen people in the company. Everybody reported to me, which ate up a lot of time. The company didn't have an organizational chart. No one really had a particular area of responsibility. One of the first things I did was to spend a lot of time with people and find out what they did and what they wanted to do. My first priority was to get people focused. I spent a lot of time cleaning up the departments, letting people know, 'Okay, you're now in charge of educational marketing. Now, let's look at the market, What do we need to do? Let's set some priorities.'

"What I have here is a lot of people with an incredible amount of energy but not a lot of business experience. They've never been through a corporate planning cycle. A lot of my job is just saying things like, 'Here's how a company works. What are you doing now? You're doing some of the important things. Now let's take it back a step and make sure we have a positioning strategy. Now let's prioritize.' As you go through the process, you build bonds with people.

"We had to learn how to work smarter. When I came, I found that a lot of people were working very hard. They would say, God, I'm working fifteen hours a day. And being exhausted and overworked has no direct correlation to output in this business.

"Another thing about building an organization which I feel really strongly about is that you can build little boxes and put people in them or you can take the people and build boxes around them. I'm a strong believer in operating according to what people do. As their interests change, or if they try something that isn't very successful, you keep shifting them until you find the right place for them.

"You get the sense that people really care about what's going to happen around here. That's an attitude that has to be fostered and developed. A lot of venture capitalists have said to me, 'Marcia, this is terrific. You've built a real team.' They adore Ann. They think this is a real special place.

"I believe that you have to empower people to make decisions and to take responsibility. Once people have some objectives and focus, I don't sit on them, or how they spend their day, or when they come in. If they're doing their jobs, they have a lot of flexibility. I don't look at what time they take for lunch. I empower them to decide how they want to set their work up, how they want to get it done. And then I judge people by results. Although I'm flexible, I do expect performance. But I've never found that I needed to carry a big stick. I don't go around making a big deal about things, but my expectations are basically met. There is a high level of performance around here. I act as a role model, but I sometimes have to tell people around me to go home when it's 5:00 p.m. Because I don't want people to work the sorts of hours I work. I want to make sure they don't burn out.

"Another norm around here is that there's always time for people. There's no doubt that we get things done. But there's always the time if somebody's kid is sick or something, that they can go home and someone else can cover. If someone's upset, had a bad day, I always check; I'm very intuitive. When I walk in in the morning, I can usually pick up when someone needs an extra moment. That's an important part of keeping people on keel. I train people to watch for what's going on and to pay attention. If someone looks really upset and you're a manager, it's your responsibility to check and see if it's work-related, something not going well, something which can't be handled. It's not hand-holding as much as a moral obligation to people. This is a very supportive environment by design. I think that when you're asking people to give as much energy and time, that the organization has an obligation to give it back.

"Ann and I are diametrically opposite. At the beginning, one of the important things was to sit down and make sure we had defined our roles so that Ann very clearly was empowered, had an area and a world and knew in what ways her specialness was invaluable to the company. What Ann saw was that my vision of the company was the same as hers. That gave her a great deal of comfort because she didn't know that in the beginning, although she had assumed it. We saw that there were certain areas of responsibility that Ann would prefer not to take care of which I have taken on. And I'm very comforted in knowing that Ann is out talking to people and generating ideas. She feels a lot of freedom because she knows that someone's tending the home fires. So she can continue to be herself. We each sense how indispensable we are to the company.

"She's one of the most charismatic, incredible people in the world. I think that she's a typical genius. She has an incredible emotional intensity. Her mind is fertile. I am much more consistently intense; classic achiever personality. After I got a sense of Ann's personality, I made sure that we maximized it. One thing I realized is that she could be all that she could be if we hired somebody to take care of things. When I hired Ann's secretary I said to her, 'Your primary responsibility in life is to take care of Ann. Make sure you ask her if she's had lunch. If she's going to a conference, make sure she has the things she needs.'

"There are some things I can't tell Ann in the hall. I need to make sure I lay it out. I'm aware that when I want to communicate with her, writing it down is the key if it's important. I take a risk when I grab her in the hall. We do have disagreements. If I have a problem I bring it up to Ann and vice versa. We talk them through and resolve them. We haven't had any nonresolvable issues.

"Before coming here, I had been a vice president at Regis McKenna in charge of consumer accounts, including Apple Computer. I'd gotten to work with Ann in January of 1982 right after they had gotten venture capital. They had come to us to work on positioning. They had no marketing strategy. It was last December when one of the board members said, 'Would you be interested in working at TLC?' He asked me what I would be interested in doing. I said that the only thing I would be interested in would be the presidency of the company. We proceeded to a five-hour interview with the board. The interview was an intensive grilling. But I knew I could be successful. I was ready to run something. I've always enjoyed running things. I was always comfortable with that. I'm obviously not a sledgehammer type of person. I prefer to nudge rather than shout.

"I was attracted to the company because it had good products and a base of people. Ann had paid a lot of attention to making sure she had the best. I looked at the market for educational software and decided we could be a winner. I also realized that it was a no-loss situation personally. If by any chance things went to hell in a handbasket, I knew I would at least have the company in shape where somebody else could take it over if I couldn't handle it. The Valley is very forgiving. As long as you have taken the risks and the chances, people are sympathetic. It's also a hungry place. If you've managed a high-growth situation, that makes you valuable somewhere else. The fact that we are mostly women here is not by design. The strong people in this company are women, and I think some people aren't willing to come in as an assistant here. I think that balance in companies is really important. I consider myself a good manager and a good person. I don't think I err towards being masculine or feminine. I'm pretty balanced in between in terms of expectations and demands. I happen to be in a female body, but pretty in the middle in terms of masculine and feminine characteristics.

"Some of the ways we differ from the typical patriarchal organization are cultural, but not gender related. We feel that the corporation has the potential for being more human. If I leave a legacy here it might be a more humane business organization. If three-quarters of our people were men, I would still operate the same way with the same culture. There may be other differences. We've thought about it many times. Sometimes we'll say, 'We'll just get some men in here to balance things out.' If it were a feminine organization, I would worry about it. But the people here are pretty well balanced. We have some more feminine-type people and more masculine-type people. But we have a commonality of purpose and a belief in what we are doing, whether we are male or female. Ask us when we're making $50 million and see if we've changed."

Exhibit 1 Landmark Dates for The Learning Company

October 16, 1979	APPLE EDUCATION FOUNDATION GRANT awarded to Advanced Learning Technology
August 14, 1980	INCORPORATED as a California corporation— Advanced Learning Technology
September 15, 1980	NSF/NIE GRANT awarded to Advanced Learning Technology
August 17, 1981	MAGIC SPELLS, MOPTOWN agreement with Leslie Grimm
November 13, 1981	NUMBER PAIR GAMES (Bumble Games, Bumble Plot) agreement with Leslie Grimm
November 17, 1981	DISCOVERY TOOL agreement with Warren Robinett
January 1982	VENTURE CAPITAL FUNDING from Melchor Venture Management
January 1982	MARCIA KLEIN joins Advanced Learning Technology
April 2, 1982	CORPORATION NAME CHANGED to The Learning Company
June 27, 1982	MARKETED FIRST PRODUCTS

Exhibit 2 Senior Management (The Learning Company Prospectus)

MARCIA KLEIN

President and CEO, brings to the company an extensive background in both marketing and education fields. Prior to joining The Learning Company, she was vice president of the consumer clients group for Regis McKenna, Inc., a high technology marketing and public relations strategy firm in Palo Alto. She was responsible for activities for several accounts, including Apple Computer, where she recently orchestrated the public introduction of Lisa and the Apple IIe computers.

Prior to Regis McKenna, Klein held various marketing and sales positions at J. Walter Thompson advertising agency, Hunt-Wesson Foods, and Procter & Gamble, as well as a teaching position at the College of Notre Dame, Belmont, California.

She holds an M.A. in education from Stanford University, an M.A. in counseling from the University of Santa Clara, and a B.A. from the University of Michigan.

ANN M. PIESTRUP

Founder and chairman of the board, is an internationally recognized authority on the application of microcomputers in childhood learning. She is in demand as a consultant on educational matters by schools, colleges, and governments. Piestrup has been involved in education as a grant recipient to adapt microprocessors to learning, teaching research, educational evaluation teacher training, and as a fifth-grade teacher.

Piestrup was a research associate with RMC Research Corporation and the American Institute for Research and

held consulting and teaching assistant positions with the University of California at Berkeley.

She earned doctoral and master's degrees in educational psychology at the University of California at Berkeley and a bachelor's degree in social sciences at Seattle University. Piestrup holds California teaching credentials at the elementary and secondary school levels. She shares credit for developing a number of computer programs for children, has published many works and is a frequent speaker at educational conferences.

Exhibit 3   Organizational Chart

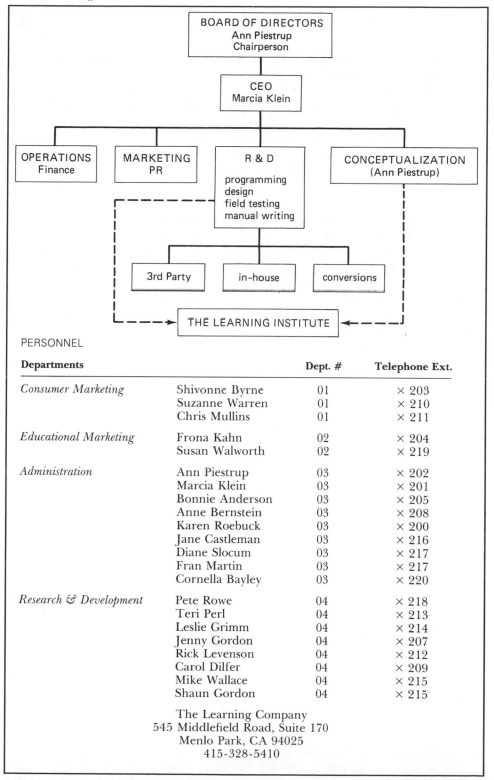

PERSONNEL

Departments		Dept. #	Telephone Ext.
Consumer Marketing	Shivonne Byrne	01	× 203
	Suzanne Warren	01	× 210
	Chris Mullins	01	× 211
Educational Marketing	Frona Kahn	02	× 204
	Susan Walworth	02	× 219
Administration	Ann Piestrup	03	× 202
	Marcia Klein	03	× 201
	Bonnie Anderson	03	× 205
	Anne Bernstein	03	× 208
	Karen Roebuck	03	× 200
	Jane Castleman	03	× 216
	Diane Slocum	03	× 217
	Fran Martin	03	× 217
	Cornella Bayley	03	× 220
Research & Development	Pete Rowe	04	× 218
	Teri Perl	04	× 213
	Leslie Grimm	04	× 214
	Jenny Gordon	04	× 207
	Rick Levenson	04	× 212
	Carol Dilfer	04	× 209
	Mike Wallace	04	× 215
	Shaun Gordon	04	× 215

The Learning Company
545 Middlefield Road, Suite 170
Menlo Park, CA 94025
415-328-5410

Exhibit 4   The Next Most Precious Gift

THE LOVE OF LEARNING

Next to your love, you can give your child nothing more precious than the confidence and the joy that comes from learning.

Now you can provide a new kind of learning experience for your child: an opportunity to develop thinking skills at a very early age, in a very natural way. At last, The Learning Company™ software truly fulfills the educational promise of the personal computer.

The Learning Company's 11 award-winning programs are as colorful, as fast-moving, as many-faceted as a child's curiosity. Your child will grasp new concepts eagerly as each success opens the door to a new challenge in logical thinking. As an adult, you will notice how skillfully The Learning Company's educators and software designers have combined sophisticated teaching techniques with pure fun.

What will you see as your child explores the wonders of The Learning Company software? Possibly a delighted three-year-old building *Juggles' Rainbow*™ in brilliant color. Perhaps an utterly fascinated five-year-old sorting out the tall thin red Gribbits and short fat blue Bibbits in *Moptown Parade.*™ A seven-year-old, a ten-year-old or even a teenager, deeply involved in designing logical kicking machines to control *Rocky's Boots.*™

What's your reward? It may be a moment of shared pride as your six-year-old shows you the solution to one of *Gertrude's Puzzles.*™ Or it may be the special satisfaction you feel when your grown-up teenager calls home from college to say that Boolean algebra seems, somehow, very familiar.

You can be sure of one thing. It will be very precious.

Exhibit 5 The Learning Company Product Line (The Learning Company Prospectus)

A major goal of The Learning Company is to create personal computer programs that have the educational and entertainment appeal that Dr. Seuss's books have for children.

The typical buyer is expected to be a concerned parent with a home computer or access to a personal computer that can be brought home, and with a child or children age three and up. These programs are priced between $29.95 and $49.95.

Juggles' Rainbow

Children develop reading and math readiness skills by playing with dancing rainbows, butterflies, and windmills. In colorful, delightful games, children learn spatial concepts such as "above" and "below," "right" and "left." Ages 3–6.

Bumble Games

Children learn fundamental math skills by playing with Bumble, a friendly creature from the planet Furrin. They learn to plot numbers and even create their own computer graphics. Ages 4–10.

Bumble Plot

Children learn advanced math skills while trapping robbers and discovering underwater treasure. They create computer graphics by plotting positive and negative numbers on increasingly complex grids. Ages 8–13.

Gertrude's Secrets

Children develop logical thinking skills in the animated world of Gertrude, the go-getter goose. They learn to categorize and recognize patterns while solving playful puzzles. And children can even create their own colorful puzzle pieces. Ages 4–10.

Gertrude's Puzzles

Children develop abstract thinking skills in Gertrude's animated world and solve complex logic puzzles using colors and shapes. Children can also design playing pieces with Gertrude's graphics editor. Ages 8–13.

Rocky's Boots

Children learn the basics of logic and circuitry in the futuristic world of Rocky's boots. They design logic machines using simulated computer circuits. Children play 39 games or create their own. Ages 9 and up.

Moptown Parade

Children develop logical thinking skills in the imaginary world of Moptown. Children learn problem-solving skills by strategically arranging colorful Moppet characters. Ages 6–10.

Moptown Hotel

Children develop advanced strategic thinking skills in Moptown's fantasy world. Children learn to hypothesize and develop strategic thinking skills. Ages 9 and up.

Magic Spells

In an adventure world of castles, demons, and wizards, children unscramble and practice spelling words. And spellers of any age can sharpen their skills by creating their own word lists. Ages 6–10.

The Role of the Founder in Creating Organizational Culture

EDGAR H. SCHEIN

How do the entrepreneur/founders of organizations create organizational cultures? And how can such cultures be analyzed? These questions are central to this article. First I will examine what organizational culture is, how the founder creates and embeds cultural elements, why it is likely that first-generation companies develop distinctive cultures, and what the implications are in making the transition from founders or owning families to "professional" managers.

The level of confusion over the term *organizational culture* requires some definitions of terms at the outset. An organizational culture depends for its existence on a definable organization, in the sense of a number of people interacting with each other for the purpose of accomplishing some goal in their defined environment. An organization's founder simultaneously creates such a group and, by force of his or her personality, begins to shape the group's culture. But that new group's culture does not develop until it has overcome various crises of growth and survival, and has worked out solutions for coping with its external problems of adaptation and its internal problems of creating a workable set of relationship rules.

Organizational culture, then, is the pattern of basic assumptions that a given group has invented, discovered, or developed in learning to cope with its problems of external adaptation and internal integration—a pattern of assumptions that has worked well enough to be considered valid and, therefore, to be taught to new members as the correct way to perceive, think, and feel in relation to those problems.

In terms of external survival problems, for example, I have heard these kinds of assumptions in first-generation companies:

The way to decide on what products we will build is to see whether we ourselves like the product; if *we* like it, our customers will like it.

The only way to build a successful business is to invest no more than 5 percent of your own money in it.

The customer is the key to our success, so we must be totally dedicated to total customer service.

In terms of problems of internal integration the following examples apply:

Ideas can come from anywhere in this organization, so we must maintain a climate of total openness.

The only way to manage a growing business is to supervise every detail on a daily basis.

The only way to manage a growing business is to hire good people, give them clear responsibility, tell them how they will be measured, and then leave them alone.

Several points should be noted about the definition and the examples. First, culture is not the overt behavior or visible artifacts one might observe on a visit to the company. It is not even the philosophy or value system that the founder may articulate or write down in various "charters." Rather, it is the assumptions that underlie the values and determine not only behavior patterns, but also such visible artifacts as architecture, office layout, dress codes, and so on. This distinction is important because founders bring many of these assumptions with them when the organization begins; their problem is how to articulate, teach, embed, and in other ways get their own assumptions across and working in the system.

Founders often start with a theory of how to succeed; they have a cultural paradigm in their heads, based on their experience in the culture in which they grew up. In the case of a founding *group,* the theory and paradigm arise from the way that group reaches consensus on their assumptions about how to view things. Here, the evolution of the culture is a multi-stage process reflecting the several stages of group formation. The ultimate organizational culture will always reflect the complex interaction between (1) the assumptions and theories that founders bring to the group initially and (2) what the group learns subsequently from its own experiences.

WHAT IS ORGANIZATIONAL CULTURE ABOUT?

Any new group has the problem of developing shared assumptions about the nature of the world in which it exists, how to survive in it, and how to manage and integrate internal relationships so that it can operate effectively and make life livable and comfortable for its members. These external and internal problems can be categorized as shown in Figure 1.

The external and internal problems are always intertwined and acting simultaneously. A group cannot solve its external survival problem without being integrated to some degree to permit concerted action, and it cannot integrate itself without some successful task accomplishment vis-à-vis its survival problem or primary task.

The model of organizational culture that then emerges is one of shared solutions to problems which work well enough to begin to be taken for granted—to the point where they drop out of awareness, become unconscious assumptions, and are taught to new members as a reality and as the correct way to view things. If one wants to identify the elements of a given culture, one can go down the list of issues and ask how the group views itself in relation to each of them: What does it see to be its core mission, its goals, the way to accomplish those goals, the measurement systems and procedures it uses, the way it remedies actions, its particular jargon and meaning system, the authority system, peer system, reward system, and ideology? One will find, when one does this, that there is in most cultures a deeper level of assumptions which ties together the various solutions to the various problems, and this deeper level deals with more ultimate questions. The real cultural essence, then, is what members of the organization assume about the issues shown in Figure 2.

Figure 1 External and Internal Problems

Problems of External Adaptation and Survival

1. Developing consensus on the *primary task, core mission, or manifest and latent functions of the group*—for example, strategy.

2. Consensus on *goals,* such goals being the concrete reflection of the core mission.

3. Developing consensus on the *means to be used* in accomplishing the goals—for example, division of labor, organization structure, reward system, and so forth.

4. Developing consensus on the *criteria to be used in measuring how well the group is doing against its goals and targets*—for example, information and control systems.

5. Developing consensus on *remedial or repair strategies* as needed when the group is not accomplishing its goals.

Problems of Internal Integration

1. *Common languages and conceptual categories.* If members cannot communicate with and understand each other, a group is impossible by definition.

2. Consensus on *group boundaries and criteria for inclusion and exclusion.* One of the most important areas of culture is the shared consensus on who is in, who is out, and by what criteria one determines membership.

3. Consensus on *criteria for the allocation of power and status.* Every organization must work out its pecking order and its rules for how one gets, maintains, and loses power. This area of consensus is crucial in helping members manage their own feelings of aggression.

4. Consensus on *criteria for intimacy, friendship, and love.* Every organization must work out its rules of the game for peer relationships, for relationships between the sexes, and for the manner in which openness and intimacy are to be handled in the context of managing the organization's tasks.

5. Consensus on *criteria for allocation of rewards and punishments.* Every group must know what its heroic and sinful behaviors are; what gets rewarded with property, status, and power; and what gets punished through the withdrawal of rewards and, ultimately, excommunication.

6. Consensus on *ideology and "religion."* Every organization, like every society, faces unexplainable events that must be given meaning so that members can respond to them and avoid the anxiety of dealing with the unexplainable and uncontrollable.

Figure 2   Basic Underlying Assumptions Around Which Cultural Paradigms Form

1. *The organization's relationship to its environment.* Reflecting even more basic assumptions about the relationship of humanity to nature, one can assess whether the key members of the organization view the relationship as one of dominance, submission, harmonizing, finding an appropriate niche, and so on.

2. *The nature of reality and truth.* Here are the linguistic and behavioral rules that define what is real and what is not, what is a "fact," how truth is ultimately to be determined, and whether truth is "revealed" or "discovered"; basic concepts of time as linear or cyclical, monochronic or polychronic; basic concepts such as space as limited or infinite and property as communal or individual; and so forth.

3. *The nature of human nature.* What does it mean to be "human," and what attributes are considered intrinsic or ultimate? Is human nature good, evil, or neutral? Are human beings perfectible or not? Which is better, Theory X or Theory Y?

4. *The nature of human activity.* What is the "right" thing for human beings to do, on the basis of the above assumptions about reality, the environment, and human nature: to be active, passive, self-developmental, fatalistic, or what? What is work and what is play?

5. *The nature of human relationships.* What is considered to be the "right" way for people to relate to each other, to distribute power and love? Is life cooperative or competitive; individualistic, group collaborative, or communal; based on traditional lineal authority, law, or charisma; or what?

In a fairly "mature" culture—that is, in a group that has a long and rich history—one will find that these assumptions are patterned and interrelated into a "cultural paradigm" that is the key to understanding how members of the group view the world. In an organization that is in the process of forma-tion, the paradigm is more likely to be found only in the founder's head, but it is important to try to decipher it in order to understand the biases or directions in which the founder "pushes" or "pulls" the organization.

HOW DO ORGANIZATIONAL CULTURES BEGIN? THE ROLE OF THE FOUNDER

Groups and organizations do not form accidentally or spontaneously. They are usually created because someone takes a leadership role in seeing how the concerted action of a number of people could accomplish something that would be impossible through individual action alone. In the case of social movements or new religions, we have prophets, messiahs, and other kinds of charismatic leaders. Political groups or movements are started by leaders who sell new visions and new solutions. Firms are created by entrepreneurs who have a vision of how a concerted effort could create a new product or service in the marketplace. The process of culture formation in the organization begins with the founding of the group. How does this happen?

In any given firm the history will be somewhat different, but the essential steps are functionally equivalent:

1. A single person (founder) has an idea for a new enterprise.
2. A founding group is created on the basis of initial consensus that the idea is a good one: workable and worth running some risks for.
3. The founding group begins to act in concert to create the organization by raising funds, obtaining patents, incorporating, and, so forth.
4. Others are brought into the group according to what the founder or founding group considers necessary, and the group begins to function, developing its own history.

In this process the founder will have a major impact on how the group solves its external survival and internal integration problems. Because the founder had the original idea, he or she will typically have biases on how to get the idea fulfilled—biases based on previous cultural experiences and personality traits. In my observation, entrepreneurs are very strong-minded about what to do and how to do it. Typically they already have strong assumptions about the nature of the world, the role their organization will play in that world, the nature of human nature, truth, relationships, time, and space.

Three Examples

Founder A, who built a large chain of supermarkets and department stores, was the dominant ideological force in the company until he died in his seventies. He assumed that his organization could be dominant in the market and that his primary mission was to supply his customers with a quality, reliable product. When A was operating only a corner store with his wife, he built customer relations through a credit policy that displayed trust in the customer, and he always took products back if the customer was not satisfied. Further, he assumed that stores had to be attractive and spotless, and that the only way to ensure this was by close personal supervision. He would frequently show up at all his stores to check into small details. Since he assumed that only close supervision would teach subordinates the right skills, he expected all his store managers to be very visible and very much on top of their jobs.

A's theory about how to grow and win against his competition was to be innovative, so he encouraged his managers to try new approaches, to bring in consulting help, to engage in extensive training, and to feel free to experiment with new technologies. His view of truth and reality was to find it wherever one could and, therefore, to be open to one's environment and never take it for granted that one had all the answers. If new things worked, A encouraged their adoption.

Measuring results and fixing problems was, for A, an intensely personal matter. In addition to using traditional business measures, he went to the stores and, if he saw things not to his liking, immediately insisted that they be corrected. He trusted managers who operated on the basis of similar kinds of assumptions and clearly had favorites to whom he delegated more.

Authority in this organization remained very centralized; the ultimate source of power, the voting shares of stock, remained entirely in the family. A was interested in developing good managers throughout the organization, but he never assumed that sharing ownership through some kind of stock option plan would help in that process. In fact, he did not even share ownership with several key "lieuten-ants" who had been with the company through most of its life but were not in the family. They were well paid, but received no stock. As a result, peer relationships were officially defined as competitive. A liked managers to compete for slots and felt free to get rid of "losers."

A also introduced into the firm a num-ber of family members who received fa-vored treatment in the form of good devel-opmental jobs that would test them for ultimate management potential. As the firm diversified, family members were made divi-sion heads even though they often had rela-tively little general management experience. Thus peer relationships were highly politi-cized. One had to know how to stay in favor, how to deal with family members, and how to maintain trust with nonfamily peers in the highly competitive environment.

A wanted open communication and high trust levels, but his own assumptions about the role of the family, the effect of ownership, and the correct way to manage were, to some degree, in conflict with each other, leading many of the members of the organization to deal with the conflicting sig-nals by banding together to form a kind of counter-culture within the founding cul-ture. They were more loyal to each other than to the company.

Without going into further detail, I want to note several points about the "for-mation" of this organization and its emerg-ing culture. By definition, something can become part of the culture only if it works. A's theory and assumptions about how things "should be" worked, since his com-pany grew and prospered. He personally re-ceived a great deal of reinforcement for his own assumptions, which undoubtedly gave him increased confidence that he had a cor-rect view of the world. Throughout his life-time he steadfastly adhered to the principles with which he started, and did everything in

his power to get others to accept them as well. At the same time, however, A had to share concepts and assumptions with a great many other people. So as his company grew and learned from its own experience, A's assumptions gradually had to be modified, or A had to withdraw from certain areas of running the business. For example, in their diversification efforts, the management bought several production units that would permit backward integration in a number of areas—but, because they recognized that they knew little about running factories, they brought in fairly strong, autonomous managers and left them alone.

A also had to learn that his assump-tions did not always lead to clear signals. He thought he was adequately rewarding his best young general managers, but could not see that for some of them the political cli-mate, the absence of stock options, and the arbitrary rewarding of family members made their own career progress too uncer-tain. Consequently, some of his best people left the company—a phenomenon that left A perplexed but unwilling to change his own assumptions in this area. As the com-pany matured, many of these conflicts re-mained and many subcultures formed around groups of younger managers who were functionally or geographically insu-lated from the founder.

Founder B built a chain of financial ser-vice organizations using sophisticated finan-cial analysis techniques in an urban area where insurance companies, mutual funds, and banks were only beginning to use these techniques. He was the conceptualizer and the salesman in putting together the ideas for these new organizations, but he put only a small percentage of the money up himself, working from a theory that if he could not convince investors that there was a market, then the idea was not sound. His initial as-sumption was that he did not know enough about the market to gamble with his own money—an assumption based on experience, according to a story he told about the one enterprise in which he had failed miserably. With this enterprise, he had trusted his own judgment on what customers would want, run his or her own company, subordinates will tolerate this kind of contradictory behavior and the organization's culture will develop complex assumptions about how one runs the organization "in spite of" or "around" the founder. If the founder's conflicts are severe to the point of interfering with the running of the organization, buffering layers of management may be built in or, in the extreme, the board of directors may have to find a way to move the founder out altogether.

The mechanisms listed in Figure 3 are not equally potent in practice, but they can reinforce each other to make the total message more potent than individual components. In my observations the most important or potent messages are role modeling by leaders (item 3), what leaders pay attention to (item 6), and leader reactions to critical events (item 7). Only if we observe these leader actions can we begin to decipher how members of the organization "learned" the right and proper things to do, and what model of reality they were to adopt.

To give a few examples, A demonstrated his need to be involved in everything at a detailed level by frequent visits to stores and detailed inspections of what was going on in them. When he went on vacation, he called the office every single day at a set time and wanted to know in great detail what was going on. This behavior persisted into his period of semi-retirement, when he would still call *daily* from his retirement home, where he spent three winter months.

While C's assumptions about how to make decisions led to a very group-oriented organization, his theory about how to manage led to a strong individuation process. C was convinced that the only way to manage was to give clear and simple individual responsibility and then to measure the person strictly on those responsibilities. Groups could help make decisions and obtain commitment, but they could not under any circumstances be responsible or accountable. So once a decision was made, it had to be carried out by individuals; if the decision was complex, involving a reorganization of functions, C always insisted that the new organization had to be clear and simple enough to permit the assignment of individual accountabilities.

C believed completely in a proactive model of man and in man's capacity to master nature; hence he expected of his subordinates that they would always be on top of their jobs. If a budget had been negotiated for a year, and if after three months the subordinate recognized that he would overrun the budget, C insisted that the subordinate make a clear decision either to find a way to stay within the budget or to renegotiate a larger budget. It was not acceptable to allow the overrun to occur without informing others and renegotiating, and it was not acceptable to be ignorant of the likelihood that there would be an overrun. The correct way to behave was always to know what was happening, always to be responsible for what was happening, and always to feel free to renegotiate previous agreements if they no longer made sense. C believed completely in open communications and the ability of people to reach reasonable decisions and compromises if they confronted their problems, figured out what they wanted to do, were willing to marshal arguments for their solution, and scrupulously honored any commitments they made.

On the interpersonal level, C assumed "constructive intent" on the part of all members of the organization, a kind of rational loyalty to organizational goals and to shared

Figure 3   How Is Culture Embedded and Transmitted?

Each of the mechanisms listed below is used by founders and key leaders to embed a value or assumption they hold, though the message may be very implicit in the sense that the leader is not aware of sending it. Leaders also may be conflicted, which leads to conflicting messages. A given mechanism may convey the message very explicitly, ambiguously, or totally implicitly. The mechanisms are listed below from more or less explicit or more or less implicit ones.

1. *Formal statements of organizational philosophy, charters, creeds, materials used for recruitment and selection, and socialization.*

2. *Design of physical spaces, facades, buildings.*

3. *Deliberate role modeling, teaching, and coaching by leaders.*

4. *Explicit reward and status system, promotion criteria.*

5. *Stories, legends, myths, and parables about key people and events.*

6. *What leaders pay attention to, measure, and control.*

7. *Leader reactions to critical incidents and organizational crises* (times when organizational survival is threatened, norms are unclear or are challenged, insubordination occurs, threatening or meaningless events occur, and so forth).

8. *How the organization is designed and structured.* (The design of work, who reports to whom, degree of decentralization, functional or other criteria for differentiation, and mechanisms used for integration carry implicit messages of what leaders assume and value.)

9. *Organizational systems and procedures.* (The types of information, control, and decision support systems in terms of categories of information, time cycles, who gets what information, and when and how performance appraisal and other review processes are conducted carry implicit messages of what leaders assume and value.)

10. *Criteria used for recruitment, selection, promotion, leveling off, retirement, and "excommunication" of people* (the implicit and possibly unconscious criteria that leaders use to determine who "fits" and who doesn't "fit" membership roles and key slots in the organization).

commitments. This did not prevent people from competitively trying to get ahead—but playing politics, hiding information, blaming others, or failing to cooperate on agreed-upon plans were defined as sins. However, C's assumptions about the nature of truth and the need for every individual to keep thinking out what he or she thought was the correct thing to do in any given situation led to frequent interpersonal tension.

In other words, the rule of honoring commitments and following through on consensually reached decisions was superseded by the rule of doing only what you believed sincerely to be the best thing to do in any given situation. Ideally, there would be time to challenge the original decision and renegotiate, but in practice time pressure was such that the subordinate, in doing what was believed to be best, often had to be insubordinate. Thus people in the organization frequently complained that decisions did not "stick," yet had to acknowledge that the reason they did not stick was that the assumption that one had to do the correct thing was even more important. Subordinates learned that insubordination was much less likely to be punished than doing something that the person knew to be wrong or stupid.

C clearly believed in the necessity of organization and hierarchy, but he did not trust the authority of position nearly so much as the authority of reason. Hence bosses were granted authority only to the extent that they could sell their decisions; as indicated above, insubordination was not only tolerated, but actively rewarded if it led to better outcomes. One could infer from watching this organization that it thrived on intelligent, assertive, individualistic people—and, indeed, the hiring policies reflected this bias.

So, over the years, the organization C headed had a tendency to hire and keep the people who fit into the kind of management system I am describing. And those people who fit the founder's assumptions found themselves feeling increasingly like family members in that strong bonds of mutual support grew up among them, with C functioning symbolically as a kind of benign but demanding father figure. These familial feelings were very important, though quite implicit, because they gave subordinates a feeling of security that was needed to challenge each other and C when a course of action did not make sense.

The architecture and office layout in C's company reflected his assumptions about problem solving and human relationships. He insisted on open office landscaping; minimum status differentiation in terms of office size, location, and furnishings (in fact, people were free to decorate their offices any way they liked); open cafeterias instead of executive dining rooms; informal dress codes; first-come, first-serve systems for getting parking spaces; many conference rooms with attached kitchens to facilitate meetings and to keep people interacting with each other instead of going off for meals; and so forth.

In summary, C represents a case of an entrepreneur with a clear set of assumptions about how things should be, both in terms of the formal business arrangements and in terms of internal relationships in the organization—and these assumptions still reflect themselves clearly in the organization some years later.

Let us turn next to the question of how a strong founder goes about embedding his assumptions in the organization.

HOW ARE CULTURAL ELEMENTS EMBEDDED?

The basic process of embedding a cultural element—a given belief or assumption—is a "teaching" process, but not necessarily an explicit one. The basic model of culture formation, it will be remembered, is that someone must propose a solution to a problem the group faces. Only if the group shares the perception that the solution is working will that element be adopted, and only if it continues to work will it come to be taken for granted and taught to newcomers. It goes without saying, therefore, that only elements that solve group problems will survive, but the previous issue of "embedding" is how a founder or leader gets the group to do things in a certain way in the first place, so that the question of whether it will work can be settled. In other words, embedding a cultural element in this context means only that the founder/leader has ways of getting the group to try out certain responses. There is no guarantee that those responses will, in fact, succeed in solving the group's ultimate problem. How do founder/leaders do this? I will describe a number of mechanisms ranging from very explicit teaching to very implicit messages of which even the founder may be unaware. These mechanisms are shown in Figure 3.

As the above case examples tried to show, the initial thrust of the messages sent is very much a function of the personality of the founder; some founders deliberately choose to build an organization that reflects their own personal biases while others create the basic organization but then turn it over to subordinates as soon as it has a life of its own. In both cases, the process of culture formation is complicated by the possibility that the founder is "conflicted," in the sense of having in his or her own personality several mutually contradictory assumptions.

The commonest case is probably that of the founder who states a philosophy of delegation but who retains tight control by feeling free to intervene, even in the smallest and most trivial decisions, as A did. Because the owner is granted the "right" to only to be proven totally wrong the hard way.

B did not want to invest himself heavily in his organizations, either financially or personally. Once he had put together a package, he tried to find people whom he trusted to administer it. These were usually people who, like himself, were fairly open in their approach to business and not too hung up on previous assumptions about how things should be done. One can infer that B's assumptions about concrete goals, the means to be used to achieve them, measurement criteria, and repair strategies were pragmatic: Have a clear concept of the mission, test it by selling it to investors, bring in good people who understand what the mission is, and then leave them alone to implement and run the organization, using only ultimate financial performances as a criterion.

B's assumptions about how to integrate a group were, in a sense, irrelevant since he did not inject himself very much into any of his enterprises. To determine the cultures of those enterprises, one had to study the managers put into key positions by B—matters that varied dramatically from one enterprise to the next. This short example illustrates that there is nothing automatic about an entrepreneur's process of inserting personal vision or style into his or her organization. The process depends very much on whether and how much that person wants to impose himself or herself.

Founder C, like A, was a much more dominant personality with a clear idea of how things should be. He and four others founded a manufacturing concern several years ago, one based on the founder's product idea along with a strong intuition that the market was ready for such a product. In this case, the founding group got together because they shared a concept of the core mission, but they found after a few years that the different members held very different assumptions about how to build an organization. These differences were sufficient to split the group apart and leave C in control of the young, rapidly growing company.

C held strong assumptions about the nature of the world—how one discovers truth and solves problems—and they were reflected in his management style. He believed that good ideas could come from any source; in particular, he believed that he himself was not wise enough to know what was true and right, but that if he heard an intelligent group of people debate an idea and examine it from all sides, he could judge accurately whether it was sound or not. He also knew that he could solve prob-

The Evolving Organization **357**

lems best in a group where many ideas were batted around and where there was a high level of mutual confrontation around those ideas. Ideas came from individuals, but the testing of ideas had to be done in a group.

C also believed very strongly that even if he knew what the correct course of action was, unless the parties whose support was critical to implementation were completely sold on the idea, they would either misunderstand or unwittingly sabotage the idea. Therefore, on any important decision, C insisted on a wide debate, many group meetings, and selling the idea down and laterally in the organization; only when it appeared that everyone understood and was committed would he agree to going ahead. C felt so strongly about this that he often held up important decisions even when he personally was already convinced of the course of action to take. He said that he did not want to be out there leading all by himself if he could not count on support from the troops; he cited past cases in which, thinking he had group support, he made a decision and, when it failed, found his key subordinates claiming that he had been alone in the decision. These experiences, he said, taught him to ensure commitment before going ahead on anything, even if doing so was time-consuming and frustrating.

A's loyalty to his family was quite evident: he ignored bad business results if a family member was responsible, yet punished a non-family member involved in such results. If the family member was seriously damaging the business, A put a competent manager in under him, but did not always give that manager credit for subsequent good results. If things continued to go badly, A would finally remove the family member, but always with elaborate rationalizations to protect the family image. If challenged on this kind of blind loyalty, A would assert that owners had certain rights that

could not be challenged. Insubordination from a family member was tolerated and excused, but the same kind of insubordination from a non-family member was severely punished.

In complete contrast, B tried to find competent general managers and turn a business over to them as quickly as he could. He involved himself only if he absolutely had to in order to save the business, and he pulled out of businesses as soon as they were stable and successful. B separated his family life completely from his business and had no assumptions about the rights of a family in a business. He wanted a good financial return so that he could make his family economically secure, but he seemed not to want his family involved in the businesses.

C, like B, was not interested in building the business on behalf of the family; his preoccupation with making sound decisions overrode all other concerns. Hence C set out to find the right kinds of managers and then "trained" them through the manner in which he reacted to situations. If managers displayed ignorance or lack of control of an area for which they were responsible, C would get publicly angry at them and accuse them of incompetence. If managers overran a budget or had too much inventory and did not inform C when this was first noticed, they would be publicly chided, whatever the reason was for the condition. If the manager tried to defend the situation by noting that it developed because of actions in another part of the same company, actions which C and others had agreed to, C would point out strongly that the manager should have brought that issue up much earlier and forced a rethinking or renegotiation right away. Thus C made it clear through his reactions that poor ultimate results could be excused, but not being on top of one's situation could never be excused.

C taught subordinates his theory about

building commitment to a decision by systematically refusing to go along with something until he felt the commitment was there, and by punishing managers who acted impulsively or prematurely in areas where the support of others was critical. He thus set up a very complex situation for his subordinates by demanding on the one hand a strong individualistic orientation (embodied in official company creeds and public relations literature) and, on the other, strong rules of consensus and mutual commitment (embodied in organizational stories, the organization's design, and many of its systems and procedures).

The above examples highlighted the differences among the three founders to show the biases and unique features of the culture in their respective companies, but there were some common elements as well that need to be mentioned. All three founders assumed that the success of their business(es) hinged on meeting customer needs; their most severe outbursts at subordinates occurred when they learned that a customer had not been well treated. All of the official messages highlighted customer concern, and the reward and control systems focused heavily on such concerns. In the case of A, customer needs were even put ahead of the needs of the family; one way a family member could really get into trouble was to mess up a customer relationship.

All three founders, obsessed with product quality, had a hard time seeing how some of their own managerial demands could undermine quality by forcing compromises. This point is important because in all the official messages, commitment to customers and product quality were uniformly emphasized—making one assume that this value was a clear priority. It was only when one looked at the inner workings of A's and C's organizations that one could see that other assumptions which they held created

internal conflicts that were difficult to overcome—conflicts that introduced new cultural themes into the organizations.

In C's organization, for example, there was simultaneously a concern for customers and an arrogance toward customers. Many of the engineers involved in the original product designs had been successful in estimating what customers would really want—a success leading to their assumption that they understood customers well enough to continue to make product designs without having to pay too much attention to what sales and marketing were trying to tell them. C officially supported marketing as a concept, but his underlying assumption was similar to that of his engineers, that he really understood what his customers wanted; this led to a systematic ignoring of some inputs from sales and marketing.

As the company's operating environment changed, old assumptions about the company's role in that environment were no longer working. But neither C nor many of his original group had a paradigm that was clearly workable in the new situation, so a period of painful conflict and new learning arose. More and more customers and marketing people began to complain, yet some parts of the organization literally could not hear or deal with these complaints because of their belief in the superiority of their products and their own previous assumptions that they knew what customers wanted.

In summary, the mechanisms shown in Figure 3 represent *all* of the possible ways in which founder messages get communicated and embedded, but they vary in potency. Indeed, they may often be found to conflict with each other—either because the founder is internally conflicted or because the environment is forcing changes in the original paradigm that lead different parts of the organization to have different assumptions about how to view things. Such conflicts often result because new, strong managers who are not part of the founding group begin to impose their own assump-

tions and theories. Let us look next at how these people may differ and the implications of such differences.

FOUNDER/OWNERS VERSUS "PROFESSIONAL MANAGERS"

Distinctive characteristics or "biases" introduced by the founder's assumptions are found in first-generation firms that are still heavily influenced by founders and in companies that continue to be run by family members. As noted above, such biases give the first-generation firm its distinctive character, and such biases are usually highly valued by first-generation employees because they are associated with the success of the enterprise. As the organization grows, as family members or non-family managers begin to introduce new assumptions, as environmental changes force new responses from the organization, the original assumptions begin to be strained. Employees begin to express concern that some of their "key" values will be lost or that the characteristics that made the company an exciting place to work are gradually disappearing.

Clear distinctions begin to be drawn between the founding family and the "professional" managers who begin to be brought into key positions. Such "professional" managers are usually identified as non-family and as non-owners and, therefore, as less "invested" in the company. Often they have been specifically educated to be managers rather than experts in whatever is the company's particular product or market. They are perceived, by virtue of these facts, as being less loyal to the original values and assumptions that guided the company, and as being more concerned with short-run financial performance. They are typically welcomed for bringing in much-needed organizational and functional skills, but they are often mistrusted because

they are not loyal to the founding assumptions.

Though these perceptions have strong stereotypic components, it's possible to see that much of the stereotype is firmly based in reality if one examines a number of first-generation and family-owned companies. Founders and owners do have distinctive characteristics that derive partly from their personalities and partly from their structural position as owners. It is important to understand these characteristics if one is to explain how strongly held many of the values and assumptions of first-generation or family-owned companies are. Figure 4 examines the "stereotype" by polarizing the founder/owner and "professional" manager along a number of motivational, analytical, interpersonal, and structural dimensions.

The main thrust of the differences noted is that the founder/owner is seen as being more self-oriented, more willing to take risks and pursue non-economic objectives and, by virtue of being the founder/owner, more *able* to take risks and to pursue such objectives. Founder/owners are more often intuitive and holistic in their thinking, and they are able to take a long-range point of view because they are building their own identities through their enterprises. They are often more particularistic in their orientation, a characteristic that results in the building of more of a community in the early organizational stages. That is, the initial founding group and the first generation of employees will know each other well and will operate more on personal acquaintance

Figure 4 How Do Founder/Owners Differ From "Professional Managers"?

Motivation and Emotional Orientation	
Entrepreneurs/founders/owners are . . .	*Professional managers are . . .*
Oriented toward creating, building.	Oriented toward consolidating, surviving, growing.
Achievement-oriented.	Power- and influence-oriented.
Self-oriented, worried about own image; need for "glory" high.	Organization-oriented, worried about company image.
Jealous of own prerogatives, need for autonomy high.	Interested in developing the organization and subordinates.
Loyal to own company, "local."	Loyal to profession of management, "cosmopolitan."
Willing and able to take moderate risks on own authority.	Able to take risks, but more cautious and in need of support.
Analytical Orientation	
Primarily intuitive, trusting of own intuitions.	Primarily analytical, more cautious about intuitions.
Long-range time horizon.	Short range time horizon.
Holistic; able to see total picture, patterns.	Specific; able to see details and their consequences.
Interpersonal Orientation	
"Particularistic," in the sense of seeing individuals as individuals.	"Universalistic," in the sense of seeing individuals as members of categories like employees, customers, suppliers, and so on.
Personal, political, involved.	Impersonal, rational, uninvolved.
Centralist, autocratic.	Participative, delegation-oriented.
Family ties count.	Family ties are irrelevant.
Emotional, impatient, easily bored.	Unemotional, patient, persistent.
Structural/Positional Differences	
Have the privileges and risks of ownership.	Have minimal ownership, hence fewer privileges and risks.
Have secure position by virtue of ownership.	Have less secure position, must constantly prove themselves.
Are generally highly visible and get close attention.	Are often invisible and do not get much attention.
Have the support of family members in the business.	Function alone or with the support of non-family members.
Have the obligation of dealing with family members and deciding on the priorities family issues should have relative to company issues.	Do not have to worry about family issues at all, which are by definition irrelevant.
Have weak bosses, Boards that are under their own control.	Have strong bosses, Boards that are not under their own control.

and trust than on formal principles, job descriptions, and rules.

The environment will often be more political than bureaucratic, and founder-value biases will be staunchly defended because they will form the basis for the group's initial identity. New members who don't fit this set of assumptions and values are likely to leave because they will be uncomfortable, or they will be ejected because their failure to confirm accepted patterns is seen as disruptive.

Founder/owners, by virtue of their position and personality, also tend to fulfill some *unique functions* in the early history of their organizations:

1. Containing and absorbing anxiety and risk.

Because they are positionally more secure and personally more confident, owners more than managers absorb and contain the anxieties and risks that are inherent in creating, developing, and enlarging an organization. Thus in times of stress, owners play a special role in reassuring the organization that it will survive. They are the stakeholders; hence they do have the ultimate risk.

2. Embedding non-economic assumptions and values.

Because of their willingness to absorb risk and their position as primary stakeholders, founders/owners are in a position to insist on doing things which may not be optimally efficient from a short-run point of view, but which reflect their own values and biases on how to build an effective organization and/or how to maximize the benefits to themselves and their families. Thus founder/owners often start with humanistic and social concerns that become reflected in organizational structure and process. Even when "participation," or "no layoffs," or other personnel practices such as putting marginally competent family members into key slots are "inef-

ficient," owners can insist that this is the only way to run the business and make that decision stick in ways that professional managers cannot.

3. Stimulating innovation.

Because of their personal orientation and their secure position, owners are uniquely willing and able to try new innovations that are risky, often with no more than an intuition that things will improve. Because managers must document, justify, and plan much more carefully, they have less freedom to innovate.

As the organization ages and the founder becomes less of a personal force, there is a trend away from this community feeling toward more of a rational, bureaucratic type of organization dominated by general managers who may care less about the original assumptions and values, and who are not in a position to fulfill the unique functions mentioned above. This trend is often feared and lamented by first- and second-generation employees. If the founder introduces his or her own family into the organization, and if the family assumptions and values perpetuate those of the founder, the original community feeling may be successfully perpetuated. The original culture may then survive. But at some point there will be a complete transition to general management, and at that point it is not clear whether the founding assumptions survive, are metamorphosed into a new hybrid, or are displaced entirely by other assumptions more congruent with what general managers as an occupational group bring with them.

4. Originating evolution through hybridization.

The founder is able to impose his or her assumptions on the first-generation employees, but these employees will, as they move up in the organization and become experienced managers, develop a range of new assumptions based on their own experience. These new assumptions will be congruent with some of the core assumptions of the original cultural paradigm, but will add new elements learned from experience. Some of these new elements or new assumptions will solve problems better than the original ones because external and internal problems will have changed as the organization matured and grew. The founder often recognizes that these new assumptions are better solutions, and will delegate increasing amounts of authority to those managers who are the best "hybrids": those who maintain key old assumptions yet add relevant new ones.

The best example of such hybrid evolution comes from a company that was founded by a very free-wheeling, intuitive, pragmatic entrepreneur: "D" who, like C in the example above, believed strongly in individual creativity, a high degree of decentralization, high autonomy for each organizational unit, high internal competition for resources, and self-control mechanisms rather than tight, centralized organizational controls. As this company grew and prospered, coordinating so many autonomous units became increasingly difficult, and the frustration that resulted from internal competition made it increasingly expensive to maintain this form of organization.

Some managers in this company, notably those coming out of manufacturing, had always operated in a more disciplined, centralized manner—without, however, disagreeing with core assumptions about the need to maximize individual autonomy. But they had learned that in order to do certain kinds of manufacturing tasks, one had to impose some discipline and tight controls. As the price of autonomy and decentralization increased, D began to look increasingly to these manufacturing managers as potential occupants of key general management positions. Whether he was conscious of it or not, what he needed was senior general managers who still believed in the old system but who had, in addition, a new set of assumptions about how to run things that were more in line with what the organization now needed. Some of the first-generation managers were quite nervous at seeing what they considered to be their "hardnosed" colleagues groomed as heirs apparent. Yet they were relieved that these potential successors were part of the original group rather than complete outsiders.

From a theoretical standpoint, evolution through hybrids is probably the only model of culture change that can work, because the original culture is based so heavily on community assumptions and values. Outsiders coming into such a community with new assumptions are likely to find the culture too strong to budge, so they either give up in frustration or find themselves ejected by the organization as being too foreign in orientation. What makes this scenario especially likely is the fact that the *distinctive* parts of the founding culture are often based on biases that are not economically justifiable in the short run.

As noted earlier, founders are especially likely to introduce humanistic, social service, and other non-economic assumptions into their paradigm of how an organization should look, and the general manager who is introduced from the outside often finds these assumptions to be the very thing that he or she wants to change in the attempt to "rationalize" the organization and make it more efficient. Indeed, that is often the reason the outsider is brought in. But if the current owners do not recognize the positive functions their culture plays, they run the risk of throwing out the baby with the bath water or, if the culture is strong, wasting their time because the outsider will not be able to change things anyway.

The ultimate dilemma for the first-generation organization with a strong founder-generated culture is how to make the transition to subsequent generations in such a manner that the organization remains adaptive to its changing external environment without destroying cultural elements that have given it its uniqueness, and that have made life fulfilling in the internal environment. Such a transition cannot be made effectively if the succession problem is seen only in power or political terms. The thrust of this analysis is that the *culture* must be analyzed and understood, and that the founder/owners must have sufficient insight into their own culture to make an intelligent transition process possible.

The Biotechnology Industry

Biotechnology was similar to the semiconductor industry in the 1950s or computers in the 1960s. Its impact on human lives would be very great but no one knew exactly when breakthroughs would occur or which companies would survive. Cetus, the first independent biotechnology research firm was established in 1971 shortly before the development of recombinant DNA techniques. Although there were about 200–300 small biotechnology firms in the United States in 1983 and a probable investment of at least $500 million in the years 1979–83, few genetically engineered products were out on the market. Proposed products included new drugs like antiviral interferons and biosynthetic human insulin, vaccines against hepatitis, low-calorie sugars, and self-fertilizing and superproductive crops. The industry's fruition seemed to lie in the late 1980s for pharmaceuticals and many health-care products and the 1990s and later for other chemical and agricultural wonders.

Despite its youth, the industry had seen both boom and bust: a frantic surge of investor interest around 1980, retrenchment when major commercial applications and quick profits failed to materialize, and then predictions of a shakeout in the field. The slow development process dismayed many business-oriented investors and managers who were used to the computer field's fast development and production.

WHAT IS GENETIC ENGINEERING?

Genetic engineering is the process of manipulating selected genes to produce entirely new microorganisms or desirable new traits in old organisms. The basic chemical constituent of genes is deoxyribonucleic acid (DNA), which serves as an instruction code directing a cell to produce specific proteins required for its biological processes. Recombinant DNA technology (often called gene-splicing or cloning) enables genetic engineers to isolate, analyze, and recombine genetic material and to design new genes not normally found in nature. Once identified, genes can be inserted into microorganisms such as bacteria and yeasts, and large quantities of the particular gene product can be generated at low cost. A second basic method, hybridoma technology, involves the fusion of two dissimilar cells to create a hybrid cell, for example, monoclonal antibodies, which the body can use to destroy invaders.

This note was prepared by Research Associate E. Mary Lou Balbaky, under the supervision of Associate Professor John Kao.

HISTORY

Most of the early work in the field was done in major universities such as Stanford, Berkeley, Harvard, and MIT; later work was done by independent companies.

After the technology for creating new microorganisms was developed, many scientists and laymen began to fear the creation of uncontrollable and destructive life forms. In 1975, 150 scientists from all over the world met to discuss ways to deal with the potential hazards of experimentation with DNA. Strong feelings among these scientists spread to public concern with DNA research. By the end of 1976, however, the "genetic monster" scare was dissipating and genetic engineers were working quite freely while adhering to certain self-imposed guidelines.

Although genetic engineering for commercial purposes was still considered something of a wild notion, venture capital funds and some eager investors were very active in setting up companies. In 1976 Herb Boyer, a major pioneer in gene splicing, and Robert Swanson, a young venture capitalist, set up Genentech to develop and produce interferons, human insulin, and human growth hormone. Biogen was formed in 1978 at first as a broker for university-based research; Molecular Genetics was formed in 1979, Genetics Institute in 1980, and many more in 1981. (*Exhibit 1* has information on some of the well-known companies in the field.)

Many large firms in the pharmaceutical, health care, chemical, and energy industries realized that genetic engineering would have a major impact on their industries. Some set up their own in-house genetic engineering facilities; others established research contracts or joint ventures with research companies. Pharmaceutical contractors included Eli Lilly, G. Searle,

Merck, Pfizer, Abbott Labs, and Schering-Plough. Chemical-company investors included Monsanto, Dow, Du Pont, and Rohm. Also energy companies such as Standard Oil of Indiana, Shell Oil, and Lubrizol invested in small firms.

In June 1980 the Supreme Court ruled that new life forms created in the laboratory could be patented. This decision helped bring biotechnology to the attention of the general investing public four months later when Genentech went public. The firm's initial offering was of a million shares at $35 a share. The price rose to $89 a share within 20 minutes and closed the day at $71. A rash of public offerings followed. Cetus went public in March 1981 and raised $119 million with no marketable products yet developed.

By 1982 disillusionment had set in; investors were beginning to demand products rather than promises. No one doubted the eventual usefulness of biotechnology, but companies and investors were finding that commercial developments were very hard to achieve. By mid-1982 no major genetically engineered products were commercially viable and only a few had been introduced. Many scientist/founders and venture capitalists underestimated the effort and specialized skills required to make a technical breakthrough, produce a product in quantity, package it, and put it on the market. Companies that had entered the field quickly with just a few million dollars and a handful of researchers were running out of money.

Commercial success required good business sense, high-quality science, selecting the right markets, and creative financing. Limited partnerships and joint ventures were considered innovative ways to stay viable over the long haul.

1983

In 1983 investors were much less receptive to new companies. As of August 1983, only a few companies had federal approval to market anything. Genentech (Eli Lilly), launched human insulin and was test-marketing a human growth hormone. Cetus and Molecular Genetics introduced products to prevent diseases in newborn pigs and calves, and there were diagnostic kits for pregnancy, venereal disease, and certain types of cancer. Time frames for the introduction of other products ranged from several years to several decades. Interferons, the much anticipated antiviral agents, would not be available in commercial quantities until 1990. The best prospects for the near term were products not requiring ingestion or injection into human patients; these products included diagnostics, animal vaccines, and monoclonal antibodies.

Industry competition was intense mainly in R&D, licensing, and the recruiting and retaining of qualified, talented personnel. The timing of the entry of a new product—especially a pharmaceutical one—into the market was important in determining success and profitability. Accordingly, the speed with which a company developed products and completed clinical testing and approval had an important effect on the company's competitive position.

Patents

Companies and universities wanted to protect their proprietary rights to processes and new microorganisms. The most common impulse was to get as many patents as possible. Hundreds of biotech patent applications were filed. Several prominent patent battles were in progress in 1983.

Outlook

The short-term outlook for the industry was not very positive, but the long-term potential looked exceptional. The Reagan administration's cutbacks in funding for education and basic science suggested that companies themselves had to take responsibility for research and training.

Exhibit 1 Well-Known Genetic Engineering Firms

Company	Start-up Date	Market Value (*Forbes*) (August 1983)	Public Stock Offering Date	Full-time Employees and PhDs/MDs	Principal Investors	Special Products (some)
Cetus	1971	$380 million	March 1981	292 Employees 46 PhD/MDs (5 Nobel Laureates)	Standard Oil of California (25%) Standard Indiana (28%) National Distillers (16%)	Blood tests for infectious diseases, etc.
Genentech	1976	$655 million	October 1980	112 Employees 40 PhDs (to double)	Lubrizol (20%) Monsanto (2%)	Interferon, human insulin, human growth hormone
Biogen	May 1978	$292 million (Cambridge) $425 million (all locations)	March 1983	(all locations) 250 Employees 79 PhDs (Nobel Prize winners)	Monsanto Schering Plough Inc. Ltd.	Factor VIII, hepatitis, vaccine, diagnostics for hepatitis
Molecular Genetics	November 1979	$175 million	March 1983	67 Employees 26 PhDs		Herpes vaccine; annual health products
Genetic Systems	November 1980	$224 million	June 1981			Monoclonal antibodies for venereal diagnostics
Integrated Genetics	February 1981	(book value) $5.6 million	July 1983	69 Employees 17 PhDs		Diagnostics for salmonella, hepatitis; diagnostics, Factor VIII, etc.
Cambridge Bioscience	March 1981		March 1983	4 Employees 6 Consultants		Chemical and food diagnostics; bacteria diagnostics

Evolution and Revolution as Organizations Grow

LARRY E. GREINER

A COMPANY'S PAST HAS CLUES FOR MANAGEMENT THAT ARE CRITICAL TO FUTURE SUCCESS

A small research company chooses too complicated and formalized an organization structure for its young age and limited size. It flounders in rigidity and bureaucracy for several years and is finally acquired by a larger company.

Key executives of a retail store chain hold on to an organization structure long after it has served its purpose, because their power is derived from this structure. The company eventually goes into bankruptcy.

A large bank disciplines a "rebellious" manager who is blamed for current control problems, when the underlying cause is centralized procedures that are holding back expansion into new markets. Many younger managers subsequently leave the bank, competition moves in, and profits are still declining.

The problems of these companies, like those of many others, are rooted more in past decisions than in present events or outside market dynamics. Historical forces do indeed shape the future growth of organizations. Yet management, in its haste to grow, often overlooks such critical developmental questions as: Where has our organization been? Where is it now? And what do the answers to these questions mean for where we are going? Instead, its gaze is fixed outward toward the environment and the future—as if more precise market projections will provide a new organizational identity.

Companies fail to see that many clues to their future success lie within their own organizations and their evolving states of development. Moreover, the inability of management to understand its organization development problems can result in a company becoming "frozen" in its present stage of evolution or, ultimately, in failure, regardless of market opportunities.

My position in this article is that the future of an organization may be less determined by outside forces than it is by the organization's history. In stressing the force of history on an organization, I have drawn from the legacies of European psychologists (their thesis being that individual behavior is determined primarily by previous events and experiences, not by what lies ahead). Extending the analogy of individual development to the problems of organization development, I shall discuss a series of developmental phases through which growing companies tend to pass. But, first, let me provide two definitions:

1. The term *evolution* is used to describe prolonged periods of growth where no major upheaval occurs in organization practices.
2. The term *revolution* is used to describe those periods of substantial turmoil in organization life.

As a company progresses through developmental phases, each evolutionary period creates its own revolution. For instance, centralized practices eventually lead to demands for decentralization. Moreover, the nature of management's solution to each revolutionary period determines whether a company will move forward into its next stage of evolutionary growth. As I shall show later, there are at least five phases of organization development, each characterized by both an evolution and a revolution.

KEY FORCES IN DEVELOPMENT

During the past few years a small amount of research knowledge about the phases of organization development has been building. Some of this research is very quantitative, such as time-series analyses that reveal patterns of economic performance over time.[1] The majority of studies, however, are cast-oriented and use company records and interviews to reconstruct a rich picture of corporate development.[2] Yet both types of research tend to be heavily empirical without attempting more generalized statements about the overall process of development.

A notable exception is the historical work of Alfred D. Chandler, Jr., in his book *Strategy and Structure*.[3] This study depicts four very broad and general phases in the lives of four large U.S. companies. It proposes that outside market opportunities determine a company's strategy, which in turn determines the company's organization structure. This thesis has a valid ring for the four companies examined by Chandler, largely because they developed in a time of explosive markets and technological advances. But more recent evidence suggests that organization structure may be less malleable than Chandler assumed; in fact, structure can play a critical role in influencing corporate strategy. It is this reverse emphasis on how organization structure affects future growth which is highlighted in the model presented in this article.

From an analysis of recent studies,[4] five key dimensions emerge as essential for building a model of organization development:

1. Age of the organization.
2. Size of the organization.
3. Stages of evolution.
4. Stages of revolution.
5. Growth rate of the industry.

1. See, for example, William H. Starbuck, "Organizational Metamorphosis," in *Promising Research Directions*, edited by R. W. Millman and M. P. Hottenstein (Tempe, Arizona, Academy of Management, 1968), p. 113.

2. See, for example, the *Grangesberg* case series, prepared by C. Roland Christensen and Bruce R. Scott, Case Clearing House, Harvard Business School.

3. *Strategy and Structure: Chapters in the History of the American Industrial Enterprise* (Cambridge, Massachusetts, The M.I.T. press, 1962).

4. I have drawn on many sources for evidence: (a) numerous cases collected at the Harvard Business School; (b) *Organization Growth and Development,* edited by William H. Starbuck (Middlesex, England, Penguin Books, Ltd., 1971), where several studies are cited; and (c) articles published in journals, such as Lawrence E. Fouraker and John M. Stopford, "Organization Structure and the Multinational Strategy," *Administrative Science Quarterly*, Vol. 13, No. 1, 1968, p. 47; and Malcolm S. Salter, "Management Appraisal and Reward Systems," *Journal of Business Policy*, Vol. 1, No. 4, 1971.

I shall describe each of these elements separately, but first note their combined effect as illustrated in Exhibit 1. Note especially how each dimension influences the other over time; when all five elements begin to interact, a more complete and dynamic picture of organizational growth emerges.

After describing these dimensions and their interconnections, I shall discuss each evolutionary/revolutionary phase of development and show (a) how each stage of evolution breeds its own revolution, and (b) how management solutions to each revolution determine the next stage of evolution.

Age of the Organization

The most obvious and essential dimension for any model of development is the life span of an organization (represented as the horizontal axis in Exhibit 1). All historical studies gather data from various points in time and then make comparisons. From these observations, it is evident that the same organization practices are not maintained throughout a long time span. This makes a most basic point: management problems and principles are rooted in time. The concept of decentralization, for example, can have meaning for describing corporate practices at one time period but loses its descriptive power at another.

The passage of time also contributes to the institutionalization of managerial attitudes. As a result, employee behavior becomes not only more predictable but also more difficult to change when attitudes are outdated.

Size of the Organization

This dimension is depicted as the vertical axis in Exhibit 1. A company's problems and solutions tend to change markedly as the number of employees and sales volume increase. Thus, time is not the only determinant of structure; in fact, organizations that do not grow in size can retain many of the same management issues and practices over lengthy periods. In addition to increased size, however, problems of coordination and communication magnify, new functions emerge, levels in the management hierarchy multiply, and jobs become more interrelated.

Stages of Evolution

As both age and size increase, another phenomenon becomes evident: the prolonged growth that I have termed the evolutionary period. Most growing organizations do not expand for two years and then retreat for one year; rather, those that survive a crisis usually enjoy four to eight years of continuous growth without a major economic setback or severe internal disruption. The term evolution seems appropriate for describing these quieter periods because only modest adjustments appear necessary for maintaining growth under the same overall pattern of management.

Stages of Revolution

Smooth evolution is not inevitable; it cannot be assumed that organization growth is linear. *Fortune*'s "500" list, for example, has had significant turnover during the last 50 years. Thus we find evidence from numerous case histories which reveals periods of substantial turbulence spaced between smoother periods of evolution.

I have termed these turbulent times the periods of revolution because they typically exhibit a serious upheaval of management practices. Traditional management practices, which were appropriate for a smaller size and earlier time, are brought under scrutiny by frustrated top managers and disillusioned lower-level managers. During such periods of crisis, a number of companies fail—those unable to abandon past practices and effect major organization changes are likely either to fold or to level off in their growth rates.

The critical task for management in each revolutionary period is to find a new set of organization practices that will become the basis for managing the next period of evolutionary growth. Interestingly enough, these new practices eventually sow their own seeds of decay and lead to another period of revolution. Companies therefore experience the irony of seeing a major solution in one time period become a major problem at a latter date.

Growth Rate of the Industry

The speed at which an organization experiences phases of evolution and revolution is closely related to the market environment of its industry. For example, a company in a rapidly expanding market will have to add employees rapidly; hence, the need for new organization structures to accommodate large staff increases is accelerated. While evolutionary periods tend to be relatively short in fast-growing industries, much longer evolutionary periods occur in mature or slowly growing industries.

Evolution can also be prolonged, and revolutions delayed, when profits come easily. For instance, companies that make grievous errors in a rewarding industry can still look good on their profit and loss statements; thus they can avoid a change in management practices for a longer period. The aerospace industry in its infancy is an example. Yet revolutionary periods still occur, as one did in aerospace when profit opportunities began to dry up. Revolutions seem to be much more severe and difficult to resolve when the market environment is poor.

PHASES OF GROWTH

With the foregoing framework in mind, let us now examine in depth the five specific phases of evolution and revolution. As shown in Exhibit 2, each evolutionary period is characterized by the dominant *management style* used to achieve growth, while each revolutionary period is characterized by the dominant *management problem* that must be solved before growth can continue. The patterns presented in Exhibit 2 seem to be typical for companies in industries with moderate growth over a long time period; companies in faster growing industries tend to experience all five phases more rapidly, while those in slower growing industries encounter only two or three phases over many years.

It is important to note that *each phase is both an effect of the previous phase and a cause for the next phase.* For example, the evolutionary management style in Phase 3 of the exhibit is "delegation," which grows out of, and becomes the solution to, demands for greater "autonomy" in the preceding Phase 2 revolution. The style of delegation used in Phase 3, however, eventually provokes a major revolutionary crisis that is characterized by attempts to regain control over the diversity created through increased delegation.

The principal implication of each phase is that management actions are narrowly prescribed if growth is to occur. For example, a company experiencing an autonomy crisis in Phase 2 cannot return to directive management for a solution—it must adopt a new style of delegation in order to move ahead.

Phase 1: Creativity . . .

In the birth stage of an organization, the emphasis is on creating both a product and a market. Here are the characteristics of the period of creative evolution:

- The company's founders are usually technically or entrepreneurially oriented, and they disdain management activities; their physical and mental energies are absorbed entirely in making and selling a new product.
- Communication among employees is frequent and informal.
- Long hours of work are rewarded by modest salaries and the promise of ownership benefits.
- Control of activities comes from immediate marketplace feedback; the management acts as the customers react.

. . . & the leadership crisis. All of the foregoing individualistic and creative activities are essential for the company to get off the ground. But therein lies the problem. As the company grows, larger production runs require knowledge about the efficiencies of manufacturing. Increased numbers of employees cannot be managed exclusively through informal communication; new employees are not motivated by an intense dedication to the product or organization. Additional capital must be secured, and new accounting procedures are needed for financial control.

Thus the founders find themselves burdened with unwanted management responsibilities. So they long for the "good old days," still trying to act as they did in the past. And conflicts between the harried leaders grow more intense.

At this point a crisis of leadership occurs, which is the onset of the first revolution. Who is to lead the company out of confusion and solve the managerial problems confronting it? Quite obviously, a strong manager is needed who has the necessary knowledge and skill to introduce new business techniques. But this is easier said than done. The founders often hate to step aside even though they are probably temperamentally unsuited to be managers. So here is the first critical development choice—to locate and install a strong business manager who is acceptable to the founders and who can pull the organization together.

Phase 2: Direction . . .

Those companies that survive the first phase by installing a capable business manager usually embark on a period of sustained growth under able and directive leadership. Here are the characteristics of this evolutionary period:

- A functional organization structure is introduced to separate manufacturing from marketing activities, and job assignments become more specialized.
- Accounting systems for inventory and purchasing are introduced.
- Incentives, budgets, and work standards are adopted.
- Communication becomes more formal and impersonal as a hierarchy of titles and positions builds.
- The new manager and his key supervisors take most of the responsibility for instituting direction, while lower-level supervisors are treated more as functional specialists than as autonomous decision-making managers.

. . . & the autonomy crisis. Although the new directive techniques channel employee energy more efficiently into growth, they eventually become inappropriate for controlling a larger, more diverse and complex organization. Lower-level employees find themselves restricted by a cumbersome and centralized hierarchy. They have come to possess more direct knowledge about markets and machinery than do the leaders at the top; consequently, they feel torn between following procedures and taking initiative on their own.

Thus the second revolution is imminent as a crisis develops from demands for greater autonomy on the part of lower-level managers. The solution adopted by most companies is to move toward greater delegation. Yet it is difficult for top managers who were previously successful at being directive to give up responsibility. Moreover, lower-level managers are not accustomed to making decisions for themselves. As a result, numerous companies flounder during this revolutionary period, adhering to centralized methods while lower-level employees grow more disenchanted and leave the organization.

Phase 3: Delegation . . .

The next era of growth evolves from the successful application of a decentralized organization structure. It exhibits these characteristics:

- Much greater responsibility is given to the managers of plants and market territories.
- Profit centers and bonuses are used to stimulate motivation.
- The top executives at headquarters restrain themselves to managing by exception, based on periodic reports from the field.
- Management often concentrates on making new acquisitions which can be lined up beside other decentralized units.
- Communication from the top is infrequent, usually by correspondence, telephone, or brief visits to field locations.

The delegation stage proves useful for gaining expansion through heightened motivation at lower levels. Decentralized managers with greater authority and incentive are able to penetrate larger markets, respond faster to customers, and develop new products.

. . . & the control crisis. A serious problem eventually evolves, however, as top executives sense that they are losing control over a highly diversified field operation. Autonomous field managers prefer to run their own shows without coordinating plans, money, technology, and manpower with the rest of the organization. Freedom breeds a parochial attitude.

Hence, the Phase 3 revolution is under way when top management seeks to regain control over the total company. Some top managements attempt a return to centralized management, which usually fails because of the vast scope of operations. Those companies that move ahead find a new solution in the use of special coordination techniques.

Phase 4: Coordination . . .

During this phase, the evolutionary period is characterized by the use of formal systems for achieving greater coordination and by top executives taking responsibility for the initiation and administration of these new systems. For example:

- Decentralized units are merged into product groups.
- Formal planning procedures are established and intensively reviewed.
- Numerous staff personnel are hired and located at headquarters to initiate companywide programs of control and review for line managers.
- Capital expenditures are carefully weighed and parceled out across the organization.
- Each product group is treated as an investment center where return on invested capi-

tal is an important criterion used in allocating funds.

- Certain technical functions, such as data processing, are centralized at headquarters, while daily operating decisions remain decentralized.
- Stock options and companywide profit sharing are used to encourage identity with the firm as a whole.

All of these new coordination systems prove useful for achieving growth through more efficient allocation of a company's limited resources. They prompt field managers to look beyond the needs of their local units. While these managers still have much decision-making responsibility, they learn to justify their actions more carefully to a "watchdog" audience at headquarters.

. . . & the red-tape crisis. But a lack of confidence gradually builds between line and staff, and between headquarters and the field. The proliferation of systems and programs begins to exceed its utility; a red-tape crisis is created. Line managers, for example, increasingly resent heavy staff direction from those who are not familiar with local conditions. Staff people, on the other hand, complain about uncooperative and uninformed line managers. Together both groups criticize the bureaucratic paper system that has evolved. Procedures take precedence over problem solving, and innovation is dampened. In short, the organization has become too large and complex to be managed through formal programs and rigid systems. The Phase 4 revolution is under way.

Phase 5: Collaboration . . .

The last observable phase in previous studies emphasizes strong interpersonal collaboration in an attempt to overcome the red-tape crisis. Where Phase 4 was managed more through formal systems and procedures, Phase 5 emphasizes greater spontaneity in management action through teams and the skillful confrontation of interpersonal differences. Social control and self-discipline take over from formal control. This transition is especially difficult for those experts who created the old systems as well as for those line managers who relied on formal methods for answers.

The Phase 5 evolution, then, builds around a more flexible and behavioral approach to management. Here are its characteristics:

- The focus is on solving problems quickly through team action.
- Teams are combined across functions for task-group activity.
- Headquarters staff experts are reduced in number, reassigned, and combined in interdisciplinary teams to consult with, not to direct, field units.
- A matrix-type structure is frequently used to assemble the right teams for the appropriate problems.
- Previous formal systems are simplified and combined into single multipurpose systems.
- Conferences of key managers are held frequently to focus on major problem issues.
- Educational programs are utilized to train managers in behavioral skills for achieving better teamwork and conflict resolution.
- Real-time information systems are integrated into daily decision making.
- Economic rewards are geared more to team performance than to individual achievement.
- Experiments in new practices are encouraged throughout the organization.

. . . & the ? crisis. What will be the revolution in response to this stage of evolution? Many large U.S. companies are now in the Phase 5 evolutionary stage, so the answers are critical. While there is little clear evidence, I imagine the revolution will center around the "psychological saturation" of employees who grow emotionally and physically exhausted by the intensity of teamwork and the heavy pressure for innovative solutions.

My hunch is that the Phase 5 revolution will be solved through new structures and programs that allow employees to periodically rest, reflect, and revitalize themselves. We may even see companies with dual organization structures: a "habit" structure for getting the daily work done, and a "reflective" structure for stimulating perspective and personal enrichment. Employees could then move back and forth between the two structures as their energies are dissipated and refueled.

One European organization has implemented just such a structure. Five reflective groups have been established outside the regular structure for the purpose of continuously evaluating five task activities basic to the organization. They report directly to the managing director although their reports are made public throughout the organization. Membership in each group includes all levels and functions, and employees are rotated through these groups on a six-month basis.

Other concrete examples now in practice include providing sabbaticals for employees, moving managers in and out of "hot spot" jobs, establishing a four-day workweek, assuring job security, building physical facilities for relaxation *during* the working day, making jobs more interchangeable, creating an extra team on the assembly line so that one team is always off for reeducation, and switching to longer vacations and more flexible working hours.

The Chinese practice of requiring executives to spend time periodically on lower-level jobs may also be worth a nonideological evaluation. For too long U.S. management has assumed that career progress should be equated with an upward path toward title, salary, and power. Could it be that some vice presidents of marketing might just long for, and even benefit from, temporary duty in the field sales organization?

IMPLICATIONS OF HISTORY

Let me now summarize some important implications for practicing managers. First, the main features of this discussion are depicted in *Exhibit 3,* which shows the specific management actions that characterize each growth phase. These actions are also the solutions which ended each preceding revolutionary period.

In one sense, I hope that many readers will react to my model by calling it obvious and natural for depicting the growth of an organization. To me this type of reaction is a useful test of the model's validity.

But at a more reflective level I imagine some of these reactions are more hindsight than foresight. Those experienced managers who have been through a developmental sequence can empathize with it now, but how did they react when in the middle of a stage of evolution or revolution? They can probably recall the limits of their own developmental understanding at that time. Perhaps they resisted desirable changes or were even swept emotionally into a revolution without being able to propose constructive solutions. So let me offer some explicit guidelines for managers of growing organizations to keep in mind.

Know where you are in the developmental sequence. Every organization and its component parts are at different stages of development. The task of top management is to be aware of these stages; otherwise, it may not recognize when the time for change has come, or it may act to impose the wrong solution.

Top leaders should be ready to work with the flow of the tide rather than against it; yet they should be cautious, since it is tempting to skip phases out of impatience. Each phase results in certain strengths and learning experiences in the organization that will be essential for success in subsequent phases. A child prodigy, for example, may be able to read like a teenager, but he cannot behave like one until he ages through a sequence of experiences.

I also doubt that managers can or should act to avoid revolutions. Rather, these periods of tension provide the pressure, ideas, and awareness that afford a platform for change and the introduction of new practices.

Recognize the limited range of solutions. In each revolutionary stage it becomes evident that this stage can be ended only by certain specific solutions; moreover, these solutions are different from those which were applied to the problems of the preceding revolution. Too often it is tempting to choose solutions that were tried before, which makes it impossible for a new phase of growth to evolve.

Management must be prepared to dismantle current structures before the revolutionary stage becomes too turbulent. Top managers, realizing that their own managerial styles are no longer appropriate, may even have to take themselves out of leadership positions. A good Phase 2 manager facing Phase 3 might be wise to find another Phase 2 organization that better fits his talents, either outside the company or with one of its newer subsidiaries.

Finally, evolution is not an automatic affair; it is a contest for survival. To move ahead, companies must consciously introduce planned structures that not only are solutions to a current crisis but also are fitted to the *next* phase of growth. This requires considerable self-awareness on the part of top management, as well as great interpersonal skill in persuading other managers that change is needed.

Realize that solutions breed new problems. Managers often fail to realize that organizational solutions create problems for the future (i.e., a decision to delegate eventually causes a problem of control). Historical actions are very much determinants of what happens to the company at a much later date.

An awareness of this effect should help managers to evaluate company problems with greater historical understanding instead of "pinning the blame" on a current development. Better yet, managers should be in a position to *predict* future problems, and thereby to prepare solutions and coping strategies before a revolution gets out of hand.

A management that is aware of the problems ahead could well decide *not* to grow. Top managers may, for instance, prefer to retain the informal practices of a small company, knowing that this way of life is inherent in the organization's limited size, not in their congenial personalities. If they choose to grow, they may do themselves out of a job and a way of life they enjoy.

And what about the managements of very large organizations? Can they find new solutions for continued phases of evolution? Or are they reaching a stage where the government will act to break them up because they are too large.

CONCLUDING NOTE

Clearly, there is still much to learn about processes of development in organizations. The phases outlined here are only five in number and are still only approximations. Researchers are just beginning to study the specific developmental problems of structure, control, rewards, and management style in different industries and in a variety of cultures.

One should not, however, wait for conclusive evidence before educating managers to think and act from a developmental perspective. The critical dimension of time has been missing for too long from our management theories and practices. The intriguing paradox is that by learning more about history we may do a better job in the future.

Exhibit 1   Model of Organization Development

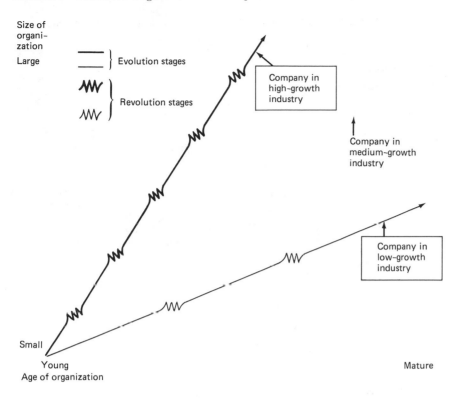

Exhibit 2   The Five Phases of Growth

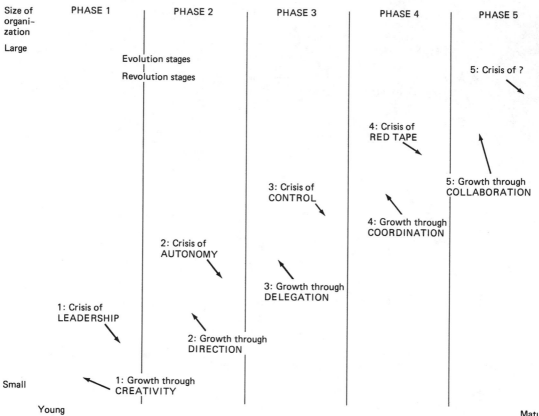

Exhibit 3   Organization Practices During Evolution in the Five Phases of Growth

Category	PHASE 1	PHASE 2	PHASE 3	PHASE 4	PHASE 5
MANAGE-MENT FOCUS	Make & sell	Efficiency of operations	Expansion of market	Consolidation of organization	Problem solving & innovation
ORGANIZATION STRUCTURE	Informal	Centralized & functional	Decentralized & geographical	Line-staff & product groups	Matrix of teams
TOP MANAGEMENT STYLE	Individualistic & entrepreneurial	Directive	Delegative	Watchdog	Participative
CONTROL SYSTEM	Market results	Standards & cost centers	Reports & profit centers	Plans & investment centers	Mutual goal setting
MANAGE-MENT REWARD EMPHASIS	Ownership	Salary & merit increases	Individual bonus	Profit sharing & stock options	Team bonus

Three Myths

MIDAS

Bacchus, on a certain occasion, found his old schoolmaster and foster father, Silenus, missing. The old man had been drinking, and in that state wandered away, and was found by some peasants, who carried him to their king, Midas. Midas recognized him, and treated him hospitably, entertaining him for ten days and nights with an unceasing round of jollity. On the eleventh day he brought Silenus back, and restored him in safety to his pupil. Whereupon Bacchus offered Midas his choice of a reward, whatever he might wish. He asked that whatever he might touch should be changed into *gold*. Bacchus consented, though sorry that he had not made a better choice. Midas went his way, rejoicing in his new-acquired power, which he hastened to put to the test. He could scarce believe his eyes when he found a twig of an oak, which he plucked from the branch, become gold in his hand. He took up a stone; it changed to gold. He touched a sod; it did the same. He took an apple from the tree; you would have thought he had robbed the garden of the Hesperides. His joy knew no bounds, and as soon as he got home, he ordered the servants to set a splendid repast on the table. Then he found to his dismay that whether he touched bread, it hardened in his hand; or put a morsel to his lips, it defied his teeth. He took a glass of wine, but it flowed down his throat like melted gold.

In consternation at the unprecedented affliction, he strove to divest himself of his power; he hated the gift he had lately coveted. But all in vain; starvation seemed to await him. He raised his arms, all shining with gold, in prayer to Bacchus, begging to be delivered from his glittering destruction. Bacchus, merciful deity, heard and consented. "Go," said he, "to the River Pactolus, trace the stream to its fountain-head, there plunge your head and body in, and wash away your fault and its punishment." He did so, and scarce had he touched the waters before the gold-creating power passed into them, and the river-sands became changed into *gold,* as they remain to this day.

Thenceforth Midas, hating wealth and splendor, dwelt in the country, and became a worshipper of Pan, the god of the fields.

DAEDALUS

The labyrinth from which Theseus escaped by means of the clew of Ariadne was built by Daedalus, a most skillful artificer. It was an edifice with numberless winding passages and turnings opening into one another, and seeming to have neither beginning nor end, like the river Maeander, which returns itself, and flows now onward, now backward, in its course to the sea. Daedalus built the labyrinth for King Minos, but afterwards lost the favor of the king, and was shut up in a tower. He contrived to make his escape from his prison, but could not leave the island by sea, as the king kept strict watch on all the vessels, and permitted none to sail without being carefully searched. "Minos may control the land and sea," said Daedalus, "but not the regions of the air. I will try that way." So he set to work to fabricate wings for himself and his young son Icarus. He wrought feathers together, beginning with the smallest and adding larger, so as to form an increasing surface. The larger ones he secured with thread and the smaller with wax, and gave the whole a gentle curvature like the wings of a bird. Icarus, the boy, stood and looked on, sometimes running to gather up the feathers which the wind had blown away, and then handling the wax and working it over with his fingers, by his play impeding his father in his labors. When at last the work was done, the artist, waving his wings, found himself buoyed upward, and hung suspended, poising himself on the beaten air. He next equipped his son in the same manner, and taught him how to fly, as a bird tempts her young ones from the lofty nest into the air. When all was prepared for flight he said, "Icarus, my son, I charge you to keep at a moderate height, for if you fly too low the damp will clog your wings, and if too high the heat will melt them. Keep near me and you will be safe." While he gave him these instructions and fitted the wings to his shoulders, the face of the father was wet with tears, and his hands trembled. He kissed the boy, not knowing that it was for the last time. Then rising on his wings, he flew off, encouraging him to follow, and looked back from his own flight to see how his son managed his wings. As they flew the ploughman stopped his work to gaze, and the shepherd leaned on his staff and watched them, astonished at the sight, and thinking they were gods who could thus cleave the air.

They passed Samos and Delos on the left and Lebynthos on the right, when the boy, exulting in his career, began to leave the guidance of his companion and soar upward as if to reach heaven. The nearness of the blazing sun softened the wax which held the feathers together, and they came off. He fluttered with his arms, but no feathers remained to hold the air. While his mouth uttered cries to his father it was submerged in the blue waters of the sea, which thenceforth was called by his name. His father cried, "Icarus, Icarus, where are you?" At last he saw the feathers floating on the water, and bitterly lamenting his own arts, he buried the body and called the land Icaria in memory of his child. Daedalus arrived safe in Sicily, where he built a temple to Apollo, and hung up his wings, an offering to the god.

Daedalus was so proud of his achievements that he could not bear the idea of a rival. His sister had placed her son Perdix under his charge to be taught the mechanical arts. He was an apt scholar and give striking evidences to ingenuity. Walking on the seashore he picked up the spine of a fish. Imitating it, he took a piece of iron and notched it on the edge, and thus invented the *saw*. He put two pieces of iron together, connecting them at one end with a rivet, and sharpening the other ends, and made a *pair of compasses.* Daedalus was so envious of his nephew's performances that he took an opportunity, when they were together one day on the top of a high tower, to push him off. But Minerva, who favors ingenuity, saw him falling, and arrested his fate by changing him into a bird called after his name, the Partridge. This bird does not build his nest in the trees, nor take lofty flights, but nestles in the hedges, and mindful of his fall, avoids high places.

ECHO AND NARCISSUS

Echo was a beautiful nymph, fond of the woods and hills, where she devoted herself to woodland sports. She was a favorite of Diana, and attended her in the chase. But Echo had one failing; she was fond of talking, and whether in chat or argument, would have the last word. One day Juno was seeking her husband, who, she had reason to fear, was amusing himself among the nymphs. Echo by her talk contrived to detain the goddess till the nymphs made their escape. When Juno discovered it, she passed sentence upon Echo in these words: "You shall forfeit the use of that tongue with which you have cheated me, except for that one purpose you are so fond of—*reply.* You shall still have the last word, but no power to speak first."

This nymph saw Narcissus, a beautiful youth, as he pursued the chase upon the mountains. She loved him and followed his footsteps. O how she longed to address him in the softest accents, and win him to converse! But it was not in her power. She waited with impatience for him to speak first, and had her answer ready. One day the youth, being separated from his companions, shouted aloud, "Who's here?" Echo replied, "Here." Narcissus looked around, but seeing no one called out, "Come." Echo answered, "Come." As no one came, Narcissus called again, "Why do you shun me?" Echo asked the same question. "Let us join one another," said the youth. The maid answered with all her heart in the same words, and hastened to the spot, ready to throw her arms about his neck. He started back, exclaiming, "Hands off! I would rather die than you should have me!" "Have me," said she; but it was all in vain. He left her, and she went to hide her blushes in the recesses of the woods. From that time forth she lived in caves and among mountain cliffs. Her form faded with grief, till at last all her flesh shrank away. Her bones were changed into rocks and there was nothing left of her but her voice. With that she is still ready to reply to any one who calls her, and keeps up her old habit of having the last word.

Narcissus' cruelty in this case was not the only instance. He shunned all the rest of the nymphs, as he had done poor Echo. One day a maiden who had in vain endeavored to attract him uttered a prayer that he might some time or other feel what it was to love and meet no return of affection. The avenging goddess heard and granted the prayer.

There was a clear fountain, with water like silver, to which the shepherds never drove their flocks, nor the mountain goats resorted, nor any of the beasts of the forest; neither was it defaced with fallen leaves or branches; but the grass grew fresh around it, and the rocks sheltered it from the sun. Hither came one day the youth, fatigued with hunting, heated and thirsty. He stooped down to drink, and saw his own image in the water; he thought it was some beautiful water spirit living in the fountain. He stood gazing with admiration at those bright eyes, those locks curled like the locks of Bacchus or Apollo, the rounded cheeks, the ivory neck, the parted lips, and the glow of health and exercise over all. He fell in love with himself. He brought his lips near to take a kiss; he plunged his arms in to embrace the beloved object. It fled at the touch, but returned again after a moment and renewed the fascination. He could not tear himself away; he lost all thought of food or rest, while he hovered over the brink of the fountain gazing upon his own image. He talked with the supposed spirit: "Why, beautiful being, do you shun me? Surely my face is not one to repel you. The nymphs love me, and you yourself look not indifferent upon me. When I stretch forth my arms you do the same; and you smile upon me and answer my beckonings with the like." His tears fell into the water and disturbed the image. As he saw it depart, he exclaimed, "Stay I entreat you! Let me at least gaze upon you, if I may not touch you." With this, and much more of the same kind, he cherished the flame that consumed him, so that by degrees he lost his color, his vigor, and the beauty which formerly had so charmed the nymph Echo. She kept near him, however, and when he exclaimed, "Alas! Alas!" she answered him with the same words. He pined away and died; and when his shade passed the Stygian river, it leaned over the boat to catch a look of itself in the waters. The nymphs mourned for him, especially the water nymphs; and when they smote their breasts Echo smote hers also. They prepared a funeral pile and would have burned the body, but it was nowhere to be found; but in its place a flower, purple within and surrounded with white leaves, which bears the name and preserves the memory of Narcissus.

How Much Land Does a Man Need?

LEO TOLSTOY

I

An elder sister came to visit her younger sister in the country. The elder was married to a tradesman in town, the younger to a peasant in the village. As the sisters sat over their tea talking, the elder began to boast of the advantages of town life, saying how comfortably they lived there, how well they dressed, what fine clothes her children wore, what good things they ate and drank, and how she went to the theatre, promenades, and entertainments.

The younger sister was piqued, and in turn disparaged the life of a tradesman, and stood up for that of a peasant.

"I would not change my way of life for yours," said she. "We may live roughly, but at least we are free from anxiety. You live in better style than we do, but though you often earn more than you need, you are very likely to lose all you have. You know the proverb, Loss and gain are brothers twain. It often happens that people who are wealthy one day are begging for their bread the next. Our way is safer. Though a peasant's life is not a fat one, it is a long one. We shall never grow rich, but we shall always have enough to eat."

The elder sister said sneeringly:

"Enough? Yes, if you like to share with the pigs and the calves! What do you know of elegance or manners! However much your goodman may slave, you will die as you are living—on a dung heap—and your children the same."

"Well, what of that?" replied the younger. "Of course our work is rough and coarse. But, on the other hand, it is sure, and we need not bow to anyone. But you, in your towns, are surrounded by temptations; today all may be right, but tomorrow the Evil One may tempt your husband with cards, wine, or women, and all will go to ruin. Don't such things happen often enough?"

Pahóm, the master of the house, was lying on the top of the stove and he listened to the women's chatter.

"It is perfectly true," thought he. "Busy as we are from childhood tilling mother earth, we peasants have no time to let any nonsense settle in our heads. Our only trouble is that we haven't land enough. If I had plenty of land, I shouldn't fear the Devil himself!"

The women finished their tea, chatted a while about dress, and then cleared away the tea things and lay down to sleep.

But the Devil had been sitting behind the stove, and had heard all that was said. He was pleased that the peasant's wife had led her husband into boasting, and that he had said that if he had plenty of land he would not fear the Devil himself.

"All right," thought the Devil. "We will have a tussle. I'll give you land enough; and by means of that land I will get you into my power."

II

Close to the village there lived a lady, a small land-owner who had an estate of about three hundred acres.[1] She had always lived on good terms with the peasants until she engaged as her steward an old soldier, who took to burdening the people with fines. However careful Pahóm tried to be, it happened again and again that now a horse of his got among the lady's oats, now a cow strayed into her garden, now his calves found their way into her meadows—and he always had to pay a fine.

Pahóm paid up, but grumbled, and going home in a temper, was rough with his family. All through that summer, Pahóm had much trouble because of the steward, and he was even glad when winter came and the cattle had to be stabled. Though he grudged the fodder when they could no longer graze on the pastureland, at least he was free from anxiety about them.

In the winter the news got about that the lady was going to sell her land and that the keeper of the inn on the high road was bargaining for it. When the peasants heard this they were very much alarmed.

"Well," thought they, "if the innkeeper gets the land, he will worry us with fines worse than the lady's steward. We all depend on that estate."

So the peasants went on behalf of their Commune, and asked the lady not to sell the land to the innkeeper, offering her a better price for it themselves. The lady agreed to let them have it. Then the peasants tried to arrange for the Commune to buy the whole estate, so that it might be held by them all in common. They met twice to discuss it, but could not settle the matter; the Evil One sowed discord among them and they could not agree. So they decided to buy the land individually, each according to his means; and the lady agreed to this plan as she had to the other.

Presently Pahóm heard that a neighbor of his was buying fifty acres, and that the lady had consented to accept one half in cash and to wait a year for the other half. Pahóm felt envious.

"Look at that," thought he, "the land is all being sold, and I shall get none of it." So he spoke to his wife.

"Other people are buying," said he, "and we must also buy twenty acres or so. Life is becoming impossible. That steward is simply crushing us with his fines."

So they put their heads together and considered how they could manage to buy it. They had one hundred rubles laid by. They sold a colt and one half of their bees, hired out one of their sons as a laborer and took his wages in advance; borrowed the rest from a brother-in-law, and so scraped together half the purchase money.

Having done this, Pahóm chose out a farm of forty acres, some of it wooded, and went to the lady to bargain for it. They came to an agreement, and he shook hands with her upon it and paid her a deposit in advance. Then they went to town and signed the deeds; he paying half the price down, and undertaking to pay the remainder within two years.

So now Pahóm had land of his own. He borrowed seed, and sowed it on the land he had bought. The harvest was a good one, and within a year he had managed to pay off his debts both to the lady and to his brother-in-law. So he became a land-owner, ploughing and sowing his own land, making hay on his own land, cutting his own trees, and feeding his cattle on his own pasture.

[1] 120 *desyatins*. The desyatin is properly 2.7 acres; but in this story round numbers are used.

When he went out to plough his fields, or to look at his growing corn, or at his grass-meadows, his heart would fill with joy. The grass that grew and the flowers that bloomed there seemed to him unlike any that grew elsewhere. Formerly, when he had passed by that land, it had appeared the same as any other land, but now it seemed quite different.

III

So Pahóm was well-contented, and everything would have been right if the neighboring peasants would only not have trespassed on his corn fields and meadows. He appealed to them most civilly, but they still went on: Now the Communal herdsmen would let the village cows stray into his meadows, then horses from the night pasture would get among his corn. Pahóm turned them out again and again, and forgave their owners, and for a long time he forbore to prosecute any one. But at last he lost patience and complained to the District Court. He knew it was the peasants' want of land, and no evil intent on their part, that caused the trouble, but he thought:

"I cannot go on overlooking it or they will destroy all I have. They must be taught a lesson."

So he had them up, gave them one lesson, and then another, and two or three of the peasants were fined. After a time Pahóm's neighbors began to bear him a grudge for this, and would now and then let their cattle on to his land on purpose. One peasant even got into Pahóm's wood at night and cut down five young lime trees for their bark. Pahóm passing through the wood one day noticed something white. He came nearer and saw the stripped trunks lying on the ground, and close by stood the stumps where the trees had been. Pahóm was furious.

"If he had only cut one here and there it would have been bad enough," thought Pahóm, "but the rascal has actually cut down a whole clump. If I could only find out who did this, I would pay him out."

He racked his brains as to who it could be. Finally he decided: "It must be Simon—no one else could have done it." So he went to Simon's homestead to have a look round, but he found nothing, and only had an angry scene. However, he now felt more certain than ever that Simon had done it, and he lodged a complaint. Simon was summoned. The case was tried, and retried, and at the end of it all Simon was acquitted, there being no evidence against him. Pahóm felt still more aggrieved, and let his anger loose upon the Elder and the Judged.

"You let thieves grease your palms," said he. "If you were honest folk yourselves you would not let a thief go free."

So Pahóm quarrelled with the Judges and with his neighbors. Threats to burn his building began to be uttered. So though Pahóm had more land, his place in the Commune was much worse than before.

About this time a rumour got about that many people were moving to new parts.

"There's no need for me to leave my land," thought Pahóm. "But some of the others might leave our village and then there would be more room for us. I would take over their land myself and make my estate a bit bigger. I could then live more at ease. As it is, I am still too cramped to be comfortable."

One day Pahóm was sitting at home when a peasant, passing through the village, happened to call in. He was allowed to stay the night, and supper was given him. Pahóm had a talk with this peasant and asked him where he came from. The stranger answered that he came from beyond the Vólga, where he had been working. One word led to another, and the man went on to say that many people were settling in those parts. He told how some people from his village had settled there. They had joined the Commune, and had had twenty-five acres per man granted them. The land was so good, he said, that the rye sown on it grew as high as a horse, and so thick that five cuts of a sickle made a sheaf. One peasant, he said, had brought nothing with him but his bare hands, and now he had six horses and two cows of his own.

Pahóm's heart kindled with desire. He thought, "Why should I suffer in this narrow hole, if one can live so well elsewhere? I will sell my land and my homestead here, and with the money I will start afresh over there and get everything new. In this crowded place one is always having trouble. But I must first go and find out all about it myself."

Towards summer he got ready and started. He went down the Vólga on a steamer to Samára, then walked another three hundred miles on foot, and at last reached the place. It was just as the stranger had said. The peasants had plenty of land: Every man had twenty-five acres of Communal land given him for his use, and any one who had money could buy, besides, at two shillings an acre[2] as much good freehold land as he wanted.

Having found out all he wished to know, Pahóm returned home as autumn came on, and began selling off his belongings. He sold his land at a profit, sold his homestead and all his cattle, and withdrew from membership of the Commune. He only waited till the spring, and then started with his family for the new settlement.

IV

As soon as Pahóm and his family reached their new abode, he applied for admission into the Commune of a large village. He stood treat to the Elders and obtained the necessary documents. Five shares of Communal land were given him for his own and his sons' use: that is to say—125 acres (not all together, but in different fields) besides the use of the Communal pasture. Pahóm put up the buildings he needed, and bought cattle. Of the Communal land alone he had three times as much as at his former home, and the land was good cornland. He was ten times better off than he had been. He had plenty of arable land and pasturage, and could keep as many head of cattle as he liked.

At first, in the bustle of building and settling down, Pahóm was pleased with it all, but when he got used to it he began to think that even here he had not enough land. The first year, he sowed wheat on his share of the Communal land and had a good crop. He wanted to go on sowing wheat, but had not enough Communal land for the purpose, and what he had already used was not available; for in those parts wheat is only sown on virgin soil or on fallow land. It is sown for one or two years, and then the land lies fallow till it is again overgrown with prairie grass. There were many who wanted such land and there was not enough for all; so that people quarrelled about it. Those who were better off wanted it for growing wheat, and those who were poor wanted it to let to dealers, so that they might raise money to pay their taxes. Pahóm wanted to sow more wheat, so he rented land from a dealer for a year. He sowed much wheat and had a fine crop, but the land was too far from the village—the wheat had to be carted more than ten miles. After a time Pahóm noticed that some peasant-dealers were living on separate farms and were growing wealthy; and he thought, "If I were to buy some freehold land and have a homestead

[2]   Three rúbles per desyatina.

on it, it would be a different thing altogether. Then it would all be nice and compact."

The question of buying freehold land recurred to him again and again. He went on in the same way for three years, renting land and sowing wheat. The seasons turned out well and the crops were good, so that he began to lay money by. He might have gone on living contentedly, but he grew tired of having to rent other people's land every year, and having to scramble for it. Wherever there was good land to be had, the peasants would rush for it and it was taken up at once, so that unless you were sharp about it you got none. It happened in the third year that he and a dealer together rented a piece of pasture land from some peasants; and they had already ploughed it up, when there was some dispute and the peasants went to law about it, and things fell out so that the labor was all lost.

"If it were my own land," thought Pahóm, "I should be independent, and there would not be all this unpleasantness."

So Pahóm began looking out for land which he could buy; and he came across a peasant who had bought thirteen hundred acres, but having got into difficulties was willing to sell again cheap. Pahóm bargained and haggled with him, and at last they settled the price at 1,500 rúbles, part in cash and part to be paid later. They had ,all but clinched the matter when a passing dealer happened to stop at Pahóm's one day to get a feed for his horses. He drank tea with Pahóm and they had a talk. The dealer said that he was just returning from the land of the Bashkirs, far away, where he had bought thirteen thousand acres of land, all for 1,000 rúbles.

Pahóm questioned him further, and the tradesman said, "All one need do is to make friends with the chiefs. I gave away about one hundred rúbles worth of silk robes and carpets, besides a case of tea, and I gave wine to those who would drink it; and I got the land for less than a penny an acre."[3] And he showed Pahóm the title deeds, saying, "The land lies near a river, and the whole prairie is virgin soil."

Pahóm plied him with questions, and the tradesman said, "There is more land there than you could cover if you walked a year, and it all belongs to the Bashkirs. They are as simple as sheep, and land can be got almost for nothing."

"There now," thought Pahóm, "with my one thousand rúbles, why should I get only thirteen hundred acres, and saddle myself with a debt besides? If I take it out there, I can get more than ten times as much for the money."

V

Pahóm inquired how to get to the place, and as soon as the tradesman had left him, he prepared to go there himself. He left his wife to look after the homestead, and started on his journey taking his man with him. They stopped at a town on their way and bought a case of tea, some wine, and other presents, as the tradesman had advised. On and on they went until they had gone more than three hundred miles, and on the seventh day they came to a place where the Bashkirs had pitched their tents. It was all just as the tradesman had said. The people lived on the steppes, by a river, in felt-covered tents.[4] They neither tilled the ground, nor ate bread. Their cattle and horses grazed in herds on the steppe. The colts were tethered behind the tents, and the mares were driven to them twice a day. The

---

[3] Five kopéks for a desyatina.
[4] Kibitkas.

mares were milked, and from the milk kumiss was made. It was the women who prepared kumiss, and they also made cheese. As far as the men were concerned, drinking kumiss and tea, eating mutton, and playing on their pipes, was all they cared about. They were all stout and merry, and all the summer long they never thought of doing any work. They were quite ignorant, and knew no Russian, but were good-natured enough.

As soon as they saw Pahóm, they came out of their tents and gathered round their visitor. An interpreter was found, and Pahóm told them he had come about some land. The Bashkirs seemed very glad; they took Pahóm and led him into one of the best tents, where they made him sit on some down cushions placed on a carpet, while they sat round him. They gave him some tea and kumiss, and had a sheep killed, and gave him mutton to eat. Pahóm took presents out of his cart and distributed them among the Bashkirs, and divided the tea amongst them. The Bashkirs were delighted. They talked a great deal among themselves, and then told the interpreter to translate.

"They wish to tell you," said the interpreter, "that they like you, and that it is our custom to do all we can to please a guest and to repay him for his gifts. You have given us presents, now tell us which of the things we possess please you best, that we may present them to you."

"What pleases me best here," answered Pahóm, "is your land. Our land is crowded and the soil is exhausted; but you have plenty of land and it is good land. I never saw the like of it."

The interpreter translated. The Bashkirs talked among themselves for a while. Pahóm could not understand what they were saying, but saw that they were much amused and that they shouted and laughed. Then they were silent and looked at Pahóm

while the interpreter said, "They wish me to tell you that in return for your presents they will gladly give you as much land as you want. You have only to point it out with your hand and it is yours."

The Bashkirs talked again for a while and began to dispute. Pahóm asked what they were disputing about, and the interpreter told him that some of them thought they ought to ask their Chief about the land and not act in his absence, while others thought there was no need to wait for his return.

VI

While the Bashkirs were disputing, a man in a large fox fur cap appeared on the scene. They all became silent and rose to their feet. The interpreter said, "This is our Chief himself."

Pahóm immediately fetched the best dressing gown and five pounds of tea, and offered these to the Chief. The Chief accepted them, and seated himself in the place of honor. The Bashkirs at once began telling him something. The Chief listened for a while, then made a sign with his head for them to be silent, and addressing himself to Pahóm, said in Russian, "Well, let it be so. Choose whatever piece of land you like; we have plenty of it."

"How can I take as much as I like?" thought Pahóm. "I must get a deed to make it secure, or else they may say, 'It is yours,' and afterwards may take it away again."

"Thank you for your kind words," he said aloud. "You have much land, and I only want a little. But I should like to be sure which bit is mine. Could it not be measured and made over to me? Life and death are in God's hands. You good people give it to me, but your children might wish to take it away again."

"You are quite right," said the Chief. "We will make it over to you."

"I heard that a dealer had been here," continued Pahóm, "and that you gave him a little land, too, and signed title-deeds to that effect. I should like to have it done in the same way."

The Chief understood. "Yes," replied he, "that can be done quite easily. We have a scribe, and we will go to town with you and have the deed properly sealed."

"And what will be the price?" asked Pahóm.

"Our price is always the same: one thousand rúbles a day."

Pahóm did not understand. "A day? What measure is that? How many acres would that be?"

"We do not know how to reckon it out," said the Chief. "We sell it by the day. As much as you can go round on your feet in a day is yours, and the price is one thousand rúbles a day."

Pahóm was surprised. "But in a day you can get round a large tract of land," he said.

The Chief laughed. "It will all be yours!" said he. "But there is one condition: If you don't return on the same day to the spot whence you started, your money is lost."

"But how am I to mark the way that I have gone?"

"Why, we shall go to any spot your like, and stay there. You must start from that spot and make your round, taking a spade with you. Wherever you think necessary, make a mark. At every turning, dig a hole and pile up the turf; then afterwards we will go round with a plough from hole to hole. You may make as large a circuit as you please, but before the sun sets you must return to the place you started from. All the land you cover will be yours."

Pahóm was delighted. It was decided to start early next morning. They talked a while, and after drinking some more kumiss and eating some more mutton, they had tea again, and then the night came on. They gave Pahóm a feather bed to sleep on, and the Bashkirs dispersed for the night, promising to assemble the next morning at daybreak and ride out before sunrise to the appointed spot.

VII

Pahóm lay on the feather-bed, but could not sleep. He kept thinking about the land.

"What a large tract I will mark off!" thought he. "I can easily do thirty-five miles in a day. The days are long now, and within a circuit of thirty-five miles what a lot of land there will be! I will sell the poorer land, or let it to peasants, but I'll pick out the best and farm it. I will buy two ox-teams, and hire two more laborers. About a hundred and fifty acres shall be plough land, and I will pasture cattle on the rest."

Pahóm lay awake all night, and dozed off only just before dawn. Hardly were his eyes closed when he had a dream. He thought he was lying in that same tent and heard somebody chuckling outside. He wondered who it could be, and rose and went out, and he saw the Bashkir Chief sitting in front of the tent holding his sides and rolling about with laughter. Going nearer to the Chief, Pahóm asked "What are you laughing at?" But he saw that it was no longer the Chief, but the dealer who had recently stopped at his house and had told him about the land. Just as Pahóm was going to ask, "Have you been here long?" he saw that it was not the dealer, but the peasant who had come up from the Vólga, long ago, to Pahóm's old home. Then he saw that it was not the peasant either, but the Devil himself with hoofs and horns, sitting there and chuckling, and before him lay a man barefoot, prostrate on the ground, with only trousers and a shirt on. And Pahóm dreamt that he looked more attentively to see what sort of a man it was that was lying there, and he saw that the man was dead, and that it was himself! He awoke horror-struck.

"What things one does dream," thought he.

Looking round he saw through the open door that the dawn was breaking. "It's time to wake them up," thought he. "We ought to be starting."

He got up, roused his man (who was sleeping in his cart), bade him harness; and went to call the Bashkirs.

"It's time to go to the steppe to measure the land," he said.

The Bashkirs rose and assembled, and the Chief came too. Then they began drinking kumiss again, and offered Pahóm some tea, but he would not wait.

"If we are go to, let us go. It is high time," said he.

VIII

The Bashkirs got ready and they all started: some mounted on horses, and some in carts. Pahóm drove in his own small cart with his servant and took a spade with him. When they reached the steppe, the morning red was beginning to kindle. They ascended a hillock (called by the Bashkirs a *shikhan*) and dismounting from their carts and their horses, gathered in one spot. The Chief came up to Pahóm and stretching out his arm towards the plain.

"See," said he, "all this, as far as your eye can reach, is ours. You may have any part of it you like."

Pahóm's eyes glistened: It was all virgin soil, as flat as the palm of your hand, as black as the seed of a poppy, and in the hollows different kinds of grasses grew breast high.

The Chief took off his fox fur cap, placed it on the ground and said, "This will be the mark. Start from here, and return here again. All the land you go round shall be yours."

Pahóm took out his money and put it on the cap. Then he took off his outer coat, remaining in his sleeveless undercoat. He unfastened his girdle and tied it tight below his stomach, put a little bag of bread into the breast of his coat, and tying a flask of water to his girdle, he drew up the tops of his boots, took the spade from his man, and stood ready to start. He considered for some moments which way he had better go—it was tempting everywhere.

"No matter," he concluded, "I will go towards the rising sun."

He turned his face to the east, stretched himself, and waited for the sun to appear above the rim.

"I must lose no time," he thought, "and it is easier walking while it is still cool."

The sun's rays had hardly flashed above the horizon, before Pahóm, carrying the spade over his shoulder, went down into the steppe.

Pahóm started walking neither slowly nor quickly. After having gone a thousand yards he stopped, dug a hole, and placed pieces of turf one on another to make it more visible. Then he went on; and now that he had walked off his stiffness he quickened his pace. After a while he dug another hole.

Pahóm looked back. The hillock could be distinctly seen in the sunlight, with the people on it, and the glittering tyres of the cartwheels. At a rough guess Pahóm concluded that he had walked three miles. It was growing warmer; he took off his undercoat, flung it across his shoulder, and went on again. It had grown quite warm now; he looked at the sun, it was time to think of breakfast.

"The first shift is done, but there are four in a day, and it is too soon yet to turn. But I will just take off my boots," said he to himself.

He sat down, took off his boots, stuck them into his girdle, and went on. It was easy walking now.

"I will go on for another three miles," thought he, "and then turn to the left. This spot is so fine, that it would be a pity to lose it. The further one goes, the better the land seems."

He went straight on for a while, and when he looked around, the hillock was scarcely visible and the people on it looked like black ants, and he could just see something glistening there in the sun.

"Ah," thought Pahóm, "I have gone far enough in this direction, it is time to turn. Besides I am in a regular sweat, and very thirsty."

He stopped, dug a large hole, and heaped up pieces of turf. Next he untied his flask, had a drink and then turned sharply to the left. He went on and on; the grass was high, and it was very hot.

Pahóm began to grow tired. He looked at the sun and saw that it was noon. "Well," he thought, "I must have a rest."

He sat down, and ate some bread and drank some water; but he did not lie down, thinking that if he did he might fall asleep. After sitting a little while, he went on again. At first he walked easily: The food had strengthened him; but it had become terribly hot and he felt sleepy, still he went on, thinking: "An hour to suffer, a lifetime to live."

He went a long way in this direction also, and was about to turn to the left again, when he perceived a damp hollow. "It would be a pity to leave that out," he thought. "Flax would do well there." So he went on past the hollow, and dug a hole on the other side of it before he turned the corner. Pahóm looked towards the hillock. The heat made the air hazy: It seemed to be quivering, and through the haze the people on the hillock could scarcely be seen.

"Ah!" thought Pahóm, "I have made the sides too long; I must make this one shorter." And he went along the third side, stepping faster. He looked at the sun: It was nearly half-way to the horizon, and he had not yet done two miles of the third side of the square. He was still ten miles from the goal.

"No," he thought, "though it will make my land lopsided, I must hurry back in a straight line now. I might go too far, and as it is I have a great deal of land."

So Pahóm hurriedly dug a hole, and turned straight towards the hillock.

IX

Pahóm went straight towards the hillock, but he now walked with difficulty. He was done up with the heat, his bare feet were cut and bruised, and his legs began to fail. He longed to rest, but it was impossible if he meant to get back before sunset. The sun waits for no man, and it was sinking lower and lower.

"Oh dear," he thought, "if only I have not blundered trying for too much! What if I am too late?"

He looked towards the hillock and at the sun. He was still far from his goal, and the sun was already near the rim.

Pahóm walked on and on; it was very hard walking but he went quicker and quicker. He pressed on, but was still far from the place. He began running, threw away his coat, his boots, his flask, and his cap, and kept only the spade which he used as a support.

"What shall I do," he thought again, "I have grasped too much and ruined the whole affair. I can't get there before the sun sets."

And this fear made him still more breathless. Pahóm went on running, his soaking shirt and trousers stuck to him and his mouth was parched. His breast was working like a blacksmith's bellows, his heart was beating like a hammer, and his legs were giving way as if they did not belong to him. Pahóm was seized with terror lest he should die of the strain.

Though afraid of death, he could not stop. "After having run all that way they will call me a fool if I stop now," thought he. And he ran on and on, and drew near and heard the Bashkirs yelling and shouting to him, and their cries inflamed his heart still more. He gathered his last strength and ran on.

The sun was close to the rim, and cloaked in mist looked large, and red as blood. Now, yes now it was about to set! The sun was quite low, but he was also quite near his aim. Pahóm could already see the people on the hillock waving their arms to hurry him up. He could see the fox fur cap on the ground and the money on it, and the Chief sitting on the ground holding his sides. And Pahóm remembered his dream.

"There is plenty of land," thought he, "but will God let me live on it? I have lost my life, I have lost my life! I shall never reach the spot!"

Pahóm looked at the sun, which had reached the earth: One side of it had already disappeared. With all his remaining strength he rushed on, bending his body forward so that his legs could hardly follow fast enough to keep him from falling. Just as he reached the hillock it suddenly grew dark. He looked up—the sun had already set! He gave a cry: "All my labour has been in vain," thought he, and was about to stop, but he heard the Bashkirs still shouting, and remembered that though to him, from below, the sun seemed to have set, they on the hillock could still see it. He took a long breath and ran up the hillock. It was still light there. He reached the top and saw the cap. Before it sat the Chief laughing and holding his sides. Again Pahóm remembered his dream, and he uttered a cry: His legs gave way beneath him, he fell forward and reached the cap with his hands.

"Ah, that's a fine fellow!" exclaimed the Chief. "He has gained much land!"

Pahóm's servant came running up and tried to raise him, but he saw that blood was flowing from his mouth. Pahóm was dead!

The Bashkirs clicked their tongues to show their pity.

His servant picked up the spade and dug a grave long enough for Pahóm to lie in, and buried him in it. Six feet from his head to his heels was all he needed.

1886

MODULE FOUR

Entrepreneurship in the Established Firm

The notion of entrepreneurship and creativity in the established organization has received considerable attention in the business world and in business schools, as established firms strive to maintain their competitive strength in a turbulent environment. Many corporations are experimenting with ways to address the tensions inherent in a need for both control and independence of action, for both continuity and change.

The evolving organization and the established organization present a study in contrasts. Whereas the evolving organization must work to reduce ambiguity and uncertainty, the established organization's challenge is the opposite. Ambiguity and uncertainty, expressed in such terms as institutional slack, flexibility, and the freedom to fail, must frequently be built into the system. Similarly, the evolving organization commonly works with a set of values which are the heartfelt and personal expression of a founder or founder team and on which an emerging corporate culture is based. The established organization, on the other hand, has a culture firmly in place. Frequently it is formalized, institutionalized, and impersonal into which life must be breathed through conscious direction of the organization's culture.

Finally, the locus of entrepreneurial activity may differ in the evolving and established firms. The evolving organization is typically driven by the vision and zeal of a formula or formulas in a situation where the organizational context is initially minimal and fluid. On the other hand, entrepreneurship in the established organization is much more a team effort which must take into account the institutional and sometimes political constraints imposed by an established structure and culture.

Two entrepreneurial roles can be differentiated in the established firm. First, we must consider the role of the middle manager entrepreneur. This is the person who assumes the career risk of pursuing a new idea within the established setting, and who serves needed resources, runs interference for the idea so it can germinate, endures the "flack" of institutional inertia and resistance. Examples of this entrepreneurial middle manager in this module are Jerry Welsh, Beth Horwitz, and Teri Williams at American Express. This figure is also discussed in Rosabeth Moss Kanter's paper on the middle manager as innovator. The second role is the entrepreneurial leader at the top of the organization. This individual, in many ways, resembles the start-up entrepreneur—creating and pursuing a vision. But the entrepreneurial leader must establish this vision by working through others, especially by finding, empowering, and championing the entrepreneurial middle manager. The cases on Lou Gerstner (American Express) and Jan Carlzon (SAS) deal with the issues and concerns of the entrepreneurial leader.

This module note will first explore in more detail the nature of the established organization in Section 1. Next, it examines entrepreneurship in the established firm in the familiar terms of task, person, and organizational context. (See Figures 4-1 and 4-2.)

WHAT IS AN "ESTABLISHED" ORGANIZATION?

"Established" refers to characteristics of size and duration. Established organizations have achieved scope and complexity in numbers of people and the interdependency and relationship among organizational subunits. A social image is helpful. A small town and an entrepreneurial start-up may share certain features: face-to-face relationships; informal communication; a living sense of how relationships have developed over time; and an appreciation of traditions and common beliefs. It is possible to know everyone in the town and "what makes them tick." People may assume multiple roles: The mayor may also teach in the local school; the town doctor may conduct the local chamber music group. People "pitch in." It is possible for each individual to feel involved in the community, based on an understanding that every person matters in relation to the whole.

Figure 4-1

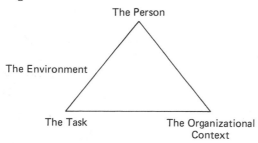

The Person

The Environment

The Task

The Organizational
Context

Figure 4-2 The Established Company—Key Issues

Person	Understanding the entrepreneur's motives, skills, and fit with organization
Task	Shaking things up: Creating slack
Organizational Context	Creating/influencing the organizational context: structure, culture
	Dealing with traditions, formality, systems, stability
Environment	Appreciating the role of environmental constraints and opportunities:
	Labor pool
	Regulation
	Availability of career alternatives to the intrapreneur

By contrast, the established firm is closer to the notion of the modern city, with its impersonal relationships, reliance on cues of status and appearance to guide communication, and substitution of style for tradition. The modern city depends on specialized roles and rules to make life manageable and predictable. People come and go with less impact on the community as a whole. Alienation and frustration can accompany the feeling of being a small cog in a large machine.

In addition to size, established organizations also share the characteristic of duration. That is, they have accumulated a significant amount of history which can affect their sense of the present and the future. As organizations mature, they accumulate shared values and beliefs. "Significant events" may also have occurred and the organization's response to them becomes an important part of its evolving identity. The sum of traditions for the established organization defines its culture: shared values and a sense of how things are to be done.

Implicit in the issue of duration are the questions of how organizations change, what their rites of passage are, and how they can maintain entrepreneurial and innovative characteristics as they grow. Successful entrepreneurship requires flexibility and quickness of response, but large organizations may tend towards inertia. This inertia can require substantial "start-up costs" when change is needed. It also implies that any motion once initiated must be maintained.

Description of the established organization has a lengthy academic tradition. Sociologist Max Weber,[1] for example, detailed the characteristics of the large bureaucratic organization, pointing out that an organization whose goals

---

[1] Max Weber, *The Theory of Social and Economic Organization* (New York: Oxford University Press, 1947).

lay in efficiency and predictability often tended to enforce the importance of formal roles, fixed rules, division of labor, specialization, and hierarchy.

In a bureaucratic organization, the sense of individual significance may disappear; a person may feel powerless. Yet it is precisely from the individual that arises all creative experience, perception of opportunity, and passion for implementation. Balancing the world of the talented individual and the collective is often the most challenging and critical task for an established organization. Only when the needs of the individual and the organization are in alignment can entrepreneurship in the established organization become a reality.

Too often the established organization resembles the bureaucracy described by Weber, in which flexibility and innovation are sacrificed for predictability and control. Large size and the weight of tradition can prove powerful barriers to change and adaptability, and challenge an organization like IBM, which, in 1986, had 375,000 employees around the world. Its scientific and technical development work was carried out in 20 research laboratories with over 2,500 people and in at least another 20 smaller centers. A senior executive at IBM once described the firm not as a powerful ship but as a fleet. How do you communicate among the ships in the fleet? How long does it take a fleet to turn around? How do you coordinate the many elements of the fleet so that they act as one?

MANAGING ENTREPRENEURSHIP IN THE ESTABLISHED ORGANIZATION—THE TASK

To begin with, many of the tasks in an established environment are similar to those of an evolving one. That is, a new idea must be generated (creative tasks) and implemented (operational/managerial tasks). At the same time, commitment must be developed for the idea (leadership/interpersonal tasks). However, in the established organization, a variety of institutional or political tasks must also be completed. Multiple stakeholders vie for influence in terms of their particular point of view, and winning support for the new idea and obtaining resources can be a delicate task when the internal entrepreneur is on a schedule and must deal with institutional inertia, conservatism, or bureaucracy.

For the manager of entrepreneurial processes in the established firm, the challenge is often less in terms of defining or structuring the task than in making sure slack or potential space exists within which the task can emerge and define itself. In many cases the would-be entrepreneur in the established environment must literally wrest control of the new enterprise from the organization. Another strategem involves hiding out—going underground until the idea is too firmly planted to be in danger of being uprooted by hostile or competitive organizational forces. The terminology used to describe the internal entrepreneurial process bears testimony to its countercultural flavor: skunkworks, bootlegging, garage.

Figure 4-3 The Middle Manager and the Leader

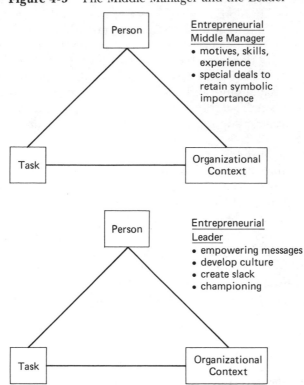

The Person

As mentioned earlier, entrepreneurship in the established firm involves a wider cast of characters than in the evolving firm. Principal among them are the entrepreneurial middle manager and the entrepreneurial leader, graphically shown in Figure 4-3.

The Entrepreneurial Middle Manager

The entrepreneurial middle manager is in the position of developing a venture within the setting of an established organization. This carries disadvantages as well as advantages. In an established environment, the choices available to the entrepreneur are shaped by institutional forces: standard operating procedures; values; customs; existing stakeholders; and organizational politics. The entrepreneur is called upon to create and nurture the new venture, shielding it from an often hostile or unsupportive environment. On the positive side, established organizations offer resources to support the new venture which are frequently difficult to find in a start-up situation. Established organizations have capital,

human resources, brand name, market position, and other assets which can speed the development of the internal venture.

The Entrepreneurial Leader

The leadership of an established organization can be a focal point for change and inculcating entrepreneurial values. Jan Carlzon, who is discussed in the Scandinavian Airlines Systems case, is an excellent example. As the source of corporate authority, the leader can recreate or protect a great deal of the informality and flexibility which often dries up as an organization matures.

For example, a leader can short-circuit layers of organizational hierarchy by expressing personal interest in a new project or initiative. Steven Jobs, founder of Apple Computer, became directly involved in the development of the Macintosh computer, which was central to Apple's strategy and hopes for future success. His role was lauded by some members of the Macintosh project team: "He was a catalyst for us. He gave us faith. He sheltered us from the corporate noise."[2]

With selective attention, the leader can also foster the careers of unusual people who had the potential of making significant contributions. For example, as discussed in American Express cases, Lou Gerstner, president of the company, brought in Jerry Walsh who, despite his lack of a previous business background, became recognized as an important creative force within the company and its industry. The leader can exert a protective influence, create unusual pathways for advancement, or give confidence and the resources to make new things happen. Leaders can also stimulate new patterns of interaction by changing the organizational structure and "shaking things up."

The leader can be a role model and personal advocate for new initiatives. The Macintosh team had this to say about Jobs: "He's a maniacal genius. His job is to stir up everything. He's a muckraker in the classic sense of the word: He will not leave anything alone. He will not allow inadequacy or compromise to exist."[3] These were important qualities to affirm for this creative team. By modeling desired behavior and talking about the importance of entrepreneurship and innovation, the leader preaches an important set of lessons to the congregation. Symbolic events, gestures, and imagery all provide opportunities for leadership to assert the importance of desired behavior.

Leaders must also demonstrate the extent of the organization's commitment to entrepreneurial activity. It is vital to differentiate fads from concerns of fundamental strategic importance. And it is critically important to insure that actions are consistent with messages communicated. Process must be managed so that expectations are not aroused which cannot be fulfilled. Once they take a position, leaders *must* deliver.

---

[2] Apple Computer segment, from *In Search of Excellence: The Video*, produced by Nathan Tyler Productions, Waltham, MA.
[3] Ibid.

Finally, managing entrepreneurship in the established environment means that the well-oiled bureaucratic fighting machine is also the opportunity-driven, nimble company. American Express is an example of a company which has become successful in both tasks: balancing the entrepreneur with the manager, the individual with the team player, structure and control with environmental uncertainty, action with planning, and opportunity-seeking with risk aversion. Achieving this balance is a central task of company leadership.

THE ORGANIZATIONAL CONTEXT

Two principal avenues by which entrepreneurship can be fostered in the large and tradition-laden organization—communication and creating slack—are described below.

Communication—Setting Clear Goals

Leadership goes hand in hand with internal communications. Many communication vehicles can affirm values and desired behavior and make the organization feel "small" again. How company leadership takes advantage of formal mechanisms such as scheduled meetings and written communiques as well as informal mechanisms such as "the grapevine" determines how influential the new messages will be.

Employees not only need to know *what* is desired but *why*, and *how* it will be achieved. When Jan Carlzon turned Scandinavian Airlines System around, he explained the company environment and strategy through a series of simple pamphlets called, "Jan Carlzon's Little Red Books." Initially pooh-poohed, these pamphlets enhanced the common understanding of new attitudes and behavior, desired values, and behaviors. Developing the courage to support others unlike one's self, offering new kinds of support, emphasizing cross-functional interaction, implementing entrepreneurship, tolerating diversity, and encouraging people to accept responsibility and authority are other examples.

Creating Slack in the Organization

Ultimately, entrepreneurship in the established corporation boils down to providing the conditions for its emergence. This involves creating an appropriate amount of slack or potential space in the system. There are a variety of mechanisms for accomplishing this goal.

Championing and empowering. In the past, artists and researchers pursued their work with the necessary freedom and resources only if they were able to secure the support of a powerful patron who would provide financial resources and a suitable work environment. Equally important was the career

protection which came from association with a proper patron. Eventually, such patronage assured a sympathetic audience for the finished product.

The modern corporate equivalent of this "patron of the arts" is the champion. Like Steven Jobs and the Macintosh, the champion shares the enthusiasm and passion of the creative team. He or she sees that entrepreneurs have the necessary resources and environment, protects them from corporate politics, and maintains their freedom to succeed or fail. The champion is also a screening device, or tester. This is important for the organization, since the champion is in an ideal position to ask such questions as: How much support should we give? How much commitment do we see? Is this a good idea? Utilizing these techniques, the champion provides an important service both to the entrepreneur and to the organization.

Making the large organization feel intimate. A large organization need not "feel" large to the entrepreneur. Many organizations have experimented with decentralizing innovation and giving the organization the feeling of an intimate and informal start-up.

When Matt Sanders was given the job of creating a new laptop computer for Convergent Technologies, he was also given the following directive, "You can have any resources you want, but you'll have to start this project from scratch." This is an example of what some call the "leaky roof" syndrome. Entrepreneurs have been known to wax nostalgic for the "good old days" when their company was so poor that it had a leaky roof or worked out of a garage. As the organization trades its leaky roof for designer skylights, it may lose some of the creative environment. Thus, attempts to replicate the leaky roof era can be important to an established company. Perhaps in the future, it will invest in garagelike spaces or buildings whose roofs are punctured.

Another approach to making the organization feel small comes from the IBM "IBU" or "independent business unit" concept. As of 1986, IBM had sixteen IBUs organized around new or emerging products. Examples of IBUs past and present include the IBM PC group, the PC software group, and various customer service functions. Each is essentially a "company within a company." Decentralization creates greater autonomy, responsibility at the local level, and at times the emergence of a useful sense of local culture. Other examples of IBUs include various corporate ventures, seed groups, and strategic business units.

A third technique for preserving organizational intimacy is demonstrated by companies like Lucasfilm, Ltd., which recognize that smallness and informality are essential to their creative success. They therefore resolve not to grow beyond a "small-town" size. Lucasfilm's dramatic success and resulting opportunities created a dilemma around growth. Their solution involved budding off separate companies and new ventures so that the firm's final organizational structure consisted of a group of small companies each no larger than 300 people.

Another avenue to smallness and the preservation of focus involves the ability of established organizations to add to their internal portfolio through diversification rather than by internal development. IBM has grown significantly by acquiring chip design and telecommunications companies rather than developing these businesses internally. Sensitivity to these acquisitions' local autonomy will allow them in time to function as elements of an overall "fleet."

A final approach is established solid, impermeable boundaries between organizational subunits, which can then develop their own identities. The Macintosh development group at Apple and videogame designers at Activision have at times enjoyed such needed privacy. The instability of such a solution is indicated by the observation that such boundaries have become highly porous at both Apple and Activision with changing business conditions and strategy.

Reward system. Obviously critical to fostering entrepreneurial and innovative behavior in the large organization, rewards reveal an organization's priorities and its assumptions about human motivation. If they are to sculpt desired behavior, however, rewards must be appropriate, fair, and flexible.

One level of reward clearly is financial incentives. Bonuses, stock options, cash gifts can all be linked to performance. There is an immediate dilemma tied to the use of financial rewards, however. First, the established company can never replicate the kind of returns an entrepreneur could realize independently. IBM, Xerox, and others are not in the business of turning their internal entrepreneurs into millionaires. Problems of fairness and equity also appear, as do the implications of creating a desire for independence. Dangers inherent in constructing what amounts to a dual ladder of financial compensation include potential conflicts between "intrapreneurs" and team players, old and young, old-timers and newcomers, scientists and managers.

Therefore, established companies must investigate sophisticated intrinsic or noncash rewards to stimulate internal entrepreneurship. Intrinsic rewards are particularly important because they bond the entrepreneur to the company and not to financial rewards which might increase a sense of freedom and mobility. Intrinsic rewards can take many forms and avoid the organizational problems of gross inequities.

For example, success can lead to changes in status within the organization. Promotion or title expansion is but one route. An interesting example that carries this a step further is the IBM Fellow's Program.[4] IBM annually screens its scientists and engineers for those who have made outstanding contributions. They are given the status of IBM Fellow for five years and free rein to follow their inclinations. IBM also has a number of recognition programs that draw attention to the accomplishments of outstanding individuals and publicizes these success stories through periodic ceremonies and internal media coverage. Another approach to recognition comes from Lotus Development Corporation, which with an interesting blend of personal recognition and marketing, made the project leader for its Symphony software part of the product's advertising campaign.

---

[4]   The IBM Fellows Program, HBS Case Services, #0-488-014, Boston, MA.

Preferred access to internal resources is another reward. Tom West of Data General has talked about the "pinball" mentality[5] of many internal entrepreneurs, meaning the entrepreneurial motivation comes from an understanding that success will earn the resources . . . which will enable further success. For the pinball player, success leads to a "free game" that extends the time of play, a motivating influence in itself.

The notion that work itself is motivating is also important. Established companies can provide greater resources, logistical support, and access to information than embryonic companies. One scientist described IBM as the "world's largest and most wonderful sandbox." There is something inherently motivating about working in such an environment.

Many firms have attempted to institutionalize the idea that success brings access to more resources. 3M rewards scientists and engineers with free time to pursue their own inclinations. Recent researchers have talked about the notion of "intracapital,"[6] whereby some companies provide an internal venture capital function for deserving projects. For institutionalized resource allocation to work, however, it must be fair and fast because new ideas need quick feedback in a competitive marketplace.

Many issues face the company designing a reward system appropriate for entrepreneurship and innovation. For example, free rein may subvert the current system. Or, creation of an entrepreneurial fast track may subvert a tenure and seniority system, with negative implications for the organization. In addition, the reward system is a reflection, conscious or unconscious, of a firm's assumptions about what is important. Therefore, tying incentives to some sense of present or future profit ensures an appropriate focus on markets and competitive environments.

The system must also include an appropriate balance between risk and reward for the internal entrepreneur; notions of responsibility and accountability thereby come into play. What do intrapreneurs have at stake? What will they lose if the project stumbles because of factors within their control and responsibility?

Implicit in these questions is the role of failure. People must be insulated from noble failures or those from uncontrollable factors. The example of an associate fired by a well-known investment bank for a typo on an internal memo shows to what extremes mistakes can be punished within allegedly rational environments. How success and failure are handled sends important signals to other intrapreneurs in the organization. But if some sanctions are not levied for laxness, then cavalier attitudes, other self-induced mishaps, or half-baked schemes may proliferate in an organization under the guise of "creativity."

Because effective team building is an important aspect of internal entrepreneurship, rewards must recognize teams as well as individuals and encourage creative people to hand over their work to managers at the appropriate time. Cooperation is essential to preventing entrepreneurial or managerial elites.

[5] Tracy Kidder, *Soul of a New Machine* (Boston: Little, Brown, 1981).
[6] Gifford Pinchot, personal communication.

However, self-selection must be accepted: Teams often form because their members enjoy working together on a project. This also achieves further decentralization.

Managing informality. Large and complex organizations must constantly search for ways to short-circuit red tape. "Skunkworks" and "bootlegging" are some recent images that found a place in the management literature. These suggest an informal underground or internal network that provides access to information and resources outside the formal organization. Such approaches require sophisticated interpersonal skills and a high degree of collegiality. A great deal of trust is required to give people such free rein.

Preserving informality means taking the time to do so. Creative thinking does not come about in a hurried, high pressured environment. It involves the conscious effort to take time, through mechanisms of retreats or protected environments referred to by some in the literature as "reservations." For example, Activision protected its creative designers in enclaves and insulated them from day-to-day business and organizational pressures. It based this decision on the assumption that creativity flourished in isolation from "business-as-usual" attitudes.

Human resource management. Internal entrepreneurship and innovation ultimately depend on good people who attract more good people. Whether internally developed or brought in, strategies to motivate, attract, and keep these people must be put into practice. Prioritizing rewards in terms of hard (money and perks) and soft (fun and challenge) elements is an important, company-specific task.

Lateral mobility and an internal free market to pursue opportunities also maintain flexibility in the people inventory within the organization. Attention to job design, career path planning, and human resource strategy all contribute to this objective.

Human resource issues must be considered at every stage: recruiting, assimilating, appraising, promoting, and training must all support company goals. HRM's importance also lies in developing and maintaining performance criteria which support company values and provide operational linkages with organizational strategy.

THE CASES

American Express TRS Company and Lou Gerstner

The American Express Travel Related Services (TRS) Company has placed entrepreneurship at the center of its current corporate philosophy, which is reflected in how it manages people and generates new ideas; it has decreased the complexity of many procedures involving people management and resource allocation. The case provides a rich opportunity for looking at a number of important issues such as: the significance of the leadership role of the CEO, Lou Gerstner, in making new things happen; the unique effects of size, complexity, and tradition on entrepreneurial and creative activity; and the key ingredients by which entrepreneurship is fostered at American Express. Discussion analyzes how successful TRS has been in cultivating entrepreneurs and considers if this method is applicable in other industries.

Jerry Welsh, Beth Horowitz, and Teri Williams: The Entrepreneurial Middle Manager at American Express

In these cases, American Express is examined from two other levels in the company. Jerry Welsh is an executive vice president at TRS in charge of the Worldwide Marketing and Communications department. Seen as a symbol of corporate intrapreneurship at American Express, he is considered a champion of new ideas. Discussion will explore the basis for his success, how he gets things done, and the nature of his relationship with the rest of the organization.

On another level, the Beth Horowitz and Teri Williams cases give the perspective of recent MBAs new to TRS to explore whether the organization is really entrepreneurial and creative for the talented new employees, and how one makes a difference at this level.

Scandinavian Airlines System

This case presents the history of Scandinavian Airlines System (SAS). SAS was heading for financial disaster until Jan Carlzon became president. He is regarded as a master turnaround artist who breathed new life and entrepreneurial energy into a bureaucratic company with many obstacles in its path, including heavy government influence, and a social system that not only makes personal financial rewards difficult to attain but which imposes stiff regulations on companies, significantly increasing their costs.

Nonetheless, SAS has developed a new entrepreneurial attitude—a primary factor accounting for its current position as the number one business airline in Europe. Morale, operating performance, and financial results have all improved under Carlzon's leadership. His role—instilling a new sense of entrepreneurial culture at SAS—is examined in such terms as personal style, charisma, and communication of leadership. Also, the tools used to effect change and to market a new sense of what he called Cultural Revolution at "The SAS" are evaluated. Discussion explores how the SAS organization changed under Carlzon, future issues, and the transferability of these lessons to other companies.

FOR FURTHER READING

BRANDT, STEVEN, *Entrepreneuring in Established Companies*. Homewood, Ill.: Dow-Jones-Irwin, 1986.

BURGELMAN, ROBERT A. and LEONARD R. SAYLES, *Inside Corporate Innovation*. New York: The Free Press, 1986.

CARLZON, JAN, *Moments of Truth*. Cambridge, Mass.: Ballinger Publishing Company, 1987.

KANTER, ROSABETH MOSS, *The Change Masters*. New York: Simon and Schuster, 1983.

NAYAK, P. RANGANATH and JOHN M. KETTERINGHAM, *Breakthroughs*. New York: Rawson Associates, 1986.

STEVENSON, HOWARD and JOSE TARRILLO-MASSI, "Preserving Entrepreneurship As Companies Grow", *Journal of Business Strategy*. Vol. 7, No. 1, 1986.

WEBER, MAX, *The Theory of Social and Economic Organization*. New York: Oxford University Press, 1947.

American Express Travel Related Services Company

In April 1985, American Express Company was enjoying a renewed spirit of corporate entrepreneurship, and performance had been impressive by almost any measure. It continued to do an outstanding job of positioning its products and services in the consumer's mind. A 1984 survey by *American Banker* revealed that people rated American Express products and services higher than those of any other financial services firm in the United States.

American Express Travel Related Services Company Inc. (TRS) was that part of the American Express Company involved in the company's traditional businesses of charge cards, travelers cheques, and travel. It was a substantial business by any measure, with more than 33,000 employees throughout the world. In 1984 its net income was $387 million on revenues of $3.62 billion. This represented 63 percent of American Express's corporate net income. TRS engaged in a wide range of activity. It was composed of five fully integrated international units—Canada, Asia/Pacific/Australia, Europe/Middle East/Africa, Latin America, and Japan—and two domestic divisions: Payment Systems, which was responsible for U.S. travelers cheque and money order activities; and Travel Services, which encompassed vacation and leisure travel, corporate and card travel, and ancillary travel related businesses; (American Express Publishing Corporation, which published *Travel and Leisure* magazine and *Food and Wine* magazine, Merchandise Sales, and Incentive Travel). TRS also owned about two-thirds of First Data Resources, based in Omaha, which engaged in transaction processing, chiefly for banks.

The output of TRS read like a business edition of the *Guiness Book of World Records*. Cards-in-Force passed 20 million in 1984, up 17 percent from 1983. In 1984 the American Express Card was issued in 28 currencies, including newly issued Korean won and Danish kroner cards. The Gold Card was available in 16 countries and carried by four million people. Customer spending on the card in 1984 was $47.6 billion. Over one million establishments accepted the American Express Card. The public purchased $15.1 billion worth of travelers cheques in 1984, up 9.1 percent from 1983; travelers cheques outstanding amounted to $2.6 billion, up 8.1 percent over 1983. TRS processed the clearing and payment on 367.5 million travelers

This case was prepared by Associate Professor John Kao.

cheques worldwide. American Express Travelers Cheques were sold through more than 89,000 outlets worldwide. Business-related travel sales were the responsibility of TRS's Travel Management Services (TMS) division; they increased 23 percent over 1983. TRS' publishing activities also prospered. Ad sales in *Travel and Leisure* grew 23 percent over 1983; paid subscribers numbered 975,000. *Food and Wine*'s paid subscriptions rose to 600,000, and sales increased 18 percent from 1983. TRS' worldwide network of travel offices grew to 1,200. Total Express Cash locations neared 4,000. And TRS had become the United States' largest wholesaler and retailer of package tours.

In 1979 TRS set aggressive financial targets: to grow its earnings at a compounded rate of 15–20 percent a year and to maintain an ROE of about 20–25 percent after tax. This had to be achieved without milking the business but while investing for the future. It required TRS to become the low-cost producer of each of its businesses, conducting marketing programs that both expanded the existing market and protected against competitive attack.

In fact, the rate of earnings growth surpassed 15–20 percent. In the first quarter of 1984, earnings were up 40 percent. TRS' ROE was 25 percent after tax for the past three years. It continued to invest in productivity. For example, $40 million were put into a new processing center for travelers cheques. In 1984 TRS spent $150 million on new investments; at the same time earnings grew by 28 percent.

To gain insight into its performance, TRS compared itself with other companies. It looked at all publicly held companies in the United States with $150 million earnings in 1979, 20 percent compounded earnings growth, and at least 15 percent annual growth. The resulting list included TRS and two other companies. Then TRS looked at companies with a 20 percent or better ROE. This time the list contained nine companies, including TRS. Only TRS met them all in the two sets of criteria.

These achievements were all the more noteworthy in light of current industry conditions. For example, *Fortune* in 1978 spoke of the card business as a maturing one: "American Express cards and travelers cheques are coming under attack. [There may be nothing] that can lessen the impact of all the new competition." Yet card net income increased nearly 300 percent in five years and Cards-in-Force doubled in five years. In travelers cheques, American Express faced 30 new competitors—firms with the strength to commit the required financial and human resources. Many were banks that had served as TRS' cheque-distribution system.

TRS attributed its success to its entrepreneurial spirit as seen in new products, services, marketing campaigns, and approaches to company development. Lou Gerstner, chairman and CEO of TRS, compared its performance to the runner breaking the four-minute mile. New questions arose: What would come next? What would be the effect of the competition, who had been inspired by TRS' success to greater efforts? In April 1985 American Express TRS stood poised for new challenges.

COMPANY HISTORY

American Express was created on March 18, 1850 through a merger of three large express firms: Butterfield, Wasson & Co.; Livingston and Fargo; and Wells and Company. Wells and Fargo are also known as founders of the famous Wells Fargo Company which, with American Express, created supply and communications links to California during the gold rush. The rise of American Express was thus linked to the headlong expansion of the United States westward during the late nineteenth century. Early express-men linked the East Coast with the expanding frontier through a variety of transportation and communication services.

The company's activities expanded rapidly: It developed foreign freight, travel, and other financial services. In 1882 it established an express money-order system to facilitate funds transfer. These instruments were issued at any company office and could be cashed at the point of delivery. If they were lost or stolen, the purchaser received a refund. Money orders were sorely needed because of the dangers of loss and theft. In fact, it was 1882 when the infamous Jesse James was finally brought to a halt. The need was also confirmed by the service's overnight success: Nearly 12,000 money orders were sold in the first six weeks of service. The company also expanded into handling foreign remittances in part in response to the demand from a new wave of immigrants wishing to send money to their families and creditors in the old countries. Foreign freight activities paralleled the rise of the United States as an exporting nation.

The company invented the travelers cheque in 1891. James Fargo, then its president, said, "It should be better than dollar bills, so that if lost or stolen, the owner would get his money refunded." Because travelers also sought a wide variety of information and support services at American Express offices besides financial transactions, the company also established a travel-information service, although it had not intended to enter the travel business at all. Fargo had stated, "I will not have gangs of trippers starting off in carabancs from in front of our offices . . . There is no profit in the tourist business, and even if there were, this company would not undertake it." Nevertheless, American Express' travel business did develop in response to demand, and a national news magazine called the company "the benevolent protector of Americans everywhere." The company took its mission very seriously. Ralph Reed, company president in the early 1950s, stated: "Throughout the world, American Express has become a symbol of the American way of life and affords the peoples of virtually all free nations an opportunity to see a typical American firm in action. . . . If by carrying the message of American democracy across the seas, American Express contributes in some measure to the spread of democratic concepts, we will be satisfied that we have lived up to our heritage from the past."

By early 1985 American Express had achieved an enviable position in the financial service industry. Dun's *Business Month* named it one of the country's five best-managed companies, based on its "bold, risk-taking thrusts into new markets . . . singular vision and an aggressive resolve to get there." Analysts described it as "unquestionably the premier company in the financial services industry."

Among its major businesses in addition to TRS were the $520 million Swiss-based Trade Development Bank Holdings S.A., active in foreign exchange, precious metals, and correspondent banking; the Fireman's Fund Insurance Company, one of United States' major property and liability underwriters and a life insurance company; IDS Financial Services, a Minneapolis-based organization specializing in financial planning that was acquired for $727 million in 1983; and Lehman Brothers Kuhn Loeb, a major investment banking firm acquired in 1984 for $360 million. It also owned a 50% interest with Warner Communications in Warner Amex Cable Communications. See *Exhibit 1* for a broad overview of the American Express Company organization.

In 1984 American Express earned $610 million on revenues of $12.9 billion. (See *Exhibits 2-4* for financial data.) The evolving mix of products and services created many new opportunities for what James Robinson, its chairman and CEO, called "cross-selling." The company happily anticipated a move to a new 51-story corporate headquarters, the American Express Tower, which would be the largest of four structures in the new World Financial Center in lower Manhattan.

THE INDUSTRY

In the mid-1980s, the financial services industry was characterized by volatility and change. The 1982 American Express annual report acknowledged these trends: "Profound changes are sweeping through the consumer financial marketplace and the institutions serving it. The combination of economic volatility, technological advances, and the deregulation of U.S. financial institutions is resulting in significant changes in the way companies and individuals manage their assets."

Even the definition of the financial services industry had evolved far beyond the limits of banking, insurance, and brokerage activity. Competition was keener and feedback from the marketplace more rapid. Lou Gerstner, chairman of TRS, remarked that American Express, with its innovations, created its own competition. The transformation of the regulatory environment and the dimensions of competition was accompanied by a profound change in the whole concept of service for such businesses. The company also had to consider maturation and saturation in such markets as the domestic travel-and-entertainment card business. The level and mix of services were seen as the only way to differentiate products in this area. Robinson explained: "What it all means is that a consumer or institution can enter American Express through one of many doors. Once there, you have access to an array of high-quality products and services that respond to your specific needs. As your needs change, we can grow with you." These thoughts were restated by Gerstner, who felt that service at American Express should feel like a huge mom and pop drugstore.

Certainly, competition in TRS' traditional card business was heating up. An estimated 42 percent of the American public had at least one credit card by the end of 1984. In that year, for example, Visa and Mastercard boasted of 130 million cards in force in the United States (about 195 million worldwide) that were accepted at some 2.3 million U.S. and 3.7 million establishments worldwide. And they had established prestige cards to compete with the American Express Gold Card.

Competing card services were aggressively marketed. In 1984 Wells Fargo Bank began giving its card customers Wells Dollars—one Wells Dollar for each $5 they charged—redeemable for discount catalogue merchandise.

One observer described deregulation of the financial services industry as "the cork coming out of the bottle." For example, traditional banking institutions were looking for diversification and offering different kinds of products to create interstate networks and to form broad alliances with money market funds and with American Express itself.

These competitive pressures led to the industry's growing awareness of the importance of creativity and innovation.

NEW INITIATIVES AT TRS

The recent history of TRS has been described as "dogged determination" to say "no" to the prospects of low growth. Large-scale investment, innovative marketing programs, and new and risky marketing initiatives in its traditional businesses paid off. These included such innovations in marketing the American Express Card as cause-related marketing, women's marketing, and graduating-students programs. Another example was an investment in a $40 million Travelers Cheque Operating Center in Salt Lake City when the travelers cheque business was described by one manager as "at its nadir."

In response to its new operating environment, TRS created a host of service innovations:

The platinum card. This was the first new charge card the company has introduced since 1966, when it began offering the Gold Card. The Platinum Card offered a wide range of services for card members who traveled and entertained frequently, including nonresident membership in private clubs throughout the world, check-cashing privileges of up to $10,000 a week at American Express Travel Service offices, a year-end summary of charges, a choice of billing dates, a special 24-hour personalized travel service, and personalized travel arrangements. It was available by invitation only to U.S. and Canadian card members who had at least two years of card membership, a good payment record, and charges averaging at least $10,000 a year. The annual fee for the card was $250. It was recently chosen by *Fortune* as one of its "products of the year."

Cause-related marketing.   This innovative marketing program that tied the use of TRS products and services to charitable donations supported more than 50 causes in the United States and abroad, including the San Jose Symphony Orchestra, Dallas Ballet, Fort Lauderdale Symphony, Cape Hatteras Lighthouse, Greater Miami Opera, Lincoln Park Zoo in Chicago, Mount Vernon Ladies Association, Tulsa Ballet, Duke of Edinburgh Awards in the United Kingdom, and the National Olympic committees of Sweden, Spain, the United Kingdom, Ireland, Brazil, Mexico, Japan, Australia, and Argentina. In a *Wall Street Journal* article, Jerry Walsh, an EVP and the concept's originator, described this campaign: "The wave of the future isn't checkbook philanthropy. It's a marriage of corporate marketing and social responsibility."

Gerstner commented that cause-related marketing motivated companies to do more for worthwhile social and cultural projects. "At first, we didn't know whether we'd found a new way to help business or just an interesting formula for giving money away. It's both. The increase in business we've seen in our cause-related markets proves the concept is as successful as any marketing program we've ever tried. We're doing good deeds, and we're also pleased with the commercial results." He also placed cause-related marketing into the context of "new directions in corporate citizenship [which] have to do with infusing a keen sense of public responsibility into every major corporate activity, from personnel to marketing to training. . . . What I'm advocating is an expansive view of business as a generous, caring citizen of the community."

Statue of Liberty campaign.   In October 1983, TRS launched the first nationwide cause-related marketing program (see *Exhibit 5*). For three months TRS donated one penny for every card transaction and one dollar for each new card member toward the restoration of the Statue of Liberty. TRS also contributed for each travel package valued at $500 or more (excluding airfare) and each purchase of travelers cheques.

The results for the statue and TRS were significant. The campaign raised $1.7 million for the statue. More significantly, *The Wall Street Journal* of June 21, 1984 reported that card usage increased 28 percent during the promotion period (compared to the corresponding period the year before) and new card applications (through a network of "Take One" application dispensers) increased by more than 45 percent (compared to the year before). Moreover, the card business had its best fourth quarter ever during this period.

The campaign was highly visible. Some 66 percent of card members were aware of the restoration, 40 percent (or 60 percent of those aware of the restoration) associated it with American Express, and 3 percent (or 7.5 percent of those aware of the restoration) said the program caused them to increase spending. This 3 percent translated into 300,000 card members.

Senior TRS management used the process by which the project was approved as an illustration of its new approach to entrepreneurial decision making. Its approval was said to have taken five minutes over lunch and to have required not a single piece of paper. Perhaps even more striking, it went from approval to launch in nine weeks.

Corporate card/TMS.   Traditionally, the American Express Corporate Card was a personal credit card issued a corporation's traveling employees that was supported by some additional MIS services. In 1982 Gerstner changed this concept in a way that, as one TRS manager said, went "against all advice and conventional wisdom." He took the Corporate Card out of the Card Division and put it into the Travel Division to create the TMS concept. TMS (Travel Management System) was a front-end to back-end system for corporations and smaller businesses to manage more efficiently the more than $80 billion they spent annually on travel and entertainment. TMS required a network of 22 Business Travel Centers in the United States that were equipped with state-of-the-art technology and electronically linked to one another. The TMS product was unique and a striking success. For example, in 1983–1985 it outsold its larger competitor nine times out of ten in head-to-head competition for the business of major corporations.

American Express card marketing.   In 1980, analysts stated that the American Express Personal Card in the United States was a mature business. Furthermore, the impending introduction of so-called "premium cards" by banks would mean inevitable erosion of market share for American Express. But the analysts were wrong. American Express continued to experience over 20 percent new-card growth in 1983 and 1984. What insiders called the "monomaniacal" search for growth in card use in a market described as mature was one example of American Express's entrepreneurial spirit and current management style.

Campaign to recruit women card members.   By year-end 1984, 28 percent of American Express card members were women, up from 10 percent in the 1970s; one in three new card applicants was a woman. TRS pitched the card to women through the "Interesting Lives" campaign. It prompted Gloria Steinem to say, "When new creativity is necessary, it shouldn't reverse roles and show winning at the expense of men. American Express, one of the best examples of previously male creativity that now makes women feel welcome and invited, knew this up front." The ads showed women leading "interesting lives" in many areas: the expert skier with a baby; the career woman traveling for business and taking her scuba equipment with her; two women engineers talking business over lunch.

Campaign to recruit college students.   To extend its message to this large but difficult-to-reach market, American Express designed a marketing strategy aimed at graduating college seniors. Those seniors with the promise of a career-oriented job paying over $10,000 a year could qualify for an American Express Card (even with no previous credit history). Combining special events, college newspaper ads, specially targeted direct-mail pieces, posters, and kiosk displays, American Express signed up over half a million card members from 1976 to 1984. During 1984 alone, the number of new cards issued to graduating college seniors increased 58 percent over 1983's total.

ENTREPRENEURSHIP AT TRS

Entrepreneurship became an increasingly visible concern at American Express. Its 1984 annual report identified entrepreneurship, quality, and integrity as part of its basic principles and saw the 21 percent compounded annual growth rate in net income that TRS enjoyed since 1979 as a "fine example of internal development and entrepreneurship." Robinson wrote in the annual report, "Entrepreneurship is important because in today's world we have to constantly look for changes in the marketplace that create opportunities for new products and services." The people of American Express closest to the marketplace would respond to those opportunities; the best ideas did not always come from the top. Gerstner stated that, "Increased competitive threats on the one hand and the need to expand rapidly or start up totally new business efforts [were] tailor-made for the entrepreneurial solution with its emphasis on aggressiveness, initiative, and bold action."

The striking level of TRS' product and service innovation was attributed to the development of an entrepreneurial culture. Welsh called this an officially sponsored counterculture, dragging into the future those who wanted to play. The entrepreneurial culture involved reconciling two spirits and styles that seemed naturally to conflict: the well-organized, carefully planned corporate style and the freewheeling style of the classic entrepreneur. TRS' culture was a continuum of values ranging from control, predictability, and ordliness to flexibility, individual initiative, and diversity.

Gerstner identified three major ways in which TRS fostered entrepreneurship.

> First, in the area of corporate culture, we began to send the message throughout the organization and to the outside world where we were recruiting that ours was a business environment which welcomed outstanding performers—even if their business backgrounds and styles were unconventional to the corporate world. We did this in ways ranging from speeches from me to very well-conceived recruitment presentations in which we warned prospective employees that Travel Related Services at American Express was an exciting place to work, but a place in which one's career was far from guaranteed. We confessed openly that we were not interested in structured training programs for new employees; nor were we interested in well-defined, predictable career paths which laid out one's career throughout years of virtually guaranteed employment.
>
> Second, we began to take risks with some very unconventional appointments . . . [which] sent a strong message to the organization and to the business world outside. That message was that we were going to sacrifice conventional qualifications and conventional organizational principles to the higher value of exercising and rewarding talent.

Third, we initiated and supported bold unconventional moves in the businesses. For example, we formed joint ventures with leading banks in the U.K. and France. American Express had never given up equity in one of its base businesses before, but this program was strategically sound and a bold competitive program. We committed tens of millions of dollars to create a T&E card market in Japan—a market that could be our second largest in five years. We merged our corporate-card and corporate travel activities to create a unique family of products that only American Express can offer corporations in controlling the billions of dollars they spend on business travel and entertainment.

Entrepreneurship at TRS was a double-edged sword: desirable because of competitive pressures and a problem because it could disrupt the orderly planning and implementation of a well-run business. But there was value in sacrificing conventional qualifications and organizational principles: the higher value of exercising and rewarding talent. Gerstner said:

> Invariably the entrepreneurial culture existing alongside the more traditional ones will, especially in the beginning, cause tension. I believe, however, that this tension can be channeled in very constructive and creative ways, for example in ways which produce feelings that the entrepreneurs and the more traditional management elements are both indispensible parts of a stronger, unified whole, or simply put, each group can feel that it is the necessary savior of the other.

Entrepreneurship at TRS also extended to the management of other companies. For example, it bought a small company earnings were growing at a 40 percent compounded annual rate. TRS structured a management incentive and environment in which the entrepreneurs who built it could continue to thrive. The company continued to grow at the same 40 percent rate in the first four years TRS owned it. In 1984, TRS sold 25 percent to the founders and the public. In doing so, it created a new incentive system for the entrepreneurs and increased the value of its investment.

Lou Gerstner

Born in 1942 in New York, Gerstner graduated from Dartmouth College in 1963 and then received a Harvard MBA in 1965. He spent 12 years at McKinsey and then joined American Express in 1978 as president of the card division. In 1979 he became CEO of American Express Travel Related Services. In 1981 he became vice chairman of the board of American Express Company. In 1983 he was named chairman of the executive committee of American Express Company.

Gerstner spoke of his style as both managerial and as a stimulus to entrepreneurship. He said that his task was to leaven necessary structure with centers of entrepreneurship led by people able to conceptualize change before other people could, who had the drive and energy to marshal resources to take advantage of that change, and who not only were willing to take the risk but love it. His management style is further described in the case "Lou Gerstner."

Jerry Welsh

The business press described Jerry Welsh as "American Express Company's blue-ribbon bet for the man most likely to dream up the next great financial services marketing idea." A marathoner, he was born in Kansas, served in the Army, and went through Officers Candidate School where he received advanced training in Slavic languages. He then spent ten years teaching Russian language and literature and doing experimental educational programs at a number of colleges, mostly in Tennessee. But the winds of a career change were in the air. As he put it, "When you made $18 thousand per year and had three children, you knew it wasn't going to fly for long." Welsh came up with a travel idea for organizing travel tours with an academic flavor to take advantage of new markets. He was unfamiliar with the business system. So in 1975 he asked a friend for some advice on where to find the appropriate travel company. The friend suggested American Express. Welsh pitched the idea there, and TRS acquired both the idea and Welsh.

Steps on his career included director of the Travel Division (1975) and director of special projects. He worked in the Card Division but left in 1980. In 1982 he became senior vice president for U.S. marketing, with responsibility for consumer products. He said he was "tired of the rap of being different, of being a conversation piece" and wanted to develop his track record. In 1984 he was EVP of worldwide marketing and communications. This was a post created for him; he was its first, and possibly only, occupant. He coordinated the activities of more than 30 marketing organizations worldwide and was responsible for worldwide advertising and promotion of all travel-related products, including the American Express Card. He was the originator of such campaigns as cause-related marketing and "interesting lives." He was a champion of the concept of managed entrepreneurship.

Exhibit 1 Organization Chart

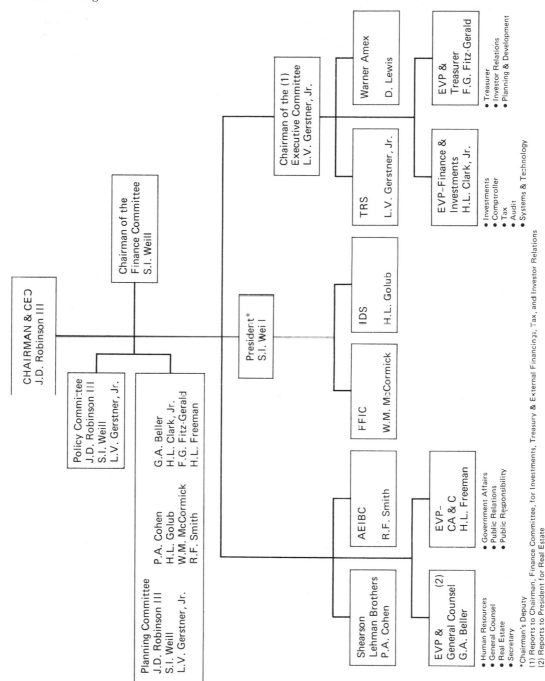

Exhibit 2 Consolidated Five-Year Summary of Selected Financial Data* American Express Company (millions, except per share amounts and where italicized)

	1984	1983	1982	1981	1980
Operating Results					
Revenues	$12,895	$ 9,770	$ 8,093	$ 7,291	$ 6,426
Percent increase in revenues	*32%*	*21%*	*11%*	*13%*	*26%*
Expenses	12,159	9,253	7,339	6,586	5,830
Income taxes	126	2	173	181	130
Net Income	610	515	581	524	466
Percent increase (decrease) in net income	*18%*	*(11)%*	*11%*	*12%*	*23%*
Assets and Liabilities					
Time deposits	$ 5,470	$ 4,071	$ 2,127	$ 1,784	$ 1,120
Investment securities:					
Carried at cost	13,449	12,766	7,163	6,446	6,026
Carried at lower of aggregate cost or market	315	211	81	148	166
Carried at market	8,566	1,709	948	917	1,235
Accounts receivable and accrued interest, net	14,802	11,497	9,204	8,191	6,825
Loans and discounts, net	7,089	6,642	4,379	3,929	3,811
Total assets	61,848	43,981	28,311	25,252	22,731
Customers' deposits and credit balances	13,262	12,511	6,810	6,218	5,818
Travelers Cheques outstanding	2,454	2,362	2,177	2,468	2,542
Insurance and annuity reserves	8,831	7,667	4,323	4,110	3,856
Long-term debt	3,839	2,643	1,798	1,293	1,293
Shareholders' equity	4,607	4,043	3,039	2,661	2,430
Common Share Statistics					
Net income per share	$ 2.79	$ 2.53	$ 3.02	$ 2.79	$ 2.59
Cash dividends per share	$ 1.28	$ 1.26	$ 1.125	$ 1.025	$ 1.00
Average number of shares outstanding	217	203	192	188	180
Shares outstanding at year end	217	213	191	188	185
Number of shareholders of record	*51,211*	*45,753*	*36,580*	*36,611*	*34,735*
Other Statistics					
Number of employees at year end					
United States	*59,420*	*53,740*	*48,533*	*43,315*	*39,475*
Outside United States	*17,027*	*16,716*	*15,472*	*14,994*	*15,556*
Total	*76,447*	*70,456*	*64,005*	*58,309*	*55,031*
Number of offices at year end					
American Express offices worldwide	*1,472*	*1,356*	*1,160*	*1,066*	*1,046*
Representative offices	*810*	*797*	*760*	*782*	*782*
Total	*2,282*	*2,153*	*1,920*	*1,848*	*1,828*

* Operating results for the year ended December 31, 1983 do not include the effect of the acquisition of Investors Diversified Services, Inc., accounted for as a purchase as of December 31, 1983. Where applicable, amounts and percentages for 1984 include the effect of the acquisition of Lehman Brothers Kuhn Loeb Holding Co., Inc., accounted for as a purchase as of May 11, 1984.

Exhibit 3

1984

	Travel Related Services	International Banking Services	Investment Services	IDS Financial Services	Insurance Services	Other and Corporate	Adjustments and Eliminations	Consolidated
Revenues	$ 3,620	$ 1,548	$ 2,280	$1,576	$4,025	$ 82	$ (236)	$12,895
Pretax income (loss) before general corporate expenses	$ 625	$ 193	$ 168	$ 95	$ (114)	$ 16	$ (18)	$ 965
General corporate expenses						(229)	—	(229)
Pretax income (loss)	$ 625	$ 193	$ 168	$ 95	$ (114)	$ (213)	$ (18)	$ 736
Net income	$ 387	$ 156	$ 103	$ 62	$ 43	$ (125)	$ (16)	$ 610
Assets	$12,542	$13,768	$22,735	$6,411	$7,735	$1,239	$(2,582)	$61,848

Insurance Services comprises the following:

	Property-Liability			Total	Life and Other	Insurance Services
	Commercial Lines	Personal Lines	Investment Income			
Revenues	$ 2,017	$ 817	$ 429	$3,263	$ 762	$ 4,025
Pretax income (loss)	$ (558)	$ (40)	$ 404	$ (194)	$ 80	$ (114)

1983

	Travel Related Services	International Banking Services	Investment Services	IDS Financial Services	Insurance Services	Other and Corporate	Adjustments and Eliminations	Consolidated
Revenues	$ 2,889	$ 1,437	$ 1,826	—	$3,784	$ (6)	$ (160)	$ 9,770
Pretax income (loss) before general corporate expenses	$ 445	$ 183	$ 326	—	$ (242)	$ (17)	$ (10)	$ 685
General corporate expenses						(168)	—	(168)
Pretax income (loss)	$ 445	$ 183	$ 326	—	$ (242)	$ (185)	$ (10)	$ 517
Net income	$ 301	$ 136	$ 175	—	$ 30	$ (117)	$ (10)	$ 515
Assets	$10,226	$13,287	$ 9,060	$5,410	$7,057	$1,095	$(2,154)	$43,981

Exhibit 3 (*Continued*)

1984	Travel Related Services	International Banking Services	IDS Financial Services	Insurance Services	Other and Corporate	Adjustments and Eliminations	Consolidated

Insurance Services comprises the following:

	Property-Liability				Life and Other	Total Insurance Services
	Commercial Lines	Personal Lines	Investment Income	Total		
Revenues	$ 1,925	$ 783	$ 437	$3,145	$ 639	$ 3,784
Pretax income (loss)	$ (609)	$ (95)	$ 452	$ (252)	$ 10	$ (242)

1982	Travel Related Services	International Banking Services	IDS Financial Services	Insurance Services	Other and Corporate	Adjustments and Eliminations	Consolidated
Revenues	$ 2,516	$ 1,025	$ 1,318	$3,356	$ 14	$ (136)	$ 8,093
Pretax income before general corporate expenses	$ 363	$ 101	$ 228	$ 220	$ (5)	—	$ 907
General corporate expenses	—	—			(153)	—	(153)
Pretax income (loss)	$ 363	$ 101	$ 228	$ 220	$ (158)	—	$ 754
Net income	$ 247	$ 60	$ 124	$ 244	$ (94)	—	$ 581
Assets	$ 8,445	$ 7,681	$ 6,351	$6,513	$ 784	$(1,463)	$28,311

Insurance Services comprises the following:

	Property-Liability				Life and Other	Total Insurance Services
	Commercial Lines	Personal Lines	Investment Income	Total		
Revenues	$ 1,947	$ 640	$ 348	$2,935	$ 421	$ 3,356
Pretax income (loss)	$ (95)	$ (22)	$ 328	$ 211	$ 9	$ 220

Exhibit 4 Consolidated Statement of Income American Express Company (millions, except per share amounts)

	1984	1983	1982
Year Ended December 31,			
Revenues			
Commissions and fees	$ 4,814	$4,037	$3,235
Interest and dividends	3,291	2,227	1,759
Property-liability premiums	2,834	2,665	2,553
Annuity premiums	739	43	34
Life insurance premiums	798	535	345
Other	419	263	167
Total	12,895	9,770	8,093
Expenses			
Provisions for losses and benefits:			
Property-liability insurance	2,142	1,966	1,491
Annuities	1,018	31	27
Life insurance	609	401	243
Investment certificates	104	—	—
Banking, credit, financial paper and other	479	402	358
Compensation and employee benefits	2,260	1,933	1,591
Interest	2,104	1,526	1,196
Occupancy and equipment	656	530	436
Commissions and brokerage	509	521	440
Advertising and promotion	490	384	313
Communications	383	315	270
Taxes other than income taxes	269	237	188
Claims adjustment services	171	236	145
Financial paper, forms and other printed matter	150	120	117
Other	815	651	524
Total	12,159	9,253	7,339
Pretax income	736	517	754
Income tax provision	126	2	173
Net income	$ 610	$ 515	$ 581
Net income per share	$ 2.79	$ 2.53	$ 3.02

See notes to consolidated financial statements.

Exhibit 5

In Addition To All The Logical Reasons For Using The American Express Card, There Is Now One That Is Unabashedly Sentimental

For 25 years now, American Express has been extolling all the eminently logical reasons why one should carry the American Express Card.

But now there is a reason that, while not based on logic, may prove to be the most compelling.

Coming to the aid of the Statue of Liberty.

For it, or rather she, stands as our greatest national symbol of freedom. That does not mean, however, that she stands free from the damage of time and the elements. And so, after almost one hundred years, she is now in urgent need of restoration.

To this end, American Express puts forward a proposition.

Each time you use the American Express Card until the end of this year, American Express will make a contribution to The Statue of Liberty—Ellis Island Foundation. That is, each time you use the Card for shopping, travel, entertainment, dining, or for any other reason, not only will you benefit, but so too will the Statue of Liberty.

While the contribution for each usage is a modest one cent, one can see that this penny, multiplied by millions, will result in a figure of which we can all be proud.

Further, for all of those who have not yet realized the logic of carrying the Card, American Express offers a further inducement: To honor each new Cardmember accepted, one dollar will be given as a donation to the Statue.

One dollar will also be donated when you book a selected travel package from an American Express Vacation Store. And, finally, a penny will also go to the Statue for each purchase of American Express Travelers Cheques.

We believe this to be an exceptionally fitting solution to a very pressing problem.

For, while it is she who stands for all of us, it seems a most auspicious moment to show that all of us truly stand behind her.

The American Express Card.

For the sake of the Statue of Liberty—Don't leave home without it.

[Contributions made through this American Express program are not tax deductible.]

Lou Gerstner

Lou Gerstner, chairman of American Express Travel Related Services Company (TRS), settled into the plush seats of the American Express Gulfstream II as it taxied for takeoff at the Fort Lauderdale airport. Only an hour earlier, he had addressed a meeting of his division's star performing sales managers. Dressed conservatively in a grey suit and regimental tie, he had worked the crowd, quietly chatting with people in a personal fashion.

In his speech he had focused on several themes. The issue for the company, he said, was "redefining excellence." He stressed the importance of having each person at the company rise to new challenges, both personal and professional. Citing Roger Bannister and his triumph in breaking the four-minute mile, Gerstner had said, "We have no peers; we have done something unique. Now what? We must now set our own standards, explore new boundaries, develop new approaches, support the self-renewing persons who feel like they're always striving for the ultimate goal."

As the plane rose to cruising altitude, he reflected on the past and pondered the future. (The rest of the case is in his words.)

IN THE BEGINNING

Entrepreneurship is not something I set out to do at American Express. I don't think I ever said, "Well, I am going to become a corporate entrepreneur." But it may be that I started out with a management style and philosophy that one could subsequently look at and call entrepreneurial. Some of it goes back to my first twelve years of full-time work at McKinsey. It was a small company with almost no hierarchy, which placed an overriding premium on problem-solving and on people—whatever their level—with good ideas.

Another concept I learned then and continue to believe very strongly is: We all succeed together. If we do something right, there is plenty of credit to go around for everybody. A team of people working together to me is so powerful that it will always beat hands-down a group of uncoordinated individuals any day, even if the individuals are a bunch of all-stars.

This case was prepared by Associate Professor John Kao.

So I was influenced by the concept of how McKinsey worked, the supremacy of good ideas is an informal structure, and by the experience of twelve years trying to get tough problem-solving done in other companies where I observed —but was not part of—the infrastructure. I carried those experiences into American Express.

I remember going to early meetings at American Express where there were three or four levels of management present. Perhaps foolishly, I started behaving as I had at McKinsey. Somebody would ask a question or say something, and I would start probing around the table. Sometimes I would go to the third-level person and talk with him or her. Naively, I showed a disregard for the structural, inherent rigidity of the system. It seems that I shocked people some, and I had to back off a little bit. People would come to me and say, "Why did you do that? Why are you questioning my subordinates?" I started out with a distrust of formal bureaucracy and a positive attitude of "let's have relatively informal problem-solving." But I wasn't sitting around consciously thinking about a management style. That was just the way I developed, so I was practicing the only behavior I knew.

It finally became clear to me after a year or two in American Express that changing the organization was a lot harder to do than I had thought. My view had been that it would take me a year to get the basic elements in place and be ready to go. In fact it took four years. Early on it became clear to me that creating an environment in which change could occur fairly rapidly was very important.

The situation I found at American Express had several key features. First, a rigid organizational structure in which there was a high degree of internal competition among operating units—a lot of internal rivalry. I don't think it was different from a lot of other companies. Rivalry between new and old product lines is natural. Second, I found pockets of resistance to the idea that the world might change—very much an attitude of "We have done it this way for years and have been successful. Don't talk to us about new competitors." In our strategic planning, we identified competitors, but we didn't always reach an internalized sense of what was going on outside that told us what we should do inside. Perhaps this phenomenon was related to the great—almost unique—success the company had enjoyed over the years.

Related to this was an enormous amount of mythology in the management structure. "Why do we do this? We do it because we always did it that way." Or "We do it because the consumer wants it." Or "We just do it." But when you started to think "Well, what do you mean the consumer wants this? Which consumer? How often? Where?" the analysis just fell apart. It was clear to me that we needed to get more external focus on what we were all about.

As I indicated, one couldn't argue with our past success. The results had been good. On the other hand, if one looked back two or three years, it was becoming clear that growth was slowing down. The competitive environment was changing rapidly. The world was talking electronic fund transfer, cashless society. Because our current chairman, Jim Robinson, saw all these things, he brought me in to be a change agent. Hell, I was 35 years old. What else was I going to be? I was not going to preside over a status-quo approach to the business.

EFFECTING CHANGE

I did three basic things. We started rebuilding the strategy and direction of each of the businesses. It took us five years. Concurrently we broke down barriers between the units. We did this in a couple of ways. The first way was to reorganize, to force change by saying we no longer had the businesses that we had for 20 years and that we had to create new ones. Instead of saying we were in the card business or the travelers cheque business, we said that we were in the "consumer financial services" business. We put those two businesses together. Then we changed things again and became the payment systems division. Then we took our overseas groups and put them together in a geographic organization. I believe in organizational change. I don't do it just for the sake of doing it, but if you consistently and regularly change the home base and the way people view the world, they tend to think more externally than they do internally.

We did another equally important thing, which was to move managers across units. You better not denigrate one of the other product lines today, because you just may be there next week. Third (and this is a constant battle and never complete), I tried to create an affinity with TRS. We should all feel a part of that organization, even though we work in card, travelers cheque, or money order. I created this by changing our compensation system so that part of the bonus for all senior managers in TRS is based on TRS' total performance.

Another thing we have done is to build up a culture that focuses on performance and pays off for performance and not for a lot of other things that it used to pay off for. In one of the divisions, longevity had previously been important; in another the politics of being on the right team was. There was a value placed on moving quickly through jobs. "How quickly can I get to the next job?" as opposed to "What have I learned and what have I accomplished?" When I arrived the average time in a job was sometimes less than a year. If you were going to be in a job for only a year, how could you possibly show performance? How could you possibly develop subordinates? How could you possibly develop a sense of how you could do this job better than anyone else?

We had to find ways of reinforcing this culture of performance. I did it through promotions and by talking about what I thought was important. We also did it in the selection of a certain kind of people. But I don't think there is an easy answer on how one changes culture. A lot of individual feathers make a critical mass of feathers.

If the CEO isn't living and preaching the culture and isn't doing it consistently, then it just doesn't happen. This is a sine qua non—this is not a sufficient condition, but a necessary one. I have been running TRS for six years, and it took four years to get over the hump, onto the down slope, and feel the sense of some acceleration. Now we are in the wonderful period of reaping a few benefits of a lot of work by our senior management team.

You have first to decide what kind of a company you want to have. If you don't have a vision you believe, you can't achieve it. People just won't believe you and you won't communicate it effectively in everything you do.

When I first joined the company, I could personally address each of the major strategies of the business. I was involved in every strategy and even the substrategies. But this company has almost tripled in size since I got here. Its complexity has gone up exponentially. I have taken on more corporate responsibilities. I can no longer act—for good or bad—in a direct, hands-on way. One of the things that was very clear to me in the study of strategic planning back at McKinsey was that if you look at the creative input to any problem-solving, the real insights and important issues are set in the early stages of problem-solving, in the phrasing of the problem, in the assumptions you choose to make, in the research methodology you pick. In the early stages, problem-solving contains an enormous potential to create insight. As you move on, all you get served up are two or three options. The real range of options has been largely filtered out months earlier.

I have a regular set of what I call "shirt-sleeve sessions." I sit back with my senior team and we agree on programs for the year—not the long-term strategy, which is already set, but the key things we are going to get done this year, perhaps the uncertainties in our current strategy. Some of it is pure implementation and some is conceptual thinking. Then I schedule a series of meetings to deal with those issues. During the year, a couple more of them come up and we just schedule them on an ad hoc basis. The meetings usually last about three hours. I don't want tight, formal presentations for 55 minutes of every hour. They are not held in my office. I go down to the conference room of one of my division presidents. These are small groups, but they cut across the organization. We might have two or three levels represented, the people who know something about the problem, not those who have to be there just to be at the meeting. We discuss in a very tough, hard-nosed, and creative problem-solving fashion without people feeling that if I criticize the solution, I am criticizing the person who developed it. I am in effect selecting key issues and inserting myself very early in the process of discussion.

Let me tell you one of the things we do that I would guess a lot of corporations would not want to do. Let's say I have decided that it is time to have a very intensive three-day meeting on our card product line strategy. We will have been tracking a lot of our thinking for three or four years. A lot of people are involved. I feel it is time to pull the group together and spend three days in a "retreat house" and bang away on the issues. I know the people I want at that meeting. There will be a dozen or more people who will be upset that they are left out of this meeting. The more vocal of them will come into my office and say, "My career is over. Why have you done this to me?" That is a problem. I will say to them, "Look, I wanted to have a small meeting. I think that you make contributions in other areas. I do not think it is critical for you to be at this meeting. You are part of the senior management team, so as the results evolve from this process, you of course will participate in reviewing them to the extent that they impact your area of business. You will have a say in them. But this is an important brain-storming session and these are the people I want to have at the meeting."

I am trying to avoid the concept of reward being associated with these meetings. In the regular shirt-sleeve sessions that last three hours, I have consciously driven out the reward. They are tough, hard-nosed meetings. A lot of people come out of there wrung out; they do not see them as a reward.

Another aspect of project management is that I strictly avoid creating tsars. Let's say there is a strategic problem. The easy thing would be to take somebody, hired either from outside or internally, and say that he or she is going to be a staff person at headquarters. All of a sudden they will have five assistants and three vice presidents, and they want to be a senior vice president. They are going to be the "head" of this process. I don't want that. One of the things I learned at McKinsey is that the busiest people are those who can get the most work done. They are busy because they are good. I keep loading onto people who have full-time jobs.

I really believe that to be successful our group has to be candid, has to be able to speak frankly and openly to each other. I require staff work as a problem-solving process, but I don't think there is a problem of unleashing people's creativity if they trust each other and have a pretty good vision of what we are trying to do.

Part of what I did was to affirm that we were going to have growth and that we needed to find it, because there was an attitude here that growth was over. The perception of capacity for growth in the marketplace has a profound effect on your ability to operate entrepreneurially. The presence of a growth market permitted me to do a lot once we got things going. It provided a lot of the needed feedback, rewards, and resources.

Another issue has to do with a constant trade-off between discipline and entrepreneurship. In a company like ours, there is a need for both. My job is to manage these trade-offs. On the discipline side, there is no question that I am a reasonably autocratic driver of the organization when it comes to strategy. I set the strategic agenda here. I am not going to let this ship get off its course. Sure, I will let some people play around with it, and I will, I hope, even be prepared to be convinced that I am going off in a wrong direction. But we have a handful of priorities here, and tough discipline toward our goals is very important to me. Now within that, I am looking for people who are very creative in developing solutions or implementing tactical programs. Because we have been successful, because we have financial resources, we are able to take a risk on a Statue of Liberty program. It is still not easy. Let me tell you, if that had fallen on its face, it would have been in *Business Week*. There would have been a lot of people who would have asked, "What are you doing? You are spending all that money for this program?" I am not saying that success insulates you from second guessing. The people responsible for the failure wouldn't have been demoted, but their bonus wouldn't have been so big. They might not have been promoted as quickly to their next job. There is a cost of failure around here. But if they come up with a big, winning idea a year later, they would be back on track. It depends on the quality of the idea as it goes through our process. If the rest of us get excited about it, it's going to work. We will do it.

CHANGE AGENTS

There are different kinds of change agents. Jerry Welsh is perhaps an extreme. He has an enormously creative mind and thinks differently from most business people. He starts with a very different set of premises about the world. We don't have a lot of those people around. I am not sure we need a lot of them. But we have other kinds of change agents. We have people who are what I would call "china-breakers." They are bulls in the china shop. They have more conventional kinds of jobs than Jerry's. They are brilliant. They have strong convictions that we ought to do something in a certain way, but they are very tough on people. They tend to be tough on their peers. So you work at supporting those kinds of people, not getting rid of them. You say, "You turkey, why do you treat people that way?" But you don't fire them. You don't let the organization kill them.

Younger people come into an organization and think they want to be entrepreneurs. But being an entrepreneur is a skill; you don't just say I want to be an entrepreneur. It is like saying I would like to shoot golf in the low 70s. That is a nice objective, but you have to have some natural and some acquired capabilities. I am delighted with all the people who have come in with these feelings, but they are going to have to show two things. First, some insights, some brilliant ideas. Second, they are going to have to have the guts to stand up and say, "Hey, I want to do this, despite the costs and risks."

There are always costs. They come as much from one's own sense of self-worth and the willingness to take risks as from institutionally imposed ridicule or a slowing of one's career. There are pockets of structural rigidity in this company that I don't even know of at the entry levels. There have to be some. There have to be some people who still think that young kids are supposed to push pencils and nothing else. You can't get all of that out of an organization.

The conditions we need to permit the real entrepreneurs to perform are: (1) a growth mentality; (2) rewarding performance right down through the organization; and (3) not "shooting" people who come up with ideas that are unusual and have some risks associated with them. If someone is responsible for building a business, then he or she is supposed to generate some good ideas and is supposed to grow them. Where are these ideas coming from? How am I going to use them? People will start looking for bright people to work with them. They will start saying, "How can I come up with some home runs?"

The way to deal with the entry level is by flow of attention from the top. In some parts of our organization, I am convinced that this works. In other parts of the organization, somewhere along the way there may be a wall. The wall may be time-driven, in that we just haven't gotten to something yet. It may be time-independent in the case of somebody who just can't operate in this kind of an environment. I don't think that every young person who comes into this company is going to become an entrepreneur overnight. Many people who come into our company are going to find the structural, classical career path far more attractive and secure. We have those opportunities, too.

HUMAN RESOURCES

When I got here, the personnel function had a formal process of evaluation. It was process-bound and held in low regard. Someone would evaluate your performance but would never tell you what it was. Supervisors would fill out the forms and of course half the time "forget" to do it because the person above did not fill them out either. It was pure paperwork. What I have tried to do is energize this activity. We still have papers to fill out. It takes a lot of time to do it. But we try to develop a system of trust and value in the process that doesn't threaten either party. By definition it can be a threat. If I am evaluating your performance, that is not exactly a Sunday stroll. We have tried to reduce the stress to a minimum and keep constructive honesty in the forefront of the people evaluation process.

Performance appraisals get done in November–December, when I meet for three days with my senior management. We review the top 150 people in the company. We talk about them. The forms are there. We discuss their performance and their potential. We discuss their salary change for the year, their bonus, their long-term capital stock awards. Everything is implemented April 1. Everyone is supposed to sit down and communicate. There is a fair amount of structure. We talk about details. That person is good at something. How can we change the organization to take advantage of that person? I have at least four senior jobs in this company, in the top 15/20, that would not exist except for the people that are in them. And do you know what? The organization understands this. Would I ever replace Jerry Welsh in his job? Probably not. I don't have anybody who could operate like Jerry.

It works both ways. Take another of my entrepreneurs. It drives him crazy that I have him in a unique job, because he wants to be one of the other guys. You say to somebody, "Hey, I want you to play a unique role in this company. I am going to reward you. You are going to get resources. You are going to get invited to meetings. You are going to be this; you are going to be paid for that. Guess what? You are *not* going to have a classical job. You are not going to run a big empire." Now the person who takes the job may feel a little bit uncertain about that position.

There is still a management dichotomy in the company. There is still the classical, safe view of the world, which is that the jobs to have in the company are managing the big P&Ls where you can produce earnings increases every month, you have 4,000 people reporting to you, and you are a division president. If you think that I have been able to eradicate that, I haven't—and I don't want to. I need that kind of traditional drive for people who prefer a more traditional career path. So my task is not just in finding, protecting, and nourishing these nontraditional people in nontraditional roles, but also nourishing them in the sense of their being supported by the rest of the organization. I also have to keep supporting them in their own view of themselves. They do not have institutional safety nets. They have much more of a personal view. To be successful, they have to do two things. They have to maintain loyalty and goodwill—not just mine, but others'. Second, they have to produce tangible benefits that are of a nonrepetitive, non-status quo kind.

That is the hardest balance a CEO can deal with, because you can't run a company the size of TRS without some very sophisticated structure and systems. The issue constantly is: How do you keep the change agents? How do you protect that kind of cleansing, productive wind blowing through the corridors?

LOU GERSTNER'S ROLE

If I left American Express tomorrow, the kind of discipline that we have built into the organization would definitely carry forward for a number of years. But the entrepreneurial side of it could falter because of its inevitable dependence on relationships. The entrepreneur constantly needs to be regenerated, nurtured. By definition, entrepreneurship does not come out of structure; it is not systematic. It is heuristic, it happens. You have to make it happen every day. It could die, because the relationships and messages stop with me. Now the next person coming in might be similarly inclined, so they would start it up again, but they would have to reaffirm relationships or create new ones. And the organization would clearly test for some time whether that person really meant it.

I am the locus of a lot, if not most, of it in supporting or nurturing entrepreneurial behavior and seeing that it happens. I am not the entrepreneur in the classic and creative sense. I am not dreaming of the Statue of Liberty. I do not want to take credit for our entrepreneurial ideas, only for the entrepreneurial environment which helps produce and develop them.

I believe that Newton's First Law of Motion applies to everything we do. Things have momentum. You have to exert forces against momentum or you can't change direction. I think that the basic force within any organization of our size is toward the bureaucratic, safe approach. In large organizations, whether they are the government or the military, nonprofit organizations or profit-making companies, there is an inevitable process that leads toward rigidity, safe bets, nonrisk-taking. Therefore the process of being a corporate entrepreneur is a constant task of changing the direction of something moving in a different direction from yours. It is important to have a sense of drive, zeal, and mission. You've got to be out there creating an atmosphere of "can do." A great deal of my time is spent communicating this value—communicating it all the time, to all levels of management.

The biggest threat of entrepreneurship comes as the company grows to a size where my ability to intercede personally, both longitudinally and latitudinally, is limited. Four years ago I could reach down pretty close to the new recruits coming in. My message would be getting to their boss's boss if not their boss. Today, the levels between me and that first level are more numerous and more difficult to pass through. The new issue that I am now struggling with is: How do I create a team of corporate entrepreneurs? I do not want a team of individuals. How do I do that? Team work is one solution. My other concern is: How do I rethink the way I make use of my time? But the fundamental problem I face all the time is our size. Our growth and complexity are making it increasingly difficult for me to do something highly personalized. Some forces have been built into our system and structure which promote entrepreneurial behavior, but for the most part this was done by me personally.

I have been spending a lot of time marketing culture. If you believe that in the absence of strong continual pressure the organization will revert back over time, the marketing has to be constant and deep and wide.

The process is highly personal, in the sense that I am unable to articulate it completely. I can say what I want done, but I can't articulate how to do it. I can't do it for other people. I can't say, "Now look, I want you to be entrepreneurial. Here is what you are going to do; now read this book." My big challenge is how to maintain our momentum while the organization grows, without spending all my energies in the process.

I worry about how to keep things going as we get bigger. In my opinion, corporate entrepreneurship requires the presence and support of unconventional people. It is not easy to figure out where to find those people. Jim Robinson, the American Express chairman, has said to me on several occasions, "Go find a few more Jerry Welshes." I don't know how to do that in a systematic way.

I think it is important to recognize that entrepreneurs or entrepreneurial behavior don't always come in packages of creative brilliance. I am really talking about forms of nonstandard, creative behavior. I think you have to tolerate a lot of that in an organization. I have worked for some big companies where I was amazed at their lack of tolerance for aberrant behavior. You have to build a system that sends the message to the members of the organization that if you perform in an extraordinary fashion, you are allowed to be different. You don't have to abide by all the rules. There are certain rules that everybody has to abide by, but there are others that you don't have to abide by if you are an extraordinary performer in one dimension.

Human Resource Management at American Express Travel Related Services Company

One of Lou Gerstner's themes during his tenure at American Express was that the quality of its people was the most important influence on the company's success. This belief grew from a perception of Travel Related Services (TRS) as involved in creating and refining service concepts whose value was, in large part, emotional and human. He referred to this as the search for humanistic, "real" service that shows a person-to-person caring only partly captured by objective measurement and numbers-oriented management.

The mission of Human resources (HR) at TRS lay in implementing this belief through programs in the areas of training, management development, and recruiting.

The HR staff facilitated development planning in harmony with five goals that Lou Gerstner articulated in a company memo in 1981.

1. Fill each position with someone with outstanding personal and professional skills so that each new employee will outperform his or her predecessor.
2. Have a healthy mix of managers (that is, "fast trackers" and "old pros") at each level to provide for sound, orderly management continuity.
3. Provide each manager with a sense of challenge, a sense of reward, a sense of personal satisfaction in his or her job; make this a place where people truly enjoy to work.
4. Push the entry level for managerial talent from the upper- and middle-management level to the lowest level so that people who have been hired at the "bottom" level and move through the organization increasingly become the main source for managerial jobs. This means increasing the number and quality of entry-level management hires.
5. Make the development of people an integral and vital part of each manager's job so that getting good results in management development is on a par with strategic, functional, and P&L result.

A new philosophy of career development evolved which was based on certain principles:

This case was prepared by Associate Professor John Kao.

Copyright © 1985 by the President and Fellows of Harvard College. Harvard Business School case 9-485-175.

1. Personal success should be measured by accomplishments, not promotion.
2. There are two equal career paths—P&L management and functional leadership.
3. Career development requires hard work and sacrifice.
4. Our future leaders will be people-builders.

Prior to Lou Gerstner's arrival in 1982, the HR function had been embryonic. Business units did all their own recruiting in an unsystematic process that involved the odd solicited resume and a good deal of old-boy, old-girl networking. There had been little formal recruiting or career planning, and retention problems were common.

In 1985, the HR function consisted of a senior vice president with a direct reporting relationship to Lou Gerstner. Four functions in turn reported to him, including compensation and benefits, management resources—which consisted of education and staffing, labor/employee relations, and an international function which also reported to the international group president at the TRS Company. Given the shifting of company businesses, HR attention was focused as much on future as on current needs. Considered a strategic function, HR saw itself as infusing culture through a variety of training and skill development activities; it consistently focused on why TRS believed in quality and service, why it marketed in a certain way, and what was valuable about how TRS does things. New approaches to recruiting included extensive on-campus efforts involving senior managers. TRS is said today to experience a 76 percent compounded annual retention rate. HR considers itself to be an evolving function in an evolving company.

THE GRADUATE MANAGEMENT PROGRAM

The Graduate Management Program (GMP) was inaugurated in 1978 as a major component of a new emphasis on hiring entry management executives to fill a growing need for management talent. Initiated by Lou Gerstner and developed and run by the HR area, it was intensively pursued from 1982 to the present, and as of 1985 had 200 alumni.

The participant pool for the GMP program consisted of two groups: "external" participants who had been hired at TRS from graduate business schools (very rarely from bachelor-level programs); and "internal" participants who were current TRS employees nominated by their managers and accepted into the program. Fifty-five percent of GMP program candidates were internally nominated.

Designed for new high-potential members of the company who might be prone to more innovative and risk-taking behavior, the GMP program was intended to provide a high exposure, enriched set of experiences: an "intensive first year of development opportunities" that supported learning on the job. The desire to provide more developmental services for this group was linked to a higher level of expectations about their potential and long-term performance. The GMPs were specially treated in a variety of ways. They were invited to periodic cocktail parties with senior executives. They could call on HR informally for advice and feedback, and like enlightened consumers, often took advantage of these problem-solving resources. HR organized periodic lunch meetings with smaller groups of ten GMPs at a time which provided an informal mechanism for people to talk about what they were doing.

The program also served as an ongoing channel of communication for alumni; there was an active effort to support the GMP network by involving alumni in current GMP activities and by inviting groups of alumni to come in and meet with newcomers.

It was envisioned that the GMP program would take up about 10–20 percent of a first-year person's time. The program involved three basic components: training, business reviews, and an issues series that might include presentations on important subjects such as new technology, new financial service markets, and changes in approaches to marketing. Key company personnel would make presentations, and the GMP group would have an opportunity to learn the inner workings of various business groups at TRS. The program depended on the participation of its members and included a personalized developmental strategy for each individual and periodic reviews.

The GMP program carried Lou Gerstner's unmistakable stamp. Letters went from his office to the GMP group. Gerstner would participate in the introductory sessions for GMPs that might involve 60–70 people. Memorizing all of their names and faces with "class cards," Gerstner would use these meetings as mass-event review sessions, addressing three to four questions to a number of people in the room in a highly personal fashion. Special functions with the chairman and GMPs were also organized, and from time to time, Gerstner would meet with GMPs in the TRS boardroom for special question-and-answer sessions.

The GMP program was deemed a success by the company. At present, GMP alumni included one international division president, three vice presidents, five to seven advanced directors, and about 20 entry-level directors. The GMPs were said to have earned a name for themselves. There were many success stories within the system, and examples of groups with GMPs that had become company "hot shops."

HR functioned as the internal placement mechanism for the GMPs. At first, they went where jobs were open, in areas where business was booming. Now the allocation process was more subtle. There had also been unsolicited requests on the part of managers to get a GMP. The HR department involved the managers who would be working with GMPs, inviting them to the overview sessions, for example. At present, a large percentage of GMP managers were former GMPs themselves.

The HR department also had to counter the perception that high-flying MBA types had limited value, that they were pushy and would take things over, and that one could get adequate people for less dollars. A hazard lay in the possibility of an "us versus them" atmosphere, especially if brighter and more high-potential people were recruited. Also, they had to counter the feeling that the GMPs might be threatening. Gerstner himself fanned those flames from time to time, with public comments that managers were now "set up."

HR allocated GMPs within TRS, but avoid the notion that they are involved in anything other than the most informal of career-planning processes. One person commented, "The company's strength is that it's not a bureaucracy. It has the flexibility of getting a superstar up quickly." Others said that the lack of a formal career-planning process could be a problem.

THE TRS MANAGEMENT CURRICULUM

The TRS management curriculum was conceived and created by Lou Gerstner in 1984 in response to senior management's desire to share cross-functional knowledge of the TRS business among their management teams. In addition, TRS had a number of issues to address in management training and development. Historically, TRS employees felt that senior management viewed management courses as useful but not essential for promotion by senior management. Managers recommended their employees for courses but would pull them out at the last minute, or would expect them to conduct "business as usual" while attending the courses. Attendance was somewhat haphazard with no systematic sequence of training courses and seminars to attend.

As originally conceived, the TRS management curriculum was designed to provide a broad overview of TRS businesses for the management teams. The curriculum was based on these major objectives:

- To enhance the management skills employees need to accomplish their work
- To ensure on going continuing education in TRS businesses and the environment in which they exist
- To support the systematic development of a unique, worldwide TRS culture and business philosophy

In direct response to senior management's objectives and taking into account these concerns, the TRS management curriculum incorporated the following:

- A series of 33 *required seminars* for each of six levels of management
- Inclusion of *TRS line and staff functional experts* on course design to ensure course relevance to the TRS business
- *Mandatory seminar* attendance as one criterion for promotion, with flexibility to avoid repetition of recent training experiences
- Seminar delivery by *TRS line and staff experts* as an additional criterion for credit

The first year was devoted to initiating, building, and testing the TRS management curriculum. TRS management education staff were supported by 100 line personnel who collaborated as key designers, facilitators, and presenters. Together, they completed the design of 20 courses; these were piloted at all domestic operating centers and at American Express Plaza.

These pilots, and subsequent participant response, growing employee support and interest, and strong management support and involvement have generated a heightened sense of anticipation and increased expectations of both quality and attendance. This momentum also meant that the requests for training greatly exceeded the available capacity.

Throughout 1985, the TRS management curriculum would be launched worldwide. It would be an active year of full delivery. Local training personnel were being trained to deliver the programs at the supervisor's and manager's levels in each of the regional businesses, and additional staff was added to ensure availability of programs to meet growing management development needs.

INCENTIVE COMPENSATION

In 1983 a new management incentive and bonus program was instituted. It was a paired compensation system, with two components. First was MERIT, which was based on past performance and related to how well one managed one's job and people in such areas as goal setting, management behavior, decision-making processes, and people planning. Second was BONUS, which was based on specific targets such as "Cards-In-Force" and "Net Income." In the case of HR, for example, a specific target might involve reaching a recruiting quota. For managers, it might have to do with whether their people achieved their ratings. Bonuses were based on challenges, not contrived goals. It was said to be common for time and resource budgets to be "stretched" by 20 percent. People lived close to the action at TRS and targets were developed by those who knew what the real numbers were. The program's objective lay in achieving challenging goals and in providing appropriate rewards.

MANAGEMENT REVIEW PROCESS

At TRS, goal-setting, performance appraisal, management development reviews, and compensation decision-making processes were integrated to support the development and motivation of the TRS management team in accomplishing business goals.

Formal evaluation was conducted once a year at the same time for all directors, vice presidents and above in the TRS Company. Senior management reviewed results for these people. (Every manager in the company had a formal performance appraisal once a year.)

The management development review process assessed the results of the previous year's development plan, highlighted key strengths and areas for development, and articulated development plan for the next year. The review process also identified an employee's career plan and management's assessment of responsibility of plan, measured the potential contribution and upward mobility of each employee, and determined the succession plan for each job.

Forms and guides were revised each year to incorporate learning. Information drawn from management development reviews was used to staff jobs throughout the year. In addition, the TRS Executive Committee approved all senior level job moves.

Jerry Welsh

When I came to American Express, I was a college professor, a Russian language and literature and comparative government scholar. I came to American Express because I was too stupid to realize you couldn't do that. I had three kids ages ten, eleven, and fourteen. I couldn't afford to send them to college.

They've been very good to me at American Express. My salary has increased five times in three years. Would I be tempted to go out on my own? Yeah, but I've scaled down my life. I don't want to scale up my life. I would go to a smaller place. Not a company, but out on my own. I don't want to make any more money. I want to scale my life back. That's partly because of my own value system of being a teacher. The only ideas I want to get have to do with the betterment of the world today. Whether I'd do it alone or with someone else, I don't know. At American Express, one of these days my string will run out. That's the way it should be. I think if you're sensitive to yourself and if you're truly yourself and with all your vulnerabilities you will become irrelevant over time, more baggage than you are an asset. I think I'm slowly becoming that and before long the cart will tip over and I'll go and do something else on my own. Not to make money, just to do something else.

You've got to remember I was 35 years old when I came to New York. If you had told me I was going to do what I'm doing now I would have said you're crazy, you've lost your mind. But I realized I had to change my life, so I changed it. I did not know what I was doing and fell into a very lucky situation. God was good to me and that was that. I don't have a very literate explanation for all this.

BUSINESS PHILOSOPHY

There are a couple of false dilemmas. One is the risk vs. risk-aversion false dilemma. There is no safety net in any corporation. Trust me. They will bag your happy ass. And the more visible the mistake is, the quicker they'll do it. There *is* no safety net. If you're hiding behind one of the pillars, that's one

This case was prepared by Associate Professor John Kao.

Copyright © 1986 by the President and Fellows of Harvard College. Harvard Business School case 0-488-013.

thing. But if you try to get visibility in the corporation, what you better do is have 33,000 employees under you. The minute you make a bad move you're *gone*. They don't fire you that day, but as my friend here said, you are gone. As you say in the South, when somebody cuts your throat with a razor you don't know it 'til you try to turn your head and it rolls off.

The next false dilemma is freedom vs. constraint. The idea that you're not free inside, but you're free outside is foolish. Unless you are well funded from your family or from an illegal business, you are not free. They've got the stranglehold on you, the banks or whoever has the purse strings. The Golden Rule is he who has the gold, makes the rule. Now inside you're as free as you want to risk, assuming you're in the right department. They'll let you go until you make a bad move and then you're gone. This stuff about you've got to be free to fail, that's just bullshit. Are you free to fail in brain surgery? Hey, let's try to get 60 percent successes. Come on. If you're one of the 40 percent you'll sue, or your heirs will sue. Nobody is free to fail.

Supervisors are not stupid. Their job is to say, "O.K., you've got a great idea. Do this, this, and this, you forgot to do this, get that done and do it." One of the things a corporation is not, is levels of idiocy. There are people there who make sure you mind the store. Are you going to be completely free? Of course not. You won't be free anywhere you are, with the blue box, with American Express' name, with 150 years of a franchise, with a $23 billion company at its current stock price. Do you think they're going to let you and me run loose in the tulips? No way. They'd be nuts if they would do that. Ted Turner wouldn't let you run free either. With Ted you'd be doing it Ted's way. With us you'll do it our way. Of course, if you're in a company with level after level of stupid people who shuffle papers, just quit.

Here is this guy Steven Jobs. What a tremendous thing he did. But he's gone. All he's got is money. He can't even get arrested. Ted Turner wanted to buy CBS. He goes to the investment bankers in New York. Why do all of them want to get in? Why don't they say, "I've got my money, I want to stay out." Why do they want in? Because that is where the power is ultimately, in these big organizations. Do you know how little $50 million is? It's nothing. There are plenty of people who have $50 million. They cannot get arrested. They can't get in the paper, they can't get an idea going, they can't get scope. That's really what I want to say, it depends on what scope and what stage you want to work on. You want a few bucks, make a few bucks. There are people in corporations making a few bucks. Go out and make a few bucks, that ain't going to make you happy. Look at Donald Trump. What does Trump talk about in interviews? Does he talk about buildings? Hell no. All he talks about is disarmament. Getting the Russians to talk. What does Ted Turner talk about? Ted Turner wants to be Secretary of State. They don't make entrepreneurs Secretary of State. I have trouble with the old entrepreneur thing because I'll tell you frankly, most people don't want to do it. You want the rocking chair kind of deal which is a lot of motion, no danger. Nobody wants to get his ass shot off.

In a big company there are a lot of things going on. It is not a laboratory. In a laboratory you have one variable. Look how many variables are swimming around American Express. How many advertising campaigns do we have? How many things are going on in the economy? You never know whether anything works or not. Everybody thinks the Statue of Liberty was a big success. Hell, let's say it was. The business went up. Was it because of that? I don't know, do you? We don't know. Let's say that was the reason. Then let's say that makes me great. Are you ready to say that? I'm ready to say it. I'm great. Now, if the business doesn't go up, does that mean it didn't work? O.K., let's say it didn't work. I think Project Home Town America, which was a much bigger idea than the Statue of Liberty, did not "work" the way the Statue of Liberty did. Some people think it failed. I think it was a brilliant success so the hell with them. So you can't tell. Sure you know when it's a disaster, but you can't tell on an incremental basis what works. Take "Do you know me." Does it work? Well something out there is working. We're going to do an advertising campaign that's going to blow everybody away in about a month. Blow them out. It's going to change the way everybody looks at advertising in America. And the point is, half the people will say, "God damn that Welsh. It's going to be a disaster, noncommercial, it's not going to sell anything. It's counterintuitive that it will sell anything." Trust me, it sells *everything*. Can I prove it? No. So, you just run as hard as you can until somebody gets you.

MANAGEMENT STYLE

I do not believe in general management. And I will urge you never to believe in it. It's like believing in the concept of perfect father, perfect husband, perfect wife, perfect friend. Let's say I'm a perfect friend. What you really mean is the kind of friend I am is going to be perfect for you. The kind of husband I am will be perfect for you. The kind of father I am, I hope, is going to be perfect for you. I do what I am doing. I do my own work. That's the way I manage my department. I let others do the paper and all of that. When the promotions are up, I don't even know about my fringe benefits, so when I interview somebody and they say to me, hey, what's the dental plan? How the hell do I know what the dental plan is? I have no idea, nor do I want to know. I don't even care. Not because I'm an entrepreneur, I never did care about dental plans even when I was a college professor, so I do not want dental plans. I do not like dental plans. I manage our department by doing what I do best which is the projects that I do. And I surround myself with people who do various projects, so I'll be doing some things with Beth [Horowitz], some things with somebody else, and they'll do things without me. The way I encourage this is to say, "Look, understand something, these standards don't come from me. Your job is not to kiss my feet. That is not your job, believe me, trust me. Who cares?" My satisfaction comes from other things than that, believe me.

So your job is to make a tremendous contribution in terms of the value you add by having great ideas, being a great implementer of ideas, being quick off the block. I like things quick, I like things to happen now. I don't want to wait, I don't want to study them. We've got to have them now, and that's the way I manage. You *know* in our department if you don't make it. We have meetings all the time. If we have one meeting at 11:00 then we want the answer about 3:00 so we have another meeting on the answer. We want to know where it is. "Well, what's the idea?" We have to come up with an idea now. That's what my department does. If we've got a problem, what's the answer, give me your idea. There are many ideas, what's yours? I don't come up with all the ideas. They do. So the thing I want is the idea. Then I want someone to go implement it. In our department, we come up with and implement it. I do my own work. I do the things I think I do best, whatever they are. I'm not interested in trying to get everybody feeling good about their job and their career and their aspirations and my aspirations. Forget all that crap. My aspirations are to be arrested for loitering, I guess. It isn't that your aspirations don't matter to me, it's that my aspirations are my personal business, yours are yours. Your career is your personal business. I'm not going to manage your career.

WORKING AT AMERICAN EXPRESS

My thing at American Express is that I got lucky. I took some risks and they *all* worked, every *one* of them, or I would not be sitting here today. I cannot afford a big mistake, even today. Nor will I ever be able to, and that's fine. That's the way I want it when the end comes, and there's an end for everything. You're thinking about the beginning, I'm thinking of the end. There's an end for all of us, not in the ultimate sense, but careerwise. You change. I'll go down, I hope not in disgrace but I'll go down, or I'll make a big mistake and I'll be gone. We'll cover it up and make it sweet and all of that, but I'll be gone and that will be good. Then I'll start the next phase.

I have developed a bit of a track record at American Express so they believe me a little now, whereas they didn't before. If you come up to my department and you have a brilliant idea I feel about you the same way they felt about me. "This is a brilliant idea. We're going to do it and give you full credit for it but we're not going to do it the way you want to do it. We're going to do it this way but everybody will still know that it's your idea. You will be chief point man. I'm here to advise you and of course be your boss and I'm telling you we're going to do it this way." Because my view is that part of being an entrepreneur or whatever we want to call people who are living by their own lights is that I'm not going down with your methodology. I'm going down with mine. If this room caught on fire right now and everybody was waiting for somebody to come up with an idea, I assure you I'd come up with an idea. The idea is to get the hell out of here through that door. And if someone said, "Nope, I'm going through the other door," I'd say, "No, don't! *This* door." Now I might be wrong but I would want to go down with my own idea. Now, if you want to go down with yours you've got to remember when you get a little credibility, the first idea you might do my way, but everyone knows it was your idea. The second idea you do it your way, the third idea you pass me. It shouldn't be frustrating to you. There is an apprenticeship about things. You have to have a track record.

I have people around me who will actually tell me to go to hell. You absolutely must have people around you from your assistants to everybody who will say, that's wrong, don't do it, you'll die, do not do this, don't. I'm very proud of the fact. People around me either care enough about me or are afraid that I'm going to wreck the ship or something, to say, "don't do this it's a bad idea." When I throw out my ideas, by the time I come to the next meeting they're all there and the bad parts are knocked out.

All of us in our department make changes together. For example, we're going to play croquet in our new building in the corridors. A couple of years ago when I suggested we play croquet in the building, that took them by surprise. But now, everybody is open to croquet so people get more comfortable with change. What can you really learn from an entrepreneur? Live by your own rules, know what the risks are, and know what you want.

The chairman of American Express said, "Jerry, where are all the people who are going to be the next group of people like you?" You can't predict who's going to be what. If you had said to me ten years ago when I was a college professor, "Oh, Jerry, you're going to be this, you're going to be that." I think that's silly. You don't know. Ten of the people here are going to do 50 times what I've done perhaps. How can we tell? How can you groom somebody to be whatever it is you are? There's no way to train anybody to be what you are, whether that's good or bad. Someone steps forward or they don't step forward. If I were my boss I would worry about this problem, but I don't because I understand the process and understand how unforgiving it is. Don't ever think there are any corporate parachutes and all that crap. That's a lie. People who get in trouble with American Express listen to all that stuff. "We will help your career. What's my career path?" The hell out of here if you don't do it right. People don't like to say that. If I fail will I be fired? Well, yeah. That's life. Life is that way. If you put the American Express name on a bad idea and bring that name down, you're gone, you are out of here. That's the way it should be.

I have the same philosophy Bear Bryant did about football which is this. You recruit the smartest people, don't care if they're girls, boys, black, white, green, transvestite, you just recruit the best people. You get rid of mediocrity, ruthlessly. Someone who is mediocre you get rid of. Bag 'em immediately! You take all excellent people. Trust me, these people are going to be pains in the ass. You say to them, here are the limits, don't go around without your clothes on, don't do anything weird that way. You work hard, you be excellent, you add value, I'll take care of you. The way I manage is simply to get rid of mediocre people.

What do I do well? I come up with ideas and ram them through. What am I going to do next year? I have no idea. I'm struggling with that myself.

What I'm certain of though is that it will be more beautiful than what I'm doing now. Absolutely confident of that, maybe I'm wrong but I'm confident. No career plans, I just don't have any of that. I do one thing well. I try to stick to that. I'm not going to try to do things I cannot do. That's a mistake you don't want to make. If you look at people who are really smart, they can do one or two things well. There's nobody who can really do a lot. It's just a myth. Life is not that way.

I would say in graduate school if you had tried to get me to sell Jell-O, I couldn't. I don't care if someone ever said to me, "Is there room in this market for another soft pudding?" There's Country Time, Shake & Bake, I don't care about it. I never cared about it. I came right from there to what I'm doing now. I never did care about it. That's why I was a college professor. How do I motivate people? They know they're lucky to be working on ideas that make a difference in the world. It's one thing to sell Pepsi, it's another thing to sell Pepsi to help people. So I think if you work in my area you're a lucky person.

But, I still make major mistakes. When I go down, and I will, it's going to be with my own problems. Everybody can play their role but with the chances we take, I'm going down in my own little red wagon.

We've come pretty far away in my group from business, I'll admit that we're the counterculture, but this still is American Express. The shareholders are still showing up. Now, we have launched things with no research. We've done all those things, but this is business, I don't need to tell any of you here that we think we've done some very good things for the business. I'm just telling you that in another environment these things could not have happened. Whether that means it's entrepreneurial or intrapreneurial, these things could not and have not happened in other places.

ENTREPRENEURSHIP

To me an entrepreneur is a person who is determined to take his/her destiny into his/her own hands and do it their way, period, with little modification. Are you going to be happy with the rewards? I mentioned people like Ted Turner. They're not happy with the rewards. If I went out and made $5 million today or $20 million, I'd still want to make big projects go . . . and you can't do that with $20 million in Nashville, Tennessee . . . You have to have American Express behind you. Are you that kind of person? Are you going to be happy with the rewards? Don't be what you're not going to be happy with when you get it. O.K.? Understand what you want. Do you want power? Influence? Do you want to be a big mucky-muck, then you've got to lay pipe to do that. If you want to be rich, go to the quickest route to get rich. The people who say they want to be rich usually want something more. All of them come back, they want to do something, they want to be Tom Wyman, president of CBS. They criticize Tom Wyman but, they all want to play golf with him. I don't want to do that, but some do.

I will tell you how to find an entrepreneur. First of all, risk is one factor. There are many others. Ability to quickly conceptualize problems and come up with solutions, take risks, and say, "Let me be the one. I'll do it." An entrepreneur would know what he'd be saying at Harvard. "Look guys, all this class participation stuff is dragging me down. I'm not too verbal, but I'll tell you what: I'm going to shoot the eyes out of whatever exam you give me, O.K.? So, I'll be showing up sometimes and I'll be out sometimes. But trust me, when the end of the day comes I'm blowing all these people away." How many people do you hear saying that? They don't want to do that. They want to say, "I was within the limits of what's safe for me, I want to be cool."

You can say entrepreneurship is where you take the big risk. But there is no parachute for you anywhere. You're gone. They will get rid of you in five minutes and they should. In Cleveland, in New York, once a year the modeling agencies have open calls. Every time this happens I always forget about it until it shows up in *The New York Times* and breaks my heart again. All of the young girls come in from Cleveland and these modeling agencies open up their doors. You want to talk about cruelty then? You've won every beauty contest in Cleveland, Ohio and you come to New York and they rip your face apart and rip your body apart and they rip you apart. You ain't got it. You're gone. That is what you're going to face, I don't care where you're going. If you want to hit the top, I don't care if you want to go make $100 million, you want to be chairman of American Express, you want to be head of the stodgiest company in the country, you're going to be looking right across at smart people who are going to say, "I'm better than you are." And the thing that nobody wants to face up to, that very few people acknowledge when they talk about risk, is losing your job, losing your little fortune. Who cares about you? You're bankrupt at 25. You lose your job. You'll bounce back. You know how many people have done that? What you don't bounce back from maybe is to put yourself on the spectrum of how smart am I, how hungry am I, how much energy do I have, how much guts do I have. We all got the rest of it. We're all straight on how to do the risk taking but when the time comes to step out and get your ass shot off, there aren't that many people stepping out.

I don't know about entrepreneurs. I don't know whether I'm one and I really don't care if I'm one. Because all I know is that I am doing what I want to do a lot.

The myth of the general manager is something I feel very strongly about. It is a myth that anybody well rounded is O.K. and the more talented you are the more vulnerable and the more eccentric and the more in trouble you are. Voltaire said, "Great minds have great vices." Absolutely right. Show me a person who is well rounded and I will show you a mediocre person. Show me a general manager, and I'll show you someone who is mediocre, who can't do anything. Unless you find general managers this way: If I'm a general manager I'll give you my strengths and surround myself with people with other strengths who are covering my ass. That is what a good general manager does. They aren't people who know a little bit about this, and sit around and analyze. That is what you've got to come to grips with, whether you want to be a "general manager." Everybody at American Express wants to be a general manager. I've never wanted to be a general manager. I think it would be a disaster to put me in as a general manager. I think I would hate to be a general manager. Who wants to do that?

What I'm really trying to say is, the brighter the person the more eccentrically developed they are. That's generally true. And you can never fully round out your flat sides. I have the same flat sides I did when I was seventeen years old and joined the army. I'm the same person I was then, but a little older. I'm the same person. Oh, when I was younger I was really wild, but I'm more soft-spoken now. I just don't believe you round out.

PERSONAL OBSERVATIONS

The tough lessons in life are to realize what your limits are, to look around at the guy next to you and say, hey, that guy is smarter than I am. That guy's got more energy than I do. That guy is better than I am. That's tough. There are about three people at American Express that are clearly smarter than I am. They're not ahead of me but they're smarter than I am. They're not going to get up earlier than I do. They're not going to charge harder than I do. But they're smarter.

I'm very hard-nosed about mediocrity and I'll tell you why. The way to wreck your boat, whether it's in your personal life or in your professional life is to be either mediocre yourself or surround yourself with those who are that way. What you need to do in the limits of human kindness is to get them out of your way. I want them all working for VISA. I want them all to be somebody else's friend. Why? You're just going to spin your wheels trying to make it. An expression in the South is, kick ass and take names. You never can make chicken salad out of chicken shit, you just can't. I wouldn't have said this 20 years ago, but some people don't have it. Don't have the courage. There are some people who just don't have any guts ,and they will sink your boat every time. So, within the limits of kindness, you put them on the street and hope that your competition hires them.

I'm a very self-centered person and in not a very good way. There are a couple of reasons for that. One, when you are in a high-intensity environment like the corporation, you have almost no personal life. You see, it's a self-fulfilling prophecy, a circular thing. When you make so many sacrifices in your personal life then of course it becomes very important. Luckily, my kids were almost grown when I came to New York. I was a college professor and I used to do a lot of things with them. Thank God, now they're grown. If I had small kids today, man I'd have guilt trip all over. You just cannot have a family and do this. I haven't. Almost my whole life is my job, and what intermingles in my personal and professional life. Is that bad? No, but it's not going to go on forever either. You have to get comfortable with the idea that you've got phases in your life. You're coming, you're going, you're gone, you're here, you're somewhere else. What happens to people is tragic. You think, "Well Jerry Welsh, boy, after him—après moi, le deluge. Nothing will be after me because I am the ultimate one." That's when you know you're in trouble. After me there will be something different, probably something better. What happens to people is they think they've got to hang on. If I leave, it will all fall apart. That's foolish. When you start thinking that way, you need to quit. I haven't come to that point yet, my personal and professional lives *are* intertwined to the extent that I'm thinking about business, about ideas a lot of my life. Do you think a person like me has a wife? If you asked all the women here, would you marry a person like me? NO WAY.

Beth Horowitz

I don't know if this relates to the definition of entrepreneurship, but I don't know another place where you can participate in major decisions and be heard like you can here.

Beth Horowitz

BACKGROUND

Horowitz' career at American Express began during her college days. A medieval and renaissance European history major, she worked for American Express during one summer in between junior and senior and for six to eight months post graduation. Her assignment was with the American Express Foundation which was responsible for Amex's philanthropic activity and reported its results to the board of directors. Then she worked with the Japan Society, a business-oriented cultural exchange organization, where she felt she might have more impact with her bachelor's degree. Enrolling at HBS in 1982, she studied international business and marketing and did a creative marketing field study. (*Exhibit 1* presents Horowitz' resume. *Exhibit 2* is an excerpt from a company entry strategy paper which she wrote for *Power and Influence* in 1984.)

The HBS career management course plus Horowitz' previous experience confirmed her decision to rejoin Amex. She felt a need to identify with a cause, and experience loyalty to an organization. She also wanted a dynamic environment with bright people, one which involved constant learning, which was filled with opportunities and in which one could spend an entire career being constantly challenged. She was attracted to the Amex environment because it was constantly changing, not highly structured. She didn't want a static work situation and felt that Amex provided a combination of small company fluidity and the resources of a large company. Horowitz felt that the company offered some opportunities which were as close to running one's own business as one could ever come in an established firm. If one developed a new idea and honed it, one might get the right to run with it.

This case was prepared by Associate Professor John Kao.
Copyright © 1985 by the President and Fellows of Harvard College. Harvard Business School case 9-487-040.

WORLDWIDE MARKETING
AND COMMUNICATION

At the time of this case, Horowitz was manager in the Worldwide Marketing group of a special department called Worldwide Marketing and Communications. Created around the talents of Jerry Welsh, WWMC was a 30- to 40-person group involved with companywide special projects, cause-related marketing activities, public affairs and communications, and enhancements to the Amex marketing function worldwide. (See the case on American Express Travel Related Services.) Under Welsh but outside of the Worldwide Marketing area were Fred Wilkinson, SVP of Communications, and Warner Canto, VP of Special Projects. At the time of this case, the Worldwide Marketing Group consisted of two VPs, two directors and five managers. This group addressed the more hard-core marketing activities which came under WWMC's purview (that is, policy development and global coordination of selected business activities). There were many who pointed to WWMC as an important enclave of entrepreneurial activity which set an example for the rest of the firm. (*Exhibit 3* presents an organizational chart for WWMC.)

Horowitz described WWMC as having a very open working atmosphere. Staff meetings, with as many as 25 people, were uninhibited. People felt free to throw ideas around and critique each other's ideas openly. Some comments were definitely off the wall. Responsibility for this atmosphere, she believed, could be attributed to the influence of Jerry Welsh, whom she described as being the source of some of the most radical and innovative ideas. He encouraged people to come up with more extreme ideas. He created the general environment of teamwork and the freedom to run with an idea and be heard. And he had the track record and credibility to back this up.

Horowitz had briefly considered employment in companies with more hierarchical environments, but felt uncomfortable about a rigid process for communicating ideas up which could kill them at a number of stages. Decision making could be further hampered by organizational size and rapid management turnover. This contrasted with the WWMC style. In her experience there was a high degree of informal communication between groups that had no formal line relationship. For example, she volunteered a few days of her time to the Project Hometown America team (a TRS national Cause-Related Marketing Program in the Special Projects area) when they needed additional personnel. She also aided the Special Projects group in assessing and selecting TRS's top 50 city markets worldwide, for use in targeting marketing programs.

Horowitz had also worked on a number of projects over which she had effective day-to-day control. She had participated in developing uniform methods for market sizing and product positioning strategy on a global basis. She had helped draft a key senior management presentation on the Amex travel business. She had also run an internal worldwide conference on a high-growth, high-potential segment of the business.

The atypical nature of WWMC was also evident in its reporting structure. Typically, MBAs started as assistant managers or managers. Higher levels included directors, vice president, senior vice president, executive vice president and division president. Horowitz had reported to VPs since she started as an assistant manager. Although this was commonplace in WWMC, it was not in many other areas of the company. She felt that in her group there wasn't the sense of people looking over one's shoulder. Rather, she went to her superiors for occasional feedback, when there was a snag, or when she was almost done with a particular project. Concerning her projects, in her words, "They're not doing it; *I'm* doing it." For example, Horowitz developed and drafted Worldwide Card Project Positioning on her own and then received feedback during the final stages. Managers at WWMC, in her view, were given a great deal of responsibility and could therefore develop rapidly. The group was not hung up on titles.

Was the company really entrepreneurial? Horowitz' answer was yes, in relation to other large companies. In her words, Amex was an established company with an "amazing" range of resources which it could commit. It had a wealth of developed management and is involved with many different businesses. Big also meant more structure but relatively little in comparison with other companies of its size. There is more opportunity for people, with less risk. Personal career risk existed, but one's decision would not destroy the company. Noble failures *could* create career problems, particularly in established businesses where there was an opportunity to compare one's performance with a predecessor. Yet even established businesses at Amex could be creative and entrepreneurial, Horowitz believed. Rewards included promotions, a change in activity, and bonuses at middle and upper management levels which could amount to a substantial percentage of salary. Sanctions included signals that one's career was not going to progress, that one would become less visible and involved in a smaller job.

While Horowitz thought she could do well as an independent business person, she had some aversion to risk. Many of her colleagues, like herself young MBAs attracted to entrepreneurial environments, wondered, however, about spending their entire careers with large companies.

Exhibit 1   Resume

---

159 Erie Street
Cambridge, MA 02139
(617) 576-6787

Permanent Address:
846 West Gate
Valley Stream, NY 11580
(516) 825-0613

Education
1982–1984   **HARVARD UNIVERSITY**   **Boston, MA**
             GRADUATE SCHOOL OF BUSINESS ADMINISTRATION
             Candidate for the degree of Master in Business Administration in
             June 1984. General management curriculum with emphasis in inter-
             national business. Tutor for first-year Finance. Member of Interna-
             tional Business, Asia, Finance, Marketing, and International Affairs
             Clubs.

1975–1979   **CORNELL UNIVERSITY**
             COLLEGE OF ARTS & SCIENCES   **Ithaca, NY**
             Bachelor of Arts degree in History, May 1979, awarded "With Dis-
             tinction in all Subjects." Concentration in Medieval and Renaissance
             Studies. Attained proficiency in French. Served as Arts & Sciences
             Ambassador, speaking to candidates for admission and giving campus
             tours. Paid researcher, summer 1978, for Cornell Corporate Respon-
             sibility Project, producing report entitled, "The University as an Insti-
             tutional Investor." Dean's List. Phi Beta Kappa.

**Work
Experience**
summer   **NEW SCHOOL FOR SOCIAL RESEARCH**   **New York, NY**
1983   Executed projects for President and for Vice President of Finance.
             Created a forecasting model for evaluation of methods for expanding
             undergraduate college. Developed a second mortgage program for
             senior faculty. Performed detailed analysis of energy use and conser-
             vation to generate savings in operation of physical plant; projected
             trends in natural gas deregulation, oil prices, and electricity rates.

1980–1982   **JAPAN SOCIETY, INC.**   **New York, NY**
             Performed marketing function for this private, American non-profit
             organization. Raised funds and coordinated special events including
             dinners honoring Prime Minister Zenko Suzuki and Business
             Roundtable Chairman Ruben P. Mettler; United States premiere of
             1982 Grand Kabuki tour. Prepared budgets, negotiated banquet con-
             tracts, coordinated security arrangements and logistics, supervised
             staff and board member participation, coordinated with Consulate
             General of Japan, wrote speeches for dignitaries. Generated over
             nine percent of Society's FY 1982 operating budget through Suzuki
             dinner. Initiated market research to increase corporate funding base.

1979–1980   **AMERICAN EXPRESS FOUNDATION**   **New York, NY**
             Prepared educational and cultural gift-matching reports for the
             Foundation's Board of Trustees. Screened requests for funding. Also
             employed at the American Express Foundation summer 1977 and
             inter-sessions 1977–78, 1978–79.

Publication *Dutch Drawings of the Seventeenth Century from a Collection*
1979   Library of Congress #79-90194. Co-authored catalogue as art history
             seminar student for Nov. 6–Dec. 23, 1979 exhibition at Herbert F.
             Johnson Museum of Art, Ithaca, New York.

Other   Italian and Japanese language courses, 1980–82. Travel through
Activities Britain, Continental Europe, and Japan. Volunteer fundraising and
             special events planning for Cornell University. Interviewed Cornell
             candidates. Invited to serve on Board of Cornell Alumni Association
             of New York City.

References Personal references available upon request.

Exhibit 2 My "Entry Strategy" at American Express (From Professor John Kao's *Power and Influence* class, April 1984)

When I enter American Express Company headquarters in New York to report for work on August 15, 1984, it will not be the first time I will have entered that building for that purpose. The first time was some seven years ago in June 1977, when as a college student seeking summer employment between my sophomore and junior years, I was sent to the American Express Foundation on a two-week temporary assignment. Two weeks stretched into nine and an invitation to return whenever I had a break in my academic schedule. I did indeed spend most of my subsequent breaks at the company, and returned for six months after college before moving on to another job in 1980. I have since remained in contact with a few of my former colleagues. Thus it was with considerable forethought and some inside knowledge that I accepted a marketing position at American Express on April 6, 1984.

My initial exposure to the company was fascinating. I worked in a small department of only six people which was headed by a senior vice president; I did not have to gaze through 20 management layers to see out into the rest of the company. At that time the Foundation was located on the 38th floor of corporate headquarters, just beneath the company's top executive floors, (39 and 40), which were spoken of in the same reverent tones that in GM were reserved for the 14th floor.

A great deal of my information filtered freely down from 40 to 38. An astute listener who was viewed as both a "bright college kid" and a harmless political outsider could pick up some valuable insights, as I did that first summer. I think I was most absorbed by the power and complexities inherent in this multinational organization. I did a fair amount of running about the 39th and 40th floors, usually to get someone's approval for something. In the process I received a fair education in power dynamics and corporate politics.

1977 was a particularly interesting time to be at the company, for it was the year that the mantle of chairman and CEO passed from Howard L. Clark (the "old guard") to James D. Robinson III, a young (early 40s) go-getter who hailed from Atlanta. Waves of excitement and apprehension rippled through the company, for it was widely known that "changes would be made." At first this meant getting rid of a great deal of management "dead wood." In the ensuing years the business world witnessed the more visible strategic changes which included an aggressive acquisitions program and the development of an almost entirely new top management team.

The company I am returning to is in many ways different from the one I first entered in 1977. Top management is young; merit supersedes seniority. The waves of excitement have grown in size and intensity; one must learn to ride them skillfully or be pulled under. I will be working in a section of Travel Related Services headed by Jerry C. Welsh, hailed in an April 1984 HBS *Bulletin* article as "a professional idea man" who can conceptualize change before others and who "loves to take risks." My position is assistant manager, marketing services," and my precise duties remain undefined since Mr. Welsh's area, reorganized just before my last interview, may be reorganized twice more before August.

Fortunately I possessed a high tolerance for ambiguity and feel a tremendous need to be creative (traits confirmed by the battery of tests I took in Career Management), so I think I am well-suited to the environment at American Express.

Exhibit 2 My "Entry Strategy" (*Continued*)

There are several reasons why I chose this position over my other alternatives (including one had offered substantially more pay):

- The self-assessment exercises in the Career Management course at HBS helped me focus my job search in areas which would satisfy my interests and provide a good fit with my personality and behavior; the marketing job at American Express came closest to the elusive "perfect fit" that I sought.
- My previous experience with American Express was very positive and, in fact, stimulated my initial interest in business school.
- I want to build a career in one company rather than "job hop," so I wanted a company that would provide many long-term learning and growth opportunities.
- I wanted a marketing-driven, multinational corporation.

Since good fit alone will not ensure a successful career, I have analyzed the position from a "Power and Influence" viewpoint and developed by "entry strategy." One of my first nonmarketing tasks will be to (re)*learn the political ropes* in the company and assess the critical interdependencies in my department. This will require a thorough diagnosis of power sources, balances, and imbalances.

Another key element of my entry strategy will be *flexibility*. I will concentrate on learning the business and will cheerfully accept the tedious assignments along with the exciting ones. The former are generally an inevitable part of one's early career, and any assignment, no matter how routine, can be made challenging if one tries to complete it in the most efficient way possible and with the fewest errors. This outlook has helped me many times face tasks I would rather not do. In striving for flexibility, I will try not to be discouraged by any temporary setbacks which may result from the ambiguous environment, such as frequent change of superiors. Instead I will attempt to move with change and use it to my advantage.

I also intend to continue my lifelong process of learning. I believe that learning is an ongoing process and not limited to periods of formal education. When one ceases to learn, to explore, and to search for new ideas, stagnation and inertia seem inevitable. I will learn from every possible source—superiors, peers, and subordinates. I will learn as much as I can about other areas of Travel Related Services and other areas of the company. I will study the competition and never lose sight of the big picture/strategic perspective so that I can meaningfully incorporate my work into the larger context of the company.

If possible, I will *develop a niche* of expertise in an area of crucial importance to the company. Perhaps I will seek an assignment in the "critical issues" area, one of several areas under Mr. Welsh. As I understand it, this area is responsible for thoroughly understanding critical issues such as credit card surcharge. I may try to volunteer for an assignment that will help me develop a niche if none comes my way. Experience has taught me that one cannot always wait to be handed projects that will lead to increased responsibilities and a more rewarding career.

During my first few years I will probably devote the greatest chunk of my time to *developing working relationships* with superiors, peers, and subordinates. The key to my *managing up* strategy will be to develop trust and credibility, particularly with my

Exhibit 2 My "Entry Strategy" (*Continued*)

immediate superior, through the flexibility, learning, and niche strategies. I will not hesitate to present ideas when appropriate, but I will also be a good listener. During the course of my recent interviews at American Express I met one senior vice president and four vice presidents who work in the area I will join. Although I will not report directly to any of them, I will attempt to maintain ties with all.

Successfully *managing laterally* may be a great challenge, given the company's reputation for hiring bright, aggressive, and independent people. Nevertheless, it will be crucial to develop a sense of teamwork, not only for the cooperation and shared information that will result, but also for the rich, personal friendships that can make work a more rewarding experience.

I assume that at first I will not have to spend a great deal of time *managing down*. However, I will make a concerted effort to develop any and all professional or clerical subordinates, by delegating work selectively and giving them the benefit of my limited experience and knowledge. I will also foster teamwork among subordinates where it will prove constructive, just as I will encourage it among my peers. I will treat my subordinates well and hope to develop close, informal relationships with them.

American Express has an exceptional one-year program for entry-level MBAs called the Graduate Management Program (GMP). Its purpose is to provide newcomers with knowledge of all areas in which the company operates, and to enable them to develop "networking" relationships with peers and high-level executives from different parts of the company. I intend to take full advantage of this program and I hope that it will prove helpful in building a strong base of relationships which will enable me to use power and influence for productive ends throughout my career at American Express.

The last part of my entry strategy concerns assessing my possible career paths in the company. *Typically*, one considers several factors in developing a game plan for advancement:

1. How have top performers advanced?
2. In which areas should I seek assignments?
3. Where can I develop expertise?
4. What contributions can I make?
5. Where is the company headed in the future and how can I make issues 2, 3, and 4 coincide with this assessment?
6. Who are the critical decisionmakers with respect to my career (personnel, immediate superior, vice presidents, Jerry Welsh).

I prefaced this section with the work "typically" because American Express is not a "typical" company. Perhaps Louis V. Gerstner, chairman and chief executive officer of American Express Travel Related Services, quoted in the recent *Bulletin* article, best expresses the atypical approach to career development at American Express:

> We have a willingness to change titles and adapt them. We have positions at the very top of this corporation that basically are created for people because that's the position they ought to have . . . That makes for a group of people who focus on getting things

Exhibit 2 My "Entry Strategy" (*Continued*)

done in new and different ways. There is no book on how to succeed at American Express . . . There is no clear career path in this company . . . There is no way you can tell a brand new recruit what is the career path between him or her and Gerstner . . . The absence of a formalized career path permits an environment in which ideas, and results, and performance, and competence are valued much more than hierarchical standing.

As I stated, American Express is not a "typical" company, and that is precisely why I chose it and why I think that I can succeed there.

Exhibit 3 Worldwide Marketing and Communications

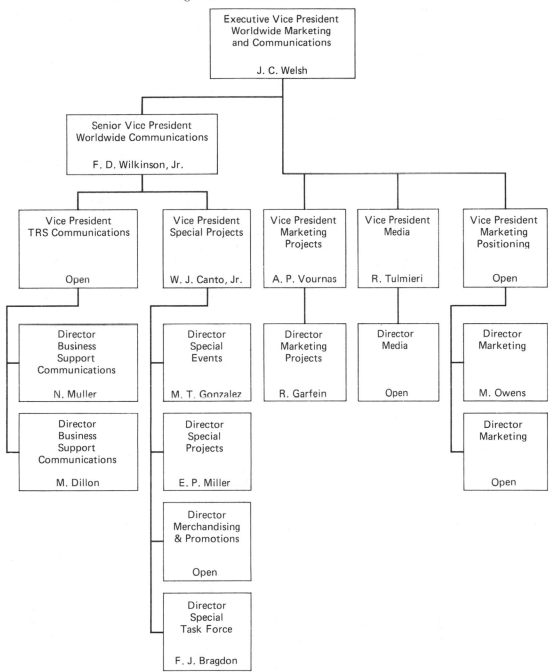

Teri Williams

> The people who do well here would be excellent entrepreneurs on their own.
>
> Teri Williams,
> director of Travelers Cheque Product Management
> American Express Travel Related Company

At this time of this case, Teri Williams was director of Travelers Cheque Product Management at the American Express Travel Related Services Company, a position that she had held for one and a half years. (See *Exhibit 1* for organization chart.) Her responsibilities included developing new travelers cheque services which would affect both consumer and seller and included the American Express Travelers Cheque with a new service delivery idea, which she oversaw from concept to implementation. This was a travelers cheque refund delivery service that would physically provide the customer replacements for lost travelers cheques within three hours. Called "Refund Express," the idea came out of a brainstorming session that Williams managed in February 1984. The service was up and running in a year. Establishing it had meant working with the American Express Travelers Cheque Operations Center, the firm's advertising group, and marketing services throughout the organization. While she had not had P&L responsibility, Williams had been involved in every aspect of bringing a service into existence and maintaining it, from conceiving strategic plans to detailing operating procedures. (See *Exhibit 2* for a description of "Refund Express.")

BACKGROUND

Williams' father was a restaurant owner; her mother was a nurse. With a degree in economics from Brown, from 1979 to 1981 she worked in corporate lending at a major financial institution in New York and then enrolled in Harvard Business School where she concentrated in marketing. During the summer between her first and second year at HBS she worked at American Express in Gold Card marketing, a program to resolicit those who had canceled their Gold Card membership. She rejoined the company following graduation from HBS in 1983. (See *Exhibit 3* for Williams' resume.)

This case was prepared by Associate Professor John Kao.

Copyright © 1986 by the President and Fellows of Harvard College. Harvard Business School case 9-487-011.

THE AMEX ENVIRONMENT

Williams thought highly of the firm's creative atmosphere; her group of "a lot of zany wild people," many new ideas flourished. She felt that these ideas were widely disseminated and openly discussed. Williams liked the company's flexible environment, and contrasted it with her previous experience in corporate lending where there had been set procedures for doing things. "If you had a better way there," she noted, "you'd have to fight an uphill battle because 'this is the way we've been doing things.'" Turf battles were not uncommon and formal and rigid definition of responsibilities was the rule.

Williams felt that individual goals were defined at American Express, but how one reached them was not. The company as a whole seemed committed to having people work on their new ideas regardless of their job description. For example, Williams had an idea for a new promotion that was not part of her job description. She was given the responsibility to implement it with the promotions department by simply approaching and talking with senior management. As she put it, "If you have ideas outside your goals, people here tend to say, 'Great, you go and do it.'" When she first arrived she thought they'd say, "Great, you stand aside . . . and I'll do it."

Williams felt there was a great deal of cross-functional and informal communication laterally and across levels. For example, she said she felt comfortable walking into her boss' office to discuss an idea. She could also talk freely with others about some important issue. Of course, she would discuss the idea with her boss first, but she didn't feel she needed his permission to discuss it with his superior officer. She felt she had a personal relationship with senior managers to whom she did not report directly. Williams thought that people in the firm were helpful. For example, the personal card people were very helpful with Williams' Gold Card information needs even though they were in different areas. In Williams' words, "They pull out information. There aren't rivalries." (See *Exhibit 4* for a description of career paths and corporate culture in the financial services area at American Express.)

START-UPS VERSUS ESTABLISHED ORGANIZATIONS

When asked to contrast start-ups and established organizations, Williams noted that an established company can have a strong and positive history. New ideas need to be consistent with this history, for example, at American Express there were strong traditions of customer service. Entrepreneurs focus on one thing, but at American Express one needed to focus on the company as a whole. The company's name was on the product and one had to have that larger point of view. Williams cited the example of her refund service which was part of Travelers Cheque, and in turn, part of American Express as a whole. Her group had debated whether to use an external courier service simply because of the risk to company reputation of using an outside vendor.

Williams also thought that an established organization might involve greater interpersonal skills than a situation in which everything starts from scratch since one is dealing with some standardized operations and an operations staff has been around for years. "One must be sensitive to their perspectives. It's important to ensure the integrity of existing operations to avoid jeopardizing existing levels of service," she commented.

In William's view, American Express was entrepreneurial when compared to most companies. It fostered the development of ideas; one was constantly asking if there's a better way to do things. That approach involved risk, however. For example, Williams said that she bet her job that the Travelers Cheque delivery service was ready for a national roll-out. She accepted the risk that she might get fired if the service didn't work. The risk was defined for her, not by an upfront monetary investment, but rather by her career investment at American Express. Like an entrepreneur, one becomes the champion of the idea, and one's ego and credibility are involved. "American Express is a large company, but feels like a small company in that people hear about your accomplishments." Noble failures were not sanctioned, but if there was a consistent record of nonaccomplishment, "you'd be fired," she said. She concluded:

> The goal of this business was to constantly think about new opportunities. It required analytical skills to build the evidence required to sell new ideas. In the entrepreneurial situation, the most important things was the feeling . . . you wanted to do something new. At American Express, things do happen because they're great ideas. The company has money and marketing experience. People who want to play it safe end up being mediocre at American Express. You have to take risks to successfully implement new ideas and succeed here. Drive and flexibility are important as well as the ability to sell your ideas. Entrepreneurship may be an overused word here but it *does* represent important skills which cannot be learned. Our company's climate is an important contributor to entrepreneurship as well. For example, there is no sibling rivalry here. The entrepreneurs at the company respect the operations people and vice versa.

Exhibit 1 AETC Business Management Organization Chart

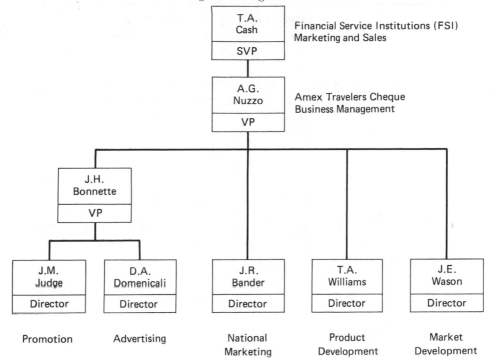

Exhibit 2 "Refund Express"

The Only Travelers Cheque Refund
Delivered Right to Your Customers
. . . In Under 3 Hours!

Here's How Only American Express—Makes It Happen.

A speedy, convenient refund is one of the reasons your customers buy American Express® Travelers Cheques. Now, by combining our vast refund network with nationwide courier services, we *bring the refund to your customers* in major U.S. cities. Vacations continue uninterrupted while the refund courier is on his way.

There's always a chance you will lose your Travelers Cheques. Now, American Express introduces an incredible new way to replace lost or stolen Travelers Cheques. In major U.S. cities, a refund can now be hand-delivered by courier, right to you, in under 3 hours from the time the loss is reported . . . and at no extra charge.

Here's how it works:

10:30 am—You discover you've lost $750 in American Express® Travelers Cheques. Don't panic.

10:35 am—Just call the toll-free Refund Hotline and arrange for a refund.

By 1:35 pm—A courier arrives at your specified, pre-arranged location, with replacement cheques. Your vacation is saved.

There's only one way to get this new refund service, ask for American Express Travelers Cheques.

American Express Refund Hotline
In the mainland U.S. 800-221-7282
In Hawaii 800-221-4950

Marketing Support

Advertising

American Express is launching this exciting and innovative refund service supported by heavy advertising. A brand new commercial will be featured during early news and prime time on all 3 networks. This spot will appear for the first time on April 12 and run for a period of six weeks. During this time 86% of your best customers will see this commercial over 5 times. It will be followed by our national campaign which will also include two new commercials.

Merchandising Material

Distinctive counter cards with take-one leaflets will be available for display at your institution. This material will help communicate the new service to your customers. The take-one leaflets are also available for use as statement stuffers. (Call your American Express representative to place an order.)

Exhibit 3 Resume

TERI A. WILLIAMS
50 W. 34th Street—#14A10
New York, New York 10001
Home: (212) 563-6740

Experience

1983– **AMERICAN EXPRESS T.R.S. COMPANY**   **New York, NY**
Present:

1984–   Director—Travelers Cheque Product Management
Present: Responsible for developing product enhancements and managing existing services for an over $9 billion business.
- Introduced a refund delivery service supported by a $5MM national advertising campaign, promotional material and public relations. Contributed to 12% sales gain YTD in 1985 vs 1984.
- Manage product development process including Synectics session, focus groups, concept testing, in-market operations testing, and full roll-out.
- Manage six managers, hired four out of six, and two secretaries. Operating budget of $500,000.

1983–84   Manager—Travelers Cheque Product Management
Implemented cost reduction programs to increase operating efficiencies. Developed and implemented a new American Express Travelers Cheque wallet which reduced production costs by $500,000 annually, yet met quality standards. Total cost reductions were $2MM annualized.

1979–81   **BANK OF AMERICA, NT & SA**   **New York, NY**

Treasury Associate, International Treasury Services. Marketed foreign exchange consulting services to corporate treasurers and international finance managers. Analyzed clients' exposure to foreign currencies. Recommended hedging and alternative financing techniques such as forward contracts, swaps and parallel loans. Coordinated computer and trading support facilities for existing customer accounts.

Education

1981–83   **HARVARD GRADUATE SCHOOL
OF BUSINESS ADMINISTRATION**   **Boston, MA**

MBA with Distinctions—Top 10%.
Member of Marketing and Finance clubs and the Afro-American Student Union. Tutored marketing and finance.

1975–79   **BROWN UNIVERSITY**   **Providence, RI**
BA in Economics. Chairperson of freshmen counseling program. Elected Brown Marshall for outstanding leadership skills by Dean and faculty members.

Personal   Raised in Bridgeport, Connecticut, family of seven. Funded college
Background   education with part-time work, scholarships and loans. Interests include travel, tennis and bicycling.

Exhibit 4 American Express Financial Services Institutions

FOCUS ON...

THE CHALLENGES AT FSI MARKETING AND SALES

MARKETING

handles all aspects of the marketing of American Express Travelers Cheque business.

National Marketing sets overall business objectives, develops business opportunities and allocates resources to meet goals.

Product Management develops methods to enhance the product, reduce costs, improve customer service, and build national acceptance for the product.

Market Development pursues non-traditional channels such as, credit unions and commercial firms, and supervises sales within the Travel Service Offices network.

Marketing Services creates advertising, designs promotional materials, and directs public relations.

within FSI manages the relationship between American Express and the participating financial institutions. Activities include coordinating the placement of Gold Card applications with financial institutions and developing programs to insure high-quality customer service.

reaches consumers with a fully-integrated financial management product that includes a checking account with a cooperating bank, a money market account, a Gold Card and brokerage services. This product package is sold to brokers around the country who in turn offer it to their customers.

SALES

The FSI multi-product sales force is an energetic group of professionals based all around the country. These field representatives sell and service customers ranging from small banks and credit unions to multi-billion dollar bank holding companies. Selling American Express financial products and services requires sophisticated selling abilities and provides diverse challenges. It is a rewarding sales experience with specific goals developed and monitored for each person.

Additionally, a team at headquarters directs the field sales force, provides support for their efforts and acts as liason between the sales and marketing functions.

AMERICAN EXPRESS Card Design and AMERICAN EXPRESS Travelers Cheque Design are both registered service marks and copyrighted properties of American Express.

BUSINESS ANALYSIS, PLANNING & DECISION SUPPORT

This area functions as the finance and planning arm of the FSI Marketing and Sales team, providing broad scale financial support, long-term strategic planning, and general systems support.

Business Analysis & Planning handles portfolio analysis, credit review, cash management, pricing, financial reporting, forecasting and budgeting. This group also develops long-term strategic plans and financial analysis for new product development.

Decision Support produces integrated, micro-computer-based MIS to support the decision-making process. Extensive modeling is used to assist marketing managers. Decision Support also provides general analytical, management science and programming support.

Marketing Information & Analysis involves mainframe MIS derived from the company's large-scale operating systems. In addition to developing and maintaining new MIS capabilities, this group is active in analyzing and drawing business conclusions from existing data.

FOCUS ON...
FSI MARKETING AND SALES

A Career Perspective

FOCUS ON...

YOUR FUTURE AT FSI MARKETING AND SALES

FSI offers you an exciting environment to put what you've learned into action. And, if you're like other people who have joined the FSI staff, you'll quickly become involved in projects that will expand your knowledge and test your capabilities.

But FSI isn't for everyone. The pace is fast and invigorating. You'll need to adapt to change quickly. And while you'll have the support of the team, you'll have to be a self-starter who recognizes opportunities and acts on them with creativity, sound business planning and follow-through.

And, perhaps most important, there is real opportunity for career growth. How far you go with FSI—and American Express—depends on you. There is no pre-determined or "typical" path. FSI is truly an entrepreneurial situation—with all the risks and rewards inherent in that term.

In fact, if we were to characterize the qualities you need to succeed on the FSI team we'd see the following:

- *Assuming ownership and taking risks*
- *Creatively effecting change*
- *Thinking analytically*
- *Having fun*

In return, you'll find yourself enjoying a highly visible position with the resources of an international leader in diversified financial services to back you up.

© 1985 American Express Travel Related Services Company, Inc.

AMERICAN EXPRESS TRAVEL
RELATED SERVICES
COMPANY, INC.
AMERICAN EXPRESS PLAZA
NEW YORK, NEW YORK 10004

FOCUS ON...

THE PEOPLE OF FSI MARKETING AND SALES

66 *Working in FSI's unstructured environment is exciting for me. You have the opportunity to see a need in an area—even if it's not within your own function—and do something about it. It's the atmosphere of team effort that makes this possible. Although there's certainly a feeling of competitiveness, everyone supports everyone else's efforts.* 99

Evelyn Tong
Assistant Manager
Business Analysis & Planning
MBA, Columbia

66 *Diversity is the key word at FSI. The people have come from a wide range of experiences which creates a stimulating workplace. The nature of the assignments are equally diverse which broadens our knowledge and brings new challenges.* 99

David Douglas Stone
Manager
Travelers Cheque Product Management
M.A. Fletcher School of Law and Diplomacy

66 *I was always interested in marketing, but I didn't want to follow the highly structured career path of a marketing position at a packaged goods company. At FSI, I saw the opportunity of a less restricted experience. And I was right. The word 'marketing' is defined in its fullest terms here. I quickly became involved in all aspects of marketing, not just a specialized portion of it.* 99

Margaret Simonetti
Manager
Gold Card Product Management
MBA, Stanford

465

Exhibit 4 *(continued)*

FOCUS ON...

THE FSI MARKETING AND SALES ENVIRONMENT

A stimulating career path, the opportunity to contribute meaningfully, rapidly. These attributes help to characterize work life as we experience it here. We agree that FSI possesses that certain "spirit."

These are not the terms you would normally associate with the working atmosphere at a company that was founded in 1850. Especially one that continues to base a sizable portion of its income on a product that was introduced in 1891.

But ask the professionals on the team at FSI* Marketing and Sales and that's what you'll hear when they describe their working experience.

THE FSI STORY

Changes in the financial environment in the early 1980's resulted in unprecedented competition for the American Express® Travelers Cheque—the product that was introduced in 1891. The revolution within the financial services industry required new business approaches, new strategies and the revitalization of products.

FSI stands for "Financial Services Institution." As the name suggests, the FSI group markets its products to banks, savings and loans and other financial services institutions. However, the group also markets through other distribution channels, including the Joint Service Office network, AAA offices, and Shearson Lehman Brothers and other brokers.

That's where FSI came in. And since then, the group has been the center of a highly-charged turn-around situation that is constantly evolving to meet the demands of a rapidly changing, highly competitive marketplace.

This group is continually assessing new ways to enhance its products to maintain their competitive edge, and developing new market outlets to further increase market share and profitability.

The dynamic strategies of FSI have enabled American Express to maintain and strengthen its leadership role with well-known prestigious products that have clear competitive advantages.

In short, FSI is *first now...and determined to be first into the future.*

THE FSI ORGANIZATION

FSI is divided into five general areas:

Travelers Cheque Business Management handles all Marketing, Research & Development and other aspects of the American Express Travelers Cheque business.

Gold Card® Product Management coordinates the American Express

marketing efforts with financial institutions participating in the Gold Card program.

Financial Services based Management markets an integrated financial management package through brokers.

Sales directs and supports field sales efforts for all products.

Business Analysis, Planning and Systems Support provides financial, analytical and systems support to the other areas of the FSI group.

Based at American Express corporate headquarters in the heart of New York City's financial district, FSI is a group of professionals with diverse backgrounds and talents working toward a common goal of excellence. And they are people who are having fun doing it.

Fewer than 80 people make up the entire professional and support staff at headquarters; approximately 100 sales representatives are in the field.

When you consider that this group generates over 10 billion dollars in sales each year, you can see how each member of the team must make significant contributions—consistently.

That's why the excitement is here!

> 66 *Working at FSI is never dull. There is continual change. Keeping up with state-of-the-art technology is especially important in my area, and requires the ability to adapt quickly. That's what makes it exciting—and fun.* 99
>
> Steve Sherman
> Director
> Marketing Information Analysis
> MBA, Wharton, University of Pennsylvania

> 66 *I was attracted to American Express because of its opportunity for growth. What I found at FSI exceeded my expectations. It's a dynamic atmosphere that encourages as much responsibility-taking as possible. And management fosters the exchange of ideas, inviting all points of view.* 99
>
> Nina Lawrence
> Assistant Manager
> Travelers Cheque National Marketing
> MBA, New York University

Scandinavian Airlines System

The rest of the industry relies on the bland leading the bland.

Anthony Sampson

The difference between good and bad service is two millimeters.

Jan Carlzon

In 1983, the Scandinavian Airlines System (SAS) was named "Airline of the Year" by *Air Transport World*. The industry's most respected journal chose SAS as the top airline in all categories including passenger service, financial management, technical management, industry service, and market development. In a press release, the company referred to this honor as the "Oscar" of the airline industry; previous winners had included Lufthansa, Japan Airlines, and Delta Airlines.

HISTORICAL OVERVIEW

The Creation of SAS

SAS was initially formed as a consortium through an agreement signed by the national airlines and governments of Denmark, Sweden, and Norway in 1946. SAS was unsubsidized and the consortium agreement stipulated that it should be run as if privately owned. The company was owned two-sevenths by Danish Airlines (DDL), two-sevenths by Norwegian Airlines (DNL), and three-sevenths by Swedish Airlines (ABA). Government and private interests shared the ownership of each national parent company, 50-50. SAS was given first choice rights on domestic routes and exclusive rights to flights outside of Scandinavia.

SAS' start-up did not occur in conditions conducive to unanimity. Norway, which had once been a province of Denmark, was given to Sweden

This case was prepared by Associate Professor John Kao, with the assistance of Jennifer Blome. Copyright © 1986 by the President and Fellows of Harvard College. Harvard Business School case 9-487-041.

in 1814 and did not become independent until 1905. World War II, in which Sweden was neutral and Norway and Denmark were occupied, divided these Scandinavian countries further. Nevertheless, SAS evolved into what some called a miniature United Nations of the air.

Technical/Production Orientation

From its origin, SAS had been led and managed by technically experienced people. This was natural, considering the high levels of travel demand that emerged after World War II: SAS, like other airlines, invested heavily in new aircraft and technically trained personnel. The major issues at that time were safety, reliability, efficiency, control, and the need to remain in the forefront of rapidly improving technology. As with other airlines, this technical orientation remained dominant with SAS through the 1970s. With the consistent industry growth, the ability to produce for the least cost and with the best technology was seen as the key to success. In fact, airplanes were said to receive more attention than customers.

Early Corporate Philosophy

Until the 1980s, the philosophy and management style of SAS closely reflected its technical orientation. Many of the company's standard operating procedures consisted of detailed instructions and checklists compiled in systematized manuals. This was a reasonable approach for those concerned with flight safety, such as pilots or aircraft technicians; it also seemed a normal and acceptable way of running a business for senior management. Thus, other areas were controlled by detailed instructions and manuals in a centralized system.

During these postwar years of high growth in a controlled environment, the common philosophy within the airline industry was: In a growing market, within the framework of a cartel, a company can be managed to profitability by general economizing and reciprocally dividing up the markets.

The conditions prevailed until the mid-1970s, which brought dramatically increased oil prices, a recessionary environment, and a stagnant travel market. There also was a shift towards deregulation and liberalization in the industry, which resulted in increased competition. The rapid rate of technical change slowed and all technology became easily accessible to all the airlines. The airline industry's response was to simplify and cut costs; all customers' needs were perceived to be the same.

The president of SAS at that time was Knut Hagrup, an aeronautical engineer. The industry's overall approach was typified by Hagrup's comments:

> There are many buds to be nipped. We must get rid of all unnecessary elements in our business and in our products. We are facing a trend towards a simplified way of living. I am quite convinced that the luxury first class air traveling during

the fifties and the sixties is over or must end because of the super crisis we now face. In the seventies so far, the service on board has been gradually simplified. Whatever will be done, we can be assured that in the foreseeable future, we will not get back to something similar to this era, when the passengers got spoiled in many respects.

SAS' response to the problem facing the industry at that time was not surprising. After all, cost cutting had been successful in the past. This time, however, cutting costs resulted in deteriorating service and highly dissatisfied employees for the established airlines, including SAS. Two SAS cabin attendants recalled:

> They always cut down on our things, like newspapers and lemons. We gave the passengers our own newspapers. It was so miserable to have to tell the passengers we didn't have any lemons that we sometimes bought them ourselves. The service just got worse and worse. They cut down on the wrong things. The passengers complained but nothing happened.
> SAS had a bad reputation. Whatever we did, it was bad. The passengers were often aggressive. When we tried to be nice and helpful they just hissed at us.

During this period, SAS was weighed down with bureaucracy. The president approved every employee hire so that adding a mechanic could take three months. The head of an airplane maintenance facility did not have enough spending authority to buy a truck. The situation was aggravated by a market that had ceased to grow, and by the entry of many new competitors in the wake of U.S. deregulation.

Hagrup's tenure as president and CEO of SAS ended with his retirement in 1978. He was replaced by Carl-Olov Munkberg, who, with many years' experience within the SAS group, was the first president with a business degree and no engineering background. Munkberg introduced a new philosophy to SAS, one that he had implemented at another company. Top management probably selected him because of his previous experience; they agreed with Munkberg that a profit-oriented management concept with delegated responsibility and authority would benefit the company.

Munkberg moved slowly in pursuing these strategies, facing opposition and resistance from the organization. The drive for change became absorbed into many working groups, into pilot projects for profit centers in restricted areas of operations, and into repeated discussions with the board about alternative organizational designs. In an effort to slash costs, 1,300 jobs were eliminated through attrition, including many positions that were closest to the customer. The lack of visible action created uncertainty and frustration; the company was perceived to be at a standstill. Munkberg strove for consensus and evolution, rather than for revolution. Enter Jan Carlzon.

JAN CARLZON

> The most rotten thing in the world is a seat which takes off unsold.
>
> Jan Carlzon, President and CEO, SAS

When Jan Carlzon was appointed president and CEO of SAS he had already experienced successful results within the travel industry and the SAS organization itself.

Carlzon's interest in entertainment values was apparent during his days at the Stockholm School of Economics where he was in charge of school parties. While there, he is said to have written a letter to the Beatles asking them to come to entertain in Sweden. This chance of a lifetime, he explained in his letter, would cost the band only the price for their plane tickets. At Vingresor, a Swedish tour company where Carlzon served as marketing manager, he set up villages in Majorca and other resorts. One of his innovations involved the creation of a separate village where parents left their children to play during the day. An ad showed some children with the caption, "It's no longer a problem to take mom and dad on a vacation."

He became managing director of Vingresor three years later, and in one year successfully turned its deficit into a profit; the middle-sized operation became one of Sweden's largest tour companies.

In 1978, Sweden's domestic airline, Linjeflyg, was in need of a new managing director. One of the airline's board members recalled of Carlzon: "I had heard him make a couple of presentations. He impressed me by his ability to communicate important problems in a very simple way. I decided to keep him in mind for the future." Carlzon was offered the position but wasn't eager to accept. He felt he was still needed at Vingresor and had more to accomplish there. Yet eventually he was persuaded to take the position.

Linjeflyg, which was losing money, was charging the same fares for rush-hour flights as for the off-peak midday departures. Carlzon cut midday fares 50 percent or more to attract families, senior citizens, and youth travelers. Demand soared. Young customers pitched tents outside the airport to wait for open seats. Like his previous success at Vingresor, Carlzon managed to turn Linjeflyg's losses into gains within the first year as director.

Carlzon was brought in to be in charge of the SAS airline division with Munkberg as president in late 1980. This arrangement proved untenable and Carlzon was made president and CEO in 1981. Said one top SAS manager, "Carlzon took the job as a challenge; he had worked within the SAS organization before and he was very much aware of the service business. He saw a chance to do the same thing he did with Linjeflyg."

Leadership Style

Jan Carlzon differed from many of his Scandinavian counterparts, most notably in his method of communicating, both with his employees and the market. Carlzon's leadership style was described as outgoing and bold; he used fun and imagination to communicate simple ideas. An article in *Fortune* magazine characterized some elements of his style. "In contrast to the stately pillars of the Scandinavian establishment, Carlzon is a self-styled exhibitionist who declares that 'all business is show business.'" (*Fortune*, May 30, 1983.)

Carlzon's showmanship style was exemplified by his introduction of SAS's makeover of the DC-9 aircraft and the new SAS uniforms:

> Dust off your disco shoes, frequent fliers—Jan Carlzon is bent on putting the go-go back into the airline business. Or so it seemed last month when SAS unveiled its new image at a Copenhagen extravaganza: Visitors toured a DC-9 spruced up with a new image and fresh logo and a remodeled interior; Carlzon, SAS' boyish president, led a company chorus line to a disco version of "Love is in the Air." What's most upbeat of all, though, is that accompanying all this flash is some 1960's-style profitability.
>
> (*Fortune*, May 30, 1983)

Carlzon also threw the largest party ever held in Sweden in 1983. Four thousand employees were entertained in a hangar with a Wild West show, discos, and limousines to take partygoers home. Despite the positive effects, Carlzon's style was a little unsettling for a few members of the organization. The *Fortune* article continued:

> A few colleagues resent the time and rhetoric Carlzon lavishes on the press. "There's an indecent amount of bragging going on," sniffs one director.

Not only did Carlzon have a flair for publicity but his employees praised his ability to listen and his openness toward people and ideas. He said of himself, "I like to meet people, but not really businesspeople . . . people who think and feel, talk and discuss." Such traits were perhaps also responsible for his success in responding to the needs of the market and employees in such positive and productive ways. One of Carlzon's top managers described the success of his leadership style:

> He has great charisma and he's a preacher . . . he's very eager to spread his ideas. He's been talking and talking and I think that was necessary to make the shift in the organization to marketing/service orientation from technical/production orientation.

THE NEW SAS

SAS' profits and its market share had been falling since the mid-1970s, but not until 1979–1980 did the real financial crisis hit. After 17 profitable years, SAS suffered a loss of $17 million in fiscal 1979–1980 on total operating revenue of $861 million. Carlzon was made president and CEO in 1981, and in the fiscal year ending September 30, 1982, SAS showed a $24.6 million operating profit, and a $48.9 million operating profit the following year. This occurred in a difficult environment for the airline industry. Worldwide losses for the industry totaled $1.7 billion in a year that saw SAS make $71 million on $2 billion in sales. In contrast, Air France lost $100 million that year, while Swissair made a relatively modest $19 million.

Later Carlzon suggested that this crisis point of 1979 was necessary for him to step in and implement drastic changes. All confidence had been lost in the then-current president Munkberg. In 1981, as president and chief executive officer of SAS, Carlzon's most immediate tasks involved influencing a new corporate philosophy, creating a new business concept, and following through with a reorganization of the company's structure.

New Corporate Philosophy

SAS' new corporate philosophy focused on a market/service orientation. Carlzon tried to make the employees aware they were in the service business, not the airplane business. *Exhibit 1* presents a new corporate credo. The new philosophy was: In a stagnating market, where market forces are set free, a company can achieve profitability by adjusting and aggressively investing in its real needs better than the competition.

Carlzon consistently stressed that an airline's only real asset is a satisfied customer. To him the market-oriented philosophy meant that "the role of SAS central management is to listen to what its 'front-line' operators are telling it, rather than the other way around, which is still the pattern in far too many organizations." (*Financial Times*, October 31, 1983.)

This front-line concentration was one of the important elements of the new organizational structure and management philosophy.

The New Structure

A decentralized organizational structure was necessary to facilitate the operation of the market/service-oriented company SAS was striving to become. Carlzon supported the decentralized structure; in his mind, the only way a company could respond to all the needs of the customer was to:

> allow the employee to utilize his or her own creativity, ingenuity, and familiarity with the situation, respond in a way they see in the best interest of the customer, and operate within a structure which gives that employee the responsibility for their actions.

The new decentralized structure called for organization along profit lines, resulting in the creation of a divisional structure. See *Exhibit 2*. Each division was responsible for organizing itself and pricing its product to show a profit. The divisions were to follow what Carlzon called a "from-the-outside-in" approach.

> Commercial decides what markets it can serve profitably and in what manner, and "buys" the necessary flight and ground services and equipment from traffic services and crews from operations. They in turn "buy" the aircraft and training from technical, and administration backs them all up.

Divisions were set up as entrepreneurial entities with the flexibility and responsibility to enhance creativity and action. It was these "entrepreneurs" who came up with many service innovations and new business ideas at SAS. *Exhibit 3* shows revenue by business area for SAS in 1984. *Exhibit 4* shows a divisional marketing brochure.

Carlzon said that the core of the SAS turnaround was changing people's sense of responsibility and authority. The implementation process was really about developing morale—changing people's minds and developing some risk taking, but essentially improving confidence and morale. The new profit centers ranged from the entire airline division to the Stockholm-London route. Now, for instance, a route manager was virtually an entrepreneur, free to decide the time and number of flights between two cities—contingent on the approval of the governments involved—and to lease airplanes and flight crews from other divisions. Managers were encouraged to go outside SAS if they could get a better deal. European airline operations, for example, bypassed SAS to lease some Fokker turboprops.

Replacing thirteen out of fourteen top executives, Carlzon brought new blood into the company's top management, people who had fresh ideas and enthusiasm. It was necessary to have top managers "who could adapt more easily to the new policy of greater decentralization and local responsibility for profits," Carlzon explained.

All management levels were substantially thinned, and 120 senior managers were sent to intensive management training seminars. Through customer sensitivity courses and education about the company's goals and strategies, 10,000 front-line people were also extensively trained, preparing them for their increased responsibility and freedom to operate as they thought best. "Front-line people are encouraged to take the initiative in dealing with customer service problems without waiting for orders from above," commented Carlzon.

Business Concept and Strategies

With the new managers in place, Carlzon and his team analyzed SAS' situation in the market. U.S. strategy consultants were hired to assess the industry's top carriers. It was very important to Carlzon to have a clear view of things; he was described as not liking to look too deeply or to make things too complicated. Once Carlzon felt he had clarified the situation, he developed a new business concept and strategies for SAS.

Carlzon's main strategy was to become the preferred airline of the frequent-flying business traveler. This market segment was selected because it was relatively stable and could afford to pay the real cost of providing an airline seat. In the past, full-fare passengers (businesspeople) had been mixed in with discount passengers who might have paid half the full fare, yet, businesspeople did not receive any additional service. By giving them better service tailored to their specific needs and separating them from discount passengers, Carlzon reasoned, businesspeople might prefer to pay the higher price. Departing radically from the traditional cost-cutting methods, Carlzon instead invested heavily in new products and services for which the market might pay a full-fare, higher-yield ticket. Carlzon's recovery plan was simple: "You've got to get the car moving before you can put on the brakes." SAS had to start making money again before it could start looking at the cost side.

When Carlzon did turn to the cost side, employees were asked to evaluate every resource with this criterion: "Would the businessperson be willing to pay for it? If not, it should be eliminated. If yes, it should be kept and perfected as well as being made as efficient as possible. While SAS employment levels continued to increase, administration costs were reduced by 25 percent, and corporate overhead was reduced by $23 million per year. Personnel were shifted to highly visible service areas where customer contact occurred, an area that had been penalized under previous SAS regimes. In Carlzon's words, "SAS consists of 50 million annual moments of truth when a customer makes a contact with an SAS employee."

The basic strategy during this time focused on the following principles:

1. Emphasis was on the full-paying passenger (Businessman's Airline).
2. Marginal capacity was filled by cargo and tourist class passengers, and a clear differentiation in prices and services were offered the tourist and business class segments.
3. Resources were concentrated and the organization designed to meet the needs of these segments.
4. Rather than operating unprofitable lines, cooperation was sought with other airlines at important junctions such as Bangkok and New York.
5. The organization was decentralized in order to become more responsive to the market.
6. Freight was marketed through a new concept of door-to-door transport with more flexible pricing.

What was going on, what had to be done, and why were communicated clearly and simply throughout the company. One way was through the distribution of Carlzon's "Little Red Books." When these books were first distributed, some employees laughed at the simply stated messages and cartoon pictures. But before long these booklets were appreciated for what they were: Carlzon's analyses and strategies presented with simplicity and imagination. His first booklet was entitled "Let's Get in There and Fight," his second, "The Fight of the Century," and his most recent book, "Now We're Going to Use Our Heads." His concentration on information, training, and education was based on the philosophy that:

> instruction restrains the ability to act, and information increases the possibilities . . . so we skipped a lot of manuals and went more for information to inform of strategies, goals, ideas, products, service, concepts, the market, and customers' needs. You can't manage air personnel from the ground by manuals. (Top SAS manager.)

Service Innovations

The company applied its emphasis on entrepreneurship and innovation to improving service. It spent a great deal of time brainstorming about passenger preferences and 160 new approaches to service were initiated (of these 140 have already been completed). As Carlzon said, "We want to be 1 percent better than the competition in a hundred ways, rather than 100 percent better in only one way."

The company took major steps to improve the customer's perception of service. It separated full fare from discount passengers, instituting separate check-ins for full-fare passengers with a guarantee delay of no longer than six minutes. Gate assignments for planes were restructured to suit passenger, not airplane, convenience. Copenhagen's Kastrup airport inaugurated a "Scanorama" business lounge which was subsequently replicated in other major gateway cities. Amenities included free telexes to anywhere in Europe; an unlimited acceptance of unstamped letters for airmailing abroad; a private meeting room with slide projector, calculator, copy machine, conference table, and a recording secretary; a videocassette recorder in the lounge with a selection of current movies; and sleeping cubicles. Callers using the lounge's international direct dial phones paid for "minutes they say they talked to the places they say they dialed."

On-board amenities were also improved. These included more leg room for customers, improved food, and free drinks. In November 1981, SAS launched its "EuroClass" full-fare service. Other airlines, such as British Airways and Air France, had introduced business class services earlier, but with a surcharge. SAS' competitive edge was to provide the improved service without adding the surcharge. The company invested in extra personnel to load and maneuver planes quickly as part of a 1981 punctuality drive, "Operation Punctuality." Carlzon himself had video monitors installed in his office where he could observe every deviation from schedule and follow it up personally. Within a year, SAS became the most punctual airline in Europe with an on-time rate of 94.5 percent, improving further to 97 percent over the subsequent two years.

To emphasize to customers and personnel alike that the new services and business image represented long-term commitments, Carlzon next gave SAS an entirely new corporate identity. He explained: "Corporate identity is a communication tool that starts with an honest evaluation of what a company is, and develops into an organized, controlled system." To complement the new services and the "business" image, planes were freshly painted and refurbished inside. SAS personnel were fitted with new uniforms designed by Calvin Klein to present a "professional" presence. See *Exhibit 5*.

This campaign proved very successful for SAS with an increase of 8 percent in the number of passengers paying full economy fare on continental flights during fiscal 1982. The time schedule for introduction of services is shown below:

EuroClass—Business Class on European flights	November 1, 1981
Improved Business Class on intercontinental services	February 1, 1982
New intra-Nordic low fares introduced	June 1, 1982
First Business Class introduced on intercontinental routes	September 26, 1982
New low fares extended to European routes	November 15, 1982
New corporate identity unveiled	April 12, 1983

Other service improvements included more nonstop flights from the Swedish and Norwegian markets to major European cities, bypassing the customary stop in Copenhagen. This was made possible by using smaller DC-9 aircraft and selling SAS's larger airbus aircraft which required stopovers to fill up their large capacity.

The price tag for these innovations was estimated at $40 million overall, including all aspects of upgraded accommodation and service for SAS' business and full-fare customers. Of this, about $15 million was spent on the new corporate identity program inaugurated in April 1983. Not every innovation was a success; for example, Carlzon supposedly wanted to change the airline's name to Royal Scandinavian but was overruled. In addition, door-to-door parcel service failed

THE FUTURE

By early 1985, the company could look back on a series of successfully achieved objectives. *Exhibits 6–8* present performance improvements from 1979–83. It spoke of a "first wave" which had transformed the company into a market service-oriented company from a technically based organization. Now SAS was focused on a new series of challenges called the "second wave," a period characterized by further deregulation and the need for creative responses to a new environment.

What lay ahead? Could momentum be maintained as SAS continued to seek excellence and expansion in its service concepts? Could Carlzon continue to motivate and inspire the individual initiative for innovation? These were just a few of the uncertainties challenging SAS in the years to come.

Regulatory Environment

SAS's regulatory environment within Scandinavia was comparable to that in the rest of Europe. Treaties and agreements were made between countries and between airline companies. International price levels and conditions were negotiated within the framework of the International Air Transport Association (IATA) and were then submitted to the relevant government agencies for approval.

As mentioned, SAS received concessions from the Scandinavian governments, and had the first choice for new routes. If they turned it down or thought there was a need for another carrier, the routes were offered to smaller airlines operating in Scandinavia.

Influenced by deregulation in the United States, European governments were coming under pressure to further liberalize and deregulate. SAS publicly indicated belief that deregulation would come, and that it was prepared. An SAS top manager explained, "It is important to be efficient in a nonregulated and deregulated environment. So we shall not depend on the monopoly, but we are going to manage as in a competitive situation."

Competition

If deregulation came to Europe, SAS would have competition from smaller airline companies that would challenge its shorter routes. Competition would also increase from the 20 bigger European airlines already flying into Scandinavia, since these airlines would be able to operate more freely. In addition, market entry would be greatly eased for new competitors.

SAS faced its toughest competition within the European market, from airlines such as Swissair, British Airways, and Air France. What would it take for SAS to remain competitive in the future? An SAS manager explained:

> We must stick to our basic pillars . . . We must have a maximum of safety. It is a basic issue for our image—people must perceive the aircraft functions well. Also, [we must] stick to the service business. We make our living by giving service to customers, not buying and selling aircraft. Third, would be excellence. We don't just offer a product line of services, but high-quality service on every point from door to door. On top of all that [we must] be economically efficient and cost effective.

Future Growth

With an action-oriented, risk-taking culture developing and amid the glow of recent success, the SAS organization would continue to develop.

In and of itself, expansion was not a strategy for the airline. Yet, striving to meet the needs of business travelers led SAS to expand routes to where they wanted to travel. It monitored the Asian market and was ready to respond with more routes or alternative gateways, if needs so demanded.

New businesses continued to develop within the SAS organization, capitalizing on the strengths and resources of SAS' market/service orientation and the existing infrastructure which facilitated the transformation of ideas into profitable service businesses. Such new companies included various "knowledge" companies selling SAS' expertise in management and training programs. Other areas in which the company shared its expertise included: technical service and maintenance, ground handling, data systems, flight crew training, management training, catering services, hotel and hospital management. It worked through such facilities as:

- The Bangkok Maintenance Center—for the airplanes and motors of other carriers.
- Fornebu Airport, Norway—SAS had a maintenance contract for Hercules and Orion aircraft with the Norwegian Air Force.
- Saudi Arabia—flight kitchen service in the airports of Riyadh and Jidda.
- SAFIG—The Saudi Arabian Flight Inspection Group involving about 30 SAS pilots and technicians who calibrated navigation and landing aids on the Arabian peninsula.
- SAS Flight Academy in Bromma, Sweden, trained pilots and technicians.
- SAS Service Courses—used by more than 50 banks, hotels, and other companies. Operated in conjunction with Time Systems of Denmark; parts of this program were sometimes referred to as "SAS Charm School."
- The rationale for SAS service—sales and service—export was threefold: SAS' image, the perception of Scandinavian quality and honesty, and the absence of colonial or political taint. Five to 100 percent of external services came from the perception of spare capacity in the company and the desire to use it productively.

SAS also worked on integrating its complementary businesses to provide businesspeople with a comprehensive service package. Such businesses as limousine service and the SAS hotels were initially developed and run independently; now, integration to provide "door-to-door" service had begun operation in some locations. With such a comprehensive system, a businessperson could be taken from office to airport and, upon arrival at destination, to a SAS hotel. His or her luggage, in the meantime, would be handled by the chauffeur and would be waiting in the hotel room. Many possibilities existed for further integration as more services were created.

Dealing With Success

I used to say that the mass media takes a person to a post and ties him to it. Then they write positive things about him, and that is like putting logs at the person's feet; and when he has received enough "good" press, he can't take it any longer. Then they light the fire and finally try to extinguish the whole person. It is like Jeanne d'Arc at the stake.

Jan Carlzon

We have had problems coping with our success. SAS' success has caused some liability to the company. When it announced operating profit of $90 million in the fiscal year ending September 1984, problems were created. SAS has pointed to its need for $114 million a year in profit to self-finance the replacement fleet it will need to bring onstream by the early 1990s. But billion kroner profit figures were a red flag to employees. Sporadic strikes occurred in Stockholm and Copenhagen on wage and manning issues, including a one-day strike by cabin attendants in May of 1984. There was another problem as well. Aviation authorities were reluctant to grant fare increases to the newly profitable SAS which they had been more willing to consider in the "underdog days" of red ink.

A Top SAS Official

Human Resource Management

In early 1985, the company contemplated its response to a second wage challenge in the area of human resource management. The company was considering innovations in career path planning, training, and compensation. Despite traditional Scandinavian job and salary security, SAS staff were concerned about wages and career progression. For example, one flight attendant remarked that good performance would lead in eight years to promotion as a purser. The company had not managed noncash compensation or rewards to maximum effect. And, while there was willingness to consider some form of employee ownership, there was also concern about a "chain letter" effect. There was debate about what types of training were desirable in the future, for which audiences, and to develop what types of skills. There was also a continuing concern about nurturing innovative and entrepreneurial attitudes, and avoiding a "box" mentality that dealt with problems from an excessively circumscribed and limited perspective.

SAS also emphasized social and humanistic values. Said one senior manager, "It's not enough to win. Is making money what life is about? The real driver under our business is changing the world." Certainly, SAS' role in Sweden and internationally was significant. In Sweden, SAS was regarded as the source of new ideas and inspiration in the business community, and Carlzon as the spokesperson for a new type of business style and philosophy. SAS' business of providing services to a variety of outside clients such as the Swedish departments of education and taxation, the post, telephone and telegraph authority, and municipal governments added to its influence. And Carlzon himself was voted Sweden's most popular individual in a survey carried out by a leading Swedish daily newspaper in 1983.

During the first phase of changing the company to a market/service orientation, training efforts were concentrated on top management and front-line personnel. Now, however, new problems arose which concerned middle-level management's understanding of their responsibilities and role in the new company. As one SAS manager said, "There was perhaps too little concentration on middle management, and so the internal resource management is what we're all working on now."

Carlzon himself recognized the importance of and the challenge in motivating middle-level managers: "The most difficult thing when you want to direct your company towards the market, and take the marketplace view of the company, is the people in middle management."

Attention was also directed to support personnel. While front line people receive positive feedback from the customers, this motivation was lacking for support personnel.

How could SAS maintain its momentum? Carlzon acknowledged the difficulty in this task as well:

> I haven't got the answer. I think that culture is one thing; rewards, of course, are a very important thing as well. You know that for Christmas last year we

sent a watch to all our employees, a watch with an airplane on the second hand, proof that we had become the most punctual airline in the world. It was a very expensive watch. We had to pay tax to the authorities, because in Scandinavia you cannot give a gift to your employees without tax if it is worth much. Stupid, you have to give rewards; people must feel that they did something. But when thinking about the problem I used to ask myself: "How the hell could I, as a front-line employee—how could I suddenly decide on not giving good service? As long as I have all responsibility and all possibility to take any action, I don't have to ask any manager's permission for what I am doing. I could never shift blame, saying that I don't get a positive response from my manager. So, the day I start to see unhappy customers around me, the only person to blame is myself, because I had all the possibilities."

But what I am afraid of is that these people working in the front line do not get this freedom to take responsibility, that too many managers on different levels start interfering again, and start to direct people by orders and instructions again. This, I am afraid of, that they might feel that these are just words coming from the top, and that our educational periods were only words, and it didn't match reality.

Exhibit 1   Corporate Credo

SATISFIED CUSTOMERS AND MOTIVATED EMPLOYEES ARE OUR GREATEST ASSETS

Consequently, the aim is to:

1. Act professionally, competently and uncompromisingly in all matters concerning safety and quality.
2. Provide individually oriented service to both customers and colleagues.
3. Keep our promises.
4. Ensure that the tasks of every colleague are meaningful.
5. Always be one step ahead in product development and make the future secure by staying profitable.
6. Have a visible, consistent management at all levels of the company.

Exhibit 2

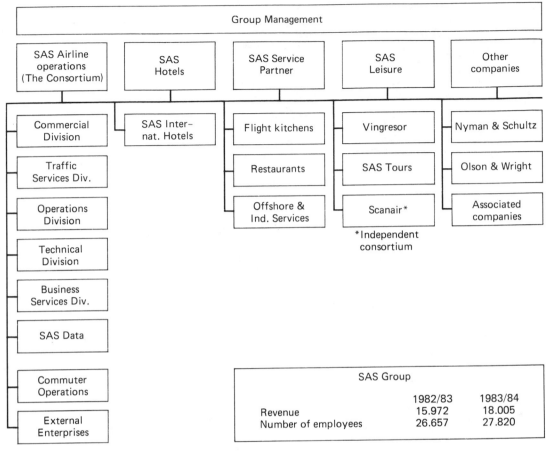

Exhibit 3 The SAS Group

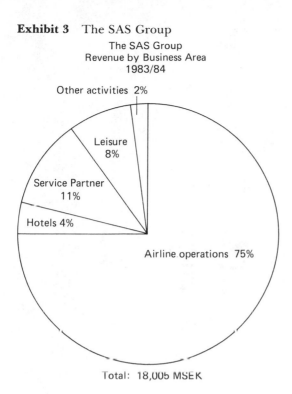

The SAS Group
Revenue by Business Area
1983/84

Other activities 2%

Leisure
8%

Service Partner
11%

Hotels 4%

Airline operations 75%

Total: 18,005 MSEK

Exhibit 4   Scandinavian Airlines System (A)

Exhibit 5 Scandinavian Airlines System (A)

Ramp personnel, loaders and mechanics will get new overalls made of durable, bright blue cotton. There's also a choice of trousers and jacket. Three different red T-shirt designs are also available in either long or short sleeves, with or without a collar. The mechanics' shirts come with "SAS Maintenance" printed on the back in bold white letters.

A fundamental change.

This brochure introduces SAS's new corporate identity program.

Our new uniforms.

Our new aircraft livery.

New interiors for our entire fleet.

Our new corporate image reflects a thoroughly and consistently applied communications system, touching everything from ticket covers to ground support equipment and reservations offices worldwide.

The transformation is already in the works. On September 25, more than 9,000 of our colleagues—those who deal directly with our customers – donned new uniforms. They represent one of the most important elements in our public image: air crews, ground staff and ticket office personnel. Some of our planes are already flying in new colors and with all-new interiors; the intercontinental fleet will be ready by early 1984. In another year, the new design program will have covered the world.

Thousands of SAS people are involved in the program. On the surface, it looks like one of the most significant investments we have made since the new SAS took shape a couple of years ago.

On the contrary!

The most important venture we've embarked on is our comprehensive investment in service.

The most important goal we set for ourselves, the most significant long-term commitment we've made, is to satisfy our customers. The most important ingredient in the "new" SAS is not our new livery or our uniforms – it's the people behind them.

The most important decision we ever made is to get in there and fight–and fight together. More than anything else, SAS represents, and will continue to be, the will to live up to the expectations of our customers, person to person, every time we meet.

The introduction of a corporate identity program should not be interpreted as merely an exercise in vanity or a cosmetic facelift. It is a visual expression of the "new" SAS, new from deep down inside.

Our new look is a direct reflection of how we see ourselves today – fresh, optimistic and totally dedicated to serving our customers. Something like the charming face on the opposite page. No matter if we are male or female, young or old, with or without wrinkled foreheads.

What's most important is what's behind that identity.

That's more vital than anything else.

Exhibit 6 Selected Financial Data, MSEK

SAS Group	82/83	81/82	80/81	79/80	78/79
INCOME STATEMENT DATA					
Traffic Revenue	**10 463.1**	8 585.9	7 003.4	6 342.2	5 544.7
Other Revenue	**5 509.4**	4 221.1	3 168.1	2 878.0	2 521.0
Operating Revenue, total	**15 972.5**	12 807.0	10 171.5	9 220.2	8 065.7
Operating Expenses before Depreciation	**14 695.7**	11 895.6	9 663.7	8 920.8	7 551.2
Depreciation	**483.1**	473.7	429.9	390.8	359.5
Operating Income after Depreciation	**793.7**	437.7	77.9	− 91.4	155.0
Financial Items (net)	**−210.3**	−145.7	−165.7	− 71.6	−56.8
Income after Financial Items	**583.4**	292.0	− 87.8	−163.0	98.2
Other Items (net)	**17.6**	156.0	36.5	99.9	49.4
Income before Allocations and Taxes	**601.0**	448.0	− 51.3	− 63.1	147.6
BALANCE SHEET DATA					
Current Assets	**5 428.4**	4 172.0	3 080.6	2 727.1	2 473.1
Fixed Assets (incl. Restricted Funds)	**3 653.6**	3 425.9	3 732.7	3 628.7	3 218.8
Total Assets	**9 082.0**	7 597.9	6 813.3	6 355.8	5 691.9
Current Liabilities	**4 551.5**	3 632.5	3 121.3	2 803.1	2 320.8
Long Term Debt	**2 299.4**	2 147.5	2 288.5	2 147.2	1 805.0
Reserves, Minority Interest	**786.3**	704.2	665.9	585.8	576.4
Equity including Income of the Year	**1 444.8**	1 113.7	737.6	819.7	989.7
Total Liabilities and Equity	**9 082.0**	7 597.9	6 813.3	6 355.8	5 691.9

Exhibit 7 Comparative Statistics: Production, Traffic, and Personnel

SAS Consortium		82/83	Change	81/82	80/81	79/80	78/79
Size of Network	(km 000)	214	+ 2%	210	224	252	264
Number of Cities Served		93	− 6%	99	105	103	102
Kilometers Flown, scheduled services	(mill.)	119.3	+ 6%	112.9	113.2	120.4	124.3
Hours Flown (airborne), total	(000)	182.1	+ 6%	171.1	171.1	180.0	185.7
Available Tonne Kms, total	(mill.)	2 331.3	− 4%	2 427.3	2 472.4	2 536.8	2 528.3
Available Tonne Kms, scheduled services		2 311.5	− 4%	2 394.9	2 450.7	2 515.9	2 483.5
Available Tonne Kms, non-sched. services		19.8	−39%	32.4	21.7	20.9	44.8
Revenue Tonne Kms, sched. services	(mill.)	1 431.2	+ 1%	1 418.3	1 415.8	1 432.6	1 435.1
Passenger and Excess Baggage		986.0	+ 2%	962.3	958.3	972.6	966.6
Freight		393.9	− 3%	404.3	407.5	412.2	425.2
Mail		51.3	− 1%	51.7	50.0	47.8	43.3
Total Load Factor, scheduled services	(%)	61.9	+ 2.7 enh	59.2	57.8	56.9	57.8
Number of Passengers Carried, total	(000)	9 222	+ 4%	8 861	8 413	8 393	8 669
Available Seat Kms, sched. services	(milj.)	17 037	0%	17 118	17 761	18 460	18 216
Revenue Pass. Kms, sched. services	(mill.)	11 159	+ 3%	10 879	10 817	10 972	10 908
Passenger Load Factor, sched. services	(%)	65.5	+ 1.9 enh	63.6	60.9	59.4	59.9
Average Pass. Trip Length, sched.	(kms)	1 219	− 2%	1 239	1 296	1 318	1 272
Traffic Revenue/Revenue Tonne Km (SEK)		7.17	+25%	5.74	4.64	4.13	3.57
Airline Operating Expenses/Available Tonne Km (including depreciation) (SEK)		4.12	+23%	3.35	2.80	2.49	2.11
Average Number of Employees		17 101	+ 4%	16 376	16 425	17 069	16 755
Revenue Tonne Kms/Empl., sched. services		83 700	− 3%	86 600	86 200	83 900	85 700
Revenue Pass-Kms/Empl., sched. services		652 500	− 2%	664 300	658 600	642 800	651 000

Exhibit 8   Scandinavian Airlines System (A)

SAS The Consortium
Intercontinental Passengers

	%-Change from Previous Year	Share of Total SAS Passengers	
	1982/83	1981/82	1982/83
First Class	−18	3%	3%
"First Business Class"	+11	24%	27%
Discounted Fares	− 3	73%	70%
Strategic action	First Business Class		

Operational and Financial Statistics for SAS Consortium

	78/79	79/80	80/81	81/82	82/83
Passenger load factor (% of seats sold)	59.9	59.4	60.9	63.6	65.5
Production available (million tonne kilometers)	2 484	2 516	2 451	2 395	2 312
Revenue passenger-kilometers per employee (km 000)	651	643	659	664	653
Number of employees at end of year	16 800	17 100	16 400	16 400	17 100
Operating result after depreciation (million SEK)	99	−111	15	316	618

The Middle Manager as Innovator

ROSABETH MOSS KANTER

When Steve Talbot, an operations manager, began a staff job reporting to the general manager of a product group, he had no line responsibility, no subordinates or budget of his own, and only a vague mandate to "explore options to improve performance."

To do this, Talbot set about collecting resources by bargaining with product-line managers and sales managers. By promising the product-line managers that he would save them having to negotiate with sales to get top priority for their products, he got a budget from them. Then, because he had the money in hand, Talbot got the sales managers to agree to hire one salesperson per product line, with Talbot permitted to do the hiring.

The next area he tackled was field services. Because the people in this area were conservative and tightfisted, Talbot went to his boss to get support for his recommendations about this area.

With the sales and service functions increasing their market share, it was easy for Talbot to get the product-line managers' backing when he pushed for selling a major new product that he had devised. And, to keep his action team functioning and behind him, Talbot made sure that "everyone became a hero" when the senior vice president of engineering asked him to explain his success to corporate officers.

Arthur Drumm, a technical department head of two sections, wanted to develop a new measuring instrument that could dramatically improve the company's product quality. But only Drumm thought this approach would work; those around him were not convinced it was needed or would pay off. After spending months developing data to show that the company needed the instrument, Drumm convinced several of his bosses two levels up to contribute $300,000 to its development. He put together a task force made up of representatives from all the manufacturing sites to advise on the development process and to ensure that the instrument would fit in with operations.

When, early on, one high-level manager opposed the project, Drumm coached two others in preparation for an officer-level meeting at which they were going to present his proposal. And when executives argued about which budget line the money would come from, R&D or engineering, Drumm tried to ease the tension. His persistence netted the company an extremely valuable new technique.

When Doris Randall became the head of a backwater purchasing department, one of three departments in her area, she expected the assignment to advance her career. Understandably, she was disappointed at the poor state of the function she had inherited and looked around for ways to make improvements. She first sought information from users of the department's services and, with this information, got her boss to agree to a first wave of changes. No one in her position had ever had such close contacts with users before, and Randall employed her knowledge to reorganize the unit into a cluster of user-oriented specialties (with each staff member concentrating on a particular need).

Once she had the reorganization in place and her function acknowledged as the best purchasing department in the region, Randall wanted to reorganize the other two purchasing departments. Her boss, perhaps out of concern that he would lose his position to Randall if the proposed changes took place, discouraged her. But her credibility was so strong that her boss's boss—who viewed her changes as a model for improvements in other areas—gave Randall the go-ahead to merge the three purchasing departments into one. Greater efficiency, cost savings, and increased user satisfaction resulted.

These three managers are enterprising, innovative, and entrepreneurial middle managers who are part of a group that can play a key role in the United States' return to economic leadership.

If that seems like an overly grand statement, consider the basis for U.S. companies' success in the past: innovation in products and advances in management techniques. Then consider the pivotal contribution middle managers make to innovation and change in large organizations. Top leaders' general directives to open a new market, improve quality, or cut costs mean nothing without efficient middle managers just below officer level able to design the systems, carry them out, and redirect their staffs' activities accordingly. Furthermore, because middle managers have their fingers on the pulse of operations, they can also conceive, suggest, and set in motion new ideas that top managers may not have thought of.

The middle managers described here are not extraordinary individuals. They do, however, share a number of characteristics:

Comfort with change. They are confident that uncertainties will be clarified. They also have foresight and see unmet needs as opportunities.

Clarity of direction. They select projects carefully and, with their long time horizons, view setbacks as temporary blips in an otherwise straight path to a goal.

Thoroughness. They prepare well for meetings and are professional in making their presentations. They have insight into organizational politics and a sense of whose support can help them at various junctures.

Participative management style. They encourage subordinates to put in maximum effort and to be part of the team, promise them a share of the rewards, and deliver on their promises.

Persuasiveness, persistence, and discretion. They understand that they cannot achieve their ends overnight, so they persevere—using tact—until they do.

What makes it possible for managers to use such skills for the company's benefit? They work in organizations where the culture fosters collaboration and teamwork and where structures encourage people to "do what needs to be done." Moreover, they usually work under top managers who consciously incorporate conditions facilitating innovation and achievement into their companies' structures and operations.

These conclusions come from a study of the major accomplishments of 165 effective middle managers in five leading American corporations (for details on the research, see the ruled insert [A].) I undertook this study to determine managers' contributions to a company's overall success as well as the conditions that stimulate innovation and thus push a business beyond a short-term emphasis and allow it to secure a successful future.

Each of the 165 managers studied—all of whom were deemed "effective" by their companies—told the research team about a particular accomplishment; these covered a wide range. Some of the successes, though impressive, clearly were achieved within the boundaries of established company practice. Others, however, involved innovation: introduction of new methods, structures, or products that increased the company's capacity. All in all, 99 of the 165 accomplishments fall within the definition of an innovative effort.

Basic accomplishments differ from innovative ones not only in scope and long-run impact but also in what it takes to achieve them. They are part of the assigned job and require only routine and readily available means to carry them out. Managers reporting this kind of accomplishment said they were just doing their jobs. Little was problematic—they had an assignment to tackle; they were told, or they already knew, how to go about it; they used existing budget or staff; they didn't need to gather or share much information outside of their units; and they encountered little or no opposition. Managers performing such activities don't generate innovations for their companies; they merely accomplish things faster or better that they already know how to do.

In contrast, innovative accomplishments are strikingly entrepreneurial. Moreover, they are sometimes highly problematic and generally involve acquiring and using power and influence. (See the ruled insert [B] for more details on the study's definitions of *basic* and *innovative* accomplishments.)

In this article, I first explore how managers influence their organizations to achieve goals throughout the various stages of a project's life. Next I discuss the managerial styles of the persons studied and the kinds of innovation they brought about. I look finally at the types of companies these entrepreneurial managers worked in and explore what top officers can do to foster a creative environment.

THE ROLE OF POWER IN ENTERPRISE

Because most innovative achievements cut across organizational lines and threaten to disrupt existing arrangements, enterprising managers need tools beyond those that come with the job. Innovations have implications for other functions and areas, and they require data, agreements, and resources of wider scope than routine operations demand. Even R&D managers, who are expected to produce innovations, need more information, support, and resources for major projects than those built into regular R&D functions. They too may need additional data, more money, or agreement from extrafunctional officials that the project is necessary. Only hindsight shows that an innovative project was bound to be successful.

Because of the extra resources they require, entrepreneurial managers need to go beyond the limits of their formal positions. For this, they need power. In large organizations at least, I have observed that powerlessness "corrupts."[1] That is, lack of power (the capacity to mobilize resources and people to get things done) tends to create managers who are more concerned about guarding their territories than about collaborating with others to benefit the organization. At the same time, when managers hoard potential power and don't invest it in productive action, it atrophies and eventually blocks achievements.

Furthermore, when some people have too much unused power and others too little, problems occur. To produce results, power—like money—needs to circulate. To come up with innovations, managers have to be in areas where power circulates, where it can be grabbed and invested. In this sense, organizational power is transactional: it exists as potential until someone makes a bid for it, invests it, and produces results with it.

The overarching condition required for managers to produce innovative achievements is this: they must envision an accomplishment beyond the scope of the job. They cannot alone possess the power to carry their idea out but they must be able to acquire the power they need easily. Thus, creative managers are not empowered simply by a boss or their job; on their own they seek and find the additional strength it takes to carry out major new initiatives. They are the corporate entrepreneurs.

Three commodities are necessary for accumulating productive power—information, resources, and support. Managers might find a portion of these within their purview and pour them into a project; managers with something they believe in will eagerly leverage their own staff and budget and even bootleg resources from their sub-

ordinates' budgets. But innovations usually require a manager to search for additional supplies elsewhere in the organization. Depending on how easy the organization makes it to tap sources of power and on how technical the project is, acquiring power can be the most time-consuming and difficult part of the process.

Phases of the Accomplishment

A prototypical innovation goes through three phases: project definition (acquisition and application of information to shape a manageable, salable project), coalition building (development of a network of backers who agree to provide resources and support), and action (application of the resources, information, and support to the project and mobilization of an action team). Let us examine each of these steps in more detail.

Defining the project. Before defining a project, managers need to identify the problem. People in an organization may hold many conflicting views about the best method of reaching a goal, and discovering the basis of these conflicting perspectives (while gathering hard data) is critical to a manager's success.

In one case, information circulating freely about the original design of a part was inaccurate. The manager needed to acquire new data to prove that the problem he was about to tackle was not a manufacturing shortcoming but a design flaw. But, as often happens, some people had a stake in the popular view. Even hard-nosed engineers in our study acknowledged that, in the early stages of an entrepreneurial project, managers need political information as much as

---

[1] See my book *Men and Women of the Corporation* (New York: Basic Books, 1977); also see my article, "Power Failure in Management Circuits," HBR July–August 1979, p. 65.

they do technical data. Without political savvy, say these engineers, no one can get a project beyond the proposal stage.

The culmination of the project definition phase comes when managers sift through the fragments of information from each source and focus on a particular target. Then, despite the fact that managers may initially have been handed a certain area as an assignment, they still have to "sell" the project that evolves. In the innovative efforts I observed, the managers' assignments involved no promises of resources or support required to do anything more than routine activities.

Furthermore, to implement the innovation, a manager has to call on the cooperation of many others besides the boss who assigned the task. Many of these others may be independent actors who are not compelled to cooperate simply because the manager has carved a project out of a general assignment. Even subordinates may not be automatically on board. If they are professionals or managers, they have a number of other tasks and the right to set some of their own priorities; and if they are in a matrix, they may be responsible to other bosses as well.

For example, in her new job as head of a manufacturing planning unit, Heidi Wilson's assignment was to improve the cost efficiency of operations and thereby boost the company's price competitiveness. Her boss told her she could spend six months "saying nothing and just observing, getting to know what's really going on." One of the first things she noticed was that the flow of goods through the company was organized in an overly complicated, time-consuming, and expensive fashion.

The assignment gave Wilson the mandate to seek information but not to carry out any particular activities. Wilson set about to gather organizational, technical, and political information in order to translate her ambiguous task into a concrete project. She followed goods through the company to determine what the process was and how it could be changed. She sought ideas and impressions from manufacturing line managers, at the same time learning the location of vested interests and where other patches of organizational quicksand lurked. She compiled data, refined her approach, and packaged and repackaged her ideas until she believed she could "prove to people that I knew more about the company than they did."

Wilson's next step was "to do a number of punchy presentations with pictures and graphs and charts." At the presentations, she got two kinds of response: "Gee, we thought there was a problem but we never saw it outlined like this before" and "Aren't there better things to worry about?" To handle the critics, she "simply came back over and over again with information, more information than anyone else had." When she had gathered the data and received the feedback, Wilson was ready to formulate a project and sell it to her boss. Ultimately, her project was approved, and it netted impressive cost savings.

Thus although innovation may begin with an assignment, it is usually one—like Wilson's—that is couched in general statements of results with the means largely unspecified. Occasionally, managers initiate projects themselves; however, initiation seldom occurs in a vacuum. Creative managers listen to a stream of information from superiors and peers and then identify a perceived need. In the early stages of defining a project, managers may spend more time talking with people outside their own functions than with subordinates or bosses inside.

One R&D manager said he had "hung out" with product designers while trying to get a handle on the best way to formulate a new process-development project. Another

R&D manager in our survey got the idea for a new production method from a conversation about problems he had with the head of production. He then convinced his boss to let him determine whether a corrective project could be developed.

Building a coalition. Next, entrepreneurial managers need to pull in the resources and support to make the project work. For creative accomplishments, these power-related tools do not come through the vertical chain of command but rather from many areas of the organization.

George Putnam's innovation is typical. Putnam was an assistant department manager for product testing in a company that was about to demonstrate a product at a site that attracted a large number of potential buyers. Putnam heard through the grapevine that a decision was imminent about which model to display. The product managers were each lobbying for their own, and the marketing people also had a favorite. Putnam, who was close to the products, thought that the first-choice model had grave defects and so decided to demonstrate to the marketing staff both what the problems with the first one were and the superiority of another model.

Building on a long-term relationship with the people in corporate quality control and a good alliance with his boss, Putnam sought the tools he needed: the blessing of the vice president of engineering (his boss's boss), special materials for testing from the materials division, a budget from corporate quality control, and staff from his own units to carry out the tests. As Putnam put it, this was all done through one-on-one "horse trading"—showing each manager how much the others were chipping in. Then Putnam met informally with the key marketing staffer to learn what it would take to convince him.

As the test results emerged, Putnam took them to his peers in marketing, engineering, and quality control so they could feed them to their superiors. The accumulated support persuaded the decision makers to adopt Putnam's choice of a model; it later became a strong money-maker. In sum, Putnam had completely stepped out of his usual role to build a consensus that shaped a major policy decision.

Thus the most successful innovations derive from situations where a number of people from a number of areas make contributions. They provide a kind of checks-and-balances system to an activity that is otherwise nonroutine and, therefore, is not subject to the usual controls. By building a coalition before extensive project activity gets under way, the manager also ensures the availability of enough support to keep momentum going and to guarantee implementation.

In one company, the process of lining up peers and stakeholders as early supporters is called "making cheerleaders"; in another, "preselling." Sometimes managers ask peers for "pledges" of money or staff to be collected later if higher management approves the project and provides overall resources.

After garnering peer support, usually managers next seek support at much higher levels. While we found surprisingly few instances of top management directly sponsoring or championing a project, we did find that a general blessing from the top is clearly necessary to convert potential supporters into a solid team. In one case, top officers simply showed up at a meeting where the proposal was being discussed; their presence ensured that other people couldn't use the "pocket veto" power of headquarters as an excuse to table the issue. Also, the very presence of a key executive at such a meeting is often a signal of the proposal's importance to the rest of the organization.

Enterprising managers learn who at the top-executive level has the power to affect their projects (including material resources or vital initial approval power). Then they negotiate for these executives' support, using polished formal presentations. Whereas managers can often sell the projects to peers and stakeholders by appealing to these people's self-interests and assuring them they know what they're talking about, managers need to offer top executives more guarantees about both the technical and the political adequacies of projects.

Key executives tend to evaluate a proposal in terms of its salability to *their* constituencies. Sometimes entrepreneurial managers arm top executives with materials or rehearse them for their own presentations to other people (such as members of an executive committee or the board) who have to approve the project.

Most often, since many of the projects that originate at the middle of a company can be supported at that level and will not tap corporate funds, those at high levels in the organization simply provide a general expression of support. However, the attention top management confers on this activity, many of our interviewees told us, makes it possible to sell their own staffs as well as others.

But once in a while, a presentation to top-level officers results in help in obtaining supplies. Sometimes enterprising managers walk away with the promise of a large capital expenditure or assistance getting staff or space. Sometimes a promise of resources is contingent on getting others on board. "If you can raise the money, go ahead with this," is a frequent directive to an enterprising manager.

In one situation, a service manager approached his boss and his boss's boss for a budget for a college recruitment and training program that he had been supporting

on his own with funds bootlegged from his staff. The top executives told him they would grant a large budget if he could get his four peers to support the project. Somewhat to their surprise, he came back with this support. He had taken his peers away from the office for three days for a round of negotiation and planning. In cases like this, top management is not so much hedging its bets as using its ability to secure peer support for what might otherwise be risky projects.

With promises of resources and support in hand, enterprising managers can go back to the immediate boss or bosses to make plans for moving ahead. Usually the bosses are simply waiting for this tangible sign of power to continue authorizing the project. But in other cases the bosses are not fully involved and won't be sold until the manager has higher-level support.

Of course, during the coalition-building phase, the network of supporters does not play a passive role; their comments, criticisms, and objectives help shape the project into one that is more likely to succeed. Another result of the coalition-building phase is, then, a set of reality checks that ensures that projects unlikely to succeed will go no farther.

Moving into action. The innovating manager's next step is to mobilize key players to carry out the project. Whether the players are nominal subordinates or a special project group such as a task force, managers forge them into a team. Enterprising managers bring the people involved in the project together, give them briefings and assignments, pump them up for the extra effort needed, seek their ideas and suggestions (both as a way to involve them and to further refine the project), and promise them a share of the rewards. As one manager put it, "It takes more selling than telling." In most of the innovations we observed, the manager couldn't just order subordinates to get involved. Doing something beyond routine work that involves creativity and cooperation requires the full commitment of subordinates; otherwise the project will not succeed.

During the action phase, managers have four central organizational tasks. The technical details of the project and the actual work directed toward project goals are now in the hands of the action team. Managers may contribute ideas or even get involved in hands-on experimentation, but their primary functions are still largely external and organizational, centered around maintaining the boundaries and integrity of the project.

The manager's first task is to **handle interference** or opposition that may jeopardize the project. Entrepreneurial managers encounter strikingly little overt opposition—perhaps because their success at coalition building determines whether a project gets started in the first place. Resistance takes a more passive form: criticism of the plan's details, foot-dragging, late responses to requests, or arguments over allocation of time and resources among projects.

Managers are sometimes surprised that critics keep so quiet up to this point. One manufacturing manager who was gearing up for production of a new item had approached many executives in other areas while making cost estimates, and these executives had appeared positive about his efforts. But later, when he began organizing the manufacturing process itself, he heard objections from these very people.

During this phase, therefore, innovative managers may have to spend as much time in meetings, both formal and one-to-one, as they did to get the project launched. Managers need to prepare thoroughly for these meetings so they can counter skepticism and objections with clear facts, persuasion, and reminders of the benefits that can accrue to managers meeting the project's objectives. In most cases, a clear presentation of facts is enough. But not always: one of our respondents, a high-level champion, had to tell an opponent to back down, that the project was going ahead anyway, and that his carping was annoying.

Whereas managers need to directly counter open challenges and criticism that might result in the flow of power or supplies being cut off, they simply keep other interference outside the boundaries of the project. In effect, the manager defines a protected area for the group's work. He or she goes outside this area to head off critics and to keep people or rules imposed by higher management from disrupting project tasks.

While the team itself is sometimes unaware of the manager's contribution, the manager—like Tom West (head of the now-famous computer-design group at Data General)—patrols the boundaries.[2] Acting as interference filters, managers in my study protected innovative projects by bending rules, transferring funds "illicitly" from one budget line to another, developing special reward or incentive systems that offered bonuses above company pay rates, and ensuring that superiors stayed away unless needed.

The second action-phase task is **maintaining momentum** and continuity. Here interference comes from internal rather than external sources. Foot-dragging or inactivity is a constant danger, especially if the creative effort adds to work loads. In our study, enterprising managers as well as team members complained continually about the tendency for routine activities to take precedence over special projects and to consume limited time.

[2]   Tracy Kidder, *The Soul of a New Machine* (Boston: Little, Brown, 1981).

In addition, it is easier for managers to whip up excitement over a vision at start-up than to keep the goal in people's minds when they face the tedium of the work. Thus, managers' team-building skills are essential. So the project doesn't lose momentum, managers must sustain the enthusiasm of all—from supporters to suppliers—by being persistent and keeping the team aware of supportive authorities who are clearly waiting for results.

One manager, who was involved in a full-time project to develop new and more efficient methods of producing a certain ingredient, maintained momentum by holding daily meetings with the core team, getting together often with operations managers and members of a task force he had formed, putting out weekly status reports, and making frequent presentations to top management. When foot-dragging occurs, many entrepreneurial managers pull in high-level supporters—without compromising the autonomy of the project—to get the team back on board. A letter or a visit from the big boss can remind everyone just how important the project is.

A third task of middle managers in the action phase is to engage in whatever **secondary redesign**—other changes made to support the key change—is necessary to keep the project going. For example, a manager whose team was setting up a computerized information bank held weekly team meetings to define tactics. A fallout of these meetings was a set of new awards and a fresh performance appraisal system for team members and their subordinates.

As necessary, managers introduce new arrangements to conjoin with the core tasks. When it seems that a project is bogging down—that is, when everything possible has been done and no more results are on the horizon—managers often change the structure or approach. Such alterations can cause a redoubling of effort and a renewed attack on the problem. They can also bring the company additional unplanned innovations as a side benefit from the main project.

The fourth task of the action phase, **external communication,** brings the accomplishment full circle. The project begins with gathering information; now it is important to send information out. It is vital to (as several managers put it) "manage the press" so that peers and key supporters have an up-to-date impression of the project and its success. Delivering on promises is also important. As much as possible, innovative managers meet deadlines, deliver early benefits to others, and keep supporters supplied with information. Doing so establishes the credibility of both the project and the manager, even before concrete results can be shown.

Information must be shared with the team and the coalition as well. Good managers periodically remind the team of what they stand to gain from the accomplishment, hold meetings to give feedback and to stimulate pride in the project, and make a point of congratulating each staff member individually. After all, as Steve Talbot (of my first example) said, many people gave this middle manager power because of a promise that everyone would be a hero.

A MANAGEMENT STYLE FOR INNOVATION . . .

Clearly there is a strong association between carrying out an innovative accomplishment and employing a participative-collaborative management style. The managers observed reached success by:

- Persuading more than ordering, though managers sometimes use pressure as a last resort.
- Building a team, which entails among other things frequent staff meetings and considerable sharing of information.

- Seeking inputs from others—that is, asking for ideas about users' needs, soliciting suggestions from subordinates, welcoming peer review, and so forth.
- Acknowledging others' stake or potential stake in the project—in other words being politically sensitive.
- Sharing rewards and recognition willingly.

A collaborative style is also useful when carrying out basic accomplishments; however, in such endeavors it is not required. Managers can bring off many basic accomplishments using a traditional, more autocratic style. Because they're doing what is assigned, they don't need external support; because they have all the tools to do it, they don't need to get anyone else involved (they simply direct subordinates to do what is required). But for innovative accomplishments—seeking funds, staff, or information (political as well as technical) from outside the work unit; attending long meetings and presentations; and requiring "above and beyond" effort from staff—a style that revolves around participation, collaboration, and persuasion is essential.

The participative-collaborative style also helps creative managers reduce risk because it encourages completion of the assignment. Furthermore, others' involvement serves as a check-and-balance on the project, reshaping it to make it more of a sure thing and putting pressure on people to follow through. The few projects in my study that disintegrated did so because the manager failed to build a coalition of supporters and collaborators.

. . . AND CORPORATE CONDITIONS THAT ENCOURAGE ENTERPRISE

Just as the manager's strategies to develop and implement innovations followed many different patterns, so also the level of enterprise managers achieved varied strongly across the five companies we studied (see the *Exhibit*). Managers in newer, high-technology companies have a much higher proportion of innovative accomplishments than managers in other industries. At "CHIPCO," a computer parts manufacturer, 71% of all the things effective managers did were innovative; for "UTICO," a communications utility, the number is 33%; for "FINCO," an insurance company, it is 47%.

This difference in levels of innovative achievement correlates with the extent to which these companies' structures and cultures support middle managers' creativity. Companies producing the most entrepreneurs have cultures that encourage collaboration and teamwork. Moreover, they have complex structures that link people in multiple ways and help them go beyond the confines of their defined jobs to do "what needs to be done."

CHIPCO, which showed the most entrepreneurial activity of any company in our study, is a rapidly growing electronics company with abundant resources. That its culture favors independent action and team effort is communicated quickly and clearly to the newcomer. Sources of support and money are constantly shifting and, as growth occurs, managers rapidly move on to other positions. But even though people frequently express frustration about the shifting approval process, slippage of schedules, and continual entry of new players onto the stage, they don't complain about lost opportunities. For one thing, because coalitions support the various projects, new project managers feel bound to honor their predecessors' financial commitments.

CHIPCO managers have broad job characters to "do the right thing" in a manner of their own choosing. Lateral relationships are more important than vertical ones. Most functions are in a matrix, and some managers have up to four "bosses." Top management expects ideas to bubble up from lower levels. Senior executives then select solutions rather than issue confining directives. In fact, people generally rely on informal face-to-face communication across units to build a consensus. Managers spend a lot of time in meetings; information flows freely, and reputation among peers—instead of formal authority or title—conveys credibility and garners support. Career mobility at CHIPCO is rapid, and people have pride in the company's success.

RADCO, the company with the strongest R&D orientation in the study, has many of CHIPCO's qualities but bears the burden of recent changes. RADCO's once-strong culture and its image as a research institute are in flux and may be eroding. A new top management with new ways of thinking is shifting the orientation of the company, and some people express concern about the lack of clear direction and long-range planning. People's faith in RADCO's strategy of technical superiority has weakened, and its traditional orientation toward innovation is giving way to a concern for routinization and production efficiency. This shift is resulting in conflict and uncertainty. Where once access to the top was easy, now the decentralized matrix structure—with fewer central services—makes it difficult.

As at CHIPCO, lateral relationships are important, though top management's presence is felt more. In the partial matrix, some managers have as many as four "bosses." A middle manager's boss or someone in higher management is likely to give general support to projects as long as peers (within and across functions) get on board.

And peers often work decisions up the organization through their own hierarchies.

Procedures at RADCO are both informal and formal: much happens at meetings and presentations and through persuasion, plus the company's long-term employment and well-established working relationships encourage lateral communication. But managers also use task forces and steering committees. Projects often last for years, sustained by the company's image as a leader in treating employees well.

MEDCO manufactures and sells advanced medical equipment, often applying ideas developed elsewhere. Although MEDCO produces a high proportion of innovative accomplishments, it has a greater degree of central planning and routinization than either CHIPCO or RADCO. Despite headquarters' strong role, heads of functions and product managers can vary their approaches. Employers believe that MEDCO's complex matrix system allows autonomy and creates opportunities but is also time wasting because clear accountability is lacking.

Teamwork and competition coexist at MEDCO. Although top management officially encourages teamwork and the matrix produces a tendency for trades and selling to go on within the organization, interdepartmental and interproduct rivalries sometimes get in the way. Rewards, especially promotions, are available, but they often come late and even then are not always clear or consistent. Because many employees have been with MEDCO for a long time, both job mobility and job security are high. Finally, managers see the company as a leader in its approach to management and as a technological follower in all areas but one.

The last two companies in the study, FINCO (insurance) and UTICO (communications), show the lowest proportion of innovative achievements. Many of the completed projects seemed to be successful *despite* the system.

Currently FINCO has an idiosyncratic and inconsistent culture: employees don't have a clear image of the company, its style, or its direction. How managers are treated depends very much on one's boss—one-to-one relationships and private deals carry a great deal of weight. Though the atmosphere of uncertainty creates opportunities for a few, it generally limits risk taking. Moreover, reorganizations, a top-management shake-up, and shuffling of personnel have fostered insecurity and suspicion. It is difficult for managers to get commitment from their subordinates because they question the manager's tenure. Managers spend much time and energy coping with change, reassuring subordinates, and orienting new staff instead of developing future-oriented projects. Still, because the uncertainty creates a vacuum, a few managers in powerful positions (many of whom were brought in to initiate change) do benefit.

Unlike the innovation-producing companies, FINCO features vertical relationships. With little encouragement to collaborate, managers seldom make contact across functions or work in teams. Managers often see formal structures and systems as constraints rather than as supports. Rewards are scarce, and occasionally a manager will break a promise about them. Seeing the company as a follower, not a leader, the managers at FINCO sometimes make unfavorable comparisons between it and other companies in the industry. Furthermore, they resent the fact that FINCO's top management brings in so many executives from outside; they see it as an insult.

UTICO is a very good company in many ways; it is well regarded by its employees and is considered progressive for its industry. However, despite the strong need for UTICO to be more creative and thus more competitive and despite movement toward a matrix structure, UTICO's middle ranks aren't very innovative. UTICO's culture is changing—from being based on security and maintenance to being based on flexibility and competition—and the atmosphere of uncertainty frustrates achievers. Moreover, UTICO remains very centralized. Top management largely directs searches for new systems and methods through formal mechanisms whose ponderousness sometimes discourages innovation. Tight budgetary constraints make it difficult for middle managers to tap funds; carefully measured duties discourage risk takers; and a lockstep chain of command makes it dangerous for managers to bypass their bosses.

Information flows vertically and sluggishly. Because of limited cooperation among work units, even technical data can be hard to get. Weak-spot management means that problems, not successes, get attention. Jealousy and competition over turf kill praise from peers and sometimes from bosses. Managers' image of the company is mixed: they see it as leading its type of business but behind more modern companies in rate of change.

ORGANIZATIONAL SUPPORTS FOR CREATIVITY

Examination of the differences in organization, culture, and practices in these five companies makes clear the circumstances under which enterprise can flourish. To tackle and solve tricky problems, people need both the opportunities and the incentives to reach beyond their formal jobs and combine organizational resources in new ways.[3] The following create these opportunities:

- Multiple reporting relationships and overlapping territories. These force middle managers to carve out their own ideas about appropriate action and to sell peers in neighboring areas or more than one boss.
- A free and somewhat random flow of information. Data flow of this kind prods executives to find ideas in unexpected places and pushes them to combine fragments of information.
- Many centers of power with some budgetary flexibility. If such centers are easily accessible to middle managers, they will be encouraged to make proposals and acquire resources.
- A high proportion of managers in loosely defined positions or with ambiguous assignments. Those without subordinates or line responsibilities who are told to "solve problems" must argue for a budget or develop their own constituency.
- Frequent and smooth cross-functional contact, a tradition of working in teams and sharing credit widely, and emphasis on lateral rather than vertical relationships as a source of resources, information, and support. These circumstances require managers to get peer support for their projects before top officers approve.
- A reward system that emphasizes investment in people and projects rather than payment for past services. Such a system encourages executives to move into challenging jobs, gives them budgets to tackle projects, and rewards them after their accomplishments with the chance to take on even bigger projects in the future.

Some of these conditions seem to go hand in hand with new companies in not-yet-mature markets. But top decision makers in older, traditional companies can design these conditions into their organizations. They would be wise to do so because, if empowered, innovative middle managers can be one of America's most potent weapons in its battle against foreign competition.

---

[3] My findings about conditions stimulating managerial innovations are generally consistent with those on technical (R&D) innovation. See James Utterback, "Innovation in Industry," *Science* February 1974, pp. 620–626; John Kimberly, "Managerial Innovation," *Handbook of Organizational Design*, edited by W. H. Starbuck (New York: Oxford, 1981), and Goodmeasure, Inc., "99 Propositions on Innovation from the Research Literature," *Stimulating Innovation in Middle Management* (Cambridge, Mass., 1982).

Insert A

The Research Project

After a pilot study in which it interviewed 26 effective middle managers from 18 companies, the research team interviewed, in depth, 165 middle managers from five major corporations located across the United States. The 165 were chosen by their companies to participate because of their reputations for effectiveness. We did not want a random sample: we were looking for "the best and the brightest" who could serve as models for others. It turned out, however, that every major function was represented, and roughly in proportion to its importance in the company's success. (For example, there were more innovative sales and marketing managers representing the "market-driven" company and more technical, R&D, and manufacturing managers from the "product-driven" companies.)

During the two-hour interviews, the managers talked about all aspects of a single significant accomplishment, from the glimmering of an idea to the results. We asked the managers to focus on the most significant of a set of four or five of their accomplishments over the previous two years. We also elicited a chronology of the project as well as responses to a set of open-ended questions about the acquisition of power, the handling of roadblocks, and the doling out of rewards. We supplemented the interviews with discussions about current issues in the five companies with our contacts in each company.

The five companies represent a range of types and industries: from rather traditional, slow-moving, mature companies to fast-changing, newer, high-technology companies. We included both service and manufacturing companies that are from different parts of the country and are at different stages in their development. The one thing that all five have in common is an intense interest in the topic of the study. Facing highly competitive markets (for the manufacturing companies a constant since their founding; for the service companies a newer phenomenon), all of these corporations wanted to encourage their middle managers to be more enterprising and innovative.

Our pseudonyms for the companies emphasize a central feature of each:

CHIPCO:
manufacturer of computer products

FINCO:
insurance and related financial services

MEDCO:
manufacturer of large medical equipment

RADCO (for "R&D"):
manufacturer of optical products

UTICO:
communications utility

What Is an Innovative Accomplishment?

We categorized the 165 managers' accomplishments according to their primary impact on the company. Many accomplishments had multiple results or multiple components, but it was the breadth of scope of the accomplishment and its future utility for the company that defined its category. Immediate dollar results were *not* the central issue; rather, organizational "learning" or increased future capacity was the key. Thus, improving revenues by cutting costs while changing nothing else would be categorized differently from improving revenues by designing a new production method; only the latter leaves a lasting trace.

The accomplishments fall into two clusters:

Basic. Done solely within the existing framework and not affecting the company's longer-term capacity; 66 of the 165 fall into this category.

Innovative. A new way for the company to use or expand its resources that raises long-term capacity; 99 of the 165 are such achievements.

Basic accomplishments include:

Doing the basic job—simply carrying out adequately a defined assignment within the bounds of one's job (e.g., "fulfilled sales objectives during a reorganization").

Affecting individuals' performance—having an impact on individuals (e.g., "found employee a job in original department after failing to retrain him").

Advancing incrementally—achieving a higher level of performance within the basic job (e.g., "met more production schedules in plant than in past").

Innovative accomplishments include:

Effecting a new policy—creating a change of orientation or direction (e.g., "changed price-setting policy in product line with new model showing cost-quality trade-offs").

Finding a new opportunity—developing an entirely new product or opening a new market (e.g., "sold new product program to higher management and developed staffing for it").

Devising a fresh method—introducing a new process, procedure, or technology for continued use (e.g., "designed and implemented new information system for financial results by business sectors").

Designing a new structure—changing the formal structure, reorganizing or introducting a new structure, or forging a different link among units (e.g., "consolidated three offices into one").

While members of the research team occasionally argued about the placement of accomplishments in the subcategories, we were almost unanimous as to whether an accomplishment rated as basic or innovative. Even bringing off a financially significant or flashy increase in performance was considered basic if the accomplishment was well within the manager's assignment and territory, involved no new methods that could be used to repeat the feat elsewhere, opened no opportunities, or had no impact on corporate structure—in other words, reflected little inventiveness. The manager who achieved such a result might have been an excellent manager, but he or she was not an innovative one.

Exhibit Characteristics of the five companies in order of most to least "entrepreneurial"

	CHIPCO	RADCO	MEDCO	FINCO	UTICO
Percent of effective managers with entrepreneurial accomplishments	71%	69%	67%	47%	33%
Current economic trend	Steadily up	Trend up but currently down	Up	Mixed	Down
Current "change issues"	Change "normal"; constant change in product generations; proliferating staff and units.	Change "normal" in products, technologies; recent changeover to second management generation with new focus.	Reorganized about 3–4 years ago to install matrix; "normal" product technology changes.	Change a "shock"; new top management group from outside reorganizing and trying to add competitive market posture.	Change a "shock"; undergoing reorganization to install matrix and add competitive market posture while reducing staff.
Organization structure	Matrix	Matrix in some areas; product lines act as quasi-divisions.	Matrix in some areas.	Divisional; unitary hierarchy within divisions, some central services.	Functional organization; currently overlaying a matrix of regions and markets.
	Decentralized	Mixed	Mixed	Centralized	Centralized
Information flow	Free	Free	Moderately free	Constricted	Constricted
Communication emphasis	Horizontal	Horizontal	Horizontal	Vertical	Vertical
Culture	Clear, consistent; favors individual initiative.	Clear, though in transition from emphasis on invention to emphasis on routinization and systems.	Clear, pride in company, belief that talent will be rewarded.	Idiosyncratic; depends on boss and area.	Clear but top management would like to change it; favors security, maintenance, protection.

Current "emotional" climate	Pride in company, team feeling, some "burn-out."	Uncertainty about changes.	Pride in company, team feeling.	Low trust, high uncertainty.	High certainty, confusion.
Rewards	Abundant. Include visibility, chance to do more challenging work in the future and get bigger budget for projects.	Abundant. Include visibility, chance to do more challenging work in future and get bigger budget for projects.	Moderately abundant. Conventional.	Scarce. Primarily monetary.	Scarce. Promotion, salary freeze; recognition by peers grudging.

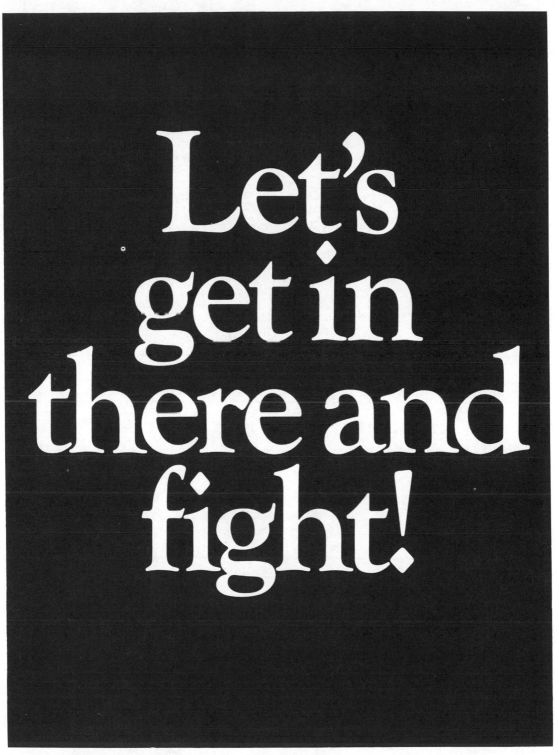

We have to fight in a stagnating market.

We have to fight competitors who are more efficient than we are. And who are at least as good as we are in figuring out the best deals.

We can do it. But only if we are prepared to fight. Side by side. We are all in this together.

Jan Carlzon

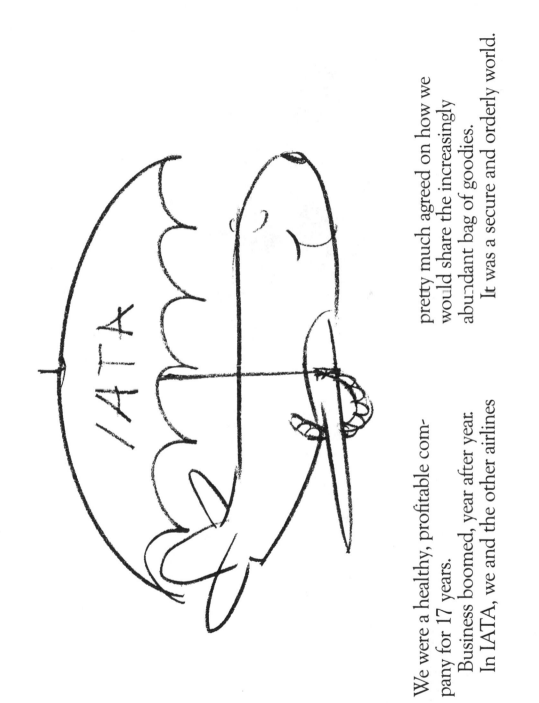

We were a healthy, profitable company for 17 years.

Business boomed, year after year.

In IATA, we and the other airlines pretty much agreed on how we would share the increasingly abundant bag of goodies.

It was a secure and orderly world.

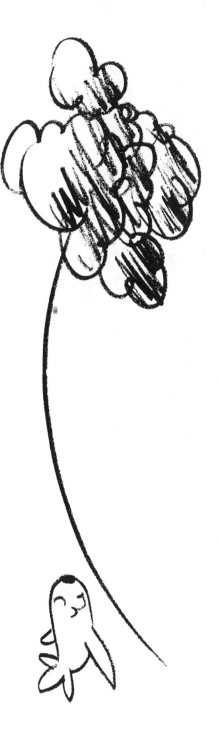

Who was to know there were storm clouds beyond the horizon?

Suddenly, bad weather struck...

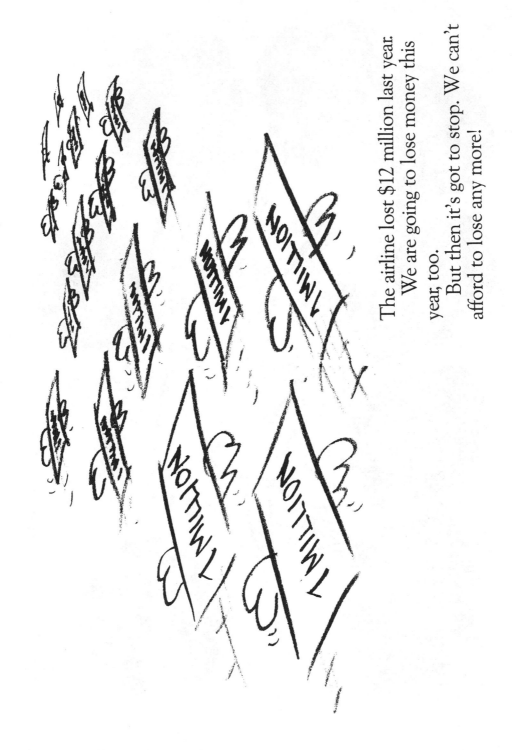

The airline lost $12 million last year. We are going to lose money this year, too.

But then it's got to stop. We can't afford to lose any more!

We are in bad shape. But we haven't reached the crisis point yet. If we were, we wouldn't know how to get our nose up again.

But we can. If we are ready to fight for our jobs and our future, we can recover.

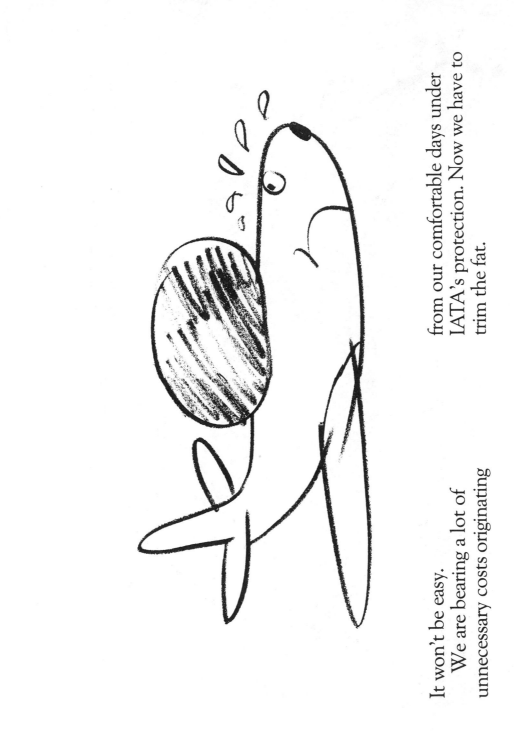

from our comfortable days under IATA's protection. Now we have to trim the fat.

It won't be easy. We are bearing a lot of unnecessary costs originating

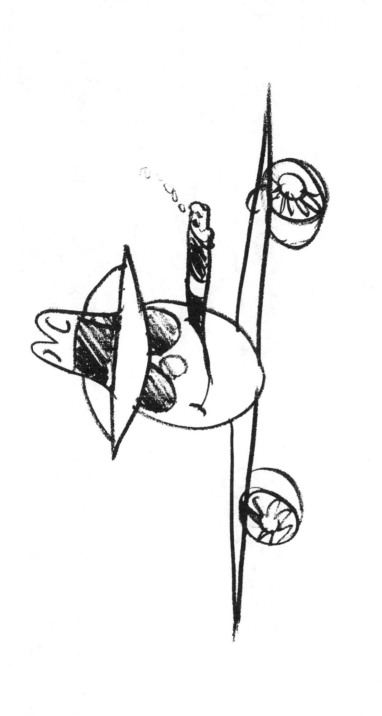

We've got some tough competition.
Like the "street fighters" from the
rough-and-tumble American

domestic market. Efficient. In shape.
Like Delta...

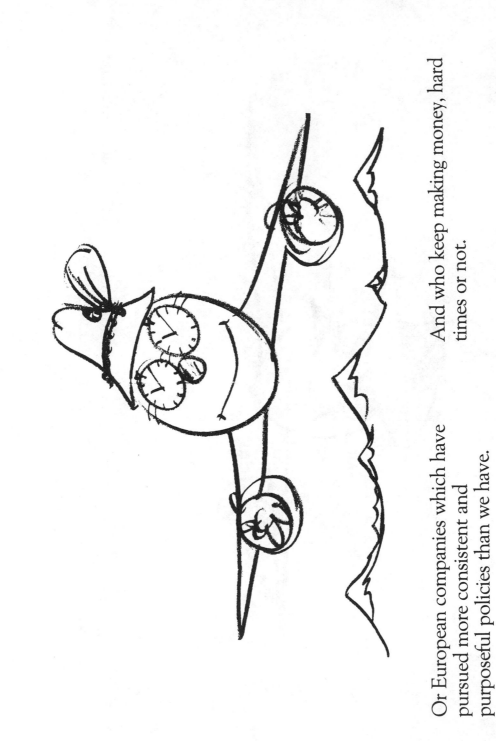

And who keep making money, hard times or not.

Or European companies which have pursued more consistent and purposeful policies than we have.

Look at the differences:

Delta has:

○ 40 % more revenue tonne-kms per employee

○ 120 % more passengers per employee

○ 14 % more available tonne-kms per pilot

○ 40 % more passenger-kms per cabin attendant

○ 35 % more passenger-kms per passenger sales employee

It is difficult to make similar comparisons in the technical and maintenance fields, but even in these areas Delta has a substantially higher productivity than SAS.

Key figures *	Swissair INTERNATIONAL	SAS INTERNATIONAL
Cabin Factor	63.6	59.3
Load Factor	59.2	57.8
Passenger revenue (USD)/RPK	0.09	0.08
Cargo revenue (USD)/RFTK	0.37	0.31
Total revenue (USD)RTK	0.79	0.73
Operating cost (USD)/ATK	0.45	0.42
Revenue-Cost Relationship (Over 100 = profit)	103.5	99.7
Average flight leg/km	1051	967

* USD = U.S. Dollars. RPK = Revenue Passenger-kilometers, RFTK = Revenue Freight Tonne-kilometers. RTK = Revenue Tonne-kilometers. ATK = Available Tonne-kilometers.
Exchange rate: one USD = 4.65 Swedish kronor.

This is what we have to do:

Right now, we look like this:

Income $1.505 million

Expenses $1.517 million

Deficit $12 million

Next year, we should look at least this good:

Income $1.517 million

Expenses $1.505 million

Profit $12 million

And in just a few years, that profit should be $120 million, at least!

We'll be in bad shape if we don't make it.

This is how we are going to do it!

We have to consolidate.

We have to be market-oriented.

We have to be more efficient.

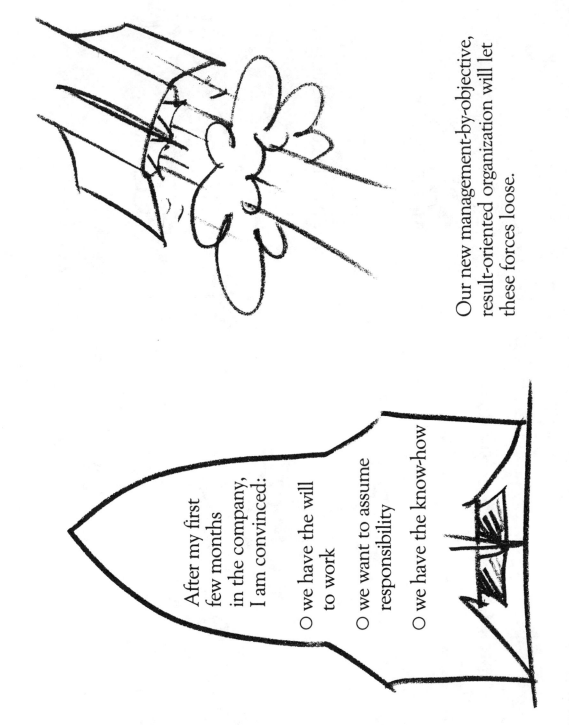

Our new management-by-objective, result-oriented organization will let these forces loose.

After my first few months in the company, I am convinced:

○ we have the will to work

○ we want to assume responsibility

○ we have the know-how

The organization will open the vents and let responsibility and authority take off all over the company. And liberate initiative and determination. So we can all take off.

The new organization won't solve any problems in itself.
It is merely a prerequisite if we are to work more efficiently.

No more friction!

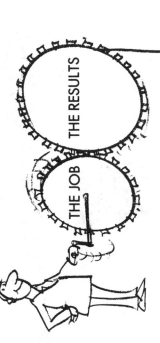

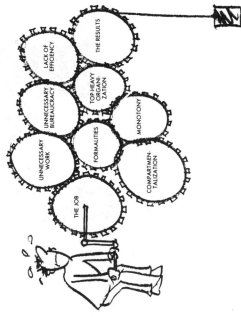

The new organization is designed to get results.

This requires efficiency.

To eliminate friction. We have to pitch in and do away with the kind of work we no longer need.

The kind that diverts our energy, time and money from important business.

The repair job is starting now, and the wheels will be ready to roll in September.

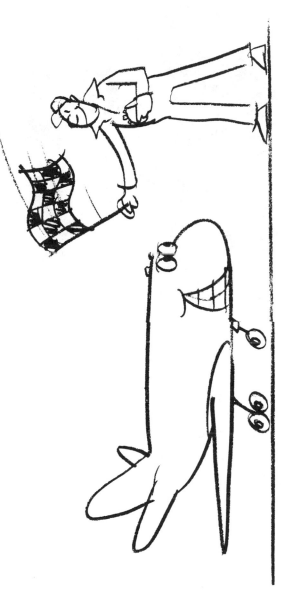

We are going to be much more punctual. Everyone can help. "Operation Punctuality" is starting soon. It's going to give everyone a chance to help make us one of Europe's most punctual airlines.

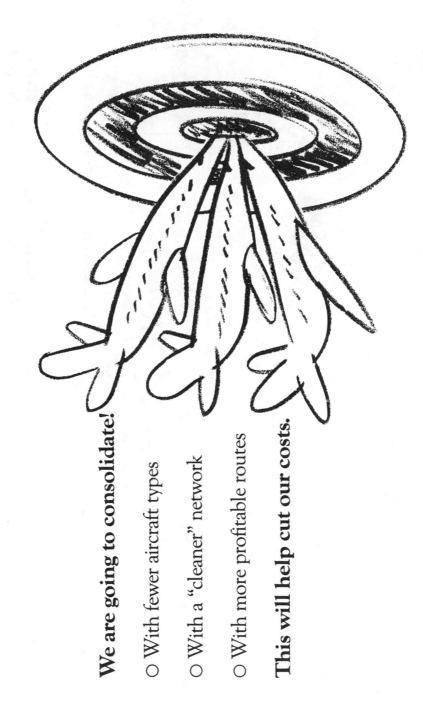

We are going to consolidate!

○ With fewer aircraft types

○ With a "cleaner" network

○ With more profitable routes

This will help cut our costs.

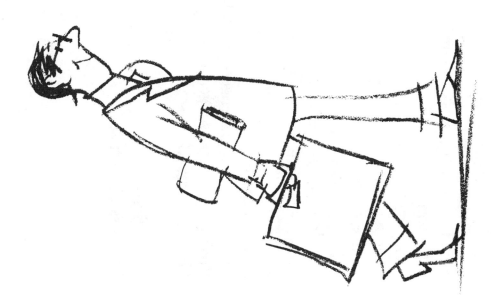

We are going to zero in on the business travel market.

○ It's big.

○ It's demanding.

○ It's where the money is.

Above all, we are going to capture the business travel market in Scandinavia – our home market. Half of it today is in the hands of our competitors.

This is what we're going to do for Business Class:

Ticket Offices.
Special phone numbers.
High-level service at ticket counters.

Check-in.
Simplified check-in for passengers with carry-on baggage only.
Separate check-in counters for Business Class.
Seat selection.
High service level, shorter lines.
Quicker check-in procedures.
Special baggage tags.

Service Lounge at Kastrup
Telephone, telex services (debited).
Ticketing (Help with rebookings).
Office space.
Coffee shop.
SAS News Bulletin Board.
Wardrobe for winter clothes.
Message Service.

Embarkation
Economy Class passengers board first.
Business Class passengers board last.
Gate manager to assist passengers.

Debarkation.
Business Class first.

Better Punctuality.

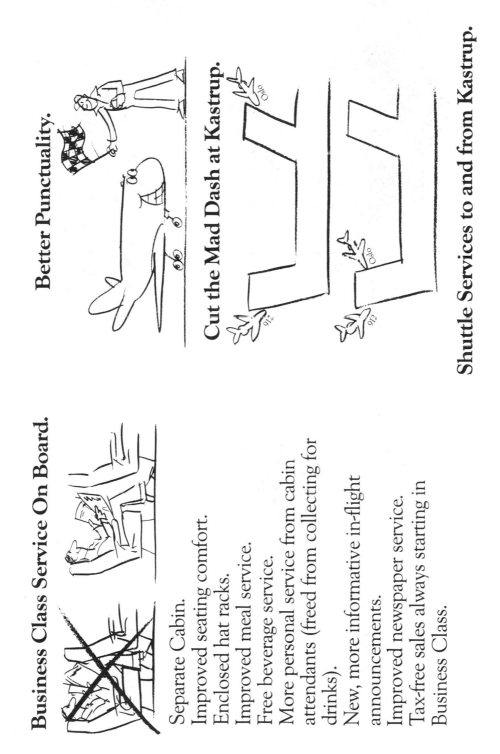

Cut the Mad Dash at Kastrup.

Shuttle Services to and from Kastrup.

Business Class Service On Board.

Separate Cabin.
Improved seating comfort.
Enclosed hat racks.
Improved meal service.
Free beverage service.
More personal service from cabin attendants (freed from collecting for drinks).
New, more informative in-flight announcements.
Improved newspaper service.
Tax-free sales always starting in Business Class.

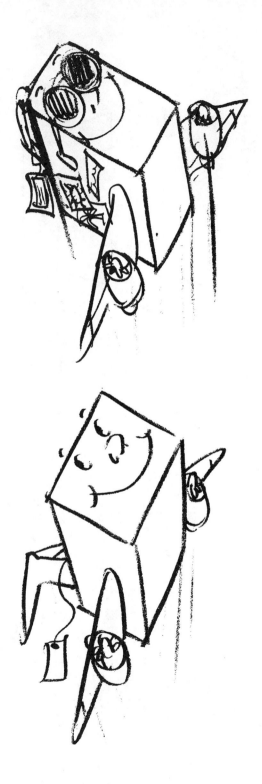

Increased cargo revenue will beef up the bottom line. Cargo marketing will be more efficient as a result-oriented sector all its own.
We are going to raise our pleasure-travel revenues as well. We've got some attractive proposals up our sleeves for the holiday market.

We are also out for better marginal business, like more profitable charters....

...that should do it.

+2%

A 2 % improvement means some $30 million. With that much in our pockets, we've taken the first step toward a new, profitable SAS.

When you put it all together...

○ We are slashing unnecessary costs.

○ We are improving our efficiency.

○ We are consolidating our operations and cutting even more costs.

○ We are tailoring our products and service for the needs of the big business travel market, to increase our income.

○ We are boosting our profitability with cargo and tourism.

○ We are grabbing every opportunity for marginal business.

○ We are going to find it's more fun to work.

We've got to help each other.

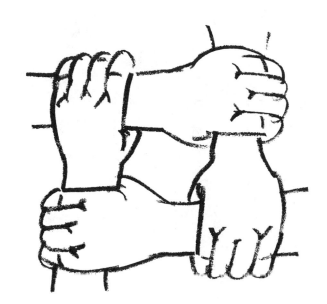

If we help each other, we can put just about anything right and spare our customers a lot of grief.

But we've got to work together!

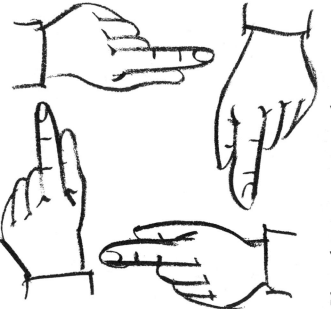

If anything goes wrong, the customer doesn't care whose fault it is. He's the one who's going to suffer anyway.

Don't wait. Start Now!

We've got a lot of projects and ideas in the works. Some will start right away, and others may take half a year to materialize. Don't wait. Make it happen, now!

○ Sell SAS. Don't miss a single chance.

○ Bend over backwards for our passengers at our stations.

○ Help your colleagues. If you don't have any personal contact with our customers, see that you help those who do.

○ On board, give your utmost in service. Don't let off a single unhappy passenger. Your friends on the ground will back you up!

○ Do whatever you can to load and unload baggage on time, so we can maintain our timetables.

○ Plan maintenance and overhaul so our aircraft will be ready to go on schedule.

○ Start today!

Bear in mind:

The only really valuable asset we have is a truly satisfied customer.

Index

DeLay, James, 199
Diamond Shamrock, 142, 144
Dickason Audrey, 106, 142–44
Differentiation, 8
Digital Equipment Corporation, 105
Directors Guild, 66–67
Disney, Walt, 79, 81, 82, 85, 209
Disney Studios, 24, 41, 43, 65
DNA research, 251, 268–69, 365–66
Dodge, Liz, 196
Dole, Sally, 263
Donkey Kong (videogame), 42–43
Draper, Bill, 253, 254
Drouin, Reńe, 31
Drucker, Peter, 95
Drumm, Arthur, 489
Dryden, Kay, 80, 87
du Toit, Derek F., 158
Duchamp, Marcel, 29
Duffy, Paula, 104*n*
Dvorak, John, 180*n*

E

Eagleton, Terence, 28*n*
EBS (program), 109
Echo and Narcissus myth, 384–85
ECO. *See* Entrepreneurship, creativity, and organization
Edelman, Barry, 262–64
Edlund, Richard, 79
Education and Technology Advisory Board (ETAB), 331–32, 340
Eisner, Michael, 24
Emerson, Ralph Waldo, 93
Empire Strikes Back, The (movie), 65, 66, 68, 84, 85
Empire Strikes Back (videogame), 47
Entertainment software for personal computers, 107, 222–23, 276–77
Entrepreneurial spirit, 1, 5
human resource management and, 10
Entrepreneurs
careers of, 103–5
case studies on, 105–77
characteristics of, 4, 5, 90, 167–68
entrepreneurial traits, 97–99
managers compared to, 98, 102–3, 360–64
personality quirks, 157–65
personality studies, 99–101
typologies of entrepreneurs, 101–2
founding, organizational culture and, 348–64
human resource management by, 8–12
tasks of, 95–97
"Entrepreneurs' disease," 184
Entrepreneurship
as behavioral phenomenon, 168
creativity linked with, 17–19
current interest in, 1–2, 166–67
definition of, 91–93, 167–68

in established organizations, 1, 4–5, 396–406
case studies, 406–531
definition of "established," 397–99
"intrepreneurship," 166
managing, 399–406
mechanisms of, 402–6
"supply-side," 167
Entrepreneurship, Creativity, and Organization (course), content of, 2–5
Entrepreneurship, creativity, and organization (ECO)
analytical framework of, 5–8
human resources' influence on, 11–12
goals and principles of, 2–5
Environment
creativity in terms of, 23
definition of, 5, 6
entrepreneurship and, 93–95
of established company, 398
as source of uncertainty, 9
Epyx (company), 277
Erickson, Robert J., 253, 256, 259–63, 266
E.T. (movie), 43, 47, 53, 77
Etak (company), 213, 214
Exidy (company), 46
Expectations, managing, 10

F

Fast food businesses, Au Bon Pain compared to, 311
Faxon, Roger, 80
Federal Express Corporation, 102
Field, Lee, 28*n*, 69*n*, 127*n*, 144*n*, 152*n*, 208*n*, 315*n*, 347*n*
Film business, 62–63
top money-making films in, 68–69
Financial services industry, 412–13
Fini, Leonor, 32
Fireman's Fund Insurance Company, 412
First Boston Corporation, 155
First Data Resources (company), 409
Flamholtz, Eric, 179*n*
Ford, Henry, 162
Ford Foundation, 131
Ford Motor Company, 131
Foreman, Carl, 63
Forget, Bernard G., 252–53, 259
Founder's role in creating organizational culture, 348–64
Fox Video Games, 58
Frankston, Bob, 237
French breads and croissants industry, 292–93
Frogger (videogame), 47
Fujitsu Computers, 21
Fuji-Xerox (company), 132
Fulop, Bob, 58
Funkhouser, Richard, 330
Future shock, 184

Managers
  entrepreneurs compared to, 98, 102–3, 360–
    64
  middle
    entrepreneurial, 400–401
    as innovators, 489–505
  women, in Japan, 139
Manzi, Jim, 224, 234–36, 238–41, 246
Market research (marketing studies)
  creativity and, 18
  Turner on, 126
Marley, Bob, 108
Martin Marietta Corporation, 336
Marvel Comics, 336
Maslow, Abraham, 15, 102n
Mattel (company), 41, 46, 47
MCA Inc., 43
MCC (Microelectronics and Computer Consortium),
    21
Melchor Venture Management, 316, 322
Micro Finance Systems, Inc. (MFS), 108, 223, 233,
    234
Microsoft (company), 276
Midas myth, 382
Middle managers. *See* Managers—middle
Midway Manufacturing Company, 44, 53, 56
Miles Laboratories, 256
Miller (videogame designer), 54
Milton, Lester, 157–58
Minnesota Manufacturing & Mining Corporation.
    See 3M
Mintzberg, H., 16n
Missile Command (videogame), 58
MIT (Massachusetts Institute of Technology), 275–
    76
MITI (Japanese Ministry for International Trade
    and Development), 21
Mitsubishi Corporation, 132–35
Model T Ford, 162
Molecular Genetics (company), 366–68
Moore, David, 99–100, 104, 160n
Morehead, Jay, 334
Motherwell, Robert, 33
Ms. Pac Man (videogame), 44
MTV (music television channel), 194, 195, 198–
    200
Munkberg, Carl-Olov, 470, 471
Museum of Modern Art, 33
Music-recording industry, background of, 194–
    95
Myths, 382–85

N

Nakamura, Masayo, 59
Namco (company), 59
Narcissus myth, 384–85
Need for control, entrepreneurs', 159–60
Neil, Bill, 82

O

Olympic licensing program, 334
"1-2-3" program, 105, 108, 110, 223, 232, 234–35,
    237
Opportunity
  "blocked," 104
  for entrepreneur, 95–96
  promoter as driven by, 168–71
Opposites, integration of, 16–17
Organization for entrepreneurship, 4, 5
Organizational context
  in ECO analytical framework, 5, 6
  the entrepreneur and, 93
  of established company, 398, 402–6
  in fostering creativity, 23
  HRM and, 11–12
  rapid growth and, 185–89
Organizational culture
  at Au Bon Pain, 306, 308
  counter-, 23–24, 399, 406
  definition of, 348
  founder's role in creating, 348–64
  Japanese, 128–29
  in rapid growth, 188–89, 190
  at SAS, 407
Organizations
  bureaucratic, 398–99
  differing views of, 7–8
  enhancing or hindering creativity in, 21–25
  entrepreneurship in. *See* Entrepreneurship—in
    established organizations
  evolving, 178–91
    case studies, 191–395
    established organizations compared to, 396–97
  growth of. *See* Growth
  human resource management in, 8–12
  life cycle of, 178–80
  redundancy in, 188
  sources of uncertainty in, 8, 9
  See also Organizational culture
Original Cookie Company, 295
Osborne, Alex F., 25
Osborne Computer Company, 180
Ozzie, Ray, 236

P

Pac Man (videogame), 42–45, 47
Painting, Beckmann on, 70–74
Paramount Pictures, 47, 84
Park, Hamish, 330
Parker Brothers (company), 47, 53
Pavailler (company), 291
PC software industry, 107, 222–23, 276–77
Pepsico, 293, 299, 336
Perkins, John, 57
Perls, Klaus, 30
Personal computer software industry, 107, 222–23,
    276–77

Personal Software, Inc., 233
Persons
   in ECO analytical framework, 5, 6
   in fostering creativity, 23
   HRM perspective for, 8–12
   rapid growth and, 189–91
Peters, Thomas, 17
Philanthropy
   of American Express, 413–14
   of Lotus, 119, 225–26, 236
Phildius, Peter P., 266, 267
Picasso, Pablo, 15
Piestrup, Ann M., 316–21, 323, 324
Pinchot, Gifford, 405n
Pizza Time Theatre (company), 210, 217
Plaque Attack (videogame), 76
Platinum Card, 413
Polaro, Bob, 58
Pollack, Dale, 79n
Pollock, Jackson, 33
Pollock, Tom, 84
Pong (videogame), 210, 217
Porter, Michael, 21, 180
Prince, George, 25n
Professional Software Technology (company), 234
Profit sharing, 119
Project, defining, 492–94
Projection, by entrepreneurs, 163
Promoters, trustees compared to, 168–76
Psychological tasks of entrepreneurs, 96–97
Putnam, George, 494

Q

Quality, as defined by Au Bon Pain, 303–5

R

Rabb, Sidney, 145
Raiders of the Lost Ark (movie), 65, 68
Rains, Lyle, 57
Randall, Doris, 490
Rapid growth. *See* Growth—rapid
Raudsepp, E., 16
Rauschenberg, Robert, 35, 38
Reagan, Ronald, 41, 327, 328, 330, 333, 343, 344
Rebay, Baroness Hilla, 32
Recruiting
   at Au Bon Pain, 315
   rapid growth and, 189–90, 265–66
Reed, Ralph, 411
Rembrandt van Rijn, 29
Resources
   commitment of, 171–72
   control of, 172–74
   human. *See* Human resource management
Return of the Jedi (movie), 65, 68, 81, 84
Revson, Charles, 97

Reward philosophy
   at Au Bon Pain, 315
   for entrepreneurship in established firms, 404–6
   of Integrated Genetics, 261–63
   promoters' vs. trustees' attitudes to, 175–76
   in rapid growth, 190
Roberts, Edward B., 159n
Roberts, Michael, 179n
Robinett, Warren, 58
Robinson, James D., III, 412, 416, 426, 433, 454
Robotics, 210–11
Rockwell International Corporation, 336
Roe, A., 15
Rosen, Ben, 234
Rothenberg, A., 16
Rothko, Mark, 33

S

Saatchi & Saatchi (advertising agency), 198–99
Sachs, John, 110
Sachs, Jonathan, 223, 224
Safeway Stores, 336
Sahlman, William, 180
Salar Corporation, 157–58
Salmonella test, 250, 264, 268
Sampson, Anthony, 468
Sanders, Jerry, 105
Sanders, Matt, 403
Sara Lee division, 293
SAS. *See* Scandinavian Airlines Systems
Satellite News Network, 122
Say, Jean Baptiste, 167
Scandinavian Airlines Systems (SAS), 397, 401, 402, 407, 468–531
   human resource management at, 480–81
   "Let's Get in There and Fight!" booklet of, 475, 506–31
Schein, Edgar H., 348n
Schlesinger, Len, 292, 300–303, 305–6, 311, 312
Schumacher, E. F., 171
Schumpeter, Joseph A., 167
Schwartz, Robert, 96
Scientific Thinking Institute, The, 318–19
Serone Laboratories Inc., 264
Sevin, Rosen, Partners, Ltd., 234
Shaich, Ron, 291–303, 306, 311–13
Shaw, Carol, 57
Shepard, Alan, 329
Silliker Laboratories, 268
Simultaneous loose-tight properties, 17
Skoultchi, Arthur I., 252, 255, 259
Smith, Fred, 97, 102
Smith, Norman R., 159n
Smith, Thomas A., 254, 257–58, 266, 267
Smith, Tom (ILM manager), 81
Sodd, Joe, 199
Software Arts (company), 237
Sotheby, Parke Bernet (auction house), 30

Wigley, Barbara, 199, 202
Wigley, Michael, 194–200, 202, 205
Wilkinson, Fred, 450
Williams, Christian, 121*n*, 127
Williams, Teri A., 397, 407, 458–67
Wilson, Heidi, 493
Wilson, Joseph C., 132
Workman, John Rowe, 124, 125
Wozniak, Steven, 105
Writers Guild, 66–67
WTBS (TV station), 121, 126
Wyman, Meade, 224
Wyman, Tom, 445

X

Xerox Corporation, 132, 330
Xerox Research Center, 59

Y

Yamamoto, Tuma, 21
Yars Revenge (videogame), 58
Young, Maggie, 87
Young Astronaut Council, 327, 330, 331, 335, 337–39
Young Astronauts Program
  local chapters of, 332–33, 337, 338, 342
Young Astronauts Program, The, 95, 192–93, 327–47

Z

Zaleznik, Abraham, 99, 100
Zork (videogame series), 275–76, 278, 286, 287